Gender
in the 21st Century

Gender
in the 21st Century

Caribbean Perspectives, Visions and Possibilities

Edited by Barbara Bailey and Elsa Leo-Rhynie

Ian Randle Publishers
Kingston

First published in Jamaica, 2004 by
Ian Randle Publishers
11 Cunningham Avenue
P.O. Box 686
Kingston 6.
www.ianrandlepublishers.com

© Office of the Principal
University of the West Indies
Mona

National Library of Jamaica Cataloguing in Publication Data

Gender in the 21st century : Caribbean perspectives, visions and possibilities / editors Barbara Bailey ; Elsa Leo-Rhynie

p. : ill. ;   cm

Bibliography : p.   – Includes index

ISBN 976-637-185-7 (hbk)
ISBN 976-637-188-1 (pbk)

1. Women in development – Caribbean Area   2. Women – Caribbean Area
2. Gender identity – Caribbean Area
I. Bailey, Barbara   II. Leo-Rhynie, Elsa

305.309729   dc 21

All rights reserved – no part of this publication may be reproduced, stored in a retrieval system, or transmitted in any form, or by any means electronic, photocopying, recording or otherwise without the prior permission of the editors or publisher.

Cover design by Shelly-Gail Cooper
Book design by Allison Brown
Printed and bound in the USA

Contents

Preface ix

Introduction xi

Foreword xxiii

THEME I: GENDER IN THE 21ST CENTURY: PERSPECTIVES AND VISIONS

Feminist Scholarship and Society — 3

1. Feminist Scholarship and Society — 5
   Joycelin Massiah

2. Feminist Activism: The CARICOM Experience — 35
   Peggy Antrobus

Pushing the Boundaries: Redefining Masculinities and Femininities — 59

3. Gender, History Education and Development in Jamaica — 61
   Verene Shepherd

4. Gender and Schooling: Implications for Teacher Education — 82
   Jeanette Morris

5. Male Marginalisation Revisited — 99
   Errol Miller

6. Old (Female) Glass Ceilings and New (Male) Looking Glasses: Challenging Gender Privileging in the Caribbean — 134
   Mark Figueroa

7. Fatherhood in Risk Environments — 162
   Wilma Bailey, Clement Branche, Jean Jackson, Amy Lee

Pushing the Boundaries: Images, Representations and Identities — 177

8. Caribbean Masculinities and Femininities: The Impact of Globalisation on Cultural Representations — 179
   Rhoda Reddock

9. Gender Politics and Media Production 217
   Marjan de Bruin

10. Masculinity, the Political Economy of the Body, and
    Patriarchal Power in the Caribbean 236
    Linden Lewis

11. 'Mama, Is That You?': Erotic Disguise in the Films *Dancehall Queen* and *Babymother* 262
    Carolyn Cooper

12. Shake that 'Booty' in Jesus' Name: The Possibilities of a
    Liberation Theology of the Body for the Body of Christ in
    Jamaica 281
    June Ann Castello

Pushing the Boundaries: New and Emerging Issues 301

13. Women and Work: Policy Implications of ILO Conventions 303
    Leith L. Dunn

14. The Challenge of Gender and the Labour Market after 30
    Years of CARICOM 333
    Orville W. Taylor

15. The Environment: Prospects for a Gender Responsive
    Approach to Policies and Programmes 348
    Winsome Townsend

16. Female Emancipation and the Sewing Machine 361
    Velma Pollard

THEME II: GENDER IN THE 21ST CENTURY: POSSIBILITIES

Bridging Epistemologies 371

17. Shifting Centres and Moving Margins: The ISS Experience 373
    Saskia E. Wieringa

18. Shifting Centres and Moving Margins: The UWI Experience 397
    Hermione C. McKenzie

Bridging Epistemologies, Constructing New Paradigms 417

19. Gender Studies: Interdisciplinary and Pedagogical Challenges 419
    Elsa Leo-Rhynie

20. Constructing Feminist Knowledge in the Commonwealth
    Caribbean in the Era of Globalisation   437
    Violet Eudine Barriteau

21. Gender Equity, Information and Communications Technologies
    and Connectivity   466
    Fay Durrant

22. Shifting the Paradigm, Erecting and Re-Erecting Boundaries:
    Case Studies from the Scientific World   478
    Grace Sirju-Charran

23. A Different Imagination: A Visual Essay   490
    Patricia Mohammed

Setting New Agendas: The Scholarship of a New Generation   507

24. Mirror Mirror: A Feminist Examination of the Construction
    of Beauty and Body Image   509
    Suzanne Marguerite Charles

25. Ambivalent Aspirations: Assertion and Accommodation in
    Indo-Trinidadian Girls' Lives   528
    Gabrielle Jamela Hosein

26. Gender and the HIV/AIDS Epidemic in the Caribbean   564
    Michelle V. Davis

Setting New Agendas: Within and Beyond the Academy   583

27. Governance, Leadership and Decision-making: Prospects for
    Caribbean Women   585
    Maxine Henry-Wilson

28. Gender, Feminism and Constitutional Reform in the
    Caribbean   592
    Tracy Robinson

29. The Caribbean Experience in the International Women's
    Movement: Issues, Process, Constraints and Possibilties   626
    Barbara Bailey

30. Bureaucratising Feminism: Charting Caribbean Women's
    Centrality within the Margins   655
    Michelle Rowley

31. Feminisms, Gender Studies, Activism: The Elusive Triad   687
    Linnette Vassell

List of Contributors 707

Index 721

Preface

This book is a compilation of most of the papers presented at the very successful Mona Academic Conference 2003. The conference has become the annual centrepiece of the campus' activities, welcoming as it does the new academic year and setting the stage for an environment in which ideas are shared, and analysis and discussion are promoted. The 2003 conference was a very special one, as it not only focused on Gender Studies, one of the most rapidly developing areas of scholarship in academia, but it also celebrated the tenth anniversary of the Centre for Gender and Development Studies (CGDS) in the University of the West Indies (UWI).

For the past 35 years, the feminist movement has spearheaded a variety of changes worldwide which have benefited women, men and children in practical ways. The changes have also resulted in the development of new and sometimes controversial perspectives, which have challenged many of the misconceptions and assumptions about women and men and their roles in society, around which families, communities and nations, as well as development policy, planning and practice, in many instances, continue to be structured.

Recognition of the need for a Caribbean perspective prompted the initiative to introduce Women's Studies in the UWI and eventually led to the establishment of the CGDS. The Centre can be proud of its institutionalisation as an interdisciplinary centre within the university, the dynamic growth of its scholarship, which is attested to by the number, variety and quality of its research and publications, as well as its outreach activities, which contribute to the development of policy nationally, regionally and internationally. The rich diversity of the papers in this volume speaks to the creativity and depth of the research undertaken by our Caribbean and other scholars and provides the academy, policy makers and practitioners in the field, with thought-provoking analyses of great relevance in terms of the formulation and implementation of policy and practice for the future.

Structured in keeping with the sub-themes of the conference, the volume addresses the interplay between feminist scholarship and society: in Pushing the Boundaries, the extent to which established beliefs are challenged is explored; the strong interdisciplinary demand of gender studies is examined in Bridging Epistemologies; and a prospective view of this area of scholarship is highlighted in the section Setting New Agendas. The record is a comprehensive one and will be a valuable reference for both academics and practitioners.

The future poses many challenges for Caribbean women and men, chief among which are the issues of poverty, violence, and the establishment of gender equity in all aspects of national and regional life. This volume of papers leaves us in no doubt that the vision which has guided the significant achievement of the CGDS over the past ten years will continue to identify the possibilities in these challenges, and makes it clear that there is strong capacity and support in the region for the teaching, research, publication and outreach which will generate ongoing change at all levels of society.

Kenneth O. Hall

Pro Vice Chancellor and Principal
The University of the West Indies, Mona Campus

Introduction

'Gender in the 21st Century: Perspectives, Visions, and Possibilities' was the theme for the 2003 Mona Academic Conference, and this volume retains it as its title. It comprises the keynote speech, plenary presentations and most of the panel presentations made at that conference which celebrated the tenth anniversary of the institutionalisation of Gender Studies within the University of the West Indies (UWI) and the establishment of the Centre for Gender and Development Studies (CGDS). It also commemorated the activism and work of the pioneers in the field who worked assiduously from 1982 onwards, as Women and Development Studies groups, carrying out research, teaching courses, seeking funding and working with agencies involved in furthering the rights of women – from policy-making groups to grass roots organisations – all having the common objective of improving the status of women's lives.

By the time the Centre for Gender and Development Studies was formally institutionalised within the UWI, the term 'gender' had entered the development and academic debate. The choice of 'gender' for the naming of the centre was deliberate and related to the insights, both scholarly and activist, that women's problems are not primarily due to their biological differences from men, but rather to 'gender' differences and the unequal relations of gender that are socially determined. It was an attempt to ensure that gender issues, as these were manifested between and among different categories of men and women, would be addressed in the Centre's teaching curricula, research and advocacy activities. Based on this, the CGDS was established in 1993 as an independent, interdisciplinary Centre with a mandate to:

(a) question historically accepted theories and explanations about society, and human behaviour;

(b) seek an understanding of the world which takes women, their lives and achievements into account; and

(c) examine the origins of power differences between men and women, and the division of human characteristics along gender lines.

At the international level, issues related to the status of women were addressed primarily by the United Nations (UN) through the Commission on the Status of Women, the Economic and Social Council, the UN World Conferences on Women and Special Sessions of the General Assembly. International Women's Year, 1975 and the Decade for Women (1975 – 1985), brought these issues to the fore and their significance has been reflected in subsequent UN conferences designed to study, plan and adopt action for the solution of major problems of world development. Added to this, in 1995 the Human Development Report published by the United Nations Development Programme (UNDP), for the first time, assessed countries according to two new human development indices, the Gender Development Index (GDI) and the Gender Empowerment Measure (GEM), which incorporated specific indices of gender equity, the starting point for mainstreaming gender in development discourse.

Recognising the dynamic context within which gender is being addressed internationally, this publication presents a wide range of issues associated with the scholarship and activism of feminism, particularly in the Caribbean. The first chapter carries the keynote address at the conference, which was delivered by the Hon. Mia Mottley, Attorney-General and Deputy Prime Minister of Barbados. Her presentation demonstrates an awareness of current thinking in terms of the mainstreaming of gender in governance and leadership, and challenges and inspires readers to identify gender justice as an integral component of social justice. She urges all in governance and leadership to recognise where structural factors and cultural influences militate against women achieving their full potential, and asks that a culture of openness, consultation and consensus be developed so as to allow women to be heard and understood, and included in development initiatives. The interaction of gender, race, and social class is emphasised, as is the need to examine problems and issues holistically, and in the context of achieving social justice.

The remaining chapters reflect the sub-themes of the conference viz:

1. Feminist Scholarship and the Society
2. Pushing the Boundaries
3. Bridging Epistemologies
4. Setting New Agendas

1. Feminist Scholarship and the Society

Feminist scholarship has historically taken its cue from, as well as informed issues addressed in, various national, regional and international forums which relate to the position and condition of women. In so doing, it has provided direction for policy and programme formation aimed at treating with social and gender inequity. Both Joycelin Massiah and Peggy Antrobus trace the significant progress and impact of feminist scholarship on the countries of the Caribbean region, and the extent to which gender issues have been brought to the forefront of consciousness and debate by three major groups: the academy, the State machinery, and non-governmental and activist organisations. These groups have focused on different areas of challenge relating to women's lives, and interact closely – linking theory, advocacy and action. In her discussion of Feminist Scholarship and Society, Joycelin Massiah focuses on the Gender and Development (GAD) strategy, and its value in addressing a range of gender problems and issues in teaching, research, activism, and advocacy. She bemoans its unintentional contribution to a reduction of the focus on women's issues as the male marginalisation concerns have emerged. The thrust of Peggy Antrobus' presentation on Feminist Activism and Society is the influence of the feminist movement in effecting change in the politics and programmes of non-governmental organisations as well as on institutions of the State. Both point to the need for the academy to provide leadership in a range of gender-related areas including policy reform and ongoing activism and advocacy to enrich the gender discourse and stimulate its continuing evolutionary development.

2. Pushing the Boundaries

The feminist movement has always 'pushed the boundaries' of accepted thought and knowledge, and has demanded and initiated change in a variety of areas. The academy has emphasised research activity and analysis of the social, economic and political setting, leading to theory building, and providing the framework within which change may be planned and executed. The controversial nature of gender studies is fully explored in this sub-theme, which addresses three areas. The first is Redefining Masculinities and Femininities. Two papers focus on education; Verene Shepherd supports the inclusion of education as part of the development discourse, and points in particular to the ongoing Caribbean debate about male marginalisation and underachievement in a society and culture that is male-dominated. Identifying the school curriculum as one of the strong influences in the development of gender identity, Shepherd looks specifically at early history texts and the hegemonic masculinity they portray, and compares these with more recent attempts by Caribbean historians to depart from the gender stereotyping and gender messages of the earlier texts. Jeanette Morris focuses on teacher education, the stereotypical view of teaching as 'women's work' and as an extension of 'mothering', and the existing school culture as a site for the reproduction of gender relations. She points to the need for change in pedagogy and curriculum as well as at the level of policy-making to counter these effects. In this section also, Errol Miller revisits his 1986 thesis on male marginalisation and reviews alternative theoretical explanations and data available since that time which challenge or support his thesis. Mark Figueroa, in contrast, presents his theory of gender privileging, which seeks to explain the distinctive and complex nature of gender relations in the Caribbean. The marginalisation of men in some areas, and of women in others, as well as the interplay of power between the marginal and central gender groups, are seen as one outcome of the gender-privileging process that Figueroa proposes. Wilma Bailey provides a possible example of gender-privileging at work in a paper in which she examines the inconsistencies and ambivalence of men's attitudes to becoming fathers. The nature of the relationship with the mother as well as the father's perception of his male identity, his ability to provide for the child in an environment of poverty and hardship result in gender relations which are typified by mistrust and tension, with all their implications.

The second area of exploration is entitled Images, Representations and Identities. Rhoda Reddock looks at gender identities and the impact which globalisation is having in the shaping and determining of such identities, of gender ideologies as well as gender relations in the Caribbean. Cultural representations originating in sites such as the local fashion and beauty industry, the music industry and gay and lesbian subcultures are explored and accommodation, acceptance, and resistance to these transforming influences are discussed. Marjan de Bruin identifies another site – media production – and examines the role of gender in the dynamics of this production. De Bruin reports on a study conducted in Jamaica, and Trinidad and Tobago in which implicit notions of masculinity and femininity influence the preferences as well as rejection of certain identities which determine what is portrayed in the media and which influence on a wide scale the perceptions of viewers and consumers of the media product. Linden Lewis, who uses a political economy argument to explore the Caribbean male body as variable capital and to demonstrate how power is used to gain access to resources and social status, pursues 'an epistemologically different approach to the study of masculinity, the body and the reproduction of patriarchy in the Caribbean'. Carolyn Cooper focuses on the female body, examining the new 'disguise motifs' adopted by women to style their bodies and, in the context of the dance hall, give them a sense of emancipation from their mundane existence as women. Rejecting the view that this celebration of the body is a devaluation of female sexuality, Cooper strongly asserts that claiming their right to sexual display and pleasure is an essential, important aspect of women's identity. June Castello's paper rounds off this section, reminding readers of the religious nature of Jamaican society, and the link between the female body and sin, especially sexual sin. The contradictions in the treatment of the female body by the Christian religion are examined in the context of a liberation theology of the body for the Church in Jamaica.

The three papers addressing New and Emerging Issues which are 'Pushing Boundaries' in feminist scholarship, analyse different aspects of women's work, the links between livelihoods and the environment and ways in which technology has contributed to women's emancipation and financial liberation. In the first of these papers Leith Dunn emphasises the need for national and regional policy development among member states of the Caribbean community to ensure consistency with international labour standards. She argues that more Caribbean nations need to ratify the main conventions of the International Labour Organization (ILO), discusses the implications of some of the conventions designed to protect the rights of women workers and urges an expansion of these policies to provide greater protection for Caribbean women, as they struggle to balance their productive and reproductive roles. Orville Taylor points to a major difficulty associated with the implementation of some of Dunn's recommendations. He identifies gaps between the regional constitutions and the international labour conventions. Using existing data and new findings from a regional research project on labour standards, he evaluates the preparedness of the region to meet the standards established by the ILO and also contained in the CARICOM Declaration of 1995, and analyses the challenges to be faced in achieving this goal. Many women the world over depend on the environment for their livelihoods, and have special needs which have to be addressed if they are to be able to work equitably with men in development. A call for gender mainstreaming in environmental organisations and programmes is made by Winsome Townsend who uses the Gender Environment and Development (GED) framework as a basis for arguing that men and women have equal yet different needs and interests in the environment. Cultural and social distinctions make gender access to, and control over, the natural resources different, yet environmental policies and programmes tend to be silent on the gender issue with the result that these differing needs and priorities are not addressed. Change is necessary to optimise development. This section ends with an interesting piece on the sewing machine, a vital source of women's livelihoods for over a century, and the impact of this technology on the psychological and financial liberation of twentieth-century women. Velma Pollard highlights the evidence of this liberation as portrayed in popular songs, calypsos, creative writing and anecdotal cases.

3. Bridging Epistemologies

The issues with which the gender discourse has been involved have been so multifaceted that they can only be satisfactorily addressed through interdisciplinary research and study. Gender is now recognised as an important tool of analysis in the generation and reconstruction of knowledge and, along with race and social class, has become pivotal to the understanding of many historical, social and political issues, and is a central consideration in any discourse on development. Further, its pervasive impact on so many areas of Caribbean life and its intersection with so many discourses has facilitated an interdisciplinary approach to the analysis of a variety of critical issues. Saskia Wieringa and Hermione McKenzie explore this theme in two different contexts: the Institute of Social Studies (ISS) in The Hague and the University of the West Indies (UWI). The experiences of these institutions are of particular relevance as there has been strong and consistent interaction between the ISS and the UWI for almost 20 years. Wieringa traces the origins of the Women and Development Studies programme of the ISS using a model of internal and external influences to demonstrate the importance of balance between these influences in the continued vibrancy of the programme. The academic context, the international nature of the student body and the multicultural staff were obvious success factors, and the changes which have characterised the transition period in which the ISS now finds itself are explored. The UWI experience is described as one which demonstrates the value of building support with influential partners while on the periphery of the academy, prior to moving into its centre. The groundwork done to establish Women and Development Studies within UWI is an important part of the history, culture and experience of the CGDS, and McKenzie explicates this in detail, providing a valuable record for the centre and the university.

Constructing new paradigms is a sub-theme within 'Bridging Epistemologies' and the papers all report on change in knowledge and knowledge systems triggered by the demands of gender studies. Elsa Leo-Rhynie examines the demand for interdisciplinarity which feminist scholarship mandated, as also the need to change the structure of existing knowledge and its method of transmission, so as to create alternative narratives and new pedagogy, which would be liberating and empowering. The paper examines the challenges posed by these imperatives and uses the introduction and institutionalisation of gender studies at the UWI as a case study in effecting some of the changes required. Eudine Barriteau argues that the advent of globalisation has shifted attention from building on Caribbean gender systems, and from the study of women's and men's lives and the theoretical frameworks which were being constructed to capture the multifaceted nature of these lived realities. She sees the shift to concern over the damaging effects of globalisation on Caribbean men's lives as another factor being proposed to divert attention from a full understanding of women's realities and the development of Caribbean feminist knowledge. The opportunities for access to information, education and democratic participation in civic governance and the enhancement of productivity now offered by the internet and other information and communication technologies are considered by Fay Durrant. Bridging the digital divide to permit the use of these technologies to increase women's participation in decision-making in the Caribbean, presents an alternative to traditional methods of meeting women's knowledge needs and must be fully explored. Grace Sirju-Charran uses case studies from the scientific world to illustrate the reassertion of 'biology' as the main explanation of the way in which life is organised. She suggests that, in light of new technologies such as genetic engineering and cloning, there is need to better understand the complex interactions among all organisms, including humans. Pat

Mohammed reports on the making of a documentary film and its use as another medium for reaching women and men. The film seeks to change perspectives of how the conquest, colonisation and cultural development of Caribbean peoples took place. Mohammed notes that, as a filmmaker, she has had to dismantle disciplinary boundaries and to disrupt existing and accepted knowledge. She expects the film to offer a new way of perceiving how gender stereotypes have been constructed and perpetuated in the Caribbean, and how data from varying and often unexpected sources can contribute to these new perspectives.

4. Setting New Agendas

The gender discourse must examine the future in terms of its place in the academy as well as its outreach. A new generation of women and men will be carrying forward the agenda of the future – what will this be? What will be the priorities and motivating forces? This new generation may not always bring entirely new concerns to the debates but may come to the same questions with new lenses and insights. Two young scholars provide readers with some insights on their concerns. Gabrielle Hosein presents a paper using data from the early 1990s, which looks at the ambivalent aspirations of Indo-Trinidadian girls' lives. The ambivalence stems from their adherence to traditional values yet a recognition of competing forces and the need to balance these. Expanded opportunities for girls challenge them to balance 'appropriate' choices with the new and divergent options that are now available to them. The ambiguous assertions are evident in areas such as marriage, family, education and employment. Michelle Davis looks at HIV/AIDS, which is a special concern, as it has changed the lifestyles of many worldwide. She warns of the dangers of the HIV/AIDS pandemic in the Caribbean and points to its gendered nature. Davis stresses the need to question women's sexuality and understand the nature of intimate relationships and the associated power issues, as well as the acts of violence which continue to be committed against women and girls, alongside the data that show that new HIV/AIDS infections are most prevalent among women.

From 2000 to 2001, CARICOM carried out an assessment of priority gender issues in the Caribbean and proposed six concerns which should be addressed. These were gender-based violence and human rights, health, economic empowerment, education, power and decision-making, and the inadequacy of national institutional machinery. In response to this, and in anticipation of other priorities, the academy must review the content of courses, promote increased participation, and seek to widen its interdisciplinary mandate to include more and varied perspectives. The papers in the section on 'Setting New Agendas, within and beyond the Academy' focus on the outreach of the CGDS and the importance of this in its future operations. The paper by Maxine Henry-Wilson is based on personal reflections and comments on prospects for Caribbean women in relation to their involvement in governance, leadership and decision-making. She explores the extent to which increased involvement of women has made a difference and ways in which new paradigms challenge previously held assumptions about women and leadership. Tracy Robinson looks at constitutional reform in the Caribbean and the gender imperatives in such reform for the twenty-first century. Noting that constitutional reform is currently on the agenda of most Caribbean countries, she points to the focus of women's activism and advocacy on changing ordinary legislation rather than on constitutional reform and litigation. She identifies the constitutional reform process as a site for the production and reproduction of gender relations as well as for articulation of the meaning of citizenship. Emphasising its potential for feminist practice, she urges engagement with the constitutional reform process. Barbara Bailey recounts the involvement of member states of the Caribbean community as well as individual Caribbean women in the women's movement, regionally as well as internationally, and highlights their significant role, particularly over the last decade, in the shaping of many of the issues identified as being critical to women of the region. Changing global, regional and local environments has generated new concerns and Bailey traces the emergence and evolution of these issues, as well as the constraints and opportunities related to Caribbean involvement in the international meetings. Recommendations for policy change in terms of ensuring the implementation of strategic objectives and action to promote gender equity, as proposed internationally are offered and discussed. Michelle Rowley looks critically at the record of policymaking in Trinidad and Tobago and notes the adherence to, and reinforcement of, historical and cultural inequities of gender relations despite expressed commitment to gender sensitivity and gender awareness. She acknowledges the impossibility of escaping issues of women's rights, women's empowerment and gender equity, given the international focus on gender issues over the past three decades. Using the Trinidadian Gender Affairs Division as a case study, however, Rowley points to the fact that women seem to be under similar, and in some instances, greater threat within the planning machinery of the State than they were 28 years ago. The dynamic interplay between the three components of contemporary feminist politics: feminisms, activism and gender studies, is examined by Linnette Vassell. She reminds readers of the outgrowth of gender studies from feminisms and activism, and warns that without continued activism, gender studies will become 'an adjunct of the academic status quo'. For societal transformation and women's empowerment to be realities, the three cannot elude each other but must seek to re-establish and maintain the synergies which typified the early years of the vision of social emancipation. Vassell's observation is timely as, reaching out from the academy, the links with the community, the region and the wider society must be sustained as it is these that will permit the work of the academy to inform policy formulation, and act as a catalyst for the design of interventions in which the various interconnections of themes and concerns are addressed holistically. The interface between the theory building of the academy with policy and programmes of the state and NGOs must be an organic link ensuring that the gender concerns identified as crucial are addressed.

This volume examines and discusses a comprehensive range of issues which are of vital interest and importance in the evolution of the gender discourse in the Caribbean and the wider world community. The perspectives and visions shared demonstrate the multi- and interdisciplinary nature of work in this area and point to the use of innovative feminist and other methodologies which have the potential to expand the knowledge base on gender issues and inform policy and interventions at various levels, in response to the varied and multidimensional challenges in which gender is the central focus.

Barbara Bailey and Elsa Leo-Rhynie
March 2004

Foreword

Keynote Address delivered at the 2003 Mona Academic Conference

At the outset, I wish to congratulate the pioneers and the persons who have since assumed the mantle of leadership in the Gender Studies Programme at the University of the West Indies and to say to you that yours has been a worthy cause and one that has inspired much of the policy development throughout the region as it relates to gender issues.

I propose to speak in brief terms in relation to the question of gender, governance and cultural values. Let us reflect on the comments made by the most distinguished Nelson Mandela on May 10, 1994, when he, in his inaugural address, said these words 'We have at last achieved our political emancipation, we pledge ourselves to liberate all our people from the continuing bondage of poverty, depravation, suffering, gender and other discrimination.' And as the world listened to those words it must have crossed the minds of many that there was a significant departure in the settlement of the new arrangements for the modern state of South Africa from those which would have been related to the settlement of our own constitutions in the birth of our modern states; because, within the context of those things which he considered being critical to fight for, having received political emancipation, was the issue of gender justice. And in the Caribbean, at the time of our independence and while we sought to enshrine certain rights within our respective constitutions, in the majority of cases there was little or no mention of gender. Today, it would be impossible for us to contemplate the settlement of a new constitution in any country of the region without specific mention of the need for gender justice and gender equity.

I start in this context because that life span of my nation and our nations collectively, really is the time frame within which the change of values as it relates to the macro framework of governments first took place. If we accept the principle of human dignity being attached to each and every single human being, there could be no reason that could cause one being to be 'lesser' than another. Indeed, history will show that those things which have been determinants, as a result of the cultural values of a people, have very often come after what was supposed to be a fair legislative framework.

The very great constitution of the United States of America, when settled, did not contemplate that people looking like me should have the opportunity to participate in equal rights and freedoms. And within our own region, a region that has been marred historically more by the extent to which it has excluded people from the process of development than included them, there remains a sensitivity to this very issue, because of that historical experience.

So I ask you to cast your minds in the context of social justice, because social justice for us in the Caribbean is the distinguishing factor, in my view, that determines our differences from other developing regions, to the question of the extent to which we want to and insist on keeping people in the centre of the development process, in spite of the many temptations to keep markets and other theories at the centre of that process.

If we accept the precept of social and economic justice as the driving force that determines why we are doing what we do in terms of governance in our society, then we must also accept that the constituent elements of social justice must be respected. It is in that light, therefore, that I would wish to engage your minds, recognising that we have not yet perfected the art of understanding fully the dignity of each human individual, and that the debate which still continues on sexual orientation in the midst of our societies, is reflective of the fact that we still believe that there are greater and lesser beings among us.

But we have come far; because 70 years ago we fought the battles that spoke to access to those basic things which guaranteed us safety from hunger, supplied us with shelter, and provided us with the capacity to work. In spite of all of this, and in spite of the absence of the specific mention of gender and other aspects of marginalised groups within our constitutions, within the period of our independence, that driving commitment to social justice has seen a legislative framework and a policy framework developed in almost every one of our countries, such that the legal vestiges of discrimination, in almost every instance, can truly be said to be a thing of the past. Where we have to continue our efforts, however, very often relates not just to the legal architecture but to the macro policy framework, to the fiscal priorities and indeed within the context of that macro framework, to the process of governance and the precepts that we respect in that process of governance.

I believe that there can be no true commitment to social justice unless those elements of our governance reflect a respect for transparency, for accountability and for the fostering of the participatory approach to gender consensus. We have tried in Barbados out of the initial framework of our social partnership, to build incrementally, such that this can be the framework that underpins the governance of our country.

Social partnership in Barbados, initially a partnership with the government, the labour movement and the private sector, forged at the time of economic hardship as an instrument of economic stabilisation, has become a mechanism for consultation in the context of economic and social transformation. Those key decisions that must be taken in respect of how we go forward as a country, reflecting the commitment to social justice and economic justice that we originally built, can be taken in that framework. So committed are we to the process, and so happy are we with the experience, that we have recently agreed that this social partnership should now be enshrined in our new constitution as a precept of governance which will govern the activities of future generations.

When our constitutions were written, they spoke in terms of the role of government and neglected the process of governance. And this is the void that must now be filled in the settlement of the new constitution. It is the deliberate and constituent effort of a people ready to frame the rules that will govern how persons in the society interact with one another. But it doesn't stop there, because we believe that the partnership of three should be widened; that elements of civil society ought to be brought to the table largely because their interests may not necessarily be reflected through the interests of government or the labour movement or the private sector. And we further recognise that to the same extent that we would wish government to remain publicly accountable for all of its actions, that there is a requirement to ensure the same transparency and accountability on the part of those in civil society as well as in the corporate sector.

It is these concerns that are driving the establishment of a legislative framework and a policy framework that will speak to the requirement of transparency and accountability within the non-governmental organisations of our nation and also, a commission that will treat with the issue of reform of commercial law, but with an important constituent part of it being governance of the corporate sector. All of these things are necessary if we are going to achieve the goal of ensuring that those entities who are currently being marginalised in our society, whether on the basis of race, class, age or gender, are allowed to participate and ensure that the processes of governance remain clear and transparent and accountable.

The point of participation is one that is key, for we do not want to continue a process that says what is best for a group without reference to members of that group who understand what is best for themselves. They must have the opportunity to speak for themselves. Thus, people as agents of their own development must be central to the process, particularly in the area of gender.

And all of this would not have been possible without the excellent advocacy that took place across the globe, and particularly within the region by pioneers like Peggy Antrobus, Joycelin Massiah and others who would have been at the front line of a movement at a time when others were not necessarily there nor prepared to go there. And the sensitisation process has resulted in the needed policy framework, which for the most part reflects the objectives of where we need to be.

But there is a bridge that must still be built between that needed policy framework and the realities of the limp existence of many of our people in our societies. It is this bridge that must be the focus of those of us who have the honour to occupy positions of leadership, whether in government, civil society or the corporate sector, at this juncture of our development. Too often the stories abound of women who continue to have no options and no choices. Too often the question of gender is perceived simply as a new name for a woman's programme that includes men's problems, without understanding that the structural imbalance that continues to exist in our society takes us away from the goal of social justice that we have set ourselves.

The question of how to get people to recognise this issue must be put on the front burner. I believe that we have a responsibility, whether in government or at the university or with women's advocacy groups or across other spheres of civil society, to begin to define for people what we truly mean by gender, in a language that people understand. There are too many of our citizens who do not understand but who truly believe that their lot in life is to carry the burdens associated with the structural imbalances. We have a duty to correct this notion, and I speak to you not just as a minister but as someone who has first of all the responsibility of representing people at a constituency level. Week in and week out, half of my work is in trying to enlarge for people the possibilities that exist in their minds. And I say so because Barbados has had a strong commitment to the development of social capital as demonstrated by free primary to tertiary education; by extra-curricular classes; by the issue of access to credit, particularly since the government has now determined that 50 per cent of the resources of the Urban Development Commission and the Rural Development Commission must go to community enterprise to empower people; by the availability of 100 per cent mortgages at 6 per cent up to $100,000 so that people, predominantly single women, can have access to owning houses and saving money instead of paying rent.

The policy that land in the country be sold at 10 cents a square foot and in town at $2.50 a square foot when the market value is 5 times that amount is in place but yet there exists a chasm between the minds of the beneficiaries and the benefits that are there for them. That chasm very often reflects a poverty of spirit, a crisis of confidence, a culture of dependency. And we ask ourselves, how can a nation or a group of nations that have done so wonderfully well in creating the legal architecture such that we have scored perfectly in removing the mere vestiges of discrimination as with race, still have people facing these difficulties, in spite of the commitment to do otherwise?

It has become popular since I have been in government for the last nine years for people to talk about culture and development issues, but for many years it was not substantial enough to occupy the attention of ministers of government because it did not deal with hardcore policy. The reality of our situation is such that there must be a marriage between the formal education process and the non-formal education process in terms of popular culture and its various agencies in order to deal with the key issue of the socialisation of our people, such that their minds may abandon that poverty of spirit, such that the crisis of confidence can be removed, and such that the culture of dependency will convert itself into a culture of interdependency. That is no easy task; because you cannot legislate it, you cannot dictate it, as what is required is an engagement of people after you have earned their trust; and trust can only be earned through a process of time and face to face engagement and is the benefit of good experience.

I genuinely believe that once we have treated the issue of recognition of the problem and a definition of the issue for our people, that there must be a sustained platform: government at the macro level, its own agency on culture, its educational platform, the university and other educational institutions, and the church, which is perhaps lagging behind all of them. I do not say so disrespectfully but out of true recognition that for the matter of women's ordination to be an issue in the late 20th century is an indication of how far the church is behind the rest of the society.

The church, the corporate sector, the labour movement, non-governmental organisations, feminist groups, must begin to recognise that advocacy at the level of sensitising governments is not sufficient. The grassroots mobilisation which, in the Caribbean, has really been the preserve of the political movement and the labour movement, must now become the preserve of those who have an agenda to change how people think about themselves and how they think about others — whether in the context of gender or race, because those two remain the most deeply located factors in terms of conditions and creativity of Caribbean people.

And I believe that everything happens in its own time; what has happened over the last 25 to 30 years was simple. But what must now happen for the next generation or two is to truly show people how they can emancipate themselves from mental slavery, and note the words, not for us to emancipate them but for them to emancipate themselves from mental slavery; and the acceptance of responsibility on the part of the individual in this effort while at the same time supporting them with the room to make choices is what is required. It is the absence of that choice, it is the absence of those options, more than anything else, that condemns our people to a life of hardship and oppression.

A lady who owns a landscape business in my constituency employing three or four people calls it a gardening business. She tells me that she cannot access the 100 per cent mortgage because it is not for people like her. Now if it is not for her who is it for? Or when a woman, aged 24, who has four or five children comes to me and says 'I want a job', it is that she wants a government job, because she believes that a government job will give her pension and it will prevent her from being fired. That is the common perception. But when you ask more questions, it turns out that she is a seamstress and she sells well-made garments at Easter, around Cropover, when the children are going back to school, and at Christmas. But in between, things do not look too pretty. Once you start to engage her, however, you realiase that what she needs is not a government job but the ability to maintain a regular income, the opportunity to get assistance to see how best she can continue to market her services within the community. The point that I am making is that these people very often see themselves as having more options and I feel strongly that the real challenge must be located in being able to alter the cultural values in our society such that we create the true spirit of the legislation into a reality for those persons whom it was intended to benefit when it was passed.

What this requires, on our part, is a clear determination of partnership; it requires a recognition that many of the marginalised classes will need some priority in the redistribution of benefits and programmes. In the same way we recognise that those who live on country land for years should have the benefit of buying the land at the subsidised rate, then we must recognise that other marginalised classes sometimes need a leg up in order to be able to walk on their own.

We also need to articulate that there is nothing wrong with difference, while acknowledging and understanding that there are differences between men and women. When I entered political life as a young person, I felt that, as a woman, there was nothing that could stop me being a politician. There was no concept of my being a woman that was a part of my contemplation in terms of becoming a politician, but experience has a way of altering the balance as well. And while I still do not feel any stumbling block in my way in terms of active discrimination, I have come to understand that whether I like it or not or whether I do not see a difference, people view me differently as a woman politician.

The mere fact that how I choose to wear my hair can become the subject of a calypso song in circumstances where a male colleague's hair will not be the subject of calypso, is indicative of those things that people consider. There is also the fact that people comment on why the four ministers who were women (there are now five) in the Barbados government are all single, without commenting on the fact that there was an equal number of male ministers who were single or speculating as to why this was the case. So that there are very real differences in how people view you. What I have also understood is that there is a difference in perspective; not better or worse, but a difference.

And governance, for it to be complete, needs the marriage of those perspectives in order to be representative of where the society is and needs to go. So then I believe, ladies and gentlemen, we have our work cut out for us. I also understand that there has been a determination that we should treat with male marginalisation as a gender issue as if women are responsible for the underachievement of men. While I do not discount the issue and the very serious problem of male underachievement, I do not believe it is totally a gender problem. It is a problem of race, it is a problem of class, a problem of poverty and a problem of the influence of negative cultural values. For the day that that young man decides to reintegrate into the society, he has options. He has options in a way that a woman with similar circumstances does not have. And that is the clearest evidence that male marginalisation is a serious sociological issue for us to confront, and it is a serious issue for us to deal with in the context of our pursuit of social justice, but it is not an issue which must put the question of the subordination of women in the Caribbean on the back burner.

The challenge ahead is very clear. We as governments must continue to broaden the process of governance, respecting the precepts of transparency, accountability and the agenda of consensus through participation. We as governments have a responsibility to do better in terms of the redistribution of benefits for those marginalised classes, whether in the context of gender, race, class, age or other forms of marginalisation. We must leave no one behind. And we have been fortunate that in the 70 years that have succeeded since the political fervour of the 1930s, each decade has carried a few more out of the pit of the despair. But we need to quicken the pace and enlarge the numbers that we carry, for what we face on a global level is a set of policy mixes that threaten to undermine our very viability to survive as independent sovereign entities capable of managing our own economic destinies. For the first time since that process of social, economic and political revolution in the thirties, we face greater difficulties at the regional and international level, in terms of maintaining that capacity for providing for ourselves and our people.

In the end it is only through reliance on the principle of people at the heart of the development process, and ensuring that the people can produce at the maximum of their ability and allow their creativity to flourish in all of its varied facets, that we will be able to steer the course and to rise above what has been the attack from the neo-liberals and the new policies and laws within the international convergence. It is a serious task at hand and for our own very survival, even if not in pursuit of the objectives of social justice, we all have a job to do.

And I say to the women's movement in particular — you cannot rely solely on the political movement or the labour movement to practise the politics of liberalisation. For their agenda will not always coincide with yours and you must develop the capacity for the politics of mobilisation, you must begin to have cells in every village and every community throughout the region, such that you can foster the trust that is necessary to treat with the minds of individuals in their homes, in the church, in their workplaces and their areas of play. Without this, we will not begin to see the major differences that we must have, both as individuals and as governments, in order to allow for this necessary control of our destiny.

There must be an engagement of the ordinary man and woman in order to change the values and the perceptions that continue to govern how women continue to be victims of subordination and men to structurally benefit and gain privilege from the women in our societies. I am not saying this in a negative way, but only because in the same way there must also be an initiation of the spirit that causes every child who looks into the mirror not to feel that their nose is too broad and that their skin is too dark. And I say this recognising that Jamaica has wonderfully enshrined in its Emancipation Park on the statue there, a strong comment: 'none but ourselves can free our minds'.

John F. Kennedy at his inauguration spoke of the need to accept the fact that we can only save the rich if we are prepared to free the poor. The book by Joanne Simpson *Celebration of Jamaican Women* says it in a better way — that at the beginning of the 21st century the trend clearly suggests that there can be no turning back from what is before us. I say to you let us move forward with confidence and with the commitment to ensure that it is not just a few people we carry each decade but that we bring all of our citizens within the framework of a society that is intent on leaving no one behind.

Thank you very much.

The Hon. Mia Mottley
Deputy Prime Minister and Attorney-General of Barbados
August 29, 2003

THEME I

Gender in the 21st Century: Perspectives and Visions

Feminist Scholarship and Society

1 | JOYCELIN MASSIAH

Feminist Scholarship and Society

Abstract

The Gender and Development (GAD) strategy adopted both in academia and among governments of the Caribbean has served to highlight the societal dimensions of gender and the consequential multifaceted policy responses required to address gender issues. But the GAD strategy has also unintentionally contributed to a decline in policy attention to women's issues as concern for the contrapuntal 'male marginalisation' has emerged. This has led to a worsening of women's situation in some Caribbean societies, though not necessarily to an improvement in men's situation. Influenced by the international development agenda, feminist scholarship in the region has adopted the GAD approach in its teaching, research, advocacy and activism. It has succeeded in improving understanding of gender among governments and NGOs; influencing some government policymaking; isolating the infrastructural requirements for successful gendered policymaking; and identifying newly emerging development challenges, which need to be addressed from a gender perspective. Among the latter are included the HIV/AIDS pandemic, human rights abuses, poverty, governance and leadership. The continued weakness of government institutional machinery, the need for gender-sensitive policy reform and programme action and the limited development and use of measures to monitor government accountability represent the main contextual challenges. CGDS can, and must, provide leadership in both sets of challenges if the key ingredient, political will, is to be activated towards the attainment of gender justice and equality in the twenty-first century in this region.

Introduction

The very first word in the title of this conference – gender – presents us with a typically Caribbean conundrum. It is a word which generates all kinds of responses: scepticism, amusement, irritation, confusion, anger; all of these and more. Those who work in the area of gender studies or gender and development studies have been at pains to define precisely what they mean. Yet they are often accused of equating gender with women. Their accusers, by contrast, provide no definition but equate gender with men quite happily. Then there is the term feminist. That generates just as much diverse reaction. Combining it with the next word, scholarship, provides an aura of respectability, though not too much clarity, for those who are unfamiliar with the phrase.

Perhaps a useful way to begin might therefore be to clarify how I choose to interpret the phrase for this presentation and to point to some of the sources of my interpretation. Let me also say that I propose to deal with the Caribbean community and not to provide an overview of the development of feminist thought generally. That task has been very effectively done by more than one of our own feminist scholars and needs no repetition. As a general working definition, I use that offered by Professor Elsa Leo-Rhynie, for whom feminist scholarship seeks:

> To identify the origins of power differences between the sexes, and the division of human characteristics along gender lines; arrive at an understanding of the world which takes women, their perceptions, their lives and achievements into account; formulate effective change strategies which would result in an acceptance of individuals as 'human'. This acceptance would be independent of gender and would reduce the power difference along gender lines (Leo-Rhynie 2002).

For the purposes of this presentation, I use the term 'feminist scholarship' to refer to that body of ideas and knowledge contained in published and unpublished material which is based on the premises contained in Leo-Rhynie's definition. In the Caribbean such scholarship, traditionally found in the social sciences, is now increasingly being found in history, law, literature and communication studies. Females connected with the University of the West Indies (UWI), either by training or employment, past or current, have been the primary producers. Most of the published material is to be found in a series of collections of essays beginning with the publication of a selection of papers from the inaugural seminar of the then Women and Development Studies Group of the UWI (see Mohammed, Patricia and Catherine Shepherd, eds. 1988). This collection has been followed in the nineties by four others: Leo-Rhynie, Elsa, Barbara Bailey and Christine Barrow (eds.), 1997; Barrow, Christine, (ed.),1998; Mohammed, Patricia, (ed.), 2002; and Barriteau, Eudine, (ed.). In Press. Also a special issue of the international journal *Feminist Review* which focused on the Caribbean was published in 1998.

In addition to these formal publications, there are also the Women and Development (WAND) Occasional Papers, now defunct, and the current Working Papers of the Centre for Gender and Development Studies (CGDS), both coming out of the UWI. Then there is *CAFRA News,* the newsletter of the Caribbean Association for Feminist Research and Action (CAFRA) and the newsletter, *Gender Dialogue,* of the Port of Spain office of the United Nations Economic Commission for Latin America and the Caribbean (UNECLAC). Although both of these are newsletters, they do contain, from time to time, useful articles written from a feminist perspective.

Other very useful sources are three recent conferences at which cutting edge presentations were made. The CGDS St. Augustine *Symposium on Caribbean Masculinities*, 1996, broke new ground in that it took on the challenge of addressing a subject which had bedevilled the feminist movement throughout the nineties. The papers are currently in press. In 2000, the United Nations system in Barbados and the Eastern Caribbean, in collaboration with CAFRA and CGDS, Cave Hill, sponsored a *Symposium in Honour of the Work of Peggy Antrobus*. This symposium represented an opportunity to examine the state of the gender discourse in the region and to project the future in terms of research, strategic planning, models for programme and project development and methodologies for implementation. A publication from that symposium is expected. In 2002, CGDS, Cave Hill, sponsored a workshop entitled *Recentreing Caribbean Feminisms* which is slated as the first in a series concerned with reviewing and assessing the state of feminism in the region. Papers from that gathering are expected in January 2004.

Taken together, these essays provide a representative statement on the current status of feminist scholarship in the region. However, there also exists other published material which appears in books and academic journals outside of the region. In addition, there is a wealth of unpublished material in the form of conference and seminar papers, theses, reports, addresses, some of them readily available, some not. So that the Caribbean may rightly claim that it has entered the global stream of literature which is probing for a better understanding of gender justice and what it entails.

For the purposes of this event, I have drawn on the published material and such of the unpublished material as came to hand during my stint at the Caribbean office of the United Nations Development for Women (UNIFEM). There I had the opportunity and the privilege of working with some of the outstanding feminist thinkers in the region. I have chosen to focus on the work of those who have tried to enhance our understanding of the nature and content of feminist thought and of those who have been trying to apply that thinking to specific aspects of development policy and planning. This is not to deny the validity of the contributions of work in other areas, it is simply in response to the stated goal of this conference to focus on 'informing policy formulation and/or revision'.

Where are feminist scholars to be found in the region? For the most part they are located within the universities, and within a growing community of independent gender consultants. But they may also be found in non-governmental organisations (NGOs), in government ministries and departments, in regional and international agencies. In those latter locations, they may not be engaged in academic type research and publication, but they do seek to apply the ideas contained in material produced by academics as well as their own feminist perspectives to the reports, plans, projects and programmes in which they are engaged. To the extent that this effort is successful, there tends to be a blurring of the lines between the academy and its clientele. An important caveat is the need to recognise that feminism and feminist thought are neither static nor isolated. Reddock's work clearly shows that changes have taken place over time both in the content and context of feminist thought in the region (Reddock 1988). Barriteau has pointed the direction in which it should go (Barriteau 2002, 2003). Yet another caveat is the growing understanding that the theories being developed in the North do not necessarily apply here and that it is important to develop a theory which speaks directly to the realities of the Caribbean situation. Barrow states that categorically:

> Imported theories, archaic, patriarchal assumptions, gender stereotypes and misconceived policies have been problematised and challenged and the process of reinterpretation and rejection through the lens of engendered indigenous knowledge is well underway (Barrow 1998, p. xii).

Barriteau's work is unyielding on the point (Barriteau 1994, 1995, 1998, 2002).

For purposes of analysis, the available material may be divided into three main groups, roughly corresponding to the location of those identified as feminist scholars, but there is some overlap between the groups. There are those works which speak essentially to general theoretical issues. The work of Eudine Barriteau, Patricia Mohammed and Rhoda Reddock falls into this group. Then there are those which seek to explain the link between gender and specific themes. They further seek ways of assisting states to address the particular issue with appropriate policies and programmes. The works of Roberta Clarke, Tracy Robinson and others on gender-based violence, of Mariana Williams on globalisation and trade liberalisation, Barbara Bailey on education, Linnette Vassell on political participation and Sonja Harris on institutional mechanisms are some examples. Then there are those concerned with activism and here the work of Peggy Antrobus, Andaiye and Honor Ford-Smith are examples.

The overarching theme of this presentation is therefore that feminist scholarship is not limited to the academy, but follows a well-established tradition among Caribbean women for collective action towards improving the lives of women of the region. The presentation is guided by the signposts of perspectives, vision and possibilities provided in the title of the conference.

Perspectives

The regional environment

Reddock defines feminism as:

> The awareness of the oppression, exploitation, and/or subordination of women within the society and the conscious action to change and transform this situation (Reddock 1998, 53).

This suggests that a feminist scholarship which merely reflects the awareness of subordination of women is not genuinely feminist. To be truly feminist, such scholarship cannot, and must not, be allowed to exist within the walls of academia or the confines of women's NGOs. If the work of feminist scholars is to be relevant to the interests and needs of the wider community, then that work must be directed to the social, economic and political issues in the region and not limited to what some have described as 'esoteric' matters. That work must also be used to define the role of gender in the formulation and execution of ameliorative policies and programmes. That feminist scholars in this region are making an effort to bridge this gap is to be commended. Whether their work is achieving the impact that it should is another matter.

But how has feminist scholarship in the region manifested itself and what have we learnt? For that, I identify three categories of feminist scholars and provide examples of their regional work to illustrate the first aspect of my perspectives.

Theorists/Academics are those in the group who engage in multidisciplinary research and teaching within the academy. This parallels the 'professional' feminists identified by Addelson and Potter in their categorisation of feminists (Addelson and Potter 1991). Work in this group has proceeded in two directions – theory building, including clarification of basic concepts, and empirical analysis of specific issues. Progress has occurred in phases. In the initial stages of the theory building phase, there was an attempt to locate the history of feminist thought and action in the region within the prevailing theoretical frameworks which dominated feminist theorising during the eighties and early nineties (Mohammed 1994). At that time, four strands of feminists were identified. The 'liberal feminists' adopted the goal of equal opportunity as a means of maximising available human resources. The 'radical feminists' were interested in the elimination of patriarchy and other hierarchical structures and the restructuring of society. The 'socialist feminists' attempted to blend the Marxist class analysis with the radical focus on patriarchy to explain the oppression of women and to call for a complete restructuring of society. 'Black feminists', and indeed feminists throughout the developing world, insisted on the recognition of other sources of oppression affecting women, citing particularly differences of culture, race and class. They were particularly critical of the assumption of homogeneity among women taken by the various other strands of feminism.

The question of where to place the Caribbean in this categorisation has occupied the attention of several scholars. In an overview of feminism and feminist thought Reddock concluded that the socialist feminist theory has made the most significant contribution to the development of feminist theory as a whole (Reddock 1988). However, Barriteau contends that, apart from its inherent theoretical inconsistencies and limitations 'socialist feminist theory is inadequate to accommodate the multiple social relations of the Caribbean woman'. She argues that Caribbean feminists need to produce theory based on the 'particularities of our experiences' (Barriteau 1994).

Interestingly, this takes us back to the Women and the Caribbean Project (WICP) which did not assume a particular theoretical stance, but which sought to extract precisely those particularities as a precursor to theory building (Massiah 1986). Out of that project came different insights into recommended future theory-building initiatives, for example, Christine Barrow's work on independence versus interdependence, Patricia Anderson's extraction of some of the components of the gender ideology, my own work on the concepts of visibility versus invisibility, and my recategorisation of the concept of work as defined by women themselves are some of the earlier efforts.

Since then, attention has shifted from women to gender and with that shift has come an urgent need for clarifying the concept of gender and gender related concepts. Mohammed and Barriteau have been the prime movers here, but it is Barriteau who has gone beyond definitions to the creation of new explanatory categories. First, she develops a feminist theory based on post-modernist thought for use in Caribbean social science research. Her theory accepts the diversity of Caribbean societies in respect of race, class and sexual identity, and examines ways in which women are affected by these differences, in different places and at different times. Basic to the theory is the distinction between the ideological and material relations of gender. The material dimension relates to how men and women gain access to and are allocated material and non-material resources within states and governments. The ideological dimension indicates how a society's ideas of masculinity and femininity are created and maintained. She argues that the ways in which masculinity and femininity are constructed reveal the belief systems about gender operating in the state and society.

Her distinction between the ideological and material relations of gender represents a critical step in the process of feminist theory building in the region. She has used this framework in her analysis of the root causes of violence against women and her examination of how women's economic relations are filtered through gender. It also marks a critical step in the process of taking Reddock's 'conscious action to change'. For it is this framework that has shaped the CARICOM Plan of Action to 2005 for mainstreaming gender into key CARICOM programmes in education, health, with particular reference to HIV/AIDS, and labour (CARICOM 2003).

While it would not be correct to affirm that a definitive Caribbean theory has emerged, it would be fair to say that the major contribution of the academics has been the clarification of the concept of gender and related terms such as gender relations, gender equity, gender justice, gender analysis, gender training, gender planning, gender mainstreaming. As used in feminist circles, gender is not about grammar; nor is it coterminous with sex. But it is about the social and power relationships between the two sexes. It therefore accommodates the need to examine the separate situations of women and men. This clarification encouraged a conceptual shift from a WID/WAD approach to research, programming and planning to a Gender and Development (GAD) approach. The advantage of this is that GAD allows a more holistic assessment of the gender situation in all of its manifestations and a more balanced approach to research, programming and planning. Significantly, it creates an opportunity for women and men to work together to facilitate a change in gender relations which can lead to the improvement of the lives of both women and men.

Unfortunately, the term is being used uncritically, particularly among males, male groups and policy-makers (male and female) concerned with possible consequences of the so-called male marginalisation. This has had severe effects on progress with furthering the strategic interests of women. So, for example, we have had cases of significant whittling away of the resources and influence of the national governmental mechanisms. Their titles have been changed from Departments/Bureaux of Women's Affairs to Departments/Bureaux of Gender Affairs without a commensurate change in mandates, policies, or resources. We have seen strong lobbies against legal reform which seeks to provide protection for women in such areas as family law, sexual harassment and citizenship – all because popular perception is that gender means women, that enough has been done for women, so now it is the turn of the men. This is not a view restricted to the general public. Much of this has to do with lack of understanding, or maybe deliberate misunderstanding, of a relatively complex concept which challenges the fundamental structuring of society.

Academic theorists have now turned their attention to this phenomenon and are currently engaged in a major programme on masculinities. We await the published material coming out of this programme.

Gender specialists are the persons who have acquired expertise in ensuring a gender perspective in programmes and projects and whose services are engaged by NGOs, national, regional and international organisations. Some function independently; others are based within the academy. Their basic training is usually in one of the social sciences which they supplement with special training in gender. In the vast majority of cases they are highly skilled and qualified, highly regarded and highly sought after. At the regional level, they have been instrumental in assisting CARICOM, UNIFEM and UNECLAC in preparations for some of the major UN Conferences, notably the International Conference on Population and Development (ICPD), the Small Island Developing States Conference (SIDS), and the Fourth World Conference for Women (FWCW). In addition, they were involved in the five-year reviews of the ICPD and the FWCW. At the national level, their work tends to be focussed on training to facilitate empowerment, project design to ensure a gender perspective and project/programme assessment. This group is thus also engaged in the production of material which expands our knowledge and understanding of the operation of gender in Caribbean societies.

In this regard, the seven priority issues identified by the region both pre- and post-Beijing and at Beijing+5 assume prominence. In the FWCW preparations five priority areas were identified – human rights with particular reference to violence against women, poverty, health in particular HIV/AIDS, leadership and decision-making, institutional development. Following Beijing, a sixth – education – was added. Following Beijing+5, a seventh – gender and trade – was added. This constitutes the group of seven priority areas which are of concern to the majority of governments of the region and the areas in which feminist scholars need to focus their attention if they wish to continue to be relevant.

Gender specialists have been applying a gender analysis in their research in each of these areas and then using their findings to work with relevant agencies at national, regional and international levels to create new approaches to addressing the particular problems which affect women. Several examples of this extension work exist. I draw attention to three – an independent consultant working in the area of institutional mechanisms, a university researcher working in education and a programme officer in an international agency working on violence against women.

In response to the growing concern about the weakening of national institutional arrangements for addressing women's affairs, the Commonwealth Secretariat sought to develop a mechanism which would strengthen those entities as well as extend the scope and impact of their work. They invited Audrey Ingram Roberts, an independent consultant, to join a panel of three to develop an innovative concept. Using her basic discipline, management studies, grafting on to it her feminist perspective and drawing on her experience of working with national and regional agencies throughout the region, she produced the concept of a Gender Management Strategy (GMS) (Commonwealth Secretariat 1999). This system was designed as a network of structures, processes and mechanisms designed to mainstream gender within an organisation. Among its objectives are the strengthening of the national machinery and the creation of an enabling environment of gender aware plans and programmes. Its major strategy is networking among key stakeholders. Its guiding principles are empowerment, integration and accountability.

The GMS was adopted by Commonwealth Ministers of Women's Affairs at a meeting in Port of Spain in 1996 and was piloted in Malta, Uganda, Jamaica, St Kitt's/Nevis, St Vincent and the Grenadines.

In the area of education, public concern with the low achievement of boys in the school system extended into concern with UWI results which reflected a higher percentage of women graduating each year. For several years now, the Chancellor has alluded to this during his graduation ceremony address at each campus. Professor Barbara Bailey, Head, Regional Unit, CGDS, was invited to prepare a project proposal to examine the causes of this phenomenon and to recommend steps for redressing the balance. As part of the project, she spearheaded the production of a Gender and Education Training Manual for use in teacher training colleges across the region (Bailey 2000). As part of the CARICOM Plan of Action to 2005, this manual will be used in a series of workshops for teacher educators and training at the in-service level. She is also working with CARICOM to produce a regional digest of Statistics on Caribbean Examination Council (CXC) Results to assist in the process of demystifying the discourse on male underachievement. She was a member of the CARICOM Gender Mainstreaming Task Force and is collaborating with CARICOM on the implementation of the education component of the programme. Here is an example of an academic feminist scholar pushing the boundaries of her research to find ways of influencing policy and programme change within a key regional institution.

In the area of Law, Roberta Clarke, Programme Officer, UNECLAC, has undertaken several initiatives in women's human rights, in particular in the area of violence against women. With UNIFEM she produced a critical assessment of the law in this regard, along with a compilation of agencies to which women can turn for help (Clarke 1998). With UNIFEM she has also worked with magistrates of the Eastern Caribbean towards a common strategy of dealing with such cases in their courts [UNIFEM, 2000]. In UNECLAC, she initiated a research project on the production of a protocol for data collection on violence against women for use by statistical authorities in the region (St Bernard 2001). She has undertaken an assessment of the implementation of Domestic Violence

Legislation in four countries in the region (ECLAC 2001). Building on that work, she has embarked on a research project which seeks to examine the relationship between gender socialisation and violence against women. Particular focus is being placed on the role of schools as socialisation agents and on state institutions which provide protective and social services. In collaboration with UNIFEM she is currently preparing an evaluation and assessment of the work on violence against women which has been undertaken in the region in the post-Beijing era. Here is an example of a gender specialist engaged in the production of knowledge in an area which the Caribbean had identified as its number one priority. She is continually trying to use that knowledge to enhance the programme of her own agency as well as to influence policy and programmes within the governments.

Each of these women has been actively involved in research and action from a feminist perspective for many years. They are excellent examples of the use of feminist scholarship to influence change in the structure of key institutions.

Activists are mostly based in NGOs, are often described as 'agitators', and are the ones who Peggy Antrobus has warned to 'be intellectually sound but be prepared to go out into the streets'.[1] CAFRA, which can be regarded as the umbrella of feminist organisations in the region, defines its role as follows:

> We are committed to understanding the relationship between the oppression of women and other forms of oppression in the society, and we are working actively for change (CAFRA Mission Statement).

Thus the role of activists was defined from early. There was the need for analysis and there was need for action. But the analysis had to come from the subjective experiences of women themselves, not from the objective analysis of statistical measurement of impact and monitoring and the like. The analysis had to be about what women's perspectives, ideas, advice on the major development issues, for example, globalisation, affecting their region. Clearly, that analysis had to be done either by the activists themselves or by those whose function is to research issues. So the link between activism and academia was apparent from the very creation of CAFRA.

Several examples of how this link has worked exist but I wish to highlight three.

The first example of this was in the preparation for the FWCW in Beijing. Discussions began with the naming of a core group – CARICOM, UNIFEM, UNECLAC, WAND and CAFRA – as the agencies charged with the responsibility for the preparations. The group developed a strategy using the principle of networking as the primary operational tool. The strategy was designed to assist the governments in the preparation of their reports, to develop a communication strategy around the 12 critical areas identified by the UN and to train delegates in conference diplomacy. A division of labour was worked out based on the principle of comparative advantage of the partners and the plan put into effect. The plan depended highly on collaboration and consensus building, involving governments, NGOs, members of the diplomatic community, universities and individual consultants. It embraced all language areas and all political ideologies of the region. It resulted in a highly cohesive presence at the conference and the inclusion of all Caribbean positions reflected in the final document.

Another example is the slogan of the UN Inter-Agency Women's Human Rights Campaign 'A Life Free of Violence: It is your Right'. The campaign was designed in response to the high levels of domestic and sexual violence against women and girls which was identified as a priority in both the pre- and post-Beijing periods. The Caribbean component, spearheaded by UNIFEM in collaboration with CAFRA, was designed and developed with a new set of partners – the Crisis Centres – and implemented in collaboration with women's NGOs and women's/gender bureaux. There were two components. A public education element consisting of a conference, schools poster competitions, schools elocution competitions, advertising slogans, campaign posters, commemoration postage stamps, radio panel discussions, newsletters, a regional tribunal on violence against women. The second component consisted of a police education programme in which a training manual was developed, a trainer of trainers workshop hosted and conducted under the leadership of CAFRA in police forces across the region. By the end of the campaign, public awareness of gender-based violence as a human rights issue was considerably heightened, some policy action occurred, including legislative reform, the creation of shelters, and the upgrading of the ability of police to address such situations. It was crystal clear that it was the concerted work of women, using the principle of comparative advantage, across the region which had been responsible. Further, it was equally clear that women were prepared to take a strong stand against not only the practice, but also against the institutional weaknesses in confronting it.

By the end of the nineties, as the region began its preparations for the Beijing+5 Assembly, there was a deeper understanding of gender and its relationship to the ongoing and emerging developmental issues of the region. There was also a better understanding of the ways in which it may have been possible to work with governments in the task of changing institutions and structures to enable the achievement of gender justice. Much of this was due to the unflagging efforts of a few progressive women's NGOs working in collaboration with WAND which provided the intellectual leadership for their activities up to the early half of the nineties.

The story of WAND and such NGOs as Red Thread, Sistren, Women Working for Social Progress, CAFRA and others is the story of women's NGO's producing material based on feminist insights and theorising for the purpose of advocacy and activism. This is the group which made the connection between macro-level frameworks and micro-level realities, which insisted on the need to address differences other than gender, and for promoting the goal of social and gender justice for all. Their strategy was built on the concept of 'critical analysis' of global trends, regional developments and the nature of development itself. By the end of the nineties, this group, with its feminist analysis and Caribbean perspective, had made an impact at the international level on each of the major development issues of the decade – environment, human rights, population and development, social development and women.

With the decline of WAND, the links between CGDS, CARICOM and UNIFEM became more critical. Under their joint leadership, there grew greater confidence in calling the governments to account, as is reflected in the book that we will be launching later. This, the third example, constitutes the next landmark in the progress of feminist scholarship in the region. The book, *Gender Equality in the Caribbean: Reality or Illusion,* was commissioned by CARICOM and UNIFEM and is co-edited by the CGDS.

This book contains seven papers, which not only analyse the situation in respect of specific thematic areas, but also chronicle the changes since Beijing, identify good practices, lessons learnt and critical gaps in achieving gender equality. The papers also examine the status of implementation of the Beijing Platform for Action (PfA) and identify indicators to monitor progress towards transforming gender inequities in the specific thematic areas. The book is unapologetic in its assertion that what is now needed is the political will to confront the prevailing gender ideology which fuels its institutions and structures and to make the necessary changes. Activists have therefore been provided with a powerful tool with which to further their activism.

The Feminist Environment

In this section, I offer the second aspect of my perspectives which relates to what I call the feminist environment. Here my concern is with the debate on the current state of feminism in the region. Feminist scholarship in the region has moved through several stages. The WICP marked the initial stage which was one of stock taking and making women visible. That was in the late seventies and early eighties. The second stage was during the latter half of the eighties when concern was focussed on contextual issues, particularly the impact of structural adjustment policies on women and the emergence of the male marginalisation thesis. Since then there has been the move from WID/WAD to GAD, as well as tentative moves towards theory building. This, the third and current stage, has mainly been the work of the nineties.

But the weakening of the women's movement in the post-Beijing era, the emergence of the male marginalisation thesis and the deterioration in certain indicators of women's situation occasioned by the growing economic difficulties being experienced in the region have given cause for pause. The Peggy Antrobus symposium devoted considerable time to assessing the status of the movement. Their conclusion was that there is need to move away from what was described as the 'crisis of confidence' and towards a strategy for re-mobilisation. That requires collective analysis of context, strategies, alliances and communication methods in order to arrive at a new vision and new goals. They call for a 'thinking core' for the revitalised movement. So, here as well, the need for intellectual clarity is recognised as being critical and the necessary cross fertilisation between academia and activism is highlighted.

In June of last year, the Cave Hill Unit of the CGDS sponsored a Workshop entitled 'Recentring Caribbean Feminisms'. In the keynote address of the opening ceremony, Eudine Barriteau issued 12 challenges facing future work. Among those challenges were included difficulties in confronting power and how it influences the choice of issues on which to work; confronting issues of race, ethnicity and class; addressing masculinities and the male marginalisation thesis; democratising the production of knowledge; and insufficient continuity between women leaders and the cadre of young new leaders (Barriteau 2002). Discussions at the workshop revealed a number of recurring concerns – difficulty in defining terms (feminist, feminism(s)), perceived disjuncture between academics and activists, an intergenerational divide and links with the state. No real solutions were offered, although a number of proposals were suggested for following up the initiative.

In her critique of feminist politics in the Caribbean, Andaiye identifies some of the weaknesses including the lack of inclusiveness, the failure to adequately address issues of race and class, the focus on analysis, limited advocacy and minimalist projects instead of emphasising the struggle against poverty. She has sounded a clear warning of the need to identify the kind of world in which we want to live, 'not in the language of isms', and rethink and revise past approaches. She proposes a global campaign 'led and waged in the interests of the poorest women, who bear the greatest burden of unwaged and low-waged caring labour which is the foundation of all economies' (Andaiye 2002).

In a recent keynote address to the opening of a summer institute on gender at the Cave Hill campus last month, I identified ten practical leadership lessons learnt which future leaders might wish to apply to the next stage. These ranged from knowing your context and drawing strength from it, through valuing the work of our predecessors, anticipating possible new issues and maintaining the vision of gender justice, to recognising the power of strong and creative leadership (Massiah 2003). To these, Peggy Antrobus has added three others – trust your own experience; always link the national, regional and international; and feminist theory and conscious raising are key.

In effect, the current status of the feminist environment in the region is one of pausing to reflect, assess, revisit and revise before proceeding to the next stage. It is interesting that the recent reflections, although occurring in different places and involving different participants, do contain some common elements including the critical ones of analysis and the relations between academic and activist. And so the issue of what is the next stage, who and how this will be conducted becomes important for feminist scholars.

It seems to me that, despite the commendable progress made in terms of knowledge, skills at advocacy and collective action, there remains a sense in which not enough impact is evident at the policy and programme level of the state. Part of the difficulty seems to be continued uncertainty about some basic concepts, for example, the movement – is there one? What is it? A women's movement? A feminist movement? How well established is it? Does it touch women throughout the region? If so, how? If not, why not? These questions were being raised in the seventies, so why are we still debating them? There continues to be the confusion over the term gender and gender related concepts. Then there are such phrases as feminist politics, feminist methodology, and feminist bureaucracy. These are terms which feminist scholars discuss among themselves, and perhaps understand among themselves. But if the objective of their work is to achieve social transformation and gender justice, then these terms have to be clearly and creatively expressed and explained in fora with decision-makers in terms which they understand. Those explanations also have to resonate with the issues with which decision-makers are struggling. That is the major task which feminist scholars face if they wish to activate that political will to confront the gender ideologies, which obstruct the achievement of gender justice, of which Eudine Barriteau speaks so eloquently.

The Influence of the United Nations

The third aspect of my perspectives relates to the link between the national, regional and international, in particular to the influence of the

United Nations (UN) system in fostering those links. Peggy Antrobus reminds that it was a 'particular kind of politics, feminist politics, [which] informed the establishment and shaped the programmes within institutions, such as the UN...' (Antrobus 2000). Indeed it was the series of world conferences on women beginning in 1975, which gave global prominence to the link between women and the major issues of equality, development and peace. In a series of thematic world conferences beginning in 1990, it became clear that, regardless of the particular focus, women were located at the epicentre of the quest for a just and sustainable development.

The efforts of the UN to promote and protect the human rights of women have taken place in four stages. The first, 1945-62, was concerned with securing women's legal equality. This period during which both the UN Charter and the Universal Declaration of Human Rights affirmed equal rights for men and women. It was also the period during which the Commission on the Status of Women (CSW) was created. During these years, women's organisations in the Caribbean were concerned primarily with charitable works, organising, maintaining contact with international developments and, towards the end of the period, ensuring recognition of women's rights in the proposed Federal arrangements. But although many of the leaders displayed a feminist consciousness, feminist scholarship as defined today had not yet appeared.

The second period, 1963-75, focused on women's development needs as expressed through the economic and social realities of their lives. In the Caribbean, this was the era marked by links with the New Left and social movements, and with the establishment of bureaux of women's affairs in two territories – Jamaica and Guyana – in response to urgings from the UN. The creation of the CSW had confirmed for Caribbean women that the issues of concern to them were also being discussed at the highest level of the UN. By the end of the period many countries had attained political independence, had joined the UN and were participating in its democratisation. They contributed to the discussion reviewing the first development decade and offered suggestions for the second. Some pioneer feminist scholars of the region contributed to the discussions. Lucille Mair, who was the Caribbean representative on the

Commission on Social Development, had pushed for greater consideration of women's issues in its deliberations. Gloria Scott gave to the world the phrase 'the full integration of women in the development effort', when she suggested an amendment to the resolution on the International Development Strategy for the Second Development Decade. This allowed women to introduce the notion of equity, which at that time was not on the development agenda. This period ended with the creation of International Women's Year in 1975 and the hosting of the first World Conference for Women in Mexico City.

The third period, 1976-85, was designated the International Decade for Women and it recognised that women were not only beneficiaries of, but also contributors to, the development process. This period witnessed the establishment, in 1979, of the Convention for the Elimination of all Forms of Discrimination against Women (CEDAW), the international Bill of Rights for women. Caribbean feminists have been members of the CEDAW committee from its inception. The second, the Mid-Decade Conference, was held in Copenhagen in 1980. The period ended with the Third World Conference for Women in Nairobi in 1985. The Nairobi conference produced the Forward Looking Strategies, detailing the constraints which continued to prevent the achievement of equality and setting out a framework for action requiring women's involvement at all levels from decision-making to implementation. For the first time, feminist scholars were invited to work with CARICOM to coordinate details on various national issues and to design a united CARICOM approach to negotiation at the conference.

The fourth period, 1986-2000, marks the period of the shift from WID/WAD to GAD and of efforts to mainstream gender. Related to the shift from WID/WAD to GAD has been the shift from integration to empowerment of women. The former was based on the acceptance of the basic status quo, the latter on a questioning of the unequal relations between men and women, government and people, developed and developing countries. Empowerment is about providing women with the skills, knowledge and ability to use their understanding of those unequal relations to improve both their practical and strategic interests. This approach was heavily promoted at the Fourth World Conference for Women (FWCW) which was held in Beijing in 1995 and a Special Session of the General Assembly (familiarly called Beijing+5) held in 2000 to assess progress since the FWCW.

Each of the three groups of Caribbean feminist scholars played a key role in the preparations of both the FWCW and Beijing+5. It was their analyses which facilitated a regional position at the two gatherings, their understanding of the conference politics which catapulted the Caribbean into a leadership position, their advice which governments, both Caribbean and non-Caribbean, sought. So that, insofar as their impact on policy can be gauged from their influence on governments at global conferences, it may be said that feminist scholars are indeed using their consciousness to promote change.

Since Beijing+5, the UN has become intensely interested in the measurement of impact, the setting of targets and the monitoring of progress towards preset time-bound goals. The Millennium Development Goals, adopted by the UN member states in 2000, incorporates commitments made at each of the various World Conferences and reaffirmed at the five-year reviews. Among the eight goals set is one concerned with women's empowerment and gender equality which the Millennium Declaration identifies not only as a goal in its own right, but as an essential component in achieving all of the other goals. The question of whether the targets and proposed indicators are relevant to the Caribbean or whether the particular indicators are adequate to measure the Caribbean reality opens up a whole new space for Caribbean feminist scholars.

Vision

I turn now to my vision for the future. A review of the work of feminists in the post-Beijing era suggests that there has been a growing sense of confidence as the three groups of scholars have begun to come to grips with the theoretical difficulties of both gender and women's gendered concerns and issues.

They have learnt how to work effectively together at several levels, in some cases creating strong bonds of unity and cooperation across the region. But there remains a sense in which there is need for closer collaboration. They have learnt how to function at the international level. But there is a sense in which there is need to widen the group which is so engaged. They have begun to understand better the implications of some of the wider issues of the women at the individual and community level. But there is a sense that very difficult issues remain to be addressed. They have begun to see some positive results of the work in which they are engaged on the lives of women.

However, there is a real sense that the situation of women may not have changed very much. Foremost among these is the fact that the contradictory situation of Caribbean women noted in the WICP as far back as 1986, continues today. The United Nations Development Programme (UNDP) has devised two measures, the Gender Development Index (GDI) and the Gender Empowerment Measure (GEM) to indicate the level and extent of gender disparities. In the Caribbean, GDIs of over 0.50 suggest that women may not be doing too badly when compared to men in terms of achievement in levels of income, health and education. But the GEM shows that disparities between men and women in participation and access to professional opportunities, political decision-making and earning power are generally wide and widening. So how did this contradictory situation come about? This perception that all is well, is against the reality that all may not be so well at all.[2] Have Caribbean women confronted this contradiction? If not, how should they? Has the feminist scholarship of the region enabled women to understand their situation and to create strategies to deal with it? If they have adopted strategies what are they, how will they affect the next generation of children and with what impact on the wider society?

These are some of the unanswered questions and they go beyond simply meeting practical needs or addressing the material relations of gender.

The next wave will, I believe, be forced to concentrate on the strategic gender needs of women, or the ideological relations of gender. That is to say what can be done to change the attitudes of those in positions of power to make them willing to confront the prevailing gender ideology and to change the structures and institutions which maintain that ideology. This will be the most difficult phase of all. For as Audrey Ingram Roberts puts it:

> Practical gains are easily swept away and strategic interests take time and are not easily met because they challenge the very core of social systems as we know them (Ingram Roberts 1991).

But even as this is being promoted, it is important to acknowledge the place of the study of masculinities and the situation of men. It is only with this knowledge that a balanced view of the gender situation is possible, that a sensitive environment for dialogue between men and women can be created and that conditions for mutual agreement on changes in gender relations can be achieved. Only then can true gender justice prevail. It is to their credit that the CGDS has introduced this as a valid topic for teaching and research in the academic curricula.

As part of the new analysis, I would wish to see a critical assessment of the impact of feminist scholarship on society generally and young women in particular. Too often now are we seeing women, of all ages, misusing the tenets of feminism to exhibit exactly the type of behaviour which the movement had criticised among men. Too often are we seeing what UWI Vice Chancellor Nettleford describes as 'the coarseness of sensibility which has crept into society' reflected in young women. We see public displays of behaviour which are demeaning to women, disrespectful to their elders, degrading to their peers and destructive of their youth. What inspires them to such behaviour? Whatever it is, there can be no denying that one result is a slow and continuous undermining of the achievements of decades of feminist work. There is an urgent need to find out what part, if any, of the message of feminist scholarship has served to encourage this. We need to find out who is hearing the messages, how they are being used, whether new messages need to be developed. For example, what is there in the existing literature to encourage women to make a better environment for themselves and their children? How to get men to understand that by preying on young women they are helping to create the conditions for losing the next generation? How to get young women to accept that life is more than about getting as much as possible from men?

These issues are part of the everyday reality of the lives of young women who are saying in increasing numbers and in an endless variety of ways that 'your issues are not ours'. In other words, while it is important to be analytical about the larger issues of theoretical constructs, institutional structures, regional development imperatives and the international development agenda, it is equally important to understand the attitudes and behaviours of our young women. And that is a task for each of the three groups of feminist scholars.

Although I have presented cases of links between the academy, activists and policy, I believe that not enough people are involved in that process; nor is enough use being made of feminist scholarship in policy making, programme development and implementation. Part of the problem is the artificial distinction made between academics and activists. Thus, even when activists are themselves engaged in research and analysis using their academic training, they refuse to admit that they are in fact being academics. And when academics use their own material as the basis for policy advice, they are reluctant to admit that they are, in fact, being activists. Another aspect of the problem is the limited involvement of policy makers in the gender discourse. There is an attitudinal aspect to this born of hundreds of years of adherence to patriarchal values. But there is also the reality of the development paradigm into which the region is tied and the resultant dependence on external agencies, policy prescriptions and development aid. There is much to be learnt by feminist scholars about how policy is made and about how and at what points it may be possible to exercise influence.

Another issue of the future has to do with the regional development thrust towards new instruments of integration. There is an urgency to these initiatives as the region races against time to ready itself for the establishment of the Free Trade Area of the Americas (FTAA) scheduled for 2005. This, together with the struggles with the World Trade Organization and other mechanisms of globalisation, makes it imperative for feminist scholars to be a voice for women, bringing a feminist perspective to the ongoing discourse and to the relevant negotiations. Although research and some advocacy is being done in this area, notably by Mariana Williams and DAWN Caribbean, there would not appear to be that level of collaboration between the academy, gender specialists, activists and CARICOM which obtains in other priority areas of the region. This needs to be corrected.

My vision is to see a strengthened network of links between the academy, the government and the NGO community across the region working together in a number of areas:

- A critical review of what has been achieved collaboratively, what are the lessons to be learnt and shared and how can those lessons be applied to assess where we are, determine where we would like to go and chart how we could get there.

- An institutionalised presence in the form of a Women's Commission located within CARICOM and entitled to a place on all of the structures created by that entity to take forward the development agenda of the region, for example, CSME, RNM, CARICOM Programme of Action etc. Perhaps the Task Force on Gender Mainstreaming could be the nucleus of a 'standing' not 'resident' entity. But whatever form it takes, there must be a mechanism within CARICOM charged with the responsibility of ensuring a gender perspective in all of the major regional programmes which the CARICOM is promoting on behalf of governments of the region.

- At the national level a mechanism with specialist planning capability which can support the work of the Gender Bureau throughout the public service. The Planning Institute of Jamaica (PIOJ) represents a kind of prototype which provides assistance to the bureau through gender training, checklists, indicators, policy analysis which takes into account the changing social and economic scenario of each country and how gender fits.[3] This allows involvement of the political directorate in the dialogue.

- More research focussed on the priority areas of the Caribbean and more creative strategies to use that research to build awareness among policy makers and to encourage genuine efforts at change. Apart from the seven priority areas there are a number of other issues in our societies which we need to understand. Among the positive features are the increasing importance of sports and entertainment in the lives of young people and the impact of that on the economies.

Among the several negative features in Caribbean societies are rising crime and violence, the HIV/AIDS pandemic, and increasing involvement in the illegal drug trade. We need to know how gender fits into all of this and how policy initiatives in these areas could be enhanced by a gender perspective.

- More work with the statistical authorities to design indicators of accountability in critical areas. But to be useful, these indicators must be developed in collaboration with gender specialists and end-users.
- More psychosocial analysis on the impact of a gender approach to development on the individual and the wider community. This is in effect a kind of self-assessment. We need to know what is right and what may be wrong about what we are doing.

My vision is based, not merely on the hope of reaching the goal of social and gender justice, but on my belief in the creativity and determination of Caribbean women.

Possibilities

In deference to the tenth anniversary of CGDS, which this conference celebrates, I shall confine my comments on possibilities to those things which the centre might be minded to do as we move to Beijing +10. I believe that the centre has been a critical partner in the regional efforts to promote and protect the rights of women and to educate on the relevance of gender to the development agenda. This has been an important contribution since it shows that the centre, as part of a regional university which is committed to collective action with critical partners, understands the needs and is willing to work along with its partners. But I believe that there is a stronger and expanded role for the centre which is to take the lead in providing academic vitality and authority to the collective. This may be achieved through the three areas in which the CGDS has been involved: research, advocacy and technical assistance. In each of these areas it is possible to identify a number of actions which may be taken. But in seeking to identify those a few questions need to be posed.

The work of the centre has proceeded, understandably, according to the interests and skills of the leadership of each unit. However, there are some areas which have remained relatively untouched even though they are of critical importance to the region. At the political level, the current regional focus is on regional integration with particular reference to the Common Market and Single Economy (CSME) and the Caribbean Court of Justice (CCJ). Yet, although gender is an important component of both initiatives, there is no work in either area coming out of the centre, as far as I am aware. Similarly, there have been scattered efforts to produce social statistics for the region, including a long-standing and uncompleted effort to produce a gender-indicators publication. Yet there has not been an initiative from the centre to identify itself as the locus of statistical and other types of information about women and gender. I ask, further, why is it that greater attention has not been paid to others of the seven priority areas besides education and to a lesser extent leadership? Why is globalisation not on the agenda? Nor HIV/AIDS? And why has a human rights approach been limited only to legal issues?

In other words, I am suggesting that now may be an appropriate time for the centre to review and redesign its programme so that it may speak more directly to the concerns of the region. This is not to say that what it is doing is not relevant, far from it. It is merely seeking a broader base for the programme and a strategy for the centre to know and show the way forward. Against this background I would wish to suggest the following:

Research

- Ongoing work should continue on the issues of education and transformational leadership.
- Establish projects on poverty, globalisation and trade liberalisation. These should be done in collaboration with DAWN Caribbean.
- Work should be initiated on gender and HIV/AIDS. This should be done in collaboration with the Caribbean Epidemiological Centre (CAREC) and should feed into the Pan Caribbean HIV/AIDS Programme in CARICOM.
- A major research programme on male issues should be undertaken as a follow up to the masculinities symposium.

Advocacy
- Work with CARICOM and NGOs and international agencies to develop and implement a regional communication programme of public education on gender and development. A key component should be designed to address the male marginalisation thesis. This should be a major programme designed to capture public imagination and secure community support.
- Collaborate with CAFRA and NGOs to develop programmes to attract young women, to increase economic and legal literacy at the community level and to utilise material from thematic research to strengthen NGO action programmes.

Technical Assistance
- Use the manual produced under the Regional Gender Training Programme to assist with institutional strengthening of Women's/Gender Bureaux.
- Recommend and assist with review and assessment of CARICOM Women's Desk and programme for mainstreaming gender in programmes of CARICOM Secretariat.
- Develop and implement strategy for participating in major meetings of CARICOM Ministers and for following up on decisions taken in respect of gender matters.

The goal of these proposals is to strengthen and expand the ability of the centre to work with its partners to reverse the apparent state retreat from policies and programmes centred on women. The strategy is to find alternative ways of working through the existing structures, without trying to usurp the functions of the partners. It calls for creativity, tact, determination and a genuine belief that feminist scholarship is not for bookshelves, but for committed action.

Management of a strategy for this purpose requires the kind of transformational leadership being promoted by the centre itself in one of its programmes. Now is the time for the centre to demonstrate that leadership. But the centre is not an autonomous unit. It is part of a regional university which prides itself on its ability to respond to the needs of its constituents. I end with a call to the university to renew its commitment to the centre as it embarks on the next stage of its development.

Notes

1. Comments made during symposium in her honour, 2000. This group equates to the 'political feminists' identified by Addelson and Potter as individuals who are members of an activist women's organisation.
2. Incidentally, it might be an apt reminder that even as the WICP had identified this contradictory situation as an inherent aspect of the gender situation of the region it had recommended 'the urgent need for a theoretical perspective for the study of women'.
3. PIOJ, in collaboration with UNDP, spearheaded the research and publication for the first Human Development Report Jamaica in 2000.

References

Addelson, Kathryn Payne and Elizabeth Potter. 1991. Making Knowledge. In *(En)Gendering Knowledge: Feminists in Academe*, eds. J.E. Haitman and E. Messer-Davidow. Knoxville: University of Tennessee Press.

Antrobus, Peggy. 2000. The Rise and Fall of Feminist Politics in the Caribbean Women's Movement, 1975-1995, The Lucille Mathurin Mair Lecture 2000, Centre for Gender and Development Studies, University of the West Indies.

Andaiye. 2002. The Angle You Look From Determines What You See: Towards a Critique of Feminist Politics in the Caribbean, The Lucille Mathurin Mair Lecture 2002, Centre for Gender and Development Studies, University of the West Indies.

Bailey, Barbara ed. 2000. *Gender Issues In Caribbean Education*. Jamaica: CARICOM Secretariat in association with the Centre for Gender and Development Studies, Regional Coordinating Unit, University of the West Indies.

Barriteau, Eudine. 1992. The Construct of a Postmodernist Feminist Theory for Caribbean Social Science Research, *Social and Economic Studies* 41, no. 2:1-43.

——————. 1995. Socialist Feminist Theory and Caribbean Women: Transcending Dualisms, *Social and Economic Studies* 44, nos. 2 & 3:25-63.

——————. 1998. Liberal Ideologies and Contradictions in Caribbean Gender Systems. In *Caribbean Portraits: Essays on Gender Ideologies and Identities*, ed. C. Barrow, 436-456. Kingston: Ian Randle Publishers in association with the Centre for Gender and Development Studies, Cave Hill, Barbados.

———. 2001. *The Political Economy of Gender in the Twentieth Century Caribbean*. Hampshire, UK: Palgrave.

———. 2002. Issues and Challenges of Caribbean Feminisms, Keynote Address at Inaugural Workshop on Recentreing Caribbean Feminisms, Centre for Gender and Development Studies, University of the West Indies, Cave Hill, Barbados.

———. 2003. 'Beyond a Backlash: the Frontal Assault on Containing Caribbean Women in the Decade of the 1990s'. In *Gender Equality in the Caribbean: Reality or Illusion*. Kingston: Ian Randle Publishers in association with the Caribbean Community, the United Nations Development for Women and the Centre for Gender and Development Studies, University of the West Indies, Mona, Jamaica.

———, ed. In Press. *Confronting Power, Theorising Gender: Interdisciplinary Perspectives in the Caribbean*.

Barrow, Christine ed. 1998. *Caribbean Portraits: Essays on Gender Ideologies and Identities*, ed. C. Barrow. Kingston: Ian Randle Publishers in association with the Centre for Gender and Development Studies, Cave Hill, Barbados.

———. 1998A. Introduction. In *Caribbean Portraits: Essays on Gender Ideologies and Identities*, ed. C. Barrow. Kingston: Ian Randle Publishers in association with the Centre for Gender and Development Studies Cave Hill, Barbados.

Caribbean Community Secretariat. 2003. Plan of Action to 2005: Framework for Mainstreaming Gender into Key CARICOM Programmes. Prepared by Andaiye. Georgetown: CARICOM.

Clarke, Roberta. 1998. *Violence Against Women in the Caribbean: State and Non-State Responses*. New York: UNIFEM in collaboration with the Inter-American Commission of Women.

Commonwealth Secretariat. 1999. *Gender Management System Handbook*. London: Commonwealth Secretariat.

Economic Commission for Latin America and the Caribbean. 2001. *An Evaluation Study of the Implementation of Domestic Violence Legislation: Antigua and Barbuda, St Kitt's and Nevis, St Lucia and St Vincent and the Grenadines*. Port of Spain: ECLAC, Subregional Headquarters for the Caribbean.

Leo-Rhynie, Elsa. 2002. Women and Development Studies. In *Gendered Realities: Essays in Caribbean Feminist Thought*, ed. P. Mohammed. Mona: University of the West Indies Press.

Leo-Rhynie, Elsa, Barbara Bailey and Christine Barrow, eds. 1997. *Gender: A Caribbean Multi-disciplinary Perspective*. Kingston: Ian Randle Publishers in association with The Centre for Gender and Development Studies, University of the West Indies and The Commonwealth of Learning.

Massiah, Joycelin, ed. 1986. *Women in the Caribbean*. Special Issue of *Social and Economic Studies* 35: 2&3.

———. 1998. On the Brink of the New Millennium: Are Caribbean Women Prepared? The Inaugural Lucille Mathurin Mair Lecture. Centre for Gender and Development Studies, University of the West Indies.

———————. 2003. Keynote Address at Opening Ceremony of The Summer Institute in Gender and Development, Centre for Gender and Development Studies, University of the West Indies, Cave Hill, Barbados.

Mohammed, Patricia. 1994. Nuancing the Feminist Discourse in the Caribbean, *Social and Economic Studies* 43:3.

———————. 1998. Towards Indigenous Feminist Theorising in the Caribbean. *Feminist Review* 59:6.

———————. 2000. The Future of Feminism in the Caribbean. *Feminist Review* 64:116.

——————— ed. 2002. *Gendered Realities: Essays in Caribbean Feminist Thought*. Mona: University of the West Indies Press.

Reddock, Rhoda. 1988. Feminism and Feminist Thought: Consensus and Controversy. In *Gender in Caribbean Development*, eds. Patricia Mohammed and Catherine Shepherd. Jamaica, Trinidad and Tobago, Barbados: The University of the West Indies, Women and Development Studies Project.

———————. 1998. Feature Address to the HIVOS/UNIFEM Meeting of Women's Organisations, organised by the Caribbean Association for Feminist Research and Action.

Roberts Ingram, Audrey. 1991. Keynote presentation for the Tenth Anniversary Celebrations of the Women's Affairs Unit, Ministry of Youth, Sports & Community Affairs, Nassau, Bahamas.

St Bernard, Godfrey. 2001. Data Collection System for Domestic Violence. Submitted to the Economic Commission for Latin America and the Caribbean, Port of Spain.

United Nations Development Fund for Women. 2000. Report of Round Table on Gender and Human Rights for Magistrates of the Judiciary of Barbados and the Organisation of Eastern Caribbean States. Barbados: UNIFEM.

2 | PEGGY ANTROBUS

Feminist Activism
The CARICOM Experience

Abstract

The paper defines Caribbean feminism, its goals and objectives, and considers the impact of feminist activism on CARICOM society over the past 30 years. It begins with an account of the context in which feminist activism emerged in CARICOM countries in the 1970s, and tracks how this kind of politics had first to be legitimised within a framework of governance that was at least open to its contestations. The paper focuses on the author's own experience to consider feminism's influence on women in leadership positions and how this changed their politics and practice. From there, it seeks to address the ways in which this leadership sought to influence the politics and programmes of women's organisations and other NGOs, government policy, key institutions and, more broadly, societal attitudes to women, taking account of the resistance encountered and support received along the way.

Antrobus argues that feminist activism working from within and outside various institutions – among them political parties, the bureaucracy, the educational system (including the university), the church, legal system, trade unions, media and women's organisations – did indeed achieve some of its objectives, although not always in ways that were favourable to its cause.

This paper recognises feminism as an ongoing dialogic process of confrontations, resolution, contradictions, and contestation that nevertheless has the capacity to transform relationships and systems that are oppressive, and attempts to draw out the implications for feminist activism in the changing context of today.

1. Introduction

I want to start by thanking the Centre for Gender and Development Studies at Mona for inviting me to speak on this topic. It is one that is dear to my heart. While the line between feminist activism and scholarship may seem too tenuous for the distinction to be made, I think it is worth trying to appreciate their boundaries if the two spheres of activity are to contribute to a common project of deepening our understanding of Caribbean women and society; and for laying the basis for the social and economic change needed to improve the lives of the majority of people in this region.

Of course, the distinction is not always an easy one, and the word 'feminist' itself carries the burden of being associated with a particular type of feminism that is considered alien and alienating to many Caribbean women. Media representations of the word as 'man-hating', 'anti-family' and more, associated with white, middle-class, North American or European women, have loaded the word with negativity, causing many women to distance themselves from it. Indeed, for many women in the Caribbean, and elsewhere, the word 'feminism' is problematic. I was one of those women. As Advisor on Women's Affairs to the Government of Jamaica, I was at pains to distinguish my work on 'integrating women in development' from the activism of North American feminism. I recall an experience in 1978 when attending a UN meeting on 'Feminist Ideologies and Structures in the First Half of the Decade'[1]. Not wanting to use the word 'feminist', I told people that I would be attending a meeting on 'National Machinery[2] for the Integration of Women in Development'. Ironically, it was at this meeting that I came to understand the meaning, and relevance, of feminism for my work[3]. After that I started using the word as often as I could, always careful to define its meaning for me.

For me, feminism is 'a consciousness of all the sources of women's oppression and a commitment to challenge and change these forces in solidarity of other women'. There are many feminisms. Distinctions have been made between liberal, socialist, Marxist and radical feminism, depending on the definition of the primary source of oppression (Jagger and Rothenberg 1984). However, for the Caribbean, as in the case of other Third World countries, these sources include the social relations of class, race, ethnicity, colonial and neo-colonial relations in which those of gender are embedded. Patricia Mohammed and Hilary Beckles emphasise this in their chapters in the Special Issue of *Feminist Review* (1998). According to Mohammed,

> Caribbean feminism cannot be viewed as a linear narrative about women's struggles for gender equality, but a movement which has continually intersected with the politics of identity in the region (Mohammed 1998, 2).

Hilary Beckles' contribution to this volume (pp. 34-56), 'Historicising Slavery in West Indian Feminisms' reinforces this by describing how the

> political fracturing of feminine identity during (slavery) defined the distances in ethnic and class position between women of different groups, thus creating the hurdles to be crossed in the post-slavery rapprochement of the feminist project (Mohammed 1998, 2).

The network of Third World feminists, DAWN, puts it this way:

> Feminism cannot be monolithic in its issues, goals and strategies, since it constitutes the political expression of the concerns and interests of women from different regions, classes, nationalities, and ethnic backgrounds. While gender subordination has universal elements, feminism cannot be based on a rigid concept of universality that negates the wide variation of women's experience. There is and must be a diversity of feminisms, responsive to the different needs and concerns of different women, and defined by them for themselves. This diversity builds on a common opposition to gender oppression and hierarchy, but this is only the first step in articulating and acting upon a political agenda.
>
> This heterogeneity gives feminism its dynamism and makes it the most potentially powerful challenge to the status quo. It allows the struggle against subordination to be waged in all arenas – from relations in the home to relations between nations – and it necessitates substantial change in cultural, economic, and political formations (Dawn 1987, 18-19).

I define this kind of feminism as 'critical Third World Feminism', and it is with this understanding that I make my presentation.

2. Feminism in the Caribbean

While a great deal can be said about differences and diversity within and between women in their organisations and movements, one thing unites all elements and that is a common opposition to women's subordination;

a common vision. This comes from feminism as a historical process manifested in many different and varied agendas depending on circumstances in which women's struggles arise. Feminist politics derives from feminist analysis, which starts with an analysis of patriarchy. Although patriarchy is mediated by race, class and culture,[4] it is nevertheless a system that privileges the practices, attributes and values associated with patriarchal concepts of masculinity while devaluing those associated with women's social role – caring, compassion, cooperation, gentleness. Patriarchy, reflected through all the structures and institutions of our world, is a system that glorifies domination, control, violence, competitiveness and greed. It dehumanises men as much as it denies women's agency. Feminist analysis recognises the role of ideology in the construction of definitions of the male and female, how the ideology of patriarchy is dispersed and reproduced through a gender ideology that lies at the centre of human socialisation, providing the framework for hierarchy, authoritarianism and dichotomies that we name 'sexism'.

In her editorial, 'Rethinking Caribbean Difference', to the Special Issue of *Feminist Review*, Patricia Mohammed sees feminism as 'an expression of sexual equality' (Mohammed 1998, 8). In regard to feminist activism, however, I want to make a distinction between feminism as an expression of sexual equality and feminism as a critical politics that goes beyond sexual equality, using critical Third World feminist theory to question the whole system of production and reproduction: many women question the value of 'equality' within a system that is fundamentally exploitative of social groups on the basis of class, race and nationality. A development process that shrinks and poisons the pie for poor people, and then leaves women scrambling for a larger relative share, is not in women's interests. (Sen and Grown 1987, 20).

Feminist theory is key to this analysis. When activism is grounded in this theory, it announces its political and philosophical origins most clearly as feminist. Feminist analysis grounded in critical third world feminist theory seeks to challenge and change structures of women's subordination, which are grounded in modes of production and reproduction that are both capitalist and patriarchal (Mies 1986).

The distinction between feminism as an expression of sexual equality and feminism as a critical politics relates to the goal of the analysis as well as to the intended action. Is the goal to challenge and change gender inequality in and of itself, or is it to use this as a point of departure, a first step, a necessary requirement – the assertion of women's agency – toward challenging and changing a variety of systems and structures that place women's lives in jeopardy? Is the action directed toward individual redress, or to the 'community' affected? My understanding of activism is that it is action taken on behalf of the community of women – battered women, women likely to be affected by structural adjustment policies, trade liberalisation, HIV/AIDS, etc.

In this chapter I try to show how feminist activism from the 1970s attempted to confront and cross the distances and hurdles described by Beckles. But in addition to these historical factors there are two others that need to be considered as we examine feminist activism in Caribbean society. One is context, the other the internal process of feminist conscientisation[5]. These interact with each other to produce the particular contribution of feminist activism to society in any period of time.

Context plays an important role in our attempts to understand the ways in which feminism is manifested in the Caribbean. The context in which first wave feminism emerged in this region was shaped by nationalism and independence struggles, while that of second wave feminism was undoubtedly influenced by the greater awareness of the international struggles, both those related specifically to women's role and status[6] as well as those related to global crises – economic, social, political and environmental – generated by the crisis in capitalist accumulation. I will address these contexts as I describe the activism manifested in those periods, but first I want to say something about the internal process of feminist *conscientisation*.

3. The Internal Process of Feminist *Conscientisation*

Women come to feminism from different paths – personal, professional and political. Many of the women involved in women's organisations or movements were influenced by leftist, nationalist or identity politics[7] and discovered their own marginalisation, *as women*, within the processes of these larger struggles. Others began the journey to feminism through personal experiences; some through discrimination in their work places. In all these situations, the experience can be the beginning of consciousness of what it is to be female in a society that privileges males (patriarchal society). Feminist theory enables these women to analyse the factors that create the situation, not just in terms of individual behaviour but also in terms of structures and relationships of power. This understanding (consciousness) of patriarchal power transforms feelings of alienation into feminist activism as part of a *political* struggle for gender equity and equality. But for third world women, an analysis of the sources of women's oppression includes an analysis of race, class and nationality (colonialism) as well, and feminist 'consciousness-raising' becomes a process of *conscientisation*. These varied experiences highlight the complexity of women's struggles in places like the Caribbean.

Another characteristic of many of those exposed to feminism is the process of personal transformation they undergo as they become aware of gender subordination. At the same time, this essentially individualistic experience seems to engender a connection to the wider universe of injustice in a way that leads to a better understanding, *experientially*, of the link between different forms of oppression, that can build lifelong commitment to the struggle against injustices of all kinds.

Feminist consciousness can be transformational: it enables women to comprehend the barriers of class, race and ethnicity, and nationality in the search for a gender identity that can be the basis of solidarity, despite these barriers. My own experience attests to this: for me, feminism has been transformational – personally, professionally and politically. The consciousness of sexism and sexist oppression is the essence of feminist activism and it is this that energises women to take action on their own behalf and on that of other women, whether or not the word 'feminist' is used.

4. External Processes: The Context of Feminist Activism in the Caribbean

4.1. The First Wave (1940s–60s)

Nationalist and independence struggles of the first part of the twentieth century provided the context within which first wave feminism emerged in this region. This feminism was in the tradition of liberal feminism but set in the context of struggles around nationalism and independence – basically struggles for Caribbean identity. Its emphasis was on welfare, family and community: improvements in areas of traditional female roles. While some might argue that this served to reinforce traditional gender relations, I would say that this was the starting point required by the situation of widespread marginalisation and exclusion of the larger community of men and women occasioned by slavery and colonialism. However, in the exercise of leadership, women had to claim equality.

In representations of identity, the focus was on the experiences of the 'creoles', the black/white/coloured populations without any reference to that of the Indo-Caribbean people who constituted a significant proportion of the populations of Trinidad and Tobago and Guyana (Baksh-Soodeen 1989, 78). Indeed, it would be more accurate to say that issues of identity were claimed for the Afro-Caribbean experience and the need to rebuild families and communities that had been shattered by the brutality of slavery. Nevertheless, this focus, along with the relative separation of Indo-Caribbean women within their families and communities in Trinidad and Tobago and Guyana, and the prejudices that kept the groups apart, suggests that the forms of involvement by women from this social group in the organising that took place in the first wave of feminist activism was neither visible nor appreciated within CARICOM.[8]

Although they did not name themselves 'feminist', the women who worked to promote these changes as part of nationalistic struggles, acted out of a consciousness of themselves as women within societies that sought to circumscribe their lives, and they acted in solidarity with other women to challenge male privilege and power where this was present. In other words, in their politics and behaviour, it is clear that many of these women can be defined as 'feminist'. Building on the legacies of the rebel women described by Lucille Mathurin Mair, women who used a variety of means for securing their freedom and that of their children, women like Amy Garvey within the Universal Negro Improvement Association (UNIA) and Elma Francois with the Negro Welfare Association (NWA), worked to organise women to play a more active role in organisations intended for the benefit of the disenfranchised.

Honor Ford-Smith notes the close connection between the anti-colonial and feminist movement in countries with a shared history of colonisation and that 'the Jamaican feminist movement in the 1930s and 1940s was nurtured within the Garvey movement', although 'the ideal image of womanhood upheld within the movement differed very little from the ideal image upheld by dominant colonial ideology in terms of the way it perceived women's position within the family, women's labour and sexuality' (Ford-Smith 1988, quoted by Mohammed ibid., 15).

The contribution of women to charitable and social welfare is part of the legacy of women's organising and activism in this region. Many crossed the barriers of class and race to build solidarity with women of a different class and/or race and ethnic group. All played important leadership, pioneering roles in social welfare and public service, family planning, education, administration, fund-raising and activities within the labour movement, as well as in the formation of political parties.

The priority given by labour unions and political parties to education, health and family welfare, issues associated with women's practical gender interests and feminist agendas, signified the importance attached to these as parts of the agendas of community or nation building by men occupying positions of leadership in these struggles. Joycelin Massiah notes one of the characteristics of the Caribbean women's movement as its inclusiveness allowing for 'a wide variety of views, styles, concepts, and approaches'. (Massiah 1998, 9). This included openness to working with men and an absence of the confrontational style that may be associated with feminist activism in other countries.

4.2. *The Second Wave (1970s–90s)*

With the efforts toward independence and regional integration in the 1960s and 1970s, a new generation of Caribbean women took leadership to ensure that women's contribution to regionalism and nation building was recognised. Early efforts to launch a Caribbean Women's Association (CARIWA), comprising members from national umbrella organisations, were undertaken by women like Audrey Jeffers, Gemma Ramkesoon and Nesta Patrick of Trinidad and Tobago, Dorothy Lightbourne of Jamaica, Phyllis Allfrey of Dominica, Rita Guy of Saint Lucia and Lady

Grace Adams of Barbados. It floundered with the demise of the Federation but was revived by Viola Burnham and Olga Byrne of Guyana, and formally inaugurated in April 1970 under the presidency of Anne Liburd of St Kitts. Again, these women may not have claimed to be feminists but their initiative to organise women and amplify their voices around the region speaks to a vision of feminist activism as an essential part of nation building, and the thrust for regionalism. Their engagement with policy-making processes also set a pattern for feminist activism in the future. It was CARIWA that ensured the inclusion of the item 'women's rights' in the clause of functional cooperation in the Treaty of Chaguaramas (Massiah ibid., 10).

The early 1970s also witnessed efforts on the part of women within socialist-oriented political parties in Guyana and Jamaica to raise issues about policies and programmes for the advancement of women. In Guyana the Women's Revolutionary Socialist Movement (WRSM) of the People's National Congress (PNC) and in Jamaica the Women's Auxiliary of the People's National Party both worked within their parties to influence the male leadership. In the run-up to the 1972 elections in Jamaica, feminists like Lucille Mathurin-Mair and Mavis Gilmore presented a paper on 'Women and Social Change' arguing for the establishment of a coordinating agency 'empowered to promote and review through the relevant ministries those urgent needs of girls and women' (Reddock 1998, 60 quoting from Henry 1986, 12). The result of these efforts was the establishment of special mechanisms (national machinery) for the 'integration' of women's concerns into national development policies. In Guyana, a Council on the Affairs and Status of Women in Guyana (CASWIG) was formed in 1973, while in Jamaica, Lucille Mathurin Mair was appointed Advisor on Women's Affairs early in 1974. In Barbados, a National Commission on the Status of Women was appointed the following year, 1975.

All of this could be seen as representing a link between local feminist activism and an international environment that was favourable to policies and programmes for the advancement of women, since it was during this period that the United Nations had announced 1975 as an International Year for Women (IWY). Indeed, Caribbean women were involved, through the UN Commission on the Status of Women, in promoting the idea of a special year, and Gloria Scott of Jamaica is credited with having proposed the inclusion of the theme of 'Development' along with 'Equality' and 'Peace' (Antrobus 2000). The processes and events of IWY and the ensuing Decade for Women provided an international environment that supported and legitimised women's activism and Caribbean women took full advantage of this.

Building on the activism of Caribbean women of the first half of the century, the UN Decade for Women took the activism of Caribbean women to another level by putting them in touch with women from other countries and backgrounds, many of them feminists. The exchange of ideas, the opportunities to engage in joint advocacy and projects built the theoretical knowledge, understanding, confidence and skills of a wide cross-section of women in the region. In a sense, exposure through UN processes and conferences drew Caribbean women into an international and global movement that was to have far-reaching consequences for human society in the region and worldwide.

The Decade for Women served as a major training and consciousness-raising exercise for Caribbean feminists – for activists and scholars alike. The activism of the decade (1975-85) was remarkable in its scope and reaches and demonstrates what is possible when women organise to change the attitudes of society toward women and to challenge the state to review its policies and programmes to ensure equal rights and opportunities for women.

The achievements of this period in CARICOM countries included:

- establishment of 'national machinery for the integration of women' in almost every CARICOM country, as well as the establishment of special programmes within regional institutions such as the University of the West Indies and the CARICOM Secretariat;
- changes in laws throughout many countries to include to equal pay legislation; the Status of Children law that removed discrimination against children born out of wedlock; legislation on rape; maternity leave legislation; and the establishment of a family court in Jamaica;
- the inclusion of domestic workers in minimum wage legislation in Jamaica;

- programmes to increase the leadership of women in the trade unions;
- the increasing activism of traditional women's organisations such as the YWCA, the Business and Professional Women's Clubs and the Soroptimists;
- the beginnings of feminist consciousness-raising among women in religious organisations.

The Centres for Gender and Development Studies within UWI have their origins in initiatives taken by the Women and Development Unit (WAND) and women involved in research and teaching on the three campuses and the University of Guyana. I leave Joycelin Massiah to provide more information about the establishment of these programmes and the scholarship that has emerged from them. However, I want to make the point that it was feminist activism that led the way and energised the development and institutionalisation of the programmes.

Regarding the work of WAND, the establishment of the unit within the then Extra-Mural Department, a space within the university with a tradition of being responsive to the needs of the communities it served, was intended to give it the autonomy and freedom to allow women across the region to define its programme. WAND used this space to:

- raise awareness of issues of concern to women through the media and educational system;
- build the capacity of key programmes[9] within the bureaucracy to be responsive to women's concerns in their design and implementation;
- design and implement pilot projects that suggested alternative approaches in programmes of community development, agricultural extension, curriculum development, (participatory) research and skills training;
- serve as a regional focal point and catalyst for women's organising;
- implement training programmes in feminist theory for its own staff and for activists;
- publish newsletters, occasional papers, training manuals, books and research, and produce video and radio programmes that shared its

vision of equality between men and women with the widest audience of men and women within CARICOM, and beyond;
- encourage the establishment of national machinery for the integration of women in Caribbean development and to strengthen the capacity of this machinery to be effective;
- support the work of individual women who were committed to gender equality; and generally to
- serve as a catalyst for change in gender relations toward gender equality.

Starting out as a fairly technical programme, WAND's activism grew with the growth in feminism in its leadership.

During this period, feminist activism resulted in more conscious attempts to bridge the gaps between middle-class and working-class women, and across racial lines, although this was not always successful (Baksh-Soodeen 1998, 81).[10] In Jamaica the black, working-class SISTREN Theatre Collective was formed by Honor Ford-Smith and Joan Ffrench, women from a different class and racial group, while middle-class women in leadership positions within the PNP and the Communist Party focused on the concerns of working class women and built strong alliances with them. Indeed, conscious efforts to build solidarity across class and race expressed itself in the collaboration between the Committee of Women for Progress (CWP), an affiliate of Jamaica's Communist Party and the PNP Women's Movement in the struggle to include domestic workers in the minimum wage legislation, and in the advocacy around maternity leave. In Trinidad and Tobago, issues of race and identity in relation to the Indo-Caribbean women began to surface. In Trinidad and Tobago the Hindu Women's Organisation was formed in the mid-1980s (Baksh-Soodeen 1998, 79).

I want to highlight the role of feminist politics and leadership in this process by emphasising its role in the transformation of programmes and organisations. While the resources and legitimacy generated by the Decade for Women gave second wave Caribbean women an opportunity to work for changes of policies and programmes for enhancing women's role in Caribbean development, it was feminist politics and leadership within political parties, the bureaucracy, the educational system (including the university), the church, legal system, trade unions, media and women's organisations, that transformed these programmes from mere tokenism to initiatives that made a real difference to women and to Caribbean society.

Transformation is a process that starts with the transformation of individuals, who then work to transform institutions. A good example of how this happened in one organisation is the way in which the feminist politics of women within the leadership of the PNP of the early 1970s led to the transformation of the PNP Women's Auxiliary into a women's movement[11] that was the moving force in the changes that took place in Jamaica in between 1972-77. As I stated in my Lucille Mathurin Mair lecture in 2000

> The success of Jamaica's national machinery for the integration of women in development in its first years was more than anything else due to the commitment, vigilance and support it received from the leadership of the women in the PNP Women's Auxiliary/Movement. These women were feminist, meaning that they had an analysis of women's subordinate position in society, and a commitment to challenge and change it, in solidarity with other women. They saw this as an essential part of the meaning of Democratic Socialism, and they understood that the women within the party would have to organise themselves to work for gender equality within this agenda. They transformed their own organisation from a Women's Auxiliary into a Women's Movement, a change that was more than semantics. They claimed autonomy within the Party, building strategic alliances with women in the other parties to fight for the inclusion of domestic workers in minimum wage legislation and for maternity leave. They insisted on supporting women as candidates over the objections of men within the Party. They held ministers accountable by calling them to report on their performance at their conferences. They were an example of feminist leadership within the national political arena – examples of transformational leadership. (Antrobus 2000).

Another example of the way in which feminist activism served to make the link between the work of traditional women's organisations, researchers, and the bureaucracy can be drawn from Jamaica's experience in addressing the issue of girls who drop out of school because of pregnancy.

> Signalled as a 'problem' by women's organisations, the
>
> [Jamaica Women's] Bureau arranged for a situational analysis [to be carried out] by the academics at UWI, [and] facilitated their access to the Ministry of Education.

The recommendations were then channelled both [formally] to the Ministry and [informally] to the women in the Party. Using their political clout they worked from within the Party to have the recommendations taken seriously while I worked within the bureaucracy ... to define the pilot project and find the funds to implement what became the Women's Centre ... the birth of the idea and the support which made it possible came from that strategic combination of NGO sensitivity and concern, academic research, bureaucratic skill, and political will. (Antrobus, 2000).

4.3. Feminist Activism and the Socioeconomic Crisis of the 'Lost Decade'

The limitations of a focus on women's equality became apparent as the Caribbean confronted the global economic crisis of the 1980s. In the same way that the limitations of independence within the structure of global capitalism could only become apparent after political independence was achieved, so too the limitations of sexual equality could only be clearly discerned when this was established. In the 1980s, the structural linkages between systemic crises of debt and deteriorating services, food security and environmental degradation, militarism, political conservatism and religious fundamentalism enabled Third World feminists, the activists and scholars that make up the DAWN network, to frame an analysis that showed more clearly the links between these and their relationship to women's subordination (Sen & Grown 1987).

Not surprisingly, feminist scholars and activists were at the forefront of the critique of structural adjustment policies[12] or, as Sen & Grown (1997) put it the 'crisis of reproduction', since

women stand at the crossroads between production and reproduction, economic activity and the care of human beings, and therefore between economic growth and human development. They are the workers in both spheres – those most responsible, and therefore with most at stake, those who suffer the most when the two work at cross-purposes, and those most sensitive to the need for better integration between the two (DAWN 1995, 21).

Feminist analysis of these policies, and the links between the policy framework and the other crises referred to above, along with the origin of this framework in political conservatism, has been a major contribution to activism in the 1990s and beyond. In fact, feminist scholarship is essential to effective feminist activism. Feminist theory can strengthen women's activism.[13] Feminist theory/scholarship reveals how the exploitation of women's time, labour and sexuality is fundamental to the continuation of the dominant political economic system. For example,

- Because women are socialised to do domestic work and take care of people, the state can transfer responsibility for family health and nutrition to the household, where the labour does not have to be paid for.
- Similarly, the market capitalises on poor women's desperate need for income, and the notion of the 'male bread-winner' to pay them the lowest wages, and treat them as a reserve labour force.
- Finally, state, market and civil society combined manipulate women's sexuality – their relations with men, children and other women, their image of themselves – in the service of the dominant ideology.

In the past few years feminist scholarship has begun to explore and reveal these links between women's subordination and the forces that perpetuate the exclusion and subordination of whole sectors of society (even whole countries and continents). Feminist analysis suggests that there can be no social transformation toward a better world for all unless patriarchy is challenged. If this analysis is to impact society, it must be carried by feminist activism, including the activism of those men whose work is also informed by feminist theory, and who see this and are willing to embark on the difficult task of challenging the ideology that dehumanises them as much as it robs women of their agency.[14]

The combination of feminist scholarship and feminist activism, of which DAWN is an example, has in fact provided the analysis that underpinned the transformation of the international women's movement of the Decade for Women into the global women's movement of the 1990s (Antrobus, forthcoming from Zed Books, 2004). In the context of the global conferences of the 1990s, global feminism emerged as a political force with an agenda for social transformation that goes beyond the focus on women's well-being to women's perspectives on every aspect of life. This shift from the 'integration of women in development' to the call for the 'empowerment of women for social change' expressed in the statement (the Bridgetown Statement)[15] formulated at WAND's tenth anniversary celebration, symbolises the transformation of women's organising by feminism that took place in second wave feminism.

5. Feminist Activism in CARICOM in the Decade for Women

Participation in the global conferences of the 1990s marked a new phase in feminist activism in the Caribbean. Armed with the holistic conceptual and analytical framework formulated by DAWN and other Third World feminist groups, Caribbean women in partnership with feminist activists from around the world were able to see and articulate the systemic links between global conferences on environment, human rights, population, social development, habitats and food security.[16] With this, global feminism made the shift from conferences 'on' women to 'women's perspectives' on global issues. It was a shift that Third World feminism has made from early in the Decade for Women, but it could be more clearly articulated outside the confines of the UN's women's conferences. Caribbean feminist activists like Joan Ffrench of Jamaica, Audrey Roberts of the Bahamas, Nelcia Robinson of St Vincent & the Grenadines, Jocelyn Dow of Guyana, Elaine Hewitt of Barbados, and myself were among those who took leading roles in these conferences.

6. The Future of Feminist Activism

If feminist leadership is crucial for changing the conditions of women's lives, then it is important to consider how this kind of leadership can be encouraged. In my own case, the experiences that have helped deepen my feminist analysis and commitment have included (a) interaction with feminist scholars and activists (b) financial support for feminist projects (c) opportunities for study and reflection. Of these, the interaction with feminist scholars and opportunities for study and reflection related to opportunities that might be provided by feminism within the academy. Here I am not speaking only of the role of feminist scholars who are also activists. I am drawing attention to the contribution that non-activist feminist scholars within the academy can make to activists outside the academy.

My own experience speaks to the ways in which feminist theory and research can strengthen activism and advocacy. What makes DAWN one of the most effective resource networks is the theoretical consistency and clarity of its analysis. This comes from its close links to scholars and researchers, including those who eschew activism. DAWN also demonstrates how the access of scholars to activists enriches scholarship, first by enabling researchers to frame the questions that can be most pertinent to processes of social and economic change; and secondly, by enabling researchers to draw on the insights of activists to provide a reality check for their conclusions. The link serves to strengthen activism as well as scholarship.

But this mutually beneficial link is not automatic. It has to be nurtured and explicitly sought by activists and scholars alike. There are structural gaps between the world of the activist and that of the scholar that must be addressed.

I can give an example of the difficulties by referring to a failed attempt to make the link. From 1992 to 1993, the new head of the Ford Foundation's population programme, wanting to shift the traditional demographic focus of their programme to draw on a broader array of social sciences and to make links between teaching, research and advocacy, reached out to a number of universities, including UWI, to formulate projects that would reflect this orientation. The selection of UWI itself was related to the fact that this institution, with its well established programmes of teaching, research and outreach located in the Centres of Women and Development Studies, the ISER and the Woman and Development Unit (WAND) appeared ideally suited as a model of the kind of work that might be produced. However, without an explicit feminist (political) commitment on the part of WADS and ISER to this project, what emerged was a traditional social science research project without any links to the feminist activism of WAND. As a result of this, the opportunity was missed by the WADS project (undertaken in collaboration with Social and Preventive Medicine) to feed into the process leading up to the International Conference on Population and Development. Feminist scholars would have had more interest in a project that had the possibility of influencing a major policy-making process than those who saw it simply as an opportunity for funding research.

If this link is to be strengthened, both activists and scholars need to be interested in working together, and to recognise the constraints inherent in their different spheres. For example, the activist must recognise the scholar's time constraints and her need, sometimes, to be more protective of her data. The scholar, on the other hand, needs to recognise that the questions of interest to the activists may not be the same as those that interest the scholar, and that the activist is working within a time frame of greater immediacy than that of the scholar. There is also the question of methodology: the activist is likely to be more interested in participatory methodologies that reduce the gap between research and action and empower participants. Finally, there are issues of the imbalance of power between the university and the community, the scholar and the activist. All of these issues need to be addressed if the links are to be beneficial to both scholarship and activism.[17] Feminist politics provides a framework within which scholars and activists might negotiate the basis for collaborative work.

At UWI, the number of scholars and activists who are interested in forging such a link limits the link between feminist activism and scholarship. If activists recognise the importance of good scholarship to their advocacy and activism the onus will be on them to make the links, but feminist scholars might also make it less intimidating to activists who might be interested in approaching the university for assistance. During my period at WAND, one of my greatest disappointments with UWI was its failure to understand that one of WAND's goals was to define a different relationship between the university and the community it was established to serve: a relationship less loaded with overtones of privilege and less encumbered by academic requirements. Feminism would have provided a basis for this understanding.

But above all the tangible impacts of feminist activism on society, there are the intangibles – women's acknowledgement of their capacities for achievement, their sense of entitlement to respect, society's greater awareness of and sensitivity to the human rights of women. Men are more involved in the care of their children and in sharing domestic work;

women have a greater self-confidence in their role in the wider society. Even 'backlash' symbolised by the spread of the 'male marginalisation' thesis can be taken as testimony to women's achievements, and an opportunity to explore the factors that serve to marginalise men that are in no way related to the perceived advancement of women.

In the small village of Rosehall in St Vincent, where WAND had implemented a Pilot Project for the Integration of Women in Rural Development (1981-83),[18] it was reported by one of the men, several years after WAND's role in the project had ended, that men had become more involved in role-sharing in the household and that violence against women was no longer acceptable.[19] While the project had focused on women's leadership by building their skills, self-confidence and capacity for decision-making and leadership, it had never directly addressed the issue of the sexual division of labour nor the problem of violence against women. Nevertheless, the noticeable increase in self-esteem and self-respect among the women of this community was clear to all. Apart from an impressive list of material improvements in the lives of the people of Rosehall,[20] I judge one of the most significant achievements of this project to be the transformation of gender relations in this community and the rise in women's leadership, along with the transformation between the community and state actors. The project also demonstrates how the whole community benefits from women's leadership and empowerment. Although the word 'feminism' was never used, and although most of the WAND staff directly involved in the project did not identify themselves as feminist activists, the conception and guiding philosophy of the project was an example of feminist activism. This was no ordinary community development project; its political objectives of 'empowering women for social change' were clear; though (for political reasons) seldom made explicit.

In the process of translating feminist consciousness into activism, activists have learned to distinguish between the material and the ideological relations of gender (Barriteau 2002). Eudine Barriteau makes this distinction to show that, while advances in women's material needs (what Molyneux terms 'practical gender interests') might be met within a policy framework of social equity based on race and class, the ideological relations of gender could cause men to resent and resist advances in terms of women's strategic gender interests. The Rosehall experience shows one way to avoid resistance. It shows how, in the process of meeting practical gender needs, women can be empowered to challenge the ideological relations of gender and so achieve strategic gender interests as well. This takes patience, but above all clarity about the fact that women's leadership is essential for the well-being of families and communities, that is if the requirements of social reproduction are to be addressed.

7. The New Context and Implications for the Future

With all its limitations, contradictions and contestations, feminism as an ongoing dialogic process of confrontation and resolution nevertheless has the capacity to transform relationships and systems that are oppressive, no more so than today. The present conjuncture of relentless neo-liberalism, virulent religious and ideological fundamentalisms, aggressive militarism and resurgent racism at the international level, with echoes within our region, has particular implications for feminist activism. The focus of this activism must be on two areas: (a) issues of trade liberalisation and its threats to the health and livelihoods of the majority of the people in this region and (b) the impacts of religious fundamentalisms and the male backlash in the context of the HIV-AIDS pandemic as well as to the threats these pose to advances in women's rights, and the continuing struggles against violence against women.

Feminist activism has a special role to play in all of these areas, not least because it is grounded in an analysis that reveals the links between these issues and women's marginalisation, subordination and exploitation. However, the analysis itself needs to be strengthened, and this can only be done by a strengthening of the link between feminist activism and scholarship. The University of the West Indies ought to consider how it might contribute to building feminist leadership in our societies.

The Summer Institute,[21] organised by the Centre for Gender and Development Studies at the Cave Hill campus for women involved in women's programmes in the region, is an example of how this might be done. It provides an opportunity for exposing these women to feminist theory and to feminist activists. This can serve to strengthen feminist activism in the wider society. While a similar distance education programme organised by the centre at Mona is valuable, especially for those who cannot leave home, a residential course provides a better opportunity for the deepening of the feminist consciousness and commitment that is essential for the strengthening of activism.

This academic conference, on the theme of Gender in the Twenty-first Century: Perspectives, Visions and Possibilities, including this Plenary on the related themes of 'Feminist Activism' and 'Feminist Scholarship' would be a fitting time to explore how the links might be strengthened.

Notes

1. The meeting was sponsored by the Asia & Pacific Centre for Women and Development (APCWD) and held in Bangkok. It owed the inclusion of 'feminism' in the title to Elizabeth Reid, Australian feminist who had been adviser to the Prime Minister of Australia during International Women's Year, and who subsequently worked on the staff of various UN programmes. I know of no other UN meeting that includes 'feminist' in the title.

2. The name of the mechanisms (structures) established within government bureaucracies to promote programmes for the advancement of women. The Jamaican Women's Bureau was one of these.

3. In her presentation, US feminist, Charlotte Bunch, spoke of her coming to feminist consciousness through her involvement in the US Civil Rights movement. It was there, as she worked for black liberation, that she discovered her own subordination as a woman. Racism and sexism have much in common.

4. Vandana Shiva makes a useful distinction between capitalist and cultural patriarchy. Cultural patriarchy is 'mediated through cultural oppression' while capitalist patriarchy 'mediates first and foremost through material exploitation and dispensability…one (capitalist patriarchy) hits right at your chances of survival; the other (cultural patriarchy) narrows the options of how much you can travel, how much of your body you can expose, etc. etc. but it doesn't get to the very basis of survival and deny it to large numbers of people, particularly large numbers of women and children all over the world'. In Cindy Duffy, and Craig Benjamin. 'Creative Principles: Fighting Capitalism and Patriarchy on a World Scale: an interview with Vandana Shiva'. In *The World Transformation: Gender, Work and Solidarity in the Era of Free Trade and Structural Adjustment*. (Shareright rhiZone, 1995), 123-133.

5. Conscientisation is a term associated with Paulo Freire and the process of social analysis that enables the poor and oppressed to link their experience to the larger structures of their oppression, especially class. It resonates with feminist consciousness-raising, but has a wider connotation in that it does not focus on a single 'source' of oppression, as feminist consciousness-raising does.
6. Within the context of the UN Decade for Women.
7. For example within the US civil rights movement, or South Africa's anti-apartheid struggle.
8. New research is revealing the presence of Indo-Caribbean women in the labour movement (Reddock and Mohammed) and that some Indian women came to the Caribbean independently of men during Indenture.
9. These included programmes in community development, education and agriculture. At that time, not much attention was given to health, or the police. Issues of reproductive health and rights and violence against women were not high on the agenda until the 1980s and 1990s.
10. According to Baksh-Soodeen, while there was general agreement on issues of violence against women, 'whenever national issues in relation to class inequalities arose, there was a decided withdrawal on the part of the new "middle-class" feminists, who could perhaps be characterized as having a radical feminist approach'. (1998: 81).
11. See my Lucille Mathurin Mair lecture (2000) for more details of this and other examples.
12. Latin American feminist scholars were the first to draw attention to the 'super exploitation' of women's time and labour that underlay this policy framework. My own paper on 'The Impact of the Debt Crisis on Jamaican Women' presented at the first meeting of the Association of Caribbean Economists in 1987 was the first feminist critique of SAPS in the region, although it was largely ignored by subsequent research on SAPS, perhaps because I am not considered a 'scholar'.
13. WAND's regional workshops on feminist theory for activists in the 1980s speaks to recognition of the importance of this, as well as its exposure of its own staff to feminist theory within the framework of internal staff workshops in the early 1990s – 'Andaiye's school', as one staff member named these efforts (they were, of course, conducted by Andaiye).
14. John Foran, who has studied and written extensively on revolutions, recognises that one of the factors that prevents revolutions from realising their dream of a more humane world is the enmeshment of leaders in 'structures of patriarchy and racism'. (Foran 2003, 269).
15. This statement is included in Rhoda Reddock's paper in the special issue of *Feminist Review* frequently cited in this presentation (pp. 70-71).
16. Interestingly, the only global conference for which the international women's movement was not mobilised was the first of these, the 1990 World Conference on Children. Whether by accident or design, the absence of a global feminist presence from this conference ensured that there was no feminist analysis or critique of the ways in which

women's ability to nurture and protect children is determined by their own ability to resist patriarchal control and domination.

17. A few years ago I was involved in a project on university-community partnerships formulated by Atlantic Canada universities with UWI, UG and universities in Indonesia. When I retired from WAND, and I had to withdraw from the project and so was unable to contribute my experience to this venture.

18. The 'project' was time-bound but the process engendered by it has continued to the present, albeit with a new generation of leaders.

19. This is captured on a videotape of the project.

20. In the period 1981-83, tangible results based on initiatives taken by women leaders included the creation of a farmers organisation in which 40 per cent of the members were women, an ongoing adult education programme defined by the community, a sewing project designed to provide school uniforms to the children of the community, a day care centre, a preschool, a library, a community centre and a bakery. As a result of the expansion of opportunities for secondary and tertiary education in the country and region, which took place around the same time, the first five young people from Rosehall went on to university. All of them had been involved in the project and credit it with their increased self-confidence and commitment to contributing to the development of their community and country. Of the five, four were women. Three went on to take Master's degrees. All returned to work in Rosehall or the surrounding villages.

21. This year's Institute is the third of this type of programme. However, it has been difficult to secure financing and its future is uncertain. Only the determination, reflecting the commitment to activism, of Eudine Barriteau ensures it continuation.

References

Antrobus, Peggy. 2000. The 2000 Lucille Mathurin Mair Lecture. Mona: University Printers.

Baksh-Soodeen, Rawwida. 1998. 'Issues of Difference in Contemporary Caribbean Feminism'. In *Feminist Review Number 59 Summer 1998, Rethinking Caribbean Difference,* ed. Patricia Mohammed. New York: Routledge.

Baritteau, Eudine. 1998. 'Theorising Gender Systems and the Project of Modernity in the Twentieth Century Caribbean'. In *Feminist Review Number 59 Summer 1998, Rethinking Caribbean Difference,* ed. Patricia Mohammed. New York: Routledge.

──────. 2002. 'Women Entrepreneurs and Economic Marginality: Rethinking Women's Economic Relations'. In *Gendered Realities: Essays in Caribbean Feminist Thought,* ed. Patricia Mohammed. Kingston: UWI Press.

Beckles, Hilary McD. 1998. 'Historicizing Slavery in West Indian Feminisms'. In *Feminist Review Number 59 Summer 1998, Rethinking Caribbean Difference,* ed. Patricia Mohammed. New York: Routledge.

DAWN. 1995. *Markers on the Way: The DAWN Debates on Alternative Development.* Platform document for the Fourth World Conference on Women, Beijing. Fiji: DAWN publication.

Massiah, Joycelin. 1998. *On the Brink of the New Millennium: Are Caribbean Women Prepared?* The 1998 Inaugural Lucille Mathurin Mair Lecture. Mona: University Printers.

Mies, Maria. 1986. *Patriarchy and Accumulation on a World Scale: Women in the International Division of Labour.* London: Zed Books.

Mohammed, Patricia, ed. 1998. *Feminist Review Number 59 Summer 1998, Rethinking Caribbean Difference.* New York: Routledge.

—————— ed. 1998. 'Toward Indigenous Feminist Theorizing in the Caribbean'. In *Feminist Review Number 59 Summer 1998, Rethinking Caribbean Difference,* ed. Patricia Mohammed. New York: Routledge.

Reddock, Rhoda. 1998. 'Women's Organisations and Movements in the Commonwealth Caribbean: The Response to Global Economic Crisis in the 1980s'. In *Feminist Review Number 59 Summer 1998, Rethinking Caribbean Difference,* ed. Patricia Mohammed. New York: Routledge.

Sen, Gita and Caren Grown. 1987. *Development Crises and Alternative Visions: Third World Women's Perspectives.* New York: Monthly Review Press.

> # *Pushing the Boundaries:*
> # *Redefining Masculinities & Femininities*

3 | VERENE SHEPHERD

Gender, History Education and Development in Jamaica

The subject of education has continued to preoccupy post-independence political regimes in the Caribbean as they seek to redress centuries of neglect by the various imperial powers. Many gains have been made, of course, especially in relation to access to education; but there is still the feeling today that the Caribbean has not achieved all of the educational goals that are so very important for developing countries. The role of education in development is increasingly being realised, however; and in Jamaica several stakeholders, including politicians, have been speaking out on this over the past two years. Education was elevated to a particularly prominent position in the public discourses during the 2001 general election campaign in Jamaica. Despite the predictable cynicism at the attention from politicians, some members of the public viewing the attention as mere political rhetoric and opportunism, none of the stakeholders in educational development in the island would disagree with Delroy Chuck's articulated view that education is a key component of development, a needed investment in nation-building, and a means of empowering a nation's people by developing their minds.[1]

Indeed, for years there has been an ongoing global debate about the role of education in development. The inclusion of education in discussions of development is quite in keeping with the UNDP's definition of human development; for human development is now viewed as a much broader concept than economic growth and is defined as 'a process of enlarging people's choices; encompassing productivity, equality of opportunity, sustainability of opportunities and empowerment'.[2]

The issues of gender and education have been of particular concern to Caribbean societies. This is not surprising. Discourses surrounding gender are familiar phenomena of the age of postmodernity. Indeed, thanks to major United Nations (UN) initiatives between 1990 and 1995, development discourses are no longer gender-neutral. It is now quite widely accepted that development planning must take gender issues into account to maximise the impact of measures and policies, and that gender as a category of analysis must be incorporated into the development paradigm. This view was reiterated by Dr Paul Robertson who, according to a report carried in the *Daily Gleaner*, stated in the 2003 Sectoral Debate on Economy and Production in the House of Representatives that the country could not continue to talk about development without understanding the dynamics of gender in the society; that one of the objectives of the government is to ensure that development encompassed everyone. Two key areas singled out for attention were the gender imbalances in tertiary education (where females outnumber males) and in employment (where female unemployment is twice that of males).[3]

Despite the gender-balanced nature of the minister's concern, and in keeping with recent regional and international trends, it is the subject of the education of males that is of particular concern to western society and that continues to preoccupy policy makers, educators and the larger society. This is reflected in the spate of research on that subject; for even the most cursory review of the literature on gender and education will reveal that there is a current preoccupation with what several researchers and observers have labelled an apathy on the part of males towards formal education manifested in the lower numbers, compared to females, participating in the educational process at both secondary and tertiary levels. The terms 'male under-achievement' and 'male marginalisation' have been bandied about generously, at times out of the original context; and there is also some concern that the 'feminisation' of primary and teacher education, the historically embedded state ideology about the occupational roles of working-class black men, and second-wave feminism, have disadvantaged men, unsettling traditional ideas about males and masculinity and denying males/boys a secure masculinity.[4]

This article will not explore the issues of male underachievement and marginalisation as there already exists a substantial body of critique of the male marginalisation/gender-privileging dialectic[5] from scholars like Barbara Bailey, Keisha Lindsay and Mark Figueroa. However, the article will intervene in the discussion about masculinity, suggesting that, whatever may be the reasons articulated for Caribbean males' insecure masculinity, history education is not one of those contributing factors. If anything, history education, as viewed through the main textbooks, bolsters hegemonic masculinity.

There are many factors that contribute to hegemonic masculinity, a term that refers to the culturally dominant form of masculinity that is constructed in relation to femininity, as well as various subordinated masculinities, for example, homosexuality. The media, the home, peer-pressure groups, school curricula, all send out clues about the preferred masculinity that young males should adopt. These give boys a role-identity, an imaginative view of themselves, on which basis they continue to aspire to hegemonic models of masculinity. As Kay Deaux and Brenda Major observe, external cues can invoke gender identity, moving it into the working self-concept.[6] Hegemonic masculinity borrows from Antonio Gramsci's use of hegemony in his analysis of class relations and has come to mean a cultural dynamic by which a group claims and sustains a leading position in social relationships.[7] Although it is now generally accepted that there are different and often conflicting images of men and masculinity, certain masculinities are clearly favoured. Masculinities that are favoured and even rewarded are dominant or hegemonic masculinity with the prevailing traits being sexism, male supremacy and dominance. Hegemonic masculinity emerges as the configuration of gender practice that legitimises patriarchy and guarantees a dominant position for men alongside the subordination of women.[8]

Admittedly, masculinity is today a contested image as different views of men, male roles and masculinity struggle for supremacy. But within Jamaican popular culture, and within the local media in particular, one sees traditional 'macho' images of men. These images also emerge in textbooks where traits related to instrumentality, dominance and assertiveness/aggressiveness, for example, are believed to be more characteristic of men than of women; while such traits as warmth, expressiveness and concern for others are thought more characteristic of women. As Mark Figueroa has argued, 'The historic privileging of the male gender has constructed maleness as dominant, appropriate to the public sphere, technologically capable, strong and hard. Femaleness has been constructed as submissive, appropriate to the private sphere, sensitive, caring and in need of protection'.[9] Many still believe that the woman's place is in the house (and they do not mean the House of Representatives); that women are more suited to inside work and that females have certain inherently physical and psychological characteristics which predispose them to non-marketable roles such as child-rearing and home maintenance. Masculinity is presented as essentialist; that is, intrinsically different natures are attributed to men and women. These attitudes find legitimacy in the larger society and are reinforced through education. When children are exposed to history education through the dominant texts on the market, then they are exposed to a kind of education that reinforces the subordination of women and contributes to how they view and treat women when they become adults. When adult men internalise these ideas and values, they pass them on to their children who then use them to structure their worlds of home, school and community and, later on in life, their world of work.

In exploring the relationship between history and hegemonic masculinity, the article will only interrogate the content of history education as taught at the Caribbean Examinations Council (CXC) lower secondary or C-SEC level – not the Caribbean Advanced Proficiency Examination (CAPE). It will expose the gender inequalities in the historiography itself as well as in the texts used to teach the subject. It must be stressed that great strides have been made since the 1970s; and that the C-SEC syllabus, especially the recent revision, stresses the need to integrate gender analysis into the history curriculum. The teachers who have been exposed to gender analysis also do their best to adhere to the demands of the syllabus; but many of us who teach know that students also need to see the information in textbooks for reinforcement; and some miss the relevant classes in which particular issues of gender are covered. But the texts used to teach the CXC history syllabus do not all provide boys with the kind of information they need to overturn their views of women as the subordinated sex; and gender stereotypes abound. Indeed, far from learning that they were marginalised, even under slavery, boys learn from history that power was invested in men at all levels of society historically and that women were assigned an inferior role in development. So while on the one hand history education possesses the potential to help to radically transform men's perception of the role of women in the society,[10] it can also serve to reinforce the ideology that contributes to the subordination of women and thus continue the gender inequalities that affect development.

The textbooks and their contents:

There are many books on the CXC history syllabus, but those that the children are most likely to use are:

1. Isaac Dookhan, *A Pre-Emancipation History of the West Indies*
2. Isaac Dookhan, *A Post-Emancipation History of the West Indies*
3. R. Greenwood and S. Hamber, *Arawaks to Africans*. Caribbean Certificate History, Vol. 1
4. R. Greenwood and S. Hamber, *Emancipation to Emigration*. Caribbean Certificate History, Vol. 2
5. R. Greenwood and S. Hamber, *Development and Decolonisation*. Caribbean Certificate History, Vol. 3
6. W. Claypole and J. Robottom, *Caribbean Story*, Bk. 1. 3rd edition
7. W. Claypole and J. Robottom, *Caribbean Story*, Bk. 2. 3rd edition
8. Bridget Brereton, *Social Life in the Caribbean*
9. Patrick Bryan, *The Haitian Revolution*
10. Douglas Hall, *The Caribbean Experience*
11. Shirley Gordon, *Caribbean Generations*
12. Philip Sherlock and Hazel Bennett, *The Story of the Jamaican People*

Of these 12 books, the two volumes by Claypole and Robottom, now in their 3rd revision, are the most popular among students and are widely used in the schools.

All of the books in the sample were published after the 1970s. It is important to note this because it was in the 1970s that, influenced by the feminist movement, issues concerning gender began to be highlighted in historical research globally, with pioneering works done by Lucille Mathurin Mair, Kamau Brathwaite and Barry Higman, and later in the 1980s and '90s, by Hilary Beckles, Bridget Brereton, Barbara Bush, Marrietta Morrissey, Rhoda Reddock, Patricia Mohammed, Verene Shepherd, Linnette Vassell, Aleric Josephs, Swithin Wilmot, Veront Satchell, Brian Moore, Michelle Johnson, Jonathan Dalby and many more University of the West Indies scholars serving to transform and 'engender' the discipline of Caribbean history.[11] The lack of gender-differentiated data in the history texts written for schools after the 1970s was thus not a function of lack of material or of a consciousness in the academy about the need for gender analysis. Those books that were revised after 1999 should also have had access to *Engendering History,* the collection of papers from the 1993 Gender Symposium hosted over 10 years ago by the Mona Department of History in collaboration with the Centre for Gender and Development Studies and *Women in Caribbean History*, a volume put out by the Department of History's Social History Project in 1999 to address the needs of the CXC syllabus; but it is not quite obvious that recent texts have made adequate use of those books or that students use such books widely, though some teachers do. This article, which relies heavily on a public Planning Institute of Jamaica lecture delivered in November 2002, tests this claim by looking at the treatment of several of the following topics in the books, beginning with colonisation, indigenous societies and political power.

Colonisation, Indigenous Societies and Political Power:

In general, in all the texts, males emerge as the authority figures and leaders in Caribbean societies, beginning with the early period of conquest, colonisation and the reshaping of indigenous societies. They dominated indigenous Caribbean and African societies and were skilful seamen, hunters, warriors, priests, kings, government and church officials and chiefs. Apart from Queen Isabella, no woman is associated with the project of New World colonisation; but students will learn a lot about

Cortes, Pizarro, Cromwell, Penn and Venables as well as about male buccaneers, pirates and privateers who were ruthless in going after profitable enterprises, despite the dangers. Conquest and colonisation were male endeavours, characterised by violence, aggressive and deceitful male behaviour and intra-European rivalry. The 'macho' image of man predominates, with indigenous Kalinago men defined by their tendency to capture and carry off Taino women, caveman-style. Indigenous women functioned in the private sphere as homemakers and as agricultural labourers providing drudge labour. Men were adventurous and in the forefront of defence and military exploits. Only Shirley Gordon's text implies that indigenous women were more than marginal to indigenous society. Most of the books suggest that 'politics' was a male preserve; for political activities were narrowly defined and interpreted. That women were a fundamental part of the political struggles, from conquest to decolonisation, remains undeveloped in all the texts.

While the African background to the Caribbean experience receives very good treatment from Claypole and Robottom and from Sherlock and Bennett, the accounts of African society serve to empower boys rather than girls; for the impression they give is that Africa was a place where women played hardly any significant roles.

Men are similarly empowered in the text by Philip Sherlock and Hazel Bennett, authors writing in the late twentieth century who do little to compensate for past discursive short-sightedness which presented the subaltern woman as mute, and recent scholarship on Caribbean women's history has mostly been ignored.

Labour, Slavery and the Plantation System:

White labour for the colonisation project was not the domain of men, but because most of the texts hardly differentiate indentured labourers by gender (except for the Irish women forcefully rounded up at Oliver Cromwell's instructions and deported to Jamaica in 1656), students are left to assume, for example from Claypole and Robottom, that the indentured 'bondservants' were male. This has implications for the foundation of a perception that work was a male domain from the beginnings of large-scale agriculture.

The books are mostly gender-neutral in their presentation of the transatlantic trade in enslaved Africans and project the image of the slave traders, black and white, as male.

Isaac Dookhan's *Pre-Emancipation History* is completely gender-blind in the discussion of the plantation system, the *raison d'être* of slavery in the Caribbean. Of course, as in most accounts of Caribbean economy, and as is shown in Claypole and Robottom, the staple is masculinised, being described, as in most other books, as 'King Sugar'. The students are not introduced sufficiently to women's role in agriculture and, as in Claypole and Robottom, the gender division of labour is marginalised. The absence of a gender perspective in Sherlock and Bennett is glaring in the sections on slavery, with the plantation slave presented as male. That men were not more physically able to do manual labour and that at the height of slavery and the plantation system, enslaved women formed the majority of workers in the field as there was an absence of gender division of labour in field tasks, are facts that remain buried. Shirley Gordon's text, however, does concede that women were the burden bearers in the society. In the absence of gender-differentiated data and based on their socialisation, students would feel that enslaved domestics were female and agricultural labourers male. Indeed, 'slaves' are primarily undifferentiated by gender in many of the discussions of plantation economy and society.

The land-holding elite and the propertied 'planter-class' are also presented as male. Slavery is said to have undermined men's role as fathers, husbands, heads of households, protectors and providers. In Claypole and Robottom we read that, 'On islands where slaves grew their own food, the man might still have a place as the provider of food but on most plantations even this position was taken away from him'.[12] That women also had provision grounds and provided for their families' needs is not mentioned, thus reinforcing this male-as-provider characteristic so associated with masculinity.

Slavery, Resistance and Heroes:

Heroes feature prominently in Caribbean history because resistance and revolt are such central characteristics of our historical experience and because the ability of Caribbean people to shape their destiny through their agency is a topic highlighted in the syllabus. The majority of the texts present the heroes as males who remain idolised even if some of them, like Toussaint, Christophe and Dessalines, are not identified with policies that empower women. As in the colonisation discourses where heroes are all male: adventurers, conquistadors, buccaneers, pirates, church leaders, humanitarians, merchants, administrators and military men, in the treatment of slavery, resistance and maroon society, we seem equally trapped in, and influenced by, a hegemonic gender-power relation of patriarchy that needs to be destabilised.

The majority of the books suggest that men played the role as hero in revolts and were the quintessential rebels, while women used more 'passive' forms of resistance and stayed away from armed revolt. Black women's fundamental political role as rebels is thus undeveloped in most of the texts and their role in the overthrow of colonial slavery is understated in Hall's text, with women being stereotypically labelled as betraying plans for slave revolts hatched by the strong defiant men. Indeed, based on the experiences that Hall selects, one could conclude that women's contribution to the development of Caribbean society was negligible. Gordon's book does portray women as leading figures (not just marginal supporters of male rebels) in resistance struggles and in maroon society. But by naming revolts after men, these authors send a signal that men were the principal activists. Apart from Nanny of the Jamaican Maroons and Nanny Grigg of the 1816 slave rebellion in Barbados, no other females are identified as 'heroes'. Thus women's role in bringing down slavery is not given sufficient prominence with even the anti-slavery activists in England being all presented as male.

The relationship between resistance and the coming of emancipation is unclear in Sherlock's and Bennett's history; but they do acknowledge that resistance was a persistent threat to the continuation of slavery. By not giving space to gender and resistance, they ensure that readers remain influenced by the 'male as hero' thesis.[13] Bryan does not include women in his discussion of maroons in Haiti and mentions women only in connection with the fact that maroon men abducted women for their compounds. He also mentions Touissaint's mother, Pauline and

Dessalines' daughter whose hand in marriage was offered to Pétion. Otherwise, his book highlights the achievements of the military commanders and male rebels associated with the Haitian Revolution and the women occupy a marginal, domestic space.

Social Groups, Social Relations and Social Life:

Most of the books comment on the importance of class and colour in Caribbean society, with some describing the dress, social behaviour of, and restrictions imposed upon, the free people of colour. The 'sexploitation' that gave rise to the coloured group is submerged in the discourse. The poor whites in Haiti are discussed in Bryan's text but in respect of their occupations only those of men are discussed. Brereton details the lifestyles of different social classes in Caribbean society, pointing out clearly that upper-class women, in contrast to those of the working and middle classes, hardly did any work for their own support, no doubt relying on the male provider and an army of women domestics.

Slavery, Family and Fatherhood:

The popular perception in the Caribbean about males and slavery is that men had no opportunity to develop fatherly attributes or paternal feelings under slavery, as slavery defeated black people's attempts to reconstruct or construct family. The view that black men were unable to be good lovers and husbands also persists. Not only were they 'naturally promiscuous', the general view goes, but slavery sanctioned domestic violence against women by elevating black men to the status of slave drivers. Orlando Patterson's early research repeated contemporary views that, 'the institution of marriage was officially condemned by both masters and slaves'; that 'the family was unthinkable to the vast majority of the population'; that 'promiscuity was the norm'.[14] These early views have no doubt influenced subsequent writers. White men's promiscuity is also not highlighted in the texts. Evidence of black men who were good husbands and fathers; and evidence of the existence of stable black families is missing from most of the texts.[15]

The role of white men in destabilising the black family and undermining black men's role as fathers and husbands is hardly discussed.

Sherlock and Bennett missed a great opportunity to educate the Jamaican school child about this fact. They mentioned the case of Thomas Thistlewood but failed to mention that he was, arguably, one of the most brutal white rapists in Jamaican slave society of the eighteenth century.

Access to Freedom:

The view that women, more than men, had the opportunity to achieve gratuitous manumission predominates in the texts. Ignored is the fact that this female dominance is only seen if domestic slaves alone are being discussed. The data on manumission as a result of 'heroic acts' during slave revolts reveal that men were favoured over women.

Men in their capacity as artisans were more economically empowered under slavery and thus were also better placed to buy their freedom through self-manumission.

The laws in Jamaica provided that enslaved people could be freed by an Act of the Assembly for loyalty (which usually meant the betrayal of other enslaved people) or for acting as Crown witness against 'rebellious slaves', or for noteworthy acts of courage. Such cases of manumission were rare in the seventeenth and eighteenth centuries, but with the spate of rebellions in the nineteenth century, they became more common, a total of 3981 between 1817 and 1829.[16]

Emancipation, Free Village and Peasantry: An Overview

The representations of male dominance are carried over into discussions of free society when men of all ethnicities became much more involved in political questions, although white men lost ground to black men in the realm of political dominance. The books all portray men of all racial or ethnic origin as dominant, authority figures in the economy, society and political life of the modern Caribbean. After emancipation, women go back to the private sphere and cement roles in the family. There is ample coverage of issues such as the rise of the peasantry, diversification, labour protests of the 1930s, trade union development, education and decolonisation. But the gender-specific roles of ordinary men and women are hardly treated. Sherlock and Bennett treat the free village and peasant movements as male enterprises, whether the subject is the black peasant or white (facilitating) missionary.

The treatment of the post-slavery issues as far as gender is concerned is particularly disappointing in the third edition of Book 2 of Claypole and Robottom. I expected much of the revisions especially because of the availability of *Women in Caribbean History* and other data on Caribbean women that would have been unavailable to the previous editions. But these revisions in the third edition that appeared this year seemed more focused on bringing the book up to date with the revised CXC (C-SEC) syllabus in terms of the extension of data beyond 1962. Details on women are added here and there but the revisions do not challenge common perceptions of femininity or masculinity. The book thus still reflects some of the sexism noted in earlier editions. On the first page of the third edition, terms like 'masters', and 'freemen' are used though the data clearly also apply to women, as in 'The British government believed the main aim of the new schools should be to train freemen to be obedient to their masters'. The book uses the word 'skilled' to apply to men who were carpenters etc., but 'semi-skilled' to apply to women who were seamstresses and cooks. This again supports the kind of hierarchy so fundamental to masculinity. Sharecroppers under the metayage system are presented as male; plantation owners and benevolent people who facilitated land acquisition are presented as male; and the voices quoted are those of empowered males. The actors in the Morant Bay rebellion of 1865 are also male. Morant Bay in fact is represented as a violent contest among black, coloured and white men. Brereton admits but does not problematise the gender division of labour and the gender discriminatory wages in the period 1838-1938. We do, however, get a clear sense from her about women's contribution to post-slavery society: as emigrants who sent back remittances (a topic that is masculinised by Claypole and Robottom); as rural and urban workers; as wives, caregivers and mothers; and generally as strong, independent women who were not confined to the private sphere. She is the exception to those who portray the man only as head of the household in a nuclear setting, though she does admit that the father had great authority in the home among rich and poor. She provides data that reinforce common beliefs about 'barren women' being pitied. Only those who study the theme, 'Social Life', an optional theme, would read these more empowering images of women into Brereton's text.

The black challenge to colonialism is a male enterprise as far as Claypole and Robottom are concerned. The students are introduced to names like Edward Blyden, J.J. Thomas and Sylvester Williams, but they learn very little about individual women. Apart from Lady Mico (Charity) no other female input in education is mentioned. Claypole and Robottom reinforce the domestic role of women and male dominance in the arena of work and politics.

Labour, Employment, Wages, Gender Ideology:

The role of the Moyne Commission in reinforcing a gender ideology steeped in the Victorian era is ignored by most of the texts. Claypole and Robottom say nothing about the new gender ideology that reinforced gender relations and marginalised women in the post-slavery period. Dookhan does discuss the Moyne Commission's recommendations after the 1930s labour protests; but he ignored the reference to the gender question that Joan Ffrench has subsequently highlighted.[17] Dookhan also treats the workers and emigrant labourers in the post-slavery Caribbean as undifferentiated beings. Claypole and Robottom present men as workers and producers of agricultural crops and as workers in the new industries like oil, tourism and bauxite. Dookhan's limited focus on gender is reflected in the discussion of education where he points to the gender-discriminatory aspects of the curricula and the tendency for subject choices to be made according to gender.[18]

Decolonisation, Trade Unionism, Independence and Integration:

In all texts, the discourse of decolonisation, federation and independence is a male discourse. Indeed, the view seems to be that men had a natural right to political leadership in post-independence regimes. In accounts of the post-slavery period, for example in Claypole and Robottom's second volume, the heroes of the 1930s labour rebellions and the black intellectuals are all male. Students learn about Marcus Garvey but not Amy Ashwood or Amy Jacques Garvey. They learn also about Felix

Hercules of Trinidad, Randolph Smith of colonial Guyana, Cyril Briggs of St Kitts; Arthur Cipriani of Trinidad and Tobago; Hubert Critchlow of colonial Guyana; Buzz Butler, (of Grenada and Trinidad & Tobago) Norman Manley and Alexander Bustamante (of Jamaica); Grantley Adams, and Clement Payne (of Barbados) but not Aggie Bernard, Edna Manley or other influential women.

Social Life, 1838-1962:

The best treatment of this topic is obviously by Bridget Brereton whose booklet targeted this theme in the syllabus. Book 2 of Claypole and Robottom gives women most visibility in the area of social life. This in itself is a stereotypical representation. Still, apart from Edna Manley in sculpture and Louise Bennett in theatre, the intellectual and artistic classes are represented by males. From Shirley Gordon we learn that within the family, men exercised social authority, even deciding if women should work outside the home or not.

The Difference that can be Made by Gender Analysis:

This article suggests that more use should be made of the existing works by historians who have employed gender analysis in their work so that the history taught in Caribbean schools will incorporate a more accurate view of men's and women's historical roles and not only anchor women to a more empowering image of their past, but also allow men to understand that women did not play a completely subordinate role historically. The interpretation of many issues and the treatment of many topics would change if a gender perspective were to be applied. For example, men were not the only rulers in indigenous Caribbean society. In some cases, as in the case of Aracaona of Hispaniola, indigenous women became caciques. Aracaona took on the chieftainship of Xaragua when her brother, Behechio died. Military roles and the aggressiveness many associate with masculinity were not confined to males. Kalinago women, for example, were a part of the indigenous society's defence system. When Columbus arrived in Guadeloupe on his second voyage, he was met by indigenous women 'armed to the teeth', who greeted him and his crew with a shower of arrows. Columbus and his crew fired on them and captured some of the women and children, including the cacique's wife who reportedly almost strangled one of Columbus' crewmen.[19] Indigenous men were also not solely confined to the public sphere, but were engaged in what society has stereotyped as 'feminine occupations'. They helped their women in agriculture and some so-called domestic roles like child socialisation, being primarily in charge of the education of boys.

Even the pirates and buccaneers, so associated with brutality, rape, 'machismo' and a lack of honour, maintained a certain code of respect towards captured white women. According to B.R. Burg, 'strains of almost childish reverence for captured females are much more apparent in their (pirates') treatment of women prisoners'.[20] It is also clear that some pirates married and had emotional ties with women. A few were female. The most famous were Ann Bonny and Mary Read born in Ireland and London respectively. Read at first enlisted in the army and fought in Flanders and Holland. She later sailed to the West Indies to seek her fortune in a Dutch vessel. The ship was captured by pirates, whom Read joined. Both Read and Bonny eventually sailed together in the crew of the experienced pirate, John Rackman, alias 'Calico Jack'. Both dressed like men and plundered and fought as aggressively as men. An English patrol vessel captured their ship in 1720. According to Charles Johnson's account, while most of the male pirates fled, both Read and Bonny faced their attackers, pistol in hand. Read was reported to have been so upset by the spineless men that she shot and killed one of her companions. When 'Calico Jack' was hanged, Ann Bonny is said to have remarked: 'If he had fought like a man, he need not have been hang'd like a dog'.[21]

European men were not the only ones associated with the conquest and colonisation of the region; white women were crucial to the colonisation project as labourers, soldiers, 'encomenderas', spouses and exploiters of subaltern peoples. In the Spanish Caribbean, women were recognised as crucial to the creation and maintenance of a stable, healthy society. On Columbus's third voyage, the crown issued a license allowing 30 Spanish women to join in the expedition. While this represented only ten per cent of the total expedition, it is important to recognise that womens' presence destabilised the representation of 'the Enterprise of the Indies' as a totally male enterprise.[22] Joining the expedition to Hispaniola in 1508 (arriving there in 1509) was Diego Columbus's wife, Doña María de Toledo, niece of King Ferdinand of Spain. With her were several married women whose husbands were members of Diego Columbus' administration as well as several 'hijasdalgo' or daughters of the lesser nobility of Castile. One of them, Doña María de Cueller, daughter of a royal treasurer, later married Diego Velázquez, the governor of Cuba. The emigration and settlement of Spanish women in Santo Domingo is said to have contributed to stable family life in the city. Thus, the image of the Spanish 'Don Juan' and of 'Don Juanism' (an obsessive exaltation of virility and a Faustian conviction of the boundless nature of the male ego)[23] needs to be tempered by accounts that suggest that many men in the Spanish Caribbean led orderly lives as family men.

Although slavery had brutal effects on enslaved people of both sexes, black men were not totally emasculated by slavery. While those who argue that black masculinity was submerged beneath white masculinity during slavery are basically correct, as what mostly defined men's masculinity in Africa (political dominance, economic power, domestic dominance) was severely affected by slavery, it is also true that slavery afforded some black men privileges denied most black women. Thus black men did not emerge from slavery as the more disadvantaged gender; and there was no single, unified masculinity under slavery. Some masculinities were marginalised but equally some were hegemonic.[24] Those black men co-opted into the white patriarchal order as slave drivers, managers, artisans and military personnel displayed hegemonic masculinity. Such social space enabled them to assert their own ideas of masculinity, which were in fact similar to white men's.

Enslaved men had a much wider range of tasks assigned to them and were less confined to field labour than enslaved females. Women were field hands, domestics, hothouse nurses, nannies, cooks, drivers of the 'pickney gang', or washerwomen. Men did field work; but they were also the skilled tradesmen, the watchmen, the couriers, drivers, pen-keepers – all tasks that gave them positions in management and supervision. Orlando Patterson reinforces this view that enslaved men often had positions of status and authority. He indicates that 'on several estates, the head Negroes had separate and better quarters and sometimes their higher status was indicated by the proximity of their huts to the overseers' residence.'[25] He also noted 'the various drivers of the different gangs and the tradesmen together formed a kind of elite among the slaves. Their superior status was recognized by the whites in such acts as giving them a much larger supply of provisions; by generally exempting them from punishment, except in unusual circumstances'; and to give them gifts when absentees came back to visit the estates. 'Their authority was so strong among the slaves that they often formed themselves into courts and settled issues arising among the generality of field slaves, even to the extent of imposing fines and other penalties on them'. The headman headed the slave elite. He was sometimes called the head driver or governor. He issued orders, administered punishment, settled disputes and reported to the overseer and owner.

While slavery infantilised men and women by placing the meeting of most of their material needs in the hands of enslavers, it also privileged men in the assigning of such material benefits. As Patterson points out, at least once a year the enslavers were bound by law to give a minimum of clothing and salted provisions to the enslaved. By the nineteenth century this allowance was being given twice a year, with extra portions at Christmas. Many headmen, as a mark of recognition, were given extra provisions. On some estates, the head driver got 20 yards of oznaburgh (a coarse kind of linen) and eight yards of baize. Less influential men received 16 and eight respectively; the women 11 and four respectively and the children, six and three respectively.[26]

Black men in positions of authority at times held the right to punish others or to get others to provide the labour for their provision grounds. As women formed the majority of field workers, they came under the heavy hand of male authority in the realm of punishment.[27] There were also females in positions of authority; though they were fewer than men. These women operated primarily, but not exclusively, in the domestic sphere. Indeed, it was not only women who functioned in the private space of domestic work. Men worked in or around the Great House as cooks, valets, grooms and gardeners.

Hidden from several of the history texts is the fact that black masculinity under slavery was not always linked to anti-social behaviour, violence and with perceived 'macho' characteristics. Indeed, it was not black men who were the main perpetrators of violence and so there was nothing essentially violent and aggressive about black men. White men, married and single, perpetrated most of the rape, promiscuity and violence in slave society. Manhood is attested by sexual prowess, large numbers of children and a provider status and white men in slave society displayed these 'masculine' traits. They had multiple partners, many children and displayed the characteristics associated with men who make poor fathers. Also, the family was not eroded totally under slavery; and fatherhood was respected. Claypole and Robottom acknowledge that Africans continued to teach respect for the authority of fathers and elders; and that on some large plantations, children did grow up having a relationship with their fathers.

Resistance was not the preserve of men, not even in the areas of military strategising and leadership as the 1831/32 'Christmas Rebellion' (called the 'Sam Sharpe Rebellion' by most historians) demonstrates; so there is no basis for the male appropriation of power on the basis that leadership roles are natural to men. Like black men, many black women opted out of the abusive and exploitative slavery system and participated in land and maritime marronage. Texts that persist in naming revolts according to male heroes therefore need to be revised, if only because they do not project sufficiently the contributions of the 'masses'.

The impression conveyed in the texts that slave ownership was a male enterprise is false. Kathleen Mary Butler and others have shown that white and coloured women bought and sold property and that such property was not necessarily acquired through their association with property-owning men.[28] As women tended to own far more female than male slaves, it was black women who suffered the greatest exploitation at the hands of property-owning women, most of them white.

Finally, while black 'male marginalisation' in the specific sense advanced by Errol Miller was indeed a deliberate characteristic of the post-slavery period, at the same time, the prevailing gender ideology reinforced male power and privileged men. A Victorian gender ideology that promoted the sex-typing of jobs, the masculinisation of the labour force, the male-as-provider ideology and the payment of gender-discriminatory wages was promoted by missionaries, employers and state officials. Such an ideology helped black men to recover their submerged masculinity under slavery and to assume a dominant position in gender relations that was never seriously challenged until the late twentieth century.

Conclusion

When children are exposed to history education through the dominant texts on the market, then they are exposed to a kind of education that reinforces the subordination of women and may contribute to how men view and treat women in their adult lives. This essay's modest proposal for the future echoes that made by Olwen Hufton; that the historical assumption regarding the two sexes should be incorporated in some way into the school curriculum so that the emergent 18-year-old has as part of his/her intellectual package a cognisance of exclusions and arbitrary categorisation attendant upon sexual identity in the past and consequently the significance and value of some hard-won victories.[29] Of course, even if change is effective in the way in which Caribbean history is represented in the textbooks, the reality is that many children, especially boys, do not progress beyond the primary school level and proceed to secondary schools where they can be exposed to this more gendered history. In addition, many boys and young men remain totally outside of the formal educational system. Public education, the home and the media will therefore have to replace the classroom to ensure that a more gender-sensitive history education reaches young males outside of the context of the classroom. Otherwise, as guest speaker Professor Michael Kimmell suggested at the 4th biennial Lucille Mathurin Mair Lecture, masculinity will (continue) to be bad for women.[30]

Notes

1. See Delroy Chuck, 'Invest in Education', *Daily Gleaner*, Wednesday, August 28, 2002, p. A4.
2. *UNDP Report, 2002.* See also *Human Development Report, Jamaica: 2000*, in UNDP Report, PIOJ, 2000, p. 15.
3. *Daily Gleaner,* Thursday, July 17, 2003, p. A10.
4. Errol Miller, *Men at Risk* (Kingston 1991); Miller, *The Marginalization of the Black Male* (Mona 1994); Miller, *Jamaican Society and High Schooling* (ISER, UWI 1990); Keisha Lindsay, *Caribbean Male: Endangered Specie?* Working Paper No. 1. October 1, 1997; Barry Chevannes, *What We Sow and What We Reap: Problems in the Cultivation of Male Identity in Jamaica*. Grace Kennedy Foundation Lecture, March 1988; Chevannes, *Learning to be a Man: Culture, Socialization and Gender Identity in Five Caribbean Communities* (Kingston, Mona 2001); Hilary Beckles, *Black Masculinity in Caribbean Slavery*. WAND Occasional Paper 2/96, Barbados, Women and Development Studies Unit, 1996; Marlene Hamilton, 'A Review of Educational Research in Jamaica', in Christine Barrow and Rhoda Reddock, eds., *Caribbean Sociology: Introductory Readings* (Kingston 1999): 685-711; Elsa Leo-Rhynie, 'Gender Issues in Education and Implications for Labour Force Participation', in Keith Hart, ed., *Women and the Sexual Division of Labour in the Caribbean* (Mona 1989): 81-87; Hyacinth Evans, *Gender and Achievement in Secondary Education in Jamaica*. PIOJ, Policy Development Unit, Working Paper No. 2, March 1999; Barbara Bailey, *Issues of Gender and Education in Jamaica: What About the Boys?* Education For all (EFA) in the Caribbean Monograph Series, No.15. UNESCO, 2000; Mark Figueroa, 'Male Privileging and Male Academic Underperformance in Jamaica', Paper Presented to the Symposium on the Construction of Caribbean Masculinity, Centre for Gender and Development Studies, Trinidad, January 11-13, 1996 and 'Making Sense of Male Experience', *YouWe*, Newsletter of the Board for Undergraduate Studies, UWI, No. 8 (May 2002): 11-16.
5. It was Errol Miller's 1991 *Men at Risk* that popularised the 'male marginalisation thesis'.
6. Kay Deaux and Brenda Major, 'A Social-psychological Model of Gender', in Michael Kimmel, ed., *The Gendered Society Reader* (New York & Oxford 2000), 85.
7. Antonio Gramsci, *Selections from the Prison Notebooks*, edited and translated by Quintin Hoare and Geoffrey Nowell-Smith (London 1971).
8. Odette Parry, 'Sex and Gender Constructions in the Jamaican Classroom', *Social and Economic Studies* 45 no. 4 (December, 1996): 77.
9. Figueroa, 'Making Sense of Male Experience', *YouWe*, 8:12.
10. Patricia Mohammed, ed., *The Construction of Gender Development Indicators for Jamaica*. PIOJ/CIDA/UNDP, 2000, p. xi.
11. See Lucille Mathurin, 'A Historical Study of Women in Jamaica from 1655 to 1844', PhD Dissertation, University of the West Indies, Mona, 1974; Mair, *The Rebel Woman in the British West Indies During Slavery* (African-Caribbean Institute of Jamaica 1975); Kamau Brathwaite, *The Development of Creole Society in Jamaica, 1770-1820* (Oxford

1971) and B.W. Higman, *Slave Society and Economy in Jamaica, 1807-1834* (Cambridge 1976). More works appeared in the 1980s and early 1990s including Barbara Bush, *Slave Women in Caribbean Society, 1650-1832* (Bloomington 1989), Hilary Beckles, *Natural Rebels: A Social History of Enslaved Black Women in Barbados* (New Jersey 1989), Beckles, *Centering Woman: Gender Discourses in Caribbean Slavery* (Kingston 1999), Marietta Morrissey, *Slave Women in the New World: Gender Stratification in the Caribbean* (Kansas 1989) and Verene A. Shepherd, et. al., eds., *Engendering History: Caribbean Women in Historical Perspective* (Kingston 1995).

12. Claypole and Robottom, Book 1, p. 107.
13. See Sherlock and Bennett, *The Story*, p. 182.
14. Patterson, *The Sociology of Slavery*, p. 9.
15. Michael Craton's and Barry Higman's works provide evidence of the existence of the black family. See Craton, 'Changing Patterns of Slave Families in the British West Indies', and Higman, 'Household Structure and Fertility on Jamaican Slave Plantations: A Nineteenth-century Example', in Hilary Beckles & Verene Shepherd, eds., *Caribbean Slave Society and Economy* (Kingston 1991), 228-273.
16. Patterson, *The Sociology of Slavery*, p. 91.
17. See Joan Ffrench, 'Colonial Policy Towards Women after the 1938 Uprising: The Case of Jamaica', *Caribbean Quarterly* 34, nos. 3 & 4 (1988): 38-61.
18. Dookhan, *A Post-emancipation History*, p. 74.
19. J.M. Cohen ed., *The Four Voyages of Christopher Columbus* (London 1988), 139.
20. B.R. Burg, *Sodomy and the Pirate Tradition: English Sea Rovers in the Seventeenth-Century Caribbean* (New York 1984), 118. Of course, racism caused them to treat non-European women with far less regard.
21. See Kris E. Lane, *Pillaging the Empire: Piracy in the Americas, 1500-1750* (New York 1998), 188 and Charles Johnson, *History of the Pyrates* (London 1724).
22. See Luis Martín, *Daughters of the Conquistadores: Women of the Viceroyalty of Peru* (Dallas 1983).
23. Martín, *Daughters of the Conquistadores*, p. 2.
24. Hilary Beckles, *Black Masculinity in Caribbean Slavery*.
25. Patterson, *The Sociology of Slavery*, pp. 54, 65.
26. Ibid., 222-23.
27. Bush, *Slave Women in Caribbean Society*, p. 42.
28. Kathleen Mary Butler, *The Economics of Emancipation: Jamaica and Barbados 1823-1843* (Chapel Hill 1995).
29. Olwen Hufton, 'Women, Gender and the Fin de Siècle' in Michael Bentley, ed., *Companion to Historiography* (London & New York 1997), 940.
30. Professor Michael Kimmell, 'Males, Masculinity and Development', 4th biennial Lucille Mathurin Mair Lecture, March 11, 2004.

4 | JEANETTE MORRIS

Gender and Schooling
Implications for Teacher Education

Abstract

The paper begins with an overview of some of the main issues and challenges to be faced in interrogating the discourses around gender and schooling. These include the debate on gender and achievement at all levels of the education system, gendered patterns of curriculum choice, the gendered nature of school culture and schooling as a site for the reproduction of gender relations. The particular gendered discourses in teacher education are examined such as the concept of female 'caring' and the shaping of teacher identity in accordance with an ideology of teaching as an extension of motherhood. Finally the implications for teacher education are discussed in terms of a shift away from the discourse of teaching as women's work and what this means for policy, curriculum change, and pedagogy for teacher educators.

Introduction

The major issues which have engaged the attention of educators and researchers concerned with gender and schooling in the Caribbean have centred around the gender differentials in educational achievement at primary, secondary and tertiary levels, the increasing phenomenon of male underachievement, linked to their lower participation and higher dropout rate, gender stereotyping in the curriculum leading to gendered career choices and the feminisation of the teaching profession which has been blamed for the alienation of male students. Much less attention has been paid to gender issues in teacher education, despite the recognition that teachers in schools and classrooms play a major role in the reproduction of gender relations by socialising their students into appropriate masculine and feminine behaviours through the hidden curriculum. This paper attempts to re-examine some of the gender and schooling issues focusing on the implications for changing current teacher education practice. It suggests that teacher educators should undertake a critical exploration of the gendered nature of teacher education (paying special attention to the gendered discourses which predominate such as the positioning of teaching as a natural extension of motherhood and the concept of feminine 'caring') and revise their curricula to increase teachers' awareness as well as equip them with skills, strategies and resources to address some of these gender issues in their daily interaction with young people in our schools.

Gender and Schooling

One of the major issues in gender and schooling centres on the decreasing participation of boys especially at the secondary and tertiary levels of the education system. Enrolment statistics for primary schools in Trinidad and Tobago for the years 1994/1995, 1995/1996 and 1998/1999 show overall a slightly larger number of boys than girls enrolled in primary school in 1994/95, 1995/96, 1996/97 and 1998/1999 (Central Statistical Office 1996; Central Statistical Office 1998). However, the breakdown by age and class suggests that boys have a higher repetition rate than girls throughout primary school and in the examination for selection to secondary school (Central Statistical Office 2003). This is also the case in Dominica (Goldberg and Bruno 1999), although for the OECS, Drayton (1995) found that enrolment for boys and girls was very similar within primary schools but became differentiated during the years of secondary schooling.

Access to secondary school has traditionally been determined in the Caribbean by an examination such as the Common Entrance Examination which allocates students to schools based on ability. This is changing and some Caribbean territories have already removed such an examination. Universal secondary education has not yet been achieved by all Caribbean states; consequently, some selection measures are applied to the placement of students in secondary schools. When this is done by means of an examination, girls score higher than boys (World Bank 1993).

Although roughly the same number of boys and girls enter secondary school, after five years there is a significant imbalance in the number of girls and boys who enter for the Caribbean Examinations Council examinations which provide certification for secondary school graduates. In 1993, 38.1 per cent of candidate entries were male compared to 68.9 per cent female entries. The corresponding figures for 1994 were 37.42 per cent male entries and 62.58 per cent female entries (Caribbean Examinations Council Headquarters 1994). This trend continues into tertiary education as the majority of students registered for 2002/2003 at the University of the West Indies, St Augustine campus, both part-time and full-time, were female (The University of the West Indies 2000/2001). On all three campuses, female graduates also outnumbered male graduates. In the case of higher degrees the trend of greater numbers of female graduates continues for all campuses. An exception to the prevailing trend is seen in the enrolment in craft courses at technical and vocational schools in Trinidad and Tobago where males far outnumber females (Central Statistical Office 1996, 2002). This points to another of the important issues related to gender and schooling which is the gender differentiation existing in relation to curriculum choice particularly in secondary schools.

An examination of the CXC candidate entries by subject and sex reveals that, by and large, boys and girls show preference for subject areas traditionally regarded as masculine or feminine. More boys are entered for the technical subjects, physics, agricultural science, art and information technology. Girls choose the humanities, business studies, home economics, integrated science and biology. Only two subjects, chemistry and geography, had almost equal numbers of candidates. From the CXC report on the administration of the 1994 examination, girls were in the majority in 21 subjects, boys predominated in 11 subjects and two subjects had fairly similar numbers for both boys and girls.

Although more girls than boys are entering for CXC examinations in science with the exception of physics, there is a trend of low entry statistics for science for both sexes. Rampersad (1999) notes that, of a male entry population of 22,700, only 19 per cent wrote biology, 16 per cent chemistry, 17 per cent physics and 10 per cent integrated science. Similarly, although the female entry was larger, approximately 36,000, only 18 per cent wrote biology, 11 per cent chemistry, 7 per cent physics and 9 per cent integrated science. It is interesting to note that although in absolute numbers more girls are sitting the examination, the picture changes when we look at the percentage of girls who enter to take science subjects. The numbers show that the percentage of the total female entry taking science subjects is less than the percentage of males for all science subjects. This suggests that there still exists a certain amount of gender imbalance as females are not accessing science subjects in the proportion that one might expect, given their numerical superiority in the examinations.

The perception that subjects are gendered is linked to traditional societal views of gender roles which define the public sphere as the man's domain and the private sphere as the woman's domain. Education was seen as the way to prepare young people for their future adult roles so that historically it oriented girls toward domesticity and boys toward the world of work. This is evident from the type of education provided when the first secondary school for girls was established in Trinidad and Tobago in 1836. The St Joseph's convent school taught its girls the rudiments of reading and writing, conversational French and the feminine arts of housekeeping. This was in response to a traditional view of woman's role as wife and mother. Indeed the provision of secondary schooling for girls was initiated by the denominational bodies as the state only provided secondary schooling for boys in the nineteenth century. As secondary schooling expanded in the early twentieth century, mainly through the denominational bodies, there was less curriculum differentiation between boys and girls, yet official policy continued to espouse education for women to fit them for a domestic role. This view is reflected in the recommendation of the Marriott-Mayhew Commission of 1933 that domestic science be introduced into the curriculum for girls. They also recommended that the curriculum for girls should be less intellectually demanding so as to free them from having to write the external Cambridge examinations. A similar view was reiterated in the Maurice Committee report (Maurice 1959) which recommended the secondary modern school as an alternative to the grammar school for the less able and also as the best kind of education for girls. In these schools, girls and boys followed similar academic courses but in the vocational areas boys studied woodwork, metalwork, leatherwork etc., while girls learned 'the special housewifely arts so essential to a girl's education' (Maurice 1959).

This view also persisted in the fifteen-year plan for educational development 1969-1983, which to a great extent shaped the present educational system in Trinidad and Tobago. Junior secondary schools were introduced with a curriculum designed to cater for the manpower needs of society. In this new curriculum, boys and girls shared the basic subject areas but followed separate pre-vocational courses. Boys were exposed to industrial arts as an introduction to technology while girls were trained in household management – a clear indication that the educational planners envisaged traditional roles for the sexes. The successor plan 1985-1990, while not explicitly stating a policy of differentiation by sex, did not change the existing curriculum of the junior secondary school so that in practice in the junior secondary schools girls and boys followed gender segregated subjects thus perpetuating a gender segregated curriculum for the majority of children in those schools. The subsequent Education Policy Paper (1993-2003) is a departure from previous policy documents in that it makes specific mention of gender in its general objectives:

> ... every child has an inherent right to an education which will enhance the development of maximum capability regardless of gender ... and that the educational system must provide curricular arrangements and choices that ensure that cultural, ethnic, class and gender needs are appropriately addressed (Ministry of Education 1993).

However, despite the recognition at the level of general goals, when more detailed objectives for the curriculum are spelt out, there is nothing to suggest what steps should be taken to ensure that equal access to all curriculum areas becomes a reality.

The new Secondary Education Modernisation Programme (SEMP) curriculum, which is being implemented in all schools in Trinidad and

Tobago, has eight core subject areas to which all students male or female are exposed. If the curriculum is implemented as it should be, all students will be exposed to technology education as well as the aesthetics which should help in reducing gender differentiated subject choice. However traditional attitudes and expectations about gender roles which are evident in the education plans and reports of the past still persist in secondary schools today and influence the subject choices made by students. These choices limit the subsequent employment opportunities open to male and female students and are the cause of unequal access to higher paying jobs. Subjects such as office procedures, shorthand and typewriting whose enrolment is predominantly female prepare these students for low-paid secretarial and clerical jobs. Male dominated technical subjects prepare students for jobs in industry and technological fields which are better paid.

Gender stereotyping in schools is not only restricted to subject areas offered in the formal curriculum but is more often found in the informal or hidden curriculum, the implicit messages that students receive from their interactions with teachers, other students, as well as from the practices and authority structures within the school.

Teachers' interactions with students show clear gender differences. Teachers appear to have different expectations for girls and boys and as a result treat them differently. Girls are expected to behave and perform better than boys so they receive more praise for their efforts while boys receive more reprimands and negative comments (Goldberg and Bruno 1999); (Kutnick, Jules et al. 1997; Morris 1992). Teachers also present both masculine and feminine stereotypes to students in their classes in the examples that they choose, and the remarks that they make. Morris (1992) describes an incident of this nature:

> In a class concerned with consumer electricity students were asked to list household appliances which used electricity. As students suggested items the teacher wrote them up on the blackboard. When a sizeable list had been compiled she turned to a group of boys saying, 'you see why you all must study hard, your wives will want these things'.

Subsequently, when interviewed, this teacher indicated that the boys were the weakest students in her class in terms of performance and that the female students performed much better. Yet her remark assumed that the boys would be the wage earners for the family. Later in the same class when asking about appliances that used considerable amounts of electricity, the example of a clothes-dryer was given. In this instance the teacher, addressing a female student, chose to use the example of drying diapers, reinforcing the stereotype of the female as the nurturant sex whose primary sphere of activity revolves around childcare within the home.

Boys interviewed felt that girls received special treatment from teachers (Morris 1992) and also felt that boys received punishment for offences which were overlooked in the case of the girls (Goldberg & Bruno 1999). Teachers seem to have internalised traditional gender stereotypes so that boys are thought to be physically stronger and more troublesome and as a result they need to be punished more severely. They also tended to give boys more manual work such as cleaning the school yard, moving furniture and running errands.

Another of the messages about gender that students receive from the way schools are organised and managed is that, although women make up the majority of teachers, they are underrepresented in positions of authority. However, this pattern is rapidly changing as in 1987 male principals of secondary schools were in the majority, 79.8 per cent (Educational Planning Division 1987). Ten years later in 1997 their majority had decreased to 54 per cent (Ministry of Education 1998) and if the trend continues there will soon be parity of numbers among secondary principals. The number of female principals, while higher than in many other countries, masks a type of gender segregation when their location in the system schools is taken into account. In 1999, of the 100 existing public secondary schools in Trinidad and Tobago, 46 were headed by women. Twenty-six were in traditional five- and seven-year schools, mainly denominational and 13 in single sex, all female schools. In the large co-educational new sector schools, junior secondary, senior comprehensive and composite, there were fewer women principals and they were more likely to be found in the junior secondary schools where students are in the 12-14 age group rather than in the senior comprehensive schools which are large co-educational schools with students from 15-18 and a mixed staff. The location of female principals in these particular school contexts shows the persistence of the gendered stereotype of educational management which sees women managers as more suitable for younger children and an all-female environment. Such stereotypes in school management convey covert messages of gender inequality to students.

These messages are also conveyed in the classroom through the textbooks used by teachers and students. Drayton (1997, 162) in her analysis of selected English language textbooks used in Barbados, points out that 'textbooks reflect, consolidate and perpetuate dominant values'; she goes on to argue that textbooks can influence children's attitude towards another person's race, gender, social class or any other attribute. Textbooks which contain stereotypes and negative images can therefore perpetuate social inequalities. Drayton found that the principal characters in the texts surveyed were males (78 per cent) compared to females (22 per cent) and concluded that, since women comprised half or more than half of the population, their under-representation clearly indicated a sexist bias (Drayton 1997, 165). When the occupations of males and females in the texts were compared the number of male occupations was significantly greater than females, a distortion of the social reality which suggests that females' contribution to the workforce is inferior to that of males. Males were also presented as natural leaders, more adventurous, more intelligent and more creative than women. Both girls and boys using texts that portray these gender stereotypes are receiving a distorted picture of reality. The portrayal of strong, superior men who must not cry, show feelings or reveal weakness is as harmful to boys as the portrayal of the weak, inferior female is to girls.

Gender stereotypes are not the only ones present in the textbooks. Class and racial stereotypes also abound such as the image of blacks as people who have never achieved or discovered anything, since the only achievements recorded in the texts are those of Europeans. Drayton concludes that 'The colour of the textbooks is white and their sex bias is male' (Drayton 1997, 179). Drayton's findings are similar to those of King and Morrissey (1988) who reviewed textbooks used by Caribbean territories to prepare for Caribbean Examinations Council (CXC) examinations in history, geography and social studies.

The major issue that has come to the forefront of the discussion on gender and schooling is academic performance. In the majority of the English-speaking Caribbean, girls' academic performance is superior to that of boys at all levels of the education system. At the primary level Kutnick, Jules and Layne found that, while Common Entrance scores for girls and boys did not differ significantly, within class scores consistently showed girls outperforming boys in Trinidad and Tobago, St Vincent and Barbados (Kutnick, Jules et al. 1997). In Dominica, girls out-performed boys in the Common Entrance examination in almost all the papers. Only in science was there gender parity (Goldberg and Bruno 1999).

At the secondary school level it has been noted that more girls enter the CXC examinations and they predominate in the majority of subjects. When the percentage of boys gaining grades one and two is compared with that of girls the picture changes to some extent. In 1994, grades one and two were considered to be passing grades. The results for that year for the subjects at General Proficiency level show that in nine of the subjects the percentage of boys gaining grades one and two was greater than that of girls. The percentage of girls was greater in eleven subjects and there were ten subjects where the percentages were nearly equal (Caribbean Examinations Council Headquarters 1994). This seems to suggest that although fewer boys than girls entered for fewer subjects, their performance in the subjects that they chose to do was not significantly different from that of the girls doing those subjects. In Dominica, the success rate for boys and girls in the CXC examinations was examined for English A and Mathematics, two subjects in great demand by employers. A greater percentage of girls achieved success in English A while the results in Mathematics were balanced with 39 per cent of boys being successful compared to 38 per cent of girls (Goldberg & Bruno 1999). Rampersad (1999), in her analysis of the performance of males and females in science subjects in CXC and Cambridge A-level examinations, came to the conclusion that examination results showed no clear supremacy of either gender in the sciences with the exception of mathematics. She notes, however, that more females than males are taking science subjects in secondary schools overall at both ordinary and advanced levels with the exception of physics.

Apart from examination performance, another indicator of academic performance in schools is the repetition rate as well as the drop-out rate. In Dominica, for 1997 and 1998, the percentage of boys repeating Forms one to four was over 50 per cent for each form. The percentage of male drop-outs was even higher, ranging from 52 per cent to 65 per cent (Goldberg and Bruno 1999). Statistics for drop-outs for public primary schools in Trinidad and Tobago for 1996/1997 and 2000/2001 also showed a greater male drop-out rate, 0.3 for males and 0.2 for females (Central Statistical Office 2003). The number of male repeaters in government/assisted primary schools for the same years was also greater than the number of females, and this was also reflected in the repeater rate which was 8.1 for boys and 5.3 for girls, an indication of males' lower academic performance (Central Statistical Office 2003).

At the tertiary level the greater number of female students who graduate suggests that females are performing better at this level also. The reasons for male underachievement in education are unclear but recently popular opinion has begun to lay the blame on women by suggesting that the feminisation of the teaching profession is responsible for boys' lack of interest in school. Other popular myths suggest that girls' success contributes to boys' low self-esteem which affects their performance. Many of these popular views are not based on relevant research data but on traditional stereotypes of gender roles.

Researchers have put forward some tentative explanations for male underachievement which focus on gender socialisation practices. Gender socialisation in the Caribbean can be summed up in the expression 'tie the heifer and loose the bull' (Brown & Chevannes 1998). This refers to the practice of monitoring and controlling daughters' activities to avoid early pregnancy which could affect their life chances, while giving boys more freedom and little or no supervision. Figueroa (1996) suggests that this privileging of males which allows them to do as they please tends to leave them without the basic skills needed for educational attainment in the Caribbean school system, such as self-discipline and time-management. Parents invest more time in developing girls' social skills and are more likely to emphasise obedience and 'manners' for their daughters, attributes which stand them in good stead in school.

Chevannes (1996) makes the point that a large part of male socialisation takes place on the street, where the prevalent behaviours and values are the antithesis of all that schools represent. On the street, survival is the name of the game and education does not serve the male well in that context.

Other researchers explain male underachievement by reference to the construction of masculinity in the Caribbean and the incompatibility of the prevailing male norms with positive attitudes to schooling. Parry (1996) cites a Jamaican principal who indicated that reading was not seen as a masculine occupation by the boys. The fact that boys read less and are less interested in books may seriously affect their educational attainment (Goldberg and Bruno 1999). Similar views were voiced by a Barbados principal who indicated that a boy who showed academic inclinations was considered a 'nerd' by his peers. This was also the opinion of teachers in St Vincent.

Economic factors are also thought to contribute to boys' lack of interest in school. Traditionally, education was a means of achieving social mobility. Chevannes (1993) points out that in Jamaica young men see that high-risk activities such as drug-trafficking or avenues such as music or sport, which in their view do not necessarily require educational qualifications, can provide wealth and all the trappings of success. In this context it is extremely difficult to convince an unemployed ghetto youth that going to school is better.

Another explanation put forward is the fact that men get jobs and can earn a living with less education than women, so that there is less motivation to make the most of their educational opportunities (Evans 1998). Also, when there are economic problems in the home, it is generally the boys who are forced to drop out of school to help support the family (Brown & Chevannes 1998).

School factors may also provide explanations for male underachievement. The treatment of boys in school has been shown to be more negative than the treatment of girls (Goldberg and Bruno 1999) and this can lower boys' self esteem and lead to frustration, alienation and eventually to dropping out of school. Some explanations posit that the feminisation of teaching and the association of schooling with female culture have contributed to boys' alienation from the schooling process. It is said that they lack male role models both at home and at school. Miller (1991) does not support this argument, pointing out that in Trinidad and Guyana, East Indian girls are also outperforming East Indian boys who generally have male role models in the home.

The research cited cannot provide definitive causes for male underachievement, however it does provide an indication of trends, since in many of the territories the observations were startlingly alike. The empirical evidence and the perceptions of teachers, students, parents and researchers point to a need for examination of teacher education curricula and practice to ensure that teachers in schools address some of the major issues highlighted such as gender stereotyping, male underachievement and the pervasive gendered nature of Caribbean schools.

Gender Issues in Teacher Education

Weiner (Weiner 1999) in a review of gender and teacher education in Europe states that 'it has been comparatively difficult to uncover gender discourses within teacher education, regardless of country or political or education system'. She identifies the factors that shape discourses in teacher education, such as the relatively low status of teachers and teacher educators, the increasing feminisation of the profession and the exclusion of a significant number of teacher educators, for example, those in teachers' colleges, from universities and research.

One of the dominant discourses in teacher education is the perception of teaching as women's work. Teaching is seen as the natural extension of motherhood, where the female's nurturing skills will be an asset. It is also seen as a profession that is compatible with a woman's own family responsibilities. This discourse emphasising female caring, according to Fischman (Fischman 2000), has attempted to produce women teachers as conservative and passive in spite of their resistance to these discourses. The discourse defining women as caregivers also helps to shape the identities of female teachers. Cammack and Phillips (Cammack and Phillips 2002) found that the choice of teaching as a career by participants in their study was related to internalisation of these discourses. Several women had planned other careers but changed their minds because it would be rebelling against what they were good at, or against a family tradition that they were born to teach. As teachers they were also constrained by these discourses to provide a level of care, service and dedication which made the difference between success and failure for their students.

Enrolment at the teachers' colleges and the School of Education, which are the main institutions for the training of primary and secondary teachers respectively in Trinidad and Tobago, shows that the number of female students exceeds that of male students (Quamina-Aiyejina, Mohammed et al. 2001; University of the West Indies 2000/2001). This mirrors the situation in the schools where female teachers outnumber their male counterparts at both primary and secondary levels (Central Statistical Office 2003; National Institute of Higher Education 2002).

The curriculum in the teachers' colleges focuses heavily on content area knowledge and to a lesser extent on pedagogy. Gender issues are dealt with tangentially in the sociology of education but no serious attention is paid to how teachers themselves perceive gender issues, no attempt is made to investigate teachers' own attitudes or to sensitise them about how, as teachers, they have a role to play in achieving gender equity in schools. In the School of Education, gender is also dealt with in sociology courses but is not infused into all areas such as school administration and subject area disciplines. This is left up to the individual lecturer, many of whom do not see gender issues as a priority. Many teachers leave teacher training, therefore, without having understood the importance of gender in the schooling process and their role in perpetuating traditional attitudes and gender stereotyping in their classrooms.

How then can teacher education prepare teachers to recognise, challenge and address the troubling issues of male underachievement, gender stereotyping, and the teacher's own role in ensuring gender equity in the classroom? To achieve this, there must be a radical change in the way teacher education is conceptualised and implemented. It implies policy changes, retraining of teacher educators, curriculum revision and changes in pedagogy and practice.

At the policy level there must be a recognition of the importance of gender equity and a commitment to do what it takes to achieve specific goals. Given this commitment, teacher educators must be sensitised to gender issues and the impact that these issues have in the classroom. They must realise their responsibility to prepare student teachers to address these issues, which are as important as teaching them lesson-planning and classroom management. Many teacher educators themselves are not equipped to address gender issues so that training of teacher educators is paramount.

Sensitisation and awareness workshops for teacher educators which will also provide them with strategies for incorporating gender into their practice should be the first step in this process. Cammack and Phillips (Cammack and Phillips 2002) suggest that teacher educators should become aware of the dominant discourses of teaching as women's work and love and service and the influence of these discourses on their own teaching. Transmitted by the academic voices of teacher educators, these discourses set up expectations and shape the behaviours and teacher identities of student teachers.

Student teachers generally start their programmes with fairly strong traditional beliefs and attitudes towards gender role stereotypes. For teacher education programmes to successfully change attitudes, students must be encouraged to question their attitudes and beliefs. Discussion about gender issues should form part of methods, and other education courses and student teachers should critically explore their own gendered histories. This critical stance should also be carried over to their teaching practice experience. Many student teachers are placed with a cooperating teacher who is usually an experienced teacher. Student teachers may model themselves more on the cooperating teacher, whom they see as knowledgeable in practical teaching, as opposed to their university or college supervisor whom they associate with the theory of teaching. It is therefore most important that cooperating teachers be also given gender sensitisation workshops so that they can model gender-fair teaching strategies for the student teacher.

In order for meaningful change to take place, the curriculum at teachers' colleges and schools of education needs revision. Bailey, Scantlebury and Letts (Bailey, Scantlebury et al. 1997) found that most university programmes were not providing student teachers with the knowledge, skills and support to address critical gender issues in the classroom. They suggest, and this paper supports the view, that all educators must begin substantive discussions regarding gender issues in education and ensure that critically examining gender issues is a key component of all education reforms.

Pedagogical practices in universities and teachers' colleges should model the gender-fair strategies that student teachers are being asked to use. Are the male student teachers encouraged to specialise in areas traditionally seen as female, for example, early childhood education, or are they being channelled into physical education, mathematics and science specialisations which are traditionally seen as more appropriate for males? In discussions related to gender issues in methods courses, are teacher educators able to put aside personal preference and teaching style in order to model gender-equitable behaviours? Are all teacher educators agreed on this, so that focus on gender is across the board and not seen as the duty only of the 'gender specialist'?

The student teachers in our teachers' colleges and schools of education are being trained to go back into the classroom and provide a better educational experience for *all* students, both boys and girls. If gender equity is not addressed in every aspect of teacher education, as advocated, our teacher education institutions will be graduating teachers who will unintentionally diminish the educational, career and economic prospects of our students as well as do untold psychological harm to many of them. As teacher educators, we cannot allow this to happen.

References.

Bailey, B., K. Scantlebury, et al. 1997. 'It's not my style: Using disclaimers to ignore gender issues in science'. *Journal of Teacher Education* 48 no.1: 29-36.

Brown, J. and B. Chevannes. 1998. 'Why man stay so: Tie the heifer, loose the bull'. Kingston, Jamaica, The University of the West Indies.

Brown, J. and B. Chevannes. 1998. 'Why man stay so: Tie the heifer, loose the bull'. An examination of gender socialization in the Caribbean. Mona, Kingston, The University of the West Indies.

Cammack, J.C. and D.K. Phillips. 2002. 'Discourses and subjectivities of the gendered teacher'. *Gender and Education* 14 no. 2: 122-133.

Caribbean Examinations Council Headquarters. 1994. Report on administration of the 1994 examination. Bridgetown, Barbados, Caribbean Examinations Council.

Central Statistical Office. 1996. Annual Statistical Digest. Port-of-Spain, Office of the Prime Minister.

Central Statistical Office. 1998. Report on education statistics 1996/1997. Port-of-Spain, Ministry of Planning and Develpment.

Central Statistical Office. 2003. Report on education statistics 2000/2001. Port-of-Spain, Ministry of Planning and Development, Republic of Trinidad and Tobago: 67.

Chevannes, B. 1993. 'The male problem: An Afro-Caribbean perspective'. *Children in focus* 5: 7-8.

Chevannes, B. 1996. 'The role of the street in the socialisation of Caribbean males'. Caribbean Studies Association Annual Conference, San Juan, Puerto Rico.

Drayton, K. 1995. 'Gender issues in education: A review of the major issues in education and of relevant Caribbean studies'. Castries, Saint Lucia, Organisation of Eastern Caribbean States.

Drayton, K. 1997. 'White man's knowledge: Sex, race and class in Caribbean English language textbooks'. *Gender: A Caribbean Multi-disciplinary Perspective*. E. Leo-Rhynie, B. Bailey and C. Barrow. Kingston: Ian Randle Publishers, 159-181.

Educational Planning Division. 1987. Statistics on public education. Port-of-Spain, Ministry of Education.

Evans, H. 1998. 'Gender differences in education in Jamaica'. World Council of Comparative and International Educational Societies, Capetown, South Africa.

Figueroa, M. 1996. 'Male privileging and male academic performance in Jamaica'. The construction of Caribbean Masculinity: Towards a research agenda – a symposium, The University of the West Indies Centre for Gender and Development Studies, St Augustine.

Fischman, G.E. 2000. 'Imagining teachers, rethinking gender dynamics in teacher education'. Lanham, MD: Rowman & Littlefield.

Goldberg, N. and R. Bruno. 1999. 'Male underachievement in Dominica: Extent, causes and solutions'. Ministry of Education, Sports and Youth Affairs, Measurement and Evaluation Unit.

King, R. and M. Morrissey. 1988. 'Images in print: Bias and prejudice in Caribbean textbooks'. Kingston, Jamaica, Institute of Social and Economic Research.

Kutnick, P.V. Jules, et al. 1997. 'Gender and school achievement in the Caribbean'. London, Department for International Development.

Maurice, J.H. 1959. Education report of the committee on general education. Port-of-Spain, Government printery.

Miller, E. 1991. *Men at Risk*. Kingston: Jamaica Publishing House Ltd.

Ministry of Education. 1993. Report of the National Task Force on Education. Port-of-Spain, Ministry of Education.

Ministry of Education, T.T. 1998. Directory of public schools in Trinidad and Tobago, Ministry of Education, Educational Planning Division.

Morris, J. 1992. 'An investigation into the processes associated with the reproduction of gender inequality in the secondary school'. Faculty of Education. St Augustine, The University of the West Indies, 166.

National Institute of Higher Education, Science and Technology. 2002. Profile of Teachers in Public Secondary Schools 1999-2000. Port-of-Spain, 47.

Parry, O. 1996. 'Boys will be boys: Why do Caribbean males underachieve?' The construction of Caribbean masculinity: Towards a research agenda – a symposium, The University if the West Indies Centre for Gender Studies, St Augustine.

Quamina-Aiyejina, L.J. Mohammed, et al. 2001. A baseline study of the teacher education system in Trinidad and Tobago. St Augustine, The University of the West Indies.

Rampersad, J. 1999. 'Patterns of achievement by gender in school science'. *Caribbean Curriculum* 7, no.1: 37-50.

The University of the West Indies. 2000/2001. *Official Statistics 2000/2001*. Kingston: The University of the West Indies, 111.

Weiner, G. 1999. A critical review of gender and teacher education in Europe.

World Bank. 1993. Caribbean Region: Access, quality and efficiency in education. Washington, DC, The World Bank.

5 | ERROL MILLER

Male Marginalisation Revisited

Just over 17 years ago, on April 30, 1986, I had the honour to deliver the first Aubrey Phillips Memorial Lecture here on the Mona Campus of the University of the West Indies as a tribute to my late mentor and colleague, Professor Aubrey Phillips. The title of that lecture was: 'Marginalisation of the Black Male'. What followed was a controversy that has persisted until the present time.

At that time, some credited me with identifying and highlighting a dimension of gender that had not previously been explored. Others accused me of obscurantism, being a male chauvinist parading in the guise of scientific research and of diverting attention from women's issues. My approach was to ignore the inducements to become embroiled in a futile man versus woman debate but to continue to research the subject, being convinced that the phenomenon highlighted was not going away but rather would become more evident and widespread over time. It is fair to say that the passage of these 17 years has vindicated that position. The phenomenon is no longer in question. The current puzzlement centres on explanation.

I therefore welcome the opportunity afforded me by this Mona Academic Conference, celebrating the tenth anniversary of the Gender Studies Unit, not only to revisit the subject of male marginalisation, but also to further advance the discussion of the subject by virtue of additional insights gained from exploration over these 17 years.

Allow me to join in the celebration and commendation of the Gender Studies Unit for having reached this milestone in the journey and to wish for the unit even greater accomplishments through full exploration of gender issues as they relate to both women and men.

In addressing the topic, Male Marginalisation Revisited, I am not going to recite empirical and statistical evidence highlighting aspects related to the phenomenon such as:

- More male babies being abandoned than female babies;
- More boys suffering from stunted growth than girls;
- The growing tendency for boys to start school later, attend more irregularly, drop out more often, repeat more grades, have lower rates of completion of schooling and lower levels of achievement than girls on most indicators of educational attainment;
- Less males than females being enrolled in and graduating from tertiary institutions;
- More boys and men becoming patients in psychiatric wards or psychiatric hospitals than girls and women;
- More men being homeless than women;
- More boys and men committing violent crimes than girls and women;
- Much larger numbers of boys and men being incarcerated in correctional institutions and maximum-security prisons.

The focus of this paper will be on expanding and refining the explanation of the phenomenon first advanced by me over a decade ago. It is important to note that male marginalisation is not restricted to Jamaica or the Caribbean or to any one racial group or any particular society; rather, it is a universal phenomenon with different degrees of manifestation and different forms of expression. It is by no means a recent phenomenon but its current forms are new expressions related to the circumstances of contemporary society. I will employ both theory and history to support these positions.

Defining Patriarchy, Gender and Marginality

While definitions seldom capture the complexity of the phenomena they seek to describe or specify, they are useful in setting the parameters of the discourse and of establishing common meaning between those engaged in dialogue. Given the widely different approaches that have been adopted towards the conceptualisation of both patriarchy and gender, it is necessary to set out as precisely as possible the ways in which these are conceived in this paper. The conceptualisation and definition of patriarchy and gender are absolutely critical to any explanation of male marginalisation. In revisiting the subject, therefore, it is critical to return to these as the starting point.

Defining Patriarchy

The seminal theoretical contribution of feminist scholarship to social theory has been that of the radical feminist in firmly placing patriarchy as an important category in social theorising and analysis. However, the problematic has become the definition of patriarchy. Weber (1947) had defined patriarchy as women and younger men being ruled by older men, who were heads of household. While a few feminist theorists have followed the Weberian definition, the more common approach has been to discard the generation difference between men in Weber's formulation, and to define patriarchy as that system of social structures and practices in which men dominate, oppress and exploit women (Dahlerup 1987; Walby 1990). In other words, the most prevalent tendency in feminist scholarship has been to adopt a narrower and more exclusive definition than the Weberian formulation.

To define patriarchy solely in terms of men's domination of women is to treat men and women as two separate undifferentiated groups that have sustained their coherence over time and across different cultures. This posture has attracted sharp criticism especially from black feminists and post-structural and post-modernist theorists. Hooks (1984), for example, argued that while white feminists have traditionally conceptualised the family and the home as major sources of women's oppression, this is not the same among blacks where the family is not a major source of women's subordination. Indeed, as more and more black women become heads of households the family and the home have become major loci of their liberation from traditional patriarchal roles.

Collins (1990) extended the line of argument advanced by hooks by observing that race, class and gender constitute three interlocking axes of oppression that are part of an overall matrix of domination. She further made the point that while most individuals have no difficulty identifying their own victimisation, they routinely failed to see how they contributed to the suppression of others. White feminists typically point to their oppression while they resist seeing how much their white skin constitutes a social privilege. Likewise African-Americans, eloquent in their analysis of racism, often persist in their perception of poor white women as symbols of white power. Failure to see gender as part of the matrix of domination leads inevitably to such contradictions in the approach to and perception of oppression.

Taking a different line, post-modernist theorists have maintained that neither men nor women are unitary categories. They argue that the categories men and women are a number of overlapping and crosscutting discourses of masculinities and femininities that are historically and culturally variable. In their view, the notion of women and men dissolves into shifting and variable social constructs which lack stability and coherence over time. Walby offered some rebuttal by her observation that the post-modern feminists draw heavily, theoretically, upon the deconstructionism of Derrida (1976), the discourse analysis of Foucault (1981) and the post-modernism of Lyotard (1978) which are all guilty of not paying serious attention to gender. Indeed, post-structural and post-modernism theorists have been no different from modern or classical theorists in their benign neglect of gender in social analysis. The weakness in the post-modernist conception of gender as highly variable, is that, as Dahlerup aptly pointed out, men's domination of society is highly uniform across cultures and throughout history.

In *Men at Risk* (Miller 1991), I approached the definition of patriarchy from the opposite direction of the radical feminists by taking a more inclusive approach to the definition of patriarchy. I argued that the main limitation of Weber's definition of patriarchy was its omission of the kinship relations, factual or fictive, that usually exist between the older and younger men and women that constitute the household. In other words, patriarchy needs to be defined as that system of reciprocal social obligations in which final authority rests with older men of the kinship collective, who exercise that authority over their individual male and female members in the overall interest of the collective.

The differences between these three sets of definitions of patriarchy are the elements included. Most feminist scholars have confined their definition of patriarchy solely to gender. Weber's definition included the elements of gender and generation. My definition includes genealogy, gender and generation and insists that recognition of genealogy is critical if the complexities of patriarchy and gender are to be better understood.

I argued that the gender and generation elements relate mainly to the internal relations of the collective while the genealogy element defines its external boundaries and relations. From one perspective, genealogy extends kinship outside of the immediate circumstances of the household or family by establishing links with other collectives through the notion of common ancestry. At the same time, by default, it defines collectives that are not kin. This is a critical consideration both conceptually and empirically.

The essence of my argument was that, conceptually and historically, patriarchy did not only involve asymmetry in power between men and women, but also shared identity, group solidarity, common bonds and mutual obligations. These differentiated patriarchal collectives from one another. Further, historically, patriarchal collectives had major difficulties with other collectives that fell outside the covenant of kinship, particularly with the men of those collectives.

When patriarchal collectives interacted outside boundaries where kinship could be established, whether factual or fictive, then one group had to submit to the hegemony of the other. Failing such compromise, violent confrontation became the means of establishing dominance. I traced the practices of genocide, where one collective sought the physical elimination of another, the killing of male captives, the castration of male captives and the almost permanent enslavement of men, as historical outcomes of conflict between collectives which did not share the covenant of kinship or where that covenant had been breached. In all of these circumstances I showed that patriarchal collectives found it easier to incorporate women of non-kin groups than the men of such groups. I maintained that the external relations with men of hostile collectives are as much an element of patriarchy as the internal relations with women of the kinship collective.

I took the position that, within the patriarchal collective generation, age in addition to genealogy moderates the relations between men in that, because age is mutable, in time the younger males succeed the older men. Genealogy and generation combine to define the younger males as potential heirs of the older men. Succession dictates male solidarity manifested in the older men grooming and apprenticing the younger men who reciprocate by waiting their turn. While genealogy and generation contribute to male solidarity within the collective through the process of succession, gender excludes women who are left marginalised within the kinship collective. Within patriarchy, therefore, women are marginalised in the internal relations of the kinship collective. However, the genealogical relations between men and women of the collective ameliorates women's marginalisation by virtue of the filial bonds and the obligation to protect and provide for them.

Further, I argued that the genealogy element, defining the external relations of patriarchy, defined non-kin men as potential threats and possible enemies. In these circumstances of relations between unrelated collectives, where the covenant of kinship did not exist, the subordination of one collective relative to the other, voluntarily or by violence, becomes the only means of establishing the bases of interaction. By definition, therefore, patriarchy includes the marginalisation of men of the unrelated collectives, in one way or another. Where the men of the subordinated groups accept the hegemony of the dominant group they have been invariably allowed to maintain patriarchal dominance within their subordinated groups. Where the hegemony of the dominant group is challenged, the group that prevails takes severe action against its challengers resulting in the elimination or marginalisation of the males of the conquered group.

The essence of my contention therefore is that patriarchy does not only involve the marginalisation of women within the kinship collective, but also that of men of unrelated collectives. Put another way, two elemental features of patriarchy are:

- The marginalisation of women within their kinship collectives, and
- The marginalisation of men of other collectives, outside the covenant of kinship, over which dominance is established by voluntary or violent means.

The implication of this definition of patriarchy is that gender cannot be understood or interpreted solely in terms of men's domination of women. Gender analysis is not simply about the asymmetry in power between men and women. A gender perspective is not only about women's issues. To understand gender as being synonymous with women is to misconstrue or misinterpret the concept of patriarchy. The point is that gender analysis cannot assume solidarity between men and women belonging to different groups in society. This is because gender operates in conjunction with the other social criteria upon which societies are organised, and that solidarity among men and women of groups sharing common identities and common bonds of belonging is much greater than solidarity of either men or women of groups with different identities and sharing no bonds of belonging.

In agreement with the line of reasoning set out above, Skjelsbaek (1997) observed that patriarchy ought to be regarded as domination of some men over subordinated men and women of groups claiming relationship of some kind, and that patriarchy is a value system of dominance which is executed by both men and women. She further commented that 'Miller thus deconstructs the inherent dichotomy of the 1960/70s definitions and opens the way for a more nuanced understanding of patriarchy'.

Defining Gender

In defining gender it is necessary to differentiate it from sex, although the essentialist position is that sex and gender are almost synonymous. This biological reduction implies that gender differences between men and women relate to size, strength, speed and stamina. These differences all favour men and determine their leadership in society. It must be noted, however, that not only is there considerable overlap between men and women in these traits, but not even among men are these physical differences the defining features of leaders in society. Indeed, they more aptly describe the physiognomy of the bodyguards of leaders. The position taken here is that while sex is biologically determined, gender is socially constructed. The two often overlap. However, this overlap is by no means total, given the regular occurrences of masculine females and feminine men, irrespective of how masculinity and femininity are defined in any particular culture.

One argument employed to support the claims of the biological construction of gender is that if gender were only a social construct, then one should expect to find such wide variations in masculinity in history and contemporary cultures that they would defy unifying categorisations. However, there are common themes associated with masculinity and femininity across widely different cultures and throughout history. Such common themes, it is claimed, can only be accounted for by biological factors operating through genetics.

In *Men at Risk,* I argued that the common themes in masculinity and femininity are not inconsistent with their social construction when gender is defined as the sexual division of power related to living, giving and life-taking. It is the universality of the life-giving and life-taking powers, and not genetic determination, that accounts for the commonality observed throughout history and across cultures.

Defining Marginality and Centrality in Society

Marginality and centrality in society can be defined in terms of the place or location of individuals or groups relative to others with respect to:

- Power: the ability to determine outcomes consistent with one's interest, even against opposition. It is the capacity to command, coerce or co-opt others to perform one's will.
- Resources: the material means by which needs, basic or otherwise, may be satisfied. This includes the mode and means of production.
- Status or prestige: the esteem or regard in which one is held; the capacity to persuade others to show deference; honour or the lack of it.
- Belief: the ideas, knowledge and values which inform, inspire and justify action.
- Culture: the acquired way of life; the habitual rules of behaviour in all fields of endeavour passed on from one generation to the next in a particular setting.

From this perspective, the egalitarian society would be one in which all individuals are located at the same position relative to one another; that is, the society in which all places are equal. In this society all individuals would corporately make all decisions, all would command exactly the same resources, all would enjoy the same status and be honoured in like manner, all would practice the same material culture that would make equal treatment of one another routine and habitual, and all would hold to and be legitimised by the belief system on identical premises. Put another way, the egalitarian society, in which all places are equal, is the ethical society marked by equity and social justice. However, the egalitarian ideal is invariably and almost universally defeated by three factors:

- The size of society. Direct participation in all decision-making is only possible in very small societies. In societies of any significant size, direct participation by all is a practical impossibility. Some hierarchical form of representation is inevitable.
- The human life cycle. Human beings pass through pre-determined biological stages of infant, child, adolescent, adult and old person. Infants, children and sometimes the aged require guardians to act on their behalf as they are unable to represent themselves.
- Individual differences. Each human being is biochemically unique. Associated with this are variations in abilities and divergence in thought processes which can potentially lead to pluralism in beliefs, lifestyles and competence.

While each in itself constitutes a formidable obstacle to equality, together their impact is devastating in their subversion of the egalitarian ideal. The interaction of these three factors undermines the establishment and the maintenance of the egalitarian society in which places are all equal. Put another way, equality of places in society is a practical impossibility. The social reality in society is the inequality of places, with places ranging from being marginal to being central and still others occupying intermediary locations.

Marginality in society is therefore not a pathological condition or a terminal social disease but rather a social fact. Marginality is part of the essence and nature of human society. The same can be said of centrality. Further, neither marginality nor centrality is fixed or permanent. This is because the fundamental contradiction in human society is that the egalitarian society, which is the only ethical basis upon which society can be established, is practically an impossibility, while the relative inequality, resulting in marginality and centrality, which is the practical reality, cannot be absolutely or permanently or ethically justified. In other words, the egalitarian society is utopian and just, while relative inequality, manifested in the centrality and marginality which is the reality in society, is inherently immoral and unjust. This is the continuing and persistent dialectic in society. The moral ideal which is just and equitable is not attainable in reality, but that which is real is inequitable, immoral and unjust.

The implications of this contradiction are twofold. First, to seek to achieve the equitable, ethical and just society is to transcend reality, that is, to take social action or construct society on utopian bases that are at variance with social facts. In other words, the equitable, ethical and just society can only be approached through revelation which transcends reality and goes beyond the facts, and logical reasoning based on those facts. Second, to accept the social reality or to be bound by reason and logic rooted in social facts is to rationalise and legitimise inequity and injustice, which is immoral and perverse.

Confronted with this dilemma, societies are continually faced with one of two basic options: either to construct society on utopian ideals that are continually and ultimately subverted by the social reality, or to construct society on realistic criteria which justify and legitimise particular inequalities in society as absolute and permanent, but which are undermined and subverted by its immoral foundations. While the first option is ethical and moral, it is unrealistic in that it disregards social reality. While the second is realistic, it is perverse in that it justifies the unjust and accepts the immoral as an inevitable aspect of society. In either case the basis upon which any society is constructed is ultimately undermined and subverted. The first option is undermined by social facts while the second option is undermined by ethical and moral principles.

As a consequence, on whatever basis any society is negotiated and constructed at a particularly time in history, it is deconstructed and re-negotiated at some subsequent time. Accordingly, the bases upon which society is organised are never permanent and are inevitably changed in the course of history. Indeed, over time, societies oscillate between the utopian and social reality poles that define the basic contradiction of societal existence. As societies construct themselves and attempt to operate on the basis of transcendental values and utopian ideals they are undermined and subverted by the social reality of inequality. On the other hand, as societies construct themselves and attempt to operate by accepting the social reality of inequality and injustice, they are undermined and subverted by the transcendental values and utopian ideals related to justice and equality. This periodic oscillation between two poles constitutes one of the major parameters for change and the renegotiation of the basis of organisation of human societies in history.

Indeed, history can be written in terms of the rise of the marginalised and the demise of the centralised. From one perspective, civilisation can be viewed as the cumulative contributions of marginalised groups in their striving to overcome marginality. Much of the energy in society can be traced to marginalised groups and/or individuals seeking to overcome marginality and striving to achieve central places.

The Social Construction of Gender and Patriarchy in Antiquity

In the final analysis, the exact nature of the social construction of patriarchy and gender is a matter of speculation. My reconstruction of the social construction of patriarchy and gender in antiquity, which is set out in Miller (1991), can be summarised as follows:

- Early humans lived in small isolated groups in relatively hostile environments of which they had very limited knowledge. Their primitive technology and shelter made them particularly vulnerable to ecological calamities. Adaptive advantage rested in group living. Hence, early humans lived in descent groups essentially to ensure survival.

- Long life constituted a scarce and treasured resource in pre-literate communities of antiquity as the aged members of the group represented the resident memory of the group and its reservoir of information and past experiences in dealing with the exigencies of living. Men lived longer than women, largely due to the risks attendant on childbearing (Lerner 1986).

- Women were engaged in childbearing and childrearing from puberty to the grave, as the average life span of females at that time was less than 30 years. Fertility and a large number of offspring was another treasured resource of kinship communes as they attempted to survive the challenges of the time. The veneration of the Mother Goddess is one of the early motifs found in cave drawings.

- In addition to dealing with bringing life into existence and preserving it, this small, autonomous, isolated group also had to deal with the issues of life-taking, as it related to the physical and ritual defence of the group. Since biology determined that women gave birth, and were perennially involved in this activity and in the preservation of the lives that were brought into being, life-taking fell by default to the men, particularly to the older men of the group.

- The separation of life-giving and life-taking powers was the original sexual division of power that separated masculinity from femininity. Women were socialised principally in relation to all the life-giving and preservation skills and knowledge, while men were socialised with respect to life-taking. Accordingly, the basic definition of femininity and its surviving common themes reside in the honing of such traits as caring, nurturing, gentleness, kindness, tenderness, co-operation, accommodation of differences, long-suffering, patience, acquiescence and passivity. Likewise, the basic definition of masculinity and its common themes resides in the development of such traits as assertiveness, decisiveness, ruthlessness, courage, valour, confrontation, toughness, conquest and the killer instinct. These latter traits are all related to the capacity to take life with impunity.

- While there was equality, and even a feminine bias, in the initial separation of life-giving and life-taking powers, in group dynamics over the long haul, life-taking proved more powerful than life-giving. While mothers were venerated for life-giving, a one-shot event, fathers were feared in that they held the power to take life on any given day. Fathers exercising the life-taking power became the final authority in all matters pertaining to the descent group. Men and women participated in the separation of sexual division of power without anticipating its long-term consequence for female marginalisation in the kinship commune.

- While the sexual division of power occurred in antiquity, the father's power to take the lives of members of the kinship commune survived well into recorded history. The Druids, the priests in Britain before the Roman conquest, had a saying which stated that all masters of families were kings in their own households: they had the power of life and death over their wives, children and slaves. Early Roman law codified this power.

Gender, defined as the sexual division of power, departs from the commonly accepted definition of gender as the sexual division of labour, women's work being restricted to the private sphere of the household and men's work being extended to occupations in the public sphere (Dex 1985 and Reddock 1994). This is not to deny that in the course of history sexual division of labour has occurred. However, this has come subsequent to, and as a result of, the prior sexual division of power. In other words, primacy is accorded to the power relations of gender and not to labour and work differences.

While the creation of patriarchy and the original construction of gender are shrouded in antiquity, with only circumstantial evidence to support contemporary speculation about their origination, including mine, the contention here is that the contemporary unravelling of gender and patriarchy is but a mirror image of the processes involved in their original construction. In this regard, three observations are necessary with respect to the definition of gender as the sexual division of power relative to life-giving and life-taking.

First, war has been, and still is, the supreme expression of patriarchy and the warrior the ultimate symbol of masculinity. Unmitigated rage, unbridled fury and unrestrained violence directed at life-taking are the quintessential and ultimate masculine modes of conflict resolution. Warriors, men most skilled and successful in taking life with impunity, are the final arbiters and authorities in deciding differences and in determining what will prevail in society. The universality of war in history and across cultures, and its virtual exclusivity as a male enterprise, testifies to the primacy and pervasive nature of life-taking in defining masculinity and in establishing final authority in societal affairs.

Second, at the root of the contemporary controversy on abortion is the question of whether women should have the right to take life with impunity. The right-to-life side of the controversy is basically that women's commitment is to give life without reservation or caveat. It asserts the primacy basis of the definition of femininity and the essence of the ancient social construction of womanhood. The right-to-choose side of the argument fundamentally changes the ancient foundation of the definition of femininity and womanhood in that it combines the life-giving and life-taking powers. In this regard, it not only changes the primary basis of the construction of femininity but it encroaches upon and threatens the very essence of the definition of masculinity. By excluding fathers from the choice, women's right to choose fundamentally changes the construction of gender. While the arguments concerning the rights of the unborn child should not be ignored, the gender definition implications of women's right to choose ought to be recognised as being at the core of the controversy. The deep passions evoked testify to the centrality of the issues being disputed.

Third, in the course of the evolution of society, the father's right to take life was transferred to the king or chief and eventually to the State. In contemporary times, the right of the State to take life has been challenged in the movement against capital punishment. In a way, this can be interpreted as a tendency toward the reform of masculinity. At the same time, there is increasing escalation of the wanton taking of life by men in gangs, terrorists, enraged lone gunmen shooting numerous unsuspecting victims for reasons hard to identify or rationalise. In a manner of speaking, the move to reform the fundamental life-taking definition of masculinity, by men and groups who have been empowered, is counterpoised, counteracted and even compromised by marginalised men seemingly reclaiming their manhood through life-taking. Mass murder, terrorism, gangs engaged in savage acts of violence, the escalation of murder, the move to abolish capital punishment and the counter-move to reinstitute it where it has been abolished, all stand in screaming contradiction. Reform and reaction to the life-taking in society is yet another example of the fundamental nature of the construction of masculinity and its continuing relevance in contemporary society.

Gender understood as the sexual division of power is key to understanding many of the great debates in contemporary society. It is also critical to the unravelling of many knotty issues related to gender issues and relationships in society, including male marginalisation.

Macro-factors Driving Societal Change

In the foregoing discussion of patriarchy and gender, I have pointed to current fundamental changes in society whereby patriarchy is being unravelled, with all the consequential issues and confusion with respect to gender roles and relationships. Before probing further, it is necessary to identify and make brief comments about the macro-factors that have been driving fundamental change in the form, nature and organisation of human society. From my perspective there are three such sets of interacting factors that can easily be identified. These are:

- Demographic changes related to the growth of human populations. Planet earth is the same size today as it was when no more than about 1,000,000 people lived in groups of 50 to 100 persons with little or no contact between them. In these circumstances, the adaptive advantage resided with group living. Today, with approximately six billion people, human populations are not only much larger but also in much greater contact by virtue of sheer numbers.

- Ecological imperatives when the land-to-person ratio and the resources for survival are the primary consideration. The living space for human groups has shrunk considerably resulting in increasing urbanisation globally. Conflict resolutions by groups putting physical distance between them by one of them moving to unoccupied and uncontested territory, have been greatly reduced. Conflicts between groups are virtually required to be resolved with both groups remaining in place.

- Knowledge and technological development that has transformed all aspects of human existence. This aspect is so well documented and accepted that it requires no further elaboration here.

Form and Nature of Societal Changes

The scope of this paper only allows me to make the briefest of sketches of the form and nature of societal changes that have evolved as a result of these interacting macro-factors. The brevity of these sketches necessitates simplification of complex phenomena. However, these are almost unavoidable in the circumstances. A fuller description and discussion is set out in Miller (2003).

The change in form and organisation can be listed briefly in historical sequence as follows:

- Relatively small isolated hunter-gatherer nomadic extended families or lineages or clans that were autonomous and virtually self-sufficient in the conduct of all human affairs.
- Larger settled lineages and clans living in subsistence farming communities made possible by the agricultural revolution driven by the emerging technology of growing crops and domesticating animals. The temple emerged not only as the first monumental structure but also as the first public space in intercourse between lineages and clans. Priests, potters and metal workers were among the first non-manual occupations. The temple was the place in which agricultural surplus was stored, redistributed and traded. Economic exchanges between lineages and clans originated in the temple where they were conducted under divine scrutiny and sealed by sacred vows. These early villages were governed by clan democracy loosely linked to the temple, in which the governor had priestly status. The structure of government consisted of a governor, a council of elders of the clans and a general assembly of all free adult males. Together they exercised political, judicial and executive power in the context of consent and consultation on various matters. Final authority rested with the general council in matters of war, with the council of elders in other matters and with the governor in terms of administrative routine carried out in the

name of the god. Temple-centred villages worshipped a pantheon of groups. In each village, however, the task of maintaining community fell to the temple. Religious bonds were the means of binding blood-related autonomous clans together in corporate living. Ritual observances and worship were therefore the first activities transferred from the private sphere of kinship, to the public sphere of corporate existence of non-kin. The blood bonds of kinship were dissolved in the solvent of ritual piety. The common gods worshipped by the clans became the glue of non-kinship solidarity that made village community possible. It must also be noted that a dynamic symbiotic, but also contentious, relationship developed between settled villages and nomadic pastoral groups.

- In time, some villages created a federation to form ancient cities in which one clan owned the government. Several important forces spurred this transformation. First, the revolution in agricultural production made possible by the invention of the metal plough, harnessing animals to draw the plough; the invention of the wheel and wheeled vehicles; and the invention of writing. This revolution in agricultural production, which occurred around 4000 BC, allowed more land to be brought under production at lower cost, and therefore generated much greater surplus that could be redistributed over larger areas and accounted for in writing. It allowed for the expansion of non-manual occupations that could supply the food-producing sector with technology and could provide more efficient public administration. This formed the basis for urbanisation. Second, as cities emerged as walled entities surrounded by a necklace of villages and hamlets, they had to be defended militarily either against invaders or by pre-emptive strikes against other cities. The most important outcome of the military defence of cities was the transformation of governance from temple-based clan democracy to royal courts ruled by warrior kings and royal lineages that owned the government. In this development, the palace joined the temple as another instrument of binding clans, lineages, tribes and castes in corporate living. Third, warriors, priests and kings, often interchangeable occupations, ruled societies through patriarchal succession.

The cooperation, competition and conflict that characterised the relationships between cities and their surrounding villages and nomadic groups can be described as follows:

- City states ruled by kings and boasting temples, writing and schools, classified themselves as civilised and the nomadic groups as barbarians.
- Imperial city states established empires guaranteeing their client cities and village protection from invasion from other cities and marauding barbarians.
- Religious empires replaced imperial cities as the foci of domination as barbarians successfully overthrew the oligarchy of cities that they conquered and were converted to universalistic religions.
- These religious empires were governed from an imperial city but exercised hegemony, in the name of religion, over cities, dukedoms, earldoms, fiefdoms, sheikdoms, chiefdoms and tribes all structured along ethnic and patriarchal lines.
- The code of conquest that was practised allowed the conquered city or village etc. autonomy over its internal affairs provided that they accepted the hegemony of their conquerors.

Over the last 400 years, nation states have broken the yoke of religious empires and established themselves as sovereign entities ruled by constitutional law.

Patriarchy in City States and Religious Empires

It is important to pause and take note of patriarchy as it was originally constructed and how it was transformed in the era of city states and religious empires. Both the ancient state and religion had the potential to alter patriarchy defined in terms of genealogy, generation and gender. Indeed, the high ethical vision of all universalistic religions declared men and women equal in the sight of god. The state and religion were premised on the notion that different kinship collectives owed primary loyalty to the state or religion and not to blood bonds. While both could be regarded as forward movements towards non-kinship forms of association, in fact they both made backward compromises to patriarchal organisation. Particular lineages, clans and tribes seized the leadership of the state and leadership of the religions and passed on these positions through patriarchal succession resulting in the emergence of royal and priestly lineages and clans. Far from transforming patriarchy, the ancient state and religion became structured along patriarchal lines.

It must be noted that competition and conflicts arose between ethnic groups, cities and religious cadres. However, because the ancient code of conquest allowed groups that accepted the hegemony of their conquerors autonomy over their internal affairs, patriarchy was preserved among both vanquished and victors. Accordingly, conflicts between lineages, ethnic groups, cities and religious groups practising the ancient code of conquest, never challenged the foundation criteria of patriarchy: genealogy, gender and generation.

On the other hand, groups that resisted the hegemony of their conquerors suffered one of the following fates:

- The physical elimination of the group, in which all members and the group itself were killed: genocide.
- The physical removal of the political and technical cadres of the conquered group and their dispersion within cities ruled by the conquerors, thus leading to at least their partial incorporation into the empire of the conquerors.
- The killing of all the male captives while integrating the women and children of the captives into the lineages of the conquerors.
- Allowing male captives to retain their lives while removing, through castration, their capacity to perpetuate their line. These eunuchs were invariably integrated into the bureaucracy of the conquerors as intermediaries between the ruling elites and commoners.
- Enslavement of the conquered group made manumission much easier for female slaves but resulted in the males of the group remaining almost permanently enslaved.

In the ancient city states and in religious empires, male marginalisation, arising as a result of rejection of the ancient code of conquest, manifested itself in loss of elite status, loss of life, loss of reproductive capacity and almost permanent enslavement. The point that must not be missed is that, in the confrontation and conflict between kinship collectives, ethnic groups, cities and religions, among the groups that lost the contest and did not accept the hegemony of their conquerors, it was the males of those groups who lost the most and whose masculinity was eliminated or seriously compromised.

The Nation State and Patriarchy

Unlike the city states of the ancient world, nation states encompass both city and surrounding countryside. Invariably, nation states comprise several cities, with none having political primacy over the others, hence the absence of any need for client relationships between cities. Also the nation embodies cities, countryside, diverse ethnic groups and different religions, while claiming autonomy and sovereignty in its relations with other nations. That is, it claims pre-eminence in allegiance and loyalty, over and beyond every other social and political entity.

Invariably, nation states are premised on the utopian values of equality, human rights, social justice, and consent as the foundation of government. Further, the fundamental unit of national organisation is the individual national, the citizen. Each national, by virtue of nationality, is entitled to equal treatment, enjoys the same rights, guaranteed the same justice and is empowered as an elector in determining the government. These transcendental values are invariably enshrined in constitutional law. Further, the State has become the principal mechanism and chief executing agency of the values of nationhood.

By virtue of its construction, the nation state constitutes a frontal attack on society organised on the basis of patriarchy, that is, on the criteria of genealogy, gender and generation. The assault has focused mainly on genealogy as tribe, clan, caste, lineage, race and family and has been relegated officially to social categories devoid of constitutional or legal content. If the ethical vision of the universalistic religions has rendered these categories immoral, then the nation state has added the adjectives unconstitutional and illegal to their meaning in the political, economic and social conduct of the nation.

In the nation state, tribe, clan, caste, lineage, race and family are conceded as having only sentimental, nostalgic and cultural meaning.

The family itself is reduced to a nurturing unit stripped of its political and economic relationships that surrounded kinship collectives in previous civilisations. On the other hand, non-kin forms of societal organisation are given positive political, economic and social meaning. These include the State replete with parliament, courts, military establishment, police force, and civil service bureaucracy and, outside of these, the political party, the corporation, the trade union, the school and the church. All of these are constitutionally and legally required to practise the utopian values on which the nation state is predicated.

At the same time, civil society within each nation carries the legacy of tribal, clan and lineage society. Kinship allegiance, clan honour, perpetuation of the lineage and patriarchal obligations continue to be the supreme values to a greater or lesser degree. In several societies, the notion of kinship has been transposed to race, with the same assumptions of blood bonds, group solidarity and mutual obligations as in lineage society. In all versions of this type of society, the family, organised on patriarchal traditions, remains the fundamental unit of social organisation. The social reality of nation states, therefore, is that of civil society organised on the basis of kinship, clan honour, perpetuation of families, patriarchal authority and filial obligations and the State predicated on the utopian values of equality, human rights, social justice and representative democracy in which sovereignty rests with the people. Further, civil society presumes the family to be the basic unit of organisation while the State is organised on the individual as the fundamental unit of its constitutional structure.

The national project, by definition, consists of transforming civil society from its ethnic roots, kinship structure and patriarchal traditions into nations in harmony with their constitutions mandating utopian values which espouse equality, justice, rights and consent. Indeed, the mobilisation of nations resides in the implementation of the transcendental values of nationhood and the promise of material progress. It must be noted that the promise of material progress implied in nationhood, particularly to the mass of the dispossessed groups, has added yet another element of meaning to the values on which nationhood is premised.

The point that must not be overlooked is that the formation of nation states has neither been the inevitable result of social evolution nor the wholehearted embrace of the high ethical vision of nationhood. Nation states have all been constructed through the processes of dynamic interaction among groups within nations, where one or two groups become the 'chief nationalists'. While leading the construction of the nation on the utopian values of equality, individual rights and social justice enshrined in constitutional law, the 'chief nationalists' invariably skew the construction of the nation in their image and garner substantial advantages to the groups to which they belong. In this context the State, controlled by the 'chief nationalists', becomes the major instrument of constructing the nation in their image and to their advantage. The greatest promise for the success of the national project, and threat to its realisation, resides in the moral conduct, or lack of it, from those groups claiming and exercising leadership in the implementation of the mandate of nationhood.

It is this tension between efforts to construct nations out of civil society rooted in ethnicity and kinship, and the acquisition and consolidation of advantage by those groups leading the construction of the nation that has effected several important societal transformations. The essence of the transformation is from kinship to non-kinship forms of association and organisation. The national ideal and creed is that nationals of all families and ethnic groups within the nation should have an equal right to participate in the parliamentary affairs of the State, to receive equal justice through its courts, and have equal access to the bureaucracy of the State including the civil service, military establishment, police force, schools and colleges, and statutory bodies. Further, all nationals, irrespective of family or ethnicity, should be unencumbered and free to become members of political parties, religions, corporations, trade unions, clubs and all other non-governmental organisations operating in the public sphere.

The practical reality is that the inequalities of civil society organised on the basis of kinship and ethnicity, and the asymmetry of the power implied in this inequality, are not automatically swept away by applying the national creed. Invariably, in the construction of the nation state backward concessions have been made to patriarchy, very similar to what occurred in the construction of the ancient city states and in the emergence of the monotheistic religions.

Some of the factors fuelling the compromise of the full implementation of the transcendental values of the national project can be listed as follows:

- The efforts of those groups (that previously held power, commanded considerable resources, were accorded high esteem and whose culture dominated the society), to retain at least some of their former positions within the nation.
- The attempts of the newly empowered groups, not only to lead the construction of the nation, but to consolidate their position in the society and nation. Indeed, the democratisation of political power has invariably brought about more upward social mobility of those controlling and administering the machinery of the State than by the mass of the people themselves.
- The formation of alliances between the old and the new guard, to their mutual benefit, which are at variance with the utopian values of nationhood.

The result of the backward concession in that patriarchy is that its defining features, genealogy, gender and generation, are carried over into the non-kinship and voluntary entities namely political parties, unions, corporations, churches, clubs, and the like.

Two additional points need to be noted with reference to the subject of this paper. First, gender is by no means primary or pre-eminent as a criterion in the organisation of societies or nations. It is embedded within other criteria. Second, gender operates in interaction with the other criteria upon which societies and nations are organised. In other words, in social and political behaviour in society and nations, the actions of men and women need to be interpreted within the context of the interactions of criteria such as class, race, religion, region, generation, ideology and any other criterion that may be involved. This is not to say that men's and women's actions are entirely predicated on the basis of locating them relative to these criteria, since individuals may affirm or oppose or adopt a non-committal stance on any issue. Rather, the identification of the criteria, and their interaction, allows the parameters and frameworks of action to be delineated.

The Transformation of Patriarchy in the Nation State

In the course of constructing the nation state from a civil society structured on the basis of kinship and ethnicity, patriarchy is transformed mainly as a result of the operations of two processes. The first process relates to partnership between the men and women of the groups holding previous advantage in the civil society and those newly empowered in the nation, in defending and preserving or enhancing and consolidating their group's interests in the nation. These groups can be labelled the dominant groups in the society and nation. The second process relates to the exclusion of men of the subordinate groups in the civil society from much of the opportunities of upward social mobility offered in the nation. Each of these processes will be discussed in turn.

The Partnership Process

The main elements of this partnership process can be listed briefly as follows:

- Easy and preferential access to and first choice of members of dominant groups to the most powerful, strategic, prestigious and lucrative opportunities available in the particular nation. This results from being in control of the mechanisms of private and public bureaucracies.
- Patriarchal rank operates in the dominant groups to determine that greatest access and first preference to these opportunities should go to older men while last choice and least preference should be accorded to younger women.
- The magnitude of opportunities available to the dominant groups outstripping the supply of men of those groups to meet the demand.
- Women of the dominant groups being recruited in these circumstances in which the supply of older and younger men of the groups is inadequate in relation to the demand.

The essence of this partnership process is that it operates in circumstances where the available opportunities to the dominant group exceed its capacity to meet the demand through its supply of men of that group. In these circumstances patriarchal closure is relaxed in the dominant group and women of the group are co-opted and recruited to satisfy the demand. Women of the dominant group are recruited to meet the shortfall or hiatus in supply of men of that group. Failure to recruit the women of the group would result in such opportunities going to the other groups competing with or challenging the dominant group for position. In other words, women of the dominant group are mobilised to assist the group to maximise its appropriation of available opportunities. In this process, the defining feature is that men and women of the dominant group are cooperating and collaborating to advance or defend the interests or position of their group. Put in the converse, men and women of the dominant groups are cooperating and collaborating to exploit or to deny opportunities to the other groups in the nation.

The fact that men of the dominant group retain most of the top positions and most strategic occupations and women of the dominant group are assigned mainly to the intermediate positions and less strategic levels in the occupational structure highlights the demarcation between senior and junior membership of the partnership. The fact that female marginalisation in the dominant group is manifest in this arrangement, is secondary to the fact that men and women of the dominant group are acting collectively in the interest of the group and against the other groups in the society. Female marginalisation within the dominant group represents an internal disagreement and quarrel. This partnership process is first and foremost a mechanism for defending and promoting the interests of the dominant group and not that of marginalising and exploiting the women of that group.

Put another way, equality of access to opportunity within the dominant group is unlikely to make any material or substantial difference to the establishment, extension or consolidation of the hegemony of the dominant group over the other groups in the society. Men and women of the dominant group are united in their intention to advance the interests of their group against that of others. It is the marginalisation of the other groups in the society that is the primary mission, not the marginalisation of women within the dominant group itself. Men and women of the dominant group are partners in advancing the interests of their group, albeit with the women being the junior and men being the senior partners. The internal quarrel within dominant groups should not obscure the solidarity of their external relations with respect to subordinate groups within their societies.

The Exclusionary Process

The second process involves the exclusion of men of the subordinate groups in society from most of the opportunities of upward social mobility. In terms of the subordinate groups, this results in most of the opportunities for upward social mobility going to women. This process has been described by Miller (1994). The core elements involved in this second process can be listed as follows:

- Conflict between the dominant and other groups in society concerning the basis on which the society is organised and challenges that arise from existing inequalities with respect to access to opportunity within the society.
- The imperative to respond to these challenges by conceding access to opportunities to the subordinate groups in the society. Concessions to such challenges are mandated by the constitutions of nations, required by the ethical vision of nationhood and usually necessary as a result of elective politics.
- Expansion in opportunities opened up to the subordinate groups and the prospect of integration into the mainstream of society.
- Control by the dominant groups of the mechanisms and gateways through which members of the subordinate groups gain access to the available opportunities for upward social mobility.
- The willingness of some segments of the subordinate groups to accept the structure of opportunity for upward social mobility as fashioned by the dominant groups.

These elements combine to shape the exclusionary process so that, in circumstances where the dominant group has control of the mechanisms governing access to institutions serving the subordinate group, and where access to the subordinate group is being expanded, the demand is increasing. In these circumstances the former prejudices the employment process in favour of females of the subordinate groups by excluding most of the males from that group. Expanded opportunities afforded to subordinate groups constitute strong incentive to their participation, given the limited scope of the opportunities for socioeconomic advancement available to them. Acceptance of the opportunities afforded means the advancement of the group by way of their daughters rather than their sons. Many members of the subordinate groups willingly accept sponsored mobility on these terms and, in so doing, participate in the gendered outcomes.

It is important to observe that men of the subordinate group are deliberately excluded from the expanded opportunities offered to their group. The basis of that exclusion is the level of threat they pose to the dominant group for political, social, economic, ideological or cultural reasons, or some combination of these. Such exclusion is heightened in circumstances of conflict between the groups, or challenge by the subordinate, in the circumstances in which the dominant group is constrained to concede some measure of expanded opportunity to their challengers by virtue of constitutional, legal or political considerations arising from the imperatives of the nation state.

Another observation that needs to be noted is that through the exclusionary process, men of the dominant groups establish alliances with women of the subordinate groups. The asymmetry of power relations dictates that the latter would be dependent on the former for maintaining their sponsored advancement in the society. Like women of the dominant group, women of the subordinate group will occupy middle-level and intermediate positions within the private and public bureaucracies and, in the process, operate as lieutenants of men of the dominant group occupying the top positions. These alliances generally earn the resentment of men of the subordinate group.

A third observation is that those women of the subordinate group who do not benefit from the sponsored mobility offered, remain the most marginalised in the society. Indeed, they continue to operate within the traditional boundaries of patriarchy. Further, many of their sons are counted among the underclass of men. In other words, it is within the subordinate group that both male and female marginalisation coincides and interacts and in a manner that reinforces the other. For example,

Gregory (1991) found that most of the street children were boys whose mothers were of low socioeconomic status who, at an early age, had entered into a series of unions with men, hoping for financial support that did not materialise.

Implications of Both Processes for the Transformation of Patriarchy

The partnership process redefines, extends and expands patriarchy within dominant groups to encompass the public as well as the private sphere. This is because their scope of authority and influence is expanded to encompass the subordinate groups. The rule of fathers in the family, lineage, or clan is extended to non-kin groups: political parties, trade unions, colleges, schools, corporations, religious organisations, the civil service etc. Accordingly, men of the dominant groups become the leaders of political parties, executives of corporations, heads of trade unions, heads of civil service bureaucracies, top officers in the security forces.

The essence of this transformation is that non-kin associations and organisations within the public sphere of the nation come to have the same structure of kinship collectives in the civil society. Patriarchy is transformed from being a feature of tribal groups and kinship collectives into new forms within non-kin associations and organisations as fathers within the groups leading the nationalist charge or holding great economic resources seize or consolidate their places in the new nation. The end result is the patriarchal state, political patriarchy, religious patriarchy, corporate patriarchy, trade union patriarchy etc., as men of the dominant group seize places in these areas within the public sphere in the nation.

The movement away from the rule of fathers in blood-bonded collectives to that of men in political parties, corporations, trade unions, colleges, schools, and other such non-kin organisations, transforms patriarchy from being the rule of fathers to rule of men. In other words, in the absence of filial relationship, the rule of fathers is transformed into the rule of men. Dahlerup (1987) noted the emergence of the patriarchal state and observed that its defining feature was that it functions in the interest of men. The position taken here is that men and women of the group controlling the mechanisms of the patriarchal state commandeer these mechanisms of the state to serve their interests and prerogatives.

While the partnership process extends the patriarchy of the dominant group from the private to the public sphere and advances or consolidates the hegemony of that group over the subordinate group in the society, by according some women of the dominant group the role of junior partner in advancing group interests in the public sphere, gender as an organising principle in society is compromised. These junior partners of the dominant group now exercise power over men of the subordinate group. At the same time, the junior position in the partnership raises the question of its justice, particularly in the context of the national creed professing equal rights and justice.

The second process, involving male marginalisation in the subordinate group, is even more radical in undermining patriarchy, in that genealogy, gender and generation are all compromised as organising principles in the society. By sponsoring the mobility of members of the subordinate group to positions previously reserved for the dominant group, genealogy is compromised. By advancing young people over older folk, generation is called into question. By skipping young women over their fathers and brothers, and prospective spouses, gender is compromised.

The net result of such sponsored mobility is that some women of the subordinate group become even more liberated from traditional patriarchal and feminine roles than their peers in the dominant group. Not only are they accorded roles in the public sphere, but they also become heads of households in their own right and not simply substitutes in one generation until male succession is restored. Patriarchy in the private sphere is reversed in a large proportion of the subordinate group as, through the process of male marginalisation, many men are without the means and symbols through which they may sustain their traditional masculine and paternal roles as prescribed by patriarchy.

The exclusionary process undermines patriarchy in the subordinate group. This is accomplished by the following:

- Breaching patriarchal rank by promoting women over their fathers, brothers and spouses.
- Undermining the material symbols by which the males of the subordinate group reinforce their authority within the group.

- Fostering matrifocal forms of socialisation in homes and schools, consistent with the structure of opportunity in which girls are most likely to succeed in accessing the socioeconomic opportunities for advancement open to the group.
- Fracturing solidarity in the subordinate group by the differential rates of incorporation of males and females into the mainstream of the society which, in the long term, results in the men being blamed for their lack of socioeconomic progress, and men resenting the advancement of females of the group ahead of themselves.

These two processes are by no means mutually exclusive. Indeed, they are highly compatible. The first process operates mainly, but not exclusively, within the dominant group, and those other groups in the society with which they establish alliances. The second process operates largely within the subordinate group in circumstances of conflict with the dominant group.

Ironically, at the same time that patriarchy is transformed and extended, by both processes, to encompass the private as well as the public spheres in the nation, it is also compromised and weakened. The factors related to this can be listed briefly as follows:

- As the authority and power of the men of the dominant groups are expanded, there is the corresponding marginalisation of large numbers of men of the subordinate groups, resulting in increased polarisation between men in the nation. While a few men become increasingly more powerful, many men become part of a highly marginalised underclass. At the same time, the position of women becomes more equalised, as many women of both the dominant and the subordinate groups come to occupy middle positions in the public and private bureaucracies in the nation. While these women are subject to the glass ceiling imposed by the men of the dominant group, the former are in a much more advantageous position than men of the underclass.
- The masculine bias in the dominant group and the underclass and the feminisation of the middle strata result in a state of flux in numerous relationships previously constructed on the basis of

patriarchal norms. Patriarchy is compromised as many young women exercise authority over fathers, several wives become the chief providers of families, many mothers become heads of households, numerous women are unable to find husbands of comparable social and economic status and therefore decide to become single parents, and large numbers of girls outperform boys in schools.

- The polarised position of men in the nation is marked by the criteria upon which the civil society is organised. For example, if the society is organised on the basis of ethnicity, religion, class, gender and generation, then the men of the dominant group will tend to belong to one ethnic group, the upper class, a different denomination or religion and be older than the men of the underclass who will tend to be of other ethnic groups, lower class, a different denomination or religion and be younger. These bases of inequality stand condemned in the national creed and constitution. Hence, the moral authority of the dominant group is undermined and diminished by charges of corruption, patronage, clientelism, nepotism, discrimination and victimisation which they cannot successfully defend given the marked disparities.

- Political, corporate, union, school and other non-kin association bonds are relatively weak compared to blood bonds assumed in kinship collectives. Given this weakness, there is the tendency for non-kin associations and organisations to fracture and disintegrate in the face of sustained resistance or gross failure to comply with their mandate.

- Confusion of roles and relationships results as traditional roles are undermined and subverted with the new roles and relationships appearing as deficits, deviations and defaults of tradition. Accordingly, there is little celebration of the changing roles and relationships but great condemnation arising from the departure from tradition.

Implications of Both Processes for Male Marginalisation

Both the partnership and the exclusionary processes contribute to male marginalisation in the subordinate groups. The partnership process contributes to male marginalisation indirectly by diverting opportunities to females of the dominant group or their clients that would otherwise have gone to males of the subordinate group. The exclusionary process contributes directly to male marginalisation in that it actively excludes these males in preference to the females of that group. The greatest impact on male marginalisation occurs when both processes are employed.

Changes in the Nature of Power in Society

In *Men at Risk*, I showed that over the long haul of history, and with the fundamental changes that have taken place in the form, nature and organisation of society, some important shifts have taken place in relation to the exercise of power. The broad dimensions of this shift can be briefly described as follows:

- The shift in the distribution of power causing power in society to become increasingly centralised. In ancient society, many men through patriarchal authority exercised absolute power over the small autonomous groups to which they belonged. In modern society, fewer and fewer men exercise absolute power over more and more people including other men. This centralisation of power has led to the marginalisation of large numbers of men who hitherto had exercised power, albeit over small groups.
- The shift in the location of power from the private to the public sphere. In ancient society, life and death, occupation, discipline of family members, sexual behaviour, education and all other matters related to group survival were the prerogative of the autonomous clan or tribe or kinship collective. Over the course of history and increasingly in the nation state, authority in these matters has tended rather to be transferred to the public sphere and to public bureaucrats in the civil service, courts, schools, parliaments, etc. Protection and provision have become the responsibility of States, especially in those states with highly developed welfare systems. The traditional role of men as protectors and providers for the kinship collective, of which they are members, has been severely eroded.
- The shift in the main modality of the idiom of power from the personalistic to the materialistic; the open and transparent exercise

of power in the personalistic idiom, replete with codes of chivalry and honour, did much for the male macho image, even if this was more in its assumptions rather than in practice. Power in the materialistic idiom is covert, disguised, impersonal and sometimes deceitful. The materialistic idiom does not inspire nearly the same allegiance or admiration as does the personalistic idiom.

The point here is that, in the transformation of power as it is located, distributed and expressed, men have been more seriously affected and in a more negative way than women. This is because patriarchy as it was constructed in nascent human society centralised large numbers of men and socialised them to expect this centralised position to be their birthright. Fundamental changes in the nature, structure and organisation of society associated with substantial shifts in the distribution, location and idiom of power has had much more substantial and negative influence on men by virtue of their centralisation in patriarchal structures.

The opposite has been true of women. Having been marginalised within patriarchal structures for thousands of years, many women have indeed been liberated from their historic marginalisation by the fundamental changes and consequential shifts in three dimensions of power. While many men may be confronted by changes that have negatively impacted their expectations and socialisation, many women are inspired by the new opportunities resulting from the emerging configuration of society and power.

In the confusion that has surrounded many of these changes, ironically, some women have not celebrated their liberation from marginalisation within patriarchy but have instead interpreted their circumstances in terms of male failure to perform their traditional patriarchal roles. Likewise, many men have not afforded themselves the opportunity to understand these changes and have instead embarked on courses of self-destruction and the destruction of others in a manner consistent with the traditional definition of masculinity in patriarchy which directs violence at anything that it does not understand or cannot control.

Concluding Comment

From the foregoing explanation it should be plain that male domination and male marginalisation are not mutually exclusive phenomena; nor are female marginalisation and male marginalisation. These phenomena are interrelated and are outcomes of the processes of domination and subordination resulting from the contest, conflict competition and confrontation between groups in society for power, resources and social advantage. In these conflicts and confrontations, gender is never the primary axis of solidarity between groups. Men and women of particular groups strive to obtain or retain dominance in society. Hence, men and women are complicit in the marginalisation of members of their own gender.

Further, much of the manifestation of male marginalisation in contemporary society is related to the transformation of patriarchy within the framework of a rights-based nation state premised on equality, social justice, democracy and the individual as the fundamental unit of social organisation. It is to be hoped that a better understanding of the processes at work will assist women and men to engage constructively and creatively and to cope with the challenges posed.

References

Collins, P.H. 1990. *Black Feminist Thought*. New York: Routledge.

Dahlerup, D. 1987. 'Confusing Concepts - Confusing Reality: A Theoretical Discussion of the Patriarchal State'. *Women and the State: The Shifting Boundaries of Public and Private*. A. S. Sassoon. London: Hutchinson, 93-127.

Foucault, M. 1981. *The History of Sexuality*. Harmondsworth, Pelican.

Gregory, Carol. 1991. 'Street Children in Jamaica' in Proceedings of the Third NGO Sector Meeting, Kingston, Jamaica. Canadian Cooperative Office November 1991.

Hartmann, Heidi I. 1979. *Capitalism, Patriarchy and Job Segregation by Sex*. New York: Monthly Review Press.

hooks, b. 1984. *Feminist Theory: from margin to center*. Boston: South End Press.

Lerner, G. 1986. *The Creation of Patriarchy*. Oxford: Oxford University Press.

Miller, Errol. 1986 and 1994. *Marginalisation of the Black Male*. Institute of Social and Economic Research, University of the West Indies, Mona.

Miller, Errol. 1990. *Jamaican Society and High Schooling*. Kingston: Institute of Social and Economic Research, University of the West Indies.

Miller, Errol. 1991. *Men at Risk*. Kingston: Jamaica Publishing House.

Miller, Errol. 2003. *The Prophet and the Virgin: The Masculine and Feminine Roots of Teaching*. Kingston: Ian Randle Publishers.

Reddock, R.E. 1994. *Women, Labour & Politics in Trinidad & Tobago: A History*. Kingston: Ian Randle Publishers.

Robertson, Roland. 1990. 'After Nostalgia? Wilful Nostalgia and the Phases of Globalization'. In *Theories of Modernity and Postmodernity*, ed. by Bryan S. Turner, 45-61. London: Sage Publications.

Rowland, Robyn, and Renate D. Klein. 1991. 'Radical feminism: Introduction'. In *A Reader in Feminist Knowledge*, ed. Sneja Gunew, 305-307. London: Routledge.

Skinner, Quentin. 1985. 'Introduction: The Return to Grand Design Theory in the Human Sciences'. In *The Return to Grand Design Theory in the Human Sciences*, ed. Quentin Skinner. Cambridge: Cambridge University Press.

Skjelsbaek, Inger. 1997. 'Gendered Battlefieds: A Gender Analysis of Peace and Conflict'. Oslo, International Peace Research Institute (PRIO), PRIO Report 6/97.

Walby, S. 1990. *Theorizing Patriarchy*. Oxford: Basil Blackwood Ltd.

Weber, M. 1947. *The Theory of Social and Economic Organisation*. New York: Free Press.

Young, Iris. 1981. 'Beyond the unhappy marriage: a critique of dual systems theory'. In *Women and Revolution: the unhappy marriage of Marxism and feminism*, ed. by Lydia Sargent. London: Pluto Press.

6 | MARK FIGUEROA

Old (Female) Glass Ceilings and New (Male) Looking Glasses
Challenging Gender Privileging in the Caribbean

Abstract

The twentieth century witnessed significant challenges to historic male gender privileging within the socioeconomic, political and cultural life of the Caribbean. Women have moved into many positions formerly occupied by men but, in doing so, women have been far more successful in the less prestigious fields and have made limited progress at the leadership levels. Meanwhile, men have been much less likely to move into female-dominated fields. In seeking to unravel the issues involved in challenging gender privileging, three case studies are explored. Two relate to leadership: first in election day activities and second in the academy. The third contrasts males' failure to move into academic fields dominated by women with a significant acceptance by males of a new body image and with it a shift into the field of personal care, a decidedly female sphere.

Introduction

It is possible to observe many significant shifts in Caribbean gender roles in the second half of the twentieth century. In fact, some of these shifts appear overwhelming when first considered. At the same time, a deeper analysis reveals a persistence of underlying gender-role stereotyping. In my paper, I look at three different spheres of activity with a view to exploring this apparent paradox. I show that, although women have moved into areas previously dominated by men, there are some areas far more resistant to change. This is in part the old story about female glass ceilings. Similarly, while men have been less likely to move into areas previously dominated by women, they too have made shifts. This is in part the story of the new looking glasses through which many men are coming to reflect their self-image. While perhaps raising more questions than answers, I seek to identify a number of key elements that need to be explained if we are to have a satisfactory analysis of gender transformations in the Caribbean.

In the first three sections of my paper, I present data on what might be loosely seen as three case studies. The first two are more closely related in so far as they deal with the issue of women taking on leadership in fields previously dominated by men. The two spheres that I cover are the running of Jamaican elections and academic work at UWI. In both cases, I look at the relative progress that women have made in terms of their share of leadership at the highest level. I contrast women's participation at different levels in these spheres and within the more and less prestigious activities related to these spheres. The third case is somewhat different as it contrasts the failure of men to move into academic disciplines dominated by women with a growing willingness by men to take on one sphere previously dominated by women. This is the sphere of personal care. The third case is also different in that the first two are presented in terms of quantitative data; the latter is more qualitative as it proved difficult to obtain hard data to illustrate the shift of male grooming patterns. I proceed by presenting each case with a minimum of discussion, after which I seek to provide some analysis of the extent to which gender privileging has, and has not, been challenged in the Caribbean.

Running Elections

Linnette Vassell (2000) has provided ample data to demonstrate the extent to which men have continued to dominate leadership roles in Jamaica. In particular, she has demonstrated the dominance that men continue to exercise at the top levels of political leadership. Before examining her data, we can note that none of Jamaica's six prime ministers has been female and the three post-colonial governors-general have also been male.[1] Table 1 presents a summary of Vassell's data compiled in 1998. The data are being used in preference to later data as they were compiled right after the 1997 parliamentary elections in which women achieved the highest ever elected representation in the nation's history. Based on this summary, 12 per cent of the Cabinet, 13 per cent of the House of Representatives, and 24 per cent of the Senate and local government councils consisted of women. This male dominance was replicated in the top leadership of the governing and opposition parties where women made up approximately 20 per cent of the executive bodies.

With the top political leadership in Jamaica so dominated by males, the uninformed observer might be excused for thinking that women play a very limited role in politics. This is certainly not the case when it comes to organising at the grass-roots level. While it is true that the vast majority of party leaders, cabinet members, members of parliament, local government councillors and top political administrators have been men, this is not the whole story. Politics and political participation involve many layers and, whereas men dominate at the top, this is not true for the entire structure. To examine the question of gender participation in politics, I have initiated a programme of research on participation in Jamaican elections, some preliminary results of which I report here. Table 2 indicates that, relative to their share of the adult population, men and women show very little difference in their willingness to register to vote, or to vote once registered. This is the first time that the male-female breakdown of voting is being looked at in any depth for a Jamaican election, as such conclusions are tentative. In addition, the sample I am using was taken for only three of the 14 parishes (municipal divisions). It will not be possible to draw definite conclusions until a representative sample is done for the entire country for a number of elections. From our sample it appears that women may be slightly less likely to vote once registered but because they represent a larger share of the adult population there is an approximately equal turnout at the polls for men and women. The different parishes seem to present moderate variations in voting patterns. Despite any differences, it is clear that women are participating at a comparable level to men. In time, I hope to extend this quantitative analysis of political participation through a study of gender and party political activism at all levels. For this paper it has not been possible to carry out this analysis based on data from the political parties but it is possible to get some good insights using data from the Electoral Office of Jamaica (EOJ).

Participation in the electoral process involves a wide variety of activities. These include administration of elections from the enumeration of voters to the final publishing of the results. Here, I am primarily focusing on what takes place on election day. Some of the roles in this process are carried out by political activists whose job it is to protect their party's candidate's interest. Other persons should not, by law, be affiliated with any party or candidate, as their jobs relate to ensuring that the elections are conducted fairly. The former group consists of scrutineers and indoor agents who are paid by the state although supplied by the parties/candidates. Scrutineers go along with the enumerators to the homes of electors to watch the enumeration exercise, while indoor agents observe during the process of polling.

The person in charge of each polling station on election day is called a presiding officer. Each presiding officer is assisted by a poll clerk. To promote good order at each polling station, a citizen is usually appointed as a 'one-day police'. There is a returning officer who, with a small staff, is responsible for the administration of the election in all the polling stations within a given constituency. The administrative head of the electoral process is the director of elections who is guided by the Electoral Advisory Committee. Although those listed above are the main persons running the elections there are others such as ballot box couriers, landlords for premises used, and cleaners and handymen who are also active in the process. The political parties also employ outdoor agents and runners whose task generally involves, among other things, seeking to ensure that party supporters come out to vote.

An analysis of participation in the electoral process reveals an overwhelming preponderance of women. The majority of those who participate in the various activities directly connected to the administration of the polling process on election day are women. The main participation by men is in the role of 'one-day police' and at the higher levels of the administrative process. The percentage of men and women involved in the different election day roles is summarised in Table 3.² While over 80 per cent of all poll clerks and presiding officers are women, nearly 80 per cent of the returning officers are men. This tendency to reserve roles that exercise leadership for men is also manifest in the fact that men make up approximately half of the supervisors who oversee polling station clusters, while those who do the work inside the polling stations are four times more likely to be women. Simply put, as you move up the hierarchy, women fall away. The vast majority of poll clerks and presiding officers are women but they represent a decreasing number as you move through the ranks of supervisors, assistant returning officers and returning officers.

Despite this limitation, it can be argued that women have made modest progress within the electoral administration. During the first adult suffrage elections held in 1944, there were no female returning officers. At that time, there were no assistant returning officers, but a number of reviewing officers were appointed in each constituency to receive submissions concerning the voters' list. In 1949, only three per cent of these were women. I have no hard data on the relative share of women as presiding officers at this time but the recollection of persons involved in politics then is that they formed a minority. By the 1970s, they had come to be a significant majority in election day administration.³ What is striking is that, in order to establish themselves as a significant fraction of the leadership within this area, women have had to completely dominate the area starting on the lower rungs. Yet, despite their dominance for at least 25 years, if not longer, the top positions are still largely held by men.

Although I do not have complete data on party activists at the grass-roots level, women represented over 80 per cent of indoor agents. This gives us some idea of the relative share of men and women in electoral organisation. Indoor agents are chosen as persons who know the voters in the polling division. Often these persons would have been involved in the enumeration exercise as scrutineers or in the party's own canvass of the area. In the grass-roots structures of the parties, the women predominate. Thus it is not surprising to discover that females accounted for 84 per cent of the indoor agents while men accounted for only 16 per cent. Women are the main ones to attend the local party meetings and keep the base-level organisations going, even where some or all of the official officers are males. Yet the base-level organisations still have a tendency to elect a disproportionate number of male officers and to send a disproportionate number of male delegates to higher party bodies. As has been noted above, male participation predominates on the security side. In the case of the formal administration of the electoral system, this is manifest in their presence as 'one-day police'. But while the official 'one-day police' are seldom called on to use physical force, there is no doubt that within the Jamaican system there is a male-dominated informal network of intimidation and violence. At the grass-roots, while women take care of much of the visible organising, men are more involved in another kind of political participation that is most clearly manifested in the garrison communities.[4]

In this way, even as gender roles have changed in Jamaican politics, the more fundamental gendered division of labour has not changed. Men continue to dominate in the spheres relating to the exercise of force. Men continue to dominate at the level of leadership. Women predominate in those activities associated with the more routine aspect of the work and women also dominate in the more static and indoor-type activities. I have no hard data to substantiate this latter point with respect to the party organisations, but persons associated with the process have suggested that, while the vast majority of indoor agents are women, there is a greater likelihood of finding men appointed as outdoor agents and even more so runners, where men often still constitute a substantial majority.

Women's move into leadership in election-day activities has not been dramatic but it has outstripped their move into political leadership. Table 4 compares the number of female returning officers with the number of MPs for selected elections from 1944 to 2002. Starting from a lower base (zero versus three per cent) in 1944, the figure for returning officers in 2002 (30 per cent) was considerably higher than that for Members of Parliament (12 per cent). Like heads of government, all those who have served as the chief administrative officer for the direction of elections have been male. The relative success in the administrative as against the political leadership can also be seen in relation to those who were appointed as the administrative and political leaders of ministries after the 2002 elections. In the administrative sphere, women held a 50 per cent share of the 16 permanent secretary posts as against their 18 per cent share of the 17 ministerial posts in the Cabinet.

Academic Leadership

On a number of indicators, women have come to predominate in the educational system. The large proportion of women who enter and pass examinations at the secondary and tertiary level has received a great deal of attention (See UWI 2002 and references). Less attention has been paid to the fact that the preponderance of women in education has not been reflected in terms of a matching presence at the highest levels in the system. This is true even when we take into account the lag time that it would take the growing number of women at the lower levels of the system to work their way to the top.

To illustrate this point, I consider the professoriate at UWI for those years for which data are readily available. Within a university, it is those who are recognised by their peers as being deserving of a chair who ultimately receive the greatest honour and respect. Those who hold the posts in the academic administration, including deans, principals and vice chancellors, often wield far more power but it is when one retires and is acclaimed as Professor Emeritus by one's peers, that one can be satisfied that one's university career has come to a most successful close. Thus, in considering academic leadership, I focus primarily on the professoriate, although the same analysis could also be made in terms of those who hold the top positions within the academic administration of the academy.

Table 5 shows that the proportion of women among the academic staff at UWI increased from 22 to 35 per cent between 1988 and 2001. During the same period, the percentage of women in the professoriate lagged far behind. For the five years between 1997 and 2001, females were, on average, just over ten per cent of the total number of professors for the three UWI campuses (UWI, various years).[5] The ratio of female professors to the total female academic staff was also much smaller than the comparable ratio for males. For the five years 1997-2001 the percentage of male academics who were professors was on average over 13 per cent, while for women the figure was on average less than three per cent. This indicates that the low representation of women within the professoriate does not simply result from the existence of a time lag after which the imbalance will be corrected as women experience promotion within the system.

To demonstrate that this is so, we can look at the available pool from which the professoriate is drawn. The bulk of UWI professors are now, and increasingly will be, graduates of UWI. Thus, we can look at the student registrations at UWI as a proxy for the number of men and women available for appointment as professors subject to an appropriate lag.[6] To determine the appropriate lag, the academic career of all those persons holding chairs at the Mona campus was reviewed. The average number of years that have elapsed since their graduation was found to be approximately 33 years.[7] Note: this is not the time between graduation and appointment to a chair, which would be, on average, shorter. Rather we need to focus on the years since graduation, as persons, once appointed, stay on for a number of years thereafter. For this paper it was not possible to conduct the analysis with respect to date of appointment to a chair. When the data become available, it will be possible to carry out a richer analysis.

Table 5 shows that the percentage of female professors has remained far below the percentage of women in the pool from which professors could have been recruited. That is, the students registered at UWI lagged by 33 years. Based on the male-female balance within this pool of students, there ought to have been three times as many female professors in 2001 than there were. Information was not immediately available on the average length of time since graduation for lecturers, but we can compare the percentage of lecturers with the pool of students lagged by 33, 23 and 13 years. We note that in the 1980s the percentage of female lecturers was still below the percentage of females registered as students – lagged by 33 years. Only after 1996 did this situation change. At no stage does the percentage of female academics come close to the percentage of female students registered – lagged by 23 years. If women are catching up in the academic field, they are doing so very slowly and they are making very heavy weather with regard to storming the highest levels of academic leadership. Some modest progress was made during the late 1990s at the lecture level. Indications are that the women will remain at more than 35 per cent of the academic staff in the future, but up to the end of the 1990s there was no indication that they would be making similar gains in terms of the percentage of chairs held.

In contrast, women have fared somewhat better in terms of appointments to the administrative and professional staff at UWI.[8] At the beginning of the 1990s, women had established themselves at the 40 per cent level in these categories. By the end of the 1990s, indications were that women could expect to be approximately 60 per cent of this category in the immediate future. Appointments at the levels equivalent to an academic professor also seem to be following a secular trend upwards. At the start of the 1990s, such appointments were below the ten per cent level. By the end of the decade they fluctuated between the low 20s and 30 per cent. If the trend continues, they may come to settle above the 30 per cent level in the near future. To achieve a 30 per cent share in the leadership in this field, women have had to become a very significant majority at 60 per cent.

Leaving aside the special case of education, which has now produced quite a few female professors (at least two of whom have been in gender studies), the arts-based disciplines have seen the next largest percentage of female professors. At Mona, over 40 per cent of the professors in arts-based disciplines were female by the end of 2003. This has been achieved in the context where, 33 years ago, close to 80 per cent of the students in arts-based disciplines would have been women. To achieve a substantial share of the academic leadership as with other areas of leadership, women will have had to almost completely dominate the field before the transformation at the top starts to take place.

Men doing Woman Things

If women have moved into leadership roles previously held by men at a slow pace, we need to question whether men have been moving into roles, formally occupied by women, in any substantial way. To illustrate that this is not happening in the academy, I compared student registrations in three fields. I chose those that might be considered as having been hardcore female and male fields over the last 30 years. The hardcore female fields are nursing and library studies, numbers for which are present in Table 6, first separately and then together. The hardcore male field I chose was engineering. Table 6 shows that women have made progress with respect to gaining entry into engineering, moving from three per cent of registrations in 1975 to 30 per cent in 2002. The relative number of men registering to do nursing and library studies has actually declined over the past three decades, starting in 1975 at ten per cent and falling to seven per cent in 2002.

Despite their reluctance to move into female dominated spheres, there is one area where men have perhaps shown a willingness to take on things formerly seen as female. In my paper (1996, 26) I noted that:

> Faced with their own limited possibilities in the last 20 years, boys have sought to take on one aspect of female privilege. This is the privilege of being pretty. Thus if the boys have taken anything from the girls it has been an enormous preoccupation with their appearance …. What has happened in Jamaica over the last decade is something qualitatively different for a society where the wearing of cologne by a man was seen as a sign of being effeminate just a generation or so ago. Jewellery including ear and other body piercing, elaborate hairstyles including chemical processing and dyeing, the latest styles in clothes and shoes as well as the use of perfumes, all unthinkable within Jamaican society a generation ago, are now the attributes of typical young males.

Unknown to me at the time, Mark Simpson (1994) was credited (WordSpy.com) with the introduction of the term 'metrosexual' into the language to describe a comparable phenomenon that he noted primarily in the major cities of the developed world. In recent times there has been a flurry of attention to this group of persons not only by the media but by the marketers anxious to sell them new grooming and cosmetic products (*The Economist*, 2003, Warren St John, 2003).[9] The rise of this and related tendencies has been seen as having positive as well as negative elements. On the negative side, 'an under-recognised form of body dysmorphic disorder' was identified in 1996 by Roberto Olivardia. This, he and his co-authors have styled as the 'Adonis complex' in a book by the same name (Harrison Pope, Katharine Philips and Roberto Olivardia, 2002). A sign of this new element is the editorial in the May 2003 issue of *Glamour* entitled 'Crazed. Insecure. Meet the new body image victims: Men'.

The same article suggests that male spending on personal care remains below a tenth of what women spend. This may be an underestimate as many personal-care products can and are being used by both men and women even where they are primarily marketed to women. Even if males are still using cosmetics, perfumes and hair-care products owned by their girlfriends, mothers, sisters and wives, there is wide consensus that the male self-care product market is growing rapidly. This has led to the launch of men's lines of personal-care products by many of the leading players in the industry. Clinique, Neutrogena, L'Oréal and Estée Lauder are just a few of the big names getting in on the act.

This has also been accompanied by a growth in the number of men's magazines dedicated to what were previously thought of as women's magazine issues and the expansion of beauty and fashion segments in the magazines (such as GQ) which have been established in the men's magazine field for some time. This new focus has been driven by, and is reflected in, the growth in advertising in these magazines by major cosmetic firms. Major sporting and entertainment figures have become cultural icons for this new grooming phenomenon. The most commonly mentioned comes from the unlikely field of British soccer known for its hard male working-class laddism. He is the captain of the English football team, David Beckham. Perhaps equally unlikely is Ian Thorpe who, although in the softer sport of swimming, hails from Australia which has been stereotyped for its 'caveman' style machismo manifested in its religious-like dedication to hard male sports. Dennis Rodman is another player in this field, perhaps not changing his hairstyle as often as Beckham, but certainly excelling in his willingness to change its colour. He, like many men of this sort, has no difficulty appearing in public fully made-up. This latter tendency has found its adherents among many of the US entertainers of African heritage, who are also noted not only for their eye make-up but also for their tendency to give their eyebrows some assistance if they were not adequately arched by nature.

It has proved difficult thus far to get hard data to assess how much this international trend is manifesting itself in the Caribbean. As noted above, it is hard to know where the growth in demand for personal products is coming from, and a brief survey of Jamaican firms suggests that insufficient research has been done in this field. More generally, the absence of a research culture in Jamaican businesses meant that I would have to dedicate far more time to this research than was available if I wished to come up with data that I was often told was in the archives. One firm did note that their main line of hair-dye for men was growing at a faster rate than the comparable product for women, and all persons interviewed agreed that there had been a noticeable growth in men's interest in personal care. This growing interest has led to the introduction of new products on the market, notably by Neutrogena and Soft Sheen.

Many Jamaican men, like their counterparts elsewhere, do not feel shy to attend beauty salons and not just for haircuts, as facials, manicures and pedicures are also on the bill. This has led to the rise of a more unisex-type operation and even the presence of the salon dedicated to the 'Totally Male', in Kingston. The local male entertainers appear, in large measure, to be following their North Atlantic counterparts. Even more striking is the growth in the male-model industry in Jamaica. The various model competitions that occur annually are attracting a larger and larger segment of males, to the point where advertisements are presenting the pictures of male and female models together.[10] While the word 'nurse', when referring to a man, is almost inevitably prefaced by the word 'male', men have apparently so entrenched themselves in the field, that the word 'model' no longer needs that preface. The local newspapers no longer display only half-naked women on their pages; we are now treated to half-naked men as well. At least for a large segment of Jamaican men, when it comes to how you look, doing what women do is not a problem.

Given the limitations of statistical data, I present a contrasting iconography to illustrate aspects of the new and old male-body images that have been presented to the Caribbean male. My first image demonstrates that there were always beautiful men but the way in which men seek to project their beauty differs. In Plate 1, contrast the natural beauty of Mohammad Ali with the tattooed, lip-coloured, multiple ear-, nose- and nipple-pierced Lenny Kravitz. In Plate 2, I contrast the presentation of the youth stars of then and now, in particular the relative simplicity of two of the Jackson brothers with the very girlie looking Omarion and Lil' Bow Wow. Plate 3 represents the bounds to which we have reached. Not many of us who grew up knowing basketballers like Kareem and Hakeem could have predicted Dennis. Finally, in Plate 4, I emphasise that the concern with male-body appearance is not always towards the kind of refined presentation evidenced by Omarion and Lil' Bow Wow, but can involve what might be considered super-macho as in Elephant Man. What is common is the projection of the image based on a level of cosmetic products that was unthinkable when the original dancehall stars like U Roy were coming of age.

Summary of Cases

In the second half of the twentieth century, women have moved into many spaces previously occupied by men. This has caused alarm in some circles as the numerical preponderance of women in certain fields, notably education, has been seen by some as a takeover. What my first two case studies show is that women have failed to take over the higher levels of fields even where they establish themselves as large majorities at the lower levels. In addition, where there is an administrative area side by side with a more prestigious sphere, women tend to make more progress on the administrative side. Thus, far from taking over, women are increasingly doing more of the routine work and may in fact be covering ground that their male superiors are responsible for. In these cases, they get neither credit nor cash in recompense, while their male bosses take the accolades. These cases also demonstrate that the failure of women to reach the highest levels is not merely due to the lag in time between their entering the field at lower levels and being promoted through the ranks to the top. Women have made progress but the old patterns of gender privileging continue to reproduce themselves. Supporting male-gender privileging is an ideological perspective that is internalised by both men and women. I have previously summarised this outlook in the following way: 'The notions that men must lead and women must follow; that men must design while women must implement; that men must develop what women must administer; that men must construct for women to maintain; men must analyse where women must feel; that men must manage the complex while women steer the routine' (Figueroa 2002, 17). This ideological perspective remains strongest in holding back women in two spheres of activity for it is seen largely as a given that women 'were incapable of mastering certain (high status) technical and scientific fields ... and that leadership was a male domain. These last two linger on, preventing women from dominating the technological fields and taking over the most senior positions' (Figueroa 2000, 76).

The UWI case demonstrates that women have in fact made more progress in entering a number of highly technical fields than they have in establishing themselves in leadership positions. The UWI case also demonstrates that, while women are making some progress in penetrating hardcore male fields such as engineering, men have shown no inclination to get involved in traditionally female fields such as nursing and librarianship. The third case indicates that there are exceptions to this rule.

Analysis of Cases

The maintenance of power in the hands of men is ultimately central to the maintenance of male privileging. Thus, it is not surprising that leadership, especially in the more important spheres, remains in the hands of men. At the same time, the privileging of men in the more important spheres alerts us to the fact that when women take over leadership in a particular field three things may be taking place. The first is that the particular area may be declining in significance and, as such, there is no great loss in handing it over. The second is where the formal positions are handed over but a shadow power of an informal (and more significant kind) is primary. Maxine Henry-Wilson refers to a similar phenomenon in terms of women becoming surrogates for men in the exercise of political power (Maxine Henry 1987). The third is where women are making some inroads into male power, and this causes men to abandon the less significant spheres in favour of retaining power in areas that are relatively more significant. Thus the strong presence of women in teaching and the civil service in Jamaica has not been accompanied by an advance of equal strength in commerce and banking.

The failure of men to move into spheres previously dominated by women is an indicator that either these fields remain low-prestige or that men have alternatives. For a woman to move into a man's field is for her to move up; for a man to move into a woman's field is for him to move down. How then do we explain the case of the shift in grooming patterns? A number of factors suggest themselves. The first is that which I put forward in 1996 and which I quoted above: that men, having seen a loss of space elsewhere, fall back on their body image as a last stand for the defence of their masculinity. Thus, the 'metrosexual' is often seen as taking care of his body not in a narrowly cosmetic way but in a manner more often associated with the maintenance of a gym-toned body. It is when this becomes an obsession that the 'Adonis complex' kicks in. Those who focus on the problem of body-image insecurity see the concern for the body not as a reclaiming of masculinity but rather a kind of victimhood similar to that which women have suffered for a long time. This body-image insecurity can be seen as being imposed by the fashion and cosmetic conglomerates in their ruthless desire for profits at the expense of the self-image of women and now increasingly men. Thus, just as the unattainable media images of the ideal woman have led to anorexia in young women, men are today being subjected to the same kind of abuse. In this manner, men are seen as losing control over their bodies as women have lost control in the past.

Another suggestion is that men are losing control of their bodies to women. It has been argued that the increased power and resources that women control places them in a position where they have a greater say in how men look. Thus, in order to relate to women and to achieve in societies where women now have greater power, men need to take more interest in their body image as this is a growing preference among women. This can be seen most directly in the need of men to take more interest in their appearance when seeking to accompany women in public. Not to pay attention to these details could reduce one's dateworthiness. An alternative perspective shows this tendency as liberating for men. Young men are seen as being more accepting of what is seen as their feminine side and are therefore less repressed than previous generations. Young men thus seem to be catching up with earlier generations of women who have, in recent years, been allowed to be more in touch with what might be considered as their masculine side. Here a caveat needs to be lodged with respect to the question of men catching up in this sphere. While it is true that men are now more concerned with personal care, women may be going to greater lengths in this field as well. As such, we may have to speak in relative terms and not just in terms of an absolute increase in male interest.

Older men, especially those who have lived through the many twists and turns since the late 1950s, are seen as ready to accept yet another new trend. They, along with their slightly younger counterparts, find that they now have significant discretionary income in a world that has become far more competitive. Like their female contemporaries, they are increasingly recognising the advantages of 'looking good'. They are therefore driving a new market for high quality and high-priced male-grooming products. A more extreme position is that this is yet another phase of male narcissism and thus in no way represents any loss of power by men. Related to this, is the view that men are actively seeking to recapture the body aesthetic in the context of a cultural milieu that had increasingly been swinging the pendulum too far in the direction of women being accepted as exclusive custodians of the body aesthetic. Here we have yet another attempt to return to the classical cannon of ancient Greece.

The re-privileging of the aesthetic of the male body can thus be read in various ways. It can be considered an indication of a loss of overall male-gender privileging, based on the advances made by women. Alternatively, it can be seen as an attempt to reassert male-gender privileging in a sphere where it had lost ground, during an epoch when it served overall male-gender privileging to have women considered mere decoration in certain circumstances. It can also be seen as a rebalancing in which men are recapturing a lost sphere in the context in which they have suffered losses to women in other spheres or, to put it positively, both men and women are doing better now that they can express both their traditionally masculine and feminine sides. Perhaps all of these tendencies are at work, making it difficult to unravel which of them may be dominant in any specific social situation that we wish to consider.

Challenging Gender Privileging

To push the boundaries and redefine masculinities and femininities, it is necessary to challenge gender privileging in a fundamental way. All societies and cultures, and the various fractions within them, have distinctive elements of gender privileging. One of the interesting aspects of Caribbean societies has been the initial clash of the notions of gender privileging in the cultures of the Europeans, Africans and Asians who were brought together in the Caribbean. The issue of gender construction in the context of these clashes has received the attention of many authors, not least of all those who focus on gender during the slave period (Rhoda Reddock 1985, Janet Monsen 1960). As Hilary Beckles has noted 'slave societies in the Caribbean facilitated a revolutionary restructuring and magnification of traditional African, European and native gender representations while producing unique features of their own (1997, 3). The particular roles in agricultural labour had their own distinct privileging in West Africa as against Western Europe. Thus, from the very outset, the presence of male and female slaves working in the field together brought with it an element of challenge to the gender privileging ideologies of both Africa and Europe. From this early beginning, various aspects of gender privileging have been challenged and re-challenged in the construction of the various Caribbean masculinities and femininities. At the same time, males have remained the dominant gender throughout our history. This does not mean that maleness was always and everywhere an advantage, nor did it rule out challenges by either gender with respect to gender privileging, including intra-gender challenges by subordinate masculinities and femininities against the respective hegemonic masculinities and femininities.

The main focus of my paper has been on women challenging for a leadership space in a sphere previously dominated by men and men challenging for a space where women have previously dominated. Given the historic dominance of the male gender, a move by women into a sphere previously dominated by men presents three aspects that come with this transformation. First, women begin to occupy a larger social space and thereby may increase their power, prestige and control of resources. At the same time, women may find themselves confined to specific roles within the new sphere, where these roles are precisely those which have less power, prestige and control of resources. Alternatively, the feminisation of a sphere can result in an overall decline in the extent to which it exercises power, prestige and the control of resources. Yet, even in the most feminised of spheres, men often retain a disproportionate position when it comes to the leadership of that sphere. In looking forward to new gender possibilities, one question immediately poses itself. How overwhelmingly feminised must a sphere become before women can come to play a significant role in its leadership? In addition, we must ask whether women can continue to take over one sphere after another without eventually coming to the point where their takeover does not lead to a decline in the power, prestige and control of resources in that sphere. Is it therefore possible to identify gender thresholds? Is there a threshold of female participation in an area beyond which we can expect to see its rapid feminisation and decline? Similarly, is there a threshold beyond which the feminisation of an area inevitably leads to female domination of the leadership of that area? Is there a threshold beyond which the feminisation of an area will no longer lead to its decline, thus opening up the possibility for genuine gender equality? Are the results different for spheres largely created by women or which have always been traditionally dominated by women? What of spheres previously dominated by women which come to be subsequently dominated by men?

With respect to the leadership, I have noted why this needs to be privileged for men in a patriarchal society. This helps us to understand why the movement of women into an area has a limited effect in shifting the balance of power between the genders. Women have made progress and indeed the balance is constantly shifting but we cannot afford to be confused by global analyses that look at overall numbers. A more refined analysis can always qualify the extent to which gender privileging is being challenged. The analysis of the possibilities for a more significant challenge to the privileging of males in leadership must take into account a very complex set of relations. As complex as these are, they appear to pale into insignificance when compared with the dynamic elements that we need to unravel in coming to terms with the new tendencies in male grooming. There are many potentially negative elements that we could point to in this development but I will not dwell on these. On the positive side, they contain an element of men coming to terms with the new gender balance. The optimist would hope that this were the dominant tendency, as both men and women will have to come to terms with new roles for both their own and the opposite gender, if the old gender privilegings are not to simply reproduce themselves over and over again.

Notes

1. The participation of women at this level has been restricted to an acting role. In recent years there has been one woman who has acted for each incumbent in these two offices for short periods of leave or absence from the island.
2. Information on one-day police was not collected as it was only available at the local level; the EOJ did not have a central register of those who served.
3. These statements are based on informal interviews with persons who were active in politics at different stages since 1944. My sample was small and unrepresentative but the informants were considered reliable. Given the level of consensus, I did not see the need to probe further.
4. For a discussion of the garrison phenomenon in Jamaica, see Figueroa and Sives (2002) and references.
5. All data on UWI are taken from UWI statistics for various years unless otherwise specified. Figures quoted here for 2001 were supplied by the Office of Planning and Institutional Research at Mona. The data published in the UWI publications constructed were not always compiled on the same bases. As such, data between years is not always strictly comparable.
6. It would be more accurate to use the graduating class but the statistics for student registrations are easier to use. They also provide a satisfactory proxy in so far as they do not greatly differ from the graduating figures and follow a very similar trend.
7. Data supplied by the Appointments Section, UWI, Mona. With full data available for the UWI, Cave Hill and St Augustine campuses, it is expected that this average will turn out to be shorter as the UWI Office of Administration has provided data to show that Mona has the lowest proportion of professorships.
8. In the past, staff of the relevant rank at UWI were classified into Academic and Senior Administrative. Those formerly in the Senior Administrative group have now been separated into Senior Administrative staff and Professional staff. This distinction has not yet been made in the compilation of statistics, hence the old designation is being used.

9. By September 22, 2003, the issue had become so hyped that MSN was highlighting, on its main page, a questionnaire 'Are you a metrosexual?', which appeared on the ESPN SPORTSNATION page: http://proxy.espn.go.com/chat/sportsnation/quiz?event_id=418.

10. See, for example *Daily Observer* Friday, August 29, 2003, p.14 and Saturday, August 30, 2003, p. 24. Interestingly, one quarter of the 40 models appearing in each of the advertisements for the 'Caribbean Model Search' are male.

References

Beckles, Hilary. 1997. 'Freeing Slavery; Gender Paradigms in the Social History of the Caribbean', Elsa Goveia Lecture, Department of History, UWI, Mona.

The Economist. 2003. 'Real Men Get Waxed: A New Male Market Emerges', July 5.

Figueroa, Mark. 1996. 'Male Privileging and Male Academic Underperformance in Jamaica'. Paper presented to The Construction of Caribbean Masculinity: Towards a Research Agenda - A Symposium, UWI, St Augustine, Centre for Gender and Development Studies, January 12, 1996, *The Construction of Caribbean Masculinity*, ed. Rhoda Reddock, forthcoming. Kingston: The UWI Press.

—————. 2000. 'Making Sense of Male Experience: The Case of Academic Underachievement in the English-speaking Caribbean'. *IDS Bulletin* 31, no. 2 (April): 68-74.

—————. 'Thinking about Gender at UWI', *You We Quality Education Forum* UWI, no. 8 (May): 16-17.

Figueroa, Mark and Amanda Sives. 2002. 'Homogeneous Voting, Electoral Manipulation and the Garrison Process in Post-Independence Jamaica'. *Journal of Commonwealth and Comparative Politics* 40, no. 1 (March): 81-108.

Glamour. 2003. 'Crazed. Insecure. Meet the new body image victims: Men'. May, p. 226.

Henry, Maxine. 1987. 'Women in Politics: Some Preliminary Findings'. Paper presented to Caribbean Studies Association Belize City.

Monsen, Janet. 1996. 'Gender Roles in Caribbean Agricultural Labour'. In *Caribbean Freedom; From Emancipation to the Present*, eds. Hilary Beckles and Verene Shepherd, 216-24. Princeton: Markus Wiener, London: James Curry and Kingston: Ian Randle Publishers.

Pope, Harrison, Katharine Phillips and Robert Olivardia. 2002. *The Adonis Complex*. New York: The Free Press.

Reddock, Rhoda. 1985. 'Women and Slavery in the Caribbean'. *Latin American Perspectives* 12, no. 1 (Winter): 63-80.

Simpson, Mark. 1994. 'Here Come the Mirror Men'. *The Independent*. November 15, 2002.

'Meet the Metrosexual'. *Salon.com*. http://archive.salon.com/ent/feature/2002/07/22/metrosexual/ (accessed July 22).

St John, Warren. 2003. 'Metrosexuals Come Out'. *New York Times*. June 22.

UWI, University of the West Indies. Various years. *Official Statistics*, UWI, Mona. 2002.

2002. *You We Quality Education Forum*, UWI, no. 8 (May).

Vassell, Linette. c2000. 'Power, Governance and the Structure of Opportunity for Women in Decision Making in Jamaica'. *The Construction of Gender Development Indicators for Jamaica*. Kingston: PIOJ/UNDP/CIDA Kingston.

Wordspy.com http://www.wordspy.com/words/metrosexual.asp

*   In writing this paper I received assistance from Shanique Green, Stacey Plummer, Ann-Marie Rose, Lorna Baxter, Marie Cobran, Pansy Young, Brigitte Collins, Al Francis and Valerie Nam, as well as the cooperation and support of Electoral Office of Jamaica (EOJ) and members of its staff (Ishiwawa Hope, Earl Simpson, Juliet Wong and Glendon Bennett). Neither the EOJ nor any of the above individuals should be held responsible for the views expressed here.

Table 1. Male and Female Participation in Political Leadership in Jamaica, 1998

Position	Total No.	M No.	M %	F No.	F %
Participation in Parliament & in Local Government					
House of Representatives	60	52	87	8	13
Senate	21	16	76	5	24
Cabinet	17	15	88	2	12
Local Government	227	173	73	54	24
Total	325	256	78	69	22
National Executive Committee: Peoples National Party					
Region 1	17	12	71	5	29
Region 2	23	18	78	5	22
Region 3	49	36	74	13	27
Region 4	45	37	82	8	18
Region 5	27	21	78	6	22
Region 6	30	25	83	5	17
Executive	49	39	80	10	20
PNP Women's Movement	6	0	0	6	100
PNP Youth Organization	6	6	100	0	0
Senators	4	3	75	1	25
Life Members	14	11	79	3	21
National Workers Union	11	10	91	1	9
Total	281	218	78	63	22
Leadership Bodies of the Jamaica Labour Party					
Central Executive	134	111	83	23	17
Standing Committee	53	43	81	10	19
Total	187	154	82	33	18

Source: Linnette Vassell (c2000)

Table 2. Male and Female Voting: 2002, Election, Jamaica Selected Parishes

	Hanover				KSAC			
	M	F	T	%F	M	F	T	%F
Population 18+	20,905	20,630	41,535	49.67%	193,520	228,353	421,873	54.13%
Voters List	19,618	19,393	39,011	49.71%	141,335	161,499	302,834	53.33%
% Enumeration	93.84%	94.01%	93.92%		73.03%	70.72%	71.78%	
Sample Votes Cast	1,137	1,075	2,212	48.60%	7,228	7,674	14,902	51.50%
95 % Confidence Margin			+ or -	2.00%			+ or -	0.77%
Total Votes Cast			24,634				166,985	
Sample % of Total			8.98%				8.92%	

Sources: Population estimates from Statistical Institute of Jamaica
Voters List from EOJ
Sample Votes Cast based on name analysis of approximately every tenth Poll Book

Note: Some books were missing and names which could not be classified were ignored
KSAC includes the parishes Kingston and St Andrew where the capital Kingston is located

Table 3. Participation in Jamaica's 2002 Election Day Administration by Gender

		M	F	T	M%	F%
1	Members of Parliament	54	6	60	90%	10%
2	Returning Officers	46	14	60	77%	23%
3	Assistant RO's	31	26	57	54%	46%
4	Supervisors	781	895	1676	47%	53%
5	Presiding Officers	1032	6018	7050	15%	85%
6	Poll Clerks	1051	6139	7190	15%	85%
7	Indoor Agents	2365	12769	15134	16%	84%

Sources: 1, 2, 3   Name analysis of samples taken from EOJ list
          4, 5, 6, 7   Name analysis of samples taken from EOJ lists
                      Sample sizes of: 648, 365, 365, and 375 respectively
                      95% confidence margin + or - 3%, 4%, 4% and 4%

Table 4. Members of Parliament and Returning Officers by Gender, Selected Jamaican Elections 1944-2002

Number Constituencies	Year	%MPs F	%MPs M	%ROs F	%ROs M
32	1944	3%	97%	0%	100%
32	1955	3%	97%	0%	100%
45	1962	2%	98%	0%	100%
53	1972	4%	96%	8%	92%
60	1980	8%	92%	8%	92%
60	1989	5%	95%	18%	82%
60	1997	13%	87%	28%	72%
60	2002	12%	90%	23%	77%

Source: Name analysis Reports EOJ (and predecessors) and EOJ website http://www.eoj.co.jm various pages

Note: Names were not always available especially 1955-1976.

Table 5. Percentage Male and Female UWI Professors, Academics and Lecturers 1988-2001 with Percentage Male and Female Students Lagged 33, 23 and 13 Years

Year	Professors			Academics			Lecturers			Students-33yrs			Year	Students-23yrs			Year	Students-13yrs			Year
	F	M	N	F	M	N	F	M	N	F	M	N		F	M	N		F	M	N	
1988	7%	93%	71	22%	78%	663	28%	72%	346	33%	67%	444	1955	35%	65%	3,038	1965	45%	55%	7,257	1975
1989	7%	93%	95	22%	78%	708	29%	71%	352	34%	66%	494	1956	37%	63%	3,259	1966	46%	54%	7,541	1976
1990	8%	92%	89	22%	78%	714	28%	72%	370	36%	64%	555	1957	36%	64%	3,614	1967	47%	53%	8,085	1977
1991	8%	92%	97	24%	76%	774	31%	69%	414	37%	63%	622	1958	37%	63%	4,216	1968	47%	53%	8,531	1978
1992	9%	91%	117	23%	77%	755	30%	70%	406	36%	64%	695	1959	37%	63%	4,627	1969	47%	53%	9,011	1979
1993	7%	93%	123	20%	80%	786	25%	75%	354	33%	67%	977	1960	38%	62%	5,016	1970	48%	52%	9,089	1980
1994	7%	93%	115	22%	78%	803	28%	72%	400	33%	67%	1,268	1961	40%	60%	5,778	1971	49%	51%	9,543	1981
1995	7%	93%	107	25%	75%	775	30%	70%	405	33%	67%	1,422	1962	41%	59%	6,326	1972	51%	49%	9,573	1982
1996	7%	93%	104	27%	73%	968	32%	68%	555	33%	67%	2,187	1963	41%	59%	6,660	1973	48%	52%	10,026	1983
1997	11%	89%	99	32%	68%	902	40%	60%	489	34%	66%	2,523	1964	44%	56%	6,928	1974	47%	53%	10,572	1984
1998	7%	93%	90	33%	67%	979	38%	62%	523	35%	65%	3,038	1965	45%	55%	7,257	1975	47%	53%	10,718	1985
1999	9%	91%	98	36%	64%	1,152	41%	59%	648	37%	63%	3,259	1966	46%	54%	7,541	1976	47%	53%	10,789	1986
2000	11%	89%	105	34%	66%	1,032	40%	60%	525	36%	64%	3,614	1967	47%	53%	8,085	1977	46%	54%	11,503	1987
2001	12%	88%	119	35%	65%	1,076	39%	61%	547	37%	63%	4,216	1968	47%	53%	8,531	1978	55%	45%	11,896	1988

Sources: UWI Statistics, various years (2001 data obtained from Office of Planning and Institutional Research Mona)

Note: No gender breakdown was published for academics in 1994 and 1995. Figures presented represent interpolations.

Table 6. Percentage of Male and Female Students Enrolled in the Fields of Library Studies, Nursing and Engineering at the UWI

Year	Library Studies			Nursing			Nursing + LS			Engineering		
	F	M	N	F	M	N	F	M	N	F	M	N
1975	83%	17%	12	92%	8%	36	90%	10%	48	3%	97%	386
1978	93%	7%	14	93%	7%	27	93%	7%	41	6%	94%	530
1981	83%	17%	18	100%	0%	24	93%	7%	42	13%	87%	585
1984	95%	5%	41	98%	2%	44	96%	4%	85	14%	86%	594
1987	94%	6%	18	94%	6%	31	94%	6%	49	13%	87%	809
1990	91%	9%	56	98%	2%	44	94%	6%	100	14%	86%	782
1993	90%	10%	94	100%	0%	11	91%	9%	105	19%	81%	1043
1996	93%	7%	110	91%	9%	23	92%	8%	133	23%	77%	1113
1999	97%	3%	140	96%	4%	26	97%	3%	166	24%	76%	1336
2002	92%	8%	191	100%	0%	38	93%	7%	229	30%	70%	1666

Source: 1975 -1990 UWI Statistics, various years, 1993 - 2002 Students Records Unit Mona
2002 Engineering Data from Office of Planning and Development UWI St Augustine

Note: UWI publications only provide gender breakdowns for all programmes in some years, hence statistics are not strictly comparable nor totals exact but the trends are clear.

Plate 1. Male Beauty, Past and Present

Mohammad Ali, 'The Greatest'

Lenny Kravitz
Musician

Plate 2. Young Stars, Then and Now

Jackson Brothers

Lil' Bow Wow

Omarion

Plate 3. Basketball Icons, What Next?

Hakeem Olajuwon

Kareem Abdul Jabar

Dennis Rodman

Plate 4. Dancehall, Contemporary and Classic

Elephant Man U Roy

Sources:

http://www.lennykravitz.com/
http://www.allposters.com/gallery.asp?aid=9518
http://valsadie.com/j5images/jbros.jpg
http://groups.msn.com/B2ksCrossingmymanomarizgallery.msnw?action=ShowPhoto&PhotoID=1009
http://bowwow4eva.cjb.net/
http://www.cattdaddy.com/nilks/bowwow.jpg
http://www.nba.com/history/players/abduljabbar_bio.html
http://www.nba.com/history/players/olajuwon_bio.html
http://pmagal.home.texas.net/hair.html
http://members.aol.com/DRConnection/photos/drjpg09.jpg
http://www.bbc.co.uk/music/profiles/elephantman.shtml
http://hosted.greensleeves.easynet.co.uk/bio/biogelephant.html
http://www.assassin-productions.fr/musique/u-roy.jpg

7 | WILMA BAILEY, CLEMENT BRANCHE, JEAN JACKSON, AMY LEE

Fatherhood in Risk Environments

Introduction. The Return of Risk

Risk analysis is fashionable and has been so for the last two decades. Although the concept is variously interpreted, the vocabulary of risk is employed by academics in almost every discipline (Douglas and Wildavsky 1982; Douglas 1990; Giddens 1990, 1991; Beck 1997; Wallace 1993; Wallace and Wallace 1995). With its new prominence the word has acquired new meaning. Until its recent reappearance, the idea of risk was neutral, involving losses or gains. Risk, then, referred to the likelihood that an event would occur and to the magnitude of the gains or losses that would be entailed (Douglas 1990). Risk assessment was a technical activity with results formulated in terms of the probability of success or failure. If a situation was associated with high risk, then it could bring massive gain or massive loss. Risk was a wager. The reincarnated risk is associated with negative outcomes.

The Risk Environment – the Inner City of Kingston

This paper is exploratory and looks at fatherhood in the context of risk taking in a risky environment. It explores the dissonance between a seeming preference for marriage as the context for reproduction and the actual conduct of Jamaican men, and suggests there are attributes of the environment that facilitate risk taking. The paper draws upon the results of two research projects. One had both research and intervention components. The research component employed a qualitative methodology, focus-group interviews among young children and adults in the inner city in the Kingston Metropolitan Area (KMA), Jamaica and examined the quality of gender relationships (the Ford study). The intervention was done by specially trained community 'change agents'. The second study was based on a quantitative survey of a sample of 714 men in the KMA as well as focus-group interviews among a subset of that sample. This study looked at men's attitudes to relationships and pregnancies (the WHO study). The paper is based mainly on this WHO study but draws upon the other because there was consistency in findings across the two studies.

Risk and Culture

Douglas (1990, 1992) argues that the change in the meaning of risk has come about because of the dangers associated with technological advances in developed countries. Culture needs a common vocabulary with which to hold powerful people – large conglomerates – accountable, and risk serves the forensic needs of this new global, adversarial culture. Risk has become a specialised word for undesirable outcome; a riposte against the abuse of power. The word *danger,* she feels would serve the same purpose but danger does not have the aura of science or a connection with objective analysis. Risk politicises danger. It is a decorative flourish on the word danger (Douglas 1992). Most cultures, she continues, develop common terms to politicise and moralise dangers. Christianity adopted the word *sin* and, in a moral world, the thought of future retribution, the prediction of punishment discouraged transgressions. Risk is used to mean danger from future damage caused by those who hold opposing views.

We see risk as danger in the works of Giddens (1990, 1991) and Beck (1997). As we enter the late modern age, a technological society, we leave security and certainty behind and must negotiate a risk society. The source of these risks is the fact that knowledge and technology are racing ahead but we do not understand the technology nor can we calculate the consequences of their malfunctioning. We are being encouraged to consider the consequences of our actions on future generations, but because we are thinking in the long term, we cannot calculate the risks of our decisions. Compounding our problems is the fact that we can depend neither on scientists with their conflicting claims nor on the politicians who make no direct decisions about technology. We live with modern risks and manufactured uncertainties and no one is responsible.

> Risks that were calculable under industrial society become incalculable and unpredictable in the risk society. Compared to the possibilities of adjudging blame and causality in classical modernity, the world risk society possesses no such certainties or guarantees.

Caribbean Studies and Gendered Risk

Men at Risk

To Beck and Giddens, mankind is at risk in an increasing technological society. To Caribbean scholars, the socioecological systems in which poor West Indian families have functioned, have placed men at risk, that is, in danger (Miller 1991; Patterson 1992; Wilson 2001). The typical household during slavery, wrote Patterson, was dominated by women even when men were present. Men had little authority, not only because the male slave lacked authority in general, but also because women had access to the earnings of their older children and were better off than men. Men were therefore emasculated, not only by the system but by their women. Those freedmen who became independent peasants in post-emancipation times were able to salvage some masculine dignity, but on the plantation a social fluidity prevailed, not as a legacy of the slave past but because of peculiar elements of the modern plantation system, among them, low wages, seasonal employment and the psychological effect of being surrounded by proud own-account small farmers. The modern lower-class urban pattern shares many of the characteristics of the slave: the causal factors being chronic unemployment, extreme inequalities and environmental incivilities.

In Miller's marginalisation thesis (Miller 1991), historically, women were the pawns manipulated by white males, who controlled the gateways to specialised institutions, to keep black men in their place. Women were allowed access to the extent that now temporarily liberated, they were totally dependent on male sponsors (Miller 1991). Power is essentially a struggle among men, and women cooperated in this conspiracy to marginalise black men, that is, to put them at risk.

Men as Risk

So there is a historical process that targets men and creates an individual by oppression. For the past three to four centuries, Caribbean men have been challenged to maintain themselves as valued products and these challenges now help to define the nature of Caribbean masculinity. A system of violence is organised around masculinity and the externals become definitive. Caribbean masculinity and risk become one as men see themselves as risk takers. 'Men at risk' becomes 'men as risk'. Boys are reared to be tough, to react aggressively to challenges, to become real men, and this identity emerges from a very early age. Examine the complaint lodged by a ten-year-old Jamaican boy against a classmate:

> This bwoy love to go on like he is a girl child when he is in class. And I have to stab him with mi pencil one time when he is touching me on mi shoulder. Bwoy is bwoy and girl is girl. If you behave like girl, dem call you bumsi, sissy. (Bailey, et al. 1997)

A touch on the shoulder is too gentle a form of communication for a boy and to emphasise his maleness, the storyteller uses his pencil as a weapon. Peter Wilson sees elements of the Puerto Rican machismo in men in the English-speaking Caribbean; machismo is a quality that manifests itself in:

> ... the ability to father children, readiness to fight, particularly in response to a challenge usually offered in the form of an insult, in drinking and in any form of activity culturally defined as the prerogative of males. (Wilson 2001, 340)

Urban 'Meltdown'

At first glance, there appears to be no link between the risk society of Giddens and Beck and the risk to men growing up in Caribbean societies. But in fact they are all seeing danger as being shaped by the pressures of social life, and risk is the forensic tool used in a discourse on the negative interaction between people and large corporations. The latest concept of a risk environment moves the action away from the larger sociocultural environment and adds greater specificity to people-environment interaction in depressed, marginalised communities. Although this concept of a risk environment was developed with the spread of HIV/AIDS in mind (Wallace 1993; Wallace et al. 1996; Aggleton et al. 1994; Wallace and Wallace 1995; Campbell 1997), it has equal significance to crime and violence and, since the real concern is with unprotected sexual intercourse in the presence of a deadly disease, it has relevance to an understanding of unwanted pregnancies. The argument is that, while there is nothing intrinsically risky about sexual intercourse, when a disease such as HIV/AIDS appears (or when a pregnancy is unwanted) and when the social and economic environment facilitates rapid partner change, the act of sexual intercourse becomes risk behaviour and the facilitating environment, a risk environment (Barnett and Whiteside 2002).

> Life lived in a risk environment affects who you are ... what you (and others) do with your body. But none of this is about 'culture' driving decisions against the grain of what is rational. People who inhabit a risk environment make decisions that are rational for them in their circumstances. However ... people may be compelled to take risks that are against their long term interests because they have little hope for the long term. (Barnett and Whiteside 2002)

Wallace and his co-workers suggest that sociogeographic networks, that is, social networks embedded in space, play a critical role in poor urban communities (Wallace 1993; Wallace et al. 1996). These networks help in the socialisation of the young, and make resources available from those who have to those who do not have. Along these networks flows the enforcement of social norms of what is acceptable and unacceptable. When a disruption of these lines reaches a critical threshold, those who can, will leave, the community is dismembered and the people disempowered. In the context of this disempowerment and urban 'melt down', a behavioural repertoire will develop to enable groups to carry out their individual and group purposes (Wallace et al. 1996).

Profile of Respondents – the WHO study

The majority (64 per cent) of the men fell in the age group 20 to 34 and 66 per cent had a secondary/high school education. They were employed mainly in manual occupations and 11 per cent were unemployed. They had an average of 2.4 children in all relationships and Table 1 shows the union status of the parents at the birth of their children. The table shows that just over 20 per cent of their children were born in marriage.

Table 1. Union status of parents at birth of children

Union Status at Birth	Children	
	#	%
Casual	292	17.1
Visiting	541	31.6
Common-Law	532	31.1
Married	346	20.2
Total	1711	100.0

Table 2. Odds ratios, confidence intervals and significance levels for factors influencing fathers' reaction to the news of pregnancy

Variable	Odds Ratio	Confidence Interval	Significance Level
Age of father			
< 20	1		
20-29	1.8	1.1 – 2.9	.015
30+	**3.2**	1.8	.000
Economic situation			
Poor	1		
Not so poor	0.8	0.5 – 1.1	.201
Fairly well off	1.4	0.7 – 2.7	.377
Union status			
Non-residential	1		
Common-law	1.1	0.7 – 1.6	.834
Married	**4.6**	2.2 – 10.0	.0001
Worker status			
Unemployed	1		
Employed	**2.2**	1.2 – 3.7	.004
Employment class			
Professional/Intermediate	1		
Skilled non-manual	1.0	0.5 – 1.9	.997
Skilled manual/ partially skilled	1.1	0.7 – 1.9	.629
Unskilled	1.6	0.8 – 3.2	.144

The News

The men were asked to reflect on how they felt when they heard the news that they were about to become a father for the first time. The period of recall was longer for the older men but with such an important event, it is unlikely that their memories would have been dulled by the passage of time. Fifty-nine per cent reported that they were happy or glad. The rest described their reaction as being worried, distressed, angry and mad. We used logistic multiple regression to estimate the effects of their socioeconomic position at the time of the birth of their children. The regression calculated the influence of the circumstances of the fathers on their reaction – happy or unhappy. The socioeconomic factors were age of father, their assessment of their economic situation, union status, worker status and employment class. Table 2 shows the odds ratio, confidence intervals and significance levels of these socioeconomic factors. Age, employment status and especially union status were significant. Those who were married were almost five times as likely as those in residential unions to be happy, and the reaction of men in common-law unions was almost identical to those in non-residential unions. So although they saw marriage as the best context for child-rearing, the majority in the sample had their children outside marriage. This was an unexpected result and we tried to explore these reactions to the news in the focus-group sessions. In some cases, we found shock and surprise among those who had a first child before they knew that they were capable of having children. The biological markers are not clear:

> My friend told me that I got a girl pregnant. I said to him 'you are a fool. I cannot breed anybody!' Five months later, I saw the belly. I said 'That's mine?' I went into shock.
>
> When she go to the doctor and tell mi seh the doctor seh so, mi never sleep dat night.

There were men who had children in caring relationships but, for the most part, they appeared to act without regard for the consequences. They took risks. This is only an example of some of the responses we received.

> 'You just want a fling wid the girl and tings happen'.

'Me see a girl and lust after her. Mi nuh really have much feelings for her. That is why some men dismiss the girl and dismiss the baby cause dem nuh have it for the girl'.

'When you don't really like a girl and she look pon yuh and she seh she pregnant, you seh "no man"'.

'When you are in a relationship with a girl that you do not like you don't really care whether or not she wants to use contraceptives'.

These attitudes accompany extremely high levels of knowledge of contraception and awareness of the health risks of unprotected sex. The men take risks in spite of their belief that 'most women sell and some of them sell disease'. What is the context in which these behaviours occur? We draw upon data gathered in the focus group sessions to define the environmental cues to risk taking.

We suggest that many urban communities in the KMA are at the stage of 'meltdown'. The internal structure of the city has taken on the familiar doughnut appearance of many western cities, having been hollowed out by the flight of productive enterprises. This has left thousands of families trapped in densely populated corroding slums, cut off geographically, economically and socially from the wider society. Moreover, the communities are fragmented internally by party political and gang affiliation and social and community structures have been destroyed. In preparing the change agents for work in their own communities for the Ford project, we asked them to outline on a map a zone of comfort within which they felt they could work freely. In some cases that comfort zone was restricted to one or two blocks within the community and those blocks effectively reflected their total living space. In such situations there is a high degree of self-interaction and, in the presence of a denuded resource base, frequent sexual contact may serve a variety of purposes – self-affirmation, resource sharing – which exaggerate risk behaviour. These conditions also facilitate an increase in criminal behaviour. What is true for the inner city holds for a number of uptown suburban enclaves which have either developed or have grown as a result of the flight from the inner city. In these suburban 'ghettos', social and economic conditions are so similar to those found around the old commercial core, that there is a tendency in the press to use the term 'inner city' in a generic sense rather than in its true geographical sense.

'Noise'

Barnett and Whiteside present the urban ghetto as a 'noisy' place. There is oral noise from 'ghetto blasters'. There is visual noise in the form of dress and there is also the push and shove of people making out and the noise of risky competition to survive under conditions of stress. (Barnett and Whiteside 2002, 82).

There is the noise of the struggle to survive and, in order to be heard one has to shout. Many of the exaggerated responses of men and women caught in these situations can be seen as attempts to communicate messages of worth above the din. The men lack education and skills, and experience difficulty in finding permanent and meaningful jobs:

> We really need training and work...and you get two days work today and you don't get any next week...
>
> We need some strong regular work to keep up with the demands.

It is perhaps ironic that much of the frustration expressed by these reluctant fathers over their joblessness, arose from the fact that they felt they were unable to fulfil what they considered to be their primary function as fathers and that was to meet the basic needs of their children:

> My responsibility as father is to make sure there is baby feeding, nappy....
>
> Right now mi feel displeased with myself. Having so much of them and not even a headway for the first one.
>
> Sometimes a man wants to do something but he can't. So him pretend like him nuh want fi do nutten.

Chronic unemployment robs these fathers of the ability to make the provisions that are central to their concept of maleness and fatherhood. The denial of the opportunities to attain these symbols of worth, trigger substitutions which can become risk behaviour.

The noise of crime

There are few inner city areas that are not being torn apart by crime and violence. This accelerates the deterioration of neighbourhoods as people are driven out by the fear of crime. Both the young children and the adults in the Ford study conveyed the paralysing effect of living with crime, of the fear of crime.

> Sometimes when dem fire shots I get frighten… [the shot] nearly catch the baby.
>
> … most of the boys live on the gully bank … all the nights sometimes they sit down … and when they see people they rob them … If ah going to the shop I have to pass the gully.

However, it was the change agents who gave a better sense of the loss of control and the effects this has on the lives of ordinary citizens. In this community there were:

> … wannabees, youngsters 14 to 19 years giving problems. They have guns and sometimes they brandish them. Last week, a man was killed right in front of my gate. They shoot him, hold up their gun and then ride off …. The police come and find no gun … a lot trying to move in that direction. To get fame they must do damage. The boys say 'lend me a piece' and they dig it up and lend him. One man now coming up as don. Everything must check with him …
>
> … older people have freedom to walk (in the community). Young men could be stopped.

Men brandishing guns control neighbourhoods and the change agents graphically described the vulnerability of young men in particular: how hitherto law-abiding youths are drawn into conflict with tragic results. Members of these communities have witnessed violent incidents in which their friends and relatives have been killed and there was a strong sense that they felt powerless to effect change. Many who had tried had been 'scalped'. It is perhaps difficult for young people, living with this ever present fear of danger and death, to ignore instant gratification and the pleasure of flesh-to-flesh contact. There is a high risk of dying and that threat is more immediate than the threat posed by HIV/AIDS or a pregnancy.

> It's like nothing deh deh. No enjoyment.
>
> … miss, some ah dem (women) don't like to use condoms.

Campbell (1997) describes a similar attitude of men working in dangerous gold mines in South Africa and feels that more attention ought to be paid to flesh-to-flesh contact as a symbol of emotional intimacy in the face of stress. Hayes (1992) feels that there is a need for a more positive attitude towards risk behaviour which, at many levels, may be beneficial in specific environments. Risk taking, he writes, implies intent but the intentions of the action are not fully appreciated once the notion of risk is associated with negative outcomes.

The noise of peer pressure

Perhaps the loudest noise emanates from their peers on the street corners where the young men gather. Street influences were especially telling in the transitional period to adulthood, when styles and attitudes were adopted as the basis for securing an adult masculine identity. This is where validation occurred. For the young men in the inner city, the street is also an attractive alternative to the female-dominated household:

> You see where I live, I can't keep out of it because…I live amongst mostly women, seen …?

The street life involves close, daily interaction among young men and the relationship is highly competitive. In the focus-group discussions, the younger participants spoke of the responsibilities and obligations of fatherhood and their inability to meet them but they said they were under considerable pressure from their peers. This peer pressure is not restricted to the inner city but there the response is exaggerated. In the following statements are some of the symbolic meanings of having a child in these situations. It is proof that the young man is in a sexual relationship. It is proof that he is potent and it elevates his status among his peers (see also Chevannes 2001). It is difficult for young men, locked out of the opportunity structure, to withstand these pressures.

> Sometimes when you nuh have a youth, a man mout you and sey yuh nuh have a girl.
>
> We push one anodda, yuh know. Cause two of us a di same age mi have two or three and you have none, bwoy, dem seh, yuh naa go on with nutten. Yuh naah work.
>
> Sometimes, you have a fren and him have a baby and you have none. You and him can't be pon the same level cause him have a baby.

There is pressure to have not just one woman. Masculinity is constructed around the man's ability to control several women. This is the compensatory dimension of men as risk. The participants freely admitted that it was 'an egotistical thing', 'Is a competition ting', 'Is really flex you ah flex'. You have to be able to 'brag and boast'. So a typical 'vocabulary' emerges and those who speak the language can send very clear messages along these 'noisy channels' (Wallace et al. 1996). Exaggerated masculinity is a behavioural code that makes sense in marginalised communities and the processes identified here are almost identical with those expressed under similar circumstances in the inner cities of New York, Africa, India and Thailand (Barnett and Whiteside 2001). Sexual acts have a biological similarity across the globe, and sexual acts may be the same. However, the role and purpose of the act may differ quite profoundly even within societies and social research must take this variability into account (Aggleton et al. 1994).

The noise of contest and conquest

This behavioural code is a means of sending messages not only to male peers. It is the means of communication within the entire social network. Men strut as much for men as for women and the sexualised man has his counterpart in the sexualised woman. A real man has to be able to read and respond to the messages (which can be explicit or suggestive) transmitted along this network. The respondents dramatise these sexual encounters and the images are strongly suggestive of power, conquest and sexual prowess. These may be casual, unplanned encounters for which they are unprepared, but they cannot back off from the challenges that are put 'eena yuh way' or miss an unexpected opportunity simply because they do not have condoms:

> … you might be out there … and a little catty can check you the said time and say she await a killer. So hear mi, 'a really long time mi nuh kill nothing'. Mi oil up and steam up and mi carry her over the ranch … yuh just want to do it and yuh don't have any protection …
>
> mi family did gaan out and mi know dem come back any time … ah do a fast thing because ah don't have time to put on protection – do a fast thing and mek she know how to spar and get the house tidy back in time …

It is important to their manhood that they make an immediate and 'appropriate' response – that they are able to 'oil up and steam up'.

The news of a pregnancy resulting from such opportunistic encounters cannot bring happiness and two considerations were uppermost in the minds of the respondents. Firstly, what would be their friends' reaction when they hear that they had fathered a child by a woman who 'run up and down like mad ants' and 'open an close her legs like scissors'? The second was the issue of paternity and this has to be seen in the context of the casual nature of sexual encounters and the general, deep-seated feelings of mistrust in gender relations. Women were not seen as being deceitful by nature. It was the result of their upbringing and the only time you can trust them is when 'you catch them from early, from dem young coming up ... and grow dem yourself ...' All the definitions of unwanted pregnancies given in the focus group sessions had to do with the regard the respondents had for women or doubts of paternity. There is a loss of face in the community when a man is given a 'jacket'. Women 'deal' with many men and give the children to the richest men. 'Children are raffled'.

Conclusion

The paper has highlighted some of the attributes of an environment that facilitates risk taking, specifically, the risk of unwanted pregnancies. It is important to specify that the focus is on unwanted pregnancies and not unwanted children; that in many cases, these reluctant fathers, because of satisfying experiences with children, discover joy as well as competence in fathering.

In urban risk environments the links in the sociogeographic network have been broken, the traditional controls that have been important in socialising the young have been removed. The control of many inner city communities is in the hands of young, male risk takers and a 'noisy' behaviour transmitting statements of individual worth is pervasive. These behaviours exist because, in the context of marginalisation, they are imbued with 'idiomatic meaning' (Wallace et al. 1996). Such behaviours carry not only the risk of unwanted pregnancies. This is the same network along which HIV/AIDS infection is propagated and therefore the potential for the rapid spread of this debilitating and deadly disease is alarming. Messages exhorting consistent condom use or abstinence (*Daily Gleaner*, July 30, 2003) will not be heard until noise-abatement measures are put in place. In other words, the causes of the meltdown in depressed areas must be addressed. Education, skills training, employment opportunities and urban renewal will rob these risk behaviours of their symbolic value.

References

Aggleton, Peter, et al. 1994. 'Risking everything? risk behaviour, behaviour change and AIDS'. *Science* 265: 341-345.

Bailey, W. et al. 1997. *Family and the quality of gender relations in the Caribbean*. Mona, Institute of Social and Economic Research.

Barnett, Tony and Alan Whiteside. 2002. *AIDS in the twenty-first century: disease and globalization*. Basingstoke: Palgrave/Macmillan.

Beck, Ulrich. 1997. 'A risky business'. *LSE magazine* 9, no. 2: 4-6.

Campbell, Catherine. 1997. 'Migrancy, masculine identities and AIDS: the psychosocial context of HIV transmission on the South African gold mines'. *Social Science and Medicine* 45, no. 2: 273-281.

Chevannes, Barry. 2001. *Learning to be a man: culture, socialization and gender identity in five Caribbean communities*. Kingston: The University of the West Indies Press.

Daily Gleaner. 2003. July 30.

Douglas, Mary and Aaron Wildavsky. 1982. *Risk and culture*. Berkeley: University of California Press.

Douglas, Mary. 1990. 'Risk as a forensic resource'. *Daedalus* 119, no. 4: 1-16.

—————. 1992. *Risk and blame: essays in cultural theory*. London and New York: Routledge.

Giddens, A. 1990. *The consequences of modernity*. Cambridge: Polity Press.

—————. 1991. *Modernity and self-identity: self and society in the late modern age*. Cambridge: Polity Press.

Hayes, M. 1992. 'On the epistemology of risk: language, and logic'. *Social Science. Social Science and Medicine* 35, no. 4: 401-407.

Miller, Errol. 1991. *Men at Risk*. Kingston: Jamaica Publishing House Ltd.

Patterson, Orlando. 1982. 'Persistence, continuity and change in the Jamaican working-class family'. *Journal of Family History* (Summer): 135-160.

Wallace, Roderick. 1993. 'Social Disintegration and the Spread of AIDS- II: Meltdown of Sociogeographic Structure in Urban Minority Neighbourhoods'. *Social Science and Medicine*, 37, no. 7: 887-896.

Wallace, Roderick and Deborah Wallace. 1995. 'US apartheid and the spread of AIDS to the suburbs: a multi-city analysis of the political economy of spatial epidemic threshold'. *Social Science and Medicine*, 41 no. 3: 333-345.

Wallace Roderick, et al. 1996. 'AIDS, violence and behavioural coding: information theory, risk behaviour and dynamic process on core group sociogeographic networks'. *Social Science and Medicine* 43, no. 3: 339-352.

Wilson, Peter. 2001. 'Reputation and respectability: a suggestion for Caribbean ethnology'. *Caribbean sociology: introductory readings*, eds. Christine Barrow and Rhoda Reddock. Kingston: Ian Randle Publishers.

Pushing the Boundaries:
Images, Representations and Identities

8 | RHODA REDDOCK

Caribbean Masculinities and Femininities
The Impact of Globalisation on Cultural Representations[1]

Abstract

This study is part of a wider study that seeks to examine issues of influence, impact and transformation in relation to the current manifestations of Caribbean Gender Ideology. The larger study seeks to examine the factors that have influenced the construction and understandings of femininities and masculinities and the ways in which these new understandings have shaped gender relations in contemporary Caribbean societies.

This particular chapter focuses on globalisation and its impact on the cultural representation of gender relations. It begins by defining globalisation and the complex ways in which it could be understood. It distinguishes between globalisation as a technologically driven force which makes communication and human interaction more accessible, and globalisation as a manifestation of globalised neo-liberal economic policy and practice. In examining the impact on gender relations in the Caribbean, focus is placed on four locations where these can be observed. These are 1) the emergence of fundamentalisms in the face of perceived cultural domination and homogenisation; 2) the beauty contest industry; 3) sport, gender and national identity; and 4) the Bollywood influence.

Introduction

Globalisation is a term that, by its sheer complexity, defies a simplistic definition, and it is one that has been subject to great contention in recent years (Robertson 1992, 182). Indeed, there is no single globalisation theory to which all of its proponents have been able to sign up (Bairner 2001, 8). Nederveen Pieterse asserts that there are numerous definitions and conceptualisations of globalisation which vary from discipline to discipline. Perceiving globalisations as plural, he argues, is crucial in comprehending globalisation as a 'multi-dimensional process, which, like all significant social processes, unfolds in multiple realms of existence simultaneously' (1993, 1). Hence, no singular or fixed definition *should* be assigned to such a multifarious process.[2]

This paper seeks to provide a preliminary exploration of the impact of globalisation on Caribbean masculinities and femininities, a subject on which there is much popular opinion and discussion. It will explore this in relation to different contexts and situations of the late twentieth and early twenty-first centuries, with specific reference to religious fundamentalisms, the beauty contest industry, the sport industry and the Indian film and music industry, examining the ways in which the continuous negotiation between the local and the global takes place and the shifting identities and realities which emerge.

So, what is globalisation? In its simplest sense, it is usually taken to refer to a *process*, rather than a fixed situation. Some argue that it should really be seen as two processes. One *structural* – related to the fast pace of developments in information and communications technology which make communication much more instant and global. The other process, which can be seen as *ideological* or *political*, is related to the hegemony of neo-liberal ideology as the only economic and political alternative. As noted by Thomas Klak (1998, 20), its power is highly ideological, in that it is advanced by its advocates as the only way to achieve economic prosperity and political democracy. The term 'globalisation' and its perceived inevitability becomes an ideological tool with which to justify a range of economic interventions including the removal of trade barriers, the removal of subsidies, cutbacks in social spending and the opening up of local markets to international trade. The assumption, here, is that this increase in global trade would be beneficial to all groups and all countries willing to take up the challenge.

Bringing both of these aspects together, it is generally acknowledged that globalisation entails the increasing free flow of people, finance, services, products, technology, images and ideas across national borders. If such a definition is to be endorsed, then it becomes evident that the Caribbean has been subject to such a process, or processes, for centuries, dating back to the era of slavery. This view is supported in a recently published article by the International Monetary Fund (IMF) which argues that globalisation is a process dating back to the nineteenth century:

> Globalisation or internationalisation, is not a new phenomenon. The period through the end of the nineteenth century was also characterised by unprecedented economic growth and global integration. But globalisation was interrupted in the first half of the twentieth century by a wave of protectionism and aggressive nationalism, which led to depression and world war. International economic and political integration was reversed, with severe consequences. Since 1945, democracy and capitalism have been embraced by an increasing number of countries – including since 1989, by most of the previously communist world. As a result, the past 50 years have been a period of growing economic and political freedom and rising prosperity. Global per capita income has more than tripled, and most of the world has experienced a major improvement in life expectancy (IMF 2001, 1).

Indeed, it is feasible to perceive the current trend of globalisation as an intensification and expansion of a process established several centuries ago (Robertson 1992, 1). A major difference, however, as Robertson states, is that the current situation has stimulated a global consciousness, where people have a significantly heightened awareness of the experiences of others (1992, 183). This is largely due to the expansion of the communications media, in particular global television, Internet technology and other technologies for fast travel and communication.

> Global communications and media have been instrumental in accelerating the compression of space and time, which is understood as an integral aspect of the globalisation process. Indeed, we can perceive the growth of global telecommunications with computer networks, satellite TV and the Internet as the technological infrastructure in the globalisation of finance, production, marketing and patterns of consumption (Girvan 2000, 18).

The proliferation of new information technologies and electronic communications has played a vital role in interconnecting people's lives and establishing the so-called 'global village', a term coined by McLuhan in the 1960s. The notion of the 'global village' is central to the ideology of globalisation as it suggests that the world is 'shrinking' in that countries and peoples are becoming more integrated, resulting in a blurring of territorial boundaries (Klak 1998, 5). Today, it is theoretically possible for everyone in the world to be connected via electronic messaging systems. The Internet is an apt example of this new technology. Provided that there is a telecommunication connection, anybody in the world can access a wealth of information.

While the Internet may aid the dissemination of information and knowledge, it too is working within specific boundaries, is subject to economic controls and hence is not objective. 'The political freedom of the Internet, as it was first envisaged, today seems something of an illusion' (Harcourt 2003, 6). Further concerns are centred on the notion that not everyone has equal access to the benefits of new communications technologies which, in turn, may result in greater disparities between members of the global community.

Global media, new information technologies and telecommunications have enabled many people in the world to become instantly connected to others. And yet, events in distant locations are quite often more easily available on television in the Caribbean than information originating from the rural areas of the same Caribbean countries, or indeed neighbouring regional capitals (Dunn 1995, xii).

Norman Girvan identifies ten features as central to globalisation:

1. A world economic order centred on the Triad of US-EU-Japan, under the political and military leadership of the US.
2. The central role of the WTO in international trade relations.
3. The construction of regional economic blocs or free trade zones.
4. Restructuring North-South trade agreements (NAFTA, FTAA, Lomé) along WTO-compatible lines; that is, replacement of the principle of non-reciprocal preferences to assist with development of weaker partners with that of reciprocal trade liberalisation to promote trade expansion and market-led growth.
5. Policies of privatisation, financial deregulation, trade and exchange rate liberalisation, fiscal and monetary orthodoxy, labour market reforms and social welfare reform, as the new orthodoxy with presumed universal applicability.

6. The alleged loss of national economic sovereignty.
7. The attainment of 'global competitiveness' as the benchmark by which all countries and producers, regardless of their resources or level of development are to be evaluated.
8. The growth of global communications.
9. The consolidation of huge concentrations of private capital; and
10. A triumphalist ideology, marked by the assumption that there is no other way to organise the world, as summed up in the phrase 'the end of history' (Girvan 2000, 67-68).

Economically, therefore, globalisation revolves around the ideas and practices of neo-liberalism which principally comprise economic liberalisation and the establishment of free trade under conditions of capitalism. The preceding two decades are of particular interest, as during the 1980s, bodies such as the International Monetary Fund (IMF) and the World Trade Organization (WTO) were instrumental in expanding trade liberalisation, and thus a competitive global market, by advising countries of the Economic South to increase market liberalisation and privatisation (Munroe-Knight 2002, 21) often as conditionalities for debt relief. Yet, as many agree, incorporation into a single global economy and the elimination of trade barriers has affected countries differentially, as 'The developing countries, mainly the least developed countries in Africa are likely to suffer significant economic marginalisation as a result of globalisation' (Benn and Hall 2000, xiv).

Today, due to the hegemony of economic and cultural liberalism and the tenets of free trade, this impact, now called globalisation, has come to be accepted as a new orthodoxy. Its discussants range from seeing it as the only true way forward for all countries, to seeing it as having benefits as well as negative effects, however it is difficult for the benefits to be equitably distributed worldwide. Generally, it has become increasingly difficult for any country to operate outside of its parameters and all have had to come to terms with it in one way or another.

In spite of widespread international criticism, the process of globalisation has continued and is now affecting almost every aspect of life. Local and national manufacturers, farmers, and even educational institutions now have to become 'globally competitive' or perish. Little attention is being paid to the proverbial 'level playing field' which used to be important for more welfare-oriented liberalism. Companies and/or countries have to become competitive in spite of historical, natural resource, human resource, cultural or economic differences.

In order to be economically competitive, firms search for cheaper and cheaper labour and open markets to minimise costs and maximise benefits, in line with an increasingly aggressive capitalist agenda. Transnational corporations, usually based in the Economic North,[3] are able to move labour and capital overseas where and when necessary to take advantage of low-wage production, in many cases using cheap female labour. However, the vast majority of these women are engaged in low-wage occupations, with little or no job security (Jain 2000, 16). This is possible through economies of scale, which smaller companies and economies are less able to implement. This exploitation of labour is evidence of a counter-argument to the notion that globalisation successfully thrusts women into an equitable position with men. Indeed some men, interestingly, are finding themselves in positions often reserved in the past for women, such as male sex workers. The explosion in popularity of the mail-order bride phenomenon is also testimony to this. Women, and increasingly men, their bodies and their sexuality are even more so today perceived as commodities. Hence, the onslaught of globalisation exacerbates inequalities at the national level, internationally, between differing states, at the social level, between men and women, and the 'haves' and 'have-nots'.

The impact of globalised communications has also had many undesirable consequences. Of particular interest recently have been the tensions between Internet consumption and women's empowerment. Ideally, according to Shade, the Internet would be used to establish active women's communities, yet there are concerns that the feminisation of the Internet has led to the privileging of women's consumption over critical analysis as consumer-oriented content has been directed at women. 'With the emergence of every new communications technology, women have been targeted as a specific audience demographic by industry, advertisers and the media themselves' (Shade 2003, 50). Shade calls for the Internet to be developed as a tool for women's activism in order to further the international women's movement (Shade 2003, 50). She argues strongly for the technology now available to be exploited to its full potential as a means of empowering its users. Yet, as Wendy Harcourt notes:

> The potential to use the Internet to guide economic, political and social practices of a nation might be there along with its subversive potential, but this potential is not necessarily one that citizens take up. This is not to undermine the many groups who have made good use of it, such as the women's movement, which seems to have found the Internet particularly suited to their needs. – [T]he failure to use the Internet as a political tool, despite many predictions and a lot of hope, is not only information overload, or the digital divide between South and North, but poses larger threats to the democratic vision of the original designers of the Web. If one remembers that the Internet was first a military invention, and the amount of money governments and then private businesses have invested in it, it perhaps should be no surprise that the 'commons' of cyberspace is not operating to foster the world's social capital in quite the way that some pioneers imagined (Harcourt 2003, 6).

It must be noted, however, that a large movement critiquing the orthodoxy and hegemony of globalisation has emerged, but so far has been unable to seriously challenge its control and influence.[4] This movement, according to Girvan, 'critiques the market-oriented, corporate-led globalisation' and advocates 'alternative ways of managing national and international exchange'. This movement, he notes, does not recommend a return to national autarchies, but rather it questions whether 'global market liberalisation will work to the benefit of all' (Girvan 2000, 68).

Globalisation and the Caribbean

The Caribbean has often been described as the most historically globalised of all regions. Indeed many of the characteristics of globalisation have been part of the historical experience of this region. This includes the movement for exploitation of cheap (sometimes unwaged) labour, the movement of people and goods, the involvement of transnational trading and manufacturing companies and the negative effects of surviving in a brutally competitive capitalist economic context. In the words of Thomas Klak:

> ... emerging global linkages come as no news to the people of the Caribbean, which historically is perhaps the most globalized of world regions. Since the 1500s, the Caribbean has been controlled by outside powers, based economically on imported labor, cleared to create monocrop landscapes...and reliant on the import of virtually everything else needed to sustain local populations (Klak 1998, 6).

Today, the region is facing new manifestations of this phenomenon. The most significant so far has been the destruction of the main agro-based plantation and peasant production systems with the removal of protective mechanisms such as the European Union quotas for preferential markets. Interestingly, these preferences were negotiated as reparations in some way for the extreme exploitation and dehumanisation of colonialism generally and the slave and post-slave era from which Europe gained so much. The current context acknowledges no such debt and calls on all countries to operate as if they are beginning from the same starting point and urges them to aim for the same conclusion.

This has been especially devastating in the banana-producing countries such as Jamaica, Dominica, Saint Lucia, Saint Vincent and the Grenadines and Grenada where the removal of preferential quotas to the European Union has compromised the banana export industry. But even in oil- and gas-rich Trinidad and Tobago, the sugar industry, livelihood for over 30,000 people, has suffered a similar fate. The theoretical argument is that the liberalisation of national markets and hence the free flow of goods, services and information will benefit everyone equally. It is interesting that, while Caribbean countries along with others in the Economic South are feeling the negative effects of this removal of protection for agricultural commodities, the United States and the European Union continue to protect their agricultural producers with large subsidies, often to the tune of $1billion per day (Watkins 2003, 6). As stated in an editorial of the *International Herald Tribune:*

> Poor and developing nations have long – and rightly – complained that while the richest countries want open markets for their manufactured goods, they rig the game when it comes to agricultural products. Now it appears that the United States and Europe are beginning to get the message. Their trade negotiators have agreed to *try* to reduce their farm subsidies and other barriers to agricultural imports. ... As

this page has been reporting in recent weeks, poor nations buy into the mantra of globalisation and free trade orthodoxy, only to find their farm products locked out of the developed nations' markets by high tariffs, or competing hopelessly against subsidized European and American goods, which sell below cost (*IHT*, 6).

Globalisation, Culture and Communication

But the opening of markets has not only been in the area of manufactured products; by far one of the most significant openings has been in the area of communications. For, although globalisation is often viewed as an economic process, it is imperative that we remember that every process, be it economic or not, impacts greatly upon human experience, and hence cannot be subject to examination in isolation. Hence, globalisation involves a myriad of cultural, social, political, psychological as well as economic effects. Speaking at a debate on 'UNESCO in a Globalising World', it was stated by the chairperson of the Executive Board that 'those who see globalisation as a purely economic process are wrong. Firstly, no human phenomenon of such scope can be limited to the sole production and consumption of goods and services ... and because even the smallest economic transaction occurs against a backdrop of beliefs and is conditioned by its socio-political context' (UNESCO Press 2000). So, how indeed have people been affected by the forces of globalisation?

One of the main critiques of globalisation has been the view that the term has largely been a misnomer and a misconception. Indeed, it can be argued that what is referred to as globalisation should be more correctly called US-isation or Americanisation, except that the United States is really only one part of the Americas. Critics point out that most of what is global television is really United States television, as are Internet communications, computer programmes and software. What contemporary globalisation has meant is that United States fashion, language, music, religion, food and ideologies, including gender ideologies, are continuously transported overseas and adopted, adapted and/or incorporated into and by countries throughout the world.

In theory, globalisation should involve the two-way or many-sided flow across borders. But yet, for the Caribbean, as well as most of the world, these ideas and values have largely originated from North America.

Satellite and cable television has been central to this process. Currently, 90 million people around the world, in 200 different countries, watch CNN (Demers 1999, 21). Much of the content broadcast on television stations around the world is from the United States of America. For example, the tiny Caribbean island of Montserrat imports 95 per cent of its television programmes (Brown 1995, 57).

But not only has the world become a market for US communication products, as a result of this it has also become a consumer of US cultural products for which the communications media are a successful marketing mechanism. This has undoubtedly led to a homogenisation in tastes and consumption habits. Yet the most crucial question remains: 'Are societies such as the Caribbean passive recipients of the output of the global North or are they engaged both in contributing to a global culture as well as in the re-interpretation and selective assimilation of received information or entertainment?' (Dunn 1995, xiii).

There has been a long-term concern over the loss of indigenous Caribbean culture to that of North America. The English-speaking Caribbean has been most susceptible as it shares common language and a history of migration with the two principle producers of media – the UK and the US, and very close geographical location to the latter. Great concern for a deepening dependency relationship and the perpetuation of 'Western' values into the Third World has been voiced (Brown 1995, 59).

For Nederveen Pieterse, however, to refer to this as 'cultural imperialism' gives little room to acknowledge the diversity of ways in which a foreign product may be interpreted or utilised. Even 'imperialism' he suggests is not an accurate term to use, as it denotes intentional and extended control over another state (Nederveen Pieterse 1993, 13). Instead, globalisation, he suggests, is complex, entailing the availability of ideas, images, products, services, technology and information virtually all over the world. To confuse globalisation, which he describes as the 'intensification of worldwide social relations', with westernisation, is to collapse globalisation theory into modernisation theory (1993, 3-4). Rather than resulting in dominant cultures subsuming others, globalisation entails an increase in the available modes of organisation. By this, he means that the increased awareness of others and communication with them has made it possible for people to assert their identities in a multitude of ways, such as, globally, transnationally, internationally, macro-regionally, nationally, micro-regionally, municipally, locally and institutionally (Nederveen Pieterse 1993, 6).

This author's definition of globalisation clearly does not endorse the view that cultural uniformity and standardisation are inevitable, arguing that a global cross-over culture, caused by 'cultural osmosis' has been in effect for centuries (1993, 8). Yet, the author reminds us that cultural hybridisation can also be inscribed with relations of power and hegemony. Heterogenisation does not necessarily mean the end of cultural hegemonies or inequalities or that one culture can dominate another. Indeed, 'Caribbean' cultures in all their manifestations are the result of unequal hybridisations and 'creolisations' as noted by Brathwaite (1977). The question remains, however, which countries or which corporations should direct and control the directions of this hybridisation process? And should the North-South pattern continue unchallenged?

Gender Ideologies and Cultural Representation

Gender ideologies are the culturally specific identities, norms, and symbols associated with social constructions of masculinity and femininity. In other words, they refer to, for example, notions of appropriate behaviours, attitudes, mannerisms for women and men, and for relations between women and men, and among persons of the same sex/gender identity. Gender ideologies are not fixed, although some aspects can be extremely pervasive and difficult to change. They are, however, dynamic and are constantly being negotiated and re-negotiated because of changes taking place in society at various levels.

Anthropologists studying relatively isolated societies could often identify specific and diverse gender ideologies and behaviours. Today however, as a result of colonial and neo-colonial cultural domination and contemporary globalisation, there tend to be greater commonalities in gender ideologies, although there is still a great deal of diversity. As noted by Holmberg: 'Phenomena, artefacts, events, language, images, sounds, music, gesture, fashion, rituals public and private, daily habits, and more can be and are sexualized, gendered, and oriented diversely, within a culture, across cultures' (Holmberg 1998, 16).

Since all means of physical transference contain communicative power, many forms of media, such as film, radio and television impinge on human consciousness. These forms of media have played a significant role in informing a sense of gender roles and gender identities, particularly through the display of sexual and gendered images.

The concept of representation has become an important one in the analysis of communication, art and media in recent times. It derives from a tradition of semiology and structuralist analysis of language and refers to the processes by which meaning is produced, the ways in which images and texts reconstruct rather than reflect the original sources that they represent (Humm 1995, 238; Marshall 1998, 565). It is argued that media images, and the communications media in all forms, produce meanings. Feminist scholarship has been particularly interested in the politics of representation and in challenging the ways in which media of all forms have constructed images and messages related to women and gender relations and constantly reconstruct and reorganise these messages.

Globalisation and the Impact on the Representation of Masculinities and Femininities in the Caribbean

Scholars of globalisation observe the ways in which representations tend towards homogenisation and stereotyping. It is also argued that the control over these representations lies in the hands of the global (read US) communications industry. It is interesting, therefore, that even those national entities involved in the representation and communication of ideas draw their inspiration, their formats and their design from the Economic North, in particular the Untied States. Local creativity in this case lies mainly in adaptation and adoption.

In an interview with the author, Trinidad and Tobago journalist Joannah Bharose noted that the entire style, format and content of the local print media have been virtually copied from the United States media. For example, in relation to the highly successful *Express Woman* Sunday magazine, she revealed:

> [T]he entire format in terms of having a light, airy magazine, that was a combination of the new favoured culture and the magazine culture. If we look at any publication,

in the UK for example, most of them come out on Wednesday – *The Guardian*, *The Times*. Except for maybe the faces, it is exactly what is coming out of those markets, page for page. The design was borrowed from several US publications. We are slaves to global trends in terms of the media because once it works up there, we don't have the money, and we don't have to exert the time and effort to do the research. Once it's tried and tested it's adopted (Bharose Interview, 14.4.03).

Joannah Bharose was one of a number of personalities involved in different ways in the 'representation' of gender ideologies in Trinidad and Tobago interviewed for this study. Others included a rapso[5] performer, also an executive member of the calypsonians' association – Brother Resistance; a beauty and dress consultant and designer – Peter Elias; and artist/designer and men's movement activist – Robert Young.

In an international market unfettered by controls or protections, by patents or even governments, the possibility of control over media messages, such as pornography, representations of acceptable and unacceptable gendered behaviour, racist and sexist messages has become increasingly difficult. The free flow of information has been one of the positives of globalisation, the inability to control or manage this information, one of its negatives. Bharose continues:

> We are slaves to whatever happens in the US market ... the American influence is really hitting at the heart of the younger, impressionable age group of our society, the teenagers and young adults. Without a doubt I think our Caribbean region, sad to say, is probably heading in the direction of a Miami or New York, in terms of, I don't want to say cultural ideas, but our ideas on living and how to live. The basic choice for jobs, food. I think because of the far-reaching influence of the larger nations, I see we're heading in the way of one large country (Bharose Interview, 14.4.2003).

In answer to the question – Is it really globalisation, or is it US-isation? Bharose responded:

> In the case of Trinidad and Tobago I really feel it's US-isation. I don't see us being influenced by Great Britain to any extent; I don't see us being influenced by the voice of culture to any extent and they are all huge powers in the globalisation process. For some reason or other we can't seem to escape the US format of globalisation. And it's sad, really sad, because there is much more out there that we can benefit from rather than from this monotone coming out of the US. And it's like when you look at the music and dress of the young people who are our future generation it gives us a clear indication of how the US influences ... But if I look at

young people I cannot tell the difference between a New Yorker and a young Trini, male or female (Bharose Interview, 14.4.03).

For his part, Brother Resistance had this to say:

> When you look at the use of the television and the cable situation and so on, what happens is that what coming in is directly from America, affecting not only our musical tastes and consumption patterns but it affecting our relations with each other. Relations of parent to children, relationships of man and woman, relationships in the wider community. It's affecting them seriously because it dictating the pace and it breaking the order, the traditional patterns that we had as a people, as a community and as a society. It mashing up them bonds.... When they say globalisation, they really mean that [Americanisation] you know. It would have been nice if it meant more cross-cultural patterns and relations between a number of different situations. We in Trinidad, for instance, don't relate with South and Central America or Latin America. We don't relate actively with Africa and India. And globalisation should have meant that a lot of these things could have become reality (Brother Resistance Interview, 24.03.03).

And Robert Young:

> There are a lot of people in countries like ours that have taken on globalisation as the new way of thinking. They want to take on whatever trends are happening, wherever ... we are open to it, but open in a way that is not a thinking way. We respond to it in an impulsive way because of all kinds of things. We have a lot of insecurities about ourselves, there is a lot of doubt. So if people say that this is right we will do it.
>
> With the opening up of the airways, and also with the lowering of import duties on clothing and other products, with things like music and fashion, it was no longer for people who have access and money. Both urban and rural areas have access. Now you can't tell if someone is from Sangre Grande or Toco,[6] everyone can look 'in'. And if you can look 'in' you *are* 'in' and try to put everyone else 'out' (Robert Young Interview, 26.03.03).

Young's opinion is slightly different from the others because he also perceives there to be a space for resistance against the onslaught of globalisation. He suggests that 'The war [US-Iraq] is promoting a space for people to say "no". The voices of dissent are rising. People are not fully accepting. People are now realizing they can say "no"' (Young Interview, 16.03.03).

There is also the argument that global culture has been hybridised through migration from Third World cultures, for example the *Latinisation* of the USA, and the *Caribbeanisation* of New York City.

Aggrey Brown, for example, asserts that 'Caribbean citizens have been willing consumers of both hardware and software' and have 'not been coerced into consumption' (Brown 1995, 52). Indeed, Brown, like Nederveen Pieterse, calls for a complete revision of the notion of 'cultural imperialism' denouncing it as a 'misdiagnosis of the situation' (1995, 52), arguing that 'the geography and history of the Caribbean can be used to its strategic advantage to participate fully in the evolution of world culture' (1995, 53). The Caribbean region, Brown notes, is accustomed to innovation, and can therefore contribute significantly to global culture. He draws on the steel pan and the current popularity of Caribbean music (reggae, in particular) to argue that 'Caribbean people need only to be reminded of and inspired by these two singular human achievements in order to make equally significant contributions to global culture via electronic media' (Brown 1995, 53-54).

> If Caribbean culture is indeed demonstrating some resilience in the face of adversity, as this study's preliminary trends suggest, and which tireless investigation can only help to elucidate, then such resilience demands the reinforcement of the modern world's most effective centre for creative cultural expression – the media (Brown 1995, 78).

In other words, Caribbean people must tap into this powerful resource in order to put their cultural products 'out there'.

The argument that Caribbean people, and Trinidadians in particular, are well acquainted with innovation is one that is also supported by anthropologist, Daniel Miller. Miller argues against the notion that a high level of consumption of United States soap operas in Trinidad and Tobago demonstrates a passive acceptance of the values attached to the messages being conveyed. In his article: 'The Young and the Restless in Trinidad: A Case of the Local and the Global in Mass Consumption', he maintains that the history of Trinidad is evidence enough to argue that Trinidadians actively and creatively appropriate artefacts in their environment. Miller also cites the steel pan as an example of a musical instrument created from disused oil drums (Miller 1992, 165). For him, this demonstrates effectively that Trinidad is not a passive victim of Americanisation. This is supported by other scholars as follows:

Not only has the Caribbean actively consumed, or chosen to consume foreign imports, rather than passively absorbing them, but it has also competently contributed significantly to a hybridised global culture, especially in terms of music. In fact, Caribbean culture is very much a part of the cultural landscape of global cities, such as New York. With almost a century of Caribbean migration to the city, one can almost describe this as the 'Caribbeanisation' of New York. This has created close links between the Caribbean and America, and involved the two-way flow of people, images, and ideologies....Hence, the argument for the 'Americanisation' of the world seems less legitimate when the very cities of the United States are becoming 'Caribbeanized'. Indeed nowhere is this transnational crossroads phenomenon more apparent than in the realm of popular music. Internationally recognized as the centre of contemporary Latin and West Indian music, New York's connections to Caribbean music reflect an ongoing process of cultural exchange that is nearly a century old....Radio, migration and music recordings assisted in the hybridisation of music forms and the incorporation of American influences on the Caribbean music. Soca itself is a blend of Trinidadian calypso and African-American soul.[7] There is much evidence to support the notion of the continual fusion of traditional island rhythms with modern American styles (Allen and Wilcken 1998, 2).

What is important to note, however, is that the globalisation of Caribbean culture is only possible through the route of the USA. Bob Marley was a Jamaican performer for many years, idolised in his own country but unknown elsewhere. His international and Caribbean recognition came with his success in North America and Britain. Most Caribbean superstars who 'make it' globally have to gain the endorsement of the US entertainment establishment, sometimes even to be accepted in the Caribbean region itself.

Additionally, the African-American media have a particular influence on the African diaspora and Economic South in particular, the impact on US black ideologies is significant in influencing consumption, identities and behaviours among people of colour throughout the world. In this globalised context, this is a grave responsibility which, however, is seldom recognised, as noted in the extract from Trinidadian fashion retailer and designer Peter Elias:

> Black men? or Indian men? Well who are their role models? Who is their identity? Black America. I had dinner last Friday in New York with the field director of BET and I scolded him for the lack of vision of their network. It's VIACOM who owns MTV and VH1, and they also own BET. It's the most profitable network. And I said 'shame on you for your lack of vision', because all of Black America, and the

Black World, aren't women with nails long like this and hair pieces that do this and talk like this and shake from their neck like this. They're not all like that. The men aren't hitting their chest on each other when they bounce. It's not all like that. All their diamonds like bling bling. I said shame on them. They must open Black America and the world to the wonderful variety. I think God blessed Black people, I don't know why. He made them a very rich race; they are very very talented but not well managed. Their amazing voices, their amazing athleticism, their compassion. Have you ever heard a gospel singer? There is nothing more beautiful. He blessed them abundantly….The whole black world is not like that. Don't show these images only, I think … (Robert Elias 8.5.2003).

Globalisation and Women's Emancipation in the Caribbean

It is interesting that, for many younger Caribbean people, the improvement in the status of women, and women's access to paid work outside the home is the result of foreign influence, which today is generally associated with globalisation. There is the view that ideas of women's emancipation and independence were brought to the region through the US media and popular culture. This is interesting as, unlike other parts of the North and South, the ancestors of the majority of Caribbean women were brought to this region for economically productive work outside the home, for the international market. This may be an accurate assessment of women's experiences in other parts of the developing world, but Caribbean women have always constituted a significant proportion of the labour market. Initially, this was enslaved labour which was eventually replaced by low-wage free and bonded or indentured labour.

The twentieth century, therefore, saw in this region, a *reduction* in the proportion of women in paid work outside the home.[8] With the replacement of plantation production by peasant production, for example, of sugar, bananas, cacao, etc., women continued to be important producers but not always the recipients of direct financial rewards. Additionally, many women involved in peasant production were often recorded as unemployed or worse yet 'economically inactive' and 'not in the labour force' resulting in many difficulties in calculating women's economic participation. Nevertheless, it is true to say that, throughout the Caribbean, paid work for women outside the home is not the result of economic globalisation or of contemporary liberating influences introduced via the Internet or cable television.

The current phase of globalisation has resulted in an increase in the number of job losses, largely as a result of the mechanisation of agriculture and the decline in local manufacturing. The consequence of such redundancy has been the large-scale outward migration, particularly of women, since the 1960s. It has been witness to the emergence of what Wiltshire refers to as the Transnational Caribbean Family, with parents, especially mothers, migrating illegally to the USA in efforts to support children. The number of Caribbean people residing in North America is more than half the number residing in their home countries.

The economic and cultural changes being experienced by the end of the twentieth and start of the twenty-first centuries, in particular the imposition of neo-liberal economic policies of the IMF and World Bank, have coincided with the challenge to patriarchal norms and attitudes by the women's movement and increasingly by individual women in Caribbean societies. One result of this has been the good use made by women, especially middle-class women, of increased opportunities for education and the resulting access to senior positions, especially in the public sector.

The increase in women's urban and white-collar employment is seen as a threat to men at a time when men's employment is becoming less secure. Women's jobs are not more secure but their identity is less defined by employment and they tend to adjust better to changes within it. This has created a context for increased violence against women, as men perceive a loss of control over women and a loss of traditional markers of masculinity. This sense of impotence and the increased visibility of some women in public life bring into sharp focus men's feelings of reduced economic security and challenge the legitimacy of their learnt role as 'provider'. This often results in serious tensions in gender relations, increased violence against women and, more recently, a backlash against the women's movement. This is reflected in the statements from the interviews below:

> The empowerment of women has proceeded at a very fast pace. I have to put it that way because some people think that women wasn't empowered before. Women were always powerful, it sounds sexist, but in terms that they were running the household. That was their role. The economy of the household, and by extension,

the wider society, the community work, the social work .... And if we move into what happening now, the empowerment has become so fast-paced in a number of other areas, professional areas in particular, and in a number of different situations and you find now that with that change, that change of rank, both sexes are having problems coming to terms with relationships. Men in particular have a problem; they don't know how to measure themselves if there is a situation where women are bringing in more money than them, or where the women might be in a situation of greater social and political influence in the community. Men have a lot of problems with that, and in making that adjustment it is causing a lot of other problems and I think that reflecting a lot in situations of domestic violence .... I see young men can only relate to young women by that – grabbing aggression, in a position of dominance, which is no longer a reality (Brother Resistance Interview, 24.3.03).

I think it has also affected ... well, men and women's relationships have always been difficult because they operate from a non-loving space. We operate love from a feeling, and it's a nice feeling, and if the nice feeling is not there, it's not love. Love is much more than a nice feeling, it operates from respect, and care and giving information and being able to give the truth. And the way the world is set up is that you can't have an equal space to build relationships. For a long time it has been unequal, women have had to limit themselves to be in a relationship with a man, and a man could just be and do what he wants. Feminism made us think that things need to be different. Some parts of feminism were marketed as man-bashing. Feminism has changed its position from radical, and man-bashing, to men have to do some work too. Women have been speaking and men haven't really been hearing because there is a kind of unawareness that you suffer from when you're the perpetrator. And so now with globalisation, and with the videos, [which] are laden with rigid, saturated sexism. And with the globalisation too is access to satellite religious stations which imposes, and is reinforced by, people trying to find truth. I think we came out of difficult spaces from having to pretend. Getting to school quickly, or church quickly. So everybody here is trying to be somebody, so you become pastor or you become a DJ. And as soon as they put a mike in your hand you get an American accent. You become somebody with a mike in your hand. The feeling of wholeness and goodness is hard because of our history, and so young men want to be inside so they do what they see or what they learn (Robert Young Interview, 26.03.03).

Indeed, the regional women's movement has been active since the late 1970s with indigenous antecedents, going back to the early twentieth century, as well as global influences from the North and the South. The indigenous and anti-imperialist imperatives of this movement born out of the radical movements of the 1970s compete with current North American influences of women's liberation, usually of a more corporate variety. For some young women, who have been brought up on this model, the two are inextricably related. As a result, many of the gains of the Caribbean women's movement over the past three decades are understood as gains of globalisation. This is reflected in the statement below by Joannah Bharose:

> I see globalisation beginning when a woman gets up in the morning and decides she is going to go out and get a job and start providing for herself, instead of depending on a man. I see it beginning when a woman decides 'I am not going to have five children, I am going to have two'. I see globalisation beginning when women say 'I am no longer dependent on someone else bringing home the bacon'. For men, it is when they recognise that, yes, women need to be treated more than just a wife or mother, or someone to look after the house' (Bharose Interview, 16.4.03).

Whatever the relationship between globalisation and women's liberation, in many parts of the world, women's efforts at emancipation are perceived as the result of 'foreign influences', usually westernisation and a challenge to local culture where women are seen as symbols and purveyors of cultural tradition and stability. This creates a basis for tension between the sexes.

Selected Issues in the Cultural Representation of Gender Ideologies in the Caribbean

This section examines four locations where the cultural contestations over the representation of gender ideologies are taking place. These are:

1) the emergence of fundamentalisms in the face of perceived cultural domination and homogenisation;

2) The beauty contest industry;

3) sport, gender and national identity; and

4) The Bollywood influence.

Fundamentalisms, Globalisation and Gender Relations

The resurgence in religious and ethnic fundamentalism has been cited as one characteristic of this era of globalisation. Where the threat of cultural hegemony is posed, there is often a 'return'[9] to fundamentalism, whether it is associated with religion, ethnicity, or nationalism. This is highlighted by Peggy Antrobus when she states:

> The cultural consequences are the ones that tended to be overlooked, except by Third World women. These include the spread of religious fundamentalism which often accompanied the adoption of the neo-liberal policy framework (economic fundamentalism)[10] and its spread through globalisation .... The spread of religious fundamentalism is strengthened by economic restructuring in three ways: firstly insecurity caused people to turn to religion; secondly loss of social services creates opportunities for religious orders to provide these services where they can indoctrinate women and children seeking assistance; finally (especially in the 1990s) Islam is seen as a counter-hegemonic force to the spread of Western culture and values. (Antrobus 2003, 4).

It is already possible to perceive this trend, as we witness the essentialising of identities in terms of religion and culture: East versus West. Ferjani notes that far from creating a homogeneous global culture where, under the rubric of 'globalisation', one would have expected the emergence of a universalist view advocating 'the international human being', we now see that 'Religion is presented as the most important determinant of civilisational identity'. As other borders, such as that of nations, gradually dissolve, religious differences increasingly play a more central role as a principle of differentiation. This results in the 'negation of the universality of the human being' and a return to fundamentalism which may pose a significant threat to the gains of women's liberatory movements (Mohammed-Cherif Ferjani 2001, 6-7).

In the Caribbean region, the process of globalisation has resulted in some dichotomous processes where the representation of women's sexualities and identities is concerned. On the one hand there is an increased commodification of women's and men's bodies through the expansion of pornography, the sex-work market, and the beauty contest industry. While on the other, there is the increased visibility of veiled women and girls, as Islamic fundamentalism becomes more widespread. This has occurred both among older established Muslim groups where women have historically never been veiled and among newer converts who also have never had a tradition of veiling. In Trinidad and Tobago even pre-pubescent girls are veiled, something which would have been unheard of until recently.

At the same time, through the globalised US media as well as continued missionary activity, fundamentalist US Christian ideology is an overwhelming presence in the Caribbean region. Some radio frequencies have become dedicated to US or US-influenced religious programming which emphasises a 'return' to a Christianity which supports women's submission, male domination, homophobia and rejects religious tolerance. In Trinidad and Tobago, US missionary activity among Hindus in the 1980s and 1990s resulted in the revitalisation of Hindu fundamentalist groups seeking to retain control over Hindu women in a context of increasing US-based and directed evangelising, ably supported by local and cable television.

Globalised Notions of Beauty – The Beauty Contest Industry

Beauty is one of those factors closely associated with femininity in most parts of the world. While it is supposed to be culturally specific, in that each culture and society can define what is beautiful in its eyes, through the globalising impact – first of European colonialism and now of United States media and popular culture – Euro-American notions of beauty have become hegemonic throughout the world. There is no greater representation of this than the beauty contest, in many ways an extension of the continuous competition against each other that women are supposed to engage in to secure a desirable male spouse.

The modern beauty contest has its origins in the United States early in the twentieth century. According to Kathy Peiss, they 'evolved from modest May Day celebrations' into the Miss America pageant by 1921 (Peiss 1998, 190). Concurrent with the development of the beauty pageant, was the evolution of the cosmetics industry with headquarters in Paris and the United States. By the end of the twentieth century, beauty contests had become an important part of popular culture internationally. US and British franchises ran international pageants such as the Miss Universe and Miss World competitions but lesser international, regional and group-specific competitions such as Miss International, Miss India Overseas and Miss Big and Beautiful also emerged as beauty contests and became a successful area for commerce and business.

US beauty pageants set hegemonic standards of beauty based on Euro-American preferences. These were of course light skin colour, straight hair, near-European phenotype, slim size (except for special competitions for larger women) and the Euro-American ideologies of girlhood and femininity. Hence, by the early twenty-first century, contestants or delegates, as they are now called at international pageants, are supposed to be young, slim, unmarried and childless and referred to as 'the girls'. These ideals, already powerful through the wide reach of United States and British cinema and television, by becoming international, drew women from every quarter of the globe into its sphere of influence.

African-American women were the first to feel the impact of this Euro-American beauty hegemony and the sense of inferiority that it brought. The iron comb, a device for straightening tightly curled African hair, was invented by Madame Walker, an African-American businesswoman who advocated this as a modern form of hair care – not hair straightening (Piess 1998, 205). Skin bleaching creams were also popularised in the United States, although Walker and her supporters did not advocate them. These practices have now spread to the African and Asian diasporas[11] and the entire world, along with the market for beauty products. During the twentieth century, the beauty industry became an important aspect of women's consumerism internationally and has expanded to include cosmetic surgery.

The notion of beauty which evolved was one where beauty was not only natural but, more importantly, had to be worked for and developed through the proper application of make-up, training, proper diet, poise, elegance etc. In the 1960s and 1970s, the beauty contest faced attacks from the revitalised feminist movement that criticised this practice as debasing women by emphasising an ultra-femininity which most women could not achieve; making women into a commodity where their bodies were reconstructed for sale like a cattle farm; emphasising women's physical attributes and not their intellectual ones; keeping women in traditional roles of femininity which were pleasing to men but were not in women's own interests and developing a homogenised notion of beauty based on the primacy of Euro-American characteristics.

The Black Power movement, popular at that time, also critiqued the contests as privileging European standards of beauty. These attacks did have some impact on the contests. More women of colour were accepted as participants in contests and increased emphasis was placed on answering the questions, many of which often dealt with issues related to women's empowerment. But this did not stop the spread of beauty contests, which spread even among men and transexual males, although never to the same degree. The success of this industry, no doubt, lies in its popularity with various people all over the world and its economic success. This, therefore, qualifies it as an important aspect of popular culture and globalised industry. It has a mass following and, even though it is criticised by intellectuals and feminists, its popular appeal and economic attraction has not diminished. Herein lies the challenge of popular culture.

In other parts of the Economic South, the critique of the globalising influence of beauty contests can also be heard. In India, for example, which has recently had much success in international contests, some of the most significant protests have taken place. While on the one hand these represent efforts to maintain national control over women's bodies, on the other it is also a resistance to what is perceived as the homogenising imperative of this Western-dominated process.

In the article 'The Ugliness of Beauty Contests: The Miss India's these days do not look very "Indian",' Khan highlights the concern among some that beauty standards all over the world are becoming aligned with what are deemed to be the 'Western' ideal. For example, the Indian winner of Miss Universe 2002 was criticised for not resembling an Indian at all. In fact, the article argued: 'rather than touting the Indian woman as the ideal beauty, these beauty pageants reward women who fit the Western standard of ideal beauty in height, weight, features and complexion' (Khan 2002). The author likens the trend to a form of neo-colonialism, in which the Western notion of beauty becomes thoroughly globalised at the expense of local concepts of beauty, and cultural values.

> Beauty contests have permeated the social fabric of Indian culture to such an extent as to be called an obsession. The ideals of beauty include fair skin and 'Caucasian features'. Promoting such standards may have a seriously detrimental effect upon those who cannot meet the homogenized criteria, this is a viewpoint echoed by many (Khan 2002).

In response to this viewpoint, others argue that the contests are simultaneously universal and local. In the Introduction to *Beauty Queens on the Global Stage: Gender, Contests, and Power*, the editors argue that the contests provide an avenue through which ideals about gender roles and norms, and notions of femininity can be conveyed (Ballerino et al 1996, 3). Beauty, they suggest is heavily linked to ideas of culture and power, and there remains a wide variation cross-culturally in what is deemed beautiful:

> Beauty contests are places where cultural meanings are produced, consumed, *and* rejected, where local and global, ethnic and national, national and international cultures and structures of power are engaged in their most trivial but vital aspects …. They connect idealized femininity with national discourses …. They are informative, deeming what is appropriate concerning women's productive and reproductive roles in society …. They can also seek to naturalize gender differences (Ballerino et al 1996, 8-9).

The authors conclude that 'Beauty pageants provide crucial insights into what happens at the intersection of local, national, and global culture'.

Beauty Contests – The Caribbean Experience

In the Caribbean, issues of colour, phenotype, hair and body shape have always been important to the beauty contest experience. During the early part of the twentieth century, at least until the Black Power revolts of the 1970s, women with strong African features were never involved. Colour, race, phenotype continued to be important influences for most of the twentieth century. This hegemony of Euro-American ideals of beauty and femininity was much more highly developed in the USA and was a powerful influence on the nearby Caribbean. According to Kathy Peiss, improving the appearance of black women (and men) was often seen as part of the larger process of the upliftment of the black race, though there were always voices of disagreement.

Whereas, in the earlier years, there was some ambivalence towards these contests based on notions of morality and female modesty, by the 1960s and 1970s Caribbean women became the first women of colour to win international beauty contests. These included Carole Joan Crawford, Miss Jamaica/Miss World, 1963; Jennifer Hosten, Miss Grenada/Miss World, 1970; Cindy Breakespeare, Miss Jamaica/Miss World, 1976; Janelle Commissiong, Miss Trinidad and Tobago/Miss

Universe, 1977; Giselle La Ronde, Miss Trinidad and Tobago/Miss World, 1986; Lisa Hanna, Miss Jamaica/Miss World, 1993; and most recently Wendy Fitzwilliam, Miss Trinidad and Tobago/Miss Universe, 1998. In today's context, it has become difficult even for women's movement activists to be critical of beauty contests.

In the year 1999, Trinidad and Tobago hosted the Miss Universe competition. This was at tremendous cost to the national purse, but it was seen as a contribution to the international visibility of the country and a showcase for the local tourism industry and economy as a whole. What became clear is that Ms Universe Inc. is a US company with local franchise holders, who compete for the franchise and the rights to host the competition at their cost. Trinidadian artist/designer/activist Robert Young had this to say about this event:

> When the government endorsed the Miss Universe competition in Trinidad, it was like a reinforcement [that] to be a woman, to be a somebody, you have to have a certain kind of femininity. And they spent $100m on that, to put somebody's globalised idea. People used to oppose beauty contests, but now those same people are involved in the industry. It is endorsed completely, this is a way for a woman to access new forms of femininity. Women got access to information. It changed a lot of things, how women should dress, how women are… and the cost of the event, the prices have gone up considerably. That was an endorsement of globalisation as the way to go, to think about women in a certain way. With the $100m endorsement from the government, poor people are getting hopeful about it. Singing Sandra changed her song, from a ghetto song, and she changed it to a marketing song for the Miss Universe pageant[12] (Young Interview, 26.03.03).

In the interview extract above, Young suggests that, by hosting the contest, the state actually endorsed beauty contests as a legitimate economic alternative for women. It could be suggested that this process was started much earlier, when Miss Universe 1977, Janelle Commissiong received the nation's highest award – The Trinity Cross. She became one of about three women to attain this award during 40 years of independence.

In an article on beauty contests in multiethnic Belize, Wilk describes beauty contests as one aspect of that society's recent thrust into 'modern' status, as evidenced by its many linkages with the US and its consumption of US goods, TV, etc. In this way, he supports the link between modernisation and globalisation rejected by Nederveen Pieterse. Beauty pageants have emerged as a very popular form of entertainment and of great interest to the public (Wilk 1996, 220). So important are they, that close links have been developed with politics, with different contests being associated with different political parties. Beauty contests, therefore, have become part of the national political struggle as well as the struggle for international recognition by small, economically challenged states.

The aim is, of course, to produce a Miss Belize who both represents the nation *and* is appropriate for the global contest of Miss World or Miss Universe. As in many other parts of the world, this is cause for much contention because of the disjuncture between local, and in this case, Belizean standards of beauty and Miss World or Miss Universe standards of beauty. In fact, those responsible for organising the national contest state that the contestants favoured by a Belizean audience would never win a Miss World/Universe competition (Wilk 1996, 226). The Belizean girls are short with big thighs and bottoms, whereas the international competitions favour tall slim girls (Wilk 1996, 227). This is something also heard in other parts of the anglophone Caribbean.

In the article 'Face of the Nation …', Natasha Barnes notes the significance of beauty contests to national identity in Jamaica, including that of the black working-class male. At the same time, she highlights the contention, conflicts and compromises which are generated in an effort to satisfy national aspirations *and* 'global' standards (Barnes 1997). Wilk (1996, 227) examines this 'collision between local standards of beauty, deeply embedded in notions of gender and sexuality, and international standards which are those of the dominant white nations of the north' arguing that 'The global standard is actually the standard of North America and Europe. The global standard wins'. Resistance to dominant global institutions does occur in that people do not passively accept that which they are exposed to from elsewhere. According to Wilk, complexity and ambiguity are inherent aspects of beauty contests … and indeed are part of their attraction. But the contention is also the result of conflict over national interests and 'global interests' (Wilk 1996, 225). However:

> Pageants forge connections between these culturally bound and local systems of aesthetics ... they build equivalence between those diverse dialogues of gender and beauty, so that gender and beauty emerge as if they were indeed universal categories .... Difference can be expressed, but only within the boundaries demarcated by the industry. Everyone on common ground. Making choices from a predetermined range of options (Wilk 1996, 218, 232).

On the one hand, beauty contests for years were used as components of national culture such as the carnival queen competitions in many islands and the Queen of the Bay competition in Belize. But especially in multi-ethnic and racially polarised societies, they can do the opposite, generating much divisiveness over definitions of local beauty or the authentic 'Face of the Nation' (Barnes 1997). Issues of power are inherent in arguments over subjective qualities such as beauty. There is contention between local ideas of beauty and international ideas. The two do not sit neatly together. Judging local representations of beauty on a large scale is bound to give rise to disagreement. Hierarchy is asserted in these cases (Wilk 1996, 229). In the end, 'The continuing lesson is that the local is subordinated to the national, and the national to the global' (Wilk 1996, 230).

Sport, Gender and National Identity

Competitive sport has often been described as a mechanism for valorising masculinity. This is illustrated in the following quotation: 'Sport has become a public forum for celebrating, displaying and reproducing masculinity' (Polley 1989, 16 cited in Townson 1997). Until recently, competitive sport performed at the national and international level was primarily a masculine activity and certainly men's sports were given greater attention, prestige and financial reward. Indeed for many women the quest for equality has been more focused on entering traditionally masculine sports than on seeking to upgrade and valorise traditionally feminine sports. Much more effort has gone into facilitating women's entry to men's sports than into encouraging men to enter women's sports. As noted by Nigel Townson:

> Undoubtedly, women are hugely under-represented in sport: in numbers playing both in professional and amateur sports; in the financial rewards; media coverage; media representation; and in sport establishments. While sport often appears as an

institution created for and by men, ironically it is women who support and service this institution. There had been various explanations for this. One is that this reflects prevailing sexist attitudes in a patriarchal society. Another suggests that it is part of a capitalist economic system which is designed to keep women as a means of cheap labour who then have little time for participation in sport (Townson 1997, 1)

Related to its role in valorising a competitive masculinity, sport has also been important in valorising national and group identity, in particular the identity of the men of that society. International competitive sport has become not only an important area of commerce and investment but also a mechanism for achieving international recognition. Unfortunately, as in most other areas of international competition, the resources and facilities available to competitors from various parts of the world are grossly inequitable, therefore equality of opportunity in sport in many countries of the economic south is a vision more than reality.

In the British colonial world, cricket, once the game of the British elite, has pride of place. Originally an aspect of elite British culture, there is sometimes some ambivalence associated with this game which has now become an important component of anglophone Caribbean popular culture. Cricket is possibly the only sport that is seriously discussed at the Caribbean Community (CARICOM) Heads of Government Meetings and which is perceived as a subject of regional importance. Soccer, or football, had increased in popularity by the end of the twentieth century, but cricket, because of its historical significance, continues to hold special meaning to the region.

One of the first scholars to recognise this link between sport and national identity was the Caribbean scholar C.L.R. James. This was most forcefully analysed in his classic work *Beyond the Boundary*, which is today seen as one of the earliest works in cultural studies. James also illustrated the ways in which the cricketing world reflected the class and colour hierarchies of the colonial context and the struggles against these hierarchies, as he notes in this extract from *Beyond the Boundary*:

> Immediately I was immersed up to the eyes in 'The Case for West Indian Self Government'; and a little later, in the most furious cricket campaign I have ever known, to break the discrimination of sixty years and have a black man, in this case Sir Frank Worrell, appointed captain of a West Indies team. I saw the beginning, the middle, but I am not at all sure that I have seen the end of violent intervention of a

West Indian crowd into the actual play of a Test match. The intimate connection between cricket and West Indian social and political life was established so that all except the wilfully perverse could see (James 1993, 225).

Possibly because of the time of James' writings, the centrality of cricket to anglophone Caribbean masculine identity and struggle for validation in the eyes of the coloniser was not explicit. In many ways, it was one example of the Empire Striking Back, where the colonised men could beat the colonisers at their own game. Aviston Downes (2004) notes the importance of sports in general and cricket in particular in the curriculum of boys', grammar schools in Barbados during the early to middle twentieth century. The language used by James reflects the conflation of masculinity with humanity which we discussed earlier, in his understanding of cricket.

International sport is an area of increasing commercial importance, investment and profit. But it is also a mechanism for national pride and international prestige. This is especially important for countries of the Economic South. But not even here is the playing field level, as countries of the North, especially the United States, have perfected sport industry research and development and many athletes of the South have little or no chance of success if they do not study or train in the North with access to 'modern' facilities and sport technology. Accepting the IMF identification of globalisation as a much older process, it is not surprising that the important disciplines of international sport such as football, basketball, shot-put, javelin, etc. are all derived from the Economic North.

According to Bairner, sport represents one of the cultural forms that have been exported and exchanged. This process was intensified during the expansion of the British empire, when some sports were taken to foreign parts. However, 'there was resistance to this tendency toward British sporting imperialism. In some countries, such as the United States, British games were transformed in such a way as to contribute to the development of unique sporting cultures' (Bairner, 2001:13).

While globalised sport means that the world ends up playing the same sports, as in the economy, issues of global competitiveness of national entities continue to be important. As has been seen in relation to other areas, even within this globalised environment, national borders remain as prominent as ever, and this is especially true in relation to sporting events. The nation remains an essential arena through which to construct identity differences concerning gender and nationality. Even in an age of satellite and of multinational sporting conglomerates, 'the 'nation' – tribal or not – remains the main unit in both sport and in communications and ... in each nation both are a part of distinctive cultural complexes' (Wilcox 1994, 20). Like food, sport is becoming both the same everywhere and increasingly different. Bairner (2001, 6) uses sport to argue that, in spite of globalisation, national sentiment will persist. Indeed he points out, national imagery is prevalent so that at many major sporting events, even in transnational events:

> Sport is one field in which national difference is celebrated and reinforced and where globalisation may have had little impact. Sport does provide us with an important arena in which to celebrate national identities ... it provides opportunities for representatives of different nations to engage with each other in honest competition ...' Nationalism in sport is unavoidable. There are virtually no other occasions in which strangers come together in emotional circumstances and share in triumphs and disappointments.... Hence, sport is very powerful in remaking national identities (Bairner 2001, 17-18).

In discussing national identity and globalisation, sport is an essential arena for the construction of certain identities, such as masculinity and social class. Briggs (2001) foresees the future of sport also as a forum for constructing gender identities as women increasingly enter the arena. Today, globalised sport has become a major arena of competing nationalisms and of representing national manhood. For countries of the Economic South, it has basically become a case of beating the white man at his own game. What is the role of women, therefore in this game of competing masculinities and nationalities?

Today, not only are sports of the North becoming the sports of choice but, for many women, success in these highly competitive areas only takes place in men's sports. While the majority of women-only sports, with the exception of netball, have disappeared, women have sought, and in some instances gained, entry into men's sports like football and basketball in their quest for equality and humanity. Today, as certain sports become globalised, women who seek sporting success have to enter these sports in order to gain recognition and support, for, as with everything else, women gain prestige by entering masculine activities; the Economic South gains prestige by excelling in the games of the Economic North, but the same is not true the other way around.

Bollywood

For Indo-Caribbean people, India presents an alternative pole of influence. As with other members of the Indian diaspora, the cultural and artistic influence of Indian music, dance and popular culture continues to be important. In virtually all areas, the emergence of parallel radio, television and cinema has contributed to this alternative cultural space, a space to which the Indian film industry, popularly referred to as Bollywood, has been a significant contribution.

Indian films were introduced into Trinidad and Tobago in 1935 by Indian engineer Ramjit Kumar. As noted by Patricia Mohammed:

> Already by 1936, the Yogi, a writer in the 'Indian News and Views Column' was requesting the appointment of two Indians on the Film Censor Board of the colony, one for the Hindi language and one for the Urdu language. He justified his request on the basis that 'There are many Indians who are interested in the importation of these films which have undoubtedly won the fancy and admiration of the entire Indian community (Mohammed 1998, 405).

Since that time, Indian movies have served as a link with the subcontinent, a purveyor of things Indian and a means of continuous rejuvenation of versions of Indo-Caribbean culture. Included in this were notions of acceptable masculinity and femininity, the 'bad woman' usually dressed in Western clothes and the 'good woman' in traditional Indian dress. These productions included much music and dance but little that was sexually explicit or suggestive of such. In the language of globalisation and international trade, these movies exploited a niche market for diasporic Indians including those in the Caribbean. With the emergence of cable television and music videos, this market has expanded but the content has also changed.

Competing on a globalised market has meant that the content of programming has undergone significant change. This is highlighted by Ghosh who noted that today, Indian films, especially those destined for the international market, have had to change, to buckle 'under the stress of globalisation' (Ghosh, Aftab 2002) supports the view that Bollywood films have become susceptible to Western influence. He notes that these changes have included the following – musically: the inclusion of hip-hop, drum 'n bass to compete with bhangra; clothes: girls and young women in miniskirts;[13] bodies: men with rippling muscles and style: Bollywood now producing romantic comedies, for example, *Bollywood Hollywood,* which are popular in Britain and now becoming packaged in a US-influenced way (Aftab 2002, 91).

In addition to appealing to a niche market of diaspora Asians, some authors suggest that Bollywood movies have also developed a mainstream audience in Britain where they often make the Top Ten charts. According to Aftab:

> Bollywood is the latest fashion in Britain. It is the most industrious film industry, producing over 800 films a year. They often have a predictable storyline, with characters varying little. Stereotypes prevail, e.g. heroic male, virginal, seemingly unattainable girl, bearded villain ... (Aftab 2002, 88).

In Britain, a new genre of British Bollywood films produced in the UK has emerged. These reflect more of the British Asian experience (Aftab 2002, 89-90).

In spite of the pervasiveness of the Indian film and music industry, there is still some ambivalence towards it, especially among young people. In a hegemonic Creole and western cultural context, enjoying this genre is not always seen as 'cool'. This is reflected in the comments by Joannah Bharose on contemporary Trinidad and Tobago:

> Yes it's very popular among the hardcore East Indian communities. And I think one of the reasons why as well is the little taboos or embarrassments certain other communities may think: 'If I am caught looking at this Indian film, what will people think?' The so-called 'cool' or 'hip' part of the Indian community would think: 'I don't want to be seen looking at this'. While they may listen to some of the music, they still have the privacy of a walkman, where they can sit down and listen to whatever they want, rather than be caught dead looking at 'Music Box'.[14] It's usually among the young, trendy kind of crowd. Let's put it this way, a lot of Indian programmes are not trendy (Bharose Interview, 16.4.03).

Research by Gabrielle Hosein on adolescent Indo-Trinidadian girls suggests that, despite the westernisation of the imagery, and the more sexually explicit and daring clothing, young women do not identify with women in Bollywood movies. They reject what they see as the less autonomous images of Indian women still evident in these movies. Rather, they identify with perceived independent white women of US television and cinema (Hosein 2003). This is interesting as Aftab suggests that this depiction of more traditional cultural values, rather than liberal values, holds some appeal for some young British Asians, as it satisfies a yearning for community where beliefs and values are respected, not ridiculed, and helps them to maintain cultural roots (Aftab 2002, 92).

Conclusion

In the discussion above, the impact of globalisation on ideologies and representations of masculinities and femininities is examined. This process, while currently experiencing widespread acceptance, is also under increasing critique and challenge. More and more governments reeling under its effects are challenging the orthodoxy, although not in the comprehensive way in which it is required. The ideological conjunction between modernisation, democracy and globalisation is such that it is difficult even for detractors to see a viable non-liberal alternative. The failure of all alternatives so far provides a challenging context within which to imagine and fashion other ways of being modern.

Notes

1. I would like to acknowledge the assistance of Nicola Swan in the preparation of this paper. This paper is a version of a larger paper entitled 'The Impact of Globalisation and the International Political Economy on the Cultural Representations of Gender Relations', prepared for the CGDS Ford Foundation funded project – Caribbean Gender Ideologies.
2. Val Moghadam refers to three aspects – economic, political and cultural globalisation (Moghadam 2000).
3. The terms Economic North and Economic South are used throughout this paper drawing on the language of the Brandt Commission to move beyond the often used language of modernisation – developing, developed etc.

4. One need only reflect on the many pieces of anti-war communication which were circulated against the US/UK War with Iraq and the international protests coordinated by Internet which had little impact on the war itself.
5. Rapso – a form of poetry/song similar to rap developed in Trinidad and Tobago in the 1980s. In the words of its major exponent, Brother Resistance, 'the rhythm of the word in the rhythm of the word'.
6. Sangre Grande and Toco – rural and semi-rural areas in the north-east of Trinidad.
7. SOCA – described by its founder Lord Shorty/later Ras Shorty I as the Soul of Calypso. He acknowledged its Indo-Caribbean influence which led him to originally name it SOKAH (Patasar 1997, 71).
8. For more on this process, see Rhoda Reddock, *Women, Labour and Politics in Trinidad and Tobago: A History*, London: Zed Books, 1994.
9. Return – this is often not the case, in many instances, these 'traditions' are invented (Hobsbawm 1983, 1).
10. Also referred to as market fundamentalism by Kari Levitt.
11. See Jack Menke, 2002.
12. This refers to a calypso by woman calypsonian Singing Sandra which highlighted the plight of young people and their parents in the urban ghettos which was adapted to market the Miss Universe contest in Trinidad and Tobago.
13. Men in the past could wear Western clothes in the Indian movies without being marked.
14. 'Music Box' – a local television programme in Trinidad and Tobago, based on Indian popular music videos.

References

Aftab, K. 2002. 'Brown: The new black! Bollywood in Britain'. *Critical Quarterly* 44, no. 3 (Autumn) 2002.

Allen, R. and L. Wilcken. 1998. 'Introduction: Island Sounds in the Global City'. In *Island Sounds in the Global City: Caribbean Popular Music and Identity in New York*, eds. Allen, R and L Wilcken, 2. New York Folk Lore Society, Institute for Studies in American Music, Brooklyn College.

Antrobus, Peggy. 2003. 'Women and Global Restructuring: Impacts on Human Security' Presentation to Women's Studies 100, Trent University, 26, March.

Bairner, A. 2001. *Sport, Nationalism, and Globalisation: European and North American Perspectives.* Albany: State University of New York Press.

Ballerino B. C. Cohen, R. Wilk, and Stoeltje, eds. 1996. *Beauty Queens on the Global Stage: Gender, Contests, and Power.* London: Routledge.

Barnes, Natasha. 1997. 'Face of the Nation: Race, Nationalisms and Identities in Jamaican Beauty Pageants'. In *Daughters of Caliban: Caribbean Women in the Twentieth Century*, ed. C. Lopez-Springfield. Bloomington and Indiana and London: Indiana University Press and the Latin American Bureau.

Benn, Denis and Kenneth Hall, eds. 2002. *Globalisation: A Calculus of Inequality: Perspectives from the South*. Kingston: Ian Randle Publishers.

Brathwaite, E. Kamau. 1977. *Contradictory Omens: Cultural Diversity and Integration in the Caribbean*. Kingston: Savacou Publications.

Briggs, A. 2001. 'The Media and Sport in the Global Village'. In A. Bairner *Sport, Nationalism, and Globalisation: European and North American Perspectives*. Albany: State University of New York Press.

Brown, Aggrey. 1995. 'Caribbean Cultures and Mass Communication Technology: Re-examining the Cultural Dependency Thesis'. In *Globalisation, Communications and Caribbean Identity*, ed. Hopeton Dunn, 52. Kingston: Ian Randle Publishers.

Brown, Hilary. 1995. 'American Media Impact on Jamaican Youth: The cultural Dependency Thesis'. In *Globalisation, Communications and Caribbean Identity*, ed. Hopeton Dunn. Kingston: Ian Randle Publishers.

Downes, Aviston. 2004. 'Boys of the Empire: Elite Education and the Socio-Cultural Construction of Hegemonic Masculinity in Barbados, 1875-1920'. In *Interrogating Caribbean Masculinities*, ed. R. Reddock. Kingston: The UWI Press.

Dunn, Hopeton. ed. 1995. *Globalisation, Communications and Caribbean Identity*. Kingston: Ian Randle Publishers.

Ghosh, Arup Ratan. n.d. 'Film Flow and Globalisation' <www.geocities.com/culturaltheoryandcinema/ffg.html>)

Girvan, Norman. 2000. 'Globalisation and Counter-Globalisation: The Caribbean in the Context of the South'. In *Globalisation: A Calculus of Inequality: Perspectives from the South*, eds. Dennis Benn and Kenneth Hall, 65-87. Kingston: Ian Randle Publishers.

Harcourt, W. 2003. 'Editorial: The Global Network Society: New Freedoms or Old Limitations?'. In *Development: Mediating Citizenship in the Global Network Society* 46, no. 1 (March): 9-16.

Hobsbawm, Eric and Terence Tanger, eds. 1983. *The Invention of Tradition*. Cambridge: Cambridge University Press.

Holmberg, Carl B. 1998. *Sexualities and Popular Culture*. California: Sage Publications, 16.

Hosein, Gabrielle. 2003. *Gender, Genderation and Negotiation: Adolescence and Young Indo-Trinidadian Women's Identities in the late 20th Century*. MPhil thesis, University of the West Indies.

International Herald Tribune. 2003. 'Editorial: Inching Toward Trade Fairness', August 16-17, p.6.

International Monetary Fund. 2001. 'Globalisation: A Framework for IMF Involvement', IMF Issues paper, 02/01, http://www.imf.org/np/exr/ib/2002/031502.htm

Jain, Devaki. 2000. 'Nuancing Globalisation or Mainstreaming the Downstream or Reforming Reform'. *Working Paper* no. 3 May, CGDS, Cave Hill, UWI.

Khan, Shireen. 2003. 'The Ugliness of Beauty Contests: The Miss Indias these days do not look or act very "Indian"'. In *Little India* 16, (April). <www.littleindia.com/india/July2k/uglybeauty.htm>.

Klak, Thomas. 1998. 'Thirteen Theses on Globalisation and Neo-Liberalism'. In *Globalisation and NeoLiberalism: The Caribbean Context,* ed. Thomas Klak. Lanham: Rowman and Littlefield.

Menke, Jack. 2002. 'Skin Bleaching in Multi-Ethnic and Multicolored Societies: The Case of Suriname'. Paper presented to the Caribbean Studies Association Annual Conference May, Nassau.

Miller, Daniel. 1992. 'The Young and the Restless in Trinidad: A Case of the Local and the Global in Mass Consumption'. In *Consuming Technologies: Media and Information in Domestic Spaces,* eds. R. Silverstone, R and E. Hirsch. London: Routledge.

Moghadam, Valentine. 2002. 'Gender and Globalisation: Female Labor and Women's Mobilisation'. *Journal of World Systems Research* 5, no. 2 (Spring): 301-314.

Mohammed, Patricia. 1998. 'Ram and Sita: The Reconstitution of Gender Identities among Indians in Trinidad through Mythology'. In *Caribbean Portraits: Gender Ideologies and Identities,* ed. Christine Barrow. Kingston: Ian Randle and CGDS/UWI.

Mohammed-Cherif Ferjani. 2001. 'World Plurality and War of Cultures'. *CODESRIA Bulletin,* nos. 3 and 4: 6.

Nederveen Pieterse, Jan. 1993. 'Globalisation as Hybridisation' *Working Paper Series,* no. 152, Institute of Social Studies, The Hague, The Netherlands, June.

Patasar, Mungal. 1997. 'The Development of Indian Music in Trinidad and Tobago'. *Caribbean Dialogue* 3, no. 4 (Oct/Dec).

Peiss, Kathy. 1998. *Hope in a Jar: The Making of America's Beauty Culture.* New York: Metropolitan Books.

Reddock, Rhoda. 1994. *Women, Labour and Politics in Trinidad and Tobago: A History.* Kingston: Ian Randle Publishers, London: Zed Books.

Robertson, R. 1992. *Globalisation: Social Theory and Global Culture.* London: Sage Publications.

Shade, L R. 2003. 'Whose Global Knowledge? Women Navigating the Net'. In *Development, Mediating Citizenship in the Global Network Society* 46, no.1 (March): 49-53.

Watkins, Kevin. 2003. 'Stumbling toward Disaster: The trade charade'. In *International Herald Tribune,* August 16-17, p. 6.

Wilcox, R. C. ed. 1994. *Sport in the Global Village.* Morgantown, WV: Fitness Information Technology, Inc.

Wilk, R. 1996. 'Connections and Contradictions: From the Crooked Tree Cashew Queen to Miss World Belize'. In *Beauty Queens on the Global Stage: Gender, Contests, and Power,* eds. B. Ballerino, C. Cohen, R. Wilk and Stoeltje. London: Routledge.

Wiltshire, Rosina. 1986. 'The Transnational Caribbean Family'. Paper presented to ISER-EC/UNESCO Sub-Regional Seminar – Changing Family Patterns and Women's Roles in the Caribbean, Barbados, November.

Interviews

Brother Resistance, March 24, 2003

Robert Young, March 26, 2003

Joannah Bharose, April 14, 2003

Peter Elias, May 8, 2003

9 | MARJAN DE BRUIN

Gender Politics and Media Production

Introduction

In my contribution – from the field of Media and Communication Studies – I will try:

a) to analyse developments in thinking and research approaches from a gender perspective and identify the contribution of Caribbean research to these new developments;

b) to briefly explore the application of the concepts of gender, professional and organisational identities in analysing the interpersonal dynamics in the production of media content;

c) to illustrate (through sharing findings of qualitative research in progress) how 'identity' at a micro- and meso-level can be operationalised, in an effort to deepen our understanding of this rather wide and frequently used concept.

All of this will, I hope, show how boundaries in thinking, conventions in knowledge and knowledge acquisition can be pushed to discover new ways of understanding and connect us with this afternoon's theme.

Focus

My main focus is the role gender plays in the dynamics of media production in newsrooms in two Caribbean countries (Jamaica and Trinidad and Tobago). In newsrooms, female and male journalists select what is presented to us as priorities – the headline stories of the day. Headline stories do the agenda setting for other national media – radio talk- and call-in shows. By deciding what is 'newsworthy', the same women and men decide what is – usually – excluded, whose voices and which images we will not hear or see, what information we will not be given – the topics that, for sometimes the most trivial reasons, do not make their way into the public domain.

The decisions on selection and treatment of content are taken by people holding gatekeepers' positions in power structures. These structures partly follow the lines of formal organograms, but for another large part, are shaped and maintained through personal and professional relationships and interactions on the work floor.

Women and men working as journalists are commonly expected to be guided by professional values while at the same time being bombarded by the interests, influences, pressures and demands of the organisation which employs them.

This paper tries to develop a conceptual framework which will allow us to analyse and understand gender in media production, serving so many different interests. The core concepts in this framework which I will explore are gender, and the professional and organisational identities which function as different frames of reference for journalists at work.

These core concepts by themselves are not new, but they have not been looked at as intersecting social and psychological mechanisms in media organisations.

Changing research foci – historical analysis

Worldwide, the Mexico Conference for the first UN decade for women, in the mid-70s, had helped to set the research agenda in at least three areas: women's under-representation in the content of news and other serious programming; trivialisation and sex-role stereotyping in content; and, women's under-representation in decision-making positions. The major driving forces behind this agenda were equity – equality of opportunity and empowerment – and political activism (Sreberny 1995, 3, 4). Both motivations were based on the assumption that a greater presence of women in media would influence the media's agenda setting, which, in turn, would cause more women's issues to be included in the public debate.

In the Caribbean, the question of media portrayal of women has long been a topic of discussion at the regional, as well as the national level. There were at least two Regional UNESCO Conferences (in 1981 and 1992) and several national conferences in various Caribbean countries between the early 80s and the mid-90s – all attended by media practitioners, educators and policy-makers. But the results of these discussions were not widely distributed and sometimes even hardly known among individuals and groups interested in the topic. Because of the absence of documentation and follow-up, the topic was almost entirely missing from the research agendas of that time – certainly in the field of media and communication studies. In gender studies, it was even worse: only recently has one of the core titles in this field included media and communication issues as a focus of attention (Mohammed 2002).

Women and their portrayal were touched on in historical studies focusing on stereotyping (Brodber 1982, cited in Anderson 1986, 294), or as a point of action for Women and Development Programmes, emphasising the need to change their portrayal (Antrobus 1991, 42). Occasionally, the topic has been included in Caribbean-wide studies, especially in the context of assessing the implementation of the Nairobi Forward-Looking Strategies for the Advancement of Women (WAND 1990). Until 1994, not much had been documented in the Caribbean on the topic of Women and Media, or Women and Communication.

In academic work, worldwide, we recognise similar developments. After a period of heavy emphasis on quality of content, described in different discourses, we now see efforts to understand the circumstances in which such content was produced. Studies of employment patterns and the division of labour in news organisations were the obvious first explorations in this direction.

Organisational dynamics and their unavoidable effects on gender relations among the producers in the newsroom were not, at any rate, included in the analysis until the late '90s.

In academic work, worldwide, the position of women in the media hierarchy and their role in the organisational production process had been the focus of research from the late '70s and early '80s but, in hindsight, one can recognise the shortcomings of this early research.

Many studies focused on women almost in isolation, as a group by themselves. Questions that occupied the minds of researchers were for instance: how many women worked in the media and how many of those occupied senior positions.

As a group, women were compared to men, but they were studied without consideration for their relations with colleagues or the wider working environment. Studies ask such questions for instance as: Do male and female gatekeepers respond differently to news stories about women? (Scott Whitlow 1977); Does sex make a difference in the lifestyle editors' treatment of Women's Pages? (Merritt and Gross 1978); What is the job satisfaction among newspaperwomen? (Barrett 1984); What are the goals and achievement orientations of women newspaper managers? (Sohn 1984) and, Which career barriers are perceived by female television news anchors? (Ferri and Keller 1986).

These interests are reflected in research done well into the '90s. Do female writers choose different subjects in their stories? (Weaver 1997); Do women differ in their ratings of media priorities? (Weaver 1997; Weaver and Wilhoit 1996); Does the greater presence of women's writings on the *New York Times* front pages have anything to do with what appeared to be a wider range of stories of special interest to women offered by this paper? (Mills 1997).

It was around that time – 1994 – that CARIMAC, in an effort to rescue forgotten histories, published its *Occasional Paper*, capturing Caribbean discussions on women and media between the early '80s and mid '90s. The study also provided baseline data on Women and Media in the Caribbean (de Bruin 1994). Caribbean material then began to appear in professional and scholarly publications, regionally as well as internationally. (Gallagher and Quindoza-Santiago 1994; Gallagher and Von Euler 1995; Jimenez-David 1996).

This research on media and gender issues in the 1990s limited itself to the same range of concerns: How many women and men work in media? What positions do they occupy in editorial departments? What is the horizontal and vertical division of labour among them, etc? The results showed that, in most of the cases, women formed a minority in the media workforce, comprised a minor fraction of middle management, especially in news organisations and were even more seriously under-represented in senior media management (de Bruin 1994; de Bruin et al 1995; Francis-Brown 1995; Nicholson, 1995).

However, the assumption that a better representation of women in the media workforce would lead to changes in their portrayal, oversimplified the connection between production and content. It neglected the influence of the working environment on the content itself as well as on the producers of this content.

These employment studies – regionally as well as internationally – did not go beyond descriptive accounts of female and male physical presence in media organisations (Burks and Stone 1993; de Bruin 1994; Gallagher 1981; Gallagher and Von Euler 1995; Gallagher and Quindoza-Santiago 1994; Jimenez-David 1996; Mills, 1997; Robinson and Saint-Jean 1998; Weaver 1997; Weaver and Wilhoit, 1996). They looked at the division of labour into 'male' and 'female' areas, also called vertical segregation – examples of gendered substructures. The emphasis was more on job and task descriptions, positions and structure than on work practices, interactions and organisational culture.

Most of these studies were done from a perspective that saw the organisation itself as a gender-neutral environment: the behaviour of women and men was seen as determined by their positions, even while reflecting the patriarchal society which structured allegedly 'gender-neutral' organisations. The belief that dynamics between gender and organisational structures and practices could play a role in reproducing gender inequity in the organisation had not yet entered the debate.

Beyond the Body Count

In Caribbean research the first studies attempting to go beyond the 'body count' appeared in the late '90s (de Bruin, 1998). They began to examine specific social practices regulated by convention and, in some cases, rules allegedly based on history and tradition – although there could hardly be traditions regarding women in areas where women had never before been admitted.

Elsewhere, also, academic discourse started to focus on gender and professional ideology, gender and journalistic culture. Concentrating only

– or mainly – on the proportion of women in the newsroom had proved to be too narrow a focus. 'Newsroom culture' and 'journalistic culture'– more specifically, gendered professional practices in the newsroom – finally became the focus of attention (Allan 1998, 1999; Carter 1998; Creedon 1993; de Bruin 2000; Kitzinger 1998; Steiner 1998; Skidmore 1998; Van Zoonen 1998; Weaver 1997, Ross, forthcoming).

Newsroom interaction between women and men journalists appeared on the agenda. Some authors suggested that the male journalist preferred to view his female colleague in terms of her sex before accepting her as a professional – sending the message that journalism and femininity did not really go together (Steiner 1998).

Only very recently has the relationship between gender and organisational dynamics been recognised as a vital factor in the production of gender inequities. This focus was not only emerging in media and communication studies but, in the mid-'90s, also began to be recognised in organisational studies. 'Women in organisations' had become – courtesy of feminist studies – an object of scholarly attention in the 80s. However, these earlier studies looked at gender mainly as 'a fixed attribute imported into workplace organisations' and not so much as a relational quality (Witz and Savage 1992, 26). After the mid-90s a steady stream of publications in organisational studies broke away from looking at the organisation as a Nobody's Land (Alvesson and Billing 1997; Gherardi 1995, Halford et al. 1997; Marshall 1993). The behaviour of employees began to be seen as the outcome of much more complex processes involving interaction and organisational practices in cultures where gender was one of the major determinants.

The analysis of gendered symbols, values, meanings and significations rather than power differences based on hierarchical positions was more and more chosen as the key to understanding relationships in organisations.

Social Identities

In exploring the role gender plays in the dynamics of media production, I use the concepts of gender, professional and organisational identity.

The choice of these concepts posed several challenges. In the first place, I am aware of the many other identities – for example, based on categories such as class, rural/urban, race, ethnicity, territory, education, political party, etc. – that could be mentioned in addition to the three categories I singled out. However, this initial limitation is a manageable starting point to the exploration of social dynamics and practices which construct identities.

Secondly, gender identity is a concept that is still demanding to be comprehensively defined, especially at the operational level. Recent Caribbean literature focusing on gender (Mohammed and Shepherd 1991; Senior 1991; Shepherd et al. 1995; Barrow 1995; Leo-Rhynie et al 1997; Shepherd 2002; Mohammed 2002) appears to be moving towards such a comprehensive description of what constitutes gender identity. In earlier literature, Anderson speaks of 'sex-role identity' (1986, 305), indicating the relevance of identification with mothering. Leo-Rhynie briefly defines gender identity in the context of socialisation and the development of identity: 'a personal recognition and general acknowledgement of oneself as part of a socially defined group – male or female, which may or may not be derived from the basic sex difference from which the group originated' (1998, 234).

The need for a comprehensive conceptual treatment of gender identity does not seem so obvious, given the fact that social identities and identification processes seem so familiar and so patent: we know that they define 'who we are, how we are supposed to feel, think, and act and in doing so, making it possible for us to live as "we" differing from "the other(s)"' (Hogg and Terry 2001, 3).

Yet, it is only by breaking this concept down into recognisable experiences that we begin to be able to observe what (gender) identity means in people's daily life and work. Gender identity, like all social identities, is a complicated construct. The reality it refers to is not fixed and static, but fluid and continuous. It can be regarded as a social as well as a personal construct: it depends on commonly shared attributes, but is also idiosyncratic. It leaves room for multiple interpretations and ambiguity. For this reason, some authors, when speaking about social identities, prefer to speak about identification instead of identity, emphasising the process (Hall 1996, 2; Van Dijk 1998, 121).

A third challenge concerns the selection of the most appropriate methodology to deal with these questions. Qualitative research has been employed in women's studies in the Caribbean and, as such, is nothing new. For instance, the Women in the Caribbean Project (WICP) in the '80s used a 'multi-level methodology'.

In my qualitative research I used open, unstructured interviews to collect data – stories, accounts, narratives – which presented me with experiences in newsroom production through the eyes of a selection of professionals. All interviews covered the same general range of issues. They all focused on the interplay between the concepts mentioned above: gender, organisational and professional identity and processes of identification in the newsroom.

However, while it has long been understood that, compared to traditional quantitative research, qualitative research is an equally valid, and in certain circumstances even better, tool to explore the world in which we live, this terrain is still treacherous.

The material from the interviews should be considered as descriptions of perceptions and not as descriptions of facts. It is not important whether the interviewee's statements are true or false: their texts give us an insight into how interactions with colleague journalists – of the other sex – at work are perceived. This approach starts from the assumption that people will try to explain the events in which they find themselves by attributing them to what they perceive to be the causes. It is in fact the basis of the psychological approach called 'attribution theory', which assumes 'that individuals engage in a search for causes of events' (Forsterling 2001, 13). These events include encounters and interactions with others.

The explanations for other people's behaviour will often be spontaneously implicit as well as explicit; they may be considered common sense, irrational and expressions of 'naïve psychology' but they form part of the process of systematically assigning meanings.

In the context of media organisations, this 'naïve psychology' illustrates 'culturally embedded sense making' in the work environments. Attribution theory states that 'individuals are reluctant to change their attributions once made, and they have trouble considering that more than one explanation is possible or that their own behaviour may be problematic'. (Canary and Spitzberg 1990, cited in Gayle and Preiss 2002). If gender and gender identity are seen as relational qualities, then the accounts of relational dynamics may inform us how and why these relational qualities are produced.

I will briefly define my core concepts of gender, professional and organisational identities and then focus especially on the interplay between these identities/identifications. I hereby use some preliminary findings from my qualitative analysis (in progress) of 19 in-depth interviews with female and male journalists working in newsrooms in the Caribbean media (Jamaica and Trinidad and Tobago).

More on identities

In their everyday life, people may take on multiple social identities to serve different functions. These identities may change priority according to circumstances and interests (Capozza et al. 2000).

People may actively strive for certain social identities by claiming membership of particular social categories. In this claiming, they will try to assume the characteristics associated with the prototypical group member – a process of 'self-stereotyping' (Deaux 2000, 5). Claiming can only be successful, if others are willing to affirm or confirm this claim, described as 'granting membership' (Bartel & Dutton 2001, 124).

Identities may also be the result of passive accretion, where people happen to have taken them on, almost incidentally, *en passant*. This may apply to organisational identity – it may come with the job. In general, people fit themselves into and, at the same time are fitted into, social categories. They 'take the cue for their identity from the conduct of others …. There is a complex mixture of proaction and reaction ….' (Weick 1995, 23).

Certain identities are imposed on people, especially identities that are based on more visible categories such as sex or race. Other authors have described this process in different discourses, emphasising the socio-historical processes that led to the establishment of certain categories or stereotypes (Guillaumin 1995).

Gender identity

Gender identity is a good example of the concept as it takes many different forms and carries many different meanings. For my purposes, I will refer to the distinction by Lorber, quoted in Ferree et al (1999, 6), with which I feel comfortable, between 'the concepts of biological sex (which refers to either genetic or morphological characteristics), sexuality (which refers to desire and orientation) and gender (which refers to social status and identity)'. The latter is also described as being a specific social version of men and women in Alvesson and Billing 1997, 215.

Gender identity, then, refers to identification with a social category associated with cultural models and notions of masculinity and/or femininity, seen as 'traits or forms of subjectivities (orientations in thinking, feeling and valuing) that are present in all persons … although to different degrees' (Alvesson and Billing 1997, 85).

Professional identity

'Professional identity' refers to a wider frame of reference – an ideology – not so much carried by the members of a specific organisation, but rather by a virtual community. Moving out of a particular organisation does not usually imply an ending of the professional identity.

Professional identities also carry a variety of connotations. International surveys showed that journalists from around the world agreed generally on only one or two professional roles as the most important ones: getting information to the public quickly and providing access for the public to express opinions (Weaver 1998, 465). Apart from those two roles, other aspects of their function showed remarkable differences between nations and cultures.

Organisational identity

Organisational identity is the collectively constructed and continuously re-negotiated understanding among the members of an organisation of 'who-we-are' (Albert and Whetten 1985 cited in Whetten and Godfrey, 1998, 35). This 'understanding' needs to be interpreted in a broad sense: some authors emphasise 'beliefs' (Pratt 1998), others emphasise a 'cognitive connection' between how the organisation defines itself and the self-definition of the employee (Dutton et al, 1994). I have pointed out elsewhere that, in the various definitions, I missed the inclusion of the emotional component – feelings, loyalty, belonging – in addition to values and beliefs. Especially, because organisational identity should be seen as a relational and comparative concept (de Bruin 2000, 229).

The constructing of gender identities at work may be seen as a process that shapes and maintains structures, such as the division of typical female and male beats when certain topics in newsrooms are assigned routinely to men and others to women. Other times, gender identification may follow structural arrangements and expectations.

Identities at work

There are multiple identities with vast differences in content and connotation. Even within apparently well-defined social identities, we discover a kaleidoscope of differences with all sorts of constantly shifting values which can be advantageous at one time and not advantageous at another.

Given the idiosyncratic nature of identities, and the advantages and disadvantages attaching to them, people may develop strategies to minimise certain socially accepted meanings attached to certain social identities. They may develop the skills of shifting one category to a lower position in their personal 'identity hierarchy' while stressing other identities instead (Deaux 2000, 9). This shifting of identities may also be seen in situations where certain identities seem to conflict with each other or in circumstances where association with another identity guarantees a greater benefit to be gained. An example of the latter may be seen when Olive Senior describes how, in conditions of poverty, 'bread-and-butter issues will have greater salience than gender issues' and therefore involvement in party politics, which can be seen as 'the means of distributing scarce resources', is, or was, more important than organising on specific women's or gender issues (Senior 1991, 164).

In media organisations, this mechanism can be seen when the invisibility of women in senior media positions may give a signal to all women in the organisation that being a woman implies hitting the glass ceiling at one time or another, '[which in turn] helps to shape the meaning and significance women attach to being female in the organisation' (Ely 1994, 205, 207). In those cases, it may not suit a woman to align with or identify strongly with 'female' and 'femininity' interests.

This variety of processes and strategies occurs at the level of interpersonal and organisational relations and can take many forms and many directions. In my analysis of interviews, I try to discover some of these forms and directions. I try to interpret journalists' narratives by observing their choice of certain identities over others, their claiming and shifting of identities, their denying identities in some conditions and asserting in others.

Sharing Insights from Work in Progress

Interviewees in my research were practising journalists in the Caribbean – ten women and nine men. Twelve worked in Jamaica, seven in Trinidad. Most of them worked in the print media, some worked in broadcasting. Most of them received some form of (educational) training and have at least a first degree. The majority were under 30 years of age and had been in the profession between four and eight years, although a few were older and more senior. The full analysis of the interviews is in progress and I will therefore simply present here some of the interim findings. In the following part I will summarise material from work in press (de Bruin and Ross, forthcoming).

Gender relations are seen by all female interviewees as a steering force in patterning newsroom interactions, even when the issues at stake are simple work or performance issues. Women perceive potential danger in interactions with male colleagues, especially with those in higher positions. A common strategy was to keep a careful distance from male colleagues. Avoiding closeness is avoiding trouble. However, this distance also means removing themselves from centres of organisational power, with the obvious danger of becoming irrelevant in the power structure – a different version of the 'glass ceiling'.

If they do not keep their distance, making themselves more vulnerable to sexual harassment, they know they can expect no organisational support. They all indicate that the gender of those in power will very likely overrule formal organisational principles: male solidarity will close the ranks and trump the issue of fairness.

When they need to bargain, for instance for payment, for overtime or transport, female journalists are unwilling to negotiate with male editors if this lessens their distance. Instead, they demonstrate a shift in priorities: the disadvantages of receiving no payment are placed second to a higher, professional goal – 'As long as it's to get the job done, even though I'm not getting reimbursed [for expenses incurred] I go ahead and do it anyway'. Emphasis on professionalism (getting the job done, meeting deadlines are sacred) – professional identification – sometimes seems to be used as a strategy for resolving gender conflicts.

This change in identity priority occurred more often. Some women journalists, who feel their lack of status in the newsroom is attributable to their sex, emphasise professional prestige and satisfaction: 'I'll get the praise from outside if it boils down to that'.

Others, who, when working on a special publication, were paid less than their male colleagues, or received no payment at all, show a similar shift. They rationalise by saying 'I get to show my stuff, my work. I can do it my way', underlining their professional identity, pushing their gender identity to a lower position.

Some women attribute the lack of professional praise from male superiors to organisational interests – a precaution against having to increase salaries.

None of the women in the male-directed organisations had much hope of upward mobility. Where the prospects for women to climb the organisational ladder are dim, it does not serve women's interest to identify strongly with other women in the organisation. What is left is individual competitive advantage, described by some as 'back-biting', seen by all as something that typically happens among women: ' … a female thing … sometimes females are the ones that hold each other down'. No one ascribed it to the organisation's lack of opportunity for women – an example of an organisational feature affecting solidarity and gender identification.

Depending on the dominant newsroom culture, it is risky for a woman to show vulnerability, express doubt or uncertainty because, as several women stated, 'If you say you can't go there or you can't do this, because you are a woman, ... or if you are afraid that something will happen to you, then you will never get the [big] story'. They suppressing their gender identity to protect their professional identity.

Outside of the newsroom itself – on assignment, or attending a seminar – other dynamics seem to be allowed. Helplessness as a prototypical feminine tactic is then sometimes recognised as being useful: 'If I'm at Parliament, and I miss something, and I ask any one of the guys, I'll get it, but I don't know if they're that friendly when it's one of my male colleagues'. And the 'backbiting' gives way to enjoying each other's company, as emphasised by several interviewees.

In the examples given above, we saw some clearly developed strategies to minimise or inflate certain identities. Other strategies focused on the shifting of identities – claiming certain identities and ignoring others.

(Over)-identification with a traditional male work ethos and professional values seemed to be useful in avoiding gender tensions and polarisation. Emphasising professional identity and playing down gender identity, in certain instances, seemed to have been a deliberate choice diminishing the potential for gender tension which comes with gender relations. In this case professional identity is used as a shield. In organisations where gender is still a steering force in newsroom interactions and often coincides with organisational power, this may lead to conflicting situations. Where professional exchange is needed, gender can still be an obstacle.

Conclusion

How does all of this show how 'boundaries in thinking, conventions in knowledge ... can be pushed to discover new ways of understanding' as stated in my introduction to this chapter?

The traditional focus on gender in (media) organisations in the past often led to an analysis of representation by numbers, by positions and power differences based on hierarchy. This focus was useful as it gave us data which we needed: an impression of what the reality of gender in organisations looked like. But at the same time, this picture was static – a still photograph instead of moving images.

Newer insights challenging this traditional interpretation are taking different angles in interpretation: they focus on the analysis of gendered symbols, values, and significations used in interactions and relationships. This more relational focus on gender includes interaction and social practices.

To really understand the value of this new orientation, this different way of thinking, one has to look for relevant concepts which can be operationalised and therefore will enable us to observe and be informed about gender experiences. It is through becoming part of these related experiences that we begin to be able to understand what (gender) identity means in people's daily lives and work.

References

Albert, S. and D. Whetten. 1985. 'Organisational identity'. In *Research in organisational behavior* 7, eds. L Cummings and B Staw, 263 – 295. Greenwich, CT: JAI.

Allan, S. 1998. '(En)gendering the Truth Politics of News Discourse'. In *News, Gender and Power,* eds. C Carter, G Branston and S Allan, 121-37. London and New York: Routledge.

Anderson, Patricia. 1986. 'Conclusion: Women in the Caribbean'. *Social and Economic Studies* 35, no. 2:291-324.

Antrobus, P. 1991. 'Women in Development Programmes: The Caribbean Experience (1975-1985)'. In *Gender in Caribbean Development,* P. Mohammed and C. Shepherd, 36–53. The University of the West Indies/ Women and Development Studies Project. Mona, Jamaica; St Augustine, Trinidad and Tobago; Cave Hill, Barbados.

Alvesson, M. and Y. Billing. 1997. *Understanding Gender and Organisations.* London: Thousand Oaks and New Delhi: Sage.

Barrett, G. H. 1984. 'Job Satisfaction among Newspaperwomen'. *Journalism Quarterly*, (Autumn): 593–99.

Barrow, C, ed. 1995. *Caribbean Portraits, Essays on Gender Ideologies and Identities,* pp. 234-252. Kingston: Ian Randle Publishers.

Bartel, C. and Dutton, J. 2001. 'Ambiguous Organisational Memberships: Constructing Organisational Identities in Interactions With Others'. In *Social Identity Processes in Organisational Contexts*, eds. M. Hogg and D. Terry, 115–130. Philadelphia: Psychology Press, Taylor and Francis Group.

Brodber, E. 1982. 'Towards a Documentation of Stereotypes'. In *Perceptions of Caribbean Women* vol. 4, Research papers WICP.

Burks, K. and V. A. Stone. 1993. 'Career-related Characteristics of Male and Female News Directors'. *Journalism Quarterly* 70, no. 3: 542–49.

Canary, D. and B. Spitzberg. 1990. Attribution biases and associations between conflict strategies. *Communication Monographs* 57:139–151.

Capozza, D. and R. Brown, eds. 2000. *Social Identity Processes, Trends in Theory and Research*. London: Thousand Oaks and New Delhi: Sage.

Carter, C., G. Branston and S. Allan. 1998. *News, Gender and Power*. London: Routledge.

Creedon, P., ed. 1993. *Women in Mass Communication*, 2nd ed. London: Thousand Oaks and Newbury: Sage.

Deaux, K. 2000. 'Models, Meanings and Motivations'. In *Social Identity Processes, Trends in Theory and Research*, eds. D. Capozza and R. Brown, 1-14. London: Thousand Oaks and New Delhi: Sage.

de Bruin, M. 1994. 'Women and Caribbean Media'. *Occasional Paper 3*. Kingston: CARIMAC.

———. 1998. 'Gender in Caribbean Media, Beyond the Body Count'. Paper presented at the 21st Scientific Conference & General Assembly of the International Association for Media and Communication Research, University of Strathclyde, Glasgow, July 26-30.

———. 2000. 'Gender, organisational and professional identities in journalism'. *Journalism-Theory, Practice and Criticism* 1, no. 2: 239-260.

———. 2002. 'Gender and Caribbean Media'. In *Gendered Realities: An Anthology of Essays in Caribbean Feminist Thought*, ed. Patricia Mohammed, 298-237. Kingston: The UWI Press, (in cooperation with University of Oklahoma Press).

de Bruin, M. with S. Francis-Brown, H. Nicholson, G. Persaud and E. Wallace. 1994. 'Women and Media in the English-speaking Caribbean'. In *Women Empowering Communication: A Resource Book on Women and the Globalisation of Media*, eds. M. Gallagher, L. Quindoza-Santiago, 65-95. London: WACC; Manila: Isis International and New York: Methuen.

de Bruin, M. and K. Ross, eds. Forthcoming. *Identities At Work*. Cresskill, NJ: Hampton Press. Denzin, Norman and Y.S. Lincoln, eds. 2000. *Handbook of Qualitative Research*, Second edition, 487-508. London: Thousand Oaks and New Delhi: Sage.

Dutton, J., J. Dukerich and C. Harquail. 1994. 'Organisational Images and Member Identification'. *Administrative Science Quarterly* 39:239-263.

Ely, R. 1994. 'The Effects of Organisational Demographics and Social Identity on Relationships among Professional Women'. *Administrative Science Quarterly* 39:203-238.

Ferree, M., J. Lorber and B. Hess, eds. *Revisioning Gender*. London: Thousand Oaks and New Delhi: Sage.

Ferri, A. J. and J. E. Keller. 1986. 'Perceived Career Barriers for Female Television News Anchors'. *Journalism Quarterly* 63:463–67.

Forsterling, F. 2001. *Attribution; an Introduction to Theories, Research and Applications*. Philadelphia: Psychology Press, Taylor and Francis Group.

Francis-Brown, S., ed. 1995. *Media, Gender and Development – A Resource Book for Journalists*. Kingston: CARIMAC/UWI.

Gallagher, M. 1981. *Unequal Opportunities: The Case of Women and the Media*. Paris: UNESCO.

Gallagher, M. with M. von Euler. 1995. *An Unfinished Story: Gender Patterns in Media Employment*. Paris: UNESCO.

Gallagher, M. and L. Quindoza-Santiago, eds. 1994. *Women Empowering Communication: A Resource Book on Women and the Globalisation of Media*. London: WACC; Manila: Isis International and New York: Methuen.

Gayle, B. and R. W. Preiss. 2002. 'An overview of Individual Processes in Interpersonal Communication'. In *Interpersonal Communication Research, Advances Through Meta-Analysis,* M.Allen, R.W. Preiss, B. Gayle and N. Burrell, 45–57. London, New Jersey: Lawrence Erlbaum Associates.

Gherardi, S. 1995. *Gender, Symbolism and Organisational Cultures*. London: Sage.

Gubrium, J. and J.A. Holstein. 2000. 'Analyzing Interpretive Practice'. In *Handbook of Qualitative Research*. Second edition, Denzin, K. Norman and Yvonna S. Lincoln, 487-508. London: Thousand Oaks and New Delhi: Sage.

Guillaumin, C. 1995. *Racism, Sexism, Power and Ideology*. London and New York: Routledge

Halford, M. Savage and A. Witz. 1997. *Gender, Careers and Organisations*. London: Macmillan.

Hall, S. 1996. 'Introduction: Who Needs "Identity"?' In *Questions of Cultural Identity*, eds. S. Hall and P. du Gay, 1-17. London: Sage.

Hogg, M. and D. Terry. 2001. 'Social Identity Theory and Organisational Processes'. In *Social Identity Processes in Organisational Contexts*, eds. M. Hogg and D. Terry, 1–12. Philadelphia: Psychology Press, Taylor and Francis Group.

Jimenez-David, R., ed. 1996. *Women's Experiences in the Media*. Manilla: Isis International; London: WACC.

Kitzinger, J. 1998. 'The Gender-Politics of News Production: Silenced Voices and False Memories'. In *News, Gender and Power*, eds. C. Carter, G. Branston and S. Allan, 186-203. London: Routledge.

Leo-Rhynie, E., B. Bailey and C. Barrow, eds. 1997. *Gender, A Caribbean Multi-Disciplinary Perspective*. Kingston: Ian Randle Publishers in association with The Centre for Gender and Development Studies, UWI, and The Commonwealth of Learning.

Leo-Rhynie, E. 1998. 'Socialisation and the Development of Gender Identity; Theoretical Formulations and Caribbean Research'. In *Caribbean Portraits, Essays on Gender Ideologies and Identities,* ed. C. Barrow, 234-252. Kingston: Ian Randle Publishers.

Marshall, J. 1993. 'Organisational Communication from a Feminist Perspective'. In *Communication Yearbook*, ed. S Deetz, 16. Newbury, CA: Sage.

Merritt, S. and H. Gross. 1978. 'Women's Page/Lifestyle Editors: Does Sex Make a Difference?'. *Journalism Quarterly* 55, no. 3:508–14.

Mills, K. 1997. 'What Difference Do Women Journalists Make?'. In *Women, Media and Politics*, ed. Pippa Norris, 41–55. New York and Oxford: Oxford University Press.

Mohammed, P. and C. Shepherd, eds. 1991. *Gender in Caribbean Development.* The University of the West Indies/ Women and Development Studies Project. Mona, Jamaica; St Augustine, Trinidad and Tobago; Cave Hill, Barbados.

Mohammed, P., ed. 2002. *Gendered Realities: An Anthology of Essays in Caribbean Feminist Thought,* 298-327. Kingston: The UWI Press (in cooperation with University of Oklahoma Press).

Nicholson, H. 1995. 'Gender as a Dynamic Concept in Media'. In *Media, Gender and Development – A Resource Book for Journalists,* ed. S. Francis-Brown. Kingston: CARIMAC/ UWI.

Pratt, M. 1998. 'To Be or Not to Be? Central Questions in Organisational Identification'. In *Identity in Organisations: Building Theory through Conversations,* eds. D. Whetten, and P. Godfrey, 171–207. London: Thousand Oaks and New Delhi: Sage.

Robinson, G. J. and A. Saint-Jean. 1998. 'Canadian Women Journalists: The "Other Half" of the Equation'. In *The Global Journalist: News People around the World,* ed. D.H. Weaver, 351–72. Cresskill, NJ: Hampton Press.

Ross, K. Forthcoming. 'Sex at Work: gender politics and newsroom culture'. In *Identities At Work,* eds. de Bruin and K. Ross. Cresskill, NJ: Hampton Press.

Scott Whitlow, S. 1977. 'How Male and Female Gatekeepers Respond to News Stories of Women'. *Journalism Quarterly* 54, no. 3:573–79, 609.

Senior, O. 1991. *Working Miracles – Women's Lives in the English-speaking Caribbean.* Barbados: UWI, Cave Hill, ISER; London: James Curey; Bloomington: Indiana University Press. Shepherd, V., B. Brereton and B. Bailey, eds. 1995. *Engendering History, Caribbean Women in Historical Perspective.* Kingston: Ian Randle Publishers; London: James Currey Publishers. Shepherd, V. 2002. *Challenging Masculine Myths: gender, history education and development in Jamaica.* Dialogue for development, lecture November 19, 2002. Planning Institute of Jamaica

Skidmore, P. 1998. 'Gender and the Agenda: News Reporting of Child Sexual Abuse'. In *News, Gender and Power,* eds. C. Carter, G. Branston and S. Allan, 204-18. London and New York: Routledge.

Sohn, Ardyth B. 1984. 'Goals and Achievement Orientations of Women Newspaper Managers'. *Journalism Quarterly* 61 (Autumn): 600–605.

Sreberny, A. 1995. 'Women, Media and Development in a Global Context'. Presentation at the International UNESCO Symposium 'Women and the Media; Access to expression and decision- making'. Toronto.

Steiner, L. 1998. 'Newsroom Accounts of Power at Work'. In *News, Gender and Power,* eds. C. Carter, G. Branston and S. Allan, 145-59. London and New York: Routledge.

Van Dijk, T. 1998. *Ideology, A Multidisciplinary Approach.* London: Thousand Oaks and New Delhi: Sage.

Van Zoonen, L. 1998. 'A Professional, Unreliable, Heroic Marionette (M/F): Structure, Agency and Subjectivity in Contemporary Journalism'. *European Journal of Cultural Studies* 1, no. 1: 123-43.

WAND. 1990. *The Involvement of Caribbean Media in the Implementation of the Nairobi Forward-Looking Strategies for the Advancement of Women.* Report of study commissioned by UNESCO.

Weaver, D. H. 1997. 'Women as Journalists'. In *Women, Media and Politics*, ed. Pippa Norris, 21–40. New York and Oxford: Oxford University Press.

———, ed. 1998. *The Global Journalist: News People around the World.* Cresskill, NJ: Hampton Press.

Weaver, D. and G. Wilhoit. 1996. *The American Journalist in the 1990s: US News People at the End of an Era*. Mahwah, NJ: Erlbaum.

Weick, K. 1995. *Sensemaking in Organisations*. London: Thousand Oaks and New Delhi: Sage.

Whetten, D. and P. Godfrey, eds. 1998. *Identity in Organisations: Building Theory through Conversations*. London: Thousand Oaks and New Delhi: Sage.

Witz, A. and M. Savage, eds. 1992. *Gender and Bureaucracy*. Oxford: Blackwell.

10 | LINDEN LEWIS

Masculinity, the Political Economy of the Body, and Patriarchal Power in the Caribbean

This chapter focuses on three intersecting dimensions of social practice that help to situate men in the Caribbean in relation to their specific social reality. In attempting to understand men and their status in contemporary society, it becomes necessary to explore masculinity, the body and the institutional phenomenon of patriarchal power. Masculinity as a gendered identity of men is both a social and an ideological practice. Though the performative dimension of masculinity cannot necessarily be reduced to men, it is upon the male body that the text of masculinity is usually inscribed and often played out to the fullest. What provides masculinity with currency is the extent to which men dominate the institutional environment in such a way as to secure power, privilege, prestige and access to valued resources. In short, patriarchal power is critical to the reproduction of masculinity in society. This chapter therefore seeks to explore the ways in which an understanding of masculinity, the political economy of the body and the exercise of patriarchal power combine to give many men advantages over women and to be in a position to reproduce these social inequalities.

Irrespective of its causes or the ways in which we might begin to assess its impact, the reality is that we are in the throes of the emergence of a regional consciousness about masculinity. This increased awareness does not mean that Caribbean men have not thought about their gendered identities as men before now, but that a number of factors have coalesced to intensify interests about men and boys, their social status and their current and future roles in society. Consciousness is always the product of specific historical and material conditions. These conditions shape the political matrix of this consciousness. Claims and counter-claims about male marginalisation in the region, the relatively poor academic performance of boys versus girls in schools, and a growing concern with boys dropping out of school, have all contributed to a greater focus on men, boys and masculinity in the Caribbean (for details concerning some of these issues see Miller 1986, 1991; Parry 2000 and Barriteau 2003). In addition, many regional governments have been responding to the Beijing Declaration to encourage men and boys to participate in the process of gender equality and transformation.

It is difficult to identify a period when there was more popular and academic discussion about men's vulnerability, their frailty, their crises or the seeming purposelessness of their presence on the streets and sidewalks of many Caribbean societies (see Barrow 1998; Lewis 1990) In addition to the reasons already advanced, this heightened consciousness has its origin in part in the shifting economic terrain, occasioned by the process of globalisation, economic restructuring and the fallout from the neo-liberal agenda in many parts of the region. The impact of these fundamental economic transformations is a profound dislocation of traditional gender roles. In this context, therefore, tensions and conflict about issues of gender have become quite commonplace in contemporary Caribbean society. If one were to go simply on this discourse, one might be led to believe that men were on the verge of extinction from this region, or at best in danger of being reduced to a second-class status. Herein lies a classic contradiction: while some argue that men are in danger or in crisis, the participation of men, as brokers of power in the region, remains resolute. How, then, can two seemingly different and conflicting tendencies inhabit the same universe of experience? Perhaps this has to do both the resilience of masculinity and with the seductive power of patriarchy.

For proof of the resilience of masculinity we need look no further than to the institutions of slavery and indentureship in the Caribbean. That men would emerge out of these two authoritarian systems, designed in part to undermine their masculinity, with any semblance of pride or dignity, is a remarkable story of the tenacity of identity, which is only now beginning to emerge in the academic literature of the region (see for example Mohammed 2002, Sampath 1993, Lewis 2003 and Patterson 1969). One of the important real strengths of masculinity is its ability to bounce back; to face tremendous obstacles yet survive, regroup and seize institutional and structural initiatives that secure power and reproduce privilege in society. The putative decline, therefore, of the masculine ideal, of the centrality of men in the public sphere, and of the general status of men, may be more hyperbolic than real.

Part of the subtext of the discourse on masculinity that has not been sufficiently theorised, is the extent to which much of the emerging consciousness of masculinity is taking place within the parameters of patriarchal rule (For contrasting views on this phenomenon see Miller 1986 and 1991; de Moya 2002; Lewis 2002 and Barriteau 2003). We have to be more careful about understanding how this discourse surrounding the fate of men in the region actually participates in patriarchal thinking. It bears repeating that masculinity is a hegemonic ideology with no particular obligation to define or justify itself. It proceeds from a normative position, so that any threat to the social order of its existence can be seen as an attempt to disrupt, destabilise and generally upset the status quo. As Pierre Bourdieu notes:

> The strength of the masculine order is seen in the fact that it dispenses with justification: the androcentric vision imposes itself as neutral and has no need to spell itself out in discourses aimed at legitimating. The social order functions as an immense symbolic machine tending to ratify the masculine domination on which it is founded (2001, 9).

If we are witnessing a heightened interest in masculinity, it is because feminist advocacy and the struggles over gender equality in the region, which have contested male privilege for the last three decades, have been succeeding in wresting some ground from the hegemony of men. Caribbean scholars should not underestimate the responses to these contestations; they may be more sophisticated than they appear on the surface.

The response of hegemonic masculinity to these challenges is not merely reactive and defensive, but involves what could be called an ontological legerdemain. It takes a certain adroitness to change the terms of a discourse from one of contesting male privilege to one in which the discursive practice revolves around the loss of status of men, their inability to compete academically, or to suffer the humiliation of being replaced socially. In short, according to this school of thought, a challenge to male privilege is tantamount to an undermining of men and masculinity. When this interpretation of social reality is then articulated in Barbados, Jamaica, Dominica, and Trinidad by heads of state or other top ranking government officials, or endorsed by those in the administration of the academy, it becomes ensconced in the public consciousness as truth. The Minister of Community Development and Women's Affairs in Dominica, Matthew Walters, in announcing the decision to change the name of his ministry to that of Community Development and Gender Affairs (incidentally, Trinidad has also changed its ministry to Culture and Gender Affairs, but with much less fanfare), lamented the deterioration in the lot of men in Dominica. Mr Walters noted: 'Men over the years have been marginalised. They have been belittled, and also have been abused' (see *Trinidad Guardian* 2000, 7). For Mr Walters, there was a connection between this declining status of men in society and the precipitation of social crisis. He states further: 'They (men) are losing their sense of belonging, their sense of responsibility. As a result of that we have an escalation in social problems in Dominica. What I want to do is take men on board' (*Trinidad Guardian* 2000, 7). Barbadian columnist Eric Lewis repeated the views expressed by Mr Walters, perhaps in more humorous fashion.

> Just now we men going to be like dinosaurs, dead and gone forever, and children will go into Museums and look at us and ask, 'Mummy what is that?' And the women will answer, 'Oh, that is a man. They use to use them back in the old time days to get children' (1997, 11).

Lewis's observation, though clearly ironic, strikes a chord with those who feel this sense of displacement and the urgency to clarify exactly what role men ought to be playing in a changing Caribbean. Let us be clear about what is happening here. This development of a popular consciousness around masculinity is not about attending to matters of social justice; it is about shoring up hegemonic male privilege from further incursions.

There is another more subtle, yet quite visible, dimension of this concern and emphasis on men and masculinity in the Caribbean, and that has to do with the issues of race and class. Discussions about the status of Caribbean men really do not apply to all men in the region. There are class and racial considerations that are encoded in the public discourse. First, the men who are most affected by economic restructuring in the Caribbean are working-class men. These are men with limited power to begin with. Middle- and upper-class men in the Caribbean are not nearly as affected by the new challenges of the economy and the fallout from the neo-liberal agenda (see Watson 2003 for a discussion of the relationship between neo-liberalism and gender). Middle- and upper-class men continue to secure participation in the operation of the apparatuses of the state, the economy and the corporate structures of the region. Solidarity with the so-called plight of working-class and economically disenfranchised men is strategically important in preserving patriarchal dividends for middle class members. Working-class men however, remain alienated from the levers of power. By virtue of their class affiliation, they are already predisposed to certain insecurities and uncertainties about reproducing themselves socially. Rather than viewing their changing economic fortunes as the product of the vicissitudes of global economic restructuring, they choose to view their economic problems as inversely related to women's advancement. They resort to scapegoating women who, themselves, are subject to the powerful regulation of capitalism. In this context, the notion of marginalisation, as articulated by their middle- and upper-class counterparts, resonates at a fundamental level. The argument here seems to follow a strange logic in which whatever the perception of progress being made by women in the region, such advancement appears to have come at the expense of men, therefore women need to be retarded so that men can reclaim the retrospective illusion of their rightful place as heads of the households and monarchs of all they survey. In the final analysis, this is too myopic a view, which in fact fails to take into account the massive scale of exploitation of women by transnational capital in Export Processing Zones and garment factories and the informal sector throughout the region. This view also seems to be ignorant of the logic of capital accumulation, whose primary objective is the expansion and reproduction of capital and the creation of surplus value. In a forthcoming article, Hilbourne Watson addresses this issue squarely when he says that the market has to 'condition gender relations because the market is the primary site of the social power of capital' (2003, 66). A failure to address this issue of the class dimensions of the discourse on masculinity in the region obfuscates the real power of capitalism to shape the terrain of social identity. Such a position leads to the erroneous idea that gender relations fall outside of social relations and occupy some autonomous space. In an era of non-essentialism, there is a noticeable silence on this question of social class in much of the academic literature of the region.

Second, when we talk about the changing status of men in the Caribbean, we are for the most part not talking about all races of men but principally about men of African descent and, in some contexts, about Indian men. Granted that men of African descent represent a majority of the population in the region, observations about groups of men idling their lives away, hanging out on street corners, unemployed, involved in drug-trafficking and other crimes, refer, for the most part, to men of African descent. Men of certain racial or ethnic groups that exist in society do not seem to be represented among this listing of miscreants. Allegations of excessive alcoholism, wife-murders, suicide and violence, are often associated with Indian men in Guyana and Trinidad. The question then becomes why does the discourse on the changing status of men in the Caribbean represent itself as a general one when in fact it may be an issue which relates only to certain racial groups of men? Would it sound too harsh to identify the problem facing men as one affecting black and Indian men predominantly? Does race raise a different kind of spectre for these perceived problems and, by extension, their policy implications and ultimate solutions? What is there about the political economy of the existence of black and Indian men that predisposes them to certain problems and challenges? Why do largely black men, but some Indian men as well, predominate in the prison populations of the Caribbean? Do other racial groups of men not have these problems or are their problems dealt with differently, not manifesting themselves publicly? To what extent does the predominance of black men among the poor, the wretched and the dispossessed, have anything to do with the problems they face? What can we say about the material conditions of existence of men of European, Chinese, Syrian, Lebanese and Jewish descent in the Caribbean, that seem, by and large, to place them outside the scope of claims of marginalisation and displacement? These are questions that force us to rethink and reconceptualise exactly what we mean by the construction of masculinity in the region and which bring us to an understanding that not all men experience masculinity in the same way. Moreover, by raising these questions about the discourse on masculinity in the region, we may begin to see how and to what extent race matters. The issue of race is particularly important to a discussion of the political economy of the male body in the Caribbean to which I would now like to draw your attention. Not only is the phenomenon of race played out on the body of the Caribbean male in specific ways to be discussed below, but it also becomes the symbolic site of material embodiment, power and sexuality. The body, therefore, is important to this investigation to the extent that it provides us with some insight into the material experiences in the lives of some Caribbean men.

The Political Economy of the Black Male Body

The discourse around the body is highly developed and quite diverse, thanks to both feminist and post-modernist theorising. There are also some very useful insights from phenomenology about the body as a vehicle through which we become conscious of the world around us. In addition, phenomenological research has pointed us in the direction of understanding how men experience their bodies in different context and historical moments (see Nancy Tuana, William Cowling, et al. 1992). Tuana and Cowling et al note: 'The world opens up to us through our bodies, and the way those bodies are marked by race, gender, sexuality or ability impacts the world we perceive and the world we create' (2000, 289).

Michel Foucault (1995) gave us much to think about in terms of the sociology of the body and deployment of the social technologies of the body, that is, the degree to which we intervene in the body, to alter its shape or appearance – to reconfigure what has always been considered 'natural' and, to some extent, unalterable. Indeed, it was Foucault who posed the question: 'What mode of investment of the body is necessary and adequate for the functioning of a capitalist society like ours?' (1980, 58). The answer to this question lies at the heart of the political economy of the body. According to David Harvey, the social geographer, different processes (physical and social) 'produce' very different kinds of bodies. Social class, race and gender among other factors all leave their impact on the body (see Harvey 2000). For Harvey, therefore, 'no human body is outside of social processes of determination' (2000, 101). How, then, are bodies produced? This question brings us back to Foucault's concern above.

We cannot think of the body without duly considering the socio-economic and political context within which the body operates. Any consideration of the body in the Caribbean must, at some point, come to terms with the role of peripheral capitalism and the impact of the neo-liberal agenda on the body of labourers. The body has to be conceptualised as a medium through which one's capacity to work is made possible. In other words, the body is the storehouse of labour power. We have to understand the body as a site of production of commodities. Harvey reminded us of Marx's understanding of the body in capitalism when he talked about exchanging one's labour power for wages. This exchange is marked in very specific contractual terms.

> Put in more direct contemporary terms, the creation of unemployment through down-sizing, the redefinitions of skills and remunerations for skills, the intensification of labour processes and of autocratic systems of surveillance, the increasing despotism of orchestrated detailed divisions of labour, the insertion of immigrants (or what amounts to the same thing, the migration of capital to alternative labour sources), and the coerced competitive struggle between different bodily practices and modes of valuation achieved under different historical and cultural conditions, all contribute to the uneven geographical valuation of labourers as persons. The manifest effects upon the bodies of labourers who live lives embedded in the circulation of variable capital is powerful indeed (Harvey 2000, 109-110).

Harvey also points to the fact that not only is the body a site of production and exchange but also a source of consumption of commodities, but given the power of persuasion, surveillance, and coercion of capitalism, there are enormous pressures placed on the site of the body for further accumulation (Harvey 2000, 111). This pressure that is placed on the body, as consumer, in the Caribbean can be seen through the manufacturing of needs that, in the words of George Lamming, 'surrender their very palates to foreign control' (1992, 284). We are all aware of the Caribbean's enormous appetite for North American commodities which necessitates frequent visits from the region to the various shopping malls in New York, Florida, Washington DC, Pennsylvania and Toronto. To live and work in a low currency area means that the labourer has to work harder to consume that which is produced in more affluent countries. In many ways, those unable to consume at this level on their own, rely on the barrels that are sent from various North American and European ports by relatives residing in the metropole. Harvey summarised this dilemma succinctly when he said:

> The evident instabilities within the circulation of variable capital coupled with the different windows on the world constructed through moments of production, exchange, and consumption place the labouring body largely at the mercy of a whole series of forces outside of any one individual's control. It is in this sense that the labouring body must be seen as an internal relation of the historically and geographically achieved processes of capital circulation (2000, 113-114).

In short, we need to be more mindful, I would argue, of the way capitalism constantly attempts, not without resistance of course, to fashion the body according to the requirements of the process of accumulation.

Why approach the question of the body from this perspective? Perhaps this approach provides some additional insights into the kind of male body that has been the subject of a growing literature on tourism, masculinity and sexuality in the Caribbean. For as long as the region has represented itself as a tropical paradise, sex has been an important part of the libidinal economy of tourism. The traditionally sexed body has been that of a woman and, hence, the female body has long been considered more central to this industry. Recently, more attention than before has been paid to the male body as the embodiment of exotic sex and sexuality (see Alexander 1998; Phillips 1999; Murray 1999 and Bindel 2003). Here again, however, the male body in question is a black body. It is not the white, Indian or Chinese body that is invested with libidinal value but rather the black male body on the beach. The black male body in idyllic tropical conditions in many ways represents the ultimate taboo for young and old North American and European white women who, after years of socialisation and preachments against such liaisons, participate in a dance of forbidden pleasure, under the cover of anonymity. Increasingly, also, many black women have been coming to the Caribbean, especially to Jamaica, 'to get their groove on', thanks to Terry McMillan's own celebrated 'island romance' that became the subject of the novel and subsequent film of the same name, *How Stella Got Her Groove Back* (1996). It is important that we note that the body is not simply a passive entity, merely waiting to be acted upon. The body is also, as Harvey counsels us, active and transformative. The body has a capacity to initiate change and ultimately to offer resistance, irrespective of the nature of the authoritarian and hierarchical arrangement that obtains within capitalism.

Elizabeth Grosz argued, quite rightly, that every body is marked by the history and specificity of its existence (1994, 142). How do we make sense of the daily solicitation on the beach articulated by or directed towards the black body? First, there are the material conditions of existence of these black male bodies. These are, for the most, part young men with limited education, few formally acquired skills, mostly unemployed and sometimes unemployable, and who live in conditions of poverty and deprivation (see Gill 1990; Phillips 1999; Murray 1999 and Bindel 2003). They come to the market place therefore owning no means of production and are therefore left with few options other than their capacity to sell sex to strangers in exchange for money, good times, the possibility of migration or some other type of material benefit. Though the body in this context consumes and exchanges in the sense discussed earlier, it does not actually produce a commodity but a service. Most men who work the beach are heterosexuals in pursuit of foreign women with enough money to make the effort worth their while. As one might imagine, there are homosexual 'beach boys' who sell sexual services to male tourists. However, given the public hostility to homosexuality in the Caribbean, these men have to be much more discrete about their liaisons. Often, they find alternative spaces to make contacts with foreign men for sexual encounters. There are known homosexual cruising spots along the Condado in Puerto Rico, areas of operation of jineteros and pingueros along the Malecón, on the main strip between calle 23 and

27 along the Vedado in Cuba, as well as on the Tata beach in Martinique, where homosexual solicitations take place. Generally, however, heterosexual men are by far the more visible agents of this practice of male prostitution in the region. Jacqui Alexander makes an important observation about the sex tourism industry in general.

> When one examines the generative scripts of heterosexual tourism and those of gay tourism, one sees that they traverse a similar imperial geography and draw upon similar epistemic frames to service an imagined 'Western' tourist (1998, 284)

Alexander argues that gay tourism ultimately participates in a process of nativisation and recolonisation, which is similar to the original colonial project and which also functions as the linchpin of heterosexual tourism.

> This form of tourism, organized as it is on sexual consumption in the 'Third World', has also become complicit in recirculating an earlier colonial myth that attempted to replace subjectivity with the sexualized 'native' body, for in this sexual narrative of consumption those providing services are never positioned as agents (1998, 294-295).

Alexander's work is very important in so far as this aspect of sex tourism has, to date, generated very little academic interest among Caribbean scholars. It is an area worthy of more research effort, not only in relation to the tourism industry but also in those national spaces where men seek out other men for sexual encounters – a phenomenon with an established practice in even the most homophobic of Caribbean territories.

The pressure exerted on the body in the context of the libidinal economy also has to do with one of the plinths of masculinity – sexual performance – a male peril worthy of no additional complications. The irony, then, is that the male body is only invested with libidinal value in so far as it is capable of producing sexual satisfaction in the specific context of the provision of these services in the tourism industry. Conversely, the tourism industry, which fully understands the economic contribution of the male body, benefits from the labour of the male body without having to make any investment in, provide protection for, or offer compensation to, the black body. Though not included in the tourism brochures, everyone knows that an important part of the tourism industry is the availability of exoticised sex. Tourism officials in Barbados once created the slogan, 'Experience the Bajan Way'. This slogan was quickly, and subversively, appropriated by 'beach boys' in that country as a metaphor for a sexual encounter with them as part of the tourist experience. Some people go to exotic places in part to consume the other sexually. The 'beach boy', the hotelier, and tourism officials are drawn into a relationship that is rooted in the dictates of market forces. There is therefore some complicity between industry stakeholders and those who sell sexual or other services, even though the former will, from time to time, inveigh against solicitation and public harassment of tourists. Julie Bindel, commenting on the response of government officials, recently reported the following in *The Guardian* newspaper:

> The Jamaican government has made half-hearted attempts to curb the behaviour of the beach boys. During the winter seasons in the later 1990s, harassment of tourists in nearby Ocho Rios and Montego Bay received such intense publicity that the government proposed to double the fines for harrassers and to establish a night court to process offenders swiftly. Nothing much has happened since, though civilian security teams patrol Negril beach day and night (2003, 3).

What then do we make of Foucault's question about the mode of investment of the body that is necessary and adequate for the functioning of capitalist societies such as those in the Caribbean? For the young men who work the beaches of the Caribbean soliciting foreign tourists, there is a definite investment in the body. From all accounts, these men are well built, muscularly toned and in good shape for the most part. Such physiques are not realised without effort. The toned body is part of the libidinal investment that 'beach boys' must make. The body then becomes part of their marketing strategy; it actually represents a site of libidinal intensity. Body-building is one of the ways to sculpt the body in desirable ways. Indeed, it is not just the men on the beach in search of foreign women who have this preoccupation with body-building. The sculpted body has replaced the flabby or rotund body in the Caribbean as that which is more desirable for men in contemporary society (see Gill, n.d.). On the question of body-building, Elizabeth Grosz has some important insights to offer here.

> Where for men (at least for many men) body building can be seen as the fulfillment of a certain notion of masculinity or even virility – in this sense, body building can be seen as an attempt to render the whole of the male body into the phallus, creating the male body as hard, impenetrable, pure muscle – it is considerably more difficult to read female body building in this way (1994, 224, fn 7).

Concerns about the body also extend to other considerations of general health. One young man in Barbados confessed to having three 'girlfriends', one from Europe, one from Canada and the other from the United States. With remarkable candour, however, he reflected: 'I don't deal with nobody else 'cause I don't want to run down my body. I got a girlfriend and a little girl here to think 'bout' (Gill 1990, 1B). The contradictions in the foregoing statement are too self-evident to warrant further comment. These men therefore understand the importance of their corporeality, and the women who seek their services are quick to point to the body as a site of attraction for them.

(Re)presenting the Black Male Body

The significance of the black male body was rather dramatically and visually brought into sharp focus recently in Jamaica, with the unveiling of Laura Facey Cooper's nude emancipation sculpture in the downtown Kingston Emancipation Park on August 1, 2003. The work of art consists of two huge bronze statues of nude, free, male and female ex-slaves, facing each other. At the base of the sculpture are the words inspired by Marcus Garvey and immortalised in song by Bob Marley, '. . . None but ourselves can free our mind'. Given the dimensions of the sculpture, all body parts appear larger than life. Though there has been some comment about the female form in this sculpture, viz. the size and trajectory of her breasts and behind, the bulk of the attention has been showered on the male form. Though the female form is nude, it is not anatomically correct. The anatomical correctness of the male form is however readily noticeable, because of its enormous, flaccid penis. The size and prominence of the man's penis notwithstanding, the public display of this phallic symbol of masculine virility, power, strength and privilege was unsettling to many church-going and morally austere Jamaicans. Moreover, given the memory of slavery and the discourse that inheres in the text of both types of body, the sculpture evoked images of the exoticised and primitivised corporeality of both forms but especially that of the male, since, at many levels, it confirmed a lot about the white stereotypical gaze at black men As Robert Connell noted, race continues to be understood as a hierarchy of bodies, and this understanding is linked directly to a hierarchy of masculinities (2000, 61).

For some weeks after the unveiling of this sculpture, the national radio talk-shows and editorial pages of the local newspapers were inundated with calls and letters that were mostly critical of the artwork. The sculpture managed to generate intense debate both in Jamaica, and among Jamaicans and the wider Caribbean community living in the United States. The work had clearly offended the sensibilities of some Jamaicans. Callers and letter-writers were concerned about the image that the sculpture projected of Jamaicans, the way such a statue represented part of a general moral decay of the nation, and many were concerned about the work's impact on the impressionable minds of children who were daily confronted by its presence on their way to and from school.

One woman's comment succinctly captures much of the discourse about this sculpture: 'It nuh look good. Dem shoulda cover them up with a loincloth or something. What the artist is saying about black people? And why dem coulden free up them mind inna dem clothes?' (Mills, 2003). Another comment that is particularly germane to this essay was: 'It merely reinforces the stereotypes of black people as sexualised beings. What does it say to people who link sex and tourism in the Caribbean?' (Mills, 2003). The commingling of sexuality and race in the sculpture remains an important subtext not only of the art itself but of the discourse surrounding the sculpture. In response to the question above, 'what does it say . . .', though this may not have been the intent of the piece, the work may speak directly to those in pursuit of intimate encounters with the sexualised and primitivised other in the Caribbean.

The Diseased Body

Jean Baudrillard, in, a recent collection of published lectures, discussed what he termed the viral economy, a space where we experience sudden intercontinental ravages, and where contagion is deeply systemic and interconnected at several levels. It is in the interstices of this new viral economy that HIV/AIDS resides. The concern here is not only with the disease itself but the nature of its global transmission. In the Caribbean, where the mainstay of the economies of most countries is tourism, this viral economy poses some invidious problems for the region, of which particular types of men, those who participate in the sex-tourism industry are perhaps the most vulnerable.

None could deny the impact of the epidemic of HIV/AIDS on the female and male body in the region. Its devastation is common knowledge. In 2003, somewhere between 350,000 and 590,000 people were living with HIV and AIDS in the Caribbean. Some 60,000 were infected during 2002 (see http://www.unaids.org for more details). According to the Deputy Director for UNAIDS in New York, Bertil Lindbald, anti-retroviral therapy coverage for people in low and middle income countries remains unacceptably low, with only 300,000 people receiving medication out of an estimated five to six million who need the therapy (see Lindbald 2003). The Caribbean has the second highest disease prevalence (2.2 per cent) in the world. Indeed, HIV/AIDS is now one of the leading causes of death in some parts of the Caribbean.

The dangers for the male body, both those engaged in sex tourism and those that are completely outside of this sphere of activity, are multiple. Caribbean men are not immune to engaging in behaviours that place them at risk for infection by this virus. The practice of maintaining multiple sexual partners increases one's chances of contracting the disease. As Lindbald noted recently, 'silence about partners outside a relationship can result in a failure of protection. We need to challenge men to be more open, honest and sensitive with regard to relationships, family, work and sexuality as well as the overall impact of the epidemic' (2003, 1). There is a certain folk wisdom among men in the region that one's masculinity is bound up with the production of children. Often these children have different mothers. If procreation is the result of these sexual encounters, then risk prevention is not a primary consideration for these men. 'Working with and persuading men to change some attitudes and behaviours has enormous potential to change the course of the epidemic and to improve the lives of their families and their partners' (Lindbald 2003, 1-2).

Moreover, men often use their power, money or other resources to negotiate condom use, or, more specially, to avoid the use of condoms which they deem to be disruptive of their sexual pleasure. For some men also, machismo impinges on their ability to seek or acquire adequate knowledge of HIV/AIDS prevention. In other cases, however, where men are in possession of adequate information about prevention, such knowledge has not necessarily been translated into appropriately responsible behaviour. Though the 'beach boy' is particularly susceptible to infection from the AIDS virus, by virtue of his sexual practice, this should not lull other Caribbean men into a false sense of security because they do not operate within the context of the sex-tourism business. When the commodification of the practice is removed from the equation of the activity of the 'beach boy', the sexual behaviour of Caribbean men in general may simply be one of degree and not substantive difference.

Recently, the prime minster of Barbados, Owen Arthur, warned delegates of the Caribbean Regional Network of People Living with HIV/AIDS that 'one of the most talented generations in the history of the Caribbean' could be destroyed by the HIV/AIDS disease (see Dear 2003). According to the prime minister, 'The great challenge that faces the Caribbean is the challenge to remove the stigma, the phobia and the discrimination that stands in the way of the society dealing with empathy with persons who are living with HIV/AIDS' (cited in the *Daily Nation*, see Dear, 2003). The issue of HIV/AIDS and its relationship to masculinity in the spread and containment of this disease needs to be fully investigated in the Caribbean.

Resistance and the Commodified Body

There is another way of looking at the body of men who work the beaches in search of female tourists. There is a sense here in which the body also resists at a more existential level. What David Scott indexes in relation to the body of whom he calls the ruud bwai (rude boy) in Jamaica, has profound resonance with the body of the 'beach boy'. One can argue that, in similar fashion to the body of the ruud bwai, the body of the 'beach boy' is transgressive in so far as it 'disrupts the dominant regime of cultural-political truth that bodies are to be educated into a particular raced/classed regime of sensibility, breeding, and conduct. It constitutes a site of internal danger to the norms of bourgeois-liberal civility' (1999, 214). The 'beach boy' operates in the sphere of the informal sector, produced through the contradictions and crises of capital. With limited prospects for functioning in the formal labour market, he survives by mimicking the rules of capitalist practice through the commodification of his own body. In this way, he reproduces himself socially, thus freeing the state of the responsibility to look after him, but without the customary protections, rights and benefits of other workers. In these adverse conditions of existence, therefore, the 'beach boy' gains access to 'employment', sustenance, entertainment, some form of pleasure, as well as the prospect of leaving the poverty of his home-country for greener pastures abroad.

To remain with the commodified body for the moment, it is fair to say that another area of libidinal investment is the hairstyle of many 'beach boys'. Through the gaze of the female tourist, the dreadlocks hairstyle has become a powerful symbol of Caribbean masculinity and virility. Often, foreigners mistake the wearer of locks to be Rastafarian, and the young men on the beach, understanding this false association, in fact turn the perception on its head to offer female tourists a taste of the exotic. Robin, a young man without locks who works the beaches deconstructs this fascination of foreign women with dreadlocks brilliantly when he says

> They grow their hair for the tourists, because they [female tourists] all want to fuck Bob Marley. No way are they real Rastas. They stink, but the women like that. They just pick up the tourists for money, but I like to give them a good time (Bindel 2003, 4).

Though one can fully appreciate what Robin observes above, the issue might not be as cut and dried. Not all women coming down to the Caribbean, especially repeat visitors, are duped by young men wearing locks and pretending to be Rastafarians. Some of these women are fully aware that these are not fully committed Rastafarians but nevertheless want to hold on to that illusion for whatever reason works best for them. Indeed these sexual liaisons may be more performative than is immediately evident to the casual observer of the phenomenon.

If, as Grosz argues, the muscular body could in some senses be considered phallic, the sex and sexuality of the body become invested with more than mere symbolic meaning. Historically, the black body has been desired because of popular stereotypes about the size of the penis. As Stuart Hall quipped, black men are believed to have penises the size of cathedrals. It is concern over this type of mythology that would subsequently generate the attention and controversy that has surrounded the Laura Facey Cooper sculpture in Kingston, mentioned above. 'Beach boys' trade on this myth, and foreign tourists participate in the illusion, or at best are curious to find out the truth. In this regard, several articles refer to female tourists being in search of the 'big bamboo' (see de Albuquerque 1999). In addition to penis size, a certain premium is placed on sexual performance. Here there is much more of a confluence of braggadocio, satisfaction and frustration.

First, there is the boasting of Caribbean men about their sexual prowess and their ability to engage in extended periods of sexual activity. Based on published reports (see Bindel 2003 and Amber 1997, among others) there may be some truth to some of these claims. Second, there are also reports about sexual dissatisfaction with some of these men whose services are exchanged for money. They are not all happy customers in the Caribbean. Some women have complained that the combination of marijuana and alcohol, taken by some men, can lead to sexual dysfunction and general dissatisfaction (Bindel 2003 and 'The Toured' 1991 'film'). One dissatisfied customer remarked: 'I have this huge Rasta with locks down his back and I ain't got nothing. I've actually had to go and find another one for my friend because she said, "This one's no good"' (Bindel 2003, 4). One woman went as far as to suggest that she had to employ corrective strategies to deal with incompetent lovers: 'After I got wise to the ways of Jamaicans, who are very much wham, bam, thank you ma'am, I made sure I taught them all how to do it properly' (Bindel 2003, 6). Here, then, is some unbridled hubris in which not only is the other consumed sexually, but the required level of sexual satisfaction can apparently only be accomplished after the imperial tutelage of a white woman. Whatever the merits of the complaints about sexual performance associated with the dimension of the tourist experience, it points decidedly to one of the hazards of this particular vocation.

Lastly, there is a common observation that runs through many of the comments of women who have visited the Caribbean in search of sun, sand and sex, that is, a number of female tourists have commented on the attentiveness of the men whom they meet on the beach. Women have expressed appreciation for the amount of time that these men spend with them, and the uncritical admiration showered on them. A number of women have indicated that size, physical flaws or age did not seem to bother the men. Many have indicated that they had not in a long time felt as desirable as these men made them feel. Some women felt as though they could not get as handsome or as well-built a man in their home countries, while some were convinced that these men had organic links to nature which they found very appealing (see Bindel 2003; de Albuquerque 1999; Phillips 1999 and Amber 1997). Though the experiences of these women may be real, the fact remains that these men they encounter are selling their services and flattery is therefore part of their sales pitch. In the end, their uncritical disposition has much to do with the way they envisage reproducing themselves socially. It is possible, therefore, that these liaisons become so fetishised that all some women see is what they want to see, and whatever relieves them of their own alienation and disempowerment at home makes them more favourably disposed to the entreaties of strange and exotic men. The political economy of desire requires much more attention than we have given it so far in the Caribbean.

Caribbean Patriarchal Power

Elsewhere, I have addressed the institutional nature of male control and domination in the Caribbean (Lewis 2000 and 2002); I will not repeat those arguments here. Instead, drawing on the insights of Sylvia Walby, this paper will address briefly four areas of patriarchal power and domination in the region that resonate with much of what has been discussed so far. These areas involve the issues of power, the state, violence and culture in the Caribbean. In a recent address at the symposium, 'The Sovereignty of the Imagination: The Writings and Thought of George Lamming', the noted Caribbean novelist, George Lamming, reminded us of the issue of power, place and social relationships. His observation is worth repeating here.

> All relations are experienced within a particular context of power. A concept of people and place does not arise out of the blue. How you come to think of where you are and how you come to think of your relationship to where you are is very

dependent on what is the character and nature of power, where you are. You yourself do not at a certain stage decide who you are, and what your relationship to where you are should be. These relations are experienced within a specific context of power (Transcript of presentation).

The relationships between men and women, and between men and men, are characterised by patriarchal power. This power is not a benign force which simply inserts itself into these relationships, but rather it grants advantages and privileges of one group of persons over another. I have had occasion in the past to point out that patriarchy is not only about male domination over females, but also the domination of hegemonic men over subordinate men of different races, classes, ethnicities and sexual orientations (see Lewis 2003). The male/male patriarchal domination is still an undertheorised area of Caribbean scholarship in gender studies. Patriarchy is viewed largely in terms of how men subordinate women, with little attention being paid to how some men dominate other men. The nature of patriarchal power is such that it is not reducible to an individual exercise, but is collective and institutional, which provides it with multiple modalities and makes it difficult to dislodge. Power, however, always elicits its own resistance and herein resides the possibility of hope for transformation in the region.

With respect to patriarchy and the state, the relations of power seem quite clear, even though the state often represents itself as neutral and universalistic. The state, however, is central to the organisation and articulation of categories of gender relations in society. As Walby noted, 'The state is patriarchal as well as being capitalist and racist. While being a site of struggle and not a monolithic entity, the state has a systematic bias towards patriarchal interests in its policies and actions' (1990, 21). Watson writes in a recent article, 'The state and capital have a direct interest in the exploitation of workers: states and capital never miss an opportunity to exploit gender and ethnicity in order to obstruct or fracture worker solidarity' (2003, 71). Women are more adversely affected by state reform measures, they assume more of the burdens of, and experience more economic and social disarticulation as a result of the impact of global restructuring (see Narayan, et al. 2000). R.W. Connell also argues that, though the neo-liberal agenda currently embraced by many Caribbean countries purports to speak a gender-neutral language of the market, its entire orientation is masculinist. 'The attack on the welfare state generally weakens the position of women, while the increasingly unregulated power of transnational corporations places strategic power in the hands of particular groups of men' (Connell 2000, 51). The fact of the matter is, as Brown argued:

> . . . insofar as state power is, inter alia, a historical product and expression of male predominance in public life and male dominance generally, state power itself is surely and problematically gendered . . . (1995, 173-174).

Indeed, given the defence of patriarchy from certain sections of the Caribbean community alluded to at the beginning of this paper, there is little surprise that as a result of the concern over the men's current status, some women in public fora have raised the concern that important resources intended to redress biases against them, might be diverted from women's issues and directed toward fixing men's problems. There is of course an irony here which is consistent with the contradictions of capitalism, and it is captured in the observation of Ellen Meiksins Wood:

> Men who are interested in maintaining old patterns of male domination have been forced to defend them against the dissolving effects of capitalism – for instance, against the effects of growing numbers of women leaving the household to enter the wage-labour force (1995, 279).

The institutional nature of patriarchy is also felt in other areas of social reality in the region. The increased incidence of violence against women and among men themselves has become a cause for alarm and immediate action in such countries as Jamaica, Guyana, Trinidad, Haiti, Dominican Republic and Puerto Rico (see Pargass and Clarke 2003 and Racine 1999). Within the generalised violence and the crisis of civil society, is a marked increase in the violence directed at women (see Lewis 2002). Walby drew our attention to the masculinist character of this phenomenon when she noted that violence should not be considered outside of an analysis of patriarchal social structures. Men in the Caribbean, like men all over the world, operate in the context of an institutional and cultural environment in which some feel that the need to control women is crucial to the reproduction of patriarchal privilege. When that control is not immediately forthcoming, they resort to violence to secure submission or compliance with their wishes.

The upsurge of violence against women in the Caribbean, especially the wave of murders of wives and partners, by men who claim to love these women, is alarming. Male on male violence, though more customary, is also increasing and contributes to the general fear and instability within civil society. Gang warfare, drug-related crimes and violence, the use of highly sophisticated weapons in the commission of crimes, and mafia-type executions, have become the popular expressions of masculinity and masculine control. The symbolic use of violence as a trope of masculinity is also well known in the region. This symbolism is evident in the deliberate design of cars owned by young men with bullet holes inserted into the windscreen and sides of the vehicle. Even though this practice may not be widespread, it is symbolic of the role and centrality of violence in the lived experiences of some Caribbean people. This simulation of a shootout suggests not only that the owner and his crew have a capacity for violence, but that they are capable of cheating death and should therefore be feared. In this context, then, violence becomes an important part of the reproduction of patriarchal power in the Caribbean, and should be addressed appropriately through analyses of the institutional context.

Lastly, there is the issue of patriarchy and the culture of the region. Culture is a medium through which we begin to understand ourselves as gendered subjects. It is the vehicle through which patriarchal domination is normalised. Since the culture shapes all of the social institutions, and men for the most part dominate the public sphere, then it stands to reason that patriarchy becomes very solidly established in the society through culture. Again, Walby is perceptive on this institutional basis of culture:

> Patriarchal cultural institutions completes (sic) the array of structures. These are significant for the generation of a variety of gender-differentiated forms of subjectivity. This structure is composed of a set of institutions which create the representation of women within a patriarchal gaze in a variety of arenas, such as religions, education and the media (1990, 21).

It is precisely through the culture that patriarchy could be defended and legitimised by appeals to authority, religion, custom and popular practice. It is in this context that we must interpret the misogyny in the lyrics of the calypso, dancehall and bachata musical forms of the region. It is also through appeals to cultural practice that patriarchal domination in the region tends to dismiss women's claims of sexual and public harassment. The culture of the region therefore plays an invaluable role in the reproduction and integration of the infrastructure of patriarchal domination, and should never be overlooked in our discussions of gender.

Conclusion

The terrain of gender relations in the Caribbean is a shifting, constantly changing set of social arrangements and practices. Occasionally, there are tensions and even serious conflicts between men and women at work, in the home and in public places in the region. Though at some level there is the need for personal accountability for one's actions, it is perhaps useful to stand back and reflect on the structural dynamics which might be at play. Clearly, political and economic factors are not the only issues that matter but one would be foolhardy to proceed as though they do not have a strong determining influence on the formation and consciousness of identity. A failure to address these structural issues reduces the discourse on gender to a vulgar and facile phenomenal form, in which issues of femininity and masculinity are viewed as occupying some autonomous social space.

The study of masculinity is still in its infancy in the Caribbean. There are many areas of this phenomenon that require careful study. George Lamming's comment, alluded to earlier, is of course appropriate in indicating that all relations are experienced within a particular context of power. One of our responsibilities, as academics, is to theorise that context of power, to explore its structural determinants and its impact on our very corporeal selves. Beyond this point, we should also be mindful of the more subtle modalities of patriarchal power and domination in the Caribbean. If we can agree that patriarchal power, domination and privilege are inherently unjust then a manifesto of social transformation becomes an urgent political necessity. It is to this political agenda that this paper was directed. Men in the Caribbean are in no danger of being marginalised or replaced by women. What they do face, however, is continuing and sustainable contestation of patriarchal power and privilege from women and progressive men. As societies with avowedly strong democratic traditions, this should not be resisted but embraced by all.

References

Alexander, Jacqui. 1998. 'Imperial desire/sexual utopias: White gay capital and transnational tourism'. In *Talking Visions: Multicultural Feminism in a Transnational Age*, ed. Ella Shohat, 281-305. Massachusetts and London: MIT Press.

Amber, Jeannine. 1997. 'Sex on the beach'. *Essence*, October, 101-104, 161-164.

Barrow, Christine. 1998. 'Caribbean masculinity and family: Revisiting "marginality" and "reputation"'. In *Caribbean Portraits: Essays on Gender Ideologies and Identities*, ed. Christine Barrow, 339-358. Kingston: Ian Randle Publishers and The Centre for Gender and Development Studies, University of the West Indies.

Baudrillard, Jean. 2002. *Screened Out*. London and New York: Verso.

Bindel, Julie. 2003. 'The price of a holiday fling'. *Guardian Unlimited*. Saturday, July 5, 1-8. http://www.guardian.co.uk/weekend/story/0,3605,990237,00.html

Bourdieu, Pierre. 2001. *Masculine Domination*. Stanford, CA: Stanford University Press.

Connell, R W. 2002. *The Men and the Boys*. Berkeley & Los Angeles: University of California Press.

———. 2002. *Gender*. Cambridge and Oxford: The Polity Press in association with Blackwell Publishers Ltd.

de Albuquerque, Klas. 1999. 'In search of the Big Bamboo'. *Transition*, Issue 77, vol. 8, no. 1 (1999): 48-57.

de Moya, Antonio E. 2002. 'Power games and totalitarian masculinity in the Dominican Republic'. In *Caribbean Masculinities: Working Papers*, ed. Rafael Ramirez, Victor Garcia-Toro and Ineke Cunningham, 105-145. San Juan: HIV/AIDS Research and Education Center and the University of Puerto Rico.

Dear, Karin. 2003. 'HIV Taking Toll'. *Daily Nation* (electronic version). Friday October 10.

Foucault, Michel. 1980. *Power/Knowledge: Selected interviews and other writings 1972-1977*, ed. Colin Gordon. New York: Pantheon Books.

———. 1995. *Discipline and Punish*. New York: Vintage Books.

Gill, Charmaine. 1990. 'Experience the Bajan Way'. *Sunday Sun*. Section B, December 23, 1990, 1.

Gill, Rosalind. 'Rethinking masculinity: Men and their bodies'. London School of Economics and Political Science, *Fathom*, http://www.fathom.com/course/21701720/session4.html

Grosz, Elizabeth. 1994. *Volatile Bodies: Toward a Corporeal Feminism*. Bloomington and Indianapolis: Indiana University Press.

Harvey, David. 2000. *Spaces of Hope*. Berkeley & Los Angeles: University of California Press.

Lamming, George. 1992. 'Culture and Sovereignty'. In *Conversations – George Lamming: Essays, Addresses and Interviews 1953-1990*, ed. Richard Drayton and Andaiye, 283-287. London: Karia Press.

———. 2003. 'Subjugation and Transcendence: Journeys to a Caribbean Utopia'. Lecture presented at The Sovereignty of the Imagination: The Writings and Thought of George Lamming Conference, held at the Mona Campus of the University of the West Indies, Kingston, Jamaica, June 5-7.

Lewis, Eric. 1997. 'Man – an endangered species'. *The Barbados Advocate*. March 14, 11.

Lewis, Linden. 2000. 'Nationalism and Caribbean masculinity'. In *Gender Ironies of Nationalism: Sexing the Nation*, ed. Tamar Mayer, 261-281. London and New York: Routledge.

———. 2002. 'Envisioning a Politics of Change within Caribbean Gender Relations'. In *Gendered Realities: Essays in Feminist Thought*, ed. Patricia Mohammed, 512-530. Cave Hill, Mona & St Augustine: UWI Press and the Centre for Gender and Development.

———. 1990. 'Are Caribbean Men in Crisis? An Economic and Social Dilemma'. *Caribbean Affairs* 3, no. 3 (July/September): 104-112.

———. 2003. 'Caribbean Masculinity Enslaved'. Paper presented to the Society for Caribbean Studies, Bristol University, Bristol United Kingdom, July 9.

———. Forthcoming. 'Caribbean masculinity: Unpacking the narrative'. In *The Culture of Gender and Sexuality in the Caribbean*, ed. Linden Lewis, 94-125. Florida: University Press of Florida.

Lindblad, Bertil. 2003. Opening Statement at the Expert Group Meeting on the Role of Men and Boys in Achieving Gender Equality. Brasilia, Brazil, October 21-24.

McMillan, Terry. 1996. *How Stella Got Her Groove Back*. New York: Viking Press. Miller, Errol. 1986. *Marginalisation of the Black Male: Insights from the Development of the Teaching Profession*. Mona: Institute of Social and Economic Research.

———. 1991. *Men at Risk*. Kingston: Jamaica Publishing House Ltd.

Mills, Claude. 2003. '"Renude" controversy'. *Jamaica Gleaner* (electronic version). Saturday, August 4.

Mohammed, Patricia. 2002. *Gender Negotiation Among Indians in Trinidad 1917-1947*. United Kingdom and Holland: Palgrave/Institute of Social Studies.

Murray, David. 1999. 'Laws of desire? Race, Sexuality, and power in male Martinican sexual narratives'. *American Ethnologist* 26, no. 1 (1999): 160-172.

Narayan, Deepa et al. 2000. *Voices of the Poor: Can Anyone Hear Us*. New York: Oxford University Press.

Pargass, Gaietry and Roberta Clarke. 2003. 'Violence against women: A human rights issue'. In *Gender Equality in the Caribbean: Reality or Illusion*, ed. Gemma Tang Nain and Barbara Bailey, 39-72. Kingston and Guyana: Ian Randle Publishers, The CARICOM Secretariat and UNIFEM Caribbean.

Parry, Odette. 2000. *Male Underachievement in High School Education in Jamaica, Barbados and St Vincent and the Grenadines*. Barbados, Jamaica and Trinidad: Canoe Press.

Patterson, Orlando. 1969. *The Sociology of Slavery: An Analysis of the Origins, Development and Structure of Negro Slave Society in Jamaica*. Rutherford, Madison and Teaneck: Fairleigh Dickinson University Press.

Phillips, Joan L. 1999. 'Tourist-oriented prostitution in Barbados: The case of the beach boy and the white female tourist'. In *Sun, Sex and Gold: Tourism and Sex Work in the Caribbean*, ed. Kamala Kempadoo, 183-200. Lanham, Boulder and New York: Rowman & Littlefield Publishers, Inc.

Racine, Marie M.B. 1999. *Like the Dew that Waters the Grass: Words from Haitian Women*. Washington, DC: EPICA Publications.

Sampath, Niels M. 1993. 'An evaluation of the creolisation of Trinidad East Indian adolescent masculinity'. In *Trinidad Ethnicity*, ed. Kevin Yelvington, 235-253. London and Basingstoke: Macmillan Press Ltd.

Scott, David. 1999. *Refashioning Futures: Criticism After Postcoloniality*. New Jersey: Princeton University Press.

'The Toured: The Other side of Tourism in Barbados' (film). 1991. Directed by Julie Pritchard Wright. Berkeley: University of California Extension Center for Media and Independent Learning.

Trinidad Guardian. 2000. 'Men belittled in Dominica – minister'. March 18, 7.

Tuana, Nancy, William Cowling, et al., eds. 1992. *Revealing Male Bodies*. Bloomington and Indianapolis: Indiana University Press.

Walby, Sylvia. 1990. *Theorizing Patriarchy*. Oxford and Massachusetts: Basil Blackwell Inc.

Watson, Hilbourne. Forthcoming. 'The globalisation of the discourse on gender and its impact on the Caribbean'. In *The Culture of Gender and Sexuality in the Caribbean*, ed. Linden Lewis, 53-93. Florida: University Press of Florida.

Wood, Ellen Meiksins. 1995. *Democracy Against Capitalism: Renewing Historical Materialism*. Cambridge and New York: Cambridge University Press.

---

* The author would like to thank Alissa Trotz, Rishee Thakur and James Rice for their comments and suggestions on an earlier draft of this paper.

11 | CAROLYN COOPER

'Mama, Is That You?'
Erotic Disguise in the Films *Dancehall Queen* and *Babymother*

Jamaican dancehall culture is commonly disparaged as a homophobic, misogynist discourse that reduces women to bare essentials: mindless bodies, (un)dressed and on display exclusively for male sexual pleasure. Approvingly gyrating to sexually explicit lyrics (usually performed by men), the female dancehall fan, as both spectacle and spectator, does appear to be complicit in the representation of her person as sex object. Even more implicated in this discourse of objectification is the female DJ who, having upstaged her male counterpart, takes control of the mike and assumes the power to represent herself verbally and dance to her own beat. The self-assertive female DJ does speak back to the male, challenging many of the chauvinist limitations that are imposed on her gender. But, somewhat paradoxically, she often speaks the very same sexually explicit body language as the male, causing short-sighted detractors to dismiss her as being even more culpable than the male DJs – and the women in the audience who take vicarious pleasure in her daring self-exposure.

The affirmation of the erotic potential of the body that is so central to dancehall culture is often misunderstood as a devaluation of female sexuality. But dancehall body politics can be permissively theorised as an articulation of self-conscious female control over the representation of her person. Woman, as sexual being, claims the right to a self-pleasuring sexual identity that may even be explicitly homoerotic. Indeed, I propose that Jamaican dancehall culture at home and in the diaspora is best understood as a potentially liberating space in which working-class women and their more timid middle-class sisters assert the freedom to play out eroticised roles that may not ordinarily be available to them in the rigid social conventions of the everyday. The dancehall, thus conceived, is an erogenous zone in which the celebration of female sexuality and fertility is ritualised.

In *Dancehall Queen* and *Babymother*, the film medium becomes a site of transformation in which the spectacularly dressed bodies of women in the dancehall assume extraordinary proportions once projected on to the screen. In both films, one set in Jamaica, the other in the UK, the styling of the body – the hair, make-up, clothes and body language that are assumed – enhances the illusion of a fairy-tale metamorphosis of the mundane self into eroticised sex object. The fantastic un/dress code of the dancehall, in the original Greek derivation of the word 'fantastic', meaning 'to make visible', 'to show', is the visualisation of a distinctive cultural style that allows women the liberty to demonstrate the seductive appeal of the imaginary – and their own bodies. In an elaborate public striptease, transparent bedroom garments become theatrical street wear, somewhat like the emperor's new clothes. And who dares say that the body is naked? Only the naive.

Both fleshy women and their more sinewy sisters are equally entitled to display themselves in the public sphere as queens of revelry. Exhibitionism conceals ordinary imperfections. In the dancehall world of make-believe, old roles can be contested and new identities assumed. Indeed, the elaborate styling of both hair and clothes is a permissive expression of the pleasures of disguise. In the words of dancehall Diva Sandra Lee: 'The extensions add a movie look to us. . . Is like a disguise. I want to look different tomorrow'.[1]

The blurb for *Dancehall Queen* locates the film's fairy tale antecedents thus: '*Dancehall Queen* is a modern-day Cinderella story, with no Prince Charming, but one very strong woman . . .'[2] The Caribbean stereotypes of the superhuman black woman and the delinquent black man meet the European fantasy of the nurturing Prince Charming; and part company. At the centre of *Dancehall Queen* is a disguise drama in which the star, Marcia, outsmarts the Don, Larry, contriving to make him believe that she is other than her everyday self – an unglamorous street vendor, pushing a heavy cart through the streets of Kingston in the unending struggle to survive. She is the work-weary mother of two children, the older of whom, Tanya, is a nubile teenager targeted for sexual abuse by Larry, the predator, disguised as benefactor.

But Marcia is not inspired to assume the dazzling disguise of Dancehall Queen in order to seduce Larry and divert him from her daughter. Nor is it the promise of sex/romance that tempts her, though she does come to enjoy her newly discovered power to arrest Larry's attention that had been so single-mindedly focussed on Tanya. It is the prize money, which guarantees a measure of economic independence, however temporary, that motivates Marcia. Furthermore, she is inspired to succeed in her bid for the crown of Dancehall Queen by her recognition of the power of costume to enable the transformation. When Marcia encounters the reigning Dancehall Queen, Olivene, in street clothes and in the glare of daylight, she is struck by the pedestrian quality of the woman. I use 'pedestrian' deliberately because in Jamaica, as elsewhere, cars are often marketed as a fashion accessory that can add immeasurable style to their owner/occupant, somewhat like Cinderella's pumpkin chariot.[3]

The glittering strobe-light world of the dance is an idealised space in which fantastic identities are possible. Once out of costume, the glamorous fairy tale princess/ hard-core Dancehall Queen often loses her appeal. Stripped of accessories, she is put to the test and found wanting. Indeed, Marcia's incredulous and malicious comment about Olivene, 'she look[s] ordinary eeh!,' signals her own recognition of the distance between the nocturnal image and the daylight reality. When Marcia herself eventually does win the crown of Dancehall Queen, it is essential that she resume her costume as street vendor in order to reclaim her own sense of identity. But she thoroughly enjoys the fairy tale fantasy of hypersexuality that the stage properties of the dancehall engender. Indeed, the persona of 'dancehall queen' permits Marcia to reclaim the sensuality that had been repressed in the drudgery of her everyday existence. As she flaunts the wigs and other accessories so essential to her new role, she is able to attract suitors like the videographer, for whom she becomes the seductive 'mystery lady'.

The camera's eye redefines Marcia as a worthy subject of attention, bedecked in all her borrowed glory. She unashamedly revels in the male gaze. No feminist anxieties of 'objectification' disturb her. Indeed, quite early in the game, when the videographer turns his camera away from her to acknowledge the presence of reigning Dancehall Queen Oilvene, Marcia gets into a huff. She wants to be the singular focus of the videographer's attention. In an illuminating essay entitled 'Is the Gaze Feminist? Pornography, Film and Feminism' Maggie Humm observes that:

> The gaze is both a metaphor in film criticism and an integral part of film discourse and narrative. Laura Mulvey first introduced the idea that men looking at women in film use two forms of mastery over her: a sadistic voyeurism which controls women's sexuality through dominating male characters, and a symbolic fetishisation of women's sexuality. Mulvey shows that cinema enables this male gaze to create the illusion, through a complicated system of point-of-view, that the male spectator is producing the gaze. The male character carries the gaze of the male spectator as his assistant. Women are objectified erotic objects existing in film simply as recipients of the male gaze. The aim, then, for Mulvey is to explain the function of film in the erotic violation of women by revealing its system of voyeuristic pleasure. To Mulvey, feminist directors have only to generate new notions of female sexuality by using *avant-garde* practices of spectator-film relationships in order to deconstruct the scopic gaze.[4]

Humm, conceding in a footnote that Mulvey has 'modified her position to give a much more sophisticated account of the gaze', does acknowledge the centrality of the latter's early work in theorising the gaze. Nevertheless, Humm argues for an even more subtle reading of the politics of spectatorship that recognises the pleasure that women as agents do take in desiring and being desired:

> Mulvey's criticism has done a lot to help us examine the question of the gendered spectator, yet, because her method derives from psychoanalytic accounts, via Lacan, of the formation of female subjectivity, it allows little scope for analysing female subjectivity in its semiotic or social discourses. Mulvey sets up too rigid a divide between visual analysis and contextual discourse. In any case, psychoanalysis has not dealt adequately with desire, since it does not read sexuality as that which must be continually produced.[5]

In Marcia's case, desire – both hers and that of the videographer – rehumanises her, putting her at centre-stage. And even after she is stripped of her disguise she remains attractive to her videographer. The persona of dancehall queen thus generates residual benefits for Marcia who now transfers to her 'real' life the embodied power which her fantasy had bestowed.

Shape-shifting and mistaken identities are familiar motifs in folk tales of many cultures. In the Caribbean, popular stories of both West African and European origin encode disguise dramas. Alice Werner's scholarly 'Introduction' to Walter Jekyll's 1907 collection, *Jamaican Song and Story*, concludes with an analysis of five stories which are classified as of the 'Robber Bridegroom' type, 'the Robber being the equivalent of an earlier wizard or devil, who, in the primitive form of the story, was simply an animal assuming human shape'. Werner elaborates:

The main incidents of the type-story are as follows:

(1) A girl obstinately refuses all suitors.
(2) She is wooed by an animal in human form, and at once accepts him.
(3) She is warned (usually by a brother) and disregards the warning.
(4) She is about to be killed and eaten, but is saved by the brother whose advice was disregarded.[6]

Though Werner observes that '[i]n the Jamaican stories it strikes one that the idea of transformation is somewhat obscured', she nevertheless does concede that various disguises *are* assumed by the Robber Bridegrooms to facilitate their duping of the gullible brides. Indeed, Werner notes that 'Rabbit', an unsuccessful suitor, 'takes no steps to change his shape, being rejected on the ground that he is "only but a meat" *i.e.*, an animal'.[7]

Dress thus becomes an essential sign of the assumed human identity. Werner summarises the argument thus:

> We are told how 'Gaulin' (Egret) and 'John Crow' provide themselves with clothes and equipages – the latter a carriage and pair, the former the humbler buggy – and this seems to constitute the extent of the disguise. Yellow Snake is said to 'change and fix up himself' – but the expression is vague. Gaulin, however, can only be deprived of his clothes (and so made to appear in his true shape) by means of a magic song. The 'old-witch' brother, who has overheard the song, plays its tune at the wedding and thus exposes the bridegroom, who flies out the door. 'John-Crow' is detected by a Cinderella-like device of keeping him til daylight, and his hurried flight through the window (in which he scraped the feathers off his head on the broken glass) explains a characteristic feature of these useful but unattractive birds.[8]

Contemporary dancehall culture in Jamaica discloses new variants of the shape-shifting motifs that are inscribed in traditional folk tales. Assuming the disguises of dancehall aesthetics, empresses of style, like Marcia, can fulfil complicated sexual fantasies. Like the animals of folk tale that deploy human dress to seduce the objects of their desire, marginalised working-class black women in Jamaica now assume the habits of seduction to full advantage. For example, in the putting on of wigs, weaves and extensions in various hues, 'picky-picky head' women go to all lengths to claim the sex appeal that is perceived to reside naturally in 'tall-hair' women, as evidenced in the dominant images of pin-up female sexiness in the mainstream media in Jamaica and elsewhere.[9]

Hairpieces do for some women what dreadlocks, and the even more fashionable 'sisterlocks', do for others. Although length and volume of store-bought hair are valorised, height is also crucial and adds another layer of constructed beauty that altogether bears absolutely no resemblance to contemporary eurocentric modes of hairstyling. Dancehall hairstyles are engineered and require sophisticated technical skills for their construction. Indeed, this dancehall hair-extension aesthetic must be acknowledged as a contemporary expression of traditional patterns of hair and body adornment in continental Africa, which have now gloriously re-emerged in the diaspora. As they flash their Rapunzel tresses, these dancehall divas, appropriating the border-crossing potential of disguise, simultaneously reinscribe and subvert the racial ideology that devalues the 'natural' beauty of African-Jamaican women and undermines their self-esteem.

In her entertaining and instructive ethnographic study, *Hair Matters: Beauty, Power, and Black Consciousness*, Ingrid Banks confronts the subject of the politics of hair head-on. In the chapter, 'Splitting Hairs: Power, Choice and Femininity' she documents the voices of women who assert their right to self-definition, and identifies the often contradictory politics of liberation that is manifested in the hairstyling choices of African-American women, and, by extension, their Caribbean sisters:

> An important critique of the self-hatred account of hair alteration is that it does not take into consideration hairstyling practices that reflect how black women exercise power and choice, as some women noted in chapter 2 ['The Hair 'Do's' and 'Don'ts'

of Black Womanhood']. The possibility that hairstyling practices, in whatever form, serve as a challenge to mainstream notions of beauty or that they allow black women to embrace a positive identity is important for two reasons: voice and empowerment. Voice is important for marginalized groups in U.S. society, and it is through voice that black women are not merely victims of oppression. Instead, black women are agents or thinking and acting beings who understand the forces that shape their lives.[10]

In the words of Flip Wilson, that irreverent African-American wit, 'When you look good, you feel good; and when you feel good you move good'.

A similarly sophisticated reading of the make-up practices of black women must take into account the many shades of meaning that the brush paints. In some instances, make-up does function explicitly to mask/erase distinctly 'African' features. Techniques for reducing the width of the nose, for example, require a subtle play of light and shade to highlight the bridge of the nose and downplay the surrounding flesh. Nevertheless, there is an element of pure artistry and empowering aesthetic pleasure in the practice of making-up that should not be denigrated. Writing out of the inter-discipline of British fashion studies, Catherine Constable, like Ingrid Banks, underscores conceptions of the mask of make-up as 'that which foregrounds its own constructedness and therefore possesses a kind of truthfulness'.[11] In the conclusion to her fascinating essay, 'Making Up the Truth: On Lies, Lipstick and Friedrich Nietzsche', she elaborates this argument:

> Once the mask is not viewed as purely patriarchal, or merely indicative of the absence of truth, it becomes a construct that can be mobilised in a variety of ways. This means that the mask can be seen to generate a wide variety of possible meanings rather than simply and reductively indicating its status as 'untruth' or the 'untruth of truth'. Furthermore, the analysis of the mask as truthful clearly has important implications for feminism in that it radically destabilises the definition of glamour as objectification. This creates a space for thinking about the radical potential of the power to hold the gaze and the ways in which that power might be instantiated by a range of female icons.[12]

The title of Banks' book clearly signifies on Cornel West's *Race Matters*. It thus asserts that what is essentially a feminised discourse – the politics of black hair – demands just as much critical attention as those more conventional domains in which the racialised politics of identity is addressed – such as is the predominantly masculine arena of sports. By thus equating 'race' and 'hair', Banks elevates a 'woman's' issue to the centre of discourse. If race matters, hair matters as much because hair marks socially constructed racial difference. In her 'Introduction: Unhappy to be Nappy', Banks observes that '[t]he research presented in the following pages is not about hair per se. *Hair Matters* illustrates how hair shapes black women's ideas about race, gender, class, sexuality, images of beauty, and power'.[13]

Cornel West's argument about the perverse consequences of racist representations of the black body in the American imaginary is especially acute when applied to black women. Though West's choice of 'refusal' unconscionably intimates that the victim wilfully embraces denigration, he, nevertheless, accurately delineates the history of trauma:

> ... [M]uch of black self-hatred has to do with the refusal of many black Americans to love their black bodies – especially their black noses, hips, lips, and hair. Just as many white Americans view black sexuality with disgust, so do many black Americans – but for different reasons and with different results. White supremacist ideology is based first and foremost on the degradation of black bodies in order to control them. One of the best ways to instill fear in people is to terrorize them. Yet this fear is best sustained by convincing them that their bodies are ugly, their intellect is inherently underdeveloped, their culture is less civilized, and their future warrants less concern than that of other peoples.[14]

In the patriarchal politics of most societies women, are required to be beautiful, unlike men who are allowed to be their natural selves, however ugly. In the derisory words of the self-important male character, Ubana, in the novel *The Joys of Motherhood*, written by the Nigerian Buchi Emecheta: '[a] woman may be ugly and grow old, but a man is never ugly and never old. He matures with age and is dignified'.[15] For many African-diaspora women, the politics of beauty is complicated by racism. Unlike their African sisters, for whom beauty was traditionally defined in indigenous terms, many African women in the diaspora are judged by standards of beauty based on non-African phenotypes. Faced with these marks of erasure, many African-diaspora women have had to settle for being sexy, instead of beautiful.

There is an old Guyanese joke about an African-Guyanese entrant in a beauty contest in the mid-sixties. The story was told to an African-Guyanese woman who worked at Fogarty's, a Georgetown store which tended to have a disproportionately high percentage of Portuguese and other light-skinned employees. The unsuccessful beauty contestant is alleged to have responded thus to a malicious question about how she fared in the competition:

> For figure and face
> I ain't mek no place
> But for bubby an arse
> Ah bus deh rass.[16]

Not all African-diaspora women share the confidence of this contestant. In fact, the beauty contest culture in Jamaica, for example, still privileges the 'browning', and occasionally the 'white' woman, as the ideal phenotype to represent this 'out of many, one people' nation in international beauty competitions.[17]

Furthermore, there is a disturbing trend in the Caribbean today for black women to bleach their skin in an attempt to approximate the standards of Euro-American ideal beauty, especially its mulatto variant. This bleaching of the skin – usually only the face and neck – is an obvious attempt to partially disguise the racial identity of the subject. The mask of 'lightness', however dangerous in medical terms, becomes a therapeutic signifier of status in a racist society that still privileges melanin deficiency as a sign of beauty. And there is decided ambivalence about the use of these bleaching agents. Some obvious bleachers, when confronted with the question, 'why yu a bleach?' [why are you bleaching?], cunningly attempt to conceal the evidence. A recurring explanation for the 'coolness' of the skin is the claim 'is because mi work in air condition office'. This adds yet another layer of disguise to the subject, for many such respondents may, in fact, be unemployed.

For me, the most alluring account of this refusal to admit that one is bleaching the skin comes from a young woman who sells in Kingston's Papine market, whose face, all of a sudden, began to assume an unusual ghostly whiteness, a vivid contrast with the rest of her body. When I nosily commented on what had happened to her face and asked her why she was bothering to bleach, she rather airily informed me that I was mistaking her for her sister. Now it is true that this young woman does have a sister who is a little darker than she, and who sometimes sells in the market as well. But I know them both well enough not to confuse them. An equally nosy man who works in the market observed in a stage whisper, 'is because she know seh she spoil up herself mek she a tell yu bout a her sister'. [it's because she knows that she's spoilt herself why she's telling you that she's her sister.] In this young woman's case, role play manifested a clear desire to deny her basic identity. She has since stopped bleaching, her natural skin colour has returned and every now and then I jokingly ask her how her sister is doing. She laughs. *With* me, I hope.

It is not only women who feel obliged to wear the mask, as the following anecdote illustrates. A panel discussion was held in December 1999 at the Mona Common Basic School where students in the Caribbean Institute of Media and Communication at the University of West Indies were screening a video on bleaching that they had made in that community as part of a research project on the theme, 'Love the Skin You're In'. At the event, a young man who had participated in the study acknowledged the fact that bleaching was harmful to the skin and said he was planning to stop. But he is a DJ who knows the value of looking good on his own terms. Let me recount his explanation, not quite *verbatim*, but as best I can recall it, for why he would continue to bleach for a little while longer: 'Christmas a come an mi ha fi look good. Mi a go gwaan bleach. An when yu see mi ready fi go out, mi a go put on one long sleeve ganzie and wear mi cap. An dem wi tink a one browning a come through'. [Christmas is coming and I have to look good. I'm going to continue bleaching. And when I'm ready to go out, I'm going to put on a long-sleeved jersey and wear my cap. And they will think that it's a browning coming through.]

First of all, I felt perversely obliged to disabuse the young man of that fantasy. No one, I told him, would ever mistake him for a browning. And, in any case, he needed to look in the mirror and see that he was perfectly handsome as a black person. Shades of Michael Jackson hover gloomily in the colonised imagination. In *Flyboy in the Buttermilk: Essays on Contemporary America*, cultural critic Greg Tate gives a 'fanciful' and 'empathetic' re-reading of the psychology of skin-bleaching in a chapter entitled 'I'm White!: What's Wrong with Michael Jackson':

There are other ways to read Michael Jackson's blanched skin and disfigured African features than as signs of black self-hatred become self-mutilation. Waxing fanciful, we can imagine the boy-who-would-be-white a William Gibson-ish work of science fiction: harbinger of a trans-racial tomorrow where genetic deconstruction has become the norm and Narcissism wears the face of all human Desire. Musing empathetic, we may put the question, who does Mikey want to be today? The Pied Piper, Peter Pan, Christopher Reeve, Skeletor, or Miss Diana Ross? Our Howard Hughes? Digging into our black nationalist bag, Jackson emerges a casualty of America's ongoing race war – another Negro gone mad because his face does not conform to the Nordic ideal.

To fully appreciate the sickness of Jackson's savaging of his African physiognomy you have to recall that back when he wore the face he was born with, black folk thought he was the prettiest thing since sliced sushi.[18]

Though I am amused by Tate's conflicted reading of Michael Jackson – 'Jackson and I are the same age, damn near 30, and I've always had a love-hate thing going with the brother'[19] – in retrospect, I do seriously wonder about the appropriateness of my intended reprimand to my skin-bleaching DJ. Not just the issue of my bad manners in pointing out the obvious, but more so the haunting question of whether or not the young man's understanding of what he was doing was much more sophisticated than I was then willing to allow. For what remains so fascinating in this young man's narrative is his rather practical sense of seasonal brownness. He knew that being brown, however achieved, was not really an essential part of his identity. Light skin colour was a fashion accessory that would stand him in good stead during the festive season. Somewhat like the bright lights that decorate the Christmas landscape, light skin colour, however fleeting, would give the DJ added visibility. The metaphor thus underscores both the elements of fantasy as well as the conscious awareness of role-play that are so subtly intertwined in these dancehall discourses of desire.

Furthermore, the DJ's metaphor of 'coming through' signals his conception of the colour line as a barrier that must be literally breached, so that he can become socially visible. And it takes a lot of cunning, Anansi-style, to make the breakthrough possible. Rupturing categories, role-play thus both emancipates and imprisons the 'real' self. In the words of Nigerian cultural critic Bibi Bakere-Yusuf:

> The black skin (or the 'racial epidermal schema' as Fanon calls it) becomes the sign of radical otherness, of impurities and degeneracy, within the European imaginary. However, through numerous efforts, the skin has often become the very vehicle by which epidermal negation is confronted, contested and negotiated by black people, in order to (re)assert their own humanity.[20]

This predilection for playing the other – i.e. playing mas' – underscores a hidden continuity between the annual rituals of carnival masquerading in other Caribbean societies and the daily gestures of dissimulation in real-time Jamaican culture and its heightened forms of expression in the dancehall. The importation of an adulterated Trinidad carnival aesthetic into Jamaican popular culture has resulted in the cross-fertilisation of traditions of role-play in which costume, dance and music are primal signifiers. And just as the Byron Lee carnival aesthetic creates a platform for predominantly upper/middle-class brown and white Jamaicans to seemingly abandon respectability, parade their nakedness in the streets and 'get on bad' i.e. pass for black, on their terms, even so everyday Jamaican dancehall culture permits the black majority to enjoy the pleasures of release from the prison of identity that limits the definition of the person to one's social class and colour.

There are, it is all too true, profound psycho-sociological underpinnings of this desire to be/play the other that cannot be simply written off as mere entertainment. Role-play both conceals and reveals deep-seated anxieties about the body which has been incised with the scarifications of history. Half a century later, Frantz Fanon's 1952 *Black Skin, White Masks* remains the classic account of this dehumanising process and its subversion:

> For several years certain laboratories have been trying to produce a serum for 'denegrification'; with all the earnestness in the world, laboratories have sterilized their test tubes, checked their scales, and embarked on researches that might make it possible for the miserable Negro to whiten himself and thus to throw off the burden of that corporeal malediction. Below the corporeal schema I had sketched a historico-racial schema. The elements that I used had been provided for me . . . by the other, the white man, who had woven me out of a thousand details, anecdotes, stories.[21]

Echoing Fanon, Bibi Bakere-Yusuf gives an incisive postmodernist reading of the mask of bleaching in African/diasporic cultures:

The erstwhile superior logic of white flesh is critiqued and exposed as part of a wider field of representation and scopic economy that tries to evade and mask its own investment in representation. Skin bleaching is therefore less a blind or bland imitation of an original and more of a practice whereby the original is presented as a construction that can be taken up, reordered, skewed and jammed in a way that becomes meaningful to the agent. For example, the very women who favour bleaching are also concerned to have full and voluptuous bodies – the antithesis of the kind of bodily figure that goes with such a phenotype. In this respect, bleaching skin can be seen as a superficial form of styling, nothing more than an appropriative aestheticisation of a bodily form, a simple borrowing from another representational regime. In this sense, bleaching certainly has little to do with a desire for dancehall women to become that which they are miming. As a superficial form of styling, bleaching can be thought of as another form of adornment, along the same lines as wearing green or pink wigs or wearing latex batty riders.[22]

This 'denaturing' impulse in Jamaican dancehall aesthetics is evident not only in the rituals of skin bleaching but also in another alarming new development – the ingestion by some women of the 'chicken pill', the hormones used in the highly mechanised production of poultry to accelerate the fattening of the goods for the market. The metaphorical colloquialism 'chick', used as a term of endearment for females, becomes all too literal in this context. Short-circuiting the process of getting the 'benefits' of eating the hormone-packed chicken itself, some Jamaican women experiment on themselves to construct the *mampi*-sized body that is so highly valorised in the culture: large breasts and bottoms. In the words of Buju Banton:

Jamaican:

Gyal, yu body good
A fatness a do it dis year
Now listen Buju Banton, massive an crew
Spread out!
Mampi size, dat a di lick
An all mawga gyal yu better get fat quick
Yu hear me?

Mampi size, dat a di lick
An all mawga gyal yu better get fat quick
No man no want no uman if yu mawga like stick
Uman, yu ha fi look fat like a mud fish
Gyal, yu body ha fi ready an copacetic

Anything come yu way yu can manage it
So if a man a form fool yu wi lick him fi six

I am a mawga man an Buju tall an skinny
An mi no waan no lickle gyal who mawga like me
Every day mi get up a cry fi di mampi
So if a heavy she heavy she ha fi kill mi
But a one thing mi know, seh Buju naa run from it [23]

English:

Girl, your body is good
Fatness is what's cutting it this year
Now listen to Buju Banton, massive and crew
Spread out!
Maxi size, that's the hit
An all meagre girls you'd better get fat quickly
Do you hear me?
Maxi size, that's the hit
An all meagre girls you'd better get fat quick
No man wants a woman if you're meagre like a stick
Woman, you have to look fat like a mud fish
Girl, your body has to be ready for action and fit
Anything comes your way you can manage it
So if a man is forming the fool you will send him packing

I am a meagre man and Buju is tall an skinny
An I don't want a skinny girl who is as meagre as me
Every day I wake and cry for a big-bodied woman
So if she's heavy, she'll have to kill me with it
But there's one thing I know, Buju is not running away from it

The dancehall thus constitutes a paradoxical social space in which the 'natural' as a marker of identity is both contested and re-instituted and sexuality, especially that of the large-bodied woman, is celebrated with abandon.

In *Dancehall Queen*, Marcia's daughter, Tanya, is incredulous when she discovers her mother rehearsing the role of dancehall queen: 'Mama, is that you?' The eroticisation of motherhood is the ultimate manifestation of the abandonment of traditional definitions of woman as desexualised caregiver. In both *Dancehall Queen* and *Babymother*, motherhood is a condition that conceals the erotic potential of the woman. The sexuality of the older woman that is usually disguised by her role as mother is released in the taking on of the persona of dancehall queen. This re-eroticisation of motherhood challenges the presumption that, after a certain age and especially after child-bearing, the woman naturally loses her sex appeal and must be replaced by a younger woman – often her very own daughter, in circumstances in which the woman's putative mate is sexually attracted to his supposed step-daughter.

Somewhat surprisingly in *Dancehall Queen* the woman is complicit in the sexual exploitation of her daughter. She functions as a pimp, procuring her daughter for Larry. Yet another layer of disguise: it is her concern for her family's economic well-being that precipitates the decision to sacrifice the daughter. But Tanya is devastated by Larry's predatory desire for her since she acknowledges him as a father figure. The enforced sexual relationship that Marcia engineers for her daughter is thus not only rapacious but incestuous. Yet, beneath the apparent heartlessness of the mother's action lies a somewhat pragmatic assessment of her daughter's options: since there is a juvenile suitor in the offing and Tanya seems likely to become sexually active, she might as well get maximum economic returns on the sexual transaction. Ironically, when Marcia herself convincingly assumes the role of Dancehall Queen, Larry's attention is deflected from Tanya who is now free to enjoy the innocent pleasures of friendship with her age-mate.

In *Babymother*, Anita struggles to claim an identity other than mother. For her, the dancehall is a creative space in which another identity as artist can be consummated. As DJ, not mere spectator, she envisions a potential identity that is obscured by the conservative gender ideology that imprisons woman in the role of supportive partner to the male star. Asserting her own power to create lyrics about her reality as babymother, Anita celebrates both her acceptance of the responsibilities of mothering as well as her escape from the constraints that motherhood often imposes on women. As songwriter and performer she is free to reflect on her own experience, thus transforming the burden of mothering into the raw material of art. The glamorisation of the male performer is now matched by the glamorisation of the baby mother as artist.

Anita's babyfather, Don Byron, a reggae superstar, refuses to support her bid to become a star in her own right. He is the quintessential robber bridegroom, the animal in human form, who intends to imprison his babymother in her rightful place within the domestic sphere. He promises Anita that he will perform a duet with her at a major show and then lets her down, revealing his true colours:

> Byron: A wa yu a do? [What are you doing?] Dis is di place fi di mother of my children. Not di stage. We don't need more than one musician in dis family.
>
> Anita: Hold on! Who are you to tell me how to be a mother? Since when please? Why shouldn't I be out there chatting the mike?
>
> Byron: Cause you're my babymother, that's why.
>
> Anita: What kind of reason is that for anything, yu dyam [damned] fool you?[24]

The pathos of Anita's struggle is intensified by the knowledge that she is valiantly attempting to do what her own mother, Rose, could not – taking on the responsibilities of bringing up a child on her own. As in *Dancehall Queen*, there is an inset disguise drama in *Babymother*. For Rose, now the successful solicitor, teenage sexual indiscretion and its usual outcome, pregnancy, had had to be disguised in the fiction of indirect affiliation. Not having been offered the expected option of marriage to her delinquent partner, and refusing abortion, the teenage mother chooses the illusion of respectability, a choice which her daughter cannot respect. Rose, passing as her daughter's sister, gives up the child to the care of her own mother because she could not cope with the very conditions of poverty that now circumscribe Anita's life:

> Rose: It was impossible you know. I was so young. Where would we be now? Mom could give you things. You would have just grown up living from hand to mouth . . .
>
> Anita: On an estate [in the projects] like this? Like Saffron and Anton?
>
> Rose: Listen, Anita, I'm really having a hard time with this.
>
> Anita: And you, a babymother like me. Yeah. Scraping food. Going nowhere.
>
> Rose: No. Yes, but . . .
>
> Anita: I'm busy, Rose.
>
> (Slams door)

Rose's story is an archetypal Caribbean tale. Another popular variant is the mother's disguising herself as the aunt of her daughter. For example, in Olive Senior's short story, 'Lily, Lily', the truth of the relationship between mother and daughter, both named Lily, is graphically foreshadowed in the daughter's intuitive reconfiguration of the family pictures she scrutinises, looking for clues to unlock the puzzle. The pun on 'gilt' encodes the politics of betrayal that is central to the disguise drama:

> When the thoughts come crowding in she returns to the mama-lily game which she played endlessly as a small child in Mama's room with the high bureau with the pictures she had to climb on a chair to look at. The pictures in the double gilt frame of Mama and Auntie Lily. Mama and Auntie Lily so alike it was hard to tell them apart, so alike when she played the game of looking from one to the other ever so fast her head spun and they merged into the one she saw in the mirror every morning of Lily-the-child, as if she were their child. She felt guilty whenever she thought this, as if she were betraying Mama whom she loved more than anyone in the world. So why, as she got older did she fancy that she looked more like Auntie Lily, wanted more and more to be with Auntie Lily, become Auntie Lily?[25]

Despite the stigma attached to teenage pregnancy or, more generally, pregnancy out of wedlock, folk wisdom acknowledges the fact that the very mother who laments the fall of her daughter into premature motherhood, especially if this pregnancy repeats the narrative of her own sexual history, is often seduced into joyous acceptance of the catastrophe when she sees the beautiful child that results from the apparent social disaster. Further, many such women quickly resign themselves to the status of premature grandmotherhood, reclaiming that estate from its conventional associations with decrepitude and asexuality.

In addition, the high level of teenage pregnancy and childbirth among working-class girls in Jamaica and the diaspora is probably matched by the high level of teenage pregnancy and abortion among middle-class girls. Class privilege, which allows varying access to abortion as a moral and economic option, masks the similarity between the sexual practices of working-class and middle-class girls. Many sexually active middle-class girls are protected from the consequences of their actions in ways that are not usually available to working-class girls.

In both *Dancehall Queen* and *Babymother*, erotic disguise functions on various levels. The trope of the 'robber bridegroom' is central to my reading of both texts. For these films are adapted reinscriptions of traditional folk tale in which both bride and groom are now robbers. Both men and women employ subterfuge to best each other. The disguise motif is not limited to the eroticised adornment of the body. Disguise enables the exploration of more profound issues of betrayal as predatory animal nature, unsuccessfully concealed by the mask of the human face, stalks its victims. In both films, the female stars are rescued from their robber bridegrooms. But the message of these cautionary tales is not just the fiction of the happy ending. Equally important is the warning that the patterns of seduction and entrapment encoded in folk tales are archetypes, surviving in the contemporary dancehall in new guises.

Notes

1. Sandra Lee, interviewed on Anthony Miller's 'Entertainment Report', broadcast on Television Jamaica, Friday, April 23, 1999. Donna Hope describes Sandra Lee thus in her MPhil dissertation, 'Inna Di Dancehall Dis/place: Socio-cultural Politics of Identity in Jamaica', University of the West Indies, Mona, 2001, 91: 'She lays claim to a legacy of urban, inner-city/downtown Kingston background and higgler/dancehall heritage that places her in a position of royalty in the dancehall dis/place. Her arrival at any dancehall event, major, minor or otherwise is heralded by an announcement over the sound system and her high status in the dancehall dis/place is consistently re-presented and legitimised by the consistent symbolising and legitimising of her presence at this event'.
2. *Dancehall Queen*, Dirs. Don Letts & Rick Elgood, Island Jamaica Films, Island Digital Media, 1997.
3. A personal anecdote will illustrate the point: One of my former students at the University of the West Indies, who works at an upmarket car sales company, tried unsuccessfully to get me to trade in my entirely trustworthy Honda Accord for an Audi A4. One of her 'compelling' arguments was that I would look so good in the car. I managed to convince her that, for me, a car is not primarily a fashion accessory.
4. Maggie Humm, 'Is the Gaze Feminist? Pornography, Film and Feminism' in eds. Gary Day and Clive Bloom, 70-71, *Perspectives on Pornography: Sexuality in Film and Literature*, (London: Macmillan, 1988).
5. Ibid., 71.
6. Walter Jekyll, ed. *Jamaican Song and Story*, London: David Nutt, 1907, xxxvi.
7. Ibid., xxxvii.
8. Ibid.
9. 'Picky-picky head,' derogatory Jamaican creole expression. The *Dictionary of Jamaican English* cites the following 1960 usage: 'when a girl's hair is very short, grows close to the scalp in little balls of fluff, very negroid'.
10. Ingrid Banks, *Hair Matters: Beauty Power, and Black Consciousness*, (New York: New York University Press, 2000), 69.

11. Catherine Constable, 'Making Up the Truth: On Lies, Lipstick and Friedrich Nietzsche' in *Fashion Cultures: Theories, Explorations and Analysis*, eds. Stella Bruzzi and Pamela Church Gibson, (London: Routledge, 2000) 191.
12. Ibid., 199.
13. Ingrid Banks, *Hair Matters: Beauty Power, and Black Consciousness*, (New York: New York University Press, 2000) 3.
14. Cornel West, *Race Matters*, (Boston: Beacon Press, 1993), 85.
15. Buchi Emecheta, *The Joys of Motherhood*, 1979; rpt. (London: Heinemann, 1980), 71.
16. For this anecdote, I am indebted to Professor Hubert Devonish of the Department of Language, Linguistics & Philosophy at the University of the West Indies, Mona, Jamaica. A rough translation of the verse: 'For figure and face I didn't place; but for boobs and arse I busted their arse'.
17. 'Browning' is Jamaican slang for 'mulatto', and is usually applied to the female.
18. Greg Tate, *Flyboy in the Buttermilk: Essays on Contemporary America*, (New York: Fireside Simon & Schuster, 1992, 95).
19. Ibid.
20. Bibi Bakere-Yusuf in email correspondence with me, January 10, 2003.
21. Frantz Fanon, *Black Skin, White Masks*, 1952; rpt (New York: Grove Press, 1967), 111.
22. Bibi Bakere-Yusuf in email correspondence with me, January 10, 2003.
23. Buju Banton, 'Gal You Body Good', Track 1, *Buju Banton Meets Garnett Silk and Tony Rebel at the Super Stars Conference*, Rhino Records, RNCD 2033 n.d.
24. *Babymother*, Dir. Julian Henriques, Formation Films, Film Four Distributors, 1998.
25. Olive Senior, *Arrival of the Snake-Woman and Other Stories*, (London: Longman Caribbean, 1989), 121.

12 | JUNE ANN CASTELLO

Shake that 'Booty' in Jesus' Name
The Possibilities of a Liberation Theology of the Body for the Body of Christ in Jamaica

Background

In the decade of the nineties when Jamaica's internationally acclaimed DJ, Beenie Man, released the hit song entitled 'Shake that Booty', a great deal of public outcry and discussion emerged. There was concern expressed about the appropriateness of the sensual focus on the body in what was purported to be a gospel album with the title 'Gospel Time Again'. The fact that the track also included a medley of traditional Jamaican gospel songs was not enough to rescue the song or the artiste from the opprobrium of those who felt that such matters were not the proper focus of the good news. This was no doubt an extension of the ritualistic confrontation of moral Jamaica with the DJ and dancehall culture. As Cooper (1994) shows in *Noises In The Blood,* much of what happens in the dancehall can be seen as the subversion of high culture by a low culture slackness that insists on the public ventilation of supposedly private female bodies. The dancehall, according to Cooper, is a space that is 'liberated from the repressive respectability of a conservative gender ideology of female property and propriety'. The body then becomes an important site for the demarcating of boundaries of propriety.

In the opening paragraph of 'Bodies and Biology', Linda Birke makes the statement that perhaps best sets out the grounds for the kind of investigation and discussion that this paper seeks to undertake. She says, 'Our bodies are ourselves: yet we are more than our bodies' (1998, 42). The body, ubiquitous form and spirit that it is, is a taken-for-granted site of discursive colonisation as various discourses, theology and feminist thought among them, have treated the body as a text on which to inscribe meanings that have been influenced by their various philosophies and these have, in turn, given shape to the particular discourses. While it has served as the testing site for all knowledge and theory, it is dismissed largely as the inferior other of the mind. It is described variously as 'a familiar form of incorporeal abstraction' (Shildrick and Price 1999), in philosophy as 'a source of interference in, and a danger to, the operation of reason' (Grosz 1994) as well as a site for the interplay of physicality and text which produces a body which is never one, never static but always multiple and fluid. The human body, whatever its interpretation, is crucial to our understanding of self and the societies we inhabit.

The struggle in Jamaica over the meanings attached to the body was relatively recently foregrounded when the 'healthy body' statues created by Laura Facey for Emancipation Park were subjected to rigorous enquiry revolving around their muted sexuality or the lack thereof. However, beyond the particular issues that have been raised by Western philosophy about the body itself are those issues that have been raised about the female body. Popular discussion in the media also focuses on the way that 'permissive' cultures such as dancehall cheapen respect for the female body and this discussion reinforces the notion of the body as a voiceless cultural script that must be invested with voice(s) and meaning(s). The Christian Church seems to be conflicted on the nature and place of the body, particularly the female body, which has been demonised and linked to sin, especially sexual sin. In Jamaica, which country can be considered at least, a religious society, if not a Christian one, congregations are, in large measure, made up of women. The Church, as the Body of Christ, articulates its mission as being that of seeking and saving the lost. Those to be saved are made up of both body and soul but it is the body that seems to present the greatest hindrance to the salvation of the soul.

This paper seeks to explore the contradictions in Christianity's treatment of the body and how the Church's construction of the female body constrains the participation of Jamaican women in the Christian faith. It also attempts to look at the possible components of a liberation theology of the body for the Church in Jamaica. It is intended to be an initial attempt at assessing these issues and, hence, does not present itself as a final or full explication. It is intended be suggestive and not conclusive. I recognise that issues of corporeality and how these are understood within religious practices and philosophy cannot be confined exclusively within the discussion of Christianity: West African Syncretic religions and Orisha should provide useful information for the investigation into such a topic. However, these will not be examined at this time in this paper.

I shall first examine the ways in which the body has been produced and reproduced in Western philosophy which will, of necessity, include discussion on the way that Judeo-Christianity has treated with the body. I shall then review the various explanations of the body offered by feminist theory, some of which follow the trends set by Western philosophy and others which set themselves the explicit task of interrogating and reconstructing matters of corporeality. I shall then make the case for a theology of the body which adopts the principles of liberation theology and try to deduce the constituent elements of such a theology.

It is useful, at this point, for me to provide the working definition of sexuality which informs the discussion in this paper. Sexuality, as we currently understand it, is linked to the term 'sex' which refers to having sex(ual) relations). The term sex is also used to refer to a category of person (as in biological sex) and to a gender. Described by Foucault as 'the truth of our being', sexuality refers to any or some of the combination of gender identity, bodily differences, reproductive capacities, needs, desires and fantasies (Weeks 2002). To the extent that gender provides the basis for differential sexual behaviour, one's gender identity contributes to the way one imagines, experiences and 'performs'[1] sexuality in terms of expressed needs, pleasurable desires and private fantasies. Bodily differences have been understood to be the basis of appropriate sexual relations as our conceptualisation of appropriate sexual relations is firmly tied to the notion of the complementarity of bodily differences. Hence man and woman become complementary and acceptable sexual partners, courtesy of the complementary accommodations of their different sexual/reproductive organs.

Weeks (2002) describes sexuality as 'a fictive unity', in view of its being a product of social and historical forces. He argues, like other social constructionists, that a sociology of sex/sexuality shows that it has changed in terms of its meaning, its constituent components and practice over historical periods and across cultural divides. It is, then, a fictive unity to the extent that we treat with it as an ahistorical and homogenous category. There are others, however, who see sexuality as located almost exclusively in our biology, as an involuntary, powerful, anatomical force which can take charge of our bodies in spite of the mind's efforts to control it.

Sexuality, then, is about bodily pleasures, practice and identity that are influenced in terms of their construction, meaning and expression by sociological and historical forces.

Sex is the truth of our being, since it has become more than just a practice, but an integral part of our identity. Importantly, that identity comes with an added value and power since all sexualities are not equal; some are more equal and, hence, more powerful than others.

To the extent that so much is said about it and so much is unclear about it, it becomes a site for contestations of power and meaning.

The Body - 'The Unspoken of Western Abstract Theory'[2]

Western philosophy since the Greeks has been preoccupied with the idea of essence, the universal features of anything, and has not focused much attention on the concrete, individual, human existence (Kierkergaard cited in Williams 1994). This has meant that Western philosophy has been intellectualistic and rationalistic, rarely concerning itself about being relevant in terms of illuminating life and revealing the truth about human existence. The body has generally been seen as a site for unruly passions and appetites that are perceived as threats to control, the pursuit of truth and knowledge. This repression and denial of corporeality seem to indicate, across many historical periods, a desire to see the intelligible as the most valued status of being. The intelligible, by definition, cannot include the corporeal; Shildrick and Price (1999) make the point that the split between the intelligible and the corporeal is interesting not merely in and of itself but, rather, because of the shift in focus that the period of the Enlightenment brought to this theorising. While the Judeo-Christian tradition, for example, saw the body as a mundane path to be walked to achieve a higher, purer and higher valued spirituality, the post-Cartesian modernist period rejected the body as obstacle to pure rational thought.

According to Grosz (1994), philosophy on finding a separate and discrete disciplinary space in Ancient Greece operated out a deep fear of the body, that is, *somatophobia*. Plato, in *The Cratylus*, claimed that the word *soma* – body – was introduced by the Orphic priests who believed that man was a spiritual – non-corporeal – being trapped in the body as in a dungeon. Matter, he further argued in his *Doctrine of the Forms*, was a denigrated and imperfect version of Idea. The body, then, in its corporeal materiality, imprisoned and betrayed the mind. This conceptualisation of mind and body along the lines of Idea and Matter, provided the justification for the mind's dominance and control of the body. Perhaps this resonates, at least superficially, with Paul's explanation to the Ephesian Church of the – natural and – divinely required model of husband as head of wife as Christ is the head of the Church. The Church is, of course, the body of Christ, fallen and sullied, for whose redemption He gave His life. The dominant husband is then associated with mind and the subordinate wife with body.

Aristotle continued this trend in philosophy by presenting maternity as merely the receptacle for the housing of being, rather than as a co-producer in the reproductive process. This understanding of the female body/womb distinguished matter or body from form and reduced the mother's role in the reproductive process to mere accommodation while the father's role was, interestingly, elaborated as moulder, provider of form. This separation set the tone for the binarisation of the sexes that is the base metaphor on which dichotomisation of the world as we experience it is founded.

Grosz goes on to explain that the distinction between matter/form is further elaborated in the distinction between a God-given soul and a mental and sinful carnality. Mind and body distinction also figures between what is immortal, mortal, and pure, what can attain morality, and what can only aspire to but never achieve it.

Descartes built on the scaffolding left by Plato and moved beyond the separation of mind and body to the separation of soul from nature. The body in this conceptualisation was seen as part of nature and governed by the laws of nature. Hence, the mind/soul had no place there in the natural world. As Grosz asserts, this 'exclusion of the soul from nature, this evacuation of consciousness from the world' was the building block upon which was constructed a science of the principles of nature that was indifferent to and assigned no value to the considerations of the subject. Scientific discussions and knowledge sought then, and still seek, to achieve impersonality which is perceived as being the same as objectivity.

We must note that the mind/body opposition created by Descartes was thus linked to the foundation of knowledge and epistemologies, over centuries, have been constructed on this understanding. The separation also accommodates a hierarchy that sets out the first named of the pair as the superior. Dualism and binary opposition have, thus, created a reality that sets mind and body apart as two incompatible and incompassable forms.

The way the Natural Sciences, particularly the Life Sciences, understand the body has its antecedents in the Cartesian conceptual framework. The body is seen as an object which functions in an organic and instrumental way. This body as object is also produced by the humanities and social sciences as reflective of attitudes and feelings but is still merely a physical object.

Another legacy of Cartesian dualism is seen in the way the body is produced as tool, as instrument at the disposal of consciousness for which it also provides housing. It is inhabited and owned by the subject who determines the uses to which it must be put. Because it is wilful and inclined toward carnality, it must be disciplined and trained.

A third legacy of Cartesian dualism is the notion of the body as a textless text in which the body is seen as a signifying medium that makes public the subject's private emotion and thought. It also receives information from outside and transmits this to the subject. The body in this way is still an object awaiting the inscription of meaning from sources external to it.

Spinoza is one of a handful of theorists who have questioned and challenged Cartesian dualism and provided alternative modes for conceptualising the body. His conceptualisation is that of a substance with many attributes that express its nature. Hence, body and mind are two such attributes which are not perceived as being incompatible but, rather, as different aspects of the same substance and, hence, cannot be separated from each other. In this conceptual framework, the body is less mechanistic and instrumental. The mind is then the idea of the body only to the extent that the body is an extension of the mind (Grosz 1994). Spinoza has, however, been criticised for failing to explain causal and other interactions of mind and body.

Feminism and the Body

Early feminist writings focused on the way that the feminine was characterised as less than fully human. This was directly related to the mind/body binary and the way that this split started the persistent association of the inferior body with the feminine. It must be noted here that there are nuances other than gendered ones which have emerged from this set of binaries – those related to race/ethnicity and socioeconomic class. The body has been associated with a gross and unthinking physicality which has been linked at some time or other to black people, people in the lower socioeconomic group, animals and slaves (Shildrick and Price 1999). This has meant that feminists have had to examine and understand the ways in which all of these dimensions intersect and articulate meaning one to the other in the (de)valuing of bodies. The important point to note in the midst of all this is that, generally, it is those who can appropriate the characteristics of being male, white, middle-class, heterosexual and healthy who have been able to rise above such gross physicality to achieve and exercise rationality. Women are still locked into their bodies and constrained from achieving such transcendence by the nature of the female body, its processes and functions.

Feminist theory's treatment of the female body falls into two broad categories: either an avoidance of it for fear of being bogged down in the defence of its indisciplined nature or an embracing of this body as part of the project of reclaiming the essence of the female. More recently, postmodern feminists have refused to deny embodiment and have seen the body as a differential and fluid construct which, mediated by history, culture among other dimensions, is never one, never fixed and always imbued with potential. This emphasis on fluidity and difference is part of the larger postmodern project of valorising difference so as to disrupt the philosophical and disciplinary tyranny of universalisms and homogeneity.

Among the group of feminist theorists who want to transcend the limits of the body are de Beauvoir, Wollstonecraft and Firestone. For them, the way to women's liberation was to be found through a disembodied subjecthood. This approach has been critiqued as conforming to a problematic masculinist conceptual framework. In the second group of feminist theorists, we find persons such as Mitchell and Kristeva who have tried to reclaim and give positive meaning to the feminine. This kind of theoretical direction was further nuanced by the work of bell hooks, Audre Lorde and Hill Collins who have shown how markers of race and sexual preference have been active agents in the production of bodies. This has also been seen in the work of our own Caribbean feminist theorists, Mohammed, Rowley and Cooper among them, who have deliberately embraced embodiment as this is shaped by gender and race. The theorists in this second group have recognised that, while the body is critical to the understanding of women's psychical and social existence, it is not acultural, ahistoric, nor is it a biological given.

The female body seems to defy any attempts to perform or conform, in an orderly way, to the husbandry of reason. This is seen especially in the reproductive processes, as part of which, according to Shildrick and Price (1999), women are able to menstruate, develop another body in the unseen and forever suspect cavity of their own body, to give birth, to lactate and, all in all, to present a dangerous volatility that seems to be the other of a seeming general self-containment and order in the male body. If we understand the dialectical relationship between language and the way we understand ourselves and our world, it would then be no surprise that there has been, in philosophy and psychoanalysis, such a close link established between women and hysteria. This is perhaps best expressed in the illustration that the Greek word which refers to the womb is *hyster*. The female body seems to leak and to overflow, transgressing the proper distinctions between self and other, to contaminate and to engulf. No wonder, then, the position adopted by many feminists of theorising the need for women's transcendence of their bodies, to become by matching and overreaching the intellectual criteria for being fully human.

Christian Theology and the Body

In speaking of theology, I wish to make the point that I refer not just to the study of the nature of God and religious beliefs, but also to the systematically developed religious beliefs and theory which seem to inform the preached gospel. I have already made the point that the theory of sexual dimorphism that separates mind from sinful body is very much a part of the Judeo-Christian religious tradition. It must, however, also be noted here that throughout much of the history of Western societies the policing of sexual behaviour and sex categories has, largely, been the purview of religious and state authorities. While this authority was yielded in the nineteenth century to the scientific and medical authorities, the Christian Church has still been a major broker in determining acceptable sexual behaviour and sex categories. As Foucault (1980) has explained, the production of knowledge is rooted in particular human histories, practices and language, and shaped by dynamics of power. The operations of power are integral in the production and reproduction of appropriate bodies. The Christian Church has been very involved in producing knowledge as this relates to determining acceptable and unacceptable sexual practices, the acceptable language of sex – in short, sexual politics.

Anne Baring asserts that the Fall of Man has been received by generations as a divinely revealed truth about the way that the human condition came about through the sin of our primal ancestors, in particular our foremother Eve. The Fall has been understood and often declaimed from pulpits as making necessary universal statements about the human nature in general and the nature of woman in particular. It has caught the Western imagination in such a way as to perhaps lay the basis for much of the misogyny that has fuelled the oppression of women.

It seems not to have made a significant impression on those who preach this that, in the Gospels, Jesus does not refer to original sin nor does He equate sexuality with sinfulness. He, in fact, protects an adulterous woman from the wrath of a self-righteously indignant crowd and hence from death by stoning. In fact, there is nothing in the Creation story that suggests that either male or female body is evil; there is, however, a focus on the man and woman both being created in the image of God.

The early Christian Church Fathers such as Jerome, Tertullian and Augustine wrote extensively about the Fall and saw sexual 'instinct' as an impediment to spirituality and purity. In fact, Augustine's Doctrine of Original Sin became the foundation of the Church's teaching that provided the justification for salvation through Christ. Being so convinced of the sinfulness of sexuality, Augustine eventually repudiated his beloved partner of 18 years, the mother of his son, because he believed that a life of sexual chastity would be better pleasing to God. This certainly seems to be cut off the same cloth as Paul's advice, in 1 Corinthians 7:8-9, to the Corinthian widows and unmarried that the unmarried state, while a good one, should be abandoned if (the bodily) passions and desires could not be controlled and, hence, they should marry since it is 'better to marry than to burn with passion'. It seems, then, that through Original Sin, the love of God and his service were set in opposition to the natural life of the body, and chastity and abstinence, corporeal sanctions, were the only remedy for this lost sense of unity. In order to cultivate the soul we have to neglect the body, for the body and matter find no common ground with spirit.

Baring further argues that the writings of the early Church Fathers demonised woman because of her descent from Eve; she was not just an inferior substance because she was created from Adam, but was also an ally of the Devil, having succumbed to temptation first. She is the gateway through which the Devil can pursue his mission in the world by causing her to tempt men into sexual relations. This theology has shaped the way men and women understand their role in the Body of Christ. Woman's eternal punishment for original sin was her (corporeal) desire for her husband and her (very corporeal) suffering during childbirth. The body has been feared, despised and, in the pursuit of a spiritual life, made to endure all kinds of misery imaginable.

This is perhaps most graphically portrayed in the way that the Church administration over the years has dealt with the story of the Virgin Birth. The body of Mary has been appropriated by the church as the ideal of corporeality for women. Her body, of course, has already been de-sexed and de-humanised. The extent to which this is seen is tracked by John Selby Spong (2001). The miraculous virgin birth seems to have been woven into theological mythology by Church Fathers over centuries. Paul, one of the earlier authors of the corpus of work known as the New Testament, does not speak of the origins of Jesus and only mentions the fact that he was born of a woman, under the law. He also recorded for us that, 'according to the flesh', Jesus was a descendant of the House of David and he names his brother, James. There is no mention of the virgin birth. Mark, the writer of the earliest gospel, also fails to record the miraculous birth but mentions Jesus' mother twice.

The virgin story entered the Christian faith in the early ninth decade through the gospel of Matthew some 55 years after Jesus' death. It reappeared in the late ninth or early tenth decade in the gospel of Luke and then disappeared in favour of the concept of Jesus' divine pre-existence in the tenth decade Gospel of John. However, the mythology of Mary, Spong explains, was destined to expand in the development of Christian history.

By the end of the second century, the virgin as feminine ideal began to grow. She then went from virgin mother to permanent virgin, hence making it necessary to transform the brothers and sisters of Jesus mentioned in the Bible to half-siblings or cousins. The Church Fathers then achieved the miraculous feat of making her a post-partum virgin and went through gymnastics to prove that her hymen remained intact during the birth of Jesus. For scriptural authority they used the text in Ezekiel (44:1) that said that when the 'gates of the city were closed only the Lord could go in and out' to validate her virginal state post-partum. By the nineteenth century her own birth was said to have been miraculous, she too, having been immaculately conceived. Mary remained untouched then by the stain of human sin that was found in the Fall of Humanity in the Garden of Eden. By the twentieth century, at the dawn of the Space Age, she was proclaimed to have bodily ascended into heaven.

Whether we impute deliberate intent to pass off mythology as miracle on the part of Church fathers or attribute heretic status to Spong, it is difficult to deny that the message of Mary, received by many congregations from many pulpits over the years, has been that both body and sexuality are evil.

But what does the Bible itself have to say about the body? The disciples are advised by Jesus in Matthew 26:41 that while the spirit is willing, 'the body is weak', reiterating the bifurcated image of body and spirit, with body as the vulnerable part of the human. While there are various injunctions that speak to the body as polluted and defiled, there are also images and instruction that speak to compatibility, even equality, of mind and body. In the New Testament we are reminded that salvation is not only for souls but also for bodies (Luke 9:2) as the disciples are dispatched by Jesus to drive out demons and cure diseases. The letter from the apostle John to Gaius and other Christians expresses the wish that the recipients would 'receive good health' and that all would go well with them even as their soul is getting along well; the resurrection body of Jesus is what the frightened and doubting disciples are invited to test for the verification of his identity. Romans 12: 4-5 uses the body and its various members to illustrate the equality and interdependence of the various members of the Body of Christ. In 1 Corinthians 6: 12-13 we see that the body and the soul are inseparably related. I must note here that, according to Christopher West (2000), Roman Catholicism does not eschew the body but presents a rather physical, sensual, even sexual, religion in the richness of the ceremonies, sacraments and symbols. Among these, West claims, is the blessing of the baptismal waters at the Easter vigil. He penetrates this liturgy and reveals that the repeated plunging of the Easter candle in and out of the baptismal font is the symbol of Christ impregnating the womb of the church, from which womb many children will be born again. He points also to the many references in the Catholic creed to begetting, conception and birth and the beatification of Mary's womb. For Roman Catholic theology, then, we are told, it is through the sensual bodily realities of the sacraments that divine life is received – the bathing of the body with water, anointing it with oil, the laying on of hands, eating and drinking of the body and blood of Christ. West also advises that the teachings of Pope John Paul II assert that we encounter God not as a super-spiritual reality but through the material (corporeal) world. It is through the incarnation, then, that matter becomes fully capable of putting us in touch with the Father.

In spite of this understanding, however, many Jamaican women have had the experience of being reminded about the body as the temple of God in such a way as to hold women more (if not exclusively) accountable for the maintenance of body purity.

How has this affected the way that Jamaican men, Christian or other, feel they should treat women? How has this affected the way in which Jamaican women in the Christian Church experience the healing and liberty that Christianity promises? These are not idle questions since the authority with which religion is invested derives from the supernatural association and our notion of divine inscrutablilty and infallibility.

This treatment of the body has certainly meant that the female body has had to undergo a particular tyranny, in worship and out, as it performs theologically prescribed Christianity. In many church denominations here in Jamaica, women must satisfy a number of criteria if their performance of Christianity is to be acceptable. They must avoid chemically processing their hair or, in some instances, keep it covered.[3] External ordinances have been set up as markers of the uniqueness of the faith lest the faith community lay itself open to charges of being part of the (feminised) carnal world. Women must not expose arms or legs or provide a hint of cleavage. They must not wear 'male' clothing, that is, trousers. They must ensure that moving to the left in the name of Jesus and moving to the right in the name of the Lord be careful and appropriate expressions of joy. They cannot shake their 'booty' in Jesus' name because to come into the presence of perfect holiness is to leave 'booty'/matter behind. They must be careful not to provide the (mostly) male church leaders and the carefully nurtured handful of men in the church with an opportunity to explain transgression in the words of their forefather, Adam, recorded in the Book of Genesis, 3: 12: 'The woman – you put here with me – she gave me some fruit and I ate it'.

This discussion is not meant to suggest that it is only men in the form of male church leaders and male believers who have understood the female body in this way. Patriarchal notions of the role and functions of the female body have been all-pervasive and many female believers and church adherents have exerted pressure on themselves and other women to conform in this way.

While many women desire the freedom to proclaim their own experience and their own vision in the world as authoritative and legitimate, rather than marginal and deviant as patriarchy would have it, many Jewish and Christian feminists recognise the painful split within that experience because, to echo the words of Elaine Showalter (cited in Tolbert 1990) we are the daughters of the male traditions of Abraham and the patriarchs, of Jesus, Paul and the Church Fathers, of our own male ministers and rabbis ... and at the same time sisters together in a new consciousness which rejects the submissive, victimised roles Western society, formed by these two great religious traditions, has forced us and generations of our foremothers, and sisters, to play.

However, in the attempt to deny, repress and obscure female corporeality, in actual fact we have centred and magnified it such that it screams its importance at us through a litany of 'musts' and 'must nots'. In fact, it is noticeable that there seems to be no similar proscription against male clothing reflected in the external ordinances. It is not my intention to suggest that the proscriptions that have been detailed here apply to all Christian denominations. I do suggest, however, that while these external ordinances set up to police female sexuality are mediated by such categories as socioeconomic class, race/ethnicity, there is still within the preached gospel and expectations of appropriate Christian behaviour, a husbandry of the female body that is driven by a notion of its volatility.

What is needed then is a way of understanding the body that extricates it from the stranglehold of such disempowering, un-liberating conceptual frameworks and theology. This is as important for theology as it is for feminism. It is equally important that this liberation exercise conform to divine instruction (by the enabling of the Holy Spirit) and not just libertarian extravagance to provide an opportunity for sexual 'letting go'.

Liberation Theology

Liberation theology is described by Gustavo Guttierez as a 'critical reflection on praxis in the light of the Word of God'. It has two basic principles: firstly it recognises a need for liberation from any kind of oppression – political, economic, social, sexual racial, religious – and, secondly, it asserts that theology must grow out of the basic Christian communities and should not be imposed from above, that is, from the infallible source book or from the 'magisterium of an infallible Church' (Hillar 1993). It is committed to explaining the theological meaning of human activities, thereby centring its praxis on the individual experience. It interprets the Christian faith out of the suffering, struggle and hope of the poor. It critiques society and the ideologies that sustain it. While it has no 'pure' theology, it sets as its explicit task, the project of changing an unjust society into a just one.

It emerged out of the critical reflection of the Church in Latin America, the society and of the ideologies sustaining both and was articulated for the first time in 1968. Its roots go deep into the religious and social movements that were sweeping the Latin American continent in the 1950s. Many of these movements and problems arose directly out of the condition of abject poverty. What is important to note is that its first concern is the recovery of God as justice (Herzgog 1976).

Liberation Theology and Feminism

hooks (2000) explains that feminism is a movement to end sexism, sexist exploitation and oppression. This sexism, frequently referred to as patriarchy, is a pervasive system in which both men and women participate in various ways. Feminism sets out to identify sexist notions lurking in a variety of fields – language, philosophy and religion among them. These fields are important since they are invested with the power to influence the way men and women construct, produce and reproduce themselves as social, political and economic beings. The body becomes a critical site for feminist interrogation since it has been the 'essence' of the argument about male superiority and female subordination. Like feminism, liberation theology both speaks and undertakes a social gospel, good news, that can impact the lives of people beyond a perceived esoteric theory to a life experience that provides opportunities for self-interpretation of their own situation and needs so as to effect a liberating praxis.

Both have relied heavily on critical self-reflection by those who are oppressed (and others) to connect faith/belief to revolutionary change.

hooks (2000) explains that revolutionary feminists raising consciousness emphasised the importance of learning about patriarchy, the way in which patriarchy became institutionalised and how it has been maintained. Paulo Freire's libertarian pedagogy which contributed much to liberation theology also speaks to the uncovering of the world of oppression by the oppressed and their commitment to transformation through praxis. Ultimately, the emerging pedagogy will be the property of all.

Both feminism and liberation theology insist on the epistemological privilege of the oppressed, be they the poor or women, since this oppression is perceived as providing a privileged standpoint and lens through which to view the world. They both assume (perhaps somewhat romantically) that the oppressed stand in a place where their point of view is not disturbed by power and its trappings (Asisi-Diaz 1989).

For both, liberation becomes a break with the present order, not a mere modification or glossing of an already flawed structure. Both strive for a Utopia, not to be found in a hereafter but rather as the outcome of new structures for the earthly here and now.

Challenges and Questions to be Considered in the Articulation of a Liberation Theology of the Body

Having pursued the discussion to this point, the questions that Elizabeth Fiorenza poses speak to this issue in a very powerful way: how do we cease to collaborate with the religious oppression and still claim a Christian birthright? This Christian birthright requires us to be part of the fellowship of the brethren who may have no problems with the restraints placed on the female body. How do we then articulate a different theology and praxis without becoming sectarian and 'worldian'?

How do women and others become religious agents and theological subjects on the foundation of the silence and denial of women and their corporeality? How does the Body of Christ reclaim the authority and resources of religion in the struggle to end patriarchal relations of subordination, oppression and repression?

At the heart of patriarchy reside the contradictions between patriarchal structures and democratic aspirations. How are these tensions to be resolved in such a way as to both ensure the integrity of the gospel and position the Church in the wider community as an effective and relevant ministry? Is the Church meant to be a democratic space or is it that human philosophies have tried to infuse this people-centred freedom into its mission of salvation? Is there any link between God's will for His people and the democratic aspirations of these people? What does this then say for liberation theology? These are questions that must be posed and considered prayerfully and thoughtfully by the Body of Christ.

I think that the beginnings of any liberation theology of the body for the Body of Christ should be the reclaiming of the important message of the Creation Story: men and women are created in *imago-dei,* the image of God. Neither male nor female bodies are inherently evil.

As an act of consciousness-raising, of uncovering oppression, I believe that Fiorenza's advice is useful. Christian women in particular and the Church, in general, must seek first to deconstruct and then reconstruct the points of tension between Christian vision and community and the patriarchal societies we inhabit. This process should seek to uncover, historically and theologically, how and why the discipleship of equals and male pyramids of subordination have together become defining characteristics of Christian identity. This process should also then see how body politics have featured in the pyramids of subordination.

Another issue that has to be confronted, as Fiorenza suggests, is the seeming contradiction between the Bible's democratic perspective of equality in the Spirit and the submission to the Word of God. I endorse her recommendation of a 'hermeneutics of suspicion' that must seek to identify patriarchal politics in the preached gospel and extricate divine instruction from cultural inscription. Out of this should emerge 'a hermeneutics of critical evaluation' that should provide a liberating vision appropriate to the needs of our times and all times. This hermeneutics should incorporate the best of liberation theological praxis, reconstruct scripture as nourishing bread (as is prescribed and described by the Word of God) and not as fossilised tablet of instruction.

This process should be guided by Spirit-led vision and the best of feminist and liberation theological scholarship. At the centre of all of this, however, must be the body, the corporeal existence and experience of women. This process must allow women to 'write through their bodies' and they must resist attempts to be driven away from them (Minh-ha 1999). Inasmuch as the body is not to be demeaned, it is not to be exalted. Like Minh-ha, I believe that there is going to be a new excitement generated through this, since the new awareness generated from experience to the life in previously deadened areas of the body will lead to a new experience. I would say it will also lead to a new liberating theology.

She further makes the point that consciousness of the body must not be the output of the accumulation of knowledge but an ongoing process to unsettle and to question all authority and order. Between knowledge and power, she asserts, is room for knowledge without power. Body politics have been, by definition, about politics/power play and epistemologies. A liberation theology of the body for the Body of Christ in Jamaica must have as its explicit project the disruption of these relations of power. In developing a liberation theology of the body, we must avoid the theoretical bind that divides the subject into discrete categories of mind and body (Grosz 1994). We must go further than just rejecting and reversing hierarchies of power as an end in itself and dislodge theories of the body from the kind of framework of inaccessible texts that are the preserve of a privileged, small social group. We should work towards avoiding making the term theory synonymous with elitism, purely mental activity, deep and/or high science, that which is disengaging. We should heed the warning of Trinh T. Minh-ha that theory oppresses when it perpetuates existing power relations and presents itself as a means to exert authority in expertise through the voice of knowledge. Knowledge itself as part of the project of Enlightenment, instead of delivering light has, very often, delivered endarkenment. This was so since its conceptual framework allowed for two degrees, one of which, darkness, had to be excluded to accommodate the other, light. We must recognise that bodies are, among other things, the products of culture, history, geography. A liberation theology of the body for the Body of Christ must then reject singular models based on the type of body by which all others are judged.

We must be very conscious that current theorising of the body allows women to become the body in a way that frees men to soar to the heights of theoretical reflection and cultural production. A liberation theology of the body then must articulate an acceptance of the embodied nature of both men and women such that they both are capable of the production of knowledge and culture.

It must confront these issues through critical self-reflection, through the desire for transformation and liberation. Herzgog (1976) warns us that in many instances theology is still doing the national henchman's job of legitimising injustice, however subtly. The liberation theology of the body as part of the 'awesome struggle over the character of personhood' must produce justice as its outcome.

Let the body's openings then, be spaces, not for scripting and remotely controlled voicing but, rather for providing the possibilities for a critical self-reflection of God's power and divine justice. Let God be truly reclaimed as justice.

Notes

1. I use the term perform here to underscore the social and learned nature of gendered sexuality
2. I have borrowed this term from Shildrick's and Price's 'Openings on the Body: A Critical Introduction'.
3. It has been argued that in the context of standards of beauty that do not include those of many black women, proscriptions against processed hair could be viewed in the light of black racial pride and uplift. However, it is my considered opinion that the matter is rarely raised in that context and is presented as an issue of vanity.

References

Asisi-Diaz, Ado. 1989. 'Mujeristas: A Name of Our Own.' http://www.religion-online.org. (accessed July 16, 2003).

Baring, Anne. 'The Myth of the Fall and the Doctrine of Original Sin'. Seminar Notes. http://www.womenpriests.org/body/baring2.htm (accessed May 06, 2003).

Birke, Linda.1999. 'Bodies and Biology'. In *Feminist Theory and the Body*, eds. Janet Price and Shildrick, 42-49. New York: Routledge.

Cooper, Carolyn. 1994. *Noises in the Blood: Orality, Gender and the 'Vulgar' Body of Jamaican Popular Culture*. London: MacMillan.

Grosz, Elizabeth. 1994. *Volatile Bodies: Towards A Corporeal Feminism*. Indianapolis: Indiana University Press.

Guttierez, Gustavo.1984. *We Drink From Our Own Wells: The Spiritual Journey of A People*. New York: Orbis Books.

Fiorenza, Elizabeth,S. 'Changing the Paradigms'. In *Christian Century Magazine*. http://www.religion-online.org (accessed July 17, 2003).

Foucault, Michel. 1980. *A History of Sexuality Vol.1*. New York: Random House.

Herzgog, Frederick.1976. 'Birth Pangs: Liberation Theology in North America'. http://www.religion–online.org (accessed July 16).

Hillar, Marian. 1993. 'Liberation Theology: Religious Response to Social Problems'. In *Humanism and Social Issues:Anthology of Essays*, eds. M. Hillar and H.R. Leuchtag. Houston: American Humanist Association. http://www.socilian.org/liberty.html (accessed July 17, 2003).

hooks, bell. 2000. *Feminism is For Everybody*. Cambridge: South End Press.

Minh-ha, Trinh T. 1999. 'Write your Body' and 'The Body in Theory'. In *Feminist Theory and the Body*, eds. Janet Price and Shildrick, 258-266. New York: Routledge.

Shildrick, Margrit and Janet Price. 1999. 'Openings on the Body: A Critical Introduction'. In *Feminist Theory and the Body*, eds. Janet Price and Margrit Shildrick, 1-14. New York: Routledge.

Spong, John Selby. 2001. 'The Virgin Mary is No Wonder Woman'. http://www.religion-online.org (accessed July 17, 2003).

Tolbert, Mary Ann. 1990. 'Protestant Feminists and the Bible: On the Horns of a Dilemma'. In *The Pleasures of Her Text*, ed. Alice Bach. http://www.religion-online.org. (accessed July 17, 2003).

West, Christopher. 2000. 'Naked Without Shame: The Scandal of the Body'.http//www.christianity.com (accessed July 17, 2003).

Weeks, Jeffrey. 2002. *Sexuality*. London: Routledge.

Williams, Lewin. 1994. *Caribbean Theology*. New York: Peter Lang Publishing Inc.

Pushing the Boundaries:
New and Emerging Issues

13 | LEITH L. DUNN

Women and Work
Policy Implications of ILO Conventions

Introduction

'Women and Work' has been one of the central issues of interest to researchers in the field of Gender Studies in the twenty-first century. This has been a persistent theme in the work of the early pioneers of the Centre for Gender and Development Studies which has been continued in the last decade. This paper presents some thoughts on how to 'push the boundaries' even further, to address new and emerging issues in the world of work. The paper therefore examines:

- The changing face of women's work in the Commonwealth Caribbean;
- Emerging opportunities and challenges this presents;
- Conventions of the International Labour Organisation (ILO) and their role in protecting women workers' rights and promoting gender equality in the workplace;
- Commonwealth Caribbean countries' adoption of ILO Conventions and the gaps to be filled in light of the emerging challenges and new areas of work;
- Policy implications of the ILO Conventions.

The Changing Face of Women's Work

In examining the long history of women and work, there is recognition that the range and scope of women's work has expanded beyond the domestic and agricultural sectors. Work has shifted from the private domestic sphere to public spaces and even further to the global labour market. New employment opportunities have emerged as a result of globalisation, trade, and advances in computer and telecommunications technologies (Dunn 1999). These opportunities include employment for women in export-processing zones in the export garment sector as well as jobs in the offshore data services sector in data entry, data processing, call centres and in software programming (Dunn and Dunn 1999).

Women's employment opportunities have also expanded because more of them are creating their own businesses. Despite this, the policy, regulatory and institutional environments are often unfriendly to women entrepreneurs (Mondesire and Dunn 1995).

As women have increasingly taken advantage of educational opportunities, there has been gradual occupational desegregation. As a result, women have been more visible in occupations and sectors that were predominantly male-dominated such as finance, construction, the fire and police service, medicine, law and engineering.

Economic pressure has increased the level of legal and illegal migration and migration has become an important source of employment for women. Unemployment levels remain higher for women than men. Many people have explored migration as an option because of their need to find alternative sources of employment. The demand for jobs has also coincided with an increased demand for teachers and nurses to fill vacancies in sections of North America and Europe. As a result, state agencies in industrialised countries have embarked on an aggressive recruitment drive in developing countries for workers in the health and education institutions.

As more women opt for overseas employment to support their families this trend is contributing to a new 'brain-drain' which has impacted negatively on national health and education sectors across the Commonwealth Caribbean. New opportunities for employment within the region will expand in 2005, with the implementation of the Caribbean Single Market and Economy (CSME) and the Free Movement of Skilled Persons. These trends will require Caribbean countries to adopt policies and legislation to protect the rights of migrant workers.

Migration is an important issue for women's rights as female migrant workers are more vulnerable to exploitation and abuse than males. The international trafficking of women and children (boys and girls) is also emerging as one of the most serious and fastest growing problems today. As expected, the Caribbean is not excluded.

Increased employment opportunities for women have been linked to greater global focus on a rights-based approach to development and the importance of rights for all human beings. As a result, most countries have ratified the United Nations Convention for the Elimination of All Forms of Discrimination Against Women (CEDAW) and ILO conventions. To varying degrees, they have adopted ILO conventions that promote basic human rights for all workers as well as specific rights for women workers. Global consensus on the Millennium Development Goals (MDGs) in 2000 also supports a rights-based approach to development. It is also an acknowledgement that the goals of poverty reduction and sustainable development can only be achieved if there is gender equality. The MDGs include the eradication of extreme poverty and hunger, the promotion of gender equality and the empowerment of women as well as combating HIV/AIDS among other goals.

Mondesire and Dunn (1995), in reviewing the participation of women in the Commonwealth Caribbean as employers and own-account workers, noted that, since 1980, there had been an increase in the number of women in decision-making positions in the private sector and women running their own businesses. For selected Caribbean countries, there had been an increase from an average of 23.5 per cent in 1980 to 32.5 per cent in 1992. Women's advancement to the highest levels of decision-making in corporations and the University of the West Indies (Pro Vice Chancellor and Registrar) was also cited. (pp. 27-29). Data demonstrating women's unequal participation in administrative and management positions were quite alarming. Sex disaggregated data for selected countries indicated, that, in 1980, there were approximately 22.1 per cent of women, compared to 77.9 per cent of males. In 1992, there was a slight improvement for women (27.9 per cent). Caribbean women's inequality at the highest levels of decision-making was consistent with global trends. For example, the ILO notes that, although some women have breached glass walls and ceilings, worldwide they hold only 1 per cent of chief executive positions. (ILO Bureau for Gender Equality website 2003). In the last decade, many Caribbean women have moved to the ranks of middle management and leadership, but relatively few hold positions as heads of corporations and board chairpersons.

Emerging Challenges

Despite these opportunities for employment, there are several challenges to the rights of women workers. One emerging challenge is that women's *participation in the labour force remains unequal*. The ILO reports that, globally, only 54 per cent of working age women participate in the labour force compared to over 80 per cent of working-age males. This demonstrates that the world is not making the most of women's talents and skills, as more women are pursuing educational courses than males.

Another important challenge is that women's unequal labour force participation has contributed to the *feminisation of poverty*. Women continue to be employed mainly in 'female' jobs that pay low wages, and require low levels of skill. The ILO estimates that women constitute 70 per cent of the world's 1.3 billion absolute poor. Poverty data for many Caribbean countries confirm a similar trend, with women being overrepresented among the poorest quintiles.

A third challenge is that sex stereotyping in occupations has persisted. The ILO notes that half of the world's labour force is employed in sex-stereotyped occupations, with women dominating those occupations which are lowest paying and least protected. A fourth issue is that, *while more women are entering paid work, more jobs have often not meant better jobs*. For women in developing regions, like the Caribbean, the majority of new employment opportunities have been in part-time jobs; work in the informal sector and in home-based work. These sectors are usually unprotected and unorganised. A fifth challenge relates to *inequality in pay*, which has persisted. Globally, women earn 20-30 per cent less than men.

Another challenge facing women is that, although more of them are creating their own businesses and these are important sources of employment, the policy, regulatory and institutional environments in many countries often remain unfriendly to women entrepreneurs. Other challenges relate to *inequalities in gender relations that persist in the workplace* and the *absence of gender-sensitive policies and practices*. These realities further undermine women's empowerment and development.

There is also the challenge that, despite ratification of ILO conventions and the adoption of equal-pay legislation, women in many Caribbean countries with more advanced educational qualifications than their male counterparts, still experience discrimination in employment and wages.

Women workers are also constrained by the *relatively limited change in the gender division of labour in the household*. Today there are many Caribbean women fulfilling multiple roles: they are single heads of households, primary breadwinners for their families, and primary caregivers for children and relatives who are elderly and sick. As a result, women still have to balance their role as workers outside the home with their domestic responsibilities.

A key emerging issue is that economic pressure is contributing to an increase in the number of *elderly women returning to the workplace*. The ILO notes that the gender gap is greying into a poverty trap and that women face a much higher risk than men of a drastic drop in living standards when they retire. The ILO also notes that women account for the majority of the population over 60 years in almost all countries. *Ageing and poverty* are also issues for Caribbean women as they are more likely than men to retire without a pension because fewer of them have been employed in positions that provide pension and health benefits. Women's increased life expectancy, which is an average of five years more than their male counterparts, presents challenges for policy-makers in the health and social services sectors.

The quality of jobs for women is also a concern and the achievement of increased work opportunities for women has not necessarily meant better quality jobs. Women are still disproportionately represented among part-time, seasonal and contract workers. This means that they have less social protection and insurance than their male counterparts and are likely to have less job security in the workplace.

Women also suffer discrimination through sexual harassment in the workplace because of patriarchal attitudes and behaviour.

Protecting the Rights of Women Workers: Global Policies

International Conventions

The global framework to protect the rights of women workers includes the United Nations Convention on the Elimination of all forms of

Discrimination Against Women (CEDAW) as well as the United Nations Convention on the Rights of the Child (CRC). Among other issues, the CRC speaks to the elimination of child labour and the need for special measures to protect the rights of the girl child. Global conferences in the last decade have evolved into a consensus on the Millennium Development Goals (MDGs).

ILO Conventions

The International Labour Organisation (ILO) is a tripartite organisation of government, trade unions and the private sector which has developed a range of conventions to protect the rights of all workers. ILO conventions complement the other UN conventions and give specific guidance on labour standards. Special conventions have been developed to promote gender equality in the workplace and to protect the rights of women workers in response to their diverse needs and responsibilities.

The ILO conventions are international treaties that are open to ratification by ILO member states. Developed though dialogue and consensus between government, trade unions and private sector groups, these conventions are *universal* in character. They are also widely accepted rules for national action that countries ratify of their own free will. The conventions are also *flexible*, which means that they can be applied to countries at various stages of development, and are drafted in a spirit of realism and effectiveness. However, those conventions that address fundamental human rights and freedoms are *not* flexible.

ILO conventions are also *viable*. The texts are prepared in tripartite technical committees and adopted by a two-thirds majority decision. Sovereign countries ratify conventions of their own free will and the expectation is that there is tripartite consultation before they are adopted. Finally, ILO Conventions are also *adaptable*. They are revised and updated periodically to adapt to a rapidly changing world.

Implications of Ratifying ILO Conventions

Countries that ratify a convention are indicating that they formally accept the convention. As a result, they are legally bound to apply the main principles and must (if necessary) adopt new laws and regulations or modify existing legislation and practice. They must also apply the convention in law as well as in practice. Conventions are often supplemented by recommendations. These are general or technical guidelines to assist implementation and are applied at a national level but are not open to ratification.

Gender Mainstreaming in the ILO

In addition to developing conventions, the ILO has also embarked on a range of gender mainstreaming measures to demonstrate its commitment to gender equality in the workplace. There has been political will at the highest level, as the Director General issued a policy statement. The organisation has also embraced gender as a cross-cutting theme across all its programmes. An action plan was developed and the Bureau for Gender Equality in the International Labour Office was established to facilitate its implementation. A methodology has also been developed to include gender concerns in planning, programme implementation, monitoring and evaluation of the ILO's work. Gender-specific development tools and indicators have been produced and disseminated. This paper has drawn on a range of the ILO publications produced. These include publications that address the ILO labour conventions. Among these are: 'Gender Issues in the World of Work: Gender Training Package (1995); 'Gender: A Partnership of Equals' (2000); 'ILO ABC of women workers' rights and gender equality' (2000). In addition, this paper draws on an ILO publication that addresses globalisation and gender (Dunn and Dunn 1999).

ILO Declarations and Conventions to Protect Women Workers' Rights

ILO conventions are guided by a number of core principles that are included in two documents: the 'Universal Declaration of Human Rights 1948 (Principles of equality and non-discrimination)' and the 'Declaration on Fundamental Principles and Rights at Work 1998'. These declarations govern all ILO member countries and are used as principles to guide labour relations even when specific conventions have not been ratified.

Listed below are a number of conventions that countries are encouraged to ratify in order to protect the rights of women workers. Given the range of occupations that Caribbean women workers now occupy, and the emerging opportunities for employment, governments are encouraged to ratify the ILO conventions which fall into 10 main categories. Details of these ILO Conventions are included in the Appendix for reference and include basic human rights, freedom of association, employment, social policy, maternity protection, night work, conditions of work, occupational health and safety, other special categories of workers and conventions of special significance.

Ratification of ILO Conventions by Commonwealth Caribbean Countries

To what extent have Caribbean countries ratified these conventions? The table below shows the Caribbean's ratification scorecard. Ratification details for each country are included in the Appendix.

Ratification of ILO Conventions: Commonwealth Caribbean (2002)

Country	Number of ILO Conventions Ratified and in force
Antigua and Barbuda	28
Bahamas	33 (30 in force)
Barbados	39 (36 in force)
Belize	42 (38 in force)
Dominica	23
Grenada	31 (26 in force)
Guyana	45 (41 in force)
Jamaica	26
St Kitts and Nevis	8
Trinidad and Tobago	17

The analysis shows that, in rank order, the countries that have ratified most conventions include: Guyana, Belize, Barbados and The Bahamas.

A review of the conventions ratified shows that relatively few of those ratified are designed to protect the rights of women workers. This suggests male-bias in the range of conventions ratified.

There are a number of core conventions which include:

- Forced labour (C29 and C105)
- Freedom of association and the right to organise (C87 and C98)
- Discrimination (C100 and C111)
- Child labour (C138 and C182)

However, only seven (7) Commonwealth Caribbean states have ratified these core conventions and these include: Antigua and Barbuda, The Bahamas, Barbados, Belize, Dominica, Grenada and Guyana.

Emerging Issues for the Caribbean

Against the background of globalisation and other factors that have shaped the face of women's work in the Caribbean, it is important to note first of all that there are gaps in the range of conventions ratified by most Caribbean countries. These omissions effectively limit the level of protection afforded to workers. Tripartite partners in each country therefore need to review and ratify all relevant conventions to protect the rights of women workers. At a minimum, countries should ratify ILO conventions to protect basic rights, employment, social policy, maternity protection, night work, conditions of work, occupational health and safety as well as conventions that address the needs of special groups, and also those that cover labour inspection and child labour.

Another issue is that countries would need to adopt policies, laws, measures and programmes to support the full implementation of the conventions ratified. For example, labour policies would need to be reviewed and engendered to address the specific needs of women workers. Collective bargaining would need to be engendered to expand the scope and range of issues covered during labour negotiation.

Special measures would also need to be adopted in recognition of the fact that gender inequality and sex stereotyping persist in the workplace and that low wages for women workers are contributing to the feminisation of poverty. Other issues that need to be addressed include the increase in migrant women workers, elderly female workers and self-employed women and children (especially girls under 18 years).

Policy implications of ILO Conventions

Economic policies are needed to address two persistent problems. The first is women's unequal participation in the labour market and the second is the need for economic growth to expand employment opportunities for both men and women. Policies must address the disproportionately higher level of unemployment among Caribbean women, who continue to experience twice the rate of male unemployment making them vulnerable to poverty. Policies will also need to ensure that women have equal access to employment, in order to reverse the tendency for women to be concentrated in 'pink ghettos' which are characterised by low wages and low skills.

Labour policies governing all sectors of the workforce also need to be reviewed to ensure that they cover a wider range of workers in existing and emerging areas of work. This review should focus specifically on the impact of globalisation and technology on women's employment in the Caribbean. Governments are therefore encouraged not only to ratify relevant conventions, but also to adopt policies that seek to maintain high standards of occupational safety and health in the emerging work spaces.

Labour policies should also be consistent with C 87 which guarantees workers freedom of association and protection of the right to organise. As such, these policies should apply to companies operating in export processing zones (EPZs) or under EPZ legislation. Similarly, the policy implications of Convention 98 which guarantees workers the Right to Organise and to Collective Bargaining strongly suggest that all labour negotiations must be engendered.

The current labour situation in the Caribbean requires a radically different approach to collective bargaining. For one, negotiations on wages, maternity leave and on collective bargaining should focus on a wide range of gender issues, women's issues and the promotion of equality. The proposed changes imply that legislation will have to be reviewed and revised and existing laws will have to be enforced more effectively.

Negotiations on wages and benefits will need to be guided by the principle of equal pay for work of equal value. Tripartite partners will also need to use a more gendered approach to job classification exercises and negotiate for benefits such as child care, housing, transportation, medical benefits as well as overtime for all workers.

Also, negotiations on hours of work should try to eliminate gender discrimination on issues such as basic hours of work and overtime. Workers should be able to negotiate on options such as part-time work, flexi-time, job sharing and night work. Similarly, labour negotiations will need to address the needs of workers with family responsibilities as well as the needs of expectant and nursing mothers. Leave negotiations will have to include not only annual leave, but also leave to fulfil family responsibilities, medical and sick leave, as well as paid leave for education and training. Occupational health and safety in the workplace would assume greater importance to ensure that policies and procedures protect workers from chemicals, hazardous substances, carrying excessive weights, from noise, poor work positions, and the negative impact of new technologies. Greater care will also need to be taken to ensure the provision of protective equipment, welfare facilities and services. Policies on HIV/AIDS in the work place will also need to be adopted to guard against stigma and discrimination. In addition they will need to ensure that workers have access to information on HIV and AIDS prevention. Measures will also have to be approved in the workplace, to establish safety and health committees and to monitor occupational safety and health.

Issues such as maternity protection and benefits, paternity leave, parental leave and care services for children and the elderly will also need to be considered. The rights of vulnerable and non-permanent workers also need to be considered as part of the collective bargaining process. These include workers who are classified as casual, temporary, task, seasonal, part-time, domestic, home-based workers and migrant workers. It should be noted that women are more likely to be found among these categories of workers.

Workplace policies will also need to promote gender equality more explicitly. To overcome the impact of past discrimination on women in the labour force, special measures will need to be adopted to give women workers a more effective voice and access to leadership positions. By so doing, they can help to influence decision-making at the highest level of labour organisations. Workplace policies should also adopt and promote the use of gender-inclusive language. Training is also needed in equal opportunities, recruitment procedures and negotiations to develop the requisite skills. Sexual harassment policies will also need to be adopted. These should include procedures for investigating, reporting, and addressing all forms of gender-based violence. Bullying should also be addressed. In the workplace, the support and promotion of gender equality in the workplace will also require the collection of sex-disaggregated data on men and women. Data on recruitment, promotion and dismissal will also be needed to monitor changes.

Consistent with ILO conventions and the ILO's core objectives of promoting decent work, Caribbean countries should engender social and economic policies as well as revise institutional mechanisms.

The aims are to:

- promote fundamental principles and rights at work;
- create more employment and income opportunities for women and men to raise living standards, increase access to legitimate income and improve income security;
- extend social protection to cover part-time and seasonal workers;
- promote social dialogue to ensure that the needs of all workers, employers and the government are addressed.

At a minimum, all countries should adopt legislation and policies to guarantee the basic human rights of all workers. They should also promote equal remuneration for work of equal value and strive to eliminate discrimination in all forms of employment, as well as to protect workers with family responsibilities. Countries should also adopt specific policies to promote gender equality and protect women against discriminatory practices in recruitment, remuneration and promotion. The promotion of gender-mainstreaming in all sectoral policies and programmes should also be adopted as a best practice and used consistently. Labour inspection polices and services should also be improved to monitor the implementation of the ILO conventions and labour standards in all sectors. This is especially important in the informal sector and other sectors in which the majority of women work. Given the growing size of the informal labour force, governments will need to adopt policies that extend labour agreements to cover non-organised workers.

Policies governing social insurance systems will also need to be reviewed and adjusted to ensure that workers in non-standard employment will have access to insurance coverage. Social safety nets will also need to be reviewed to guarantee minimum standards of protection for vulnerable groups such as the working poor, the long-term unemployed and single-parent households. This is particularly important as the majority of these households are headed by women.

Education policies will also need to be reviewed to reform the education system. Among the changes required is the need to review the curriculum and expand career counselling programmes. This would help to encourage more girls to study in disciplines that were previously male-dominated. In principle, this should provide them with access to occupations with higher levels of remuneration. Career counselling should also be expanded to encourage girls to enter sectors and industries where labour demand is expected to grow rather than to focus on traditional low-wage areas of work for women that are often saturated. Education policies in the Commonwealth Caribbean also need to take account of the current reality that girls are doing better than boys at all levels of the educational system. Guided by research, education policies must therefore address the gender and social disparities in the education system to promote gender equality and equity and address the differential needs of males and females.

Policy frameworks governing childcare programmes and the care of the elderly also need to be strengthened to facilitate women's employment outside the household.

Child labour is also an emerging issue that needs appropriate policies, laws and programmes. It has been on the agenda of the ILO since that organisation was established in 1919 and ILO Conventions 29 (forced labour), 138 (Minimum age for work) and 182 (Worst forms of child labour) have been adopted. The Worst Forms of Child Labour (WFCL) include the involvement of children in modern day slavery, prostitution and pornography, illicit activities and hazardous work.

Policies to address this problem in the Caribbean can be guided by child labour research conducted by the ILO, the University of the West Indies and other institutions in the last decade. These include studies by Crawford-Brown (1996), Dunn (2002), Degazon-Johnson (2002), Williams (2000), and Wint and Madden (2002). Policies should also be guided by recent studies on sex work and tourism in the Caribbean which have also established a link with child labour in the region. These include: Campbell, Perkins and Mohammed (1999), Dunn and Dunn (2002), Kempadoo (ed.) (1999); and Campbell and Campbell (2000).

These and other global studies show that girls below the age of 18 years are more likely to start working at an earlier age and to be paid less than males for similar types of work. They are also likely to be working in sectors and activities that are 'hidden', 'invisible' and unregulated. This makes them more vulnerable to sexual exploitation and other forms of abuse such as incest, prostitution and pornography. Girls are also more likely to be taken out of school to assume responsibilities for housework and childcare. Policies to address child labour should also be linked to national efforts to address the HIV/AIDS pandemic given the increased exposure through prostitution.

Against this background there is an urgent need for all Caribbean countries to ratify Conventions 138 and 182. Policies, legislation and programmes must also be introduced to eliminate child labour and rehabilitate working children and their families. The Government of Jamaica indicated its intention to ratify these two conventions and to adopt the Draft Child Care and Protection Act at an early date.[1] Despite the delays, the Jamaican government has, in recent years, supported several research studies on child labour in prostitution, the tourism sector, fishing and the informal sectors. These have been done in collaboration with the ILO's International Programme for the Elimination of Child Labour (IPEC) with funding from the US Department of Labour. Research findings were used to establish a national child labour programme which is housed at the Ministry of Labour. This is being implemented with the support of a small ILO national team in partnership with the Ministry of Labour, trade unions, the Jamaica Employers Federation, NGOs and teacher training institutions. The

GOJ/ILO/IPEC Country Programme has included a public education campaign, training for labour inspectors, research and intervention programmes in two tourism and fishing communities. The aim is to rehabilitate and support working children and their families. The specific needs of girl children are also being addressed in this ILO country programme.

In conclusion, therefore, tripartite committees in ILO member countries across the Caribbean region should be more proactive in identifying and filling gaps in the range of conventions ratified. They should assess new risks in the workplace and adopt policies to protect both the female and male workers. These workers are affected by emerging issues such as globalisation and new trade regulations, the extensive use of technology and computers, the exposure to HIV/AIDS in the workplace and child labour. Efforts should also be made to strengthen the policy framework, institutional structures and public education programmes to promote gender equality in the workplace.

As we embark on the twenty-first century, Caribbean countries are being challenged to 'push the boundaries' by creating a more enabling policy environment that will promote gender equality in employment as well as support the implementation of ILO conventions. All Caribbean countries are therefore urged to adopt a national gender policy and mainstream gender in all sectors and programmes. Gender mainstreaming could result in more family-friendly policies in the workplace, a reduction in sexual harassment and the promotion of gender equality. Policy action on the ILO conventions is seen as critical to achieving the millennium development goals. This is particularly needed to eradicate extreme poverty and hunger, promote gender equality and women's empowerment, improve maternal health, and combat HIV/AIDS.

Adopting a 'rights-based approach' to policy development and programming would enable countries to achieve greater economic prosperity. This approach can also lead to greater equality in participation of men and women at the highest levels of decision-making. It could also result in a creative dynamic workforce of men and women equipped to meet the challenges of globalisation in the twenty-first century.

Note

1. ILO Conventions 138 and 182 were ratified in July 2003. The Childcare and Protection Act was passed in 2004.

References

Dunn, H.S. and Dunn, L.L. 2002. *People and Tourism: Issues and Attitudes in the Jamaica Hospitality Industry*, Kingston: Arawak Publications.

Dunn, H.S. 2000. *Telecommunications and Information Technology: Their impact on Employment and Trade Unions in the Caribbean* (with an Introduction by Lloyd Goodleigh), Jamaica: Friedrich Ebert Stiftung.

Dunn L.L and Dunn, H.S. 1999. *Employment, working conditions and labour relations in offshore data service enterprises: Case studies of Barbados and Jamaica.*

Multinational Enterprises Programme. *Working Paper* no. 86. Geneva: ILO.

International Labour Office. 2000. *Gender: A Partnership of Equals.* Geneva: ILO Bureau for Gender Equality.

International Labour Office. 2000. *ABC of women workers' rights and gender equality.* Geneva: ILO.

International Labour Office. 1994. *Promotion of Equality of Opportunity and Treatment for Women Workers: An ILO Manual for Asia and the Pacific*, ILO East Asia Multidisciplinary Advisory Team (EASMAT), ILO Regional Office for Asia and the Pacific, Bangkok.

Kempadoo, K. ed. 1999. *Sun Sex and Gold: Tourism and Sex Work in the Caribbean.* Oxford: Rowman and Littlefield.

Momm, W. ed. 1999. *Labour Issues in the context of economic integration and free trade – A Caribbean Perspective.* Port of Spain: International Labour Organization Caribbean Office.

Mondesire and Dunn. 1995. *Towards equity in development: A report on the status of women in sixteen Commonwealth Caribbean countries.* Guyana: CARICOM.

Tokman, V.E. 1999. 'Globalisation and adjustment: new challenges for Latin America'. In *Labour issues in the context of economic integration and free trade – A Caribbean perspective*, Port of Spain: ILO Caribbean Office.

APPENDICES

APPENDIX 1: ILO Conventions

1. Basic Human Rights

C 100	Equal Remuneration, 1951
R 90	Equal Remuneration, 1951
C 111	Discrimination (Employment and Occupation), 1958
R 111	Discrimination (Employment and Occupation), 1952
C 156	Workers with Family Responsibility, 1981
R 156	Workers with Family Responsibility, 1981

2. Freedom of Association

C 87	Freedom of Association and Protection of the Right to Organise, 1948
C 98	Right to Organise and Collective Bargaining, 1949
C 141	Rural Workers' Organisations, 1975
R 149	Rural Workers' Organisations, 1975

3. Employment

C 122	Employment Policy, 1964
R 122	Employment Policy, 1964
R 169	Employment (Supplementary Provisions), 1984
C 142	Human Resources Development, 1975
R 150	Human Resources Development, 1975
C 158	Termination of Employment, 1982

4. Social Policy

C 117	Social Policy (Basic Aims and Standards), 1962

5. Maternity Protection

C 3	Maternity Protection, 1919
C 103	Maternity Protection (revised), 1952
R 95	Maternity Protection, 1952
C 110	Plantation, 1958 (and Protocol, 1982)
R 12	Maternity Protection (Agriculture), 1921

6. Night Work

R 13	Night Work of Women in Agriculture, 1921
C 89	Night Work Women (Revised) 1948 and Protocol, 1990
C 171	Night Work, 1990
R 178	Night Work, 1990

7. Conditions of Work

C 45	Underground Work (Women), 1935
R 102	Welfare Facilities, 1956
R 116	Reduction of Hours of Work, 1962
C 140	Paid Educational Leave, 1974

8. Occupational Health and Safety

R 4	Lead Poisoning (Protection of Women and Children), 1919
C 13	White Lead (Painting), 1921
R 114	Radiation Protection, 1960 Supplements C 115
C 127	Maximum Weight, 1967
R 128	Maximum Weight, 1967
C 136	Benzene, 1971
R 144	Benzene, 1971
C 170	Chemicals, 1990
R 177	Chemicals, 1990

9. Other Special Categories of Workers

C 159	Vocational Rehabilitation and Employment (Disabled Persons), 1983
R 169	Vocational Rehabilitation and Employment (Disabled Persons), 1963
C 169	Indigenous and Tribal Peoples, 1989

10. Conventions of Special Significance

C 4	Night work (Women), 1919
C 81	Labour Inspection, 1946 (Article 8)
C 95	Protection of Wages, 1949
C 102	Social Security (Minimum Standards), 1952 (Part V111)
C 118	Equality of Treatment (Social Security), 1962 (Articles 2 & 4 Maternity Benefits)
C 129	Labour Inspection (Agriculture), 1969
C 138	Minimum Age, 1973
C 149	Nursing Personnel, 1977
C 157	Maintenance of Social Security Rights, 1982
C 168	Employment Promotion and Protection Against Employment, 1988
C 182	Worst Forms of Child Labour, 1999 and R 190, 1999

APPENDIX 2: Caribbean Ratification of ILO Conventions

Antigua and Barbuda

Member since 1982

28 Conventions ratified and in force

C. 11	Right of Association (Agriculture) Convention, 1921 (No. 11)	2.02.1983
C. 12	Workmen's Compensation (Agriculture) Convention, 1921 (No. 12)	2.02.1983
C. 14	Weekly Rest (Industry) Convention, 1921 (No. 14)	2.02.1983
C. 17	Workmen's Compensation (Accidents) Convention, 1925 (No. 17)	2.02.1983
C. 19	Equality of Treatment (Accident Compensation) Convention, 1925 (No. 19)	2.02.1983
C. 29	Forced Labour Convention, 1930 (No. 29)	2.02.1983
C. 81	Labour Inspection Convention, 1947 (No. 81) excluding Part II	2.02.1983
C. 87	Freedom of Association and Protection of the Right to Organise Convention, 1948 (No. 87)	2.02.1983
C. 94	Labour Clauses (Public Contracts) Convention, 1949 (No. 94)	2.02.1983
C. 98	Right to Organise and Collective Bargaining Convention, 1949 (No. 98)	2.02.1983
C. 100	Equal Remuneration Convention, 1951 (No. 100)	2.02.1983
C. 101	Holidays with Pay (Agriculture) Convention, 1952 (No. 101)	2.05.2003
C. 105	Abolition of Forced Labour Convention, 1957 (No. 105)	2.02.1983
C. 108	Seafarers' Identity Documents Convention, 1958 (No. 108)	2.02.1983
C. 111	Discrimination (Employment and Occupation) Convention, 1958 (No. 111)	2.02.1983
C. 122	Employment Policy Convention, 1964 (No. 122)	16.09.2002
C. 131	Minimum Wage Fixing Convention, 1970 (No. 131)	16.09.2002
C. 135	Workers' Representatives Convention, 1971 (No. 135)	16.09.2002
C. 138	Minimum Age Convention, 1973 (No. 138) Minimum age specified: 16 years	17.03.1983
C. 142	Human Resources Development Convention, 1975 (No. 142)	16.09.2002
C. 144	Tripartite Consultation (International Labour Standards) Convention, 1976 (No. 144)	16.09.2002
C. 150	Labour Administration Convention, 1978 (No. 150)	16.09.2002
C. 151	Labour Relations (Public Service) Convention, 1978 (No. 151)	16.09.2002
C. 154	Collective Bargaining Convention, 1981 (No. 154)	16.09.2002
C. 155	Occupational Safety and Health Convention, 1981 (No. 155)	16.09.2002
C. 158	Termination of Employment Convention, 1982 (No. 158)	16.09.2002
C. 161	Occupational Health Services Convention, 1985 (No. 161)	16.09.2002
C. 182	Worst Forms of Child Labour Convention, 1999 (No. 182)	16.09.2002

The Bahamas

Member since 1976

33 Conventions ratified (30 in force)

C. 11	Right of Association (Agriculture) Convention, 1921 (No. 11)	25.05.1976
C. 12	Workmen's Compensation (Agriculture) Convention, 1921 (No. 12)	25.05.1976
C. 14	Weekly Rest (Industry) Convention, 1921 (No. 14)	25.05.1976
C. 17	Workmen's Compensation (Accidents) Convention, 1925 (No. 17)	25.05.1976
C. 19	Equality of Treatment (Accident Compensation) Convention, 1925 (No. 19)	25.05.1976
C. 22	Seamen's Articles of Agreement Convention, 1926 (No. 22)	25.05.1976
C. 26	Minimum Wage-Fixing Machinery Convention, 1928 (No. 26)	25.05.1976
C. 29	Forced Labour Convention, 1930 (No. 29)	25.05.1976
C. 42	Workmen's Compensation (Occupational Diseases) Convention (Revised), 1934 (No. 42)	25.05.1976
C. 45	Underground Work (Women) Convention, 1935 (No. 45)	25.05.1976
C. 50	Recruiting of Indigenous Workers Convention, 1936 (No. 50)	25.05.1976
C. 64	Contracts of Employment (Indigenous Workers) Convention, 1939 (No. 64)	25.05.1976
C. 65	Penal Sanctions (Indigenous Workers) Convention, 1939 (No. 65)	25.05.1976
C. 81	Labour Inspection Convention, 1947 (No. 81)	25.05.1976
C. 86	Contracts of Employment (Indigenous Workers) Convention, 1947 (No. 86)	25.05.1976
C. 87	Freedom of Association and Protection of the Right to Organise Convention, 1948 (No. 87)	14.06.2001
C. 88	Employment Service Convention, 1948 (No. 88)	25.05.1976
C. 94	Labour Clauses (Public Contracts) Convention, 1949 (No. 94)	25.05.1976
C. 95	Protection of Wages Convention, 1949 (No. 95)	25.05.1976
C. 97	Migration for Employment Convention (Revised), 1949 (No. 97) Has excluded the provisions of Annexes I to III	25.05.1976
C. 98	Right to Organise and Collective Bargaining Convention, 1949 (No. 98)	25.05.1976
C. 100	Equal Remuneration Convention, 1951 (No. 100)	14.06.2001
C. 103	Maternity Protection Convention (Revised), 1952 (No. 103)	14.06.2001
C. 105	Abolition of Forced Labour Convention, 1957 (No. 105)	25.05.1976
C. 111	Discrimination (Employment and Occupation) Convention, 1958 (No. 111)	14.06.2001
C. 117	Social Policy (Basic Aims and Standards) Convention, 1962 (No. 117)	25.05.1976
C. 138	Minimum Age Convention, 1973 (No. 138) Minimum age specified: 14 years	31.10.2001

C. 144	Tripartite Consultation (International Labour Standards) Convention, 1976 (No. 144)	
C. 147	Merchant Shipping (Minimum Standards) Convention, 1976 (No. 147)	16.08.1979
C. 182	Worst Forms of Child Labour Convention, 1999 (No. 182)	3.01.2001
		14.06.2001

Denunciation (as a result of the ratification of Convention No. 138)

CC. 5	Minimum Age (Industry) Convention, 1919 (No. 5) Denounced on 31.10.2001	25.05.1976
C. 7	Minimum Age (Sea) Convention, 1920 (No. 7) Denounced on 31.10.2001	25.05.1976
C. 10	Minimum Age (Agriculture) Convention, 1921 (No. 10) Denounced on 31.10.2001	25.05.1976

Barbados

Member since 1967

39 Conventions ratified (36 in force)

C. 11	Right of Association (Agriculture) Convention, 1921 (No. 11)	8.05.1967
C. 12	Workmen's Compensation (Agriculture) Convention, 1921 (No. 12)	8.05.1967
C. 17	Workmen's Compensation (Accidents) Convention, 1925 (No. 17)	8.05.1967
C. 19	Equality of Treatment (Accident Compensation) Convention, 1925 (No. 19)	8.05.1967
C. 22	Seamen's Articles of Agreement Convention, 1926 (No. 22)	8.05.1967
C. 26	Minimum Wage-Fixing Machinery Convention, 1928 (No. 26)	8.05.1967
C. 29	Forced Labour Convention, 1930 (No. 29)	8.05.1967
C. 42	Workmen's Compensation (Occupational Diseases) Convention (Revised), 1934 (No. 42)	8.05.1967
C. 50	Recruiting of Indigenous Workers Convention, 1936 (No. 50)	8.05.1967
C. 63	Convention concerning Statistics of Wages and Hours of Work, 1938 (No. 63) Excluding Part III	8.05.1967
C. 65	Penal Sanctions (Indigenous Workers) Convention, 1939 (No. 65)	8.05.1967
C. 74	Certification of Able Seamen Convention, 1946 (No. 74)	8.05.1967
C. 81	Labour Inspection Convention, 1947 (No. 81) Excluding Part II	8.05.1967
C. 86	Contracts of Employment (Indigenous Workers) Convention, 1947 (No. 86)	8.05.1967
C. 87	Freedom of Association and Protection of the Right to Organise Convention, 1948 (No. 87)	8.05.1967
C. 90	Night Work of Young Persons (Industry) Convention (Revised), 1948 (No. 90)	15.01.1976

C. 94	Labour Clauses (Public Contracts) Convention, 1949 (No. 94)	8.05.1967
C. 95	Protection of Wages Convention, 1949 (No. 95)	8.05.1967
C. 97	Migration for Employment Convention (Revised), 1949 (No. 97) Has excluded the provisions of Annexes I to III	8.05.1967
C. 98	Right to Organise and Collective Bargaining Convention, 1949 (No. 98)	8.05.1967
C. 100	Equal Remuneration Convention, 1951 (No. 100)	19.09.1974
C. 101	Holidays with Pay (Agriculture) Convention, 1952 (No. 101)	8.05.1967
C. 102	Social Security (Minimum Standards) Convention, 1952 (No. 102) Has accepted Parts III, V, VI, IX and X. As a result of the ratification of Convention No. 128 and pursuant to Article 45 of that Convention certain parts of the present Convention are no longer applicable.	11.07.1972
C. 105	Abolition of Forced Labour Convention, 1957 (No. 105)	8.05.1967
C. 108	Seafarers' Identity Documents Convention, 1958 (No. 108)	8.05.1967
C. 111	Discrimination (Employment and Occupation) Convention, 1958 (No. 111)	14.10.1974
C. 115	Radiation Protection Convention, 1960 (No. 115)	8.05.1967
C. 118	Equality of Treatment (Social Security) Convention, 1962 (No. 118) Has accepted Branches (b), (c) and (e) to (g)	14.10.1974
C. 122	Employment Policy Convention, 1964 (No. 122)	15.03.1976
C. 128	Invalidity, Old-Age and Survivors' Benefits Convention, 1967 (No. 128) Has accepted Parts II and III	15.09.1972
C. 135	Workers' Representatives Convention, 1971 (No. 135)	25.04.1977
C. 138	Minimum Age Convention, 1973 (No. 138) Minimum age specified: 15 years	4.01.2000
C. 144	Tripartite Consultation (International Labour Standards) Convention, 1976 (No. 144)	6.04.1983
C. 147	Merchant Shipping (Minimum Standards) Convention, 1976 (No. 147)	16.05.1994
C. 172	Working Conditions (Hotels and Restaurants) Convention, 1991 (No. 172)	22.06.1997
C. 182	Worst Forms of Child Labour Convention, 1999 (No. 182)	23.10.2000

Denunciation (as a result of the ratification of Convention No. 138)

C. 5	Minimum Age (Industry) Convention, 1919 (No. 5) Denounced on 4.01.2000	8.05.1967
C. 7	Minimum Age (Sea) Convention, 1920 (No. 7) Denounced on 4.01.2000	8.05.1967
C. 10	Minimum Age (Agriculture) Convention, 1921 (No. 10) Denounced on 4.01.2000	2.10.1978

Belize

Member since 1981

42 Conventions ratified (38 in force)

C. 8	Unemployment Indemnity (Shipwreck) Convention, 1920 (No. 8)	15.12.1983
C. 11	Right of Association (Agriculture) Convention, 1921 (No. 11)	15.12.1983
C. 12	Workmen's Compensation (Agriculture) Convention, 1921 (No. 12)	15.12.1983
C. 14	Weekly Rest (Industry) Convention, 1921 (No. 14)	15.12.1983
C. 16	Medical Examination of Young Persons (Sea) Convention, 1921 (No. 16)	22.06.1999
C. 19	Equality of Treatment (Accident Compensation) Convention, 1925 (No. 19)	15.12.1983
C. 22	Seamen's Articles of Agreement Convention, 1926 (No. 22)	15.12.1983
C. 26	Minimum Wage-Fixing Machinery Convention, 1928 (No. 26)	15.12.1983
C. 29	Forced Labour Convention, 1930 (No. 29)	15.12.1983
C. 42	Workmen's Compensation (Occupational Diseases) Convention (Revised), 1934 (No. 42)	15.12.1983
C. 58	Minimum Age (Sea) Convention (Revised), 1936 (No. 58)	15.12.1983
C. 81	Labour Inspection Convention, 1947 (No. 81)	15.12.1983
C. 87	Freedom of Association and Protection of the Right to Organise Convention, 1948 (No. 87)	15.12.1983
C. 88	Employment Service Convention, 1948 (No. 88)	15.12.1983
C. 89	Night Work (Women) Convention (Revised), 1948 (No. 89)	15.12.1983
C. 94	Labour Clauses (Public Contracts) Convention, 1949 (No. 94)	15.12.1983
C. 95	Protection of Wages Convention, 1949 (No. 95)	15.12.1983
C. 97	Migration for Employment Convention (Revised), 1949 (No. 97)	15.12.1983
C. 98	Right to Organise and Collective Bargaining Convention, 1949 (No. 98)	15.12.1983
C. 99	Minimum Wage Fixing Machinery (Agriculture) Convention, 1951 (No. 99)	15.12.1983
C. 100	Equal Remuneration Convention, 1951 (No. 100)	22.06.1999
C. 101	Holidays with Pay (Agriculture) Convention, 1952 (No. 101)	15.12.1983
C. 103	Maternity Protection Convention (Revised), 1952 (No. 103)	6.03.2000
C. 105	Abolition of Forced Labour Convention, 1957 (No. 105)	15.12.1983
C. 108	Seafarers' Identity Documents Convention, 1958 (No. 108)	15.12.1983
C. 111	Discrimination (Employment and Occupation) Convention, 1958 (No. 111)	22.06.1999
C. 115	Radiation Protection Convention, 1960 (No. 115)	15.12.1983
C. 135	Workers' Representatives Convention, 1971 (No. 135)	22.06.1999
C. 138	Minimum Age Convention, 1973 (No. 138) *Minimum age specified: 14 years*	6.03.2000

C. 140	Paid Educational Leave Convention, 1974 (No. 140)	22.06.1999
C. 141	Rural Workers' Organisations Convention, 1975 (No. 141)	22.06.1999
C. 144	Tripartite Consultation (International Labour Standards) Convention, 1976 (No. 144)	6.03.2000
C. 150	Labour Administration Convention, 1978 (No. 150)	6.03.2000
C. 151	Labour Relations (Public Service) Convention, 1978 (No. 151)	22.06.1999
C. 154	Collective Bargaining Convention, 1981 (No. 154)	22.06.1999
C. 155	Occupational Safety and Health Convention, 1981 (No. 155)	22.06.1999
C. 156	Workers with Family Responsibilities Convention, 1981 (No. 156)	22.06.1999
C. 182	Worst Forms of Child Labour Convention, 1999 (No. 182)	6.03.2000

Denunciation (as a result of the ratification of Convention No. 138)

C. 5	Minimum Age (Industry) Convention, 1919 (No. 5) Denounced on 6.03.2000	15.12.1983
C. 7	Minimum Age (Sea) Convention, 1920 (No. 7) Denounced on 6.03.2000	15.12.1983
C. 10	Minimum Age (Agriculture) Convention, 1921 (No. 10) Denounced on 6.03.2000	15.12.1983
C. 15	Minimum Age (Trimmers and Stokers) Convention, 1921 (No. 15) Denounced on 6.03.2000	15.12.1983

Dominica

Member since 1982

23 Conventions ratified and in force

C. 8	Unemployment Indemnity (Shipwreck) Convention, 1920 (No. 8)	28.02.1983
C. 11	Right of Association (Agriculture) Convention, 1921 (No. 11)	28.02.1983
C. 12	Workmen's Compensation (Agriculture) Convention, 1921 (No. 12)	28.02.1983
C. 14	Weekly Rest (Industry) Convention, 1921 (No. 14)	28.02.1983
C. 16	Medical Examination of Young Persons (Sea) Convention, 1921 (No. 16)	28.02.1983
C. 19	Equality of Treatment (Accident Compensation) Convention, 1925 (No. 19)	28.02.1983
C. 22	Seamen's Articles of Agreement Convention, 1926 (No. 22)	28.02.1983
C. 26	Minimum Wage-Fixing Machinery Convention, 1928 (No. 26)	28.02.1983
C. 29	Forced Labour Convention, 1930 (No. 29)	28.02.1983
C. 81	Labour Inspection Convention, 1947 (No. 81)	28.02.1983
C. 87	Freedom of Association and Protection of the Right to Organise Convention, 1948 (No. 87)	28.02.1983
C. 94	Labour Clauses (Public Contracts) Convention, 1949 (No. 94)	28.02.1983
C. 95	Protection of Wages Convention, 1949 (No. 95)	28.02.1983

C. 97	Migration for Employment Convention (Revised), 1949 (No. 97) *Has excluded the provisions of Annexes I to III*	28.02.1983
C. 98	Right to Organise and Collective Bargaining Convention, 1949 (No. 98)	28.02.1983
C. 100	Equal Remuneration Convention, 1951 (No. 100)	28.02.1983
C. 105	Abolition of Forced Labour Convention, 1957 (No. 105)	28.02.1983
C. 108	Seafarers' Identity Documents Convention, 1958 (No. 108)	28.02.1983
C. 111	Discrimination (Employment and Occupation) Convention, 1958 (No. 111)	28.02.1983
C. 138	Minimum Age Convention, 1973 (No. 138) *Minimum age specified: 15 years*	27.09.1983
C. 144	Tripartite Consultation (International Labour Standards) Convention, 1976 (No. 144)	29.04.2002
C. 169	Indigenous and Tribal Peoples Convention, 1989 (No. 169)	25.06.2002
C. 182	Worst Forms of Child Labour Convention, 1999 (No. 182)	4.01.2001

Grenada

Member since 1979

31 Conventions ratified (26 in force)

C. 8	Unemployment Indemnity (Shipwreck) Convention, 1920 (No. 8)	9.07.1979
C. 11	Right of Association (Agriculture) Convention, 1921 (No. 11)	9.07.1979
C. 12	Workmen's Compensation (Agriculture) Convention, 1921 (No. 12)	9.07.1979
C. 14	Weekly Rest (Industry) Convention, 1921 (No. 14)	9.07.1979
C. 16	Medical Examination of Young Persons (Sea) Convention, 1921 (No. 16)	9.07.1979
C. 19	Equality of Treatment (Accident Compensation) Convention, 1925 (No. 19)	9.07.1979
C. 26	Minimum Wage-Fixing Machinery Convention, 1928 (No. 26)	9.07.1979
C. 29	Forced Labour Convention, 1930 (No. 29)	9.07.1979
C. 50	Recruiting of Indigenous Workers Convention, 1936 (No. 50)	9.07.1979
C. 64	Contracts of Employment (Indigenous Workers) Convention, 1939 (No. 64)	9.07.1979
C. 65	Penal Sanctions (Indigenous Workers) Convention, 1939 (No. 65)	9.07.1979
C. 81	Labour Inspection Convention, 1947 (No. 81) *Excluding Part II*	9.07.1979
C. 86	Contracts of Employment (Indigenous Workers) Convention, 1947 (No. 86)	9.07.1979
C. 87	Freedom of Association and Protection of the Right to Organise Convention, 1948 (No. 87)	25.10.1994
C. 94	Labour Clauses (Public Contracts) Convention, 1949 (No. 94)	9.07.1979

C. 95	Protection of Wages Convention, 1949 (No. 95)	9.07.1979
C. 97	Migration for Employment Convention (Revised), 1949 (No. 97) *Has excluded the provisions of Annexes I to III*	9.07.1979
C. 98	Right to Organise and Collective Bargaining Convention, 1949 (No. 98)	9.07.1979
C. 99	Minimum Wage Fixing Machinery (Agriculture) Convention, 1951 (No. 99)	9.07.1979
C. 100	Equal Remuneration Convention, 1951 (No. 100)	25.10.1994
C. 105	Abolition of Forced Labour Convention, 1957 (No. 105)	9.07.1979
C. 108	Seafarers' Identity Documents Convention, 1958 (No. 108)	9.07.1979
C. 111	Discrimination (Employment and Occupation) Convention, 1958 (No. 111)	14.05.2003
C. 138	Minimum Age Convention, 1973 (No. 138) *Minimum age specified: 16 years*	14.05.2003
C. 144	Tripartite Consultation (International Labour Standards) Convention, 1976 (No. 144)	25.10.1994
C. 182	Worst Forms of Child Labour Convention, 1999 (No. 182)	14.05.2003

Denunciation (as a result of the ratification of Convention No. 138)

C. 5	Minimum Age (Industry) Convention, 1919 (No. 5) Denounced on 14.05.2003	9.07.1979
C. 7	Minimum Age (Sea) Convention, 1920 (No. 7) Denounced on 14.05.2003	9.07.1979
C. 10	Minimum Age (Agriculture) Convention, 1921 (No. 10) Denounced on 14.05.2003	9.07.1979
C. 15	Minimum Age (Trimmers and Stokers) Convention, 1921 (No. 15) Denounced on 14.05.2003	9.07.1979
C. 58	Minimum Age (Sea) Convention (Revised), 1936 (No. 58) Denounced on 14.05.2003	9.07.1979

Guyana

Member since 1966

45 Conventions ratified (41 in force)

C. 2	Unemployment Convention, 1919 (No. 2)	8.06.1966
C. 11	Right of Association (Agriculture) Convention, 1921 (No. 11)	8.06.1966
C. 12	Workmen's Compensation (Agriculture) Convention, 1921 (No. 12)	8.06.1966
C. 19	Equality of Treatment (Accident Compensation) Convention, 1925 (No. 19)	8.06.1966
C. 26	Minimum Wage-Fixing Machinery Convention, 1928 (No. 26)	8.06.1966
C. 29	Forced Labour Convention, 1930 (No. 29)	8.06.1966

C. 42	Workmen's Compensation (Occupational Diseases) Convention (Revised), 1934 (No. 42)	8.06.1966
C. 45	Underground Work (Women) Convention, 1935 (No. 45)	8.06.1966
C. 50	Recruiting of Indigenous Workers Convention, 1936 (No. 50)	8.06.1966
C. 64	Contracts of Employment (Indigenous Workers) Convention, 1939 (No. 64)	8.06.1966
C. 65	Penal Sanctions (Indigenous Workers) Convention, 1939 (No. 65)	8.06.1966
C. 81	Labour Inspection Convention, 1947 (No. 81) *Excluding Part II. Has ratified the Protocol of 1995.*	8.06.1966
C. 86	Contracts of Employment (Indigenous Workers) Convention, 1947 (No. 86)	8.06.1966
C. 87	Freedom of Association and Protection of the Right to Organise Convention, 1948 (No. 87)	25.09.1967
C. 94	Labour Clauses (Public Contracts) Convention, 1949 (No. 94)	8.06.1966
C. 95	Protection of Wages Convention, 1949 (No. 95)	8.06.1966
C. 97	Migration for Employment Convention (Revised), 1949 (No. 97) *Has excluded the provisions of Annexes I to III*	8.06.1966
C. 98	Right to Organise and Collective Bargaining Convention, 1949 (No. 98)	8.06.1966
C. 100	Equal Remuneration Convention, 1951 (No. 100)	13.06.1975
C. 105	Abolition of Forced Labour Convention, 1957 (No. 105)	8.06.1966
C. 108	Seafarers' Identity Documents Convention, 1958 (No. 108)	8.06.1966
C. 111	Discrimination (Employment and Occupation) Convention, 1958 (No. 111)	13.06.1975
C. 115	Radiation Protection Convention, 1960 (No. 115)	8.06.1966
C. 129	Labour Inspection (Agriculture) Convention, 1969 (No. 129)	19.01.1971
C. 131	Minimum Wage Fixing Convention, 1970 (No. 131)	10.01.1983
C. 135	Workers' Representatives Convention, 1971 (No. 135)	10.01.1983
C. 136	Benzene Convention, 1971 (No. 136)	10.01.1983
C. 137	Dock Work Convention, 1973 (No. 137)	10.01.1983
C. 138	Minimum Age Convention, 1973 (No. 138) *Minimum age specified: 15 years*	15.04.1998
C. 139	Occupational Cancer Convention, 1974 (No. 139)	10.01.1983
C. 140	Paid Educational Leave Convention, 1974 (No. 140)	10.01.1983
C. 141	Rural Workers' Organisations Convention, 1975 (No. 141)	10.01.1983
C. 142	Human Resources Development Convention, 1975 (No. 142)	10.01.1983
C. 144	Tripartite Consultation (International Labour Standards) Convention, 1976 (No. 144)	10.01.1983
C. 149	Nursing Personnel Convention, 1977 (No. 149)	10.01.1983
C. 150	Labour Administration Convention, 1978 (No. 150)	10.01.1983
C. 151	Labour Relations (Public Service) Convention, 1978 (No. 151)	10.01.1983
C. 166	Repatriation of Seafarers Convention (Revised), 1987 (No. 166)	10.06.1996
C. 172	Working Conditions (Hotels and Restaurants) Convention, 1991 (No. 172)	20.08.1996

| C. 175 | Part-Time Work Convention, 1994 (No. 175) | 3.09.1997 |
| C. 182 | Worst Forms of Child Labour Convention, 1999 (No. 182) | 15.01.2001 |

Denunciation (as a result of the ratification of Convention No. 138)

C. 5	Minimum Age (Industry) Convention, 1919 (No. 5) Denounced on 15.04.1998	8.06.1966
C. 7	Minimum Age (Sea) Convention, 1920 (No. 7) Denounced on 15.04.1998	8.06.1966
C. 10	Minimum Age (Agriculture) Convention, 1921 (No. 10) Denounced on 15.04.1998	8.06.1966
C. 15	Minimum Age (Trimmers and Stokers) Convention, 1921 (No. 15) Denounced on 15.04.1998	8.06.1966

Jamaica

Member since 1962

26 Conventions ratified and in force

C. 7	Minimum Age (Sea) Convention, 1920 (No. 7)	8.07.1963
C. 8	Unemployment Indemnity (Shipwreck) Convention, 1920 (No. 8)	8.07.1963
C. 11	Right of Association (Agriculture) Convention, 1921 (No. 11)	8.07.1963
C. 15	Minimum Age (Trimmers and Stokers) Convention, 1921 (No. 15)	26.12.1962
C. 16	Medical Examination of Young Persons (Sea) Convention, 1921 (No. 16)	26.12.1962
C. 19	Equality of Treatment (Accident Compensation) Convention, 1925 (No. 19)	26.12.1962
C. 26	Minimum Wage-Fixing Machinery Convention, 1928 (No. 26)	8.07.1963
C. 29	Forced Labour Convention, 1930 (No. 29)	26.12.1962
C. 50	Recruiting of Indigenous Workers Convention, 1936 (No. 50)	26.12.1962
C. 58	Minimum Age (Sea) Convention (Revised), 1936 (No. 58)	26.12.1962
C. 64	Contracts of Employment (Indigenous Workers) Convention, 1939 (No. 64)	26.12.1962
C. 65	Penal Sanctions (Indigenous Workers) Convention, 1939 (No. 65)	26.12.1962
C. 81	Labour Inspection Convention, 1947 (No. 81) *Excluding Part II*	26.12.1962
C. 86	Contracts of Employment (Indigenous Workers) Convention, 1947 (No. 86)	26.12.1962
C. 87	Freedom of Association and Protection of the Right to Organise Convention, 1948 (No. 87)	26.12.1962
C. 94	Labour Clauses (Public Contracts) Convention, 1949 (No. 94)	26.12.1962

C. 97	Migration for Employment Convention (Revised), 1949 (No. 97) *Has excluded the provisions of Annexes I to III*	26.12.1962
C. 98	Right to Organise and Collective Bargaining Convention, 1949 (No. 98)	26.12.1962
C. 100	Equal Remuneration Convention, 1951 (No. 100)	14.01.1975
C. 105	Abolition of Forced Labour Convention, 1957 (No. 105)	26.12.1962
C. 111	Discrimination (Employment and Occupation) Convention, 1958 (No. 111)	10.01.1975
C. 117	Social Policy (Basic Aims and Standards) Convention, 1962 (No. 117)	4.01.1966
C. 122	Employment Policy Convention, 1964 (No. 122)	10.01.1975
C. 144	Tripartite Consultation (International Labour Standards) Convention, 1976 (No. 144)	23.10.1996
C. 149	Nursing Personnel Convention, 1977 (No. 149)	4.06.1984
C. 150	Labour Administration Convention, 1978 (No. 150)	4.06.1984

Saint Kitts and Nevis

Member since 1996

8 Conventions ratified and in force

C. 29	Forced Labour Convention, 1930 (No. 29)	12.10.2000
C. 87	Freedom of Association and Protection of the Right to Organise Convention, 1948 (No. 87)	25.08.2000
C. 98	Right to Organise and Collective Bargaining Convention, 1949 (No. 98)	4.09.2000
C. 100	Equal Remuneration Convention, 1951 (No. 100)	25.08.2000
C. 105	Abolition of Forced Labour Convention, 1957 (No. 105)	12.10.2000
C. 111	Discrimination (Employment and Occupation) Convention, 1958 (No. 111)	25.08.2000
C. 144	Tripartite Consultation (International Labour Standards) Convention, 1976 (No. 144)	12.10.2000
C. 182	Worst Forms of Child Labour Convention, 1999 (No. 182)	12.10.2000

Trinidad and Tobago

Member since 1963

17 Conventions ratified and in force

C. 15	Minimum Age (Trimmers and Stokers) Convention, 1921 (No. 15)	24.05.1963

C. 16	Medical Examination of Young Persons (Sea) Convention, 1921 (No. 16)	24.05.1963
C. 19	Equality of Treatment (Accident Compensation) Convention, 1925 (No. 19)	24.05.1963
C. 29	Forced Labour Convention, 1930 (No. 29)	24.05.1963
C. 50	Recruiting of Indigenous Workers Convention, 1936 (No. 50)	24.05.1963
C. 65	Penal Sanctions (Indigenous Workers) Convention, 1939 (No. 65)	24.05.1963
C. 87	Freedom of Association and Protection of the Right to Organise Convention, 1948 (No. 87)	24.05.1963
C. 97	Migration for Employment Convention (Revised), 1949 (No. 97) *Has excluded the provisions of Annexes I to III*	24.05.1963
C. 98	Right to Organise and Collective Bargaining Convention, 1949 (No. 98)	24.05.1963
C. 100	Equal Remuneration Convention, 1951 (No. 100)	29.05.1997
C. 105	Abolition of Forced Labour Convention, 1957 (No. 105)	24.05.1963
C. 111	Discrimination (Employment and Occupation) Convention, 1958 (No. 111)	26.11.1970
C. 125	Fishermen's Competency Certificates Convention, 1966 (No. 125)	14.12.1972
C. 144	Tripartite Consultation (International Labour Standards) Convention, 1976 (No. 144)	7.06.1995
C. 147	Merchant Shipping (Minimum Standards) Convention, 1976 (No. 147)	3.06.1999
C. 159	Vocational Rehabilitation and Employment (Disabled Persons) Convention, 1983 (No. 159)	3.06.1999
C. 182	Worst Forms of Child Labour Convention, 1999 (No. 182)	23.04.2003

14 | ORVILLE W. TAYLOR

The Challenge of Gender and the Labour Market after 30 Years of CARICOM

Introduction

A decade ago, in a not well-publicised article (Taylor 1993), the problematic was raised that despite the 'men at risk' arguments advanced by the then topical publication, of the same name, by Errol Miller (Miller 1991), women were still at risk. In Miller's work, the evidence was that men in the anglophone Caribbean and CARICOM on the whole, have been consistently under-represented in higher education. On the other hand, Taylor demonstrated that women were persistently lagging behind men in the political arena, industry and the labour market. What, therefore, has emerged is a paradox relating to gender that is reflected in the ambivalent way that statutes in the Caribbean have developed to address the issue of discrimination on the basis of sex. As a result, discriminatory practices can exist and are allowed, if not supported, within statute.

It is the argument of this paper that Caribbean legislation dealing with gender equality is ambiguous, flawed and likely to lead to problems as the region moves towards a Caribbean Single Market and Economy (CSME). In order to discuss the issue, it is necessary to explore the notion of gender-equality, basing it in concrete concepts or at least recognised standards. The bias in this paper is towards the oldest set of international standards related to fundamental human rights and labour, those of the International Labour Organization (ILO).

Historical Review of International Standards Related to Gender

Pre-existing its sister organisation, the United Nations, by almost three decades, the modern ILO was established as part of the agenda of the 1919 Paris Peace Conference, in the aftermath of World War I and given full effect by Part 13 of the Treaty of Versailles. Its nine-point Labour Charter, embodied within the peace treaty, includes the principles of equal pay for equal work and equitable economic treatment for all workers.

Between 1919 and 1939, 67 conventions and 66 recommendations were developed by the organisation. By 1944, the ILO, at its meeting in Philadelphia, adopted the famous Declaration of Philadelphia, which re-affirmed its objectives. This declaration embodies the following principles:

1. Labour is not a commodity;
2. Freedom of expression and association are essential to sustained progress;
3. Poverty anywhere constitutes a danger to prosperity everywhere;
4. All human beings, irrespective of race, creed or sex, have the right to pursue both their material well-being and their spiritual development, in conditions of freedom and dignity, of economic security and equal opportunity. (ILO 2000, 6)

Being older than the UN it set the pattern for the United Nations Charter and the Universal Declaration of Human Rights.

The ILO's 1998 Declaration on Fundamental Principles and Rights at Work synthesises the abovementioned elements and forms part of a universal social pillar that supports democracy, transparency, equity and development. In summary, there are four essential principles by which all member nations of the ILO are bound. These comprise the following elements: (i) freedom of association and the right to collective bargaining, (ii) protection from all forms of forced or compulsory labour, (iii) the abolition of child labour and (iv) the elimination of all forms of discrimination in employment and occupation (ILO 1998). All of these are covered by basic human rights conventions of the ILO. These are Conventions 87, 98, 100, 111, 29 and 105, and 138 and 182, which address Freedom of Association, Collective

Bargaining, Equal Remuneration, Discrimination, Forced Labour and Child Labour.

Apart from being good benchmarks, ILO standards epitomise the essence of what is basic to the human condition. Interestingly, the ILO outlined a set of minimum conditions in its 1998 Declaration on Fundamental Principles and Rights at Work. This declaration forms part of a universal social pillar that supports democracy, transparency, equity and development. In this regard, the declaration presents what it considers a global consensus to which all countries, irrespective of their levels of economic development or cultural values, are bound. Regardless of how many conventions it has ratified, a country is expected hold to an obligation to 'respect, promote, and realize the…fundamental principles and rights' (ILO: 1998). Thus, it is irrelevant whether a country has ratified conventions. As long as it exists as a sovereign state, it is bound by the principles outlined above and must bring its practices in conformity with them.

Core labour standards are not directly enforceable. However, they have the potential of being important elements in the levelling of the playing field in international and regional trade. As this paper evolves it will be seen how they operate regionally and in the context of the topic of the subject.

For the purposes of this essay, there are two ILO conventions that speak to the fourth provision. These are Convention 100, which deals with equal remuneration, and Convention 111 which addresses discrimination. Within the anglophone Caribbean, there is close to unanimous ratification. The Bahamas, Barbados, Belize, Dominica, Guyana, Jamaica, St Kitts and Nevis, St Vincent and the Grenadines and Trinidad and Tobago have all ratified both of these conventions. Antigua and Barbuda has not ratified Convention 100, while Grenada has yet to ratify Convention 111.

Notwithstanding this, however, it is really irrelevant whether the conventions have been ratified. According to the Constitution of the ILO, all member nations are bound by these core conventions. Thus, being basic human rights conventions, they are already binding on the regional governments. The question then is: to what extent have the individual countries, and the regional entity on the whole, put in place the necessary framework to give effect to them?

CARICOM: A Brief Snapshot of Its Evolution

In determining the place that gender issues have occupied on the agenda of CARICOM, it is important to first take a concise look at the institution, its genesis and development.

Britain's colonies in the English-speaking Caribbean, on the verge of independence, came together in 1958 and the West Indies Federation was formed. Intended to be a political and economic union, much as the European Union is today, it lasted four years until the withdrawal of Jamaica in 1962.

Three years later in 1965, Antigua and Barbuda, Barbados and Guyana signed a treaty, forming the core of the Caribbean Free Trade Association (CARIFTA). On May 1, 1968, regional heads of government, meeting in Barbados, unanimously agreed that CARIFTA was to come into effect.

In furtherance of this process, in April 1973 at the Commonwealth Caribbean heads of government conference in Guyana, it was accepted that a Caribbean Community and Common Market (CARICOM) should be created. July 4, 1973 saw the signing of the Treaty of Chaguaramas in Trinidad and Tobago and CARICOM became a reality. For the next three decades a number of developments took place, some of which threatened either to break or consolidate the union. Nonetheless, by 1989, an agreement to put in place a Caribbean Single Market and Economy (CSME) was signed at Grand Anse, Grenada. Members of the CSME are members of the community, which is a confederation of independent states united as a system of regional governance, and the common market, which is an area where goods and services may pass across national boundaries without restriction or preference. More significant is the commitment towards the free movement of labour, as part of the endeavour to unify the regional markets. There is thus the understanding that there would be standards relating to both trade and social issues.

Over the next two decades, two other regional neighbours of the non-anglophone Caribbean were admitted. Suriname was admitted as a full member of the community and the common market in 1995 and Haiti joined as a member of the community in 1997 with the ultimate goal of becoming a full member of both the community and common market.

The significance of the CSME is that it intended to fulfil the promise of being a seamless economic union constituting a free-trade area and, to a lesser extent, a coherent political union of sovereign states. What is notable is that CARICOM does not only have rules and guidelines that relate to regional trade, but more important than that, it has a number of human resource provisions. Unlike the world at large, which has a World Trade Organization (WTO) with enforceable standards related to trade and an ILO with unenforceable labour standards, the CSME has protocols which relate to trade and labour issues, within which gender issues are often subsumed.

If one is to assume that gender issues form part of a regional human resources thrust in the CSME, then it is logical to seriously examine whether they occupy a firm place on the agenda.

Is CARICOM Gender-Sensitive?

Article 10 of the 1973 agreement mandated a Standing Committee of Labour Ministers whose charge is to formulate policies to fulfil the community's objectives concerning labour. Within the scope of the committee were matters related to gender. Seven years later, there was the meeting of officers of CARICOM Women's Bureau. This led to research being carried out over the next few years on the status of women.

Coupled with the work of the Women and Development (WAND) Project, a number of findings were published including a double volume of the leading West Indian academic journal *Social and Economic Studies (SES)* in 1986. Apart from the scholarly work, several policy documents were also published.

By the beginning of the 1990s, there was the commitment to model legislation to correct gender disparities in CARICOM. The areas covered by the model statutes include citizenship, domestic violence, inheritance, sexual offences, sexual harassment and equal pay.

Thus, the scope of the work linked the entire range of concerns related to gender. The intention was to address women's concerns holistically, in society on the whole and specifically within the labour market.

Clearly influenced by the work and standards of the ILO in which all CARICOM nations participate, the regional labour officials met in Saint

Lucia in 1993 and agreed upon the Declaration of Labour and Industrial Relations Principles. This declaration was oriented towards a 'general Labour and Industrial Relations Policy to which the region aspires, taking into account international labour standards'. (CARICOM 1999, ii) Eventually, the declaration was adopted at the 13th meeting of the Committee of Ministers of Labour in the Bahamas in 1995. A year later, the community developed the Agreement on Social Security and, in 1997, the Charter of Civil Society was adopted. Reinforcing the initial Chaguaramas Treaty, the charter declares that 'the governments of the member states share a common determination to fulfil the hopes and aspirations of their peoples for full employment and the improvement of living and working conditions'. At present, there is universal commitment to regional labour and social security standards. Within the realm of labour relations are four pieces of ILO-influenced draft harmonisation legislation, all either directly or indirectly related to gender. These are, termination of employment, recognition of trade unions, occupational health and safety and equality of opportunity and treatment.

From all of the foregoing there is little to argue against CARICOM's nominal commitment towards ensuring gender equality. There have been several protocols and agreements and a number of documents have arisen out of the deliberations over the years. What is less clear, however, is just how much of these regional norms have been translated into national policy.

Nominal Commitment but Regional Unevenness

Table 1. National Implementation of Model Legislation

MEMBER STATES	TERM OF EMP	REG. OF T.U.	EQUALITY	OCCUP. HEALTH
Antigua & Barbuda	X	X	X	
Bahamas				
Barbados	X	X	X	
Belize	X	X		
Dominica	X	X	X	X
Grenada	X	X	X	X
Guyana	X	X		
Haiti				
Jamaica				
St Kitts & Nevis				
St Lucia	X		X	
St Vincent				
Suriname				
Trinidad & Tobago				

Table 1 above indicates that, across the region, there is about a 50 per cent rate of implementation of the model legislation at the national levels. With respect to the model statute on gender, four nations have implemented it. Apart from this, several countries have statutes that deal with freedom from discrimination in employment and remuneration. Therefore, Jamaica, for example, has an Equal (Pay for Men and Women) Act of 1975 (EEPMWA) and Trinidad and Tobago has an Equal Rights Act of 2000.

Yet, ironically, it is not the absence of equal pay or other protective legislation that raises the problems with which this paper is attempting to grapple. Rather it is precisely because the various countries have statutory instruments in place to accord equal treatment across gender lines that the disparities arise. Although generally overlooked, it must be recognised that the Constitution in any state is the supreme statute. Therefore, if there is any legislation which is in place that does not conform to this supreme statute, it could be unconstitutional.

As incredible as it may sound, some of the regional constitutions do not guarantee freedom from discrimination based on sex or gender. A prime example is that of the largest country (by population) Jamaica. Section 13 outlines fundamental rights and freedoms, which include freedom of association, freedom of expression, and freedom of movement among others. Section 24(3) explicitly protects the freedom from discrimination. The section lists the bases upon which the protection revolves and these include race, place of origin, political opinions, colour or creed. Nothing in the entire constitution mentions freedom from discrimination based on sex. The omission is even more glaring when one considers that 'race' is not a scientifically recognised phenomenon, and social scientists have long recognised that it does not exist as a measurable phenomenon. Moreover, in Jamaica, there is no official data which incorporate race, and nothing relating to it appears on one's passport, birth certificate or any other document issued by the state. Yet, one is protected from discrimination based on this malleable category, while the most obvious of differences among persons does not form the basis for protection.

Nonetheless, there are countries whose constitutions do guarantee freedom from discrimination based on sex. Section 1 of the Grenadian

Constitution outlines a set of fundamental rights and freedoms which include a 'right to work'. It guarantees freedom from being prevented from exercising this right based, among others, on sex. Section 13 (3) defines the term 'discriminatory' to mean 'affording different treatment to different persons attributable wholly or mainly to their ... sex whereby persons of one description are subjected to disabilities or restrictions'.

The link between the Grenadian constitution and other statutes is logical. Grenada has a two-year-old Employment Act. The Act bears the signature of the ILO in that it, in two short sections, does what the earlier regional statutes failed to achieve. First, Section 26 prohibits discrimination. This does nothing more than the constitution. However, Section 27 states, 'Every employer shall pay male and female employees equal remuneration for work of equal value'. Of course, it will then be a challenge to see how the value of work is determined. None the less, this is miles ahead of other territories.

By contrast, Jamaica has an older EEPMWA which addresses equal pay for equal work. The statute is well intentioned and begins as follows, 'An Act to eliminate discrimination between the sexes in the payment of remuneration for the doing of similar work and to provide for matters incidental thereto' (EPMWA, 1). However, the text of Convention 100 on Equal Remuneration defines its subject matter as such, '(b) the term equal remuneration for men and women workers for work of equal value refers to rates of remuneration established without discrimination based on sex' (C.100: 1). Consequently the Jamaican Act falls short, as the ILO has indicated since 1989, because in addressing equal pay for equal work it allows for the gender distinctions along occupational lines to persist. Therefore, female-dominated occupations can legally be recompensed at a lower rate than their male equivalents, even though they may be of greater economic value.

A deeper examination of statutes demonstrates other areas of discrimination. An interesting piece of legislation, which is still on the books in Jamaica, is the Women (Employment of) Act 1942 amended in 1961. Under this Act, women are not allowed to work at night, defined as the period between 10 pm and 5 am. Categories of female workers excluded from this prohibition include, managerial and supervisory staff, factory workers, and the Fire Brigade. However, no reference is made to the military, constabulary, correctional services or the private security industry.

This Act also prohibits a woman from working in excess of ten hours in any 24-hour period. Here there are no exclusions; the ceiling on the number of hours a female employee may work is absolute. It should be pointed out that this legislation is not being enforced. Nevertheless, it remains in effect.

What is curious is the possible basis for such a legislation. Of note is the fact that it was enacted in the 1940s during World War II when there would have been a need to maximise the use of all sources of labour. To place restrictions on female labour is not only inefficient but is clearly prejudicial and paternalistic, taking from women the right to choose.

Thus, as it stands, there is still reason to believe that there is insufficient statutory protection in CARICOM against discrimination based on sex within the labour market.

Labour Market Outcomes

From official statistical data such as those provided by Jamaica's Statistical Institute of Jamaica (STATIN), there is a general asymmetry in the labour market along gender lines. Women have lower labour-force participation, higher unemployment levels and lower incomes on the whole. As an example, of all Jamaican males, 26.3 per cent are outside of the labour force. For females the figure is 33.6 per cent (STATIN 2002). Unemployment rates for women are close to double those of males. A sample of unemployment rates across CARICOM shows the male/female differentials as follows: Bahamas 6.0 to 9.7 per cent; Barbados 8.7 to 12.1 per cent; Guyana 6.2 to 14.3 per cent; Grenada 11 to 22 per cent; Saint Lucia 12.6 to 20.7 per cent and Suriname 7.2 to 17 per cent (ILO 2004).

Furthermore, despite equal-pay legislation, women are paid on the average between 60 and 75 per cent of the wages paid to similarly qualified male counterparts. The ILO data suggests that the trends for The Bahamas and Jamaica are regional. However, uneven data collection systems hinder the production of more detailed data. According to the

ILO data, females in Trinidad and Tobago earn around 75 per cent of male salaries, the data for The Bahamas show a similar relationship (ILO 2004). For Jamaica, the overall unemployment rates show 10.7 for males and 21.1 per cent for females (STATIN 2002).

Doubtless, then, using these standard data it is not difficult to see that there is some divergence in the rates of income and employment between the sexes. The question is, however, whether these data are not only accurate but whether they fully capture female economic activity?

It should be noted that female work is more likely to occur in the informal sector and is less accounted for. Therefore, female unemployment is likely to be less than is officially recorded. The under-reporting and recording of female work have been pointed out in earlier works (Taylor 1993).

Notwithstanding this reservation, there is little arguing against the fact that male salaried work is higher than female, both in employment and wage rates. But does this truly reflect the full dimensions of social inequity in the labour market and in society on the whole?

The Other Side of the Discontinuity: Are Women Getting a Double Benefit?

A deeper examination of the statute on the books of a number of CARICOM countries points to part of the reason why some constitutions do not have protection against sexual discrimination. The truth is there are other laws which are designed to be biased towards women. The aforementioned Women (Employment of) Act seems to have been originally intended to protect women from the hazards of night work which their male counterparts faced. This reflects the thinking of the ILO in its infancy as it adopted Convention 3 in 1919.

Article 3 of the 1919 Night Work Convention reads 'Women without distinction of age shall not be employed during the night in any public or private industrial undertaking, or in any branch thereof, other than an undertaking in which only members of the same family are employed' (Convention 3:1). Clearly, though, the reality of work has long evolved past this and the ILO has since adopted more recent instruments such as the Night Work Convention of 1990 which does not prohibit night work by females. The reality is though, that in practice this enjoinment does not generally occur.

However, there is another structural inequity which is enshrined in statute and enforced by the courts. Legislation related to the custody and maintenance of spouses and children are clearly pro-female. The Jamaican Children (Guardianship and Custody) Act (CGCA) of 1958 accords equal right to each parent to appeal to the courts regarding custody of the child. However, there is no connection between the custody of the child and his/her maintenance. Section 6 explicitly states,

> Where the Court ... makes an order giving custody of the child to the other, then whether or not the mother is residing with the father order that the father shall pay to the mother towards the maintenance of the child... (CGCA, 6)

The ancient Maintenance Act of 1881, amended in 1988, reinforces the primacy of the female. Section 2 makes the obvious statement that 'every man is hereby required to maintain his own children...' (Maintenance Act, 3). However, it then goes on to declare that his responsibilities include 'every child whether born in wedlock or not, which his wife may have living at the time of her marriage with him'. What this means is that not only has he legal responsibility for the progeny of the relationship but also for all of the offspring of his mate even if he did not father any of them.

Even more remarkable, if there is a divorce for whatever reason, including the deceit or unfaithfulness of the woman, the hapless husband has to continue to support her and her children financially even after he has taken on another wife and has produced biological offspring of his own. There is no equivalent provision in the Act related to the obligations of women.

In the same breath, there is no requirement for paternity to be established. As long as a male was cohabiting with a woman at the time of birth the Act infers fatherhood and dictates maintenance. Therefore, if a man takes in a pregnant female, as common West Indian parlance states 'tek her wid di belly', the child is legally his and it is his duty to maintain it.

A man's obligation to maintain does not stop with his children. Section 11 asserts that 'every man shall be liable and is hereby required to maintain his wife, irrespective of her being able to maintain herself' (Maintenance Act, 10). The Act is unequivocal in that it speaks of a unidirectional duty. Therefore, if a man is in a faithful relationship with his wife and she is the main breadwinner, earning twice his income, he has to give her financial maintenance.

Although perhaps necessary during the epoch when it was promulgated, this statute is repugnant to the concept of true gender equality. On the one hand, females seek true gender equality in the labour market and society in general. On the other hand, there is the asymmetric maintenance relationship.

To advocate gender equality in the labour market while systematically skewing the balance towards women in other social legislation is inconsistent, paradoxical and disingenuous. For feminists or pro-feminists to argue that women are to be treated as equals to men in the labour market but be given economic advantages in other spheres runs in the face of parity.

If the law recognises that a man of equal talent and qualification should be paid no more than his female counterpart – which is just – it must at the same time equally apportion the economic responsibility. A man who is earning the same as his equivalently qualified spouse, living in the same household, where they employ domestic workers to perform their routine tasks cannot, on the basis of justice and social equity, be asked to assume greater financial responsibility for the children.

Even more so, a woman cannot claim independence while declaring that her husband has a duty to take care of her needs. However, these are the underlying ideologies. Therefore, where the law and social policies make the assumption of a male-headed household, and one finds biases in the administration of social protection programmes, one cannot then seek to promote gender equality in the labour market.

Labour Market Outcomes: Men at Risk Re-visited 2002

Returning to Miller's findings in 1992, there is still a basis for the men at risk concern. Within tertiary institutions, the ratios of females to males is at least 4:1. This has been the consistent pattern among University of the West Indies graduates since the mid-1990s.

Within the labour market, eleven per cent of females are professionals with degrees while only five per cent of males are in this category. Eight per cent of women fall in the category 'vocational with certificate', compared with half that proportion for males. In the employed labour force the gender disparities are similar. Professional women comprise 25 per cent of employed females, while only 13 per cent of men fit the profile (STATIN 2002).

While it is true that the data in the professional group obscure the fact that female-dominated occupations such as nursing and teaching skew the balance and conceal the smaller numbers of women in the managerial and higher level decision-making positions, it cannot be denied that the under-representation of males should set off alarms.

Given that women are becoming more qualified, and at a faster rate, than males who are still in critical positions of power and who are earning more than they are, there is space for the suggestion that society will become increasingly run by a reducing 'androcracy' comprising a small group of qualified men holding on to power. However, a real concern must be how a smaller group of under-qualified individuals is going to cope with the unequal burden of maintenance.

Still, the picture is not simple. Despite the advantage that women have in the processes of human resource development and in the custody and maintenance statutes, there is in fact still some degree of inequity. In Jamaica, for example, the majority of households classified as poor were female-headed. This figure was an overwhelming 66.1 per cent of families (SLC 1998, 104). Among the poor, male unemployment is 8.8 per cent while for females it is 11.5. Thus, this suggests that women may indeed bear a greater burden in practical terms.

Yet, the scenario is even more confounding when one considers that, despite the fact that more female-headed families are poor, more males are paupers. The same data from the Survey of Living Conditions (SLC, 1998) records a human poverty index of 26 for males compared with 17 for females. This trend has continued throughout the 1990s with a mean for the period of 28 for males and 20 for females.

What all of the above data demonstrate is that there is no simple set of demographic factors related to economic disparities between the sexes. In making assumptions based on only one set of these will lead to flawed policies and may ultimately exacerbate conditions.

Conclusion

There is no simple solution or analysis. Without a doubt, gender equality is not an option but an imperative. True gender equality in all spheres is an essential feature of development and should occupy an important place in any national policy.

Core labour standards of the ILO and regional norms are important guidelines which can establish consistent patterns across the region and eventually the world. It is desirable that, in any international or regional trade scenario, gender clauses should be included as part of basic human rights provisions.

However, what is missing at the national level is a coherent approach among the policy-makers to first of all establish, at the ideological level, what the underlying philosophy is. Gender equality means just that. If true parity is to occur, then the existing legislative framework must be re-examined. It is clear that, despite the desired commitment towards true gender equality and, in particular, female empowerment, there has been some degree of conceptual ambivalence. Not enough thought has been put into what is really meant by gender equality. Thus, it is not surprising that there is so much discord among the statutes and policies.

To achieve true equality in the treatment of both sexes, there must be an attack on the attitudes in society that feed the notions of female dependence. Male/female equality in the labour market is underlined by a progressive ideology epitomised in the ILO's Conventions and Recommendations. On the other hand, the biases in the other social legislation are underpinned by a set of cultural perennials that are steeped in the traditions of female subordination and inferiority. Dependence and equality are incompatible goals. At present, the statutory framework relating to gender may very well reinforce gender biases. Nonetheless, the legal instruments appear to have conflicting philosophies both within specific nations and across the region among member states.

In concluding, I quote the ILO documentation and re-affirm,

> gender equality is more than a question of securing equal treatment of men and women in the formal sense. It is the matter of taking into account, in an appropriate way, gender roles in society, roles which differ between societies and have in recent years undergone immense change. Social protection schemes should be designed, on the one had to guarantee equality of treatment between men and women and, on the other hand, to take into account different gender roles and serve as a tool for the promotion of gender equality. (ILO 2001, 37)

References

CARICOM Secretariat. 1999. *Declaration of Labour and Industrial Relations Principles*. Georgetown: CARICOM Secretariat.

CARICOM Secretariat. 1997. *Charter of Civil Society*. Georgetown: CARICOM Secretariat

CARICOM Secretariat. 1996. *Agreement on Social Security*. Georgetown: CARICOM Secretariat.

Children (Guardianship and Custody) Act of Jamaica 1958.

Constitution of Grenada 1973.

Constitution of Jamaica 1962.

Employment Act of Grenada 1999.

Employment (Equal Pay for Men and Women) Act of Jamaica 1975.

Equal Rights Act of Trinidad and Tobago 2000.

International Labour Organization. 2004. *Caribbean Labour Statistics*. Port of Spain: International Labour Organization. http://www.ilocarib.org.tt/system_links/link_databases.html

International Labour Organization. 2001. *Social Security: A New Consensus*. Geneva: International Labour Organization.

International Labour Organization. 1998. *Declaration on Fundamental Principles and Rights at Work*. Geneva: International Labour Organization.

International Labour Organization. 1990. *International Labour Standards: A Worker Education Manual*. Geneva: International Labour Organization.

International Labour Organization. 1990. *Night Work Convention*. Geneva: International Labour Organization.

International Labour Organization. 1951. *Equal Remuneration Convention 100*. Geneva: International Labour Organization.

International Labour Organization. 1919. *Night Work Convention*. Geneva: International Labour Organization.

Maintenance Act of Jamaica 1881.

Miller, Errol. 1991. *Men at Risk*. Kingston: Jamaica Publishing House.

Planning Institute of Jamaica. 1998. *Survey of Living Conditions*. Kingston: Planning Institute of Jamaica/Statistical Institute of Jamaica.

Statistical Institute of Jamaica [STATIN]. 2002. *The Labour Force*. Kingston: The Statistical Institute of Jamaica.

Taylor, Orville. 1993. 'Women and Work: They are still at Risk.' *Caribbean Labour Journal* 3 no. 2.

Tutnjevic, Tamara. 2002. *Gender and Financial/Economic Downturn*. Geneva: InFocus Programme on Crisis Response and Reconstruction, International Labour Organization.

Women (Employment of) Act of Jamaica 1942.

15 | WINSOME TOWNSEND

The Environment
Prospects for a Gender Responsive Approach to Policies and Programmes

Abstract

The Gender, Environment and Development (GED) framework posits that women and men have an equal stake in the environment and that there are different gender needs and interests related to the environment. Environmental policies and programmes should therefore take account of the cultural and social differences between men and women and, especially, the differences in the extent to which men and women have access to, and control over, resources.

An analysis of environmental policies and programmes in Jamaica indicates that, for the most part, these policies are gender blind and are either not, or only superficially, responsive to gender issues. However, a contextual analysis of various national initiatives gives hope that there are good prospects for gender responsiveness in environmental policies and programmes.

The paper presents a case for gender mainstreaming in our environmental organisations and programmes.

The Rationale for Gender Considerations in Environmental Management

Environmental Management: A Resource-focused versus a System Approach

Various reasons may be put forward towards the cause of protecting natural resources (water, land, air, biodiversity). These reasons may speak to their intrinsic value, such as their aesthetic appeal in their pure and natural state, or to the health benefits to be derived from their natural unpolluted products, or their consumptive/exploitative value. Similarly, the approach to the management of natural resources runs along the spectrum from wanting to keep all areas as wilderness, to recognising the earth as the home of humans whose job it is to conquer and dominate, to the further recognition of the importance of all species co-existing in a physical and biological system.

The traditional approaches that have been taken in managing the environment have tended to be resource-focused and not system-focused. A system-focused approach will encompass not only the physical attributes but the social as well, including the important role and responsibility of humans.

Since the United Nations Conference on Environment and Development (UNCED) held in 1992, some attempts have been made to include people in environmental management. This was spurred on by terms such as 'participation' and 'community-involvement' which were included in the various discourses and documentation. However, this has translated into a catering to 'people', a term which has been used to a large extent as a homogeneous set without much attention being paid to differences arising from ethnicity, class, culture and gender.

Gender-based Interests and Needs in the Environment

Jamaica relies heavily on its natural resources for the livelihood of the population. The following is a list of the various uses made of the basic natural resources of Jamaica: Land of wood and water:

Land

1. Housing
2. Farming
3. Industrial use
4. Recreational activities

Wood

1. Charcoal burning
2. Fuelwood (cooking)
3. Furniture making

4. Housing construction
5. Lumber production
6. Furniture making
7. Craft making

Water
1. Washing clothes, bathing, general cleaning and other domestic usage
2. Manufacturing
3. Recreation
4. Fishing

It must be recognised that the various activities cited above effect a high extractive and consumptive burden on our environment. In addition, men and women have different interests and needs related to the activities. This has been brought about by the different gender roles assigned to men and women in the society. For example, women may have a greater interest than do men in the domestic usage of water while men may have a greater interest than do women in the recreational usage of water. Similarly, access to land is gender biased. Since the interests and needs related to the environment are gendered, the different activities of women and men may impact differently on the environment and conversely the lives of women and men may be impacted on differently by the environment.

Various linkages have been made between poverty and the access to, reliance on and destruction of natural resources. In Jamaica, as is true elsewhere, women form the poorest group. Clearly, women and men have different vulnerabilities with regard to how their lives are impacted upon by the environment.

For any environmental management policy or programme to be effective, the above issues need to be borne in mind from the earliest stage of policy or programme formulation. Of course, this approach needs to be carried through to the implementation stage. It is not enough to have a people-centred approach, which treats people as a united mass with common concerns and needs; a gendered approach is critical to environmental conservation or mitigation.

Gender Analysis of Some Key Environmental Policies

Gender analysis was carried out on eight (8) policies related to the environment and natural resources to determine the extent to which gender was taken into consideration in development of these policies.

The National Land Policy, 1996

The National Land Policy has the goal of establishing the framework for the proper planning, management, development and use of land. This policy does not mention gender although for over a decade, the issue of women's access to land and shelter has been raised as a concern in the national Policy Statement on Women. Additionally, one of the themes for the international Habitat Agenda is 'providing adequate shelter for all'. The Global Campaign for Secure Tenure has been designed to fulfil the commitments of governments to this Habitat Agenda and identifies the provision of secure tenure as a vital element in the promotion of housing rights. The Settlement Strategy which complements the Land Policy draws the link between lack of shelter and poverty but lacks sex-disaggregated data related to land issues and does not recognise the need for this data or the need to address gender with regard to issues such as rural to urban drift, male/female headed households, or access to land for shelter or farming.

The Draft Watershed Policy, 2003

The main goal of this policy is to promote integrated protection, conservation and development of land and water resources in watersheds for their sustainable use, and for the benefit of the nation as a whole. This policy mentions women in one of its guiding principles 'Local participation and community involvement in watershed management is very essential. NGOs, youth and women must be included in the planning and implementing interventions.' However, this principle is not reflected in any of its seven Specific Policy Goals nor their related objectives; neither is it reflected in its Implementation Plan.

Although the connection is made with regard to security of tenure and watershed degradation, the gender aspect of this is not mentioned. Additionally, the access of men and women to the different products or resources of watersheds, such as water and forest woods, is not considered, nor is the impact of women's and men's livelihoods or lack thereof on watershed management dealt with.

The Draft National Biodiversity Strategy and Action Plan, 2001

The goals of this document are to conserve biodiversity; promote the sustainable use of biological resources; facilitate access to biological resources; promote developments in biotechnology and benefit sharing; develop guidelines for the safe handling of living modified organisms; enhance resource management capability, public awareness and education and community empowerment; promote local and regional cooperation and collaboration in implementing the Convention on Biological Diversity and the National Biodiversity Strategy and Action Plan.

Although population pressure and poverty are both linked to threats to biodiversity conservation, and the document identifies cultural attitudes to natural resources as an issue, pointing out that many rural communities continue to use traditional knowledge about medicinal and other plants, gender issues are not addressed in the various 'Gaps and Challenges' identified and they are not addressed in any of the many strategic directions nor the Action Plan.

The Policy on a National System of Protected Areas, 1997

The goals of this policy are economic development; environmental conservation; sustainable resource use; recreational and public information; public participation and local responsibility; and financial responsibility.

Although this policy promotes a participatory approach to the establishment of protected areas, it does not at all address the issue of gender. This gender-blindness is also reflected in the various guidelines related to the management of protected areas.

The Beach Policy for Jamaica (Draft), 2001

The purpose of this policy is to remove any vestige of real or implied discrimination against Jamaicans in the use and enjoyment of their national heritage; to expand beach-related recreational opportunities for both local residents and all segments of the tourism market; to protect the traditional rights of fishermen to access the foreshore and the sea, and beaching rights on their return from sea; and to establish guidelines on the leasing and monitoring of the near shore-bed for mari-culture use.

Not only is this policy gender-blind in not addressing issues related to any difference in how men and women use the beach, especially fishing beaches, it is also gender-biased in its use of language, for example, the use of 'fishermen' and 'himself' instead of 'fisher folk' and 'him/herself'.

Policy on Ocean and Coastal Zone Management in Jamaica, 2001

The goals of this policy are to promote sustainable development; conserve the ocean and coastal resources and ecosystems; collect baseline data and research; utilise the role of science and traditional knowledge for integrated coastal zone management; and provide the conditions of governance required for effective integrated coastal zone management.

This policy is seeking to encourage the recognition of the basic linkages between sustainable management of coastal and marine resources, poverty alleviation and protection of the marine environment. In addition, it is seeking to encourage community-based participatory approaches in coastal planning and management planning, and in conservation of critical habitats; to develop an integrated decision-making process including all sectors; to promote compatibility and a balance of uses in order to achieve wider participation at all levels in integrated coastal and marine management.

Guiding principle 3.8, in addressing equitable distribution of environmental resources states,

> Coastal resource management should be designed to benefit all segments of the population, including present and future generations. Compensation should be awarded to those who unavoidably incur costs or damages as a result of programme or project implementation. In assessing impacts, cultural as well as economic consequences must be considered. Compensation measures and/or mitigation costs should be included in the financing plan. Public rights of access should be rigorously protected. Where access rights cannot be guaranteed, mitigation options need to be negotiated. Agreement on mitigation should precede project or programme approval. Where environmental loss or degradation is an unavoidable consequence of programme or project actions, mitigation measures must be undertaken to restore or create comparable environmental values.

Guiding Principle 3.9 states: 'Recognition should be accorded to traditional rights and use patterns.'

It must be noted, however, that the lofty guiding principles and intentions stated above do not translate into a recognition regarding the role of gender in ocean and coastal zone issues and management. There is one small saving grace, however. Under Strategy 4.1.4 – Develop sustainable agricultural practices, an action is proposed to 'perform assessment of: population size, *gender* (my emphasis) distribution, location, migration, literacy, economic activities and income. This suggests small hope for sex-disaggregated data relating to agricultural practices.

Draft National Policy and Strategy on Environmental Management Systems (EMS), 2001

Action 3.2.1 states: 'Conduct analyses to determine attitudinal, ethical, cultural and *gender* (my emphasis) issues related to the implementation of environmental management systems.' Additionally, this action is cross-referenced to two other actions relating to identifying courses and programmes for staff, the training of auditors, and building capacity in the public sector to implement EMS respectively.

This policy clearly recognises that gender may affect the implementation of environmental management systems by putting forward the intention to carry out analyses in this regard. However, the policy does not go far enough to indicate any action to ensure that gender considerations will be incorporated in either the promotion or the implementation of EMS.

Jamaica Water Sector Policy, 1999

This policy is guided by the following core principles:

i. Ensure integrated and informed management of the country's water resources. Development of water resources will not be done sectorally.

ii. Ensure water for public supply will receive priority in the allocation of resources.

iii. Ensure water is used as efficiently as possible, including promotion of conservation. Where possible the conjunctive use of surface and ground water will be implemented. Demand management must be implemented.

iv. Ensure implementation of measures to restore and enhance the quality and quantity of usable water and protect the aquifers, watersheds and other sources of water. The following shall be the specific focus of strategies designed for water pollution prevention and control:

- Maintenance of ecosystem integrity through the protection of aquatic resources from negative impacts caused by development and natural processes;
- Protection of public health against disease vectors and from pathogens;
- Ensuring sustainable water use and ecosystem protection on a long-term basis;
- Implementing 'the polluter-pays' principle.

The focus of the policy will also be on developing mechanisms to ensure compliance, including public education, incentives and sanctions.

This policy is gender blind as gender is not discussed or even mentioned.

In general, the environmental policies analysed above do not adequately address gender. Indeed most do not address gender at all. It should be noted that these policies, to a large extent, are people-centred in that they speak to community issues or acknowledge the role and/or needs of humans. According to Rowan Campbell (2003), there are two mantras to remember: any policy which has a human dimension or is in any way people-centred provides opportunities for inclusion of a gender focus or perspective and, any policy or strategy that includes an element of capacity building has the potential to ensure that equitable numbers of men and women benefit from the capacity building. Rowan Campbell further suggests that these hooks or entry points should be exploited in introducing gender into environmental policies.

A More Gender Responsive Approach to Environmental Policies and Programmes

As indicated in the section above, because of the critical link between gender and the environment, it becomes imperative that gender considerations be integrated into environmental management. Additionally, it has been proposed that many of the environmental polices analysed do have entry points where gender considerations may be incorporated. It is worth considering what approach should be taken in ensuring more gender-responsive environmental policies.

The Traditional Approach to Addressing Gender

Historically, the approach taken in trying to achieve this objective has been a specialisation approach. Moser (1993) indicated that the specialisation approach often sees the creation of a specially designed unit (often a women's unit) to deal with gender issues. Usually, gender specialists are employed to this unit to provide expertise to others and to monitor the issue. In addition, gender-specific tools are developed.

Like many other countries, Jamaica adopted this specialisation approach. As early as 1976, Jamaica established a Bureau of Women's Affairs to address the acknowledged imbalance between men and women, which affected women negatively. Jamaica has received many plaudits from the international arena because of its early action in this regard. Much of the work of this bureau has been focused on training and support for some categories of women. However, various studies have pointed to the ineffectiveness of the bureau specifically because of the wide responsibility given to it without the benefit of any functional linkages to other departments.

In addressing gender concerns in environmental management, therefore, Jamaica might draw from the lessons learned and not adopt the specialisation approach. In this regard, a more integrated approach needs to be employed.

The Need for Gender Mainstreaming in Environmental Organisations

Since adopting the Rio Declaration on the Environment and Development in 1992, Jamaica has taken a number of steps to accede to, ratify and put in force various international treaties and conventions that address protection of the environment and prevention of pollution.

The Beijing Platform of Action (1995), endorsed by United Nations member countries, has called attention to the need for gender mainstreaming. In this regard, the United Nations Development Programme (UNDP) has been working in collaboration with over 130 countries in mainstreaming gender analysis into, and developing links between, the different thematic areas – poverty eradication, employment creation and sustainable livelihoods, regeneration of the environment, and good governance.

The definition of gender mainstreaming provided by the UNDP Gender in Development Programme emphasises the need to take account of gender concerns in all activities and in organisational procedures.

The document: *Mainstreaming the Gender Perspective into all Policy and Programmes in the United Nations System* (1997) gives the following definition of gender mainstreaming:

> Mainstreaming a gender perspective is the process of assessing the implications for women and men of any planned action, including legislation, policies or programmes, in any area and at all levels. It is a strategy for making women's as well as men's concerns and experiences an integral dimension in the design, implementation, monitoring and evaluation of policies and programmes in all spheres so that women and men benefit equally and inequality is not perpetuated. The ultimate goal is to achieve gender equality. (Section I. B. paragraph 5)

According to Moser (1993), various strategies need to be employed in gender mainstreaming. That is, institutionalisation of gender considerations within the existing organisational structure; putting in place gender-aware generalists who will integrate a gender and development perspective into work; implementing extensive training in gender awareness/planning and establishing gendered changes in the planning procedures and the development of new methodological tools.

The above makes the case for taking an integrated approach in the incorporation of gender considerations in environmental management by mainstreaming gender considerations in environmental organisations. This means that not only should our environmental policies and programmes articulate gender responsiveness, but that our environmental organisations should systematically integrate gender considerations at all levels and throughout their operational procedures.

Some Good Prospects for Mainstreaming Gender Considerations in Environment Management

A few initiatives, outlined below, have taken place recently at the highest governmental levels, which should facilitate the process of mainstreaming gender considerations in environmental management. Although few in number, they are significant because of the level of influence at which they have been promulgated.

The Cabinet Office Guidelines include a requirement for prior analysis of all submissions for gender considerations. This should be seen as an attempt to begin the implementation of the governments' commitment to gender mainstreaming at the decision making level. Although this will not cover existing environmental policies, it provides the opportunity for gender to be considered in any revision to these policies and also to be addressed in any new environmental policy.

Some of the major developmental agencies operating in Jamaica have been assisting the Jamaican government in mainstreaming gender in the project cycle. For example, the Canadian International Development Agency (CIDA) is working with the Planning Institute of Jamaica (PIOJ) in developing a gender analysis framework for all Government of Jamaica projects. In addition, some projects have been providing training opportunities in gender awareness both at the policy level and implementation level.

The National Environment and Planning Agency, an executive agency of the Government of Jamaica with overall responsibility for environmental management, has recently commissioned a gender analysis of national environmental policies and has held preliminary discussions regarding the mainstreaming of gender in an umbrella environmental policy to be developed, the National Environmental and Planning Policy and Strategy.

Finally, and most significant to this Mona Academic Conference, the University of the West Indies has recognised the importance of the link between gender and the environment and thought it worthy of inclusion in the discussions at this forum.

References

Canada. 1996. Gender-based analysis: A guide for policy-making. Status of Women, March.

Earth Summit. 1992. The United Nations Conference on Environment and Development. London: The Regency Press Corporation.

Faidutti, R. n.d. 'Learning from women's experience'. In *Gender and Food Security: Environment.* FAO/19321.

Government of Jamaica. 1996. National Land Policy of Jamaica. July.

Government of Jamaica. 2000a. A Beach Policy for Jamaica: A policy for the Management of the Beach, Foreshore and Floor of the Sea, November.

Government of Jamaica. 2000b. Jamaica Water Sector Policy Strategies and Action Plan, Ministry of Housing and Water, November.

Government of Jamaica. 2002a. Ocean and Coastal Zone Management Policy in Jamaica. The National Council on Ocean and Coastal Zone Management.

Government of Jamaica. 2002b. Towards a National Policy and Strategy on Environmental Management Systems (Ems) [Draft White Paper], National Environmental and Planning Agency, Ministry Of Land and Environment, September.

Government of Jamaica. 2002c. Towards a National Strategy and Action Plan on Biological Diversity in Jamaica [Draft White Paper], June.

Jamaica's Environment 2001, Environment Statistics and State of the Environment Report. Statistical Institute of Jamaica, National Environment and Planning Agency, Kingston, October.

Leach, M. 1995. 'Editorial: Gender Relations and Environmental Change'. *Institute of Development Studies Bulletin* 26, no. 1:7-8.

'Mainstreaming Gender in the Policies, Programmes and Projects of IUCN'. IUCN Work Programme 1998-2000. http://www.iucn.org/themes/spg/Gender/GenderWorkplanE.html

May, Elizabeth. 1994. 'Women: The Resource Managers'. *Our Planet,* vol. no. 4:23-24.

Ministry of Environment and Housing. *Jamaica National Environmental Action Plan (JaNEAP) 1999-2000.* Natural Resources Conservation Authority.

Moser, C.O.N. 1993. *Gender Planning and Development: Theory, Practice and Training.* New York. Routledge, 230

Palmer, I. 1995. Ladies in Limbo, Retooling the Machine. UNDP Report.

1997. Policy for the National System of Protected Areas. Government of Jamaica.

Razavi, S. and C. Miller. 1995. 'Gender Mainstreaming: A Study of Efforts by the UNDP, the World Bank and the ILO to Institutionalize Gender Issues'. *Occasional Paper* No. 4. UN Fourth World Conference on Women. August.

Rowan Campbell, D. 2003. Gender Gap Analysis in Environmental and Physical Planning Policies. National Environment and Planning Agency. April.

Shah, M.K. and P. Shah. 1995. Gender, Environment and Livelihood Security: an Alternative Viewpoint from India. *IDS Bulletin* 26, no. 1:75-82.

'Social Considerations of Development'. 1991. United Nations Conference of Environment and Development National Report on Jamaica.

Towards a Watershed Policy for Jamaica, Green Paper No 2/99. Natural Resources Conservation Authority, Ministry of Environment and Housing.

United Nations Environment Programme (UNEP). 1999. *Global Environment Outlook 2000: UNEP's Millennium Report on the Environment*. London: Earthscan Publications Ltd.

'Women and Environmental Issues.' 1995. National Report on the Status of Women in Jamaica, March. Jamaica National Preparatory Commission for the Fourth World Conference on Women, Beijing, China, September.

16 | VELMA POLLARD

Female Emancipation and the Sewing Machine

Abstract

'… Miss Caroline
tell me how you spend your time
I spend all my time
around the Singer machine…'

These lines from a popular song of the nineteen forties sum up what was for many women then a new reality. This paper identifies the sewing machine as an important element in the psychological and financial liberation of the woman, here the Caribbean woman of the twentieth century. Evidence in support of this claim will be offered predominantly from Caribbean creative writing where artists have noted the importance of that invention in the lives of their mothers and in the achievements of their families.

Lorna Goodison, foremost Jamaican woman poet, makes the point that wherever she has read the poem 'For My Mother (May I Inherit Half Her Strength)' people have claimed it, sometimes with tears. In the USA, in Italy, all over the world they empathise with her mother and see their own parents and grandparents in her task of bringing up nine children on humble resources. An important aspect of that exercise was the sitting at the Singer machine and sewing:

> When I came to know my mother …I knew her as the figure who sat at the first thing I learned to read: 'SINGER', and she breast-fed my brother while she sewed;

and she taught us to read while she sewed and she sat in judgement over all our disputes as she sewed (Goodison 1986, 46).

This paper sees the sewing machine as the technological invention that most liberated the woman in the early twentieth century. While this liberation might apply to women of many nations, the focus here is on the Caribbean woman. Selected Caribbean texts are quoted to support this claim. The intention is not to undermine the efforts of generations of female artists whose thimbled fingers made awesome creations for male and female alike down the centuries before the invention of the machine. Rather, it is to underline the psychological and economic advantages that accompanied this machine which allowed for greater output in shorter time. Because of the machine, mother could work in what may be described as her personal factory without having to relinquish the tasks at home that demanded her attention. Because of it she could sometimes earn enough to give her a sense of independence.

Isaac Singer is the man whose name has come to be associated with the machine. But Singer's true genius was in marketing. The machine that he marketed from the 1850s improved only slightly upon one painstakingly constructed by Elias Howe whose own work benefited from other inventions going as far back as Weisenthal's in 1755.[1] As much is owed to Singer's skill as a marketer as to the genius of the early inventors.

Psychological

Days stitched seamlessly end to end, a tapestry that is the metaphor for what could well be seen as an unenviable life is what Goodison describes as her mother's experience. And that is one way of remembering it. But I want to focus here on the positive aspects of it, the psychological and the economic benefits of the operation even as we re-read Goodison's description. The psychological gains relate to the children. They have the privilege of a mother at home. The machine becomes the focal point for a kind of bonding that is invaluable in the making of the secure individual. Goodison underlines the unchanging nature of the location and the multiplicity of tasks operated from there. The adverbial phrase 'while she sewed' or its alternative 'as she sewed' forms a background to the activities which are foregrounded artfully in a kind of call-response sequence, a feature so popular in Caribbean song and verse. The lines may be reconstructed in this way:

> she breast-fed my brother
> (while she sewed)
> she taught us to read
> (while she sewed)
> she sat in judgement…
> (as she sewed)

Goodison's universal poem speaks for many Caribbean families. My discussions with people now in their fifties and sixties have confirmed this. They speak fondly of homework supervised by mother as she sewed. And in those instances where mother's academic experience was not enough to allow her to help with homework, the fact that the two sat together like two adults at the dining table, one over the machine the other over the book made for a kind of inspiration to the younger one to keep on reading as the older kept on stitching.

The most touching example of the effect of this bonding that I know of is my friend the heart surgeon who dedicated an academic paper in an international journal to his mother. His colleagues had tried more and more chemicals to have the body *not* reject the newly transplanted heart. He saw the physical configuration and thought of his mother making a 'godet' while he, a young boy, pedalled the 'foot machine' she could no longer manage because she was ill. He replicated that V slit, repaired the space and the heart stayed. The operation was his but the inspiration and the efficiency had been hers, hence the dedication.

Economic

The economic gains relate to the family unit as a whole and how it was able to maximise slender resources. Tangible and visible contributions did not always result from mother's sewing. The savings were in fact the gains. Recurrent expenses were only on cloth and thread. With luck, a mother might sew clothes for children not her own, growing up, for some reason, without a sewing mother. She might charge a small sum for this service. When mother works at home, her household chores are taken care of between bouts of sewing or, put another way, there are bouts of sewing between her household chores. There is no output for transportation to take her to some factory location to earn a living. She does not have to find street-presentable clothes to go to work every day. If money measures were put on all these, it could add up to quite a sum. The examples below suggest this.

Olive Senior, in a chapter entitled 'Making Do' in *Working Miracles*, a text concerned with the lives of Caribbean women, writes about survival strategies employed by these women. Included in that text is a Barbadian woman's description of her experience, taking care of her sons' wardrobes with commendable ingenuity: 'It wasn't very easy. Sometimes my skirts, I would cut them, heavy material-drill and things like that – and turn them into pants for them [her children]. Sometimes they look good, sometimes they don't…'[2]

Another in that same group, commenting on her mother's many-faceted life, says: 'She did selling. She used to do a little sewing too, a little hand machine you know…' (Senior, 130).

Today, mother goes out to a factory (perhaps of many sewing machines); wastes valuable time on the bus; perhaps experiences the raw anger of other travellers reacting to their own situations and becomes rattled. Neither body nor spirit is at peace. And somebody must watch her children, for a price. Day-care centres, half-day kindergartens are meant to try to 'patch' the tear that is the result of her working outside the home.

Senior, illustrating in fiction what she knew from factual research, draws a mother character who did the 'sewing and baking and doing the accounts' while the household helper 'did all the heavy work' (Senior 1995, 185). In fact, there is an occasion on which she allows mother, the kind householder/employer to correct the inappropriate appearance of the helper, Desrine's daughter, with the minimum loss of time:

> The minute she arrived, Mother dear took one look and sent Muffet and Sadie down to Mr Chin to buy yards of cambric and rushed to her sewing machine so the child could be 'decently clad', she told Desrine. Mother Dear would not allow Manuela to leave the yard until she could be enveloped in dresses which made her look not quite so much like a ripe juicy starapple ready to burst out of its skin. (p. 172)

Both the literary examples above are from the work of Jamaican women. But comment on the sewing machine runs right through the literature of the Caribbean. Brathwaite of Barbados, in *Mother Poem*, writes about woman's ways of 'keeping she body an soul-seam together and includes … taking up sewing since she was fourteen' (Brathwaite 1977, 38). Walcott of Saint Lucia, in *Another Life*, speaks pages in two terse lines within the reconstruction of his mother's past: 'Maman/Only on Sundays was the Singer silent…' (Walcott 1973, 11). And from within the francophone tradition, Aimé Cesaire of Martinique mentions 'mother' and 'Singer' in one breath, in an easily recognised context:

> … and my mother, whose limbs in the service of our tireless hunger, pedal, pedal, day and night, I am even awakened at night by those tireless limbs which pedal the night by the bitter punctures in the soft flesh of the night made by the Singer machine my mother pedals, pedals for our hunger day and night… (Cesaire 1947, 1971,52)

These references are not meant to be exhaustive but they indicate the place of the sewing machine, more specifically the Singer sewing machine as part of the household landscape of the Caribbean of a certain period. Today, women are allowed to get married without being able to use a sewing machine far less to have to own one.

Without meaning to simplify a really complex matter I want to suggest that the demise of the sewing machine as a *sine qua non* of every household and the necessity for every girl to learn to sew, has contributed to the delinquency among children, discussed in the media almost daily. Mother now, like father, takes the minibus to work and sits all day in a factory. Children come home to unsupervised nests and do their homework only if they feel like it.

Emancipation

There is a kind of paradox in the notion of emancipation marked by slavery to a location described so well in the Goodison extract quoted at the beginning of this paper and in the lines of an early pop song quoted in the Abstract where Miss Caroline says: 'I spend all my time around the Singer machine'. The emancipation then is not physical but hugely psychological. Woman is free here from total dependency on man and what he can provide. The fact that her intake is not large sums of money becomes insignificant beside her notion of personal freedom: freedom from being a slave to worry about what is happening to her children while she is at work; freedom in some cases to handle her own small sums. In addition she earns the respect of man because he too depends on her contribution for the maintenance of a certain financial level in the family account. Her services are savings. She helps to clothe the children and sometimes to clothe himself. She can make shirts or at least turn collars to make the shirts last (people wore shirts with collars then).

Perhaps this commentary overstates the case. It does not mention other ways in which women gained financial liberation: taking in washing; keeping a kitchen garden and selling the produce. Perhaps I may be attributing more to the sewing machine than it deserves. But it *is* significant that Caribbean writers of both sexes record the sound of the Singer machine as part of their consciousness when they recall fictive or real childhoods:

> Maman
> only on Sundays was the Singer silent.

Notes

1. This information was taken from the web at http://www.austral.addr.com/old_machines/sewing_machine1.htm
2. My own memory of summer holidays from elementary school includes my mother undoing skirts and re-pleating them on the other side to look fresh and almost new when school resumed.

References

Brathwaite, E.K. 1977. *Mother Poem*. Oxford: Oxford University Press.

Cesaire, A. 1971. *Cahier D'un Retour au Pays Natal (Return to My Native Land)* translated by Emile Snyder. Paris: Présence Africaine.

Goodison, L. 1986. 'For My Mother (May I Inherit Half Her Strength)'. In *I Am Becoming My Mother*. London: New Beacon Books Ltd.

Senior, O. 1991. *Working Miracles: Women's Lives in the English-speaking Caribbean.* Cave Hill: Institute of Social and Economic Research.

_____. 1995. 'Zig Zag'. In *Discerner of Hearts.* Toronto: McClelland and Stewart Inc.

Walcott D. 1973. *Another Life.* London: Jonathan Cape.

THEME II

Gender in the 21st Century: Possiblities

Bridging Epistemologies

17 | SASKIA E. WIERINGA

Shifting Centres and Moving Margins
The ISS Experience

Introduction

The Institute of Social Studies (ISS) in The Hague has offered Women's Studies to a student body of mainly Third World mid-career participants since 1978. From 1982 onwards, the ISS also offered an MA degree to those who wanted to specialise in this field, although at present the MA is no longer in Women and Development, but in Development Studies. Between the mid-1980s and mid-1990s, Women's and Gender Studies at ISS was at its best: there was a sufficient number of highly qualified staff who offered a broad-based, attractive, innovative programme of Women's and Gender Studies to a motivated student body. It ran a number of interesting projects, of which the collaboration with the UWI was the longest and most successful. The programme was represented at senior academic level and enjoyed managerial support. At present the status of Women's and Gender studies at the ISS has declined. This paper reflects on the 25 years of history of Women's and Gender Studies at the ISS and attempts to chart a perspective for Women's and Gender Studies at the global level for the future. The concept of the 'triangle of empowerment' developed elsewhere (Vargas and Wieringa 1998) is used to analyse the growth and decline of the programme, in terms of both the internal dynamics of the programme as well as the dynamics within the ISS and the changing relation of the staff of the W&D programme with ISS management.

Other issues dealt with in this presentation are first the tension between Women's and Gender Studies, particularly the power struggles over the definition and relevance of these concepts. In the second place, the epistemological basis of Women's Studies and its relation to practice is discussed with reference to women's movements and the world of gender planning. Thirdly, comments are made on the development of the field of gender and development studies in general, and, its relation with other approaches in Women's Studies based on liberalism, historical materialism, or, more recently, post-structuralist and postmodernist theories.

Women's Studies has always been regarded as a global phenomenon, albeit with historical, sociopolitical and regional specificities. In that sense, the 'centre' can be understood as western Women's Studies, that is, the metropole from which liberal, historical materialist, post-structuralist and postmodern theories on power, discourse theory, embodiment, representation and performativity emerged and in which they took centre stage. Through teaching, research and project work at the ISS, there has been an attempt to feed experiences from the 'margins' into the work done in the 'centre', and the other way round, to inspire teaching and research with women from the 'marginal' centres of this world with insights from metropolitan centres, and therefore to blur the distinctions between 'centre' and 'margin' as defined in this way. Feminist epistemology teaches us that theory should be built on women's experiences. Globally valid theories therefore can only be built on women's experiences worldwide. The continued involvement and commitment of the ISS to the strengthening of Women's Studies globally, as here in the UWI, and a recent initiative to set up a network of Asian women's studies, called Kartini, are testimony to this.

Triangulation, with its emphasis on fluidity between the poles, rather than the binary thinking embedded in dialectical models, seems to be an apt way to analyse processes of change. This concept was first elaborated in an analysis of women's movements and public policy. In that analysis, distinguishing poles were the women's movement, bureaucracy and the world of politics, and it was argued that if there was a synergy between women's organisations, femocrats and feminist politicians, remarkable gains could be made. The 'triangle of empowerment' was conceptualised as follows:

> The metaphor of a triangle does not mean that actors inhabit fixed and stable positions....The triangle should not be imagined as a construction with three sharply defined angles connected by straight lines. It is located in specific historical and socio-political time and not in abstract space. Its dynamics tend to be contradictory, partial and ambivalent rather than linear. Relations between its three angles are mediated by sometimes converging and sometimes conflicting interests. (Vargas and Wieringa 1998, 4).

For the purpose of this paper, I suggest two triangles may be distinguished and used to analyse the development of the Women's Studies programmes: an internal and an external one. The internal triangle consists of students, younger feminist staff and senior staff, while the three angles of the external triangle of empowerment of the Women's Studies programme are defined as vision, strategy and institutional support. Vision refers to the underlying perception of what Women's and/or Gender Studies should be, and therefore what is the mission of the programme. The concept of strategy should be looked at from two angles – that of the achievement of the mission, and the strategy necessary to set up and maintain the programme. Institutional support is needed at two levels: that of colleagues and that of management. An underlying level of analysis is that of the different manifestations of power relations as they operated at the ISS. For the purpose of this paper I will only refer to the two most visible layers, the manifest and the latent levels of power (Lukes 1986). As I will suggest, a struggle waged in the manifest layer of power can be subverted if conflicting interests from the latent layer intervene, which in the case of academic institutions is often hidden behind supposedly neutral academic language.

History of the Programme

The Institute of Social Studies was founded in 1952 as a Centre for Development Studies in a decolonising world. From the start, teaching at the ISS has been heavily biased towards economic processes. In 1975, for the first time, attention was paid to women's issues. Mia Berden, a Senior Lecturer in Labour Studies at the ISS, attended the 1975 Conference of the International Women's Year in Mexico. On the basis of discussions held with women from the Third World during the Tribune this ISS staff member organised a workshop at the ISS in the summer of 1977. The focus of the workshop was the link between the budding Women's Studies programmes in the West and the needs and aspirations of women in the Third World. Many Third World women in Mexico felt that western Women's Studies did not and could not adequately reflect their own histories and experiences. They wanted a space to discuss these issues among themselves.

In response to this, in 1978/79, the first two courses were offered on Women and Development within an existing programme at the ISS, the Master's degree programme of Comparative Development Studies. In 1979/80 these courses expanded into a sub-specialisation on Women and Development open to MA participants at the ISS. An ISS recommendation followed that women's studies should not be offered separately, but that teaching on women's issues should be integrated (nowadays called 'mainstreamed') to all other programmes. Female students at ISS protested vigorously, arguing that a separate place to study women's issues should be provided (Truong 1989). The ISS management accepted the students' arguments. Finally, in 1982 the first 15 MA students arrived, and in 1983/4 a full-fledged Master's programme of 15 months was offered.

The establishment of the programme did not go smoothly. The internal triangle worked well, however there were tensions at the level of the external triangle. Most attention was paid to building the vision on which the programme was based. Fortunately, there was some support from management, especially from the then Rector, but the drive and energy needed to institutionalise Women's Studies, coupled with a vision that was looked at with suspicion as being 'too feminist', alienated various staff members. The strategy was to push forward, rather than go slowly and take as many people as possible on board. This inevitably led to some tensions.

The first few years were characterised by considerable resistance against the idea of Women's Studies, particularly from the side of the conservative economists, rural planners and administrators who have always formed the majority of ISS staff members. One of the major theoretical foci of those years was the epistemological work done to uncover male biases in mainstream social sciences. Some ISS staff members probably felt that their work was being criticised. The cliché that feminists are a bunch of aggressive women was embraced and fostered by this group of conservative staff members (including some women). Second, the influence of the students who fought for their own programme was considerable, but this was not always appreciated by other staff members. Third, gender expertise was not considered a requirement by management to add ISS staff members to the team. Being a woman was felt to be sufficient. The first coordinator of the programme strongly protested, arguing that she wanted experts in Women's Studies, not just women academics with other qualifications. This again alienated a few staff members, and since they were defeated at the manifest level of power, some took this underground to the more latent level. Fourth, as indicated above, when the first MA students arrived, all three senior staff members had left and a junior academic, together with Mia Berden, had to shoulder the burden of teaching new courses, confronting the antagonism of conservative and alienated staff members, and of finding ways to attract qualified staff members. Starting from such a weak position made the programme very vulnerable during the early years.

However, the programme soon expanded. New staff members were recruited: Rhoda Reddock, Thanh-Dam Truong, Amrita Chhachhi and later Renee Pittin. Apart from Renee Pittin, all the others still had to do their PhDs at the time. The commitment to building the field of Women and Development Studies and the enormous workload this entailed was greater than the urge to finish PhDs. At that time, this was not uncommon. Women's Studies, as a new field of studies, was built everywhere by young enthusiastic scholars who had recently graduated. There was an enormous demand for teaching, and the staff worked hard to fulfil that demand, neglecting other requirements of academic life, such as research and publishing. In these early years of Women's Studies, young staff members exhausted themselves both in building this new field, and in catering to the demands of the many enthusiastic students who flocked to this new discipline.

Each new appointment at the ISS women's programme only took place after a long struggle with junior academics having to fight 'from below' and wage long battles for their views to reach the ears of the management. The growth of the women's movement worldwide however gave us a legitimacy that was often only grudgingly acknowledged. This period culminated in the appointment of a full-time professor, Geertje Lycklama. With her on board the programme acquired the necessary stability, both within the staff group itself, and in relation to ISS management.

The internal triangle was restored. There was synergy between the senior and the younger staff; the students were committed. Now that junior staff were represented at the most senior level, they could engage in various teaching, research and project activities and concentrate more on completing their PhDs. Geertje Lycklama stimulated the research work of the younger academic staff, contributed to the development of the teaching programme, and proved to be a great strategist. This period of growth lasted from the mid-1980s until the mid-1990s. Teaching was consolidated (see Truong 1989, Wieringa 1992) and the Women's Studies programme acquired a strong position within the ISS. This also was the period when the external triangle of empowerment operated with most synergy. The vision continually kept developing as new work on Gender and Women's Studies became available and was supported by many scholars and activists from outside. Strategies, in line with this vision, were used to sustain the programme, along with moderate institutional support.

However, Women's Studies was never fully accepted in other parts of the ISS curriculum, and it was therefore possible to overcome only partially the resistance to a feminist vision and Women's Studies. This was partly due to the fact that the Women's Studies staff was overburdened. Teaching entailed intensive methods and staff had many other obligations. We also were not aware that much latent dissatisfaction was lurking in the dark. Resistance to the feminist vision was no longer expressed openly, but appeared in another guise. Staff associated with the Women's Studies programme was painted as consciously creating an 'island' position for themselves, although their involvement in many activities in other parts of the Institute proved otherwise. Although there were a number of colleagues, both male and female, who genuinely supported the Women's Studies programme, and with whom we cooperated well, there were others who were indifferent and, in many ways, hostile to the programme. Although seminars, for instance, were always open to outsiders, very rarely did other staff members attended.

One of the major strategies at the time was to create a large outside network. Through the student body, we helped build a global network of Women and Development specialists. This became evident during the Fourth Women's World Conference in Beijing and the NGO Forum in Huairou in 1995, which was attended by many past students. We also engaged in a number of projects to help set up Women and Development studies elsewhere. The project with the UWI was our first and longest and so far our most successful one. In the mid-1980s, we were also involved in a project on the training of women from SWAPO, the Namibian Resistance Movement, in preparation of their independence, which took place in 1990. After that we were invited to help set up Women's Studies at the University of Windhoek, Namibia, in which we were able to cooperate with staff members from the UWI. This south-south cooperation was highly effective. Other projects on setting up academic women's studies in which we were involved included Yemen and Sudan. The most recent initiative in this regard was in Bangladesh. Other Women's Studies Centres with which the ISS built intensive links of cooperation include the Asian Institute of Technology in Thailand, Ochanomizu University in Tokyo and the University of Indonesia in Jakarta.

When Geertje Lycklama retired, the decline of the programme started, partly as a result of various national and international constraints. However, the major factors were internal to the Institute and prevented the succession of the professorship of the programme to go smoothly and this adversely affected the programme. The hostility that had long lain dormant was now expressed in racist, sexist and homophobic attitudes. The discourse used in this regard was academic, but the sentiments expressed in this discourse were often of a non-academic nature. Resentment against feminism as a movement, deeply ingrained conservative neo-liberal attitudes of a great many staff members, and male chauvinism all played a role, at times explicitly, but usually more implicitly.

With Geertje Lycklama's departure from the programme, the internal triangle disintegrated, and the tenuous external triangle, which we had established during the preceding decade, crumbled as well. The strategy of building an international network did not help to prevent the breakdown of these synergies. The internal network of allies proved to be weaker than had been realised. The new management was not as supportive of the programme, and particularly painful was the open resistance of some female ISS staff members. Dean's theory, which we extensively discussed in the classroom, that solidarity among women is not built along lines of affinity but of reflection, that it cannot be assumed but must be constructed in often painful struggles, was particularly relevant to the ISS experience (Dean 1996).

It was assumed that female staff members in other departments of the Institute would be supportive of The Women's Studies Programme. Some were, but others were resentful of the programme either out of competition, or because strong patriarchal allegiances existed at the ISS, female solidarity was weak. Those associated with the Women's Studies programme did not move along the maternal/erotic axis along which patriarchal cultures attempt to mould women. It is only via that axis that patriarchy supports and rewards women. We wanted to be accepted on the basis of our work and our feminist vision and therefore felt that we had built a strong programme, with a solid international reputation, for which we were recognised externally (see for instance Staudt 1998). The resistance to the programme was often personalised because the ISS is a small institute, characterised by a culture of distorted communication and unclear structures of hierarchy and responsibility.

Major Achievements

The difficulties the Women's Studies programme experienced do not negate the considerable success that we achieved over its 25 years of existence and which are discussed in this section of the paper. Recommendations coming out of the first workshop held at the ISS, following the 1975 Mexico Conference, informed the vision and principles on which teaching has been built. Although these principles have continuously been amended and expanded in response to major changes at the global and local levels as well as the development of Women's and Gender Studies globally, the core principles remained more or less intact. A basic principle was the insistence that Women's Studies entailed a change of paradigm with its own epistemological and theoretical emphases and the idea that one could just 'add women' (or the analytical category of gender) to existing theories (Harding 1991) was resisted. Women's Studies is not just 'better', for more complete treatment of (inclusive of women's experiences) the social sciences, but is an academic field in its own right. The second principle undergirding the programme was the relevance of theory to local development processes and the theoretical and epistemological link between women's agency and activism and Women's Studies. A third principle has been an emphasis on the mutual interdependence between the 'centre' and the 'margin', and a reversal of the hierarchies contained in this distinction and the stimulation of Women's Studies in regional centres.

Although the emphasis on topics may have differed, teaching and research ran along parallel lines. The following areas were singled out for specific attention within a holistic approach: an analysis of the histories of women's movements and organisations; women's labour; body politics and gender policy and planning (see also Lycklama 1985; Truong 1989; Wieringa 1992). From the start of the programme two basic theoretical pillars have been emphasised: gender analysis and feminist epistemology. The first allowed us to see women's subordination not as something related to women only, but as embedded in social relations of power, often linked to institutions. The second stimulated us to analyse 'malestream' science, to insist that all knowledge is partial and engaged (Mies 1979), that feminist analysis requires a 'double vision' (Kelly 1984), should pay attention to issues of race (Collins 1991) and is always already situated (Haraway 1988). Later, this analysis was enriched with discourse analysis and deconstruction (Weedon 1987), postcolonial studies (Spivak 1999), and representation (Butler 1990 and 1993). From the start, teaching was challenging and participatory, stimulating participants to engage in a critical dialogue with each other and with us about their experiences, thus putting them in a wider theoretical and analytical perspective.

Based on these pillars, several hundred participants have been trained, who in many cases have been actively engaged with and have contributed to the women's movements in their countries in various ways: academically, or via the NGOs in which they participate(d), or bureaucratically via the agencies in which they work(ed). We are proud of our student body and have often received feedback that indicates to us that our teaching has made a difference.

The network of alumnae has formed the basis of various projects for stimulating Women's Studies that the ISS has engaged in, such as at the UWI. We have incorporated elements of our teaching formula in the various Women's Studies projects to which we have contributed directly, and also via our students who are engaged in developing curricula in other universities or Women's Studies Centres. In this way, we have contributed to building the field of Women, Gender and Development Studies globally.

Women's Studies staff at the ISS also built up a solid research record in the areas we focused on. The first research project we implemented was the Women's History Project, in which research was carried out in five countries (India, Indonesia, Peru, Somalia, Sudan) and one region (the Caribbean) (Wieringa 1995a, see also 1988). Other research topics in the 1980s included women's labour (Chhachhi and Pittin 1996a and b, Reddock 1984, Mohammed 1993), migration (Lycklama et al. 1994) and body politics (Truong 1988). These topics were continued during the 1990s (Chhachhi forthcoming, Wieringa 2002a, 2003, Wieringa and Blackwood, 1999). Attention was also paid to issues of gender policy and planning (Lycklama 1987, Lycklama, Vargas and Wieringa 1998, Wieringa 1994 and 1998a). Recent research topics include human security (Truong forthcoming 2004), human trafficking (Truong 2003a and b), women's sexual empowerment and HIV/AIDS (Wieringa 2002b, 2003b) and the development of gender indicators (Wieringa 1997, 2000, Charmes and Wieringa 2003).

Recently, the ISS and the University of Amsterdam have been involved in setting up a network of Women's Studies Centres and women's organisations in Asia. This network is called Kartini, after the pioneering Indonesian feminist, and was conceived during a visit to Japan by Dr Truong. After two years of preparation it was formally established in Manila, in May 2003. In this case, the relation between the 'centre' and the 'margin' is reversed. The Asian women's and gender studies centres and the women's organisations form the core, the two European institutes play a more distant role. The central programme of teaching and research has been established on the priorities voiced by the Asian centres. These include various forms of fundamentalism (religious, economic), gender, violence and conflict resolution, and embodiment and sexual rights, as well as the development of women's studies in the region. Kartini has two coordinators, one in Asia (Manila) and one in Europe (Amsterdam).

Dilemmas

The history of the Women's Studies programme at the ISS has been characterised by various dilemmas, most of which are inherent to Women's Studies programmes elsewhere, especially when they are embedded in hierarchical institutions. The first dilemma relates to the supposed controversy between Women's and Gender Studies. The programme was always called a programme of 'Women and Development Studies'. We have always maintained that our vision and politics are feminist, based on an awareness of women's subordination and the struggle towards greater gender justice. The focus of our work has been on research and teaching that feed into efforts to reduce women's subordination. We have always used gender analysis as the most critical tool to understand the relations of oppression women are confronted with. From the very first courses we included gender analysis as well as the analysis of intersecting relations of power, such as those based on class and race. Although our understanding of gender evolved (Braidotti 1991, 2002, Haraway 1991, Scott 1989), we have never dealt with women's issues in isolation, and lately, we have incorporated fascinating new work on masculinities, particularly in the supervision of PhD candidates. This is also one of the topics included in a new course on HIV/AIDS, and the regulation of human sexuality that was developed but never offered. In spite of this, we have often been accused of neglecting gender analysis and even of being 'old fashioned' because we did not call ourselves a 'gender programme'. A compromise has now been reached; the programme is renamed 'Women, Gender and Development'.

This controversy is based on the early WID (Women in Development) approach in gender planning (Moser 1989) which tended to focus on women's issues to the neglect of other relations of power. We have not only critiqued the WID approach, but we have also criticised the adherents of the GAD (Gender and Development) approach, where they ignored a feminist perspective, and focused on socioeconomic issues, neglecting body politics and sexuality (Lycklama 1987, Wieringa 1994, 1998a). Gender analysis and theories of power and empowerment have therefore always been central components of the programme (see also Wieringa forthcoming). I suggest that the perceived dilemma between Women's and Gender studies is not so much related to the content of the programme, but is more linked to the power relations surrounding our work and who has the right to define the content of our teaching and research.

The second dilemma we faced was a strategic issue: the choice between autonomy versus integration. From the start of the programme pressure was exerted on the programme staff to integrate into mainstream teaching. Until the restructuring process some years ago, ISS had seven teaching programmes. It was felt that Women's Studies should be integrated into the other programmes and that it should not be treated as a separate programme. We maintained that we needed a strong core programme, in which there should be space for theory building and epistemology (see also Lycklama 1985, Wieringa 1992) but we also made considerable efforts to link up with the other programmes in the Institute. In fact, we spent a substantial amount of time integrating gender into courses on human rights, the informal sector, the labour programme and rural planning, as well as in general and introductory courses. We also regularly invited staff members from other programmes to teach in the courses we offered. Yet the idea that we had isolated ourselves persisted.

With the restructuring of the ISS, which resulted in the establishment of four staff groups, women's studies was initially split over two staff groups. The programme and the majority of women's studies staff members were linked to staff group three, while two other staff members joined group two, as their research interests coincided more closely with ongoing work in that staff group. It soon became clear that this resulted in a considerable weakening of the programme, with the two members in staff group two being unable to effectively fight for gender issues to get a central place, on a par with other topics, on that staff group's agenda. Recognising the failure of this experiment, we regrouped into one staff group, number three. The fear we had from the beginning, that 'mainstreaming' of gender concerns means a considerable weakening of the programme, was therefore justified.

In spite of efforts to join forces with staff members from other groups, the idea that women's studies staff were isolationists, wary of cooperating with men, persisted. Staff members from other groups were invited to join in research (such as the project on gender and sustainable development) and in projects. Certain elements of the programme have always been open to students from other parts of the ISS, and, as indicated above, public seminars were always open to staff and students from all areas of study at the ISS, and several PhD supervision committees included men.

The perceived isolation of the Women's Studies programme has been more fiction than reality. We often discussed the reasons behind this stereotyping of the programme but have never been able to effectively break through this discourse. A related issue is that reaching out to other programmes was considered to be our responsibility. Although there was a growing number of staff members who had a genuine interest in gender issues, the majority never considered it their responsibility to read up on Women's Studies; we were supposed to enlighten them.

Another strategic issue is that we never succeeded in enlisting the solidarity of most other female staff members at the Institute. Firstly, there were very few of them; and secondly, some of them still felt alienated because of the tensions surrounding the establishment of the programme. A call to all female staff members to support the setting up of a gender audit was initially rejected by several of them, although it was subsequently carried out. This lack of support was surprising, as the lopsided, male-dominated hierarchical structure of the Institute gave serious cause for concern, and there were only a few women who had been promoted to the senior academic ranks.

Part of these difficulties also originated from the tension between the core staff of Women's Studies, and some staff members who tried to work on gender issues in other programmes of the ISS, the 'extended' staff. The 'extended' staff members faced various constraints in their own programmes and at times felt very isolated. We were not always able to help them, being so caught up in our own work. This led to some resentment on their part and prevented all of us from strategising effectively to promote Gender Studies in all ISS programmes.

Based on these experiences, I would conclude that it is vital to have a core programme that is solely devoted to the paradigm of Women's Studies, to its epistemology and its theories. However, this core should not be isolated, but should be surrounded by specific focal points at other parts of the Institute. So the dilemma of a choice between autonomy and integration is a false one; a combination of both integration and autonomy is the most fruitful solution. What is required is both theoretical and epistemological autonomy, and integration with other fields of study. However, such a structure can only work effectively when it is embedded in a sympathetic environment, and this was lacking at the ISS, especially in the last years. In this regard, the views of programme staff and of management differ sharply. Management felt that it had facilitated the programme by devoting sufficient time and resources to ensure continued delivery.

The third dilemma was the controversy between so-called 'applied' science and the more fundamental forms of science. This is an issue related to the vision dimension of the external triangle. Gender planners and practitioners are sometimes accused of being 'too theoretical', of not equipping our students with the more practical knowledge they need to tackle women's subordination in their countries which, in this view, was often limited to women's socioeconomic oppression. This view was sometimes expressed by colleagues within the ISS as well. On the other hand, Women's Studies specialists, especially in the metropolitan centres, feel that they are sometimes dismissed as not relevant, as only dealing with practical matters, which were usually seen as being less important than issues associated with purely philosophical debates. These criticisms became stronger as Women's Studies became more dominated by post-structuralist and postmodernist theorists.

Again, I would like to argue that this is not an either/or issue. Its echo is found in debates in development circles between those who argue that the main issue in the 'South' is poverty, not body politics, that sex is the major hang-up of a decadent west and has no relevance to the great majority of people living in the South. In our view, poverty and body politics are not isolated phenomena (Truong 2000, 2003a and b, Wieringa 1998, 2002 a and b, 2003a and b). Poverty is related to violence, including gender violence, to migration, trafficking, the increased vulnerability of marginalised groups to diseases such as the infection by HIV. These are all gendered phenomena which have a bearing on women's bodies and sexualities. Those who ignore the imbricating relations between body and sexual politics on the one hand and socioeconomic and political processes on the other hand are also unable to discuss the context of such critical present-day issues as human trafficking and the consequences of the HIV/AIDS pandemic. It is important to analyse the relations between these phenomena and how socioeconomic processes impact cultural contexts in which women's bodies are the major battlefields.

Conservative, neo-liberal economists at the ISS have always been opposed to our insistence on the relevance of theory for the analysis of gender issues and our attention to issues related to sexual politics. My work on women's same-sex relations took place outside of any ISS context (Blackwood and Wieringa 1999). Even though every year lesbian and gay students complained of the homophobia at the Institute and their isolation and fear of exposure, it was not possible to pay attention to their concerns. Lately the fear of 'radical feminism', which has been noted since the early days of the programme, has been replaced by unease with issues related to homosexuality.

Constraints

In the 25 years of the existence of the Women's Studies programme, critical changes took place at the international and national level that affected our programme. Some international developments, such as the series of Women's World Conferences and other important global events, such as the ICPD (International Conference on Population and Development) conference (Cairo 1994) and the follow up meetings provided legitimacy and acted as a stimulus. The gradual establishment of gender desks and the mainstreaming of gender issues in all major international development agencies, from the World Bank to the smaller religious-oriented development agencies, in development departments of foreign ministries, in national ministries and in other places were also important contributing factors. Many ISS alumni worked in these organisations, and ISS staff carried out some consultancies, and engaged with them in a critical dialogue. However, there was also a problematic side to this development. Many gender planners and development agencies happily embraced the concept of gender in order to replace feminism, as feminism was seen to be too controversial. 'Gender' was perceived to be more neutral, less threatening. It didn't draw attention to women's bodies, with its fluids, its pleasures and humiliations, and to sexual politics. Consequently many of those issues were ignored. We were very critical of this shift and insisted that the concept of gender keep its critical, feminist edge (Wieringa 1994, 1998a, Charmes and Wieringa 2003). The growing influence of neo-liberal and unilateralist tendencies of the one remaining superpower of the world, the US, are also greatly damaging to the support of work that is based on a vision towards peace, gender, racial and social justice.

National developments also influenced the Women's Studies programme at the ISS and in some cases contributed to its problems. When the programme was set up, following the rise of student and social activist movements of the late sixties, Dutch academic life was in its most democratic phase. Recently those social movements, including the women's movement, have lost much of their social relevance. Women's emancipation is no longer a fashionable topic and the position of Secretary of State for Women's Emancipation has been discontinued. At the same time, universities have become more hierarchical, and in many universities, Women's Studies departments are under threat.

The major constraints that the ISS Women's Studies programme faced, however, were internal to the Institute, and related to both the internal and external triangles. The first issue, related to the internal triangle, and which is common to many women's studies programmes all over the world, is the enthusiasm, commitment and consequently high expectations of participants. In the early years of the programme, this was the first time that many students could discuss problems, frustrations and painful experiences about which, up until that time, they had had to be silent. They tended to see the programme as providing them with an opportunity to solve injustices in their private and work lives. On the one hand, this stimulated the staff; but, on the other hand, this created heavy demands on our time and energy. In addition, the Institute, and academic life in general, also made heavy demands on our time, so that staff was often overworked and exhausted. The second issue is that the balance between the two corners of the triangle related to staff got seriously upset when Geertje Lycklama left the programme.

The critical issue, however, was the institutional hierarchical culture related to the external traingle. As mentioned before, the Institute is dominated by conservative economists, rural planners and administrators, most of them white, older men. Not only were many of them hardly interested in Women's Studies, but they also held sexist, racist and homophobic views and formed an impenetrable 'old boys network' in which some women corroborated, provided they played the games along the maternal/erotic axis (Pateman 1988). The male colleagues who were supportive of Women's Studies, were mostly younger and in lower academic ranks.

The major need of the programme after Geertje Lycklama left the Institute was the appointment of a good professor, according to a fair procedure, who would be supportive of the work. Her departure created the opportunity for a backlash in which many latent tensions surrounding the programme could be expressed. This resistance, which was often personalised, typically got expressed in an academic guise. In the Dutch academic culture there is no automatic promotion to a professorial rank according to specific criteria. Every vacancy at the rank of professor and associate professor has to be filled in an internationally open procedure. Internal candidates are given no preference. On the contrary, they are more vulnerable, as their possible weaknesses are known, while those of the external candidates only become known after acceptance. This situation was exploited: the post was advertised on two occasions, and on both an external candidate was appointed, although there were two internal candidates.

Several factors played a role in these decisions. A core group of conservative economists, who focus on quantitative, 'objective' methodologies considered the work of the internal candidates to be unscientific, political, and emotional, although their level of familiarity with the work of the internal candidates was uncertain. Their lack of knowledge, coupled with their position of power made it difficult for the internal candidates to plead their case successfully. The rejection of the internal candidates was perceived as being based on an aversion to radical feminism which the candidates were thought to support. Other, more subjective factors, also played a role in the selection process as they do in any other academic setting. The candidate who was selected after the second procedure was a neo-liberal American academic, with a specialisation in International Relations.

A strategic discussion could have informed the direction of the new teaching programme. The field of Women's Studies has greatly expanded, and much more in depth work is going on in various areas than used to be possible before. A central feature of the ISS programme has always been its global character; which could have been maintained while making the focus more specific. The Hague is located in a unique surrounding, with the major international courts within its borders. A global programme focusing on women's rights might have been a viable development, incorporating the expertise of all staff and topics such as labour rights, social security and entitlements, sexual rights and international relations. This would have been of interest to international agencies and women's organisations.

The new professor rewrote the programme so that large areas of the Women's Studies programme have been made redundant, while new initiatives were considered irrelevant to the programme. The vision of the programme has thus changed with minimal consultation with the staff that has been working with it for 20 years. The link between theory and practice is no longer maintained. The rather broad base of the teaching programme has been replaced by a narrow emphasis on a relatively small field of studies, international relations.

Challenges for the Future

For a Women's/Gender Studies programme to be successful there should be sufficient synergy between the three angles of both triangles of empowerment presented: the internal triangle, with senior staff, younger staff and students, and the external triangle, consisting of the vision of the programme, the strategies employed and the institutional culture in which the programme is located.

At the UWI, it appears that all three angles of the triangle of internal relations are in harmony. UWI has a strong and committed student body, highly qualified younger staff, and a very supportive group of 'older wise women' who have always strongly supported the Gender Studies Centre. On the other hand, the stability of the triangle of internal relations at the ISS seems to be under threat.

Looking at the external triangle, there are various problematic and challenging issues at both institutions. The link between the women's movement and Women's Studies has been weakened in favour of an emphasis on academic work. Epistemologically, the link between women's organisations and Women's/Gender Studies is an important one. This does not mean there is no space for more 'fundamental' research. There clearly is a great need for continued work of feminist philosophy and epistemology. However the practitioners in these fields of study should allow themselves to be inspired by work that originates from movements both locally and globally.

Within the regions there is a clear need for careful training and research on the themes that are specific to those regions. The dialogue between activists, researchers and trainers is an important one. In various countries such as India, those dialogues are held. It is important that the experiences gained there are analysed and shared with larger, supranational audiences. South-south cooperation should be stimulated by universities, national governments and by national and international donor agencies. Our experience indicates that the dialogue between and among policy makers, practitioners and academics is vital, but that the rhythms of each should be maintained.

There is also a growing need for theoretically well-trained gender experts. It is becoming clear that superficial courses do not provide enough background for gender experts to make a meaningful input. My own work on developing the African Gender and Development Index has taught me how intellectually challenging such 'practical' work can be, and how much critical feminist-inspired analysis can offer to the field of gender planning and policy. There is a wide array of short gender courses but many of them fail to teach their participants an acceptable standard of critical gender analysis. For activists and researchers in women's organisations or staff at gender desks, more specialised training must be offered. Gender training can be offered at various levels. MA and PhD training will remain important, but besides those courses, more specialised courses should be offered, such as gender and human rights, gender and fundamentalisms, gender and livelihood, gender, culture and sexuality, the gender dimension of HIV/AIDS etc. Some of these courses will have more relevance for particular regions than others.

The third angle of the external triangle is institutional support. Based on the ISS experience, it is important to consider the dynamics of the institution within which a Women's Studies programme is offered. Location of the programme is important and cannot be ignored. If there are strong patriarchal and other types of biases operating, all kinds of undercurrents may occur leading to latent power games which may undermine the smooth operation of women's studies programmes or courses. Universities can be surprisingly conservative bulwarks. In such cases, it is important that the internal triangle is in harmony, so that pressure can be exerted easily at the management level. The 'bottom up' approach that was adopted at the ISS made the programme very vulnerable. Also commitment to our vision sometimes blinded us to finding strategies that might have eased the path to find more support for that vision within the Institute.

Dutch academic and social culture has also been challenging. The Netherlands has an extremely low percentage of female professors and little experience with women's leadership. The housewife ideology, which was very strong until the last decades of the past century (Outshoorn and Swiebel 1998), has not facilitated the respect for strong women who refuse to accommodate themselves to the maternal/erotic axis mentioned above.

Conclusion

The ISS women's studies programme has a record of interesting research, committed teaching and solid project work. During the last 25 years, hundreds of students were trained. At present the programme is facing difficulties associated with a transitional phase. The internal synergies and the dynamics between the two triangles are threatened. New balances will have to be found, both within and outside of the ISS, because Women's/Gender Studies as a field of study keeps expanding, while women's subordination remains firmly entrenched.

References

Braidotti, Rosi. 1991. *Theories of Gender*. Utrecht: University of Utrecht.

———. 2002. *Metamorphoses: Towards a Materialist Theory of Becoming*. Cambridge: Polity Press.

Butler, Judith. 1990. *Gender Trouble: Feminism and the Subversion of Identity*. New York and London: Routledge.

———. 1993. *Bodies That Matter: On the Discursive Limits of 'Sex'*. New York and London: Routledge.

Charmes, Jacques and Saskia Wieringa. 2003. 'Measuring Women's Empowerment: An Assessment of the GDI and the GEM'. *Journal of Human Development* 4, no. 3: 419 – 435.

Chhachhi, Amrita and Nandita Shah, Sujata Gothoskar and Nandita Gandhi. 1999. 'Structural Adjustment, Feminisation of Labour Force and Organisational Strategies'. *Gender and Politics in India,* ed. N. Menon, 145-77. Oxford: Oxford University Press.

Chhachhi, Amrita and Renee Pittin. 1996a. *Confronting State, Capital and Patriarchy: Women Organising in the process of Industrialization*. London: Macmillan.

———. 1996b. 'Multiple Identities, Multiple Strategies: Confronting State, Capital and Patriarchy'. *Confronting State, Capital and Patriarchy: Women Organising in the process of Industrialization*, 93-130. London: Macmillan.

Chhachhi, Amrita. 1994. 'Identity Politics, Secularism and Women: A South Asian Perspective'. *Forging Identities: Gender, Communities and the State,* ed. Zoya Hasan, 74-95. Delhi: Kali for Women.

———. 1991. 'The State, Religious Fundamentalism and Violence Against Women in South Asia'. *Towards Women's Strategies in the 1990's: Challenging Government and State,* ed. G. Lycklama. London: Macmillan.

———. Forthcoming. *Eroding Citizenship: Gender and Labour in Contemporary India*. Phd thesis.

Collins, P. Hill. 1991. *Black Feminist Thought: Knowledge, Consciousness and the Politics of Empowerment.* New York and London: Routledge.

Dean, Jodi. 1996. *Solidarity of Strangers: Feminism after Identity Politics.* Berkeley: University of California Press.

Haraway, Donna. 1988. 'Situated Knowledges: The Science Question in Feminism as a Site of Discourse and the Privilege of Partial Perspective'. *Feminist Studies* 14, no. 3: 575-99.

—————. 1991. '"Gender" for a Marxist Dictionary: The Sexual Politics of a Word.' *Simians, Cyborgs and Women; The Reinvention of Nature,* 127-149. London: Free Association Books.

Harding, Sandra. 1991. *Whose Science? Whose Knowledge? Thinking from Women's Lives.* Buckingham: Open University Press.

Kelly, Joan. 1984. *Women, History and Theory: The Essays of Joan Kelly.* Chicago and London: University of Chicago Press.

Lukes, S., ed. 1986. *Power: Readings in Social and Political Theory.* Oxford: Basil Blackwell.

Lycklama à Nijeholt, Geertje. 1985. Women's Studies as a Strategy for Change: the ISS Experience. Paper presented at Nairobi Forum, p. 14.

—————. 1987. 'The Fallacy of Integration: the UN Strategy of Integrating Women into Development Revisited'. *Netherlands Review of Development Studies* 1.

Lycklama à Nijeholt, Geertje, Virginia Vargas and Saskia Wieringa, eds. 1998. *Women's Movements and Public Policy in Europe, Latin America and The Caribbean.* New York: Garland Publishing, Inc.

Lycklama à Nijeholt, Geertje, Noeleen Heyzer and Nedra Weerakoon eds. 1994. *The Trade in Domestic Workers, Causes, Mechanisms and Consequences of International Migration.* London: Zed Books.

Lycklama à Nijeholt, Geertje, ed. 1991. *Towards Women's Strategies for the 1990s Challenging Government and the State.* London: Macmillan.

Mies, Maria. 1979. *Towards a Methodology of Women's Studies.* The Hague: Institute of Social Studies.

Mohammed, Patricia. 1995. Social History of Post-Migrant Indians in Trinidad from 1917 to 1947: A Gender Perspective. The Hague: Institute of Social Studies. PhD thesis.

Moser, C.O.N. 1989. Gender Planning in the third world: Meeting Practical and Strategic Needs. *World Development* 17, no. 11:1799-1825.

Outshoorn, Joyce, and Joke Swiebel. 1998. 'Feminism and the State in The Netherlands'. *Women's Movements and Public Policy in Europe, Latin America and the Caribbean,* eds. Geertje, Lycklama, Virginia Vargas and Saskia Wieringa, 3-25 New York: Garland.

Pateman, Carole.1988. *The Sexual Contract.* Cambridge: Polity Press.

Reddock, Rhoda. 1984. Women. Labour and Struggle in 20th Century Trinidad and Tobago: 1898–1960. The Hague, Institute of Social Studies. PhD thesis.

Rothchild, Cynthia and Scott Long. 2000. Written Out: How Sexuality is Used to Attack Women Organizing, A Report of the International Gay and Lesbian Human Rights Commission and the Center for Women's Global Leadership. San Francisco and New Brunswick.

Scott, Joan Wallach. 1989. 'Gender, a Useful Category of Historical Analysis'. *Coming to Terms: Feminism, Theory, Politics,* ed. E. Weed. New York: Routledge.

Spivak, Gayatri. 1999. *A Critique of Postcolonial Reason.* Cambridge and London: Harvard University Press.

Staudt, Kathleen. 1998. *Policy, Politics and Gender: Women Gaining Ground.* West Artford: Kumarian Press.

Sylvester, Christine. 2002. 'Global Development'. *Dramaturgies/Gender Stagings.* The Hague: Institute of Social Studies, 22.

Truong, Thanh-Dam. 1988. *Sex, Money and Morality: The Political Economy of Prostitution and Tourism in South East Asia.* London: Zed Books.

——————. 1989. Feminist Studies in International Education: The Experience of the Women and Development Programme at the Institute of Social Studies, The Netherlands. Paper presented at International Seminar on Women's Studies, Saitama, p. 14.

——————. 2000. 'A Feminist Perspective on the Asian Miracle and Crisis: Enlarging the Conceptual Map of Human Development'. *Journal of Human Development* 1, no. 1:159-164.

——————. 2003a. 'The Human Rights Question in the Global Sex Trade'. *Responding to the Human Rights Deficit,* eds., Karin Arts and Pascal Mihyo,185-201. Kluwer Law International.

——————. 2003b. 'Gender, Exploitative Migration and the Sex Industry: A European Perspective'. *Gender, Technology and Development* 7, no. 1:31-52.

——————. Forthcoming. Towards a vision of Human Security: a Buddhist perspective. *Religion, Violence and Visions of Peace,* eds. Gerrie Ter Haar and James Busuttil. Brill: Leiden.

Vargas, Virginia and Saskia Wieringa. 1998. 'The Triangle of Empowerment, Processes and Actors in the Making of Public Policy for Women'. *Women's Movements and Public Policy in Europe, Latin America and the Caribbean* eds., Geertje, Lycklama, Virginia Vargas and Saskia Wieringa, 3-25. New York: Garland.

Weedon, C. 1987. *Feminist Practice & Poststructuralist Theory.* Oxford: Basil Blackwell.

Wieringa, Saskia E. ed. 1988. *Women's Struggles and Strategies.* Aldershot: Gower.

——————. 1992. 'The Women and Development Programme at the Institute of Social Studies', the Hague, Holland. *Australian Feminist Studies,* no. 15, (Autumn).

——————. 1994. 'Women's Interests and Empowerment; Gender Planning Reconsidered'. *Development & Change,* vol. 25/4 (October): 829-849.

——————. 1995a. *Sub-Versive Women: Women's Movements in Africa, Asia, Latin America and the Caribbean.* New Delhi: Kali for Women, London: Zed Press.

——————. ed. 1997. Report on Workshop on Gender Indicators. The Hague, January.

Wieringa, Saskia E., G. Lycklama and V. Vargas, eds. 1998. *Women's Movement and Public Policy in Europe, Latin America and the Caribbean.* New York: Garland.

Wieringa, Saskia E. 1998a. 'Rethinking Gender Planning: A Critical Discussion of the Use of the Concept of Gender'. *Gender, Technology and Development* 2, no. 3: 349-373.

———. 1998b. *Kuntilanak Wangi: Organisasi-Organisasi Perempuan Indonesia Sesudah 1950*. Jakarta: Kalyanamitra, Pusat Komunikasi dan Informasi Perempuan.

Wieringa, Saskia E. and Evelyn Blackwood, eds. 1999. *Female Desires: Same-Sex Relations and Transgender Practices Across Cultures*. New York: Columbia University Press.

Wieringa, Saskia E. 2000. Towards Gender Equality in Indonesia: The Relevance of Global Instruments and Discourses in a National Context. Seminar presentation. ISS. p. 23

———. 2001. From Women's Labour to Sexual Politics: Twenty Years of Teaching and Research in Women's Studies. Paper presented at Women's Studies Conference, Dalian, p.17.

———. 2002a. *Sexual Politics in Indonesia*. Basingstoke: Palgrave/MacMillan.

———. 2002b. 'Gender, Tradition, Sexual Diversity and AIDS in postcolonial Southern Africa'. *Challenges for Anthropology in the 'African Renaissance', A Southern African Contribution,* eds. Debie Lebeau and Robert J. Gordon, 124-137. Windhoek: University of Namibia Press.

———. 2003a. 'The Birth of the New Order State in Indonesia: Sexual Politics and Nationalism'. *Journal of Women's History* 15, no. 1:70-92.

———. 2003b. HIV/AIDS and Women's Sexual Empowerment. Manual prepared for the Indonesian Women's Federation, Jakarta.

———. Forthcoming. Measuring Women's Empowerment. University of Amsterdam, mimeo, p. 26.

18 | HERMIONE C. MCKENZIE

Shifting Centres and Moving Margins
The UWI Experience

Introduction: Waking Up to Women's Issues

As the work of someone who, for many years, has been closely associated with the development and teaching of gender-related courses on the Mona campus of the University of the West Indies, this presentation is inevitably autobiographical and indeed I enjoy this aspect. But I also want to explore more deeply the place of gender studies in the academy and the prospects and possibilities for the future.

I will begin with the first United Nations World Conference on Women in Mexico City in 1975, although my interest in gender studies began long before then. For that 1975 conference, the late Dorian Powell and myself, both members of the then Department of Sociology, were asked to prepare a background paper for the Jamaican delegation to the conference. In the early 1970s, Dorian had been working on census data relating to women, specifically on their occupations and their fertility, and I had been writing on women and family structure, so we produced a joint paper which we entitled, 'The Status of Women in the Jamaican Family Structure'. Our paper tried to document the status and roles of women in the range of family types which existed in Jamaica, our women's fertility patterns according to family type, and tried to give an overview of the experiences of women in their family situations.

Of course we had not attempted such a background paper before and I do not know if the delegation was able to use our paper in their conference participation. But the experience of writing this paper stimulated our ideas on the possibilities of working specifically on gender analysis, and on the importance of disaggregated social data for both women and men. It also gave us useful experience in linking our academic work with the growing gender movements both locally and internationally. The point is that, although we and other university scholars had been studying data on women, before 1975 we had not been very conscious of the international developments relating to women, nor of the groundswell which the women's movement would create.

In the early 1970s had come the establishment of the Women's Desk/Bureau in Jamaica (Henry-Wilson 1989). Writing with some insider knowledge, as an influential member of the People's National Party, Maxine Henry-Wilson describes the internal processes by which the idea of a Women's Bureau was conceptualised and presented to the People's National Party (PNP) government, which had been elected in 1972, and the way in which this Women's Bureau was developed and established in 1973. The Bureau was first headed by Lucille Mathurin Mair who had been one of the original conceptualisers, and later in 1975 by Peggy Antrobus. Then in 1975 came the United Nations International Women's Year and the United Nations World Conference on Women in Mexico City.

Neither Dorian nor I attended the Mexico City conference. Later we learned about the NGO Tribune, established at the Mexico City conference by groups who were not official delegates to the conference but who came anyway to assert their interest and identity. Of course this most interesting development, renamed the NGO Forum, became a parallel feature of all the subsequent United Nations World Conferences on Women, providing 'an opportunity for networking and for a less restrained and more dynamic engagement among women' (Steady 1995).

To us in the academy, the opportunities provided by the NGO Forums for unofficial participation in the World Conferences were invaluable. At Nairobi, in 1985, Florence Howe of Women's Studies International, among others, organised special academic panels on developing Women's Studies teaching programmes, while at Beijing in 1995 the NGO Forum became a massive symposium. In 1975, few of us had detailed knowledge of the international developments and the international network of women's interests, but increasingly the world movements affected and strengthened our local activities.

After International Women's Year, 1975, and the further Declaration by the United Nations General Assembly in December 1975 of a United Nations Decade for Women, 1976-1985, the years of the 1970s buzzed with activity. By 1977, Joycelin Massiah was developing the Women in the Caribbean Project and a Jamaican team including myself, Dorian Powell, Erna Brodber, Victoria Durant-Gonzalez, and others who participated from time to time, began making regular visits to the Institute of Social and Economic Research (ISER), Cave Hill campus, where Joycelin was Director. There we met with other colleagues from Cave Hill and St Augustine for consultations, discussions, planning, and finally to initiate the field research which was conducted largely in Barbados, St Vincent, and Antigua, although several smaller pieces of exploratory research were also carried out in Guyana and Jamaica.

Also in 1977 in Jamaica, a very important United Nations Seminar on the Integration of Women in Development in the Caribbean was held, under the joint auspices of what was then the University of the West Indies Extra-Mural Department (now the School for Continuing Studies), more specifically under the sponsorship of the Social Welfare Training Centre, which was then managed by Sybil Francis, in collaboration with the Jamaica Women's Bureau. Out of that seminar came the resolution and recommendation to establish the Women and Development Unit of the University of the West Indies (WAND), which was established in Barbados in 1978 (Massiah 1986).

Looking back over those years, I reflect most of all on our easy intra-regional mobility and the extent to which staff members from the three main university campuses cooperated, as well as the representatives of the University Centres in the non-campus territories. As academic researchers, we travelled often to Cave Hill; and the data collectors, among whom were Jean Jackson and Margaret Bernal, travelled all over the Caribbean. WAND activities spread far and wide over the English-speaking Caribbean. We attended conferences and participated in discussions on the status of women and their needs in the region, wherever a meeting or a conference was held.

We from Jamaica travelled under financial constraints in this period because of Jamaican foreign exchange restrictions whereby each traveller could take only US$55 out of the country. Once we arrived at our destination, we survived through sponsored hotel accommodations and per diem allowances. But we always had a narrow survival margin. Some time near the end of the Women in the Caribbean Project, our Caribbean airline, BWIA, had a major strike of several weeks. Our Jamaican group travelled from Barbados to Trinidad, I think by British Airways, and then we were due to fly by ALM via Curacao to Jamaica. We overnighted in the airport because we had no money for a hotel. We had friends in Port of Spain who might have offered us a bed for the night, but at that period the Trinidad telephone system did not work well. The telephone produced numerous 'wrong numbers'. So at about 11.00 p.m., after calling our friends several times and each time getting a different sleepy, angry voice saying 'Wrong Number!' we gave up and decided to endure the night sitting in chairs at the airport. I think that Caribbean readers will understand what I mean when I talk about the bonds of 'shipmates'.

Finally in September 1982, we had a very lively and important Regional Conference in Barbados where we presented the final results of the Women in the Caribbean Project to our funders, our stakeholders, and to a wide range of international gender specialists, and after four long years the project was over.

But not over from the point of view of the academy! According to Massiah, 'this Conference brought together policy makers, administrators of women's programmes, and researchers: to assess the project, to discuss its findings, to identify ways of implementing recommended programmes, and to advise on further activity' (Massiah 1986). It also marked an important occasion whereby the Institute of Social and Economic Research at Cave Hill provided a forum and meeting place where interested women academics from across the UWI system were able to meet to discuss common issues and concerns.

The findings of the Women in the Caribbean Project generated intense and often heated debates about the appropriate theoretical frameworks for studying Caribbean women, and about the meanings of what we had found. In Olive Senior's 1991 summary, the cultural expectation regarding motherhood is central to an understanding of the lives of Caribbean women, because the choices they make in terms of childbearing will ultimately influence all their other interactions with society: their schooling, their job opportunities, their personal autonomy, their relations with men, their participation in the wider society, and in political and public life. 'In some ways, it is women's failure to appreciate these interactions and to alter their behaviour accordingly that contributes to their continued subordination.' (Senior 1991, 188)

Olive Senior summarises some of the other research findings of the project by noting that, despite the ideal image of man as protector and provider which women say they hold, women do not really look to men as their guardians and protectors. But they acknowledge them as head because it 'looks better' as they fulfil societal norms. This adherence to gender-role stereotyping and social norms, argues Senior, is actually part of woman's strategy: her style is based on cunning, guile and subversion to get what she wants from men. Because men are aware of this, male-female relationships are often marked by mutual distrust and antagonism.

Another emphasis of the research findings was the strong economic role of women, not always officially quantified. While women with the highest levels of education are making breakthroughs in the system, the majority of women are still found clustered in low-paid feminine occupations, teaching, nursing, clerical/secretarial work, and services. The rapid entry of a few women into high levels of the workforce of some countries also masks their continued subordination and exploitation.

The overall context of Caribbean economies, buffeted by many adverse conditions, small, open and exposed to metropolitan cultures, was also seen as an important factor in the survival struggles of Caribbean women. This held particular relevance for a focus on Women and Development strategies.

Following on the above exposure of some of our research findings, the next step, coming from Peggy Antrobus, then Director of WAND, from Joycelin Massiah at the Institute of Social and Economic Research at Cave Hill, from Lucille Mathurin Mair of the United Nations who attended that final Conference in 1982 in Barbados, was the idea of establishing further academic studies on women at each of the three campuses of the University of the West Indies.

Lucille Mathurin Mair has written on the strategy to establish Women's Studies at university level as a way of entrenching this new focus at the highest echelon of a country's educational system, from whence it would influence both societal knowledge and national policy developments (Mathurin Mair 1988). Joycelin Massiah also has emphasised the need for a sound intellectual basis for any generalisations about women and their social conditions, both to guide policy and to strengthen women's activism (Massiah 1986). In the Caribbean context, the need for informed, relevant teaching on women and development issues was regarded as urgent.

The next initiative took the form of a regional steering committee convened by WAND and ISER Cave Hill, both in Barbados, which agreed to seek to establish 'campus groups' *within the existing institutional framework of the University*, to undertake research, teaching, and outreach. The comprehensive plan emphasised that 'the programme should be a Women and Development Studies Programme rather than a Women's Studies Programme'. It laid out ideas for research and teaching methodologies, as well as the key elements of a Women and Development Studies curriculum. It put forward suggestions for ways in which these campus groups could use existing university provisions and facilities to support their Women and Development activities. How did these ideas work out in practice?

Take Off: The Women's Studies Working Group, Mona

In some ways, the connection of the steering committee to the campus groups was perhaps not as explicit as it might have been. At Mona, an enthusiastic group came together in December 1982, at a meeting convened by Marlene Hamilton, to form the 'Women's Studies Working Group'. I remember particularly men like Mark Figueroa and 'Wenty' Bowen being part of the original group.

At Mona, we operated much more like a collective than the formal academic sub-structure envisaged in the steering committee plan. Indeed, even after Joycelin published the details of that document in a 1986 article (Massiah 1986), I am not sure that we quite followed that structure. I remember a teleconference with Joycelin, when I explained to her that we had a 15-member committee, with everyone taking on whatever tasks were necessary; she responded somewhat conservatively that the Mona structure sounded very different from the formal structure of President/Coordinator, Secretary/Treasurer which the other campus groups were evolving.

We did have two volunteer 'coordinators', both Research Fellows at the Institute of Social and Economic Studies (ISER), Mona, namely Judy Soares, now Director of WAND, and Najma Sachak, a Tanzanian economist who had come to the Mona campus with her French husband. In outlining this situation, I reflect that the important role of the ISER, now Sir Arthur Lewis Institute for Social and Economic Studies (SALISES), both at Cave Hill and at Mona, in developing this project may have been related to the greater ability of research staff as opposed to teaching staff to take on these additional activities. I also reflect that we instituted a shared coordinator role without necessarily apprehending all the theoretical benefits of what we were doing. Years later, reading theoretically about women organising, I encountered propositions about shared leadership which indicated the value of women supporting each other, and the value of shared tasks for women already doubly burdened by jobs and domestic responsibilities. Our Mona Working Group initiated the idea of shared tasks spontaneously, on a pragmatic basis, even before exploring the theories (Women's Crisis Center, Ann Arbor 1979).

At later periods of the Mona group's history, we continued to have shared positions, as for example when we had voting for a particular post and two candidates gained an equal number of votes. We asked them to share the tasks and it worked out very well.

As time went on, we had a more formalised coordinator post. The university administration later agreed to allow 30 per cent release time to each designated coordinator, to be devoted to Women and Development Studies duties. Coordinators at various times were Elsa Leo-Rhynie, myself, Carolyn Cooper, Alafia Samuels, Hilary Hickling, Barbara Bailey, and Veronica Salter. I apologise if I have omitted anyone, I have not yet researched all the group's documents.

Those early years were very instructive to us in seeing gender not as just another academic subject but as a pervasive analytical tool to explore every discipline in the academy, and this generated a great amount of energy.

We genuinely began as 'study groups'. We had lunchtime meetings, about once every two weeks, and we always had a generous supply of local and visiting speakers. I remember the visit of Dr Filomina Chioma Steady, an outstanding Ghanaian anthropologist who was then the head of the United Nations Branch for the Status of Women, based in Vienna. She had been in Cuba at a conference and came over to visit Jamaica because she wanted to meet our group. I remember the African-American writer Gloria Hull, who spent a period as Visiting Scholar at Mona, and Barbara Smith, publisher of Kitchen Table Press. I remember Rev. Barbel von Wartenberg, married to Rev. Phillip Potter, former General Secretary of the World Council of Churches, and living at the United Theological College. She talked about hermeneutics and the interpretation of Scripture from a woman's perspective. Today, I am told that Rev. von Wartenberg is a Bishop in her Lutheran Church in Germany. Several female theological students, now all ordained ministers, were also part of our group.

The campus groups at the other two campuses, Cave Hill and St Augustine, were no less active. We communicated with each other by regular teleconferencing and by written correspondence, and we became close colleagues in the gender enterprise. Perhaps this presentation is an appropriate place to suggest that we need to jointly compile the collective history of our three campus groups during that formative period.

'Working Group' to Women and Development Studies Group

In response to Joycelin's proposals, we at Mona did change our name to the Women and Development Studies Group. At first, we were reluctant to do so because we liked the idea of being a 'Working Group'. With that original name we saw ourselves as on the cutting edge, as flexible, as open to all possibilities. But we also understood the functionality of

'Women and Development': based on the findings of the Women in the Caribbean Project, we were both exploring our gender identities, as women and men, and exploring the gendered development issues of our society.

The community outside the university responded to our group in a very positive way. Groups like Sistren Theatre Collective actually assigned members to attend our meetings, so they could share in the self-exploration and self-knowledge that we were developing. And, from 1983, we developed an annual one-day seminar where we invited women's groups in the community to network with us.

To me, our community linkages represented an important strength of our Women and Development Studies Group, and it was one which created very positive public attitudes towards the university. We learned from the community and they learned from us. We did not take on any community projects as such, but we had an easy interchange between 'town' and 'gown'. And then, in 1988, as an offshoot of our annual networking seminar, we found ourselves involved in launching the Association of Women's Organisations of Jamaica (AWOJA). Lucille Mathurin Mair, who was by then Director of the Regional Women and Development Studies Unit based at Mona, was enthusiastic and supportive. She helped us to obtain a grant from the Canadian International Development Agency (CIDA) to assist this new entity. Dr Alafia Samuels was at that time the Coordinator of the Mona Women and Development Studies Group.

AWOJA was essentially an umbrella association for women's organisations, so although in later years I joined AWOJA as an individual member, the core of AWOJA were the delegates from each organisation. We individual members were just a small support group, while the strength of AWOJA was its organisational membership. At one point, AWOJA had as many as 120 organisations in its membership.

In the formal world of the university administration, two different approaches evolved. One approach sought to establish Women and Development Studies on each campus as formal Sub-committees of Academic Board, and this was implemented at Cave Hill and St Augustine. For a period, the Regional Coordinator of the Women and Development

Studies Programme was attached to the Office of the Vice Chancellor. This was an attempt to integrate Women and Development Studies into the formal structure. At Mona, on the other hand, a university document in 1985 commented that we needed 'tightening up'. This was because we were an open, collective group with community as well as university linkages. But the strength of our group, as reflected in the comments by Filomina Steady already quoted, was in 'the opportunity for networking and for less restrained and more dynamic engagement among women'.

We were dynamic and innovative, inspired by a vision. We were very highly respected as a pioneering group bringing gender perspectives and gender scholarship to the academy and to the wider community. When Archbishop Tutu visited Jamaica in 1988, the Office of the Prime Minister asked us to hold a function for his wife and daughter because, in preparing for the visit, they had asked to meet with a gender group. When the then Director-General of UNESCO, Federico Mayor, visited Jamaica, he asked to meet with a gender group. By then the University's Women and Development Unit was well established and I was the acting Director, so I was drawn into all the high-level meetings because he had requested it.

The strength of the gender initiatives of the group made it easy to move to the next stage of institutionalisation, the establishment of a coordinating body, a University Women and Development Studies Unit, and the coming of its first Director, Dr Lucille Mathurin Mair.

We have all reflected on the extent to which our initiatives at the University of the West Indies were part of both a regional and a worldwide gender revolution. From its inception, the thrust to establish Women and Development teaching programmes at the UWI garnered support from regional sources and from international funders such as the Carnegie and Ford Foundations. The grant funding received by us in our early years is worthy of further documentation and analysis, and it is an as yet unaccomplished task. But in our thrust towards institutionalisation, the Project of Cooperation in Teaching and Research in Women and Development Studies, undertaken cooperatively between the University of the West Indies and the Institute of Social Studies at The Hague, and funded by the Netherlands Government, was a most important development.

The details of that institutionalisation process, from 1986 to 1996, are too massive to be presented here. Also, they deserve a separate endeavour. But in looking at the development of gender programmes at the University of the West Indies, the project mentioned above was a watershed. It supported the introduction of a focal administrative point for the Women and Development Studies thrust – a coordinating unit – and also supported a range of academic activities which strengthened the intellectual content of the Women and Development programmes.

The main activities supported, in addition to the administrative base, were a series of high-level seminars, starting with the Inaugural Seminar on Gender in Caribbean Development at St Augustine in 1986 and moving on to a series of Interdisciplinary and Disciplinary seminars in the Humanities, Social Sciences, Law, Natural Sciences, and Agriculture. These seminars drew together scholarship both from within and outside the region, provided a broad base for discussion and analysis of the Caribbean from a gender perspective, and most importantly provided a wealth of published material to form a strong foundation for the academic advancement of Gender Studies. The project also supported visiting fellowships to The Hague for academics and graduate students, the development of outreach activities to non-campus territories, and a short-term Certificate Programme in Gender Studies to meet the needs of persons unable to complete a full-length university programme. Dr Rhoda Reddock, a member of the St Augustine Women and Development Studies Group who had completed her doctoral studies at the Institute of Social Studies at The Hague, served as a Regional Project Officer. The funding was comprehensive but carried an important proviso: the UWI had to commit itself to continue a programme of Women/Gender and Development Studies when the project came to an end.

From the beginning, Dr Lucille Mathurin Mair's personal prestige, coming from the position of the highest post held by a woman in the UN system, and her administrative experience, were outstandingly important in establishing the unit. Tasks like obtaining accommodation for the unit (again obtained from the Institute of Social and Economic Research at Mona) and setting up a secretariat were accomplished in a very short time. And she immediately began to implement the planned programme of developmental seminars, starting with the Inaugural Seminar on Gender in Caribbean Development at the St Augustine campus in 1986 and moving on to the series of Interdisciplinary and Disciplinary seminars in the Humanities, Social Sciences, Law, Natural Sciences, and Agriculture, as already described above.

In 1989, Dr Mathurin Mair became a Minister of State in the Jamaican Ministry of Foreign Affairs, leaving behind the coordinating role which she had so effectively played. She was succeeded by Dorienne Rowan-Campbell, followed by this writer in a temporary capacity, and then by the first Professor of Gender and Development Studies, Elsa Leo-Rhynie, after whom came Professor Barbara Bailey. The beginning of formal 'institutionalisation' may be said to have begun with the establishment of the Chair in Gender and Development Studies in 1991, and by 1993 the Centre for Gender and Development was formally established within the university system. The critical elements of 'institutionalisation' were:

(a) the placing of gender studies within the university's routine administrative and budgetary structure;

(b) The establishment of a Regional Coordinating Unit in Gender and Development Studies, and three Campus Units, each headed by a Senior Lecturer. In 1993, the Units for Gender and Development Studies were renamed as the Centre(s) for Gender and Development Studies;

(c) The provision of sessional fees for lecturers in the interdisciplinary courses.

I cannot say much about the period after 1993 and institutionalisation. After institutionalisation, different actors entered the scene, and perhaps the main work of the Women and Development Studies Group was accomplished. Over time, the activism of the group diminished. Today, although many former members of the group are still on campus, the group has ceased to function as an entity. Further, institutionalisation did not necessarily produce a 'happy ever after' ending. Indeed, the gender issues in the society and in the university continue to be challenging.

Establishing the Academic Programme in Gender Studies

Ultimately, although the Women and Development Studies Unit provided invaluable support for the institutionalisation of gender studies in the academy, it was the academic members of the Women and Development Studies Group, the accredited teachers of the university, who had to establish a teaching programme in Women's/Gender Studies. And here the interdisciplinary character of gender studies became a point for debate, because where could gender studies be based in the existing structure? We at Mona were able to find an interdisciplinary niche in the then Faculty of Arts and General Studies, which began to offer 'inter-departmental courses' identified with the course code 'AR'. The initial offerings within this framework were (i) a course on Literature and Ideas in the Caribbean, and (ii) two gender courses entitled, 'Introduction to Women's Studies, Parts I and II'. Two additional courses were later added to these interdisciplinary offerings, the latter entitled, 'Gender in Caribbean Culture, Parts I and II'.

It took us seven years, from 1983 to 1989, to find that interdisciplinary niche, and it was not easy. Indeed, to get those first courses introduced we used a methodology which came from our knowledge of the academic system. The St Augustine Women and Development Studies Group, led by activists like Marjorie Thorpe and Bridget Brereton, was able in 1986 to gain acceptance of a faculty course in the (then) Faculty of Arts and General Studies entitled 'Introduction to Women's Studies, with special reference to the Caribbean'. We followed the university regulation which stated that any course approved by the university for teaching on one campus could be adopted by other campuses, and by dint of impassioned negotiation by our Faculty of Arts and General Studies at Mona, we were able to start teaching the same course. Again, the collectivity of the Women and Development Studies Group was important, because different members of the group with different areas of specialisation undertook the teaching of different modules within the broad framework of the course (as did the members of the St Augustine group).

But there was another stream of academic activity from the campus groups which made an impact on the establishment of gender studies in the academic curriculum, and this was the development by individual scholars of gender-related courses in their area of specialisation. Up to now, I have information only on what happened on the Mona campus, but again this is an area on which we can combine and compile our campus information.

Many of the first courses introduced were postgraduate courses such as 'The Image of the Female in Literature', in the (then) Department of English, 'French Caribbean Women Writers and the Novel Form', in the (then) Department of French, and the first gender course, 'Gender Roles in Education' introduced by Professor Marlene Hamilton in the School of Education.

But undergraduate courses also took hold. Pioneers like Dr Elizabeth 'Betty' Wilson in what was then the Department of French, developed her own course 'Francophone Women Writers: Perspectives on Women's Issues in Literature'; Dr Claudette Williams in the then Department of Spanish presented 'Women Writers of the Spanish Caribbean', and later added another course 'Spanish American Women's Narrative'; Professor Carolyn Cooper developed 'African/Diaspora Women's Narrative' and later added 'African-American Women's Writing'. Perhaps the most eloquently named course was Professor Verene Shepherd's 'Women and Gender in the History of the English-Speaking Caribbean', a blend of two separate but highly complementary issues which expresses clearly the often confused concepts of 'women' and 'gender'.

My own longstanding commitment to the issues of development, the need to situate gender issues within the context of development and underdevelopment, led me to design a two-semester course, 'Gender and Development in Caribbean Society'. One of my learnings from participating in the Women in the Caribbean project was that we could not study gender without also understanding the socioeconomic context of gender relations. We also could not study the gendered strategies of survival without reflecting on the linkages between these strategies and the processes of development in small and fragile economies. These perceptions have led to an expansion of studies such as that of Lynn

Bolles (1985) on women and household behaviour during the years of the structural adjustment crisis in Jamaica, and a plethora of similar studies elsewhere throughout Latin America and the Caribbean. The fundamental challenges of globalisation and its gender impacts have now become an even larger area of study.

In addition to all the above-named gender courses, many lecturers also introduced gender modules or components into other existing courses. Later, the Centre for Gender and Development Studies further added a course entitled 'Sex, Gender and Society' to the Social Sciences curriculum.

Conclusion

From lively, diverse and informal groups of academics on the three campuses, to a strong and committed Centre of Excellence on each of the campuses of the university is a tremendous movement, and it seems that the anniversaries come in threes: 1973, 30 years ago, the launching of CARICOM and the beginning of the preparations for International Women's Year, which was approved by the United Nations General Assembly in December 1972; 1982-83, the founding of the Women's Studies Groups on the three campuses; 1993, the formal establishment of the Centre for Gender and Development. Congratulations to us all.

Because the (appropriate) title for this conference is 'Gender for the 21st Century', it is worthwhile to make a balance sheet and to summarise some lessons learnt which might help to guide new pioneers as they venture into the future. Indeed I know as a parent that one cannot guide the next generation: it is inevitable that they want to strike out on their own and they will have to learn by experience. But one cannot resist trying.

Our perception, when we embarked on the gender-studies enterprise many years ago, was that we would bring a new and comprehensive approach to academic work. One of my strong personal influences has been Adrienne Rich's evocative feminist thinking on the nature of the academic enterprise. Especially in a university like our own, where high proportions of our students are female, gender scholarship should both focus on the kind of university likely to dynamically nurture both men and women as well as on the cultural and social factors which currently bring more women than men into the university. These are overarching issues. I am well aware of the studies being done on 'male marginalisation'. But these need to be balanced by studies on the pressures upon women to seek certification as the only way to get a foot in the door. They must be balanced too by studies on the legitimising functions of *education* as one of the few accepted ways in which females are permitted to excel.

We are proud to belong to a well-organised and powerful structure such as the University of the West Indies, but as the years have gone by, we have seen that it is easy for gender studies to be assigned merely a restricted place in the system. There has to be constant critical analysis of the extent to which women's and gender issues subjects, which should be central to the functioning of the university and the society, become pigeonholed in a corner. Gender analysis and gender advocacy have to be ongoing and dynamic parts of our development strategies, in both the academy and the society.

One area where there is no male marginalisation is in employment at the University of the West Indies. In preparation for this paper, I studied the academic staff statistics for the Mona campus up to 2002. They were astonishing. In 1985, 72 per cent of the academic staff were male; in 2002 the figure was 57 per cent. So female employment has improved. But in 1985, 90 per cent of the professors were male, in 2002, 84 per cent; in 1985, 81 per cent of the senior lecturers were male, in 2002, 73 per cent; in 1985, 64 per cent of the lecturers were male, in 2002, 53 per cent. Finally, in 1985, 57 per cent of the assistant lecturers were male, and in 2002, 29 per cent.

What does this mean? It means that female employment has improved at the lower end of the scale, but the upper reaches remain relatively unchanged. I wish to present this discussion not as a critique of the university, but rather as a challenge to gender analysis. Is it that the older established staff members (like myself) are still there, and it takes time for change to work through the system? Is it that women are just poorer performers, academically?

A look at our current graduate enrolment programmes, including our PhD programmes, reveals the opposite. Overwhelmingly in the graduate enrolments of the Mona campus, there are more females than males. Only in a few programmes in the Medical Sciences and in Management is there a fairly equal balance between men and women. The overall conclusion, therefore, is that although women appear to be better prepared by high-level academic preparation for academic qualification, they are not yet achieving this.

And the above observation leads to the comment that, although the Gender and Development Studies activities at UWI have developed more gender awareness in the academy and we have also fashioned a commendable academic curriculum, there is still a burning need to reduce tokenism and to translate that curriculum content into everyday attitudes and practices.

Finally, an important aspect of this paper's analysis of the development of gender teaching and research over the past 20 or so years, has been the creative interaction between individual scholars in their teaching and research and the work of the Gender and Development Units/Centres. I know that good avenues of cooperation continue to exist, and I identify these as critical factors in the ongoing development of the gender studies movement in the university, and its fluid interaction with community and societal needs, which ultimately is the purpose of the University of the West Indies.

As a postscript, I wish to share an experience travelling by air from London to Beijing for the 4th United Nations World Conference on Women in 1995. Sitting next to me was a young woman, also en route to Beijing, who knew nothing of a World Conference happening there. She was going to China as a tourist, to join a two-week expedition up the Yangtze River.

She said to me, very respectfully, 'I am not at all interested in the women's movement. I appreciate what you older women have done, and I am thankful for the opportunities which I have today. But I see no necessity for me to become an activist. Enjoy your conference'.

Of course I did not leave it there. I made no effort to persuade her to join a movement, but I did try to convince her that there were still many unresolved gender issues, and as Peggy Antrobus said yesterday, many forces trying to turn back the clock and reverse some of the international agreements which we have so painfully negotiated over the past 20 or so years.

Arising from the above experience, however, I want to suggest an important task for this early twenty-first century period. We need a narrative of the gains for Caribbean women, both in international law and conventions and in Caribbean law, over (say) the past 30 years. I could give many examples, but I will give just one of immediate relevance. Minister Mia Mottley pointed out, in her opening speech that, worldwide, the Caribbean as a region was the first to achieve region-wide ratification of the Convention on the Elimination of All Forms of Discrimination Against Women. Many educated Caribbean women today can speak very knowledgeably about 'CEDAW'. But how many women in the street know what commitments their governments have made on their behalf by ratifying 'CEDAW'?

The gains must be documented and disseminated, and this is one very important way in which we of the twentieth century can give a legacy to the twenty-first century.

References

Bolles, A. Lynn. 1985. 'Economic Crisis and Female-Headed Households in Urban Jamaica'. In *Women and Change in Latin America,* June Nash and Helen Safa, 65-83. South Hadley, Massachusetts: Bergin and Garvey Publishers.

Henry-Wilson, Maxine. 1989. 'The Status of the Jamaican Woman, 1962 to the present'. In *Jamaica in Independence*, ed. Rex Nettleford, 229-253. Kingston: Heinemann Caribbean.

Massiah, Joycelin. 1986. 'Establishing a Programme of Women and Development Studies in the University of the West Indies'. *Social and Economic Studies*, no.1 (March):151-197.

Mathurin Mair, Lucille. 1988. 'Women's Studies in an International Context'. In *Gender in Caribbean Development,* eds. Patricia Mohammed and Catherine Shepherd, 1-9. Mona: The University of the West Indies Women and Development Studies Project.

Minnich, Elizabeth Kamarck. 1998. 'Transforming Knowledge'. In *Issues in Feminism: An Introduction to Women's Studies*. 4th edn., ed. Sheila Ruth, 448-463. Mountain View, California: Mayfield Publishing Company.

Rich, Adrienne. 1979. 'Towards a Woman-Centered University'. In *On Lies, Secrets, and Silence,* ed. Adrienne Rich. New York: Norton.

Senior, Olive. 1991. *Working Miracles: Women's Lives in the English-speaking Caribbean.* Cave Hill, Barbados: Institute of Social & Economic Research, University of the West Indies.

Steady, Filomina Chioma. 1995. 'The United Nations and Women: An Alliance of Fifty Years'. In *Women and the United Nations: Reflections and New Horizons,* eds. Filomena Steady and Remie Toure, 13-25. Rochester, Vermont: Schenkman Books, Inc.

University of the West Indies. *Statistics/Official Statistics,* varying years. Prepared by Office of Planning & Institutional Research, Mona Campus.

Women's Crisis Center, Ann Arbor. 1979. 'Organizing a Women's Crisis-Service Center'. In *Strategies of Community Organization: A Book of Readings.* 3rd edn., Fred M. Cox et al., 478-483. Itasca, Illinois: F.E. Peacock Publishers, Inc.

---

*   I gratefully acknowledge the assistance of Ms Nicola Patterson, Office of Planning & Institutional Research, Mona Campus, who provided some of the University statistics.

Bridging Epistemologies, Constructing New Paradigms

19 | ELSA LEO-RHYNIE

Gender Studies
Interdisciplinary and Pedagogical Challenges

Abstract

Feminist scholarship has always transcended disciplinary boundaries. Its concern has been with the myriad facets of the lives of women and their relationships with men, the family, the community, the workplace and the state, as well as with using new methods to fully explore dimensions of power and influence in these settings, dimensions which cross gender, race and social class lines. Massiah (1986), in reviewing the beginnings of the movement to establish a programme in gender studies at the UWI, notes that an important feature of this initiative was:

> *…an interdisciplinary mode of operation, to make the connections between separate branches of knowledge, thereby contributing to a better understanding of the whole.*

The imperative of interdisciplinarity was strongly intertwined with the need to change the existing structure of knowledge and its method of transmission in order to create alternative narratives and a new pedagogy, which would be liberating and empowering. Thus, interdisciplinarity was not merely a modification of concepts and boundaries of knowledge but also a critical assessment and reconstruction of such knowledge. Using that knowledge to develop, in the academy and beyond, new insights and generate new personal and political meaning has been a major task of the gender studies programme.

The challenges presented by these imperatives and the methods used to address them over the period of the introduction and institutionalisation of gender studies at the University of the West Indies are presented and critically assessed.

> *Throughout history, new disciplines have been created at the intersection of old ones as new problem solving methods are needed* (Stark and Lattuca 1997, 355).

Introduction

Gender studies had its origins in the political activism of feminists, in which the concerns were with power and influence in the lives of women and their relationships with men, the family, the community, the workplace and the state. As feminist scholarship developed, it was very clear that these concerns transcended disciplinary boundaries; scholars could not study gender roles without also considering the historical and cultural nature of the origins of these roles, and the theorists who were examining gender identity and issues of sexuality had to draw from medicine and psychology as well as from sociology and anthropology. Changing historical, social, and political contexts were important factors in the study of the origin and practices related to gender socialisation, as well as in understanding literary texts. Given the broad concerns of persons working in the area, the limitations of existing methods of enquiry became evident, as did the need for new methodologies to fully explore dimensions of power and influence which cross the lines of gender, race and social class.

The complex 'trans-disciplinary' nature of gender studies led to the use of the term 'interdisciplinary' as a relevant descriptor of the fledgling scholarship. This created problems for acceptance by the academy, however, as the demand was that of proving gender studies to be a discipline in order for it to be recognised as equal to other disciplinary areas of study offered.

Interdisciplinary areas of study such as environmental studies have also faced difficulties in establishing their legitimacy within the academy, but the issue of gender has been an emotive one, challenging as it does concepts of power and hierarchy which typify many aspects of the structure of the academy, and presenting as part of this challenge a novel epistemological paradigm. Scholars committed to gender studies have had to overcome the suspicion of this new area of knowledge; suspicion which persists despite all attempts to establish its legitimacy.

The interdisciplinary challenge

The term 'interdisciplinary' has been defined as:

> An adjective describing the interaction among two or more different disciplines. This interaction may range from simple communication of ideas to the mutual

> integration of organizing concepts, methodology, procedures, epistemology, terminology, data and organization of research and education in a fairly large field. (Centre for Research and Innovation 1972, 25-26 quoted by Lattuca 2002, 712).

This very comprehensive definition allows for a range of interactions within and across disciplines, and is based on the integration of knowledge across a fairly large field.

The process of establishing gender studies as an interdisciplinary field has been an evolutionary one. Most persons who now work in gender studies came to that area from disciplinary backgrounds. When confronted with the myriad aspects of knowledge with which they had to cope in understanding the feminist literature, sociologists, psychologists, historians, educators and scientists all pushed the boundaries of their disciplines to embrace new concepts, new methodologies and a new epistemological viewpoint. This was essential so that they could grasp, be properly analytical and, where necessary, be critical about the material which was now part of their area of scholarship. This experience forced scholars to question certain disciplinary concepts, to redefine traditional categories of analysis and also rethink existing paradigms which had strong disciplinary bases. Lattuca (2002), drawing on the work of Dressel and Marcus (1982) describes disciplines as systematic ways of organising and studying phenomena and identified five components as framing the concept of a discipline.

(i) Substantive component – the assumptions, variables, concepts, principles and relationships of the discipline;

(ii) Linguistic component – the symbolic language which allows elements to be identified and relationships defined and explored;

(iii) Syntactical component – the search for organising processes around which the discipline develops;

(iv) Value component – commitment about what is worth studying and how it should be studied;

(v) Conjunctive component – the discipline's relationship to other disciplines.

These factors all shape the way in which members of a particular discipline 'view' their world.

The objective of most academic disciplines is to produce scholars steeped in the content and methodology of that discipline and who will be committed and loyal to the five components which define it. This is achieved through clear statements about what constitutes the particular discipline, and also by specifying certain courses as being essential for the student to be considered to have qualified for a 'major' or a 'specialisation' in a particular field of study. The field of study tends to be narrowly concentrated on the components of the particular discipline with the option of a few elective, out-of-faculty courses being the concession to 'broadening' students' educational experience.

These disciplinary 'tribes of academe' (Becher 1989) have been criticised by feminist and other interdisciplinary scholars as being limiting and untrue to the nature of knowledge and knowing and the requirement of openness and interconnectedness in learning. Relke (1994) comments that the disciplinary model of academic organisation reflects:

> a perception of knowledge as a fragmented group of hostile nation states, surrounded on the curricular level by the barbed wire of course prerequisites, and defended by an academic border patrol, heavily armed with credentials, who guard against unlawful trespass.

Study within disciplines restricts and compartmentalises knowledge; interdisciplinary studies seek to link and integrate knowledge across disciplinary boundaries. Proponents of interdisciplinarity argue that reality is multifaceted and not experienced in an ordered and structured manner in keeping with the disciplinary model; disciplinary learning results in the development of partial and often distorted images of reality; yields half-truths, as it emphasises one area of enquiry and knowledge with little thought to the inclusion and integration of relevant knowledge from other disciplines. In many instances, there can be a total disconnect between what is taught in some disciplines and the reality of students' lives and experiences. It can be further argued that, in higher education, learning as a continuing process of students questioning their experiences outside the academy, and their experiences in their courses of study, within or across faculties, is not facilitated in the disciplinary mode (Pring 1975).

The importance of integration of knowledge is addressed by L. Dee Fink (2001) in a proposed taxonomy of higher level learning. The taxonomy emphasises recognition of the important connections, similarities, interactions that need to be made between the foundational knowledge (key facts, concepts, formulae, relationships) within a discipline as well as across disciplines. The human dimension of learning is also stressed; learning about self and others, changes in feelings, opinions, interests, attitudes, values about learning and life, with an emphasis on long-term, self-directed learning. The interdisciplinary nature of gender studies fosters this type of integration.

Achieving interdisciplinarity therefore involves:

- Deconstruction of the existing established disciplinary structures and boundaries through a thorough critique of how they were built up and the assumed artificiality of their 'separateness';
- Bringing together the work of analysts and critics in different fields and using a compare and contrast type of conversation to point to the areas where integration is possible;
- Employing the tools of different disciplines (theories, methodologies) to arrive at deeper more textured meaning of existing phenomena or to explain particular dimensions of new concepts;
- Developing tools specially suited to the interdisciplinary field of study, which can enhance the understanding obtained using existing tools from other disciplines and also extend understanding of those disciplines in different and novel ways.

The processes involved in achieving interdisciplinarity can be used to facilitate and enhance work within, between or among disciplines, and they are particularly relevant when used to address the development of interdisciplinary programmes such as gender and development studies. Recent work by researchers in higher education (Boyer 1990, Fink 2001) highlights the scholarship of integration and emphasises the value of interdisciplinary and multidisciplinary learning. Relke (1994) comments on the significant influence of interdisciplinary feminist scholarship:

> What is unique about feminist interdisciplinarity is that a scholar outside a given discipline can have a significant impact on the development of scholarship within that discipline. For example... historians have from time to time learnt something of their craft from literary scholars, while scientists have helped to teach philosophers

how to do feminist philosophy. Feminist art historians have shown feminist sociologists better ways of doing sociology, and feminist psychologists have suggested new theories for the reading of women's literary texts. This is disciplinary interdependence and mutual fostering, a phenomenon that goes a step beyond integration. This can be partly accounted for by the fact that women's studies is as much the product of cultural REVolution as it is of disciplinary EVolution.

Scholarship in women's and gender studies has transformed disciplinary fields of knowledge and how they are studied by demonstrating the bias that often exists in the formation and construction of that knowledge. The contribution of women to the West Indian historical record, for example, was largely unresearched and undocumented before the work of Lucille Mathurin Mair, and other Caribbean historians who have investigated and recorded women's significant role in many facets of Caribbean life over past centuries. This research and documentation has resulted in a significant redefinition of both the objects of study in history as well as the methods to be used in that study.

The questions raised by gender are not confined, however, to a particular discipline, as they are complex, multifaceted questions which reach across and beyond disciplines. The inadequacy of discrete disciplines to respond to these multifaceted questions led to questioning and critically assessing the methods used in the production of certain types of knowledge, the politics and the ethics of these methods, the choices made in terms of what is omitted and what is included. This critical assessment is shared with students, who are encouraged to consider these issues even as they relate to the content of the programmes in which they are themselves engaged – who made the choices of the content? The texts selected? The method of assessment? On what basis? What special institutional and personal biases led to that configuration? The process is one of reflexivity, which has become a method widely used in educational and other programmes to stimulate critical thinking and develop a reasoned understanding of how the world is organised and how knowledge of that world is produced. Students of gender make the world – and individuals' experiences of that world, whether orally recounted, or documented in books and magazines or other media – sources of information which must be critically examined along with those recommended texts and readings which are provided with their course outlines. This approach opens up the possibilities for research and new methods of obtaining data which are not discipline-bound and which encourage independent learning.

Interdisciplinarity thus becomes a process of clearing the hurdles of disciplinary language, disciplinary methods, disciplinary content, of effecting 'translation' of these disciplinary concepts into the interdisciplinary discourse and through a process of 'dialogue' across disciplines, achieving a broader, more comprehensive and more complete view of specific problems, promoting an integration and a synthesis, which provide a comprehensive base for the search for solutions.

A major criticism of interdisciplinary learning is that it does not allow sufficient depth of knowledge and learning in any one area, and so the student tends to have a superficial grasp of many concepts in different disciplines but is not 'grounded' in any one – even though there may be criticisms as to the arbitrary nature of that one. Friedman (1998) comments thus: 'If the danger of disciplinarity resides in potential overspecialisation, the danger of interdisciplinarity rests in potential superficiality. Disciplinarity offers depth but also insularity; interdisciplinarity offers scope but also rootlessness.' (p. 312)

The process of criticism, important as it is, must be accompanied by respect for the intellectual rigour and the historical underpinnings of each discipline, and the work of those who ensured that the components identified as representative of a discipline were sufficiently established for the area of study to be acknowledged and recognised.

Marilyn Boxer (2000) recounts her experience as a young academic in the 1970s facing a curriculum committee to consider the establishment of a minor in Women's Studies at her college, and her consternation at the opening question from the chair of the committee: 'Is Women's Studies a discipline?' She interpreted the question as a mechanism to 'discipline' her and her colleagues who sought to disturb the academic community with this new and contentious area of study. After three decades of scholarship and massive volumes of literature, this question continues to be asked by persons seeking to bring Women's Studies or Gender Studies 'in line' with the traditional disciplines. One of the demands of most universities is that, upon institutionalisation, an interdisciplinary programme conforms to the disciplinary demand of structure and organisation – the observation of the five components pertinent to a discipline and the somewhat arbitrary demarcation of the discourse of this scholarship into this 'disciplinary' framework.

Interdisciplinary and multidisciplinary learning are now being emphasised in the literature on learning in higher education. This value has been declared by many universities but the structures to permit this have not changed sufficiently to permit true interdisciplinary collaboration, partnership and learning. The result is that the term 'interdisciplinary' has become a handy descriptor, referring in most instances to a collection of courses, which implies that they are integrated in some way, but this integration may not actually be realised. Romero (2000) has warned, referring to graduate degree programmes in women's studies, that the institutionalisation of these programmes may result in the construction of a women's studies discipline that is very similar to traditional disciplines, emphasising research over teaching and, certainly, over activism. This danger exists for programmes at the undergraduate level as swell.

The significant challenge of feminist theory to patriarchal theories of knowledge and its impact in the rethinking and transformation of disciplinary discourse – in science, in sociology, in education, in literature, law and history, as well as research methodology, has led to gender studies becoming what Lattuca (2002) refers to as a 'community of practice' with its own ways of knowing, its own methodologies of research and its own pedagogical demands.

The pedagogical challenge

Pedagogy has been defined as: 'the transformation of consciousness that takes place in the intersection of three agencies – the teacher, the learner, and the knowledge they together produce' (Lusted 1986, 3).

That intersection, in an interdisciplinary gender studies programme, must be linked to the critical stance which governs the programme's development and structure. Traditional methods of teaching which are teacher-centred and which stress the power of the teacher as expert, as knower, as dispenser of knowledge, and the student as seeker and passive recipient of knowledge from the teacher, have to be critically examined and changed. Given the feminist stance against oppressive and dominating experiences in the society, the lecture room and tutorial encounters must reflect a difference in the use of power through the objectives set, the teaching methods employed and the methods of assessment used. Thus students' opinions, their criticisms, their questions which challenge the teachers' views and those of other students, must be encouraged, and the resulting participatory mode is expected to develop that analytical capacity and trigger the evaluative ability so important in challenging the status quo and effecting the transformation sought.

Interdisciplinary learning demands intellectual flexibility; the textual material required in the interdisciplinary curriculum is from varying disciplines and students and lecturers may not have the background knowledge of those disciplines to readily understand the concepts, language and methodology of the work. This makes teaching and learning more difficult, but also more satisfying, particularly when these are set within a clear and coherent set of objectives and can be seen to contribute to the achievement of these objectives. The reproduction of gender identities and roles as inequity and as power relationships, for example, requires historical, sociological, psychological, political and cultural learnings to fully comprehend the problem and seek to fashion solutions.

The use of personal experience in teaching has been a major focus. This is closely linked to the origins of the feminist struggle – the practical problems of women in the field and the strength of the interdisciplinary thrust was fed by the knowledge and interaction with women's lives, so that theories and analyses could draw on real life experiences. Socialisation was not just a theoretical concept, it was observed; domestic violence and the trauma it produces was known because of the close connection between those teaching about power in sexual relationships and those who witnessed or shared the experience of the wilful and traumatic expression of such power. This enhances learning as it emphasises the situated nature of knowledge, and the different locations from which individuals speak – as students and teachers. It also allows students to develop the skills of analysis which permit an assessment of how these experiences have been influenced by people, events and situations. Thus they can develop a sense of self-understanding, an integrated sense of personal identity and the way in which this identity determines how persons locate themselves in the family, the workplace, the community and the world. There is a risk involved, however, that experience becomes authority, and rather than using experience to start new conversations, they become the only conversations. The use of experience, while valuable, must be accompanied by the critical analysis of the relationship which exists between experience and knowledge. Also, if interdisciplinarity is about the 'translation' of, and 'dialogue' across existing disciplines, then there must be discussion among students who bring their varying perspectives to the classroom. Discussion groups allow students to understand the collective nature of the learning process and the different perspectives from which a problem or an issue can be approached. Students often find the reflexive process and the 'unlearning' of previous teaching and learning methods, as well as the practice of sharing their experiences and arguments, intimidating and yet stimulating and liberating.

Enriching learning through the use of new pedagogical methods is both complex and challenging. Paulo Freire (1972) spoke of developing 'critical consciousness' and his views of education as the 'practice of freedom' found resonance with feminists who emphasised the need for education to liberate and transform the patriarchal domination of society. Questions have been raised, however (hooks 1988), about the effectiveness of education in achieving change in certain areas. Self-understanding does not necessarily lead to change; women who demonstrate the ability to think critically, to be analytic, to espouse strong feminist views, for example, remain in relationships in which they continue to experience the very conditions they openly denounce. Despite an understanding of patriarchy, despite their experience and critical analysis of male dominance and male privileging, they remain powerless to change this in their personal lives, at the workplace, in the community and the society. How can the message of gender be made more liberating?

The Experience of the University of the West Indies (UWI)

Meeting the interdisciplinary challenge: creating a context

Massiah (1986), in reviewing the beginnings of the movement to establish a programme in gender studies at the UWI, notes that an important feature of this initiative was an interdisciplinary mode of operation, to make the connections between separate branches of knowledge, thereby contributing to a better understanding of the whole.

The trigger and stimulus for the new initiative was the Women in the Caribbean project, directed by Dr Joycelin Massiah and spanning the late 1970s and early 1980s, a project which was interdisciplinary in scope and innovative in implementation. It was an initiative of the United Nations Decade for Women (1975-1985) and explored new research methodologies in documenting the lives of women across the English speaking Caribbean. The innovative use of photography and video, which was bold new research technology at the time, to permit the actual reporting from the women themselves of statements of their lives and experiences provided a rich source of data and forced new approaches to analysis, and different ways of communicating the message. At the same time, the Women and Development Unit (WAND) of the University of the West Indies was newly established in 1977 as an arm of the Extra Mural Department (now School of Continuing Studies). Dr Peggy Antrobus was the first Tutor Coordinator of this Unit, and both she and Dr Massiah recognised the vital importance of getting the messages from the research and from the outreach projects of WAND into the university curriculum. The strategy developed was that of forming, on each campus, Women and Development Studies (WDS) groups to promote the findings of the project across the region and also to see to their inclusion in relevant disciplinary courses. The strength and cohesiveness of these groups was achieved through meetings, seminars, formal and informal, campus based and regional, in a spirit of collaboration and partnership.

Funding to support the work of these groups in the Caribbean was sought and obtained from a number of sources, but chiefly from the Ford Foundation and the Government of the Netherlands. The intent was the introduction of a programme of Women's Studies in the university and central to the groups' strategy was the staging of a series of three interdisciplinary and seven disciplinary seminars between 1986 and 1994. These yielded over 120 papers, covering a range of topics, using a variety of methodologies, and all indicative of a surge of interest in, and the intent to be part of, the initiative to explore the historical and contemporary status of women, and most importantly to contemplate the societal gender systems which had governed the status of women and men over the years. Even in the disciplinary seminars, the thrust tended towards interdisciplinarity. Mathurin Mair (1988), in the Foreword to the publication of papers from the first interdisciplinary seminar, commented that as seminar participants become involved:

> with the analytical tools of various disciplines, they are articulating a gender focussed critique of development theories and models which promises in time to penetrate academia and to inform processes of national and regional planning. (p. x)

The work of the WDS groups served as a catalyst for the penetration of academia and for the exciting and dynamic growth of scholarship in the area of gender and development in the region. The papers from the first interdisciplinary seminar were published in the volume *Gender in Caribbean Development* which is now in its second edition and still in use as a valuable source book for students and those seeking an introduction to the issues of gender and development. The tradition was continued after the formation of the CGDS, with the publication, in 1997, of another edited volume, *Gender: A Caribbean Multi-disciplinary Perspective*, which contains a selection of papers from the other interdisciplinary and disciplinary seminars. The sharing and collaboration involved in the development and staging of the seminars and the networks which developed as a result enhanced the work of each participant and, in turn, the work of the various disciplines; academics who hitherto had not thought of gender as a field of enquiry now found it a fertile source of new information and research. The work thus became 'both transformative and generative' (Lave 1997).

The CGDS was to be a new structure within the academy, with a unique interdisciplinary mission. It was important, therefore, to devise an appropriate alternative model for approval, offering and administration of its courses and programmes rather than being forced to fit into the structure developed for faculties and which was inappropriate to the Centre's objectives. Special arrangements had to be put in place to allow for the reporting which is a well-established part of the disciplinary faculty structure. The formation of Boards of Studies on each campus has satisfied this objective; the Boards include representatives from different disciplinary areas, the library and the student body, and reflect the Centre's concerns with knowledge in its broadest sense.

Meeting the interdisciplinary challenge: making the Centre work

The CGDS, in its interdisciplinary thrust, has tried to overcome difficulties which are not only administrative and bureaucratic but also academic. Team-teaching, cross-listing of courses, cross-campus teaching, seeking and obtaining agreement for joint appointments to the CGDS as well as to a disciplinary area, and the designation and listing of lecturers who work in gender from a disciplinary perspective as 'associate lecturers' are all strategies which have been employed to ensure the interdisciplinary thrust, but also the maintenance of autonomy. The further education of lecturers through staff fellowships, of graduate students through study grants and the contributions of visiting lecturers, initially from the Institute of Social Studies in the Hague and also from each campus, were sponsored, from 1986, by successive projects of the Netherlands government, and allowed for a sharing and cross fertilisation of concepts and experiences which enriched teaching, and enhanced understanding of the scope of the concerns which were part of the gender and development initiative.

Difficulties persist even ten years after institutionalisation. The Centre's autonomy is frequently challenged, attempts are made to include the Centre as part of one or other disciplinary area, the Centre is often omitted from mailing lists which contain information sent to faculties which is also relevant to its activities, problems even arise in providing computer codes for courses offered by the Centre and which are not faculty based. Although the UWI Strategic Plan 2002-2007 lists one of the core values of the institution as 'cultivating multidisciplinary and interdisciplinary collaboration', none of the stated strategies addresses how this is to be achieved, and the difficulties involved in sustaining an independent interdisciplinary Centre within the UWI persist.

Because the Centre has been able to obtain significant external grant funding to support some of its activities; demonstrate innovative and highly visible scholarship; meet the requirement by several funding agencies that projects include a consideration of gender, it has been able to overcome the conservatism of some sectors in the university and establish its legitimacy.

Meeting the pedagogical challenge

In the late 1980s, intent on having the message disseminated, the women and men who were members of the WDS groups developed a course called 'Introduction to Women's Studies' and, despite the lack of status of the WDS groups in the official university structure, negotiated its approval through the then Faculty of Arts and General Studies, which facilitated its administration. It was taught, starting first at St Augustine in 1986, then at Cave Hill in 1987 and last at Mona in 1989, without compensation, by teams of WDS members and colleagues who recognised the validity and significance of feminist scholarship and who brought their diverse theoretical frameworks, disciplinary understandings and methodological approaches to knowledge generation and knowledge sharing to Women's Studies' classrooms. Although this was valuable, and provided a welcome introduction to gender through a consideration of many themes – in literature, education, history, law, religion and science – integration was difficult and the pedagogy utilised varied with each presenter. Some of the students' satisfactions and the lecturers' difficulties were documented by Kathleen Drayton and Elaine Fido following the first year (1987/1988) of offering 'Women's Studies: an introductory course' as a university course at the Cave Hill campus. The course was open only to students in the Faculty of Arts and General Studies. The following are excerpts from that report:

Student satisfaction:

It (the course) made me more aware of the contradictions regarding women in my own society…it also made me speak out more vigorously against these contradictions in other group discussions.

> I had a traditional upbringing wherein I saw myself as being subservient to the male. I no longer see myself in that light. I see us as equals. I value myself now for what I am and not what society wants me to be.

Lecturers' difficulties:

> The students' questionnaires this year show that they sensed a gap in our ability to cross over disciplines.

> We sometimes felt that we might have been relying on students to make the links between the different areas of knowledge which we as teachers should have been doing.

> Women's Studies requires us to retrain ourselves as scholars and teachers so that we are able to deal at an undergraduate level at least with knowledge and skills which do not fall into our primary area of competence.

The issue of integration was a persistent and troubling one, but once the CGDS was established, the faculty member appointed on each campus was able to facilitate that integration and also to ensure that the pedagogy was in keeping with that expected in a programme which challenged power relations in a number of different settings, including classrooms. New courses, developed and taught by faculty attached to the CGDS, have consciously sought to address both the interdisciplinary and the pedagogical demands and have attracted students from most faculties. A minor in Gender Studies is now offered on all three campuses; cross-campus teaching persists and allows for the considerable expertise from each campus to be made available to students on all three campuses.

At the same time, traditional disciplines have not remained static; they have had to adapt over time to accommodate new thinking and contemporary issues. Many have had to become more interdisciplinary in their approach, and gender is now a component of many courses, and is even completely integrated in some instances in the humanities and the social sciences. Thus, the work of gender studies has exerted a significant impact on the rethinking and transformation of disciplinary discourse, its pedagogy, as well as its research methodology.

Research has flourished and the research findings have fed, naturally, into the teaching carried out by each of the campus units, and into the curriculum design and development process involved in the preparation of new undergraduate courses. Ongoing research has informed new courses, such as 'Men and Masculinities in the Caribbean'; those which comprise the taught Master's programme in Gender and Development; the offering of a concentration in this area to students from the Consortium Graduate School of the Social Sciences (discontinued when the Consortium became part of the newly formed Sir Arthur Lewis Institute for Social and Economic Studies); and the supervision of graduate and undergraduate research. Research at the Masters and Doctoral levels encourages the depth of analysis necessary to add new empirical data to the current record and also to further challenge and critique existing theory.

Teaching and research activities have not been limited to the intramural programme; the CGDS has honoured its commitment to reach out to the various stakeholders in spreading the theoretical and interdisciplinary message of gender to agencies and organisations regionally. The offerings of the summer Certificate in Gender and Development Studies (1992, 1994, 1996 and 1998 and 2003), included the development and on going review of curricula. The new certificate by distance, introduced in 2003, has been a major project in curriculum building, partnership and collaboration to develop material for the distance mode yet retain the pedagogical demands of a programme in gender. The Gender in Policy and Planning course, which also involved curriculum design and development carried out within the Centre, has been of benefit to many policy makers, and that programme, along with the significant consultancy work of the CGDS undertaken internationally with the United Nations and other agencies, regionally with CARICOM and Caribbean Women's groups, and locally with Bureaux of Women's Affairs and other government agencies have been 'informing processes of national and regional planning', as envisaged by Mathurin Mair. Some of these projects not only involve the Centre in interesting and valuable research, they also ensure the outreach which is a major component of the mission of the Centre, and extends the theoretical analysis to the work of activists.

Conclusion

Gender Studies is still being asked if it is a discipline. The appropriate response is probably that it is an 'interdisciplinary discipline'; satisfying the criteria of a discipline with an extensive, significant and coherent body of literature, with foundations in the language, theories and methodologies which reflect the disciplinary origins of the feminists who have contributed to its development. But it remains uncompromisingly interdisciplinary, in opposition to the artificial boundaries imposed around disciplinary bodies of knowledge, and using its own language, its own theories and its own methodologies to direct its research, its teaching and its outreach. The permeability of interdisciplinary work and its dynamic nature make it unique and critical to knowledge building. In Gender Studies, therefore, interdisciplinarity and disciplinarity are not mutually exclusive; both are relevant institutionally as well as in scholarship. As Relke (1994) observes:

> Women's studies is the interdiscipline par excellence. Gender also cuts across all other interdisciplinary programs in a way that virtually no other interdisciplinary theme does. Moreover, women's studies has its own discourse, its own burgeoning body of scholarship, its own highly sophisticated array of interconnecting theories, and its own set of methodologies. Hence, it's also what I can only call a megadiscipline.

The dynamism of scholarship in gender studies ensures its persistence and growth within the academy. Its interdisciplinary nature and its special pedagogy, methodologies for research and insistence on reflexive thought and critical analysis, will continue to influence societal change as the CGDS commits to producing active thinkers, researchers and learners, equipped to initiate and effect change within the network of regional and international educational institutions, governments and non-governmental agencies.

References

Boxer, Marilyn J. 2000. 'Unruly knowledge: Women's Studies and the problem of Disciplinarity'. *NWSA Journal* 12, no. 2 (Summer).

Boyer, Ernest. 1990. *Scholarship Reconsidered: priorities of the professoriate.* Princeton, NJ: The Carnegie Foundation for the Advancement of Teaching.

Drayton, Kathleen and Elaine Fido. 1988. *Evaluation: Women's Studies – an Introductory Course.* The University of the West Indies, Cave Hill Campus. Mimeo.

Dressel, P. and D. Marcus. 1982. *Teaching and Learning in College.* San Francisco: Jossey Bass.

Fink, L. Dee. 2001. 'Higher Level Learning: the first step toward more significant learning'. In *To improve the Academy: resources for faculty, instructional and organizational development* 19, eds. Devorah Lieberman and Catherine Wehlberg. Bolton, MA: Anker Publishing Co. Inc.

Freire, Paulo. 1972. *Pedagogy of the Oppressed*. Harmondsworth, Middlesex: Penguin.

Friedman, Susan Stanford. 1998. '(Inter)disciplinarity and the question of the Women's Studies PhD' *Feminist Studies* 24, no. 2: 301-325.

hooks, bell. 1988. *Talking back: thinking feminist, thinking black*. Toronto: Between the Lines.

Lattuca, Lisa. 2002. 'Learning interdisciplinarity: sociocultural perspectives on academic work'. *The Journal of Higher Education* 73, no. 6 (November/December).

Lave, J. 1997. 'The culture of acquisition and the practice of understanding'. In *Situated cognition: social, semiotic and psychological perspectives,* eds. D. Kirshner and J. Whitson, 17-35. Mahwah, NJ: Erlbaum.

Leo-Rhynie, Elsa, Barbara Bailey and Christine Barrow, eds. 1997. *Gender: A Caribbean Multidisciplinary Perspective*. Kingston: Ian Randle Publishers.

Luke, Carmen and Jennifer Gore, eds. 1992. *Feminisms and critical pedagogy*. New York: Routledge, Chapman and Hall, Inc.

Lusted, David. 1986. 'Why pedagogy?' *Screen* 27, no. 5: 2-14.

Massiah, Joycelin. 1986. 'Establishing a programme of Women and Development Studies in the University of the West Indies'. *Social and Economic Studies* 35, no. 1: 151-197.

Mathurin Mair, Lucille. 1988. Foreword. In *Gender in Caribbean Development,* eds. Patricia Mohammed and Catherine Shepherd. UWI Women and Development Studies Project.

Mohammed, Patricia and Catherine Shepherd, eds. 1988. *Gender in Caribbean Development*. UWI Women and Development Studies Project. Second Edition (1999). Kingston: The Press, UWI.

Pring, Richard. 1975. 'Curriculum integration'. In *Curriculum Design*, eds. M. Golby, J. Greenwald and R. West. London: Croome Helm in association with Open University Press.

Relke, Diana M.A. 1994. 'Feminist pedagogy and the integration of knowledge: toward a more interdisciplinary university'. Paper delivered to the Vice-President's Colloquium Series, University of Saskatchewan, February 14, 1994.

Romero, Mary. 2000. 'Disciplining the feminist bodies of knowledge: are we creating or reproducing academic structure?' *NWSA Journal* 12, no. 2 (Summer).

Stark, Joan and Lisa Lattuca. 1997. *Shaping the College curriculum: academic plans in action*. Massachussetts: Allyn and Bacon.

20 | VIOLET EUDINE BARRITEAU

Constructing Feminist Knowledge in the Commonwealth Caribbean[1] in the Era of Globalisation

Abstract

Resistance in the anglophone Caribbean academy and society to grapple with questions on women's ontology continues to find new crutches for old misogynies in recent developments in Caribbean political economy. The social, economic and cultural effects of globalisation are now being offered as the latest patriarchal devices to argue against continuing feminist inquiries into women's subjectivities. Caribbean feminist scholarship is poised at a critical juncture. Having built on the earlier research that gave visibility to women's lives, one aspect is involved with critiquing theoretical frameworks whose assumptions do not fully comprehend the multiple and differing realities for Caribbean women and men embedded in Caribbean gender systems. Simultaneously Caribbean feminists are creating new models and contributing new knowledge about women's lives. It is precisely at this epistemological juncture that the ravages of globalisation, particularly its alleged deleterious effects on Caribbean men (in isolation from examining any effects on Caribbean women), are being held out as reasons that feminist inquiries should cease to focus on women's subjectivity. The commitment to continuing to contribute to feminist epistemology from a Caribbean perspective is being asked to take a back seat to investigating men's gender identities and their alleged economic and civic marginalisation. This paper maintains that these positions are but another strand of the same, resilient, enduring arguments that are unwilling to accept women's right of being, women's ontology without attaching some set of pre-qualifying conditions. This paper analyses developments and setbacks in generating Caribbean feminist knowledge against this background.

The net effect of globalisation, trade liberalisation, privatisation, and market driven policies on the small, open economies of CARICOM[2] has been to create new tensions and insecurity in the society. The promise of increased jobs, improved market access, new technologies, and financial and other resources to alleviate poverty has not materialised. In spite of modest macroeconomic growth in most of the region, there is a new class of poor people in many countries. The gap between the relative few who were poised to benefit from globalisation and those who were not has increased divisions (Andaiye 2003).

The post-colonial state's primary area of intervention for women in the public arena is in the economy. It does not take the lead in public discourse on women. When it becomes involved, it is usually drawn into dialogue and interventions by interest groups. As the economic expression of liberal ideology, capitalism requires a critical mass of both skilled and unskilled workers – women and men. The industrialisation by invitation variant of development requires cheap, easily manipulated sources of labour. In the Caribbean that translates into women workers (Barriteau 1998a, 445).

Introduction and Overview

This paper is not a case study of the effects of globalisation on Caribbean feminist scholarship or on women or men. It is about the subject matter of feminist philosophy, specifically about women's right to a good life. I use globalisation as my entry point into a recurring, troubling question, why is the sate reluctant to address women's ontology? Although it may seem that I pose my concern in a utility versus rights discourse, I am not at all interested in validating either side of that dichotomy. I seek answers to my question from the perspective of justice. I think answers have to be sought along a continuum of responses that recognise that, not only do women have a right to exist, but they have a right to a good life unencumbered by the need for any set of pre-qualifying conditions. Therefore the question of an ethics of justice should animate the State in its gender relations with women.

While I am arguing for women's right to be, and criticising either the need to or the practice of rationalising the state's focus on women by utilitarian claims, I am not positioning my analysis in a utility versus rights discourse. While I want Caribbean states to recognise women's autonomy and agency in every dimension of women's lives, I underpin my arguments for this by resorting to the concept of justice, particularly gender justice, rather than the concept of rights. I argue that it satisfies a condition of gender justice for the states to abandon the position that women need to satisfy a set of criteria to qualify for the state's attention or to benefit from its considerable resources. Women are not allowed to engage the state as full citizens without satisfying a set of qualifying conditions. Simultaneously, states assume men have *a priori* rights and access to the resources of the state.

The concept of gender justice is pivotal to the question of women's existential right to be. Gender justice is an ideal but it can be defined as a societal condition in which there are no asymmetries of access to, or allocations of, status, power and material resources in a society. In a gender system characterised by gender justice there will be no hierarchies of gender identities, or of the meanings society gives to masculinity and femininity (Barriteau 1998b, 192).

To work towards gender justice not only means closing the gaps and removing the injustices exposed by gender analysis but actively promoting conditions in which women and men are not penalised or do not receive undue privilege for the gender identities with which they 'clothe' their biological, physiological selves (Barriteau 2003d).

There are several occurrences happening simultaneously that are outgrowths of adjustments in neo-liberal ideologies and all are significant to women's lives in developing countries. Because of the confluence of political, economic and cultural factors shaping the Caribbean's post-Columbian, historical origins, the region constitutes an ideal testing ground to assess the effects of these developments. Additionally, the region's experiences with changing relations of gender can illustrate what may happen in a number of developing countries when they satisfy some of the minimum criteria the United Nations (UN) uses to assess progress on human and gender development indices.

I intertwine contradictions in four strands of occurrences that impact on the continuation of feminist knowledge production in the Caribbean, my metaphor for engaging with the question of women's right of being. These are:

- Utilitarian arguments – Focus on WID. The origin of the focus on Women in Development/Developing countries in economistic, utilitarian arguments about investment in women is a means of prioritising development;
- Rampaging globalisation – As the ongoing permutation of neo-liberal, capitalist economic relations – globalisation – is disrupting economies and social relations in many developing countries, the ravages of globalisation is seen as producing great hardships for Caribbean economies and men;
- Imploding UN sponsored, global feminism – that is as developed and supported by UN agencies and generally institutionalised in developing countries as women's/gender bureaux and WID\GAD programmes, global feminism has reached its limits;
- Resurgence and resilience of patriarchal relations in state structures – The reluctance of Caribbean states to engage with women's ontological right to be.

The implications are that feminist activism and feminist scholarship may be incapable of dealing with the resurfacing resistance to questions about women's right-of-being. The WID discourse or UN feminism never equipped women's bureaux to tackle the resilience of patriarchal relations or its reassertion within state structures. The emphasis was on gaining expanded opportunities in the public sector and negotiating the incremental openings states allowed for these. These developments throw into sharp relief the very limited character of what was attempted. Women's lives in developing countries are being squeezed by the limitations of UN informed, state sponsored feminism and rampaging globalisation. Into this milieu I insert the recurring question on women's ontology.

As I observe recent developments in the fragile political economy of Caribbean countries, I find myself increasingly occupied with how these occurrences are being addressed at the level of the Caribbean state to destabilise the question about women's right of being. I examine the vulnerability of producing feminist knowledge against the backdrop of adverse economic and social changes in the Caribbean's experience of globalisation. The ravages of globalisation are interpreted as having deleterious effects on Caribbean economies and men. Mine is not a new concern. In the Caribbean context, I recognise that what I am doing is continuing to refine and trying to extend an argument that I began some years ago (Barriteau 1996, 1998). Here I continue to reflect on, theorise and politicise the reactions to Caribbean feminist scholarship and feminism and the particular problem globalisation now poses to continuing to create feminist knowledge about women (Barriteau 2003a).

In the Caribbean, the discourse on the relevance of studying women or designing policies for women has never been pursued as a discourse of rights.[3] From its inception, examining women in Caribbean societies has been a discourse on utility. It has never been about women's freedom but more about what needs to be done to reduce the obvious inequalities between women and men in the public. Whether in terms of generating policy or studying women's lives towards generating new knowledge, the focus on women in developing countries has been structured on utilitarian arguments. The discourse on utility holds that, 'positive action is justified in light of societal consequences' (Teigen 2002, 5).

I explore and locate the latest example of the ongoing resistance in contemporary Caribbean society to recognising women's right to a good life. I maintain that the ravages of globalisation, particularly its alleged more deleterious effect on men, offers to Caribbean states a perfect excuse for continuing to refuse to engage with the central question of women's existential right to be. The refusal to engage with women's right to be is embedded in powerful gender ideologies that are treated as if they are unrelated to material relations of gender. I hypothesise further that the origin in economic arguments of a discourse on women in developing countries also has obscured society's inherent and unresolved difficulty with accepting women's right of being unencumbered by justificatory claims. Attempting to locate action on behalf of women in materialist interventions, while refusing to address ideological relations that view women as subordinate citizens, leaves a very wide path for retreat when material relations of gender are altered.

A Critical Juncture

In post-colonial countries, the desire to improve efficiency and to want greater benefits to accrue to individuals and societies from developing the human and social capital of all citizens seems such an obviously worthwhile goal that the complications posed for women were not readily discernible. There continues to be a school of feminist thought (primarily in UN sponsored spaces, the WID/WAD/GAD field), that argues for resources to be allocated to women as a way of improving life in developing countries, rather than women having a right to a good life as an end in itself. Those who make those arguments do not perceive an inherent contradiction. To advocate that the state and society pay attention to women's lives because it is for society's well being underscores why there will always be a need to devise new reasons to support a flawed argument. There is an embedded contradiction. Women's intrinsic right to a good life becomes secondary to countries demonstrating that they have achieved some objective measure of working towards gender equality and therefore can scale back.

The comparatively high ranking of Caribbean countries on the Human Development Index (HDI) and the Gender Development Index (GDI) underscores the flawed character of the utilitarian argument. Most Commonwealth Caribbean countries ranked relatively high on the United Nations Development Program, UNDP's, indices introduced in 1995 to assess countries' efforts to promote gender equality.[4] Concurrently these countries started to experience the rapid economic and social changes characterising late twentieth century processes of globalisation. Even before reflecting on the significance of the second feature I theorised that Caribbean states would retreat from an emphasis on improving conditions for women:

> But if things are so wonderful for Caribbean women, (and some material conditions are much better than in other parts of the world), why is there such an outpouring of ridicule, contempt and fear of the gains that women have made? The comparatively high ratings of Caribbean countries on the GDI and GEM have not altered gender ideologies that view women as subordinate to men and that have become overtly misogynist (Barriteau 1998a,450).

I theorised that Caribbean states had never been fully committed to promoting women's freedom, and commitment to gender equality was driven by the international community, specifically donor funding, and supported by the activism of the indigenous women's movement.

By 2002 not only had most Caribbean countries declined in the world ranking assigned by the UNDP, but several disappeared from the measurement. Barbados, which had been leading in the region in the years 1995-1999 (and continues to lead on the HDI), has not turned up on the GDI, for the past three years. Even with declines in world ranking, part of which may be due to the UNDP's recalculating its indices in 1999, as a region the Caribbean looks very good on these measurements.

Once countries obtain some of the measures the UNDP advocates to achieve equality, for example, when women attain higher levels of literacy, x percentage of UN sanctioned participation in the political process, or measurable declines in childbirth morbidity,[5] it becomes very difficult to insist that the state maintain an interest in women's lives. The state can demonstrate it has met its targets. This situation becomes compounded when these objectively measurable goals are achieved against a background of rapid and adverse changes in local economies.

In the Caribbean the latest phase of globalisation witnessed a decline in agricultural production of bananas and sugar, the loss of preferential access to European markets for bananas, the booming, illegal sub-sector of drug running,[6] the blacklisting of several Caribbean countries as illegal tax or money-laundering havens,[7] and governments paying greater attention to encouraging service sectors to replace the marked decline in agricultural exports. Social activist and analyst Andaiye states that

> WTO rules that have threatened preferential market access for the main, often the only export crops of some states, and depressed commodity prices for rice, sugar, bauxite and gold, have led to new and increased insecurities in the job market and the society as a whole, and raise the question of the long-term viability of some of the smaller states (Andaiye 2003, 3).

What distinguishes all these developments is that social commentators and some UWI academics have interpreted these as an attack on men's rights which Caribbean society ranks as higher and more valuable than women's rights. Men, like women, do have a right to the state and societal resources and to the state's actions to protect their interests. But this has never been in doubt. Caribbean state structures, like others elsewhere, are androcentric and masculinised. Their evolution in anti-imperialist, post-colonial, nationalist struggles often masked their profoundly, patriarchal character. The notion of men's rights enjoying pre-eminence is widely held. What is new is how the economic, political, social, and cultural transitions Caribbean countries are experiencing are posited as more harmful to men, the modal citizens, and therefore attention to women's issues should cease. Of course this position conveniently ignores known statistical facts such as the Caribbean having the highest level of female-headed households with a regional average of 42 per cent (Barriteau 2003c).

It is also true that where these economic changes represent job losses it is primarily (though not exclusively) in sectors where male employment predominates. The growth in service-oriented economic activities are also in areas Caribbean gender ideologies define as women's work.[8] Yet these observations require further probing. The position that globalisation is more harmful to men also ignores the fact that in the region female unemployment is historically and consistently higher than male unemployment. For example, in Barbados in 1998, the male unemployment rate declined to a single digit figure of 8.3 per cent for the first time in the 1990s (a major achievement for a Caribbean economy), while female unemployment remained above 15 per cent because of job losses in the informatics, electronics, and textile industries, leaving the national unemployment rate at 11.8 per cent (Barriteau 2001, 45; Central Bank 1999, 8).

A summary of Andaiye's analysis of labour force participation by sex in the region in the late 1990s is even more telling. She observes:

1. In Grenada, St Lucia and Trinidad and Tobago, the data show a relatively small gap between males and females, varying between one to two percent in favour of males.

2. In St Vincent and the Grenadines, male unemployment was three times that of females in the poorest quintile, but the reverse was true among the higher quintiles, presumably comprising those with higher education and more marketable skills.

3. In Barbados, Belize and Jamaica, unemployment was higher among women, the gap being between two to three times greater in favour of women.

4. In Grenada, due to a downturn in markets for bananas, nutmeg and cocoa, there was increased unemployment, especially among women, and the rate of unemployment for women was 63 percent compared to 36.9 percent for men; women were 48.6 percent of the labour force and two-thirds of the employees in the nutmeg industry.

5. In Jamaica there was a reduction in employment in female dominated sectors, particularly for women under 25 in 1998, when overall unemployment was 15.5 percent, the figure was 23 percent for women and 10 percent for men.

6. Only in Saint Lucia was male unemployment reported to have increased and female unemployment to have decreased, and the reason offered was the effect of trade liberalisation and economic downturn; it is not clear why St Lucia should be different form the other countries in this regard (Andaiye 2003, 8-9).

These observations are critical because they are in direct contradiction to the popular understandings of where women are in location to poverty levels and economic activity in the region. Again to make this point is not to argue that men are not experiencing economic marginalisation. One could argue from the days of the forced labour of indigenous peoples, slavery and indentureship, Caribbean working class men, like working class women, have always had and continue to have their labour power exploited. The flash points of social upheaval and resistance to indifferent colonial state structures throughout the post emancipation Caribbean (such as the nineteenth century Jamaican Morant Bay Rebellion and the riots and protests throughout the 1930s) all received their impetus from the grinding poverty and social and political alienation experienced by men and women. The massive protests Caribbean men and women resorted to, acted as a pressure valve to relieve the economic and political deprivation they experienced and which provides solid evidence of their longstanding economic marginalisation (Barriteau 2003c).

Andaiye also points out that, in the context of globalisation, the economic sectors that have been disrupted typically employed men. These sectors are now being replaced by those which employ women under a host of physically and financially debilitating conditions. The zero-sum reading of marginalisation that is so attractive and which suggests all men lose power and resources to women does not apply. Men's losses are not women's gains. As she states, 'the jobs in which women are employed in the new export sectors are insecure and vulnerable to the sudden flights of investors in search of cheaper labour, few labour restrictions, less enforcement of codes, larger labour pools and advantages of scale, and higher incentives' (Andaiye 2003, 19). For example, the increase in female unemployment in Barbados in 1998 is directly due to the factors she identified (Central Bank of Barbados 1999, 8; Barriteau 2001, 45).[9]

Yet the ensuing debate in the public domain is that governments cannot justify a focus on Caribbean women because Caribbean men are being marginalised[10] and in fact are being sacrificed to feminist agendas and globalisation processes (Miller 1991, 1994).

The Male Marginalisation Thesis 'posits the notion that men have *a priori* rights to the resources of the state as clients and citizens' over and above women (Barriteau 2003d). It argues, not only should activities on behalf of women be abandoned if men are experiencing hardships, but the very activities themselves are interpreted as men being further marginalised (Barriteau 2003d). The main scholar of this thesis, Professor Errol Miller, implicates international development institutions, UN agencies and the World Bank for contributing to the marginalisation of black men in Jamaica and posits that what is happening to Jamaican men will become the experiences of all males of subordinate groups in patriarchal societies (Barriteau 2003d):[11]

> Certainly UNESCO, the World Bank, USAID, and CIDA, which aided and assisted successive Jamaican governments since 1962 in expanding education, cannot stand aloof from the fact that their interventions have left black males in Jamaica more marginal in the Jamaican society than their grandfathers were. The full implications of this are still to be experienced. The recency of these interventions makes it still early to realize fully the entire extent of the social repercussions for family life, employment, religion, relations between the sexes, and the social structure (Miller 1994, 124-31).

Miller's work is used by many in the region to advocate limited access to public resources for women. Supporters of this thesis 'recommend a return to single sex schools, closing women's bureaux, excluding girls from extra-curricular programmes, and blaming women for high divorce rates and a variety of social ills' (Barriteau 2003d). The thesis both theorises and politicises the deep rooted myth that men's misfortunes originate from women's transgressions (Koven & Michel 1993, 1).

Points of Departure

1. Globalisation and the Origins of the Women-in-Development Discourse

For nearly 30 years an impressive body of feminist scholarship has focused on the multiple identities, subjectivities, and experiences of Caribbean women or women in developing countries.[12] However, beyond feminist circles within the academy and a nascent woman's movement, there is no widespread acceptance of women's intrinsic right of being. Simultaneously feminist scholarship has not threatened nor dislodged the powerful belief that women's existence should serve larger societal goals. The overarching end becomes economic growth, and even when ameliorative measures are vigorously pursued for women these are treated as a means to a larger end.

Indigenous feminist contributions to the contrary, creating feminist knowledge in developing countries has never fully escaped its origins in an economistic type of *raison d'être*. Ester Boserup (1970) followed by liberal feminist scholars, Washington, DC-based WID specialists, and development experts justifiably focussed international attention on the marginalised location of women in the processes and structures of development – that is in the Western understanding of what constitutes development (Tinker and Bramsen 1976, Tinker 1990). This attention created a flurry of remedial and corrective measures that reallocated resources, yielded new policies, and additional fields of investigation. The subjectivity of women in the Caribbean and other regions of the developing world seemed to have been legitimated. It was not.

The new scholarly and programmatic enterprise was held together by the central idea that to ignore women was to subvert the very goal that developing countries sought, an efficient, smooth, upwardly arching, path to development. The work of Boserup and others clearly indicated that if the holy grail of development was higher level of exports, greater productivity, higher GNPs and GDPs, stronger savings and investment functions, and a healthier, more literate and skilled labour force, then it would be worth a country's while to pursue these goals by fully incorporating women into development policies and programmes. It was a powerful, well-meaning argument. It combined scholarship with the strategy of lobbying for the representation of women's interest in developing countries. Even though it was not confined to this, the discipline of women's studies/feminist studies gained prominence in developing countries as the women and development discourse.

But herein lies the complexity. The genesis of the women and development discourse is in economic arguments about the utility of including women and is firmly located in the post-war, anti-colonial, nationalist climate of the late 1960s. Development scholars' systematic attention to, and critique of, modernity's fascination with economic development (Chilcote 1981; Bodenheimer 1971; Wilber and Jameson 1979; Gendzier 1985; Blomstrom & Hettne 1984) coincided with the maturation of development scholarship in the Caribbean[13] and other areas of the South. Internationally, the birth of the non-aligned nations in world politics at the Bandung conference in 1955, quickly followed by eight other conferences by 1986 (Lundestad 1986, 258-9), officially set the development agenda for developing countries. A focus on women was incrementally added to this agenda but was not conceptualised as part of the original mandate.

Boserup's revealing study and the first United Nations conference on women in Mexico City in 1975 both occurred during the second United Nations sponsored Decade of Development. Regionally and nationally, pro-independence leaders pursued nationalist agendas and agitated for political independence, without having that post colonial agenda include tackling the power dynamics inherent in the social relations of gender. Most of these leaders prioritised the relations of class and race without even symbolic gestures being paid to disrupting inherited patriarchal practices and power that they allowed to continue unchallenged.

The very reason that enabled post colonial/nationalist leaders to ignore relations of power in gender is the same reason that now enables the early twenty-first century state to retreat from engaging with issues that seemingly promote women's autonomy and agency. There was never a commitment to do so. The political will of the emerging independent state did not include involvement with questions of women's full citizenship. Scrutinising the absence of attention given to the subject of women's economic, political, social, and cultural citizenship during this strong, nationalist phase of development provides some clues, but still leaves some grey areas. Until the Women in the Caribbean Project, (WICP) in the late 1970s, any desire for information on women had to be satisfied by sifting through the mid-twentieth century anthropological studies on Caribbean family forms. 'From the 1950s to the 1970s there has been an unexplained lapse [in a focus on women] between the early studies of West Indian or Caribbean family structures and the latter multi-disciplinary approaches used by the Women in Development Project' (Barriteau 1994, 70-1).

The work of Caribbean historians, economists, and political scientists fed into creating structures and policies for emerging independent states. For example, the work of Caribbean and international sociologists and anthropologists of West Indian family structures threw into sharp relief the social and economic conditions of Caribbean women (Clarke 1957; Smith 1955, 1962; Braithwaite 1957). Still, by the time the newly minted, independent Caribbean countries entered the UN system, the latter was already driven by the idea that women had to be deliberately included in the processes of development.[14] For several reasons this was a welcome occurrence. Previously not enough attention had been paid to the often-debilitating conditions under which the majority of women managed to survive or desperately tried to keep family life viable.

Besides the absence of a political will on the part of Caribbean states to validate women's civic autonomy and relevance, the proponents of the utility and efficiency rationale for a women's focus did not anticipate that the argument could be inverted. They did not enquire, if investing in women would promote efficiency, growth and societal well-being, what would be the rationale if efficiency and growth was reversed and societal well-being endangered due to exogenous factors such as globalisation processes? How could feminists continue to argue for the centrality of women in development agendas when the stated development agenda was in jeopardy – especially after the state had invested in women? How would that argument be constructed when those opposed to women's well-being could highlight the flawed construct and existing widespread material deprivation?

An unfortunate consequence of the intent to bring women into the processes of development is that the justification for this focus is always mediated through an instrumentalist lens. In Commonwealth Caribbean societies, as elsewhere in the South, interest in women's lives has been in proving why it is beneficial to families and societies to have public policies and programmes target women. Well-meaning feminists and development experts marshalled the arguments that prove the savings to society of investing in women. They demonstrated the benefits to children of having literate, skilled mothers (Cornia 1987). We proved the deleterious effects of structural adjustment policies on women and families (Bolles 1983; Beneria and Feldman 1992; Sparr 1994; Ffrench 1994; Barriteau 1996). We revealed the improvement in primary health care if mothers were trained and understood how new knowledge and practice would benefit their children's lives. We invested programmes and extensive studies in underscoring why focusing on women was beneficial, cost-effective, and made good economic sense. In the United States liberal feminists successfully lobbied foreign policy makers to insist that a focus on women become a qualifying condition for receiving development aid (USAID 1978). Several developing countries complied by establishing women in development programmes.

A troubling, cumulative effect of all these measures is that it leaves questions about women's ontology and women's right of being unexamined and external to the Women and Development discourse. But the consequences of this lacuna are far greater than the suggestion of an unfortunate omission and lack of attention to an underlying philosophical query. Caribbean states and societies have never wrestled with the basic idea that women have a right to a political, civic existence unencumbered by notions of meeting a set of utilitarian criteria to qualify to receive the energies and resources of the state. The contradiction Carole Pateman identifies as existing at the heart of liberalism's democratic theory and practice, sets the agenda for the post-colonial Caribbean state. 'Liberalism has built into itself a contradiction between the ideals of individual freedom and equality in the public sphere and the assumption that women are naturally subject to men in the family' (Pateman in Birte Siim 1988, 162). Women need to satisfy a set of criteria to qualify for the state's attention because they are not allowed to engage the state as equal citizens. The state requires reasons to invest in women in the public domain because the unstated understanding is women's citizenship is circumscribed by their subordinate status in the private.

On the occasions when some occurrence in civic society forces the State to stare into the eye of this turbulence, there has always been a retreat based on circular arguments (Robinson 2000, 2003 Forthcoming).[15] The impact of globalisation is now forcing the issue. It has brought the discourse and popular debate to a critical juncture and has established a point of departure in the women and development discourse that has implications for constructing feminist knowledge beyond the boundaries of this discipline.

2. *Globalisation, Male Marginalisation and Feminist Theorising*

The pre-eminent feature that would mark perceptions of how the decade of the 1990s affected women centred on Caribbean men. Specifically it centred on the idea that Caribbean men are in crisis and that they are being marginalised by the activities of Caribbean states, the women's movement, and the decisions and lifestyle choices of individual women who may or may not be part of any organised women's networks (Barriteau 2003c).

The Caribbean women's movement or Caribbean feminists have not stated that Caribbean men do not experience gendered relations nor that they do not face debilitating economic and social conditions. It is altogether a different matter to attribute the adversities in men's lives to deliberate actions on the part of Caribbean women, aimed at destroying men's lives and deliberate policies on the part of Caribbean states to aid in this.

The decade of the dominance of 'Miller's Male Marginalisation Thesis' coincided with the decade of the dominance of the discourse and practice of globalisation. In the 1990s, globalisation brought heightened homogenisation and control of capital, labour and service markets, the withering away of key sectors of industrialised economies, and the simultaneous mushrooming and imploding of new economic activities, primarily services catering to or dependent on information technologies. Caribbean economies remain plugged into the world economy as providers of services, agricultural produce, light manufacturing and mining for a few countries (Griffith 1997,176). In the Eastern Caribbean countries of Dominica, Saint Lucia, St Vincent and the Grenadines, and to a lesser extent Grenada, banana exports to the United Kingdom, facilitated by quotas under successive African, Pacific and Caribbean ACP, trade agreements, withered away.[16] Ironically, the region witnessed an almost simultaneous growth in a parallel, illegal, extremely dangerous but extremely lucrative economy of drug running.

Conventional economic analysis assesses these conditions without paying any attention to how these influence changes in how women and men experience relations of gender in the region. Traditional gender analysis[17] still does not engage sufficiently with new conditions in Caribbean political economy, for example to isolate how issues of globalisation introduce comparative disadvantages for men and women.

The decade of the 1990s began inauspiciously without any visible signs of the coming efforts to shift from a concern with the multiple challenges women encounter and juggle with as citizens, workers and caregivers within families, to a focus on Caribbean men in deep crisis and increasingly being rendered powerless by individuals, institutions and Caribbean states. If, in terms of state interests, we can declare that the 1980s belonged to Caribbean women, the decade of the 1990s was dominated by debates on the ideas that Caribbean men were in crisis and that they were increasingly marginalised in their homes, their workplaces, and in the policies and practices of states. For the first time there was a sustained interest in exploring how men experienced their lives in both the private and public domains in relation to real or perceived changes for women. This was a significant and welcome point of departure in examining men's gender identities. However, it stultified at the point of showing men as victims of an emasculating, all-powerful women's movement and indifferent, feminist-controlled state systems (Barriteau 2003c).

The discourse on equality, justice and rights of the decade of the 1980s coalesced around the idea that Caribbean women were finally achieving many of the elusive goals that were being sought since the post independence period but pursued in a much more focused manner from 1975 onwards. In the 1980s, Antigua-Barbuda, Dominica, Bahamas, Saint Lucia, St Kitts-Nevis, and St Vincent and the Grenadines joined Jamaica, Barbados, Trinidad and Tobago, Grenada and Belize in institutionalising state mechanisms to monitor gender inequalities affecting women (Barriteau 2001, 22). Several countries introduced legislation to remove the more obvious aspects of institutionalised discrimination against women.

By 1985, there was a general sense that through legislation and policy, Caribbean states were attempting to correct the adversities women had endured since the beginning of the twentieth century and extending as far back as the beginning of post-Columbian Caribbean society. Women increasingly participated in the labour force in larger numbers. This was influenced by expanded educational opportunities and the diversification of Caribbean economies. The latter began in the 1960s with various industrialisation strategies of development. Access to new educational resources enabled some women to begin to gain jobs in professions that were once historically and traditionally male dominated.

A politicised, organised women's movement, evident in the growth of several women's organisations and NGOs with an explicit concern for women's well being, became very vocal and very visible. They represented another phase of women organising. What marked these organisations as different from earlier organisations is that they problematised and politicised a wide range of issues affecting women's lives. So whereas earlier organisations taught women relevant and necessary economic and political skills, the more recent organisations politicised the issues women faced and insisted on holding Caribbean states and societies responsible for taking measures to alter these. The earlier and more recent women's organisations employed complementary approaches with the central concern of promoting positive developments for women and society. The Caribbean Association for Feminist Research and Action, CAFRA, was the best expression of this more recent type of organisation (Barriteau 2003c).

Changes within civil society were reinforced by changes in the academy. Within the University of the West Indies (UWI) a women's studies programme emerged out of Women and Development Studies groups. These groups were themselves an outcome of the Women in the Caribbean Project, WICP, 1979-1982, and the establishment of the Women and Development, WAND, in the School of Continuing Studies, UWI in 1978. These significant developments at the UWI generated a definitive body of research, the full contribution of which has been insufficiently appreciated. The feminist activism of WAND's developmental work in communities in the Eastern Caribbean was another source of translating goals for Caribbean women into programmes and practices.

Internationally, the three United Nations world conferences on women called attention to deplorable conditions existing for women and the 1985 Nairobi Conference developed 'Forward Looking Strategies' for monitoring the improvement of these.

However, by the end of the 1980s the philosophy that had informed these strategies was now being questioned. A few of the major actors began to display uncertainty about the outcomes of their policy leading to an eventual re-examination of their philosophy to correct conditions of inequality for women. They began to question whether economic and social adversities affecting men[18] were not exacerbated by women's expanded labour force participation. There was a fear that Caribbean states had gone too far in promoting gender equality. Public commentators began to suggest that Caribbean states had surrendered much to the interests of women at the expense of men and the first rumblings of 'men in crisis' and Errol Miller's 'The Marginalisation of the Black Male' were being heard (*Daily Gleaner,* 15 August 1989, A:6). By the beginning of the 1990s, the first signs of slippage of commitment and policy confusion were surfacing (Barriteau 2003c).

The belief that women are *and should be* intrinsically subordinate citizens in any state system is an organising principle in western political philosophy. It is the same philosophical construct we experience in neo-liberal ideologies of the market, the state and relations of gender. It is at the heart of the rush to back-pedal on utilitarian commitments to women in the face of growing economic adversities. The idea of women's subordinate citizenship status reoccurs throughout western philosophical thought and is a foundational tenet for contemporary gender ideologies. For example, as a subset of the Male Marginalisation Thesis, the current intolerance of girls in coeducational school systems and the endemic blaming of female teachers for the academic failure of boys is rooted in the belief that boys should have a superior public education compared to girls (Figueroa 1997, 5). Yet, this is a very ancient belief which merely resurfaces in the decade of the 1990s. It is first expressed in the political philosophy of classical antiquity and revealed in Plato's *Republic* (Sterling and Scott 1985). It is re-echoed and expounded upon in Jean Jacques Rousseau's eighteenth century treatise on *The Education of Emile*. Rousseau argued that the presence of women in public life undermines masculine excellence (Lange 1991, 102). In fact, Rousseau argued three centuries ago that women should be educated 'to please men' (Gatens 1991, 120). Rousseau's work was instrumental in shaping Western and, by extension, Caribbean educational philosophy. Rousseau reinforces the belief that boys alone should be educated and that boys can only have a superior education if they are taught in single-sex schools, away from girls (Rousseau 1972).

Developments and Setbacks in Generating Feminist Knowledge

Research on Caribbean women has evolved from the early programmatic focus on bringing women in to justifying the usefulness of this approach to the region's well-being. In the academy, the discipline shifted from being called women studies to gender studies with insufficient attention paid to what was being lost in that transition and to the politics of creating feminist knowledge (Barriteau 2003b forthcoming). At the level of the Caribbean state, interest changed from offering programmes on women to programmes to promote gender equality. Mari Tiegen captures my concern when she states:[19]

> Arguments for gender equality are primarily expressed as a simple resource argument: due to the fact that the talent potential in the population is equally distributed between women and men, male dominance will necessarily lead to a failure to capitalize on all available human resources (Tiegen 2002,5).

The United Nations Development Programme, Human Development Report for 1995 extends this:

> In no society today do women enjoy the same opportunities as men. This unequal status leaves considerable disparities between *how much women contribute to human development* and how little they share its benefits (my emphasis UNDP 1995, 29).

The new terminology on gender equality is also widespread in the Caribbean, but it indicates no epistemological shifts towards an understanding of women's existential rights. It is merely the 1990's sophisticated restatement of the early utilitarian position. The basic themes of human life that Andrea Nye names as the subject matter of philosophy, the identity of the self, the nature of reality, the possibility of knowledge, are yet to be fully accepted as relevant in creating Caribbean feminist knowledge (Nye 2002, 102). The statement by CARICOM Secretary-General in the foreword to the region's mid-decade report prepared for the Fourth World Conference on Women underscores my point:

> Many of the issues that this report addresses – the political representation of non-independent territories, escalating crime linked to increasing acts of violence against women, poverty and unemployment – are the very ones that impinge on CARICOM's agenda for change. *Only if there is social stability can our region achieve the economic goals we have set* (my emphasis, Edwin Carrington in Mondesire and Dunn 1995, I).

The title of the report, 'Towards Equity in Development: A Report on the Status of Women in Sixteen Commonwealth Caribbean Countries', leaves no doubt as to the hierarchical and lesser ranking of women's well-being against the larger and seemingly more relevant goals of development. The report goes on to note that, 'over the last two decades, strategies have changed from integrating women into development to empowering women to contribute to the development process and ensuring gender equity' (Mondesire and Dunn 1995, 5). Many believed that something fundamental and qualitative had happened in what was really a programmatic shift. In the 1970s, women were brought into development to serve development goals. In the 1990s, women 'were being empowered to contribute to the development process'. In the twenty-first century, women's existence in developing countries is still required to serve the development agenda. This situation constitutes another barrier to constructing feminist knowledge about women based on exploring their subjectivities free from the need to prove the usefulness to society of focusing on women. Justifying an interest in women in developing countries in utilitarian arguments, specifically the returns to society from investing in women, facilitates a retreat of that support when resources are scarce. This offers another barrier against constructing feminist knowledge. It creates another hurdle to facing women's right of being.

At the beginning of the twenty-first century the situation Caribbean women face is paradoxical. If we use the standard UN indicators such as the HDI, the GDI, and the Gender Empowerment Measure (GEM) we might conclude there is no cause for concern. Yet, in between the spaces and gaps uncovered by these useful indices are fundamental fault lines that suggest an ongoing sustained and sustainable commitment to women's political and economic well being has shifted and is continuing to be in a state of flux (Barriteau 2003c).

Towards an Ethics of Justice

Using the arguments about the ravages of globalisation on the region enables Caribbean states and societies to once again step away from feminist claims for the recognition of women's full citizenship and freedom. It ensures that men remain the modal citizens while women's political and economic relevance occupies a secondary position. Yet this situation is potentially an exciting development for feminist theory building and feminist activism.

The early discourse on women in developing countries did not conceptualise women as having multiple identities while facing competing realities. The women Caribbean states sought to integrate into development processes were homogeneously constructed. Not only was there no recognition of differences among the types of women emerging in post-colonial societies, the early policies did not acknowledge competing identities and multiple self interests in women of similar socioeconomic backgrounds. Contemporary developments create new points of departure ripe for examination and new theorisation. Dominican women are among the group of persons hardest hit by the loss of access to banana markets in Europe. Andaiye reports that, in Dominica, women own 21 per cent of the banana producing farms, although 61 per cent of these are less than two acres (Andaiye 2003, 11). To make matters worse, the banana sector of the economy employed more than 30 per cent of the workforce and contributed 60 per cent of export earnings (Andaiye 2003, 3). Who is the woman in banana farming in Dominica and what are her needs? Of all the contending identities potentially available in the women and development discourse, the policies coalesced around women as low-skilled workers and reproducers of the labour force.

The rationale for women receiving the attention of the state and having a right to claim public spaces has to be de-linked from two problematic positions; connections to utilitarian arguments, and the need for a rationale in the first place. The factors currently impeding centralising women's subjectivities and seeking to constrain ongoing feminist investigations can be summarised as:

- the justification that state and society's interest in women be mediated through utilitarian arguments;
- the unwillingness of the state to negotiate the contradictions between viewing women as subordinate in the private domain and seeking to introduce measures premised on moving towards objectively defined criteria for achieving gender equality in the public.

These mask a fundamental issue: the right of women to traverse the public and private domain and to operate freely in both, whether economies are in decline or experiencing exceptional growth. Since Caribbean political institutions and philosophical antecedents are so firmly anchored in liberal political ideology, feminist theorists should continue to expose and 'reject the artificial separation of the public and private spheres of society'(Barriteau 1994, 274). As a way of exposing the flawed basis of the utilitarian arguments and the reticence of the state to renegotiate the ideological fault lines between the private and the public, feminists should continue to examine how the latter conceptualisations of the organisation of society overlap and reconstitute each other (Barriteau 1994, 274). There is a public exploitation of women in the private domain. This exploitation in turns uses women's reproductive work in the so-called private to underpin productive activity in the public (Barriteau 1994, 274). The continued exploitation is serviced by perpetuating myths such as 'Caribbean women the miracle workers':

> The mythology surrounding the latter view is particularly painful. While it publicizes the resourcefulness of Caribbean women it pays insufficient attention to the considerable material and psychological costs women absorb in carrying the responsibilities abdicated by the state, men, and in some cases adult children (Barriteau 1994, 296).[20]

Perhaps the crisis of globalisation may finally force Caribbean states and societies to grapple with questions of women's autonomy, agency and freedom.

Notes

1. By Commonwealth Caribbean I refer to the independent, anglophone island states and British Dependencies within the Caribbean sea, and the Central and South American countries of Belize and Guyana. These countries share a common historical, political, cultural and economic legacy. While I view the Caribbean as a geographic and political reality, including many language groupings and political cultures, for the purposes of this analysis I confine myself to the countries which share a familiar history and political economy.

2. Refers to the countries forming the Caribbean Common Market established by the Treaty of Chaguaramas , July 1, 1973. Originally independent, anglophone Caribbean countries, and Montserrat, a British dependency. Suriname was admitted to full membership in 1997 and Haiti in 2002. The British dependencies of Anguilla, the British Virgin Islands, and Turks and Caicos Islands are Associate Members.

3. Neither am I arguing it should be.

4. The main measure of this is the Gender Development Index which concentrates on the same variables the UNDP used to construct its Human Development Index, HDI, but compares and takes note of differences in the achievement of women and men to determine a country's progress on efforts to attain gender equality.
5. As has happened in the anglophone Caribbean.
6. The Caribbean island states link North America and South America. The many channels, beaches, islands and coves are used by drug smugglers as attractive transhipment points to the lucrative North American and European markets, in a sense mimicking centuries old trading routes. The Post Columbian Caribbean was born out of European expansion and globalisation. From the fifteenth century onwards Europeans used the islands and its channels to fight over the spoils of the region. Today, formal economies survive by offering tourism services while many informal economic activities revolve around the political economy of drug running.
7. On February 17th, 2003, the Financial Action Task Force, FATF, of the OECD countries removed Grenada from the list of blacklisted countries (officially known as Non-Cooperative Countries and Territories, NCCT) accused of facilitating money laundering by not ensuring that the state has the required regulatory and legislative framework to monitor such practices. Grenada's clearance now leaves St Vincent and the Grenadines as the only Commonwealth Caribbean country included in the latest list of ten countries worldwide so listed. Both Caribbean countries were once heavy exporters of bananas to the United Kingdom under the preferential access once granted to members of the African Caribbean and Pacific countries. See, 'Thanks to anti-money laundering system Grenada in the clear', *The Barbados Advocate*, February 17th 2003: 10.
8. See Carla Freeman's work, *High Tech and High Heels in the Global Economy*... 2000, for interesting and relevant analysis in regard to this point.
9. The Central Bank's report on economic activity for 1998 states, 'The surge in construction activity had a significant impact on the male unemployment rate which fell approximately 2 percentage points to close the year at an estimated 8.3 per cent. In contrast, several jobs usually held predominantly by females in the informatics, electronics and textile industries were lost as companies streamlined their operations. Consequently, the female unemployment rate remained above 15 per cent', see Central Bank of Barbados, 1999.
10. Miller means that men, especially working-class men, are deliberately made politically, economically and socially powerless in relation to all women.
11. For an extensive critique of and rebuttal of the Male Marginalisation Thesis, see, Lindsay 1997 and Barriteau 2003d.
12. A representative sample includes, Tinker & Bo Bramsen 1976; Steady 1981; Nash & Fernandez-Kelly 1983; Social and Economic Studies 1986; Sen & Grown 1987; Momsen & Townsend 1987; Mohammed & Shepherd 1988; Hart 1989; Tinker 1989; Bush 1990; Senior 1991; Mohanty, Russo & Torres 1991; Senior 1991; Beneria & Feldman 1992; Momsen 1993; Reddock 1994; Safa 1995; Shepherd, Brereton, & Bailey 1995; Marchand & Parpart 1995; Barrow 1998.

13. George Beckford's theorisation of plantation economy, The New World School of political and economic analysis, Walter Rodney's theorisation of the development of underdevelopment are examples of this.
14. In this analysis I am not interested in exposing the falsity of this notion that women were marginal to development. Women have always been incorporated into development policies in very specific and circumscribed ways. Liberal feminists and others either miss or misinterpret the ways in which women's roles have always been central to western notions of development in developing countries. See Barriteau 1994, 2001, 2003 forthcoming.
15. In the chapter, 'Beyond the Bill of Rights: Sexing the Citizen', Tracy Robinson 2003, provides ample evidence of the Caribbean state's retreat from engaging with women's full citizenship.
16. The European Union succumbed to charges of unfair trade practices brought to the World Trade Organisation by the United States on behalf of its banana interests in Latin America.
17. I have been asked by my colleague Laura Parisi whether I define traditional gender analysis as liberal feminism. It is tempting to attribute to liberal feminism all the subsequent confusion existing in the name of gender analysis, except I think it is a blend of several theoretical and programmatic approaches.
18. As well as continuing to affect women, a fact generally overlooked.
19. She is speaking in relation to Norway but the observations are quite relevant to the Caribbean and other parts of the world. One effect of the United Nations World Conferences on Women is to introduce increased homogenisation in planning, programmes and policy statements at the national level. These are sometimes adopted or introduced even when there is inadequate capacity and understanding of the issues involved in the national machineries. See Harris 1999; Barriteau 2001, 2003c.
20. As I have stated elsewhere these types of conditions needs investigation and analysis. Many Caribbean women continue to provide reproductive and nurturing services for their adult offspring as a *responsibility*. This feeds the myth of the miracle mother (who is indeed exceptional) while the exploitative and dependency aspects of these arrangements are frequently ignored. See Barriteau 1994, 295-6.

References

Andaiye. 2003. 'Smoke and Mirrors: The Illusion of Women's Growing Economic Empowerment in the CARICOM Region, Post-Beijing'. CARICOM and UNIFEM Beijing Plus Five Regional Report to the United Nations. CARICOM Secretariat, Georgetown, Guyana.

Barriteau, Violet Eudine. 2003a. 'Confronting Power and Politics: A Feminist Theorizing of Gender in Commonwealth Caribbean Societies'. *Meridians: feminism, race, transnationalism* 3, no. 2: 57-92.

_____. 2003b. 'Theorizing the Shift from "Woman" to "Gender" in Caribbean Feminist Discourse: The Power Relations of Creating Knowledge'. In *Confronting Power, Theorizing Gender: Interdisciplinary Perspectives in the Caribbean*, ed. Eudine Barriteau. Mona: UWI Press. In Press.

_____2003c. 'Beyond a Backlash: The Frontal Assault on Containing Caribbean Women in the Decade of the 1990s'. CARICOM and UNIFEM Beijing Plus Five Regional Report to the United Nations. CARICOM Secretariat, Georgetown, Guyana.

_____. 2003d. 'Requiem for the Male Marginalization Thesis in the Caribbean: Death of a Non-Theory'. In *Confronting Power, Theorizing Gender: Interdisciplinary Perspectives in the Caribbean*, ed. Eudine Barriteau. Mona: UWI Press. In Press.

_____. 2001. *The Political Economy of Gender in the Twentieth Century Caribbean*. London and New York: Palgrave International.

_____. 1998a. 'Liberal Ideologies and Contradictions in Caribbean Gender Systems'. In *Caribbean Portraits: Essays on Gender Ideologies and Identities*, ed. C. Barrow, 436-456, Kingston: Ian Randle Publishers in association with Centre For Gender and Development Studies, Cave Hill.

_____.1998b. 'Theorizing Gender Systems and the Project of Modernity in the Twentieth Century Caribbean'. *Feminist Review*. Rethinking Caribbean Difference, no. 59 (Summer): 187-210.

_____. 1996. 'Liberal Ideology and Contradictions in Caribbean Gender Systems'. Centre for Gender and Development Studies, University of the West Indies, Cave Hill, March, mimeo.

_____. 1994. 'Gender and Development Planning in the Post Colonial Caribbean: Female Entrepreneurs and the Barbadian State.' PhD dissertation, Howard University.

Barrow, Christine, ed. 1998. *Caribbean Portraits: Essays on Gender Ideologies and Identities*. Kingston: Ian Randle Publishers in association with Centre For Gender and Development Studies, Cave Hill.

Beneria, Lourdes and Shelley Feldman, eds. 1992. *Unequal Burden: Economic Crises, Persistent Poverty and Women's Work*. Boulder: Westview Press.

Blomstrom, Magnus and Bjorn Hettne. 1984. *Development Theory in Transition. The Dependency Debate and Beyond: Third World Responses*. London: Zed Books.

Bodenheimer, Susanne J. 1971. *The Ideology of Developmentalism: The American Paradigm - Surrogate for Latin American Studies*. Beverly Hills: Sage Publications.

Bolles, Lynn. 1983. 'Kitchen Hit by Priorities: Employed Working Class Jamaican Women Confront the IMF'. In *Women, Men and the International Division of Labour*, eds. June Nash and M. Patricia Fernandez Kelly, 138-160. Albany: State University of New York Press.

Brathwaite, Lloyd E. 1957. 'Sociology and Demographic Research in The British Caribbean'. *Social and Economic Studies* 6, no. 4: 523-71.

Central Bank of Barbados. 1999. *Annual Report 1998*. Barbados: Central Bank of Barbados.

Chilcote, Ronald H. 1981. *Theories of Comparative Politics: The Search for a Paradigm.* Boulder: Westview Press.

Clarke, Edith. 1957. *My Mother who Fathered Me: A Study of the Families in Three Selected Communities in Jamaica.* London: Allen and Unwin.

Cornia, Giovanni A. 1987. 'Adjustment at the Household Level: Potentials and Limitations of Survival Strategies'. In *Adjustment with a Human Face: Protecting the Vulnerable and Promoting Growth.* eds, Giovanni A. Cornia, Richard Jolly and Frances Stewart, 90-104. Oxford: Clarendon Press.

Ffrench, Joan. 1994. 'Hitting Where it Hurts Most: Jamaican Women's Livelihoods in Crisis'. In *Mortgaging Women's Lives: Feminist Critiques of Structural Adjustment.* ed. Pamela Sparr, 165-182. London: Zed Books Ltd.

Figueroa, Mark.1997. 'Gender Differentials in Educational Achievement in Jamaica and Other Caribbean Territories.' Paper presented to Conference on Intervention Strategies to address Male Under Achievement in Primary and Secondary Education, Port of Spain, Trinidad and Tobago, November.

Freeman, Carla. 2000. *High Tech and High Heels: Women, Work, and Pink Collar Identities in the Caribbean.* Duke University Press: Durham and London.

Gendzier, Irene L. 1985. *Managing Political Change: Social Scientists and the Third World.* Boulder, Colorado: Westview Press, Inc.

Griffith, Ivelaw. 1997. *Drugs and Security in the Caribbean: Sovereignty Under Siege.* Pennsylvania: Pennsylvania State University Press.

Harris, Sonja.1999. Study on Gender Mainstreaming in Caribbean Subregional countries. ECLAC-CDCC Third Caribbean Ministerial Conference on Women, Port of Spain, Trinidad, October.

Hart, Keith, ed. 1989. *Women and the Sexual Division of Labour in the Caribbean.* Mona, Jamaica: Consortium Graduate School of Social Sciences, University of the West Indies.

Koven, Seth, and Sonya Michel. 1993. Introduction: 'Mother worlds'. In *Mothers of a New World: Maternalist Politics and the Origins of Welfare State,* eds. Seth Koven, and Sonya Michel, 1-42. New York: Routledge.

Lange, Lynda. 1991. 'Rousseau and Modern Feminism'. In *Feminist Interpretations and Political Theory,* eds. Mary Lyndon Shanley and Carole Pateman, 95-111. Pennsylvania: Pennsylvania State University Press.

Lindsay, Keisha. 1997. Caribbean male: An endangered species? *Working Paper,* no. 1, ed. Patricia Mohammed, 1-20. Mona, Jamaica: Centre for Gender and Development Studies, University of the West Indies.

Lundestad, Geir.1986. *East, West, North, South: Major Developments in International Politics 1945-1986.* Oslo: Norwegian University Press.

Miller, Errol. 1991. *Men at Risk.* Kingston: Jamaica Publishing House.

———. 1994. *Marginalization of the Black Male: Insights from the Development of the Teaching Profession.* 2d ed. Kingston: Canoe Press, University of the West Indies.

Mohanty, Chandra. T. & A. Russo and L. Torres, eds. 1991. *Third World Women and The Politics of Feminism*. Bloomington & Indianapolis: Indiana University Press.

Momsen, Janet. 1993. *Women and Change in the Caribbean*. Kingston & Bloomington: Indiana University Press.

Mondesire, Alicia and Leith Dunn.1995. 'Toward Equity in Development. A Report on the Status of Women in Sixteen Caribbean Countries'. Caribbean Community (CARICOM) Secretariat Georgetown, Guyana.

Nash, June and MP Fernandez-Kelly. eds. 1983. *Women, men and the International Division of Labour*. Albany: State University of New York Press.

Nye, Andrea. 2000. 'Its Not Philosophy'. In *Decentering the Center: Philosophy for a Multicultural, Postcolonial, and Feminist World*, eds. Uma Narayan and Sandra Harding, 101-109. Bloomington: Indiana University Press.

Parpart, Jane L. and Marianne Marchand. 1995. 'Exploding the Canon: An Introduction/Conclusion'. In *Feminism, Postmodernism, Development*, eds. Marianne H. Marchand and Jane L. Parpart, 1-22. London and New York: Routledge.

Parpart, Jane L., M. Patricia Connelly and V. Eudine Barriteau. 2000. *Theoretical Perspectives on Gender and Development*. Ottawa: International Development Research Centre.

Reddock, Rhoda. 1994. *Women, Labour & Politics in Trinidad & Tobago: A History*. London: Zed Books.

Robinson, Tracy. 2003. 'Beyond the Bill of Rights: Sexing the Citizen'. In *Confronting Power, Theorizing Gender: Interdisciplinary Perspectives in the Caribbean*, ed. V. Eudine Barriteau, Mona: UWI Press. In press.

_____. 2000. 'Fictions of Citizenship, Bodies without Sex: The Production and Effacement of Gender in Law'. *Small Axe* 7: 1-27.

Safa, Helen. 1995. *The Myth of the Male Bread Winner: Women and Industrialization in the Caribbean*. Boulder: West view Press.

Sen, G. and C. Grown. 1987. *Development Crises and Alternative Visions: Third World Women's Perspectives*. New York: Monthly Review Press.

Senior, Olive. 1991. *Working Miracles: Women's Lives in the English-Speaking Caribbean*. Bridgetown: Institute of Social and Economic Research, University of the West Indies.

Siim, Birte. 1988. 'Towards a Feminist Rethinking of The Welfare State'. In *The Political Interest of Gender*, eds. Kathleen B. Jones & Anna G. Jonasdottir, 160-186. London: Sage Publications Ltd.

Steady, Filomina Chioma, ed. 1981. *The Black Woman Cross-Culturally*. Cambridge, MA: Schenkman Publishing.

Shepherd, Verene, B. Brereton, and B. Bailey, eds. 1995. *Engendering History: Caribbean Women in Historical Perspective*. Kingston & London: Ian Randle & James Curry Publishers.

Smith, M.G. 1962. *Kinship and Community in Carriacou*. New Haven: Yale University Press.

_____. 1953. 'Some Aspects of Social Structure in the British Caribbean'. *Social and Economic Studies* 1, no. 4.

Social and Economic Studies 35, no. 2. 1986a. Kingston, Jamaica: Institute of Social and Economic Research, University of the West Indies. Special issue on the Women in the Caribbean Project.

Social and Economic Studies 35, no. 3. 1986b. Kingston, Jamaica: Institute of Social and Economic Research, University of the West Indies. Special issue on the Women in the Caribbean Project.

Sparr, Pamela. 1994. *Mortgaging Women's Lives: Feminist Critiques of Structural Adjustment*. London: Zed Books Ltd.

Sterling, Richard W. and William C. Scott. 1985. *Plato The Republic: A New Translation*. New York: W. W. Norton and Company.

Teigen, Mari. 2002. 'The Universe of Gender Quotas'. *NIKK Magasin*, no. 3: 4-8.

Thanks to anti-money laundering system, Grenada in the clear. 2003. *The Barbados Advocate*, February 17th: 10.

Tinker, Irene, ed. 1990. *Persistent Inequalities: Women and World Development*. New York: Oxford University Press.

Tinker, Irene and Michelle Bo Bramsen, eds. 1976. *Women and World Development*. Washington: Overseas Development Council.

United Nations Development Program. 2002. *Human Development Report 2002*. New York: Oxford University Press.

———. 2001. *Human Development Report 2001*. New York: Oxford University Press.

———. 2000. *Human Development Report 2000*. New York: Oxford University Press.

———. 1999. *Human Development Report 1999*. New York: Oxford University Press.

———. 1998. *Human Development Report 1998*. New York: Oxford University Press.

———. 1997. *Human Development Report 1997*. New York: Oxford University Press.

———. 1996. *Human Development Report 1996*. New York: Oxford University Press.

———. 1995. *Human Development Report 1995*. New York: Oxford University Press.

21 | FAY DURRANT

Gender Equity, Information and Communications Technologies and Connectivity

Moving towards the Information Society

As the Caribbean moves towards the information society we are increasingly impelled to define and adopt a variety of new means of identifying, organising, disseminating and using information. Advances in the uses of information and communications technologies (ICTs) are having economic, social, and political impacts on our society (Mark et al), and there are implications for all groups to ensure that these impacts make positive contributions to the move towards gender equity. It is not yet possible to precisely predict the future social and economic implications of the adoption and proliferation of new information and communication technologies, and there is undoubtedly the need to study and assess the extent of these impacts on the social, economic and political dimensions of our society. In the light of advances towards the information society there are indications that information and communications technologies are facilitating the development of new paradigms including the achievement of gender equity (Ngenge), based on new opportunities for connectivity and interaction.

This paper reviews briefly the potential contribution of information and communication technologies to the development of the information society; the scope and expansion of these technologies; the state of research and analysis in some of the major areas – education, household and small business applications, employment and governance; and the facilities which exist for providing access to the general public. As new opportunities and directions emerge, there is a need to pay special attention to the impact of the current process of information and communication technological change on gender equity. Some changes will be required to strengthen the potential for social development in a gender equitable manner. It is argued that such an approach should avoid some of the weaknesses that have been noticed in the traditional media with respect to gender equity.

There is already some evidence that information and communication technologies have been transforming our economies and the lives of citizens. The outstanding example is the Internet which, as the 'network of networks', now provides access to global inter-connectivity and enables people to access information and communicate with people of like interests across great distances. Local examples of electronic networking based on the Internet include the Jamaican and Guyanese Sustainable Development Networks which have supported the development of several telecentres and enable small enterprises to display their offerings on the Internet and to promote their businesses locally and globally.

Appropriate implementation of ICTs can greatly improve communication and exchange of information via social and economic networks which, in turn, provide the basis for major advances in development. ICTs also have the potential to offer many opportunities to reduce or eliminate the differences among the population, and to enable the achievement of sustainable development.

The Digital Opportunity Task Force in its Genoa Plan of Action of 2001, stressed the importance of ensuring that access to the Internet and related networks will facilitate the dissemination of local knowledge, the development of new production and marketing processes and the implementation of electronic-based public information services, as well as increased access to basic social goods and services. When properly applied, ICTs can make an important contribution to sustainable development. Conversely, if misapplied, they can result in the marginalisation of sectors of the society according to class, gender, or geographical location.

Towards Gender Equity

The achievement of advances towards gender equity, in this context, requires identification of the issues and features which differentiate the ways in which men and women are trained to use ICTs and the ways in which they adapt to the processes involved. Wawa A. Ngenge, National Coordinator of the Cameroon Sustainable Development Network Programme, advocates that 'gender equity is the promotion of a set of actions, attitudes, and assumptions that affects opportunities and creates expectations about individuals, regardless of gender, and that is transmitted through, or affects access to, the new ICTs'. (1999, p. 7) In the present context, both genders must therefore have equal opportunities in accessing, using, developing, achieving and learning through the use of ICTs. Men and women should therefore be able to maximise access to information via ICTs and to expect equitable treatment in information that is transmitted through ICTs. Education and training in the use of ICTs at primary, secondary and tertiary levels can also be expected to remove some of the barriers and to open opportunities for learning and for additional scope in jobs and careers.

The Scope of Information and Communications Technologies

The term 'information and communications technologies' reflects an extension of information technology, the convergence of computing and communications technologies, and the dominant role being played by communications technologies.

ICTs are embedded in networks and services that affect the local and global accumulation and flows of public and private knowledge. In general terms, ICTs cover Internet service provision, telecommunications equipment and services, information technology equipment and services, media and broadcasting, libraries and documentation services, commercial information providers, network-based information services, and other related information and communication activities. Of particular note in these developments is the rapid growth of wireless components, the relative strength of the various technologies, telephones – fixed and mobile – radio, local and cable television, pagers, the Internet, and synchronous and or asynchronous communications channels and work spaces which increasingly facilitate interaction.

Research and Analysis

While research on gender issues has developed a well established research trajectory, the issue of gender with reference to information and communications technologies is relatively new, and researchers are in the process of developing an analytical framework. Regional and global studies of gender and ICTs have recognised the importance of reducing gender imbalances in access to and use of information and communications technologies in a development context.

Looking at the situation in developing countries, a recent study (2001) by Nancy Hafkin and Nancy Taggart seeks to identify means of helping women and men to overcome the digital divide. This study attempts to understand the complex relationship between gender, information and communications technologies and development, to accelerate development and increase gender equity. Hafkin and Taggart advocate that 'the many opportunities offered by information and communications technologies need to be seized deliberately because the cost of not doing so is too high'. They recommend that these technologies can certainly contribute to women's empowerment and aid in the search for solutions to women's problems.

The trends identified in this study show that opportunities in traditional manufacturing are being eliminated and that women are being required to make the transition to jobs which require greater capability for working with information and communications technologies. Jobs such as data entry at the low end of the scale and functions such as medical transcription are now being carried out in the Caribbean, but these are becoming expendable as the scanning and communications technologies advance and become increasingly more available at lower costs.

Hafkin and Taggart have identified obstacles to access as: lack of literacy, education and training, language capabilities, time, the high cost of access, remote geographical locations, social and cultural norms, and the lack of computer and information management skills.

As there is a gender imbalance in the number of women in some of the key areas of computer engineering, systems design and analysis, education for the information society was also seen as being required in a range of roles including: users, designers and managers of systems, management of information and of Internet content.

Poor and marginalised men and women often fail to gain access to infrastructure for connectivity. Competition has tended to result in improved and expanded communications facilities in commercially viable areas, but in many instances rural dwellers, and particularly the rural poor, may find that there are technical obstacles to gaining access to the national grid.

In this study, Hafkin and Taggart proposed engendered approaches to policies for ICT development, the analysis of disaggregated information as the basis for decision-making, and analysis of gender-specific impacts of policies.

The United Nations International Research and Training Institute for the Advancement of Women (INSTRAW, 2003) in a collaborative research project on Gender and ICTs, also undertook a global analysis of the factors which lead to access or obstacles to ICTs, to determine how women and men operate in this environment, to promote adequate policies and regulation, and to identify ways in which ICTs may be used to empower women.

The background papers which compose this research project cover gender neutrality, woman-centred design of technological environments, engendering management, empowering women for public policy making, and the use of ICTs to bridge the digital gender gap. These papers provided the basis for discussion in four email-based online seminars with 325 participants from more than 50 countries.

In recognition of the capacity of ICTs to achieve advances towards the information society, the seminar concluded that 'health, water, food, education, and ICTs are not in opposition to each other, rather that ICTs can be a tool to provide information on health and food as well as serving as a carrier for education for women and girls'.

To achieve the longer-term objectives of the INSTRAW research study, the seminar recommended several areas of research and action. It concluded that achievement of gender equity will be supported by the development of sex-disaggregated data on the status of the gender digital divide, and research into the use and benefits of ICTs from a gender perspective. Such information should therefore be linked to development activities, and provide the basis for increased involvement in the ICT policy making process and the development of advocacy strategies to address the needs of women in access to and use of ICTs.

The European Union's programme on Information Society Technologies has supported a number of reviews of the research on gender and ICTs. The studies of Ireland, Italy and the United Kingdom have been treated here as being representative of the package of national literature reviews.

The study on the production and consumption of ICTs in Ireland (MacKeogh et al.) shows that, while gender differences in consumption of ICTs are levelling off in younger age groups, older women are considered 'late adopters'; age and socioeconomic status have also compounded educational disadvantages in the ICT sector.

The literature review of levels of use, expertise and access to ICTs in Italy (Fortunait and Marganelli) examines differences between men and women. It was found that European women have made a choice by entering the information society more through mobile phones than through computers and the Internet.

The study on the United Kingdom (Faulkner) which covers information technology, electronics and communication, seeks to identify reasons for gender exclusion and the possible gender inclusion strategies. It found that, while similar proportions of girls and boys study subjects related to information technology, fewer girls actually qualify. While the women in these jobs are found to be better educated than the men, their status and level of pay was found to be lower than that of the men.

In relation to Internet use, Graeme Wearden, in reporting on the Nielsen Net Ratings Survey of May 2003 indicates that the gender gap still exists in Europe in relation to the use of the Internet. The survey found that of the ten sites most used by women five were shopping sites, one gaming, one travel, one finance, one education and one was a portal. This distribution may be a signal of the direction which the Internet may take in the Caribbean, and where the emphasis on shopping and gaming may increase disproportionately as compared to accessing information for development activities.

In an activity supported by the Commonwealth of Learning, researchers sought to identify barriers encountered by women in the use of ICTs for open and distance learning in the Caribbean. A 1999 survey (Fehr and Leach) of use and potential use of ICTs, identifies gender differentials of access to technologies, costs of access, the need of technical training and the development of infrastructure.

Research on gender and ICTs in the Caribbean has used surveys of the literature and extracts from global surveys to identify gender issues and barriers to women's participation in the information society.

Further examination of this issue in relation to the Caribbean, requires exploration of the barriers and potential barriers identified in earlier research, and some of the applications which now exist. Connectivity depends initially on access to ICTs, and the availability of the hardware and software. Access to ICTs would therefore include access to computers, application software, modems, Internet connections and peripherals. Access may assume that each person would purchase his or her own computer, software and peripherals and will negotiate access via an Internet Service Provider. Access may be from home or the workplace, home office, school or college, public library or telecentre. An assessment of access to ICTs should therefore include connectivity via any of these facilities. Access in much of the research has been based on consumption of computers, but it should be recognised as a more complex variable based on the variety of possible access points mentioned above.

There is of course a logical connection between access and cost of hardware and software. The costs of access will therefore range from the most costly personal computer with related peripherals and a subscription to an Internet Service Provider, costing between US$1,500 and US$2,500, to pay on demand usage of public facilities with hourly rates of US$2-3 per hour. Given that per capita incomes are in the range of US$2,786 in Jamaica, US$9,653 in Barbados and US$6,921 in Trinidad and Tobago, it would seem that personal computer ownership would be outside the scope of the majority of the population in the CARICOM region.

Development of access points in the workplace, home office, school, college, pubic library or telecentre now offer new opportunities for individuals and groups without personal facilities.

As ICTs are relatively new in education and training, there is need to consider not only training in the access to these technologies but preparation for different roles including the ability to use, create, design and manage ICTs. The introduction of Information Technology and Computer Science as subjects of the Caribbean Examinations Council (CXC) is an important step in providing certification and encouraging the development of capabilities of users of ICTs. Assessment of the uptake of this subject by boys and girls and the relationship to the working environment will depend on the analysis of data on performance, disaggregated by gender.

The ability to function as systems administrators, database managers and webmasters must be developed. Such training is provided in universities and colleges in the Caribbean and in the specialised training institutions which are being developed throughout the region. It has not yet been possible to obtain data on the gender balance in these roles in the Caribbean. In assessing the situation, it is worthwhile considering the findings of the study by Wendy Faulkner (2000) on the United Kingdom. There, training alone was found to not be enough to achieve the advancement of women in these areas. It was found that educational qualifications did not ensure the advancement of women, rather, in some cases, women with higher qualifications than men were found to be working at lower levels than their qualifications would suggest.

Much of the effort to date has been aimed at training women to use ICTs for social and economic empowerment, but the expansion of the roles to development of systems and creation of information adds a new dimension which needs to be further explored and studied.

Development of infrastructure is closely related to policy formulation. The participation of women in policies to guide the development of infrastructure is still an area which has not yet had adequate attention. In preparation for the World Summit on the Information Society, there has been some recognition that the Action Plan resulting from the summit should include measures to reduce the disparity in access to and use of information and communications technologies by women and men.

In a study done in 2002 for UNDP, Gillian Marcelle seeks to determine ways of exploiting ICTs as tools for the advancement of women and for gender equity. The study found that, while there is rapid diffusion of ICTs, uptake is influenced by elements of gender bias. Marcelle contends that ICTs can provide affordable communication and serve as tools for organising the global women's movement, collection and dissemination of gender-related information, monitoring and protection of women's rights and the integration of women producers within global production systems

Local Applications

An important issue in the development of policies and strategies to reduce the digital gender gap, is understanding not only the quantity but also the quality of participation by men and women in the use of ICTs.

In the Caribbean we have seen the introduction of telecentres which enable communities to achieve connectivity. These telecentres are in libraries, in community centres, NGOs, post offices and educational institutions. The Sustainable Development Network originally supported by the United Nations Development Programme (UNDP), national governments and other agencies, has telecentres in Haiti, Jamaica, and Guyana. Groups such as ISIS in St Lucia operate similar services. The public libraries in the Caribbean have also begun to offer public access to the Internet. The Jamaica Library Service, the National Library of Jamaica and the National Library of Trinidad and Tobago, for example, offer public Internet access.

As the data systematically collected are quantitatively oriented, there is not yet a comprehensive picture of the gender balance of the user groups who come to these telecentres, and how they use or obtain the information required for the sustainable development of their economic and social initiatives.

Eliminating Existing Barriers

Elimination of the existing barriers to the achievement of gender equity in the exploitation of ICTs for development requires the assurance that the information content transmitted is relevant to the objectives of achieving gender equity, and to the improvement of women's livelihood. The scope of this content would be based on incorporation of evaluated women's knowledge, wisdom and experience, and the use of participatory methods to design and develop the content and learning systems in order to enhance the lives of women. Use of traditional communications methods and local language content may also be expected to aid in overcoming literacy barriers through the appropriate design of ICTs and gender-appropriate learning strategies and instructional designs.

Incorporating the use of ICTs into the activities of women's livelihood will thus require the participation of such stakeholders as public librarians, healthcare workers, disaster prevention workers, community groups and small business associations. In cooperative initiatives such as the example of SisterNet studied by Ann Bishop et al, public librarians, the future clients, members of SisterNet and the healthcare providers collaborated in the design and development of a web-based information system on healthcare (Bishop et al. 2001).

With over 17,573 Internet hosts in the Caribbean (ITU, 2001), and the increasing commercialisation of the Internet, it can be expected that there will be an increase in the development of shopping sites and the targeting of women as consumers. While we do not yet have data on the use of the Internet by women in the Caribbean, we certainly hope that the attributes of this 'network of networks' will also facilitate access to applications and services, email, e-commerce and e-government and other features which may be expected to contribute to sustainable development.

Conclusion

The research and study done so far on the issue indicate that ICTs are tools which can advance the achievement of a gender balance. They can facilitate the development of social and economic networks and enable increased productivity. There is, however, the need for more research to determine why high diffusion is not matched by high uptake, and to develop greater understanding of the opportunities presented by ICTs and the ways in which they can contribute to gender equity.

References

Association for Progressive Communication. 2003. Women's Networking Support Programmes. *Gender Evaluation Methodology for Internet and ICTs* http://www.apcwomen.org/gem/all_about/index.htm_ April 2003 (accessed July 20, 2003).

Bishop, A.P., I. Bazzell, B. Mehra and C. Smith. 2001. 'Afya: Social and Digital Technologies that Reach across the Digital Divide'. *First Monday*, volume 6, number 4 (April), at http://firstmonday.org/issues/issue6_4/bishop/index.html (accessed July 20, 2003).

——————. 2000. 'Socially Grounded User Studies in Public Library Development'. *First Monday*, volume 5, number 6 (June) at http://firstmonday.org/issues/issue5_6/bishop/ (accessed July 20, 2003).

Checklist for Addressing Gender-related Barriers to ICTs Extract from *Gender Issues and Barriers to Information and Communications Technologies*. Summary Meeting Report, Ottawa, June 24-26, 2002.

Digital Opportunity Task Force. *Digital Opportunities for All: Meeting the Challenge Report of the Digital Opportunity Task Force (DOT Force) including a proposal for a Genoa Plan of Action*. 2001. http://www.dotforce.org/reports/DOT_Force_Report_V_5.0h.html (accessed July 20, 2003)

Durrant, Fay. 2002. *Community Telecentres – Focus on the Caribbean. Project for establishment of two multipurpose community telecentres in Jamaica*. Final report. February. (UNESCO Contract No.891.046.1) Unpublished.

Faulkner, Wendy. *Women, gender and ICT: Evidence and reflections from the UK*. IST-2000-26329 SIGIS. http://www.rcss.ed.ac.uk/sigis/public/D02/D02_part3.pdf. (accessed July 20, 2003).

Fortunati, Leopoldina and Annamaria Marganelli. *A Review of the Literature on Gender and ICTs in Italy*. IST-2000-26329 SIGIS. http://www.rcss.ed.ac.uk/sigis/public/D02/D02_part6.pdf. (accessed July 20, 2003).

Gender Issues and Barriers to Information and Communications Technologies : summary meeting report. 2002. IDRC, COL, New Zealand Agency for International Development. June. http://www.col.org/wdd/GenderIssuesICT_Report.pdf (accessed August 20, 2003).

Hafkin, Nancy and Helen Odame Hambly. *Gender, ICTs and Agriculture : a situation analysis for the 5th Consultative Expert Meeting of CTA's Observatory Meeting on ICTs and Agriculture in the Information Society*. http://www.agricta.org/observatory2002/background_paper.pdf (accessed July 20, 2003).

Hafkin, Nancy and Nancy Taggart. *Gender, Information Technologies and Developing Countries: an Analytical Study*. Academy for Educational Development. http://www.usaid.gov/wid/pubs/hafph.pdf (accessed July 20, 2003).

Identifying Barriers Encountered by Women in the Use of ICTs for Open and Distance Learning in the Caribbean. 1999. Report prepared by Helena Fehr and Jenny Leach, Commonwealth of Learning, Bridgetown, Barbados. http://www.col.org/wdd/BarriersICT_Caribbean_report.pdf (accessed July 20, 2003).

International Labour Organization. 2001. *World Employment Report 2000-1: Life at work in the Information Economy.* Geneva.

International Telecommunications Union. 2000. Telecommunication Development Bureau. Task Force on Gender Issues: *A catalyst for womens' advancement in Information and Communications Technologies.* 3rd Meeting of the Task Force on Gender Issues. Report of Working Group 6. Geneva. TFGI 3/9 – E. http://www.itu.int/ITU-D/gender/pdf/3rdMeeting/TFGI-3-9.pdf (accessed July 20, 2003).

International Telecommunications Union. 2003. Telecommunication Development Bureau. Work Group on Gender Issues: 2nd Meeting of the Working Group on Gender Issues, *WSIS Draft Action Plan and Section II: based on discussions with the Working Group of Sub-Committee 2.* Proposed amendments from WSIS Gender Caucus and UNIANWGE (WSIS/PC/DT-3 revised). 7-9 July. http://www.itu.int/ITU-D/gender/pdf/2ndMeeting/ (accessed July 20, 2003).

Leon, Osvaldo, Sally Burch and Eduardo Tamayo. 2001. *Social Movements on the Net.* Agencia Latinoamericana de Informacion, Quito.

MacKeogh, Carol and Pascal Preston. *Literature Review and Statistical Data relating to Gender in the Production and Consumption of ICT in Ireland.* IST-2000-26329 SIGIS. http://www.rcss.ed.ac.uk/sigis/public/D02/D02_part5.pdf (accessed August 20, 2003).

Marcelle, Gillian. *Transforming Information and Communications Technologies for Gender Equality.* Gender in Development Monograph Series #9. New York. UNDP. http://www.undp.org/gender/resources/mono9.pdf (accessed August 20, 2003).

Mark, June, Janet Cornebise and Ellen Wahl. 1997. *Community Technology Centers: Impact on Individual Participants and Their Communities.* Education Development Center, Inc. and National Science Foundation April.

Ngenge, Wawa. *A Gender Equity and New Information And Communication Technologies. (ICT)* http://www.sdnp.undp.org/sdncmr/fawecam/ngenge.htm (accessed July 20, 2003).

Pastore, Michael. *Internet Gender Gap Remains in Canada.* http://cyberatlas.internet.com/big_picture/geographics/article/0,,5911_737081,00.html (accessed August 20, 2003).

United Nations International Research and Training Institute for the Advancement of Women. (INSTRAW) *Overcoming the Gender Digital Divide: Understanding ICTs and their Potential for the Development of Women.* Synthesis Paper Virtual Seminar Series on Gender and ICTs. Prepared by Sophia Huyer and Tatjana Sikoska. April. http://www.un-instraw.org/docs/gender_and_ict/Synthesis_Paper.pdf (accessed July 20, 2003).

Wearden, Greame. 2003. *Europe's online gender divide, slow to close.* ZDNet UK, June 24, news.zdnet.co.uk/business/ (accessed August 20, 2003).

WSIS Gender Caucus World Summit on the Information Society. 2003. *National Gender Programmes: A Practical Guide.* http://www.genderwsis.org/sourcebook/sourcebook.pdf (accessed August 20, 2003).

22 | GRACE SIRJU-CHARRAN

Shifting the Paradigm, Erecting and Re-Erecting Boundaries
Case Studies from the Scientific World

Abstract

In spite of the numerous critiques of modern Western science by philosophers and feminists, including feminist scientists, the norms and culture of Science remain unchanged and scientific knowledge, particularly in the field of Biology, has been increasing by leaps and bounds in a linear and reductionist manner, so that at the present time the understanding of all life on this planet has been reduced to a small segment of the DNA molecule – the gene. The majority of questions currently asked in Biology are centred on the gene and it seems that the paradigm 'our biology is our destiny' has begun to take centre stage once more as the major explanation for the way in which life on this planet is organised. This reductionist approach to both the creation of scientific knowledge and the understanding of complex problems has its genesis in the seventeenth century with Bacon and Descartes and now appears to be approaching its limit. Can there be a smaller unit of analysis than the gene for understanding the nature of living organisms? An analysis of the new technologies of genetic engineering and the cloning of human cells suggests that in order to halt our journey into another 'brave new world' we need to adopt a holistic approach and begin to understand life as a complex interaction between molecules and organisms, including humans.

A Personal Journey or 'The Personal is Political'

> ...focusing on groups or species, for instance, may blind us to the richness of the individual experiences (Lynda Birke 1994)

The earliest memory I have of my childhood is when I was about two years old, standing in a garden watching baby goats eating grass and innocently enquiring of my elder siblings 'why are the goats eating grass?', expressing great concern in my intonation, and adding by way of justification for posing the question, '… because the goats will die.' What surprised me then was the reaction of my audience. They laughed hilariously, did not respond to my question and furthermore felt that it was noteworthy enough to report to my mother. What surprises me now is that, in spite of the remarkable progress made through research in the biological sciences, we still know so little about the behaviour of animals (including humans). From a Darwinian perspective, the possible explanation for goats eating grass might be that they had acquired certain anatomical and physiological adaptive characteristics which enabled them to get their nourishment from that source. The social scientist's explanation might be that baby goats learnt (were socialised) to eat grass from observing that their parents ate grass; and from a gender perspective, it could be argued that baby goats learnt to eat certain species of grass, and not others, from their mothers.

In spite of the claims of science that its superior methodology gives to it the reputation of being able to provide 'one true story', there are many instances when only a partial understanding of the phenomenon is possible. However, if a multi-disciplinary approach were adopted, such that all the explanations were considered together, then it might be possible to get somewhat closer to the truth.

With the discovery of DNA in the early 1950s and the development of powerful molecular tools in the 1970s which facilitated the mapping of genes at the turn of this century, for several organisms (including humans), claims are now being made that biology holds the potential to settle once and for all the nature/nurture debate. However, unless a less reductionist approach is adopted in framing the questions and explaining the data, the debate will continue.

An Overview of the Critiques of Science

> *Man's* place in the *physical* universe is to be its *master* ... to be its *king* through the *power he* alone possesses ... (Willard Libby, Nobel Laureate [my emphasis])

In spite of the laudable goals of science to discover new knowledge and new ways to improve the quality of human lives, post-Kuhnian, post-colonialist and feminist critiques of science have challenged its claims of being objective, neutral, value-free and apolitical in the methods used for attaining such knowledge. These critics have provided numerous examples to demonstrate that science was value-laden not only in the formulating of research questions, but also in the metaphors and models it uses and in the narratives it constructs. Sandra Harding (1998) posited that the scientific enterprise in seventeenth century Europe was an integral part of and facilitated colonial expansion and development. In the same publication she cited two examples which demonstrated that politics and culture greatly influenced the conduct of science. The first pointed out that the approach taken to conduct research on cancer, which focused on genes and lifestyle and ignored the environment, was political since a focus on the influence of the environment on cancer would have had implications for governments, multi-national corporations and the military. The second example cited was the study done by Sharon Traweek (1988) which demonstrated that the different cultural models of organising work in America and Japan influenced the type of research conducted by high-energy physicists in these countries. More important than the influence of culture and politics on the creation of scientific knowledge, however, is its epistemological framework of 'othering', that is, the setting up of binaries or dichotomies in which one of the pair is generally more highly valued than the other, thus leading to a hierarchy, and its reductionism (the tendency to reduce phenomenon to its smallest part, then to translate the information obtained to the whole).

These characteristics of dichotomising and reductionism have facilitated the erecting, shifting and re-erecting of boundaries.

Circumscribing Boundaries: 'Othering'

> I want to write Natural History to see if some other stories are possible; ones not premised on the divide between Nature and Culture... (Donna Haraway 1995)

My experience in 'othering' had begun at the tender age of two, I was discovering that in the early stages of life baby goats and baby humans were alike in that they both got nourishment from their mothers' milk; however, at a later stage in life, differences could be observed: on being weaned, goats ate grass while humans had apple sauce and mashed potatoes, I had begun to recognise differences and to begin to erect boundaries, to put into one category all those animals that ate grass and in the other, humans.

The works of Merchant (1980), Jordanova (1989) and Schiebinger (1993), cited by Nina Lykke (1996), critiqued the dualistic way of thinking which characterises modern western science and which results in categories of beings described as 'other than' and often seen as inferior to the 'knowing subject'. Nature, body, woman were objects of study by the 'knower', identified as white-skinned, bourgeois 'man of science'.

This creation of boundaries is one of the key processes used for interrogating nature. It is a fluid process which depends to a large extent on the researcher and the research questions being asked. When they do get constructed, they can be shifted or dismantled altogether depending on the goals set by the researcher.

Construction of boundaries results in the partitioning of knowledge about nature into discrete packets representing the disciplines such as physics, chemistry, biology and the sub-disciplines, physical, inorganic and organic chemistry; botany, zoology, biochemistry, cell biology, microbiology, genetics, and, more recently, the sub-sub-disciplines: molecular biology and molecular genetics.

While maintaining the boundaries of these disciplines is important for prescribing the guidelines of what questions can be asked and what methods can be used, thus regulating who can access the profession, at the same time it inhibits multi- and inter-disciplinary approaches. Nevertheless, even the most hard core scientist will admit that such uni-disciplinary studies are meaningless in the newer areas of environmental and natural resource management and in the older area of ecology (re-packaged as environmental biology). Feminist methods and participatory research methods have now provided us with some tools to make that quantum leap from reductionist, uni-disciplinary approaches to a more holistic, multi-disciplinary approach. A recent study on the Nariva Swamp in Trinidad, in which I had participated, involved also the participation of an agriculturalist, zoologist, botanist, microbiologist, economist, and gender specialist. The data gathered differed markedly from that obtained in an earlier study carried out by a team of biologists even though both groups had the same goal of arriving at a management plan for the sustainable use of this fragile ecosystem. The biologists were concerned with documenting all the life forms present in that ecosystem with a view to identifying those that were endangered. The multi-disciplinary team, on the other hand, sought to find out whether men and women interacted differently with the natural resources and to incorporate these differences into any management plan to be developed.

Shifting Boundaries

> It is sometimes appropriate to talk about women as a group, sometimes not (Londa Schiebinger).

A key element of the scientific method is the tendency to generalise or universalise in order to arrive at laws that would allow us to predict. In order to do this, boundaries are created by grouping together objects based on a number of arbitrary similarities. However, these boundaries do not remain fixed: many universities have broken down the boundaries around zoology and botany and re-erected new ones to re-create biology. The new boundaries surrounding molecular biology are slowly being shifted to incorporate aspects of biochemistry, genetics, cell biology and microbiology.

Shifts can also take place within defined boundaries. Vandana Shiva, in the publication 'Biopolitics', edited by V. Shiva and I. Moser (1995), points out that when scientists apply for a patent for a transgenic plant, they claim that it is novel and not a product of nature, however, in counteracting the concerns raised by environmentalists about the potential ecological impact of lateral transfer of genes to wild species, the argument shifts to state that there is nothing new or unnatural about these genetically modified plants. Shiva argues that this inconsistent shifting demonstrates a subjective, opportunistic approach in a discipline which claims objectivity.

In the introduction to the book entitled *Between Monsters, Goddesses and Cyborgs...Feminist Confrontations with Science, Medicine and Cyberspace*, Nina Lykke advocates for a broadening of the space from which feminists can confront science and technology and suggests that it could be strategically placed in the unstable boundaries between the virtual/artefactual and nature. She uses the metaphor of the monster to represent the 'boundary phenomena in the interdisciplinary or hybrid grey zone between the cultural and natural sciences'. In this zone, the established borders between the sciences could be challenged.

Reductionism

> By reductionism we mean the belief that the world is made up of atomized fragments, which associate mechanistically to make larger systems;... (Vandana Shiva 1995).

When it was time to pursue a PhD, I chose to work on the tuberisation of sweet potato root instead of extracting and characterising the 'Viagra-type' compounds from the bark of the 'bois bandé tree offered to me by my chemistry professor. Little did I realise then that, had I opted to pursue the latter project, I would have had a better experience with the reductionist approach. We were trying to understand why some roots tuberised (grew in size and accumulated starch) while others remained fibrous, or 'frustrated' and proposed that the data obtained would increase the tuber yield in sweet potato. We studied a few enzymes, the key one being peroxidase. Not only was this a ubiquitous enzyme, catalysing a number of reactions in the cell, but also its proposed role in tuberisation was to influence the quantity of the growth hormone responsible for one of the components of the tuberisation process – cell expansion. The other components include cell division, a process controlled by a different plant hormone, transport of assimilates in the form of sucrose from the leaves to these tuberising roots, and entry of these assimilates into starch-storage cells in order to get converted into starch, a process requiring several enzymes.

It was not until the mid-1970s, deep into my PhD research project, that it suddenly dawned on me that the data I was gathering would not provide the answer to improving the yield for the farmers. I came to the stark realisation that the activities of an enzyme obtained by grinding the tissue to a liquid, centrifuging and purifying, then measured in a test tube, was so far removed from its natural location that it might be meaningless. And just as suddenly my interest and enthusiasm for the project waned. My disillusionment with the ability of the scientific method and its linear, hierarchical and reductionist approach to provide solutions to complex problems had begun with the realisation that very often the sum of the parts did not translate to the whole. Much later, when I had the opportunity to assess the impacts of the green revolution and to critique the more recent 'gene revolution' technologies of genetic engineering and cloning of human cells, I came to understand how difficult it is to predict the way research results will be used by society and how they may influence its evolution. Very often, the results of scientific research redound to the benefit of one sector of the society while at the same time disadvantaging another.

Fox-Keller (physicist), Ruth Hubbard and Anne Fausto-Sterling (biologists) have traced the reductionism of the study of living organisms to their genes to post-World War II when physicists fresh from the Manhattan project exported their paradigm that life is a simple mechanistic project whose mystery can be solved by reducing it to its smallest unit – the gene. It has been argued that it is this intrusion of physics into biology that has led to the term biotechnology and genetic engineering, and to the notion that life can be reduced to a molecule which can be manipulated.

The new techniques of molecular biology have reduced the study of life to the study of reproduction and gene control, reinforcing the notion once more that 'our biology is our destiny'. In this current period in the history of biology, nature has taken precedence over nurture as an explanation for human behaviours. The search is on for genes responsible for alcoholism, depression, violent tendencies, sexual orientation, cancers and obesity, among many others. Yet, on the other hand, the tools of molecular biology have the capacity to unify all experimental biology, a phenomenon that failed to materialise with several central technologies, for example, microscopy and cell culture. It is ironic that such extreme reductionism could result in transgressing the boundaries not only between the sub-disciplines of cell biology, genetics and biochemistry, but also the carefully delineated boundaries that define a species. With the use of these molecular tools to unravel the DNA of several unrelated species, data are being obtained which reveal that only a few genes which distinguish humans from not only primates, the species to which we show greatest resemblance in evolutionary terms, but also from the lowly worm (*c. elegans*) with which, it is presumed, we have very little in common. This suggests that there are many factors (of which genes are only one), which determine the characteristics of a species and indeed of an individual.

At the same time, embryologists are using this unifying molecular approach to grapple with the question of what controls the differential expression of genes in cells (which all contain the same DNA) to make them into liver cells or kidney cells or brain cells. Furthermore, the natural variation Darwin observed in several characteristics, for example, shape of beak in birds, the infinite variation in height, shape of nose, slant of eyes, markings on the thumb, texture of hair in humans – all of which contribute to our uniqueness as individuals – continues to elude our enlightenment. What seems clear is that the reductionist explanation, which attributes these characteristics solely to genetic make-up, is inadequate.

Nevertheless, it is the general feeling among scientists that molecular tools and greater understanding of the DNA molecule will provide the answers to facilitate the understanding and controlling of a number of illnesses including cancers. Bonnie Spanier (2001) points out that, while a number of non-genetic factors including environmental factors influence the disease, the focus is on trying to understand why some cells behave abnormally and to adopt an approach to devise a treatment which would act at this molecular level. Focusing on genes obscures all the complex cell-to-cell interactions; all the reactions taking place at the cell surface and the role played by receptor molecules, all of which may precede the involvement of genes.

In the epilogue entitled 'Beyond Reductionism' of Shiva and Moser's (1995) publication *Biopolitics*, Shiva argues that the 'dominant paradigm of biology characterised by genetic engineering is being pushed to new levels of reductionism, threatening to eliminate diversity and pluralism in...nature and culture' but 'at the same time, newly emerging approaches to biology focus on the complexity of life forms, replacing predictability with unpredictability and certainty with uncertainty in the engineering of life'. She sees the possibility of shaping biology by new movements that are 'ecological, feminist and culturally plural, that challenge biotechnology at epistemological, ethical, ecological and economical levels'.

Anthropomorphism – Crossing boundaries

> It is those beliefs about what animals can or cannot do that are marshalled in any argument about whether or not other species possess abilities akin to ours (Lynda Birke 1994).

Another feature of the scientific method is its use of models and analogies. In biology, it is common to transfer characteristics of human beings to other animals (anthropomorphism) or to explain observations made on other species using human values and behaviours (anthropocentrism). Experiments done on rats and gorillas for human applications belong to the former, while the earlier studies in primatology which interpreted the behaviours of male and female primates on the basis of gender stereotypes in human societies (Haraway 1991) belong to the latter.

Bats are mammals which, like humans, have a monthly oestrous cycle. Research on foetal implantation is being carried out on these animals in order to get information which can be used in understanding human pregnancies. Feminists have critiqued both the anthropomorphism and the destructive means used to get the information.

A female student involved in the killing of pregnant bats to get at their foetuses was severely traumatised. There is as yet no counselling programme in place to deal with this kind of trauma. The ethics of using animals for research is the subject of the book *The Taming of the Shrew* by Lynda Birke (1994).

In my childhood innocence, I had expected baby goats to behave exactly like human beings, that is, to eat potatoes and not grass. In my later years, I have learnt to recognise the similarities and appreciate the differences between dualistic divides, for example, human/other; man/woman. I have learnt to analyse critically the unequal emphases placed on the overt differences and similarities and to recognise that there may be covert ones. I have learnt how tempting it is to conflate experimental data; how easy it is to ignore the distance between data and hypothesis, and I have learnt to question the assumptions (hidden or stated), put forward to close that distance.

Interrogating Boundaries – Accommodating Other Stories

> ...in science, just as in art and in life, only that which is true to culture is true to nature (Ludwick Fleck 1935).

> ...a new, different Science ideology ... less objectifying, less dualistic, less deterministic, less repressive (Renee Heller 1996).

Londa Schiebinger (2001), in her analysis of the impact of gender studies of science on the practice and methods of science, calls for a 'sustainable science' which she describes as one which resembles other new directions in feminist science theory, such as Donna Haraway's 'situated knowledge', Sandra Harding's 'strong objectivity', Carolyn Merchant's 'partnership ethic' and I would add Evelyn Fox-Keller's 'atomic individualism' (Fox-Keller 1996). Schiebinger (2001) lists a number of gender analysis tools which could be used to critique Western science and this suggests that these may be refashioned and some discarded, depending on the analytical circumstances. These tools include, *inter alia,* gender analyses of priority settings for research; the populations chosen to be the objects of research; the scientific language, analogies and metaphors used; the criteria used for determining what needs explanation and what counts as evidence. In this chapter, while it is acknowledged that setting boundaries cannot be avoided, it suggests that boundaries are mobile and therefore need to be deconstructed allowing for the creation of new spaces including the space between boundaries (cf Donna Harraway's imagery of cyborgs, goddesses and monsters), which would allow interrogation using new methods and approaches, including multi- and inter-disciplinary approaches, asking different questions and accommodating 'other' stories.

'Pristine' science, while it can provide a useful dimension, cannot on its own, arrive at the 'truth' about nature. Knowledge obtained within the boundaries of the scientific method must be extrapolated beyond the walls, using all the tools available as well as new ones in explaining the evidence.

Adequate recognition must be given to what is popularly referred to as indigenous knowledge systems, to naturopaths, and to other 'knowers' including women.

Each research institution should establish a strong bio-ethics committee that would use tools of gender analysis to evaluate research proposals, having established defined criteria of acceptability of methods; predictability of the results; how the results will be used; whether the outcome would be an improvement on what exists; and the differential impact of the research results on all pockets of society.

References

Birke, Lynda. 1994. *Feminism, Animals and Science: The Taming of the Shrew*. Buckingham, Philadelphia: Open University Press.

Fox-Keller, Evelyn. 1996. Language and Ideology in Evolutionary Theory: Reading Cultural Norms into Natural Law. In *Feminism and Science*, eds. Evelyn Fox-Keller and Helen E. Longino. Oxford, New York: Oxford University Press.

Haraway, Donna. 1991. *Simians, Cyborgs and Women*. London: Free Association Books.

Harding, Sandra. 1998. *Is Science Multicultural? Postcolonialisms, Feminisms and Epistemologies*. Bloomington and Indianapolis: Indiana University Press.

Heller Reneé. 1996. 'The Tale of the Universe for Others'. In *Between Monsters, Goddesses and Cyborgs: Feminist Confrontations with Science, Medicine and Cyberspace*, eds. Nina Lykke and Rosi Bra dioti. London and New Jersey: Zed Books.

Jordanova, L. 1989. *Sexual Visions. Images of Gender in science and Medicine between the Eighteenth and Twentieth Centuries*. London and New York: Harvester Wheatsheaf.

Lykke, Nina and Rosi Bradiotti, eds. 1996. *Between Monsters, Goddesses and Cyborgs: Feminist Confrontations with Science, Medicine and Cyberspace*. London and New Jersey: Zed Books.

Merchant, Carolyn. 1980. *The Death of Nature, Women, Ecology and the Scientific Revolution*. Berkley: Harper and Row.

Schiebinger, Londa. 1993. *Nature's Body: Gender in the Making of Modern Science*, Boston: Beacon Press.

Schiebinger, Londa. 2001. 'Creating Sustainable Science'. In *The Gender and Science Reader*, eds. Lederman, Muriel and Ingrid Bartsch. London and New York: Routledge.

Shiva, Vandana and Ingunn Moser, eds. 1995. *Biopolitics: A Feminist and Ecological Reader on Biotechnology*. London and New Jersey: Zed Books.

Spanier, Bonnie. 2001. 'Foundations for a "New Biology" Proposed in Molecular Cell Biology'. In *The Gender and Science Reader*, eds. Muriel Lederman and Ingrid Bartsch, 272-288. London and New York: Routledge.

Traweek, Sharon. 1998. *Beamtimes and Lifetimes: The World of High Energy Physicists*. Cambridge, London: Harvard University Press.

23 | PATRICIA MOHAMMED

A Different Imagination
A Visual Essay[1]

Inventing Meaning

What is the value of revisiting images of the past? What questions do they answer, if any, and can they enrich our understanding of ourselves?

Curator and art historian, Petrine Archer-Straw, observes of the Caribbean region in *Photos and Phantasms* that 'our visual perception of the past remains vague'.[2] Literary stereotypes have not generally countered the colonial constructions of the native as the simple primitive who must be tamed by the European hand. Visual images have not always been kind to us and may be upsetting to revisit, as if cauterising old wounds. As Archer-Straw has commented, some may object to the questionable theories of race in Harry Johnston's photography, even while the same photographs capture scenes in everyday life in the Caribbean at the turn of the nineteenth century that would have been lost to us without his camera and eye.

One of the ways in which we can step outside the debate of whether these images are good or bad, worthwhile or valueless, whether they configure self-hate or reveal hidden truths, might be to consider that they can serve different masters and be applied to different purposes. European views of the Caribbean underwent reinterpretations from the fifteenth to the twentieth centuries, as still happens today. Let us turn the lens on Europe itself, differently. Mimi Scheller pointed out in her recently published book, *Consuming the Caribbean*, that the European representations of the Caribbean served a far more valuable purpose for the old world, even while taxonomies were being created of the new.

First the discovery of 'novel, curious and disturbing information about the New World'[3] forced European intellectuals to re-scale the world itself, and enabled new material exchanges, if largely exploitative relations, between distant places and people. Scheller's interpretation reinforces that made by J.H. Elliot in his thought-provoking book *The Old World and the New 1492-1650*. Elliot also argued that in traditional Europe, assumptions about the nature of man, geography, theology and history were profoundly challenged by this remarkable encounter with new lands and peoples.[4]

Second, the 'discovery' of a part of the world, the existence of which they had not known before, 'contributed to an epistemic shift in European visual representations of the natural world'.[5] Natural images such as plants and animals had served an emblematic or epigrammatic function, webbed into allegorical meanings, an atavistic strain inhibiting further growth of knowledge and ideas. The only way we can understand, in retrospect, the enormous mental realignments that human society would undergo from the late fifteenth century is to imagine that such a shift can only possibly take place now if we were to discover new life forms on another planet, thus compelling a complete reassessment of ourselves and our understanding of human existence. It is good to remember that it was the New World that gave meaning to the old, that an unacknowledged symbiosis between old and new began, and that along with this came a change in perception of self and other. It is time to make a different sense of the meanings that this visual legacy holds for us, by interpreting our own genealogies through these images and subverting those thrust glibly on us. This essay visualises patterns in this shift.

The Sublime, the Scenic and Outlines In-between

At the time of the Renaissance, when it was important for Italy to recapture the former glory of Rome, the classical myths became popular among the educated. Sandro Botticelli's *The Birth of Venus* was painted for the villa of Lorenzo de Pierfrancesco de Medici in Castello, a member of the educated classes, and of the rich and powerful Medici family. The story of the birth of Venus rising from the sea was a classical symbol of the way in which the divine message of beauty came into the world. Botticelli's Venus is depicted as emerging from the sea on a shell driven by the wind gods on the left, a shower of roses blowing around her in the winds which drive the shell to the shore, where she is received by a character said to be one of the Horae shown on the right of the painting. The horae or hours were Greek goddesses of the seasons, this one possibly the nymph of spring as she wears around her neck a garland of myrtle, appropriate to birth, and a sash of pink roses. The wooded shore on the left is verdant, heralding the spring and rebirth of Italian glory.

Sandro Botticelli, *The Birth of Venus*, c 1485 - 86

Germán Arciniegas in *Caribbean: Sea of the New World* makes an insightful connection between the Italian High Renaissance and the encounter with the Caribbean. He suggests that Botticelli's *Birth of Venus* represented not just the return of the Greek Venus, or glory to the coasts of Italy, but coincides with the discovery of America or, as he phrases this, 'to be more exact, of the Caribbean sea....[I]n the very year of the death of Lorenzo the Magnificent, 1492, Columbus reached Guanahané. What did the men see from the bridges of the three caravels? Copper-coloured Indian girls peering fearfully out through the tangled jungle. The Caribbean Venus walked naked, as the gods had sent her into the world'. A depiction of this latter event, illustrated here, and produced both after the event and possibly after the invention of photography, largely dispenses with allegory. Nonetheless, the stylised flora, the naked natives against the variously clothed visitors, the cross borne by the priestly figure, the flag, a sword touching the earth, and the prostrations of the sailors are themselves iconic of conquest and conversion. Columbus is the central figure kneeling on the ground. There is already a conflation of land and church and an assumption of rightful power at the first port of entry.

Interpretation of The Landing of Columbus on the Island of Guanahane, October 12, 1492
Painting by Dioscore Puebla. Source: Courtesy, Ramsay Antiques, Nassau

Unlike Botticelli's allegorical Venus, this painting represents the reporting of an event, no doubt gleaned from travellers' tales, and drawing on the countless other artistic interpretations which have imagined this moment. While the event occurred in history, it is the imagination of the painter and sketchers of the time which filtered this through to court and wider society. This one is not a very sophisticated or particularly good painting, although executed long after the art of perspective itself was established. The Renaissance concept of perspective absorbed not only the scholars but the artists. The painting titled *The Hunt in the Forest* by Florentine artist Paolo Uccello (1397-1475) would influence the idea of depth and three-dimensional perception from then on, in the art form of painting, with the later parallel discovery of oil allowing this to be further realised on a flat surface by the next century. Yet, in this painting there is little recession and depth. The figures lie on a flat plain, placed across from right to left. What is most interesting here, however, is that the painter views the scene from the land, not the sea. It is ironically, on the one hand and in one sense, an aboriginal point of view.[6] But like the family photographer, he is still outside of the scene, positioning his lens in the foreground and oblivious to the relations between and among the sitters.

If the narrative of discovery was the dominant discourse of the fifteenth to the seventeenth centuries, from the eighteenth to mid-nineteenth centuries there was an 'exponential growth of the system of slavery in which Europeans consumed enslaved human bodies in the coerced production of both plantation commodities (for overseas consumption) and domestic and sexual services (for local consumption)…'.[7] It is no coincidence that an early iconic reference to Botticelli's Venus is transferred to the slave trade and its carriage by the eighteenth century in Thomas Stothard's *The Voyage of the Sable Venus from Angola to the West Indies* (1793). Some of the symbols from Botticelli's painting are repeated here, particularly that of the shell as vessel. By 1793, the source of winds and currents is more comprehended by geographers of the time. The iconography of the cartographer, the latter having become a key player in navigation and conquest, is evident in the cherubs or putti-like figures who represent the wind gods and also who appear protective of the sable Venus on her journey. A similar stance is also evident in the tritons in the lower right and left who guide the vessel. There is an attempt here to transform the image of the African slave trade from terror and abject abuse to a harmless and leisurely voyage across the Atlantic.

In *Blind Memory*, a more recent reading of this image, Marcus Wood notes:

> Here, the black slave woman's experience of the middle passage is presented as a version of the Birth of Venus. The rape of slave women is reconstructed in terms of a triumph of the slave Venus over the slave owners and traders who are ironically portrayed as her powerless victims … the slave ship is transformed into a beautiful scallop shell pulled by frolicking dolphins.the antithesis in the sea world to the flesh eating sharks who followed the ships.[8]

Barbara Bush points out that, in eighteenth- and nineteenth-century Europe, images of black women were lauded in poetry such as Isaac Teale's 'Sable Queen', in such flowery depictions as 'O Sable Queen!

Thomas Stothard: 1793, *The Voyage of the Sable Venus from Angola to the West Indies*

Thy mild domain,/ I seek, and court thy gentle reign/So soothing, soft and sweet/Where meeting love, sincere delight, Fond pleasure, ready joys invite, And unbrought raptures meet'.[9] This poem, she writes, was 'one of the more pleasant contemporary images of the black woman' and 'despite the unflattering picture painted by white men, in practice the physical appearances of black women failed to repel them sexually'.[10] Carolyn Cooper challenges this ambiguous placement of the Sable Venus in the milieu of slave society. 'Is she simply a helpless victim in a racist/sexist society, or does she exercise some complex measure of control over her own sexuality and that of the black man and of the Massa?'[11] Such varied readings are valuable in a contemporary re-presentation of the iconic Sable Venus.

Thus can we have Bryan Edwards using both Stothard's Voyage of the Sable Venus and Isaac Teale's poem, 'The Sable Venus' in 1796 to lyrically introduce the African-Atlantic slave trade in his book, *The History, Civil and Commercial, of the British Colonies in the West Indies*. It is useful to revisit Bryan Edward's employment of Stothard's 'Sable Venus' in light of German Arciniegas's reading of the parallel relationship between Renaissance Europe and the Caribbean encounter. Edwards, a British-born planter with civil and commercial interests in Jamaica who was unapologetic of slavery and colonisation, is uncritical of this image whose intention is to convey the glorious rebirth of Western civilisation on the shores of the Caribbean. Although he has dwelt in Jamaica, he seems unaware of the different imagery which has been introduced into the Caribbean as a result of African slavery. Instead, in the neo-classical style of the period, he supports the conflation of the Sable Venus with the Grecian variant.

Look closely again at both Venuses. Although the Sable Venus holds the strings to the sea horses, it is not a free-flowing lock of golden hair which adorns her neck like that of her counterpart, but a decorously placed slave band. Compare this rendition of the slave band to that depicted by Richard Bridgens (1821-1825) which demonstrates both the decorative as well as controlling devices on the African male and female body in Trinidad, the former a cultural embellishment of the body, the latter a metallic imposition designed to constrain.

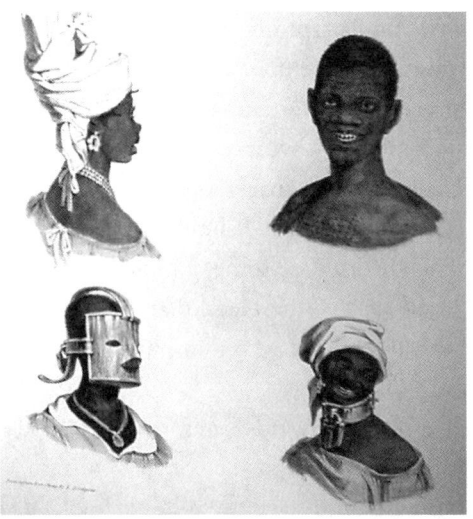

Richard Bridgens, Trinidad, 1821 Plate 20: Negro heads with Punishments
Courtesy: Collection J. Chin Aleong, Trinidad

Agostino Brunias (1773-96) *The West India Washerwoman*, Oil on canvas
Courtesy: Print of the National Library of Jamaica

Let us take these iconographic readings of the female body as they also demonstrate the process of colonisation one step further. By doing so, I do not mean to imply that these images are reducible one to the other; rather that we can also interpret them as texts of a narrative we shall continue to decode. David Brett admits that 'while the visual can and does often "trivialise" certain social experiences', particularly from the stance of the text-based historian, such social experiences are in fact inscribed and integrated into the habits of visualisation and may also be decoded.[12]

In the latter part of the eighteenth century, 20 years before Bryan Edwards[13] published his book, there came to the Caribbean the Italian-born as well as Italian- and British-trained painter, Agostino Brunias. Brunias arrived in Dominica in 1773 as the painter of Sir William Young, first Governor to Dominica after the Treaty of Paris was signed between the British and the French. He was one of the first painters in the tradition of oils who painted *en plenier* or in front of the subject, to have interpreted the Caribbean, in particular the region which is referred to as the Lesser Antilles. His *West India Washerwoman*, is in my view, evocative of the two previous depictions of Venus, resoundingly neo-classical in style.

She is central in the image; her stance is very similar to the two Venuses above. Modesty forbids her nakedness to be completely exposed, but, in the new sexual freedoms which the European scripts of primitivism have deemed fitting of this region, she stands, in the midst of similarly bare-breasted women folk. Instead of winds and nymphs, or Triton and dolphins, still at the heart of the composition, the white head wraps of the black washerwomen and the whitened, washed clothes placed on the river stones, encircle her protectively. In doing so, Brunias recreates the shape of the shell motif of both Venuses. It is also a painterly device to ensure that the eye is led to and focuses on the central object. Like the Sable Venus, her neck is encased, this time in decorative fashion. This Venus is no longer white or black. She is olive-skinned, mulatto, hybridity of the painting also colluding with hybridity of the Venus herself and in this painter's eyes the hybridity of the region which his paintings begin to signify.[14]

I am further convinced that Brunias was deliberate in his analogous Venus here because of a more subtle yet clever device. While the other (black) women are busy with the activity of clothes washing, the mulatto's head is thrown back in a narcissistic pose which assumes that the gaze of the onlooker is directed only to her, drawing the viewer to see her as she sees herself. It is a very telling pose of woman's presence, wonderfully described by John Berger in his *Ways of Seeing*. 'She is painted as being, before anything else, a takeable and desirable woman. She is still the compliant object of the painting-method's seduction'.[15] The painter is, at this time generally male. Thus, for Berger, the surveyor of woman in herself is male. There are feminist disagreements with his interpretation that women have the power to reject being objectified, or that the surveyor of woman is only male. To add to this stereotype of woman's complicit objectification, look closely also at the clothes paddle which she has in her right hand and at the position of the paddle held by the black woman on her left. It is not just a functional object casually thrown into the painting. The line of her face and eyes suggests that she may also look downwards into a mirror to see herself reflected. The paddle represents, in shape as well, the image of the mirror. Between the teachings of Christianity and Greek mythology, the mirror symbolised a warning against the sin of vanity – particularly when it is placed in a woman's hand in paintings. An early Roman mosaic shows Venus at her toilet, a conception of woman as embodying vanity. But mirrors also have a double-sided interpretation, offering also a moment of reflection. Thus the minimal outline of a handheld mirror representing the symbol of Venus, and womanhood, was adopted as the emblem of the second wave feminist movement.

The bodies and shapes of the black women in the painting are obscured. We barely see their faces, they are presented largely in profile, and their skin colour absorbs physical form. Perhaps it is a problem of both paint and painter at the time. While the introduction of oil paints allowed the luminosity and texture of skin, the challenges of painting darker skin had not been commonly addressed in painting. The shapeless and featureless representation is a gross disservice to the roles which black women also performed as workers, mothers, wives and, equally, desired sexual partners.

Deliberately or inadvertently, Brunias has positioned the mulatto woman as the new desirable femininity in the Caribbean, in relation to black and white femininity. This theme of hybridity and the centrality of the mulatto figure is recurrent in several of Brunias's paintings to make it worthy of further attention. Among these are illustrated here the *Barbados Mulatto Girl*, and an untitled painting attributed to Brunias, the latter of a black woman serving the seated mulatto and white woman. Although colour in the sixteenth century possessed few of the connotations it would later acquire, the painter illustrates by the last quarter of the eighteenth century that a colour differentiation had emerged. Brunias's relationship to the Caribbean is important in reading his work. Eventually, when his assignment as court painter had ended, and despite his repatriation, to our knowledge he returned and remained for the rest of his life in the island of Dominica.[16] While it is very likely that Brunias is simply reflecting scenes of Caribbean life in paintings geared for his patron, his paintings are also geared for a British public. As a minor artist, he continued to exhibit his work in galleries in England. Being one of the few artists who actually painted in the region in the eighteenth century, his paintings were reproduced for print publications, and through the method of engraving. Thus, one of his paintings also provides fodder for Bryan Edwards's book, an engraving of the *Pacification of the Maroons* in Jamaica being illustrated by the parallel scenario which took place in St Vincent between the Black Caribs or Garifuna and the British soldiers in 1763. The majority of his paintings are lyrical and unproblematic of social differences, thus encouraging the popular lure and allure which the Caribbean held, as a space of innocence, simplicity, fertility and abundance. Unintentionally, or perhaps deliberately, such paintings would have further exercised the European imagination, particularly on the subject of hybridisation, prefiguring debates on racial purity and confronting the unspoken subject of interracial desire.

Barbados Mulatto Girl, Agostino Brunias
Oil on Canvas. Courtesy: National Library of Jamaica

Untitled painting attributed to Agostino Brunias, Oil on canvas
Courtesy: National Library of Jamaica

West Indian Woman[17]

It is possible that the similarities between Brunias's painting of the *Washerwoman*, set in the Lesser Antilles, and Stothard's *Sable Venus* are no doubt purely coincidental and only linked by the fact that there are Renaissance influences on both sides – Brunias being Italian trained, Stothard, drawing on an Italian renaissance painting. Nonetheless,

Brunias's painting of the West India washerwoman prefigures, if not actually, creates the foundation for another iconic symbol of the Caribbean as natural, primitive and picturesque – the quaintness of women washing clothes in a stream. This scene would possibly have been strange or unusual to the more urbanised European eye. By the twentieth century, it would have been evocative of rurality, an image and nostalgia of a past. Women gathered at the riverside, doing the family or employer's washing, their own clothes drenched by the water, clinging to their bodies (the basis of the contemporary wet T-Shirt competitions). This idea of an earthier, native method of carrying out a domestic chore which brings the doer nearer to nature, must have presented itself as a scene worthy of interest to viewers, to be communicated to those visitors who did not actually make their way to the region. The detail extracted from James Hakewill's *Bridge over White River* in Jamaica is an early successor to Brunias's theme of the West India Washerwoman, executed between 1821 and 1825, as does this detail from Michel Jean Cazabon's *Santa Cruz River* in Trinidad (1849).[18]

Detail from *Bridge over White River*, James Hakewill 1821-1825
Courtesy: West Indies Collection, Main Library, UWI, Mona

Extract of Cazabon, Santa Cruz River 2 (detail) 1849, watercolour 370 x 270 mm

Forrest, 1904 *Washing Day in Jamaica* in Frank Bullen's *Back to the Sunny Seas* between pp 124 and 125

Courtesy: West Indies Collection, Main Library, UWI, Mona

Jas Johnson, *Washing day at the White River*, 1903
Courtesy: West Indies Collection, Main Library, UWI, Mona

Adolphe Duperly, *Washing day at Port Antonio*, 1905
Courtesy: West Indies Collection, Main Library, UWI, Mona

Postcard, *Washing day Dominica*, BWI circa 1920
Courtesy: Collection J. Chin Aleong, Trinidad

Washing in a Stream in Saint Lucia, 2001, Photo by Author

This scene of women washing clothes in a river persisted as a subject for illustrations, postcards and photographs: in the visiting photographer's Jas Johnson's MD portfolio of Jamaican scenes – *Washing Day at the White River* (1903), as an illustration by Forrest in a Frank Bullen's travelogue *Back to the Sunny Seas* (1904); in the Jamaican-born Adolphe Duperly's photograph of *Washing Day at Port Antonio* (1905), and in an early postcard of the British West Indies, *Washing Day in Dominica* (circa 1920). The last photograph is my own take on the subject in St Lucia in 2001, a deliberate foil to the recurrent theme I had encountered in research. This photograph, unlike the three previous ones, is not contrived or staged. The river is also not collusive, no white rush of water foaming like the soapsuds which Jas Johnson's photograph suggests (or has been amended to suggest). The detritus of modern civilisation is strewn around, the flow is sluggish, it is the dry season and the water level is low. The moment of this photograph is stolen, furtive, a swift passage over the bridge by car and flicker of the digital camera. The gentleman in the photograph caught my eyes and there is a hint of resentment, but distance ensures that this does not develop into an angry scene. Perhaps they are correct to react thus. Our souls have already been extracted by a different lens.

Woman selling fruit and vegetables in Kingstown, St Vincent 2004. Photo by Author.

I am always hesitant to focus my camera onto activities which have constituted the conventional picturesque in the region, although I find these activities to be particularly so and would like to capture such scenes on film: not because they make good photographs for postcards, or quaint copy for travel magazines but because I am interested in the natural rather than the native, and perhaps like the legacy of some of the painters of the past, they may capture passages of time and activity. But this time, to define form more studiedly, to flesh out the features, and to compose the insider stories they tell.

Notes

1. This essay draws on the research carried out for a book now near completion entitled *Imaging the Caribbean* which also informed the segment of the film 'A Different Imagination'. The latter comprised the actual presentation at the Mona Academic Conference, August, 2003.
2. Petrine Archer-Straw, *Photos and Phantasms, Harry Johnston's photography of the Caribbean* (London: The British Council Royal Geographical Society, British Council, 1998), 9.
3. Mimi Scheller, *Consuming the Caribbean* (London and New York: Routledge, 2003), 25.
4. J.H. Elliot, *The Old World and the New 1492-1650* (Cambridge: Cambridge University Press, 1970).
5. Mimi Scheller, *Consuming the Caribbean*, 43
6. My acknowledgement to Rex Dixon, British born and trained painter who has lived in the region for two decades now and has an insider/outsider view of the images I employ here. His comments have been very helpful in writing this essay.
7. Mimi Scheller, *Consuming the Caribbean*, 22.
8. Marcus Wood, *Blind Memory: Visual Representations of Slavery in England and America 1780-1865* (London: Routledge, 2000), 21.
9. Verse cited from Carolyn Cooper, *Noises in the Blood: Orality, Gender and the Body of Jamaican Popular Culture* (Warwick: Warwick University Caribbean Studies; London: Macmillan Education Limited), 23. Cooper's endnote 15 discusses the full provenance of the poem, attributed to one Rev. Teale.
10. Barbara Bush, *Slave Women in Caribbean Society 1650-1838* (London: James Currey), 11.
11. Carolyn Cooper, *Noises in the Blood: Orality, Gender and the Body of Jamaican Popular Culture* (Warwick: Warwick University Caribbean Studies; London: Macmillan Education Limited, 1994), 29.

12. David Brett, *The Construction of Heritage* (Cork, Ireland: Cork University Press), 11.
13. Bryan Edwards was English born but inherited considerable property in Jamaica and emigrated there. He became a member of the Jamaica Assembly and later the Council. He was not Jamaican born however and, for this reason perhaps, retained a different stance to that of the Creole born Jamaican planters. (Abrahams and Szwed p50).
14. In fact there are two different versions of the West India washerwoman engravings after Brunias.
15. John Berger, *Ways of Seeing* (England: Penguin, 1972), 92.
16. Much of the information on Brunias's life is due to the wonderful research by the scholar and historian from Dominica, Lennox Honeychurch.
17. Just to assure the contemporary reader of this essay that similar treatment interpreting masculinity is carried out in the manuscript *Imaging the Caribbean*; here the focus is more so on femininity.
18. Cazabon also treats the theme of the washerwoman in another painting not included here entitled *La Blanchisseuse*.

Setting New Agendas:
The Scholarship of a New Generation

24 | SUZANNE MARGUERITE CHARLES

Mirror Mirror
A Feminist Examination of the Construction of Beauty and Body Image

Abstract

She does not know her beauty. She thinks her brown glory, she thinks her brown body has no glory. If she could dance naked under palm trees and see her image in the river, she would know. Yes! She would know. But there are not palm trees in the street, and dishwater gives back no images. (Nina Simone 1964)

Situated within the global context of corporeality, this paper explores the constructions of body image and beauty and attempts to discuss the extent to which feminist thinking has affected these constructions. It examines how the body and beauty have been historically interpreted and considers the potential of corporate eugenics to further influence the understanding of and pressures placed on the female body.

Using an interdisciplinary approach, it examines how personal agency is applied and/or abdicated in determining and creating beauty and preserving the integrity of the human spirit.

She Does Not Know Her Beauty

The body has had a long, curious and contentious history, which to date remains unsettled. When Descartes announced, 'I think therefore I am', not only did he establish the body as that which the mind and soul had comprehensively vacated, but he established a binary understanding of the body, which placed mind over matter, establishing a supremacy of intellect and reason over the sensory and emotive. The Cartesian view

– which still plagues corporeal analysis today – allows the body to be considered in only one way, with variations on the theme.

The Cartesian View sees the body as:

1. An object of the Life Sciences, where the body is understood in terms of organic and instrumental functioning, which takes up from the well held Christian concept that the human body is simply part of a natural mundane order, a vessel in which the superior intellect and spirit is housed.
2. An instrument or tool at the disposal of consciousness, the latter governing the former.
3. A signifying medium, a vehicle of expressing what is essentially private (such as thoughts, ideas and beliefs) in a public space.

The Cartesian approach would be unproblematic – albeit limiting – if the binary did not, in addition to separating mind and soul from the body and ordering them hierarchically with the former at the top, lay the groundwork for the qualities associated with each, to be embodied into different bodies, male and female.

Ffrench (1989) posits that the basis of the Cartesian divide can be traced through an analysis of the nomadic stage of human existence. She suggests that, whereas early humans lived in harmony with nature, when humans confronted food shortages, nature was no longer experienced as friend but as something to outwit and over which to develop techniques of control. Ffrench contends that, as the ability to control nature became increasingly important to human survival, so did the ability to control women, who were seen in almost a monolithic association with nature. Additionally, the more control humans gained over nature, the more they separated themselves *from* nature, physically and psychologically. The necessity of control of the one by the other led to a binary understanding of the vessels in which each set of qualities was housed and ultimately to the *necessity* of male control over female body.

Both Tong and Ffrench (1989) cite this *necessity* to control as the genesis of patriarchy, a hierarchical (binary) system, which values *power-over*. The interpretation of the mind versus the body can be seen as the force which creates and maintains the categories of self and other – of which De Beauvoir (1990) speaks – and which prescribes a framework of understanding, where everything considered natural or close to nature is to be controlled by those considered close to the mind.

Today, this control has extended to all aspects of life, including women's health, career choices, and particularly their sexuality and their reproductive cycles, which make them uniquely women and by extension natural. As more and more technology is developed around when, how and what a women should conceive, reproductive choice has taken on new meanings to embrace the 'enhancing' of the genetic make-up of a future child, away from the reproductive rights more akin to the basic human right to decide if and when to prevent or terminate a pregnancy.

In so doing, a double burden is placed on women's bodies not only to produce but to produce a particular type of human being and body. Rotania (2002) suggests that:

> The use of these technologies poses new dilemmas for women's self-determination and for human society as a whole, both as regards to the final separation of sexuality and reproduction (cloning is practised without sexual intercourse and thereby human reproduction is made a laboratory practice) and to the possibility of manipulating future generations.

While new technologies act as aids to women's oppression, it is noteworthy that women's control over their responses to their cycles has always been denied. A case in point is the fact that conditions such as PMS (pre-menstrual syndrome) and menopause were not traditionally regarded as medical conditions, and now that they are, are seen as more problematic than empowering. Northrup, in her 'Women's Bodies, Women's Wisdom' (1998), maintains that PMS only became a serious concern for the medical fraternity, post-1980s, less than a good 20 years ago. Before then, *feminine woes* such as PMS were encapsulated into a neo-Freudian, *that-time-of-the-month* approach where some sort of cosmic force – akin perhaps to full-moon madness – gripped women and relieved them of the little control that they did have and the responsibility for their behaviours, where women were at their hysterical best.

Angier (2000) suggests, however, that while PMS is often used as a derogatory slur for female irritability, it is experienced by many as a state of heightened awareness, activity, intellectual clarity and feelings of well-being and ought to be regarded simply as a biological, hormonal and physiological change, and part of a woman's reproductive cycle that makes her uniquely woman.

Unfortunately, the syndrome continues to be regarded in the same way as is post-partum depression, which, until recently, was not taken sufficiently seriously (quite possibly because of its uniquely feminine roots), with deleterious effects. After all, why should research funding be directed at the causes of women's *natural* hysteria, when so many old men need to get a 'hard on'?

Additionally, if we changed the approach to women's health and did not use it as a source of ridicule, how could women's unique *woman-ness* be used as the control panel from which female oppression is orchestrated and patriarchy maintained?

Relying, therefore, on essentialism, naturalism and biologism, misogynist thought is created and maintained, and women are duly confined to the biological requirements of reproduction on the assumption that, because of their biology, they are somehow more corporeal and more natural than men and therefore more in need of control. Biology becomes destiny.

She Thinks her Brown Glory, She Thinks her Brown Body has no Glory

Allen (1998), in her work on Caribbean bodies, suggests that a binary approach to understanding humanity has created numerous other binaries, such as race, class and age, to which humanity is now subjected. Allen's point seems valid, as we have seen in the Caribbean a dichotomous understanding of mind and body, where one race and class represented the mind and another, the body and brawn over which the mind had control. Slavery, indentureship and colonialism have all shaped the way in which the Caribbean body has been understood, subsequent to the racialisation of bodies that created a reality in which a particular body type determined the way in which one spent one's day. Given the social and economic gains of being in possession of a particular type of body, historically and contemporarily, we see that division fiercely enforced, almost to the point of believing that the one could never be found in combination with the other, thereby never allowing the privileges accessed by the one to become accessible to the other.

There is little gainsaying that the Caribbean was built on control of the human body, doubly so for the black female body, which was used both as a body to labour and as a body in labour to reproduce the systems that facilitated the economic survival of the region.

But while the burden of the divide between mind and body is more easily evidenced through the lived realities of women, men in the Caribbean have also experienced the dynamics of the binaries established particularly through race and class, to the extent where even governments are now encouraging others – even if tacitly so – to come to the Caribbean to get their own piece of the big bamboo.

It is important to highlight the fact that the burdens placed on men's and women's bodies get played out in different ways, but continue to contribute to males' ability to have *power-over*. For, while women's burden lies in the control of their physical bodies as an end in itself, men's burden lies in the control of their bodies as a means to an end, where demands are made on the male body to reflect cultural meanings manifest through male sexuality. In this instance the burden becomes one of male sexual ability in which particular parts of the body – read penis – are imbued with meanings that speak to a power that eventually surpasses simple sexual ability, but speak to general *power-over*, of women as well as of everything else denied this body part. Phallic worship is not incidental.

Noteworthy too within the Caribbean context is the fact that this kind of male sexuality has been racialised to the extent that only one type of body is expected to have this kind of sexual *power-over* as a direct result of the possession of that particular type of body. In the Caribbean, big bamboo only comes in black.

The dynamic is multifaceted, for while this kind of (black) sexuality has *power-over* women, it still lacks the socioeconomic power of the mind, which is a horse of a totally different colour. In fact, this sexuality is a way of limiting the body, in which race and class have been constructed with such a dialectic, that the powers conferred to each are never interpreted to be found in combination.

In this way the body stops being a physical unit but becomes a medium through which ideology is made manifest by the privileges accorded to or denied each kind of body.

A closer examination of (our Caribbean) history proves useful in identifying the source of our beliefs. Despite our own Caribbean legacy, it is interesting to note that the use of colour as a mark of social distinction is – historically speaking – a relatively new concept.

Ancient civilisations did not make social distinctions based on physical appearance, but distinguished people according to customs and religion. An absence of colour-consciousness can be traced as far back as the Greco-Roman tradition, which 'for all its faults and failures never made colour the basis for judging a man' (Snowden 1983)

In fact, scientific racial classification began in 1735 with Carolus Linnaeus, who classified humans into four races, based mostly on continental separation and later on skin colour. His four groups were:

1. *Americanus*: reddish, choleric, and erect; hair black, straight, thick; wide nostrils, scanty beard; obstinate, merry, free; paints himself with fine red lines; regulated by customs.
2. *Asiaticus*: sallow, melancholy, stiff; hair black; dark eyes; severe, haughty, avaricious; covered with loose garments; ruled by opinions.
3. *Africanus*: black, phlegmatic, relaxed; hair black, frizzled; skin silky; nose flat; lips tumid; women without shame, they lactate profusely; crafty, indolent, negligent; anoints himself with grease; governed by caprice.
4. *Europeaeus:* white, sanguine, muscular; hair long, flowing; eyes blues; gentle, acute, inventive; covers himself with close vestments; governed by laws.

Subsequent to this classification, scientists such as Georges Cuvier and Charles Darwin continued the attachment of hierarchy to race and colour in their research, where the Europeaeus and Africanus races were polarised, with the former being regarded as superior to all others (Smedley 1993). It was such characterisations that persisted in institutions such as slavery and colonialism – which have left the Caribbean with a heritage of colour privilege, prejudice and shame.

The Caribbean black woman's beauty misconception and self-rejection was first internalised during the time of slavery. A black slave woman's outlook on her distinctive African features was negative and self-defeating, in dramatic contrast to attitudes to European (Caucasian) features, which were considered extremely desirable. In her eyes, her skin was too dark, her hair too kinky and short, and her backside too broad. Because skin shade was an inevitable indicator of the quality of life, and a good barometer of potential for economic, social, and political survival, black women adopted – or attempted to adopt – the white beauty standard.

Some enforced on other black women a skin-colour caste system that said lighter skin was more beautiful than darker skin. Thus, while dark-complexioned women rejected the inferiority of their skin, lighter-complexioned women flaunted themselves, pleased for coming closer to achieving the superior white standard of beauty. Desperate to be white, many black women rubbed urine and lye on their skin, hoping the abrasion would take away their dark colour. This rarely worked and often resulted in chemical skin peeling. It is unfortunate, however, that despite the abolition of slavery over 150 years ago, the beauty misconceptions that were acquired during bondage still enslave black females.

Franz Fanon (1976) conceptualised this historical desire to most closely approximate to a white standard of beauty in *Black Skins, White Masks*. Fanon suggested that the denigration of all things black during slavery and colonialism has left a legacy that is as well and alive as it was during the first years of Emancipation. He writes:

> The effective disalienation of the black man entails an immediate recognition of social and economic realities. If there is an inferiority complex, it is the outcome of a double process – primarily economic, subsequently, the internalisation – or better the epidermalisation – of this inferiority.

This consensual agreement to assume – and accept – one's ugliness as well as the cultural standards of others as superior (Fanon's internalisation of an inferiority complex), is well examined in Toni Morrison's *The Bluest Eye*. Through her protagonist, Pecola Breedlove, Morrison shows the illusory nature of the social construction of beauty, and examines the psychological trauma that accompanies the futile labours to assume alien standards of beauty while rejecting one's own, convinced of its inferiority. She writes:

> No one could have convinced them that they were not relentlessly and aggressively ugly…Mrs. Breedlove, Sammy Breedlove and Pecola Breedlove – wore their ugliness, put it on, so to speak, although it did not belong to them … you looked at them and wondered why they were so ugly … then you realised that it came from conviction. Their conviction. It was as though some mysterious, all knowing master had given each one a cloak of ugliness to wear and they accepted it without question.

Through the course of the novel, we learn that Pecola is obsessed with blue eyes.

She prays for them constantly, and is convinced that by making her beautiful the blue eyes will change her life. Morrison, however, questions the cultural ideals that allow Pecola – a young black girl – to yearn for blue eyes, and subverts the idea of beauty or standards of beauty, creating a beauty icon that is not even human. To reinforce this mechanical, non-human (and therefore humanly impossible) aspect of the ideal eye (ideal beauty), Pecola's new blue eyes are not described with colours within the human range, her eyes are blue 'like streaks of cobalt and more blue than the sky itself'.

It is instructive as well, that, at the novel's end, Pecola, with her imagined bluest eyes is a lunatic, speaking to an imaginary friend who assures her of the blueness of her eyes, while she – Pecola – is 'searching the garbage'.

Interestingly the Caribbean interpretation of the body provides the basis for its own critique. For if the mind supersedes the body, how then can bodily traits identified as male versus female, young versus old or race x versus race y, be used to determine the quality of mind that a body possesses and the aptness to govern. It seems that would attribute to the body the kind of power that a Cartesian approach not only denies it has, but of which the approach contends it is incapable. One then is left searching for an alternative explanation.

This alternative is perhaps best explored by Gatens (1997) who offers that the body does not have a truth or a true nature, since it is a process and its meanings and capacities will vary according to its context. Gatens makes her point by highlighting how the body is a product of its environment. She makes the comparison between the body of a woman confined to the role of wife or domestic worker and the body of a female Olympian which have little in common, simply because of the different contexts in which they operate. She argues that biological commonality – the fact of the bodies both being women's bodies – fails to account for the diversity of these two bodies. Gatens suggests that by drawing attention to the context in which bodies move and recreate themselves, we draw attention to the complex dialectic between bodies and their environments.

One can reasonably conclude, based on Gatens's focus between the body and the environment that traditional associations between the female body and the domestic sphere and the male body and the public sphere have created and maintained the historical effects of a particular type of body related to a particular sphere. It is as Derrida says 'There is no nature, only the effects of nature'.

De Beauvoir (1990) makes the point that woman is shut up in a kitchen or in a boudoir and astonishment is expressed that her horizon is limited. Her wings are clipped and it is found deplorable that she cannot fly.

In offering her perspective, Gatens accomplishes two important things:

1. Firstly a feminist perspective on viewing the body where bodies are not sexed, aged or raced, but are appreciated for what they are in the context within which they exist, and are not given extra credit for things which are largely incidental.

2. She also creates a forum through which the body is regarded as a concept to be read in relation to what supports and surrounds it.

Additionally, its interpretation and presentation (from private to public) is sufficiently problematised to raise the appropriate questions of culture and society (particularly in the West) which have sought historically to control, trap and manipulate the body, to the extent that radical feminists were once, and may still be, willing to forsake the body (perceived as the root of all women's evil) in a well-meaning, but misguided attempt to bring the mind under the control of matter. I say misguided simply to say that to reduce either mind to the body or body to the mind, is to leave their interaction unexplained, and thereby open to the same Cartesian analysis of which feminists ought to be wary.

Gatens also offers new definitions about how the body has been understood and how it is interpreted through the agents of society. Her point is emphasised when she suggests that any conceptualisation of the body must refuse singular models, based on one type as the norm by which all others are judged.

She contends that there is no *one* mode that is capable of representing the human in all its richness and variability. She goes on to suggest that a plural multiple field of possible body types must be created in which no one type can take on the coercive role of singular, norm or ideal.

Indeed Gatens's approach prompts one to ask essential questions. If one takes as a point of departure in the discussion of the creation and attendant effect of binaries, Ffrench and Tong's analysis of nomadic man and the separation of mind over matter, interesting dynamics appear. If both men and women – as human beings – engaged in the separation process of mind over matter to ensure survival, two questions readily present themselves:

1. If women were so closely associated with nature, was it that women were less human than men and sought to continue an alliance with nature to the detriment of their own survival?
2. Is it that the conceptualisation of women being closer to nature, because of their reproductive abilities, is a farce and is intentioned only, as De Beauvoir suggests, to clip her wings?

Angier (2000) provides an interesting response to both when she suggests that the historical understanding of woman and woman's body as weak is a fallacy. Based on the work of anthropologists Adrienne Zihlman and Nancy Tanner, Angier argues that the survival and welfare of prehistoric man was largely dependent on plant food gathered by women and not heroically captured by men. She challenges the widely held belief that while men literally 'brought home the bacon or the antelope, women sat slack-jawed around the fire, merrily lactating'.

In making such a challenge, Angier boldly puts questions to a society and to a culture, which has traditionally, and it now seems erroneously, accepted corporeal interpretations as universal and unchangeable fact. This challenge to interpretations of the body is crucial to any understanding of beauty.

If She Could Dance Naked Under Palm Trees and See her Image in the River, She Would Know. Yes! She Would Know

Keats in his first book of *Endymion* claimed that 'A thing of beauty is a joy forever'. Keats, however, seems oblivious to the fact that historically – particularly for women – beauty, in its conceptualisation and in particular its attainment, has been neither enduring nor joyous.

Beauty has been for women at best problematic, producing feelings of ambivalence as well as raising questions of inherent self-worth, and at worst lethal, often the source of unconscious self-contemptuous and health-threatening behaviour.

George Santayana, nineteenth century Spanish-American philosopher, defined beauty as 'pleasure regarded as the quality of a thing'. More recently, however, science has stepped in to supply a less fanciful definition of the term. Stephen Marquart – oral and maxillofacial surgeon attached to UCLA – defines beauty as 'The quality or combination of qualities in something that evokes in the perceiver a combination of strong positive emotion and a high degree of attraction' (Marquart 2003).

Wheat (2003) highlights the fact that beauty is a 'strange concept' that has aspects of personal aesthetics, as well as deep psychological and cultural elements. She asserts that 'westerners are suffering from eating disorders in order to be thin and beautiful ... all over Africa, the Caribbean, much of the Pacific and elsewhere thin is considered ugly'.

Noticeably, by not citing specific qualities of beauty, each of these definitions gives personal agency and cultural preference in the determination of what beautiful is, mirroring Gatens's admonition that the conceptualisation of the body must refuse singular models, based on one type as the norm by which all others are judged.

The importance of Gatens's advice is obvious if one considers that, if the concept of beauty is limited to only certain phenotypic globally-accepted features, one of which is a light or pale complexion, immediately three things can reasonably be expected to happen:

1. A significant percentage of society is eliminated from the definition of beauty;

2. Certain groups of men and women are either made pariahs or given privileges, for looking a particular way, which is at best incidental;
3. In order not to be socially ostracised, an approximation to the desired preferred standard must be attempted.

The situation becomes especially disquieting when one considers the power of culture and socialisation to shape society particularly given the fact of globalisation, which has led to a marked acceleration of a 'world culture' and cultural hegemony, which allows one cultural view to dominate, while suppressing any other ways of constructing, understanding or explaining reality. By eroding cultures of less dominant world powers, a consequent lack of diversity emerges, beauty standards not excluded.

What this will ultimately mean is that people of ethnically diverse backgrounds will be constantly bombarded by only particular images and interpretations of beauty, which they internalise and subsequently attempt to imitate in order to match the dominant culture. This bombardment is infinitely easier given the ease of access to global media networks.

These repercussions are further magnified when one throws into the mix the dynamics of germline engineering and genetic manipulation, where – based on a globalised standard and understanding of beauty – serious challenges can be made to the diversity of humanity, as groups who have been historically targeted and disempowered can be genetically erased.

While evolutionary psychologists agree that the attraction to bodily characteristics is biologically innate, as early humans were attracted to physical traits which were perceived as indicators of good genes, they also agree that, in more modern times, beauty standards have surpassed their pragmatic usefulness of ensuring survival of the fittest and the promulgation of the best genes, and have taken on social attachments and interpretations of prosperity, kindness, intelligence and honesty. Singh (2003) maintains that 'the Scientific properties of attraction ... can be explained by the simple will to produce viable offspring'. For women this meant a waist to hip ratio of 0.7, as it suggested fertility. A smaller waist suggested youth and, indirectly, greater fertility. For men, a more muscular physique with wider shoulders and a waist to hip ratio of 0.9 was considered most attractive.

Daniel Hamermesh (Professor of Economics at the University of Texas), in his studies on appearance discrimination, suggests that because beauty has come to be associated with intelligence, diligence, integrity and other socially valued character traits, attaining beauty standards could potentially translate into up to a 12 per cent difference in total lifetime earnings, as well as marrying partners with higher earning power and potential. Thus any person with an appearance flaw starts out in both the public and private sphere with a serious handicap (2001).

Little wonder then, given the social benefits to be reaped by being what society dictates is beautiful, that women are prepared to attain standards of beauty at any cost.

The costs and stakes rise even further when one considers the available possibilities of germline engineering. Darnovsky (2000) suggests that:

> If germline engineering were to become a common upscale practice, the effects on 'unenhanced' children could be devastating. Their senses of themselves and their life chances could be irrevocably altered. Human germline engineering could encode existing prejudices into the very bodies of future generations. The Council of Responsible Genetics notes: The Standards for what is genetically desirable will be those of society's economically and political dominant groups. This will only reinforce prejudices and discrimination in a society where they already exist.

It is important to note that the burden of beauty falls unequally on the shoulders of women and the desire to be beautiful at any cost is a good reflection of the patriarchal nature of many societies in which men hold power over women. Freedman (1986) posits that

> Girls are socialised to estimate their identity through the indicator of male attention … the connection between appearance and worthiness for females [is] deeply ingrained [and] remains throughout a woman's life, making her continuously insecure about her appearance and consequently about herself.

Freedman argues that:

> to be female is to be presented with an ideal and to measure your self and self-worth against it. As a result a woman suffers feelings of self-consciousness, and of being 'on display'. The shame she is made to feel for her shortcomings is a private emotion that she is forced to endure in silence, perceiving her body as abnormal.

Freedman's thesis implicitly points to the importance placed on how the female body is to be used, that is, in a heterosexual way, as women are not encouraged to be beautiful for themselves or each other, but to be beautiful to ensure male attention. Ann Kaplan (1983) suggests that this desire to support male voyeurism is not new and that in fact centuries of Western art have made the female body an object of aesthetic pleasure for the male spectator. She contends that the visual arts have traditionally conspired to cast femininity – as witnessed in the female body – as a performance, which takes place primarily in the context of heterosexuality, and in which the female body is inevitably situated in relation to man's *power-over*.

In addition to being socialised to accept and prepare for their bodies being 'on display', women are socialised to value youth, presumably because of its indicative ability of fertility, which allows for the female body to be considered closer to nature and for patriarchal structures to remain intact. Kathy Sudomier, writing under the pseudonym Kathy McMeel (1969) highlights the pressures placed on women to remain youthful, both through product development and the ways in which products were marketed. She admonishes:

> You dirty old ad men make me sick. . . . (You) are using chicks to peddle damn near everything. And you aren't using your chicks man, you're using ours. . . the teens and the twenties, man, they seem to be what turns you on . . . You're putting your own daughters out on the street to hustle for you.

The insanity, absurdity and obscenity of this frenetic chase for youthful beauty is revealed as one realises that the ideals for which women are taught to strive are largely unattainable, despite their most assiduous efforts. Even the models on whom beauty standards are based – who generally are statistically exceptional in their appearance – require professional stylists and make-up artists spending hours doing their hair and make-up, along with talented photographers to airbrush all physical flaws away.

It seems that, like Sisyphus, women are eternally condemned to push a boulder uphill, knowing full well that it will roll down again. Some do attempt however, to delay dealing with the reality that it is futile to try to meet these beauty standards or to toy with their mental health. By continuing to assign resources to a system in which one cannot win is against the better societal goal of healthy, strong and confident women.

However, one way in which to challenge this system, which fosters self-contempt, low self esteem and poor body image, is to question the origins of society's most deeply held beliefs and modify them accordingly. In this instance, questions also need to be asked vis-à-vis the identification of those who actually benefit from women's low body esteem, and ask who is paying to put these messages of insecurity out to women.

But There are No Palm Trees in the Street and …

The popular media have been instrumental in inculcating, what I identify – with Naomi Wolf (1992) – as the Beauty Myth(s): that beauty is a universal standard; that beauty is not culturally specific; and that one should be rewarded for beauty

Forbis (1994) argues that dictates to attain largely unattainable beauty standards are an expression of wider social control, usually experienced in a patriarchal society. She posits that:

> One primary means of directing marginalization of women has been to affect a total control of the body….What it means to be a woman according to the dominant patriarchal system involves constructing the appropriate surface presentation of self….These rules are learned through images.

Cashman (2003) maintains that these 'learned images' are the ones that are constantly repeated by the media, with the effect of ingraining the desire to achieve unattainable standards in all women. She suggests that:

> Communications media, along with the cosmetic and advertising industries, have become a 'global culture machine' and are responsible for the establishment of a Western model of beauty that is referred to by women all over the world …
>
> > The sociological explanation for the feminine susceptibility to the promises of happiness through body improvement is sought in the sexualisation of the female body by the media in order to sell products…in short, mass culture, through cultural icons, media, and the invention of body-altering methods used for discipline, creates a standard control over the [female] body … and in doing so ensure male dominance … in a pursuit of control over her physical being, a woman in essence forfeits her psychological well-being.

This 'global culture machine' is a direct consequence of the process of globalisation and the development of cultural hegemony. Antonio Gramsci (1971) who coined the term suggests that, in many instances, hegemony is achieved by consent, based on the creation of self-contempt through brainwashing, often under the guise of effective socialisation.

Gramsci suggests that critical thinking about its cultural processes should allow a society to question the origins of its most deeply held beliefs and modify them accordingly.

The fundamental questions to be asked include *inter alia*:

1. Who has been excluded from the possibility of attaining beauty and why?
2. What psychic price has been paid by those deemed outside cultural standards of beauty?
3. How can this be changed?

And Dishwater Gives Back No Image

While it is generally agreed that ethnic minorities have borne the burden of being excluded from the possibility of attaining global standards of beauty disproportionately, all persons have been victim to the capitalist motives of buying just one more jar of hope.

Voukelatos and Harris (2001) suggest that:

> Capitalist society forces women into roles that are usually unachievable and oppressive. In a sexist society, women are prevented from doing things they would otherwise do, or are made to feel bad or as if they are an outcast when they try. The beauty industry has been a major profiteer from the oppression of women. This is a multi-billion dollar industry that creates and preys on women's insecurities. The beauty myth creates a largely unattainable ideal of the 'perfect' woman. Women feel forced to invest copious amounts of time and money in the impossible attempt to achieve the 'perfect' body, which advertisers and the beauty industry promise will boost their self-esteem and improve their lives.... However, the beauty industry's version of the 'ideal' body weight and shape and one that best promotes good health do not necessarily correlate.... Aside from the profits generated by this con, the beauty myth has the added advantage for the powerful in this sexist society of keeping women focused on the extra bit of flab on their thighs and the wrinkles on their face rather than realising that a society that makes women feel bad about such meaningless things has to be changed fundamentally.

Cashman asserts that the men behind these economic interests depend on women's propensity towards feelings of ugliness. Indeed, it is the complete obsession with one's looks, accompanied by a complete dissatisfaction with how one looks that drives the beauty industry.

Not only does such a system compromise women's economic power, it compromises their power of self-definition and reduces them from the role of active participant in the creation of themselves to the passive recipient of a construct that often fits them ill, if at all.

The economic gains are rarely measured against the psychic price women are left to pay, including fad dieting, dissatisfaction, depression and any number of eating disorders, the most serious of which – Body Dysmorphic Disorder – is an excessive preoccupation with an imagined, or minor defect of a localised facial feature or body part, resulting in decreased social, academic and occupational functioning. The disorder which is characterised by a distorted perception of the body, often leads to self-destructive behaviours aimed at improving the appearance of the body.

While one cannot, with conscience, advocate massive exodus from Jenny Craig to Sara Lee, it must be stressed that this undue emphasis on the exterior, which denies women possession of their uniqueness, can only create a quiet desperation. Like Pecola, we may all be headed for lunacy. Even if one admits (like Hamermesh) that looks do matter, the pressures placed on women need to be removed in a way that allows them freedom of choice in how to value their beauty at any age and size, without constructing ways of meaning and understanding, where

> fashion, cosmetics, and 'feminine hygiene' ads ... encourage men to expect women to sport all the latest trappings of sexual slavery – expectations women must then fulfil if they are to survive ... and wearing clothes and beauty aids is not so much consumption as work ... a woman's job in this society is to be an attractive sexual object, and clothes and make-up are tools of the trade (*A Redstocking Sister* 1971).

This pattern of quiet desperation to which Cashman alludes can only be changed through continually questioning and, consequently, reinventing cultural codes that are more inclusive and which do not seek the control of woman through that which identifies her as such, her body. It also calls for a redefinition of beauty and the removal of systems of privilege attached to particular interpretations of beauty.

The change, in addition to engaging in further study and analysis around the theme of personal agency in the creation and understanding of beauty, ought to generate an understanding that beauty begins with health, physical and emotional, which widens the definition of beauty to necessitate a positive body image, where one is able to celebrate and appreciate natural body shape and complexion, while fully cognisant that one's physical appearance says very little about one's character and value as a person to society.

References

Books

Angier, N. 2000. *Woman: An intimate geography*. USA: Knopf Publishing Group.

De Beauvoir, S. 1990. *The Second Sex*. USA: Random House.

Gatens, M. 1997. Corporeal Representation in/ and the Body Politic. *Writing on the Body*, ed. K. Conboy, 80-90. New York: Columbia University Press.

Grosz, Elizabeth. 1994. *Volatile Bodies: Toward a Corporeal Feminism*. Indiana: Indiana University Press.

Smedley, Audrey. 1993. *Race in North America: Origin and Evolution of a Worldview*. San Francisco: Westview Press, Inc.

Snowden, Frank M. 1983. *Before Color Prejudice: The Ancient View of Blacks*. Cambridge, MA: Harvard University Press.

Wolf, N. 1992. *The Beauty Myth*. New York: Anchor Books.

Online References

Cashman, Ellie. 2003. Society, Self-Esteem, and Women. http://www.wesleyan.edu/synthesis/culture-cubed/cashman/was_research.html.

Craig, Steve. 1998. Feminism, Femininity, and the "Beauty" Dilemma: How Advertising Co-opted the Women's Movement. A Paper presented at the Southwest/Texas Popular Culture/American Culture Association Conference Lubbock, Texas, January. http://www.rtvf.unt.edu/people/craig/pdfs/beauty.PDF (accessed June 12, 2003).

Darnovsky, Nancy. 2000. Human Germline Manipulation and Cloning as Women's Issues. http://www.ourbodiesourselves.org/clone2.htm.

Elder, R. The Science of Attraction. http://www.emory.edu/COLLEGE/HYBRIDVIGOR/issue1/attraction.htm (accessed June 12, 2003).

Forbis, M. 1994. This is My Body: Gender, Tattooing and Resistance in the United States. MA thesis, Temple University, May. http://astro.temple.edu/~ruby/wava/forbis/forbis-three.html.

Freedman, R. 1986. Beauty Bound. Lexington, MA and Toronto: Lexington Books, 130-131. http://www.temple.edu/anthro/forbis/forbis-three.html.

Marquart. Beauty Analysis. http://www.beautyanalysis.com/index2_mba.htm (accessed June 12, 2003).

Race: Is It a Valid Issue? http://www-personal.umich.edu/~jonmorro/race.html (accessed June 12, 2003).

Rotania, A. 2002. More Voices Against Human Cloning: Paradigms of a New Feminism? *Women's Global Network for Reproductive Rights*, 75. http://www.klaever.nl/open_document.asp?id=137&site_id=157 (accessed June 12, 2003).

Sterndale, Maurice. Dysmorphic Disorder. http://www.hypnos.co.uk/hypnomag/sterndale.htm.

Voukelatos, Maria, and Lauren Carroll Harris. Body Image and Women's Oppression. http://www.greenleft.org.au/back/2001/445/445p9.htm.

West Seifert, Melinda. 2001. Appearances count — to the point of bias? *Austin Business Journals,* Week of July 23. http://austin.bizjournals.com/austin/stories/2001/07/23/focus3.html (accessed June 12, 2003).

Wheat, S. Just in the Eye of the beholder? http://europa.eu.int/comm/development/body/publications/courier/courier183/en/en_042_ni.pdf (accessed June 12, 2003).

25 | GABRIELLE JAMELA HOSEIN

Ambivalent Aspirations
Assertion and Accommodation in Indo-Trinidadian Girls' Lives

Abstract

Adolescent Indo-Trinidadian girls' aspirations suggest simultaneous adherence to and departure from demands of 'appropriate' womanhood. Their views reflect a cross-cutting range of reasons for which girls are valued and the pleasures of succeeding at belonging in divergent spaces. The challenge of finding the 'right' balance creates feelings of ambivalence about managing competing imperatives. Girls work out tensions among ideals both across *and* within *different spheres of their lives and may, therefore, differently negotiate divergent spheres and hold to particular ideals that, nonetheless, they contest in practice.*

There appear to be shifting combinations of 'appropriate' assertion and accommodation. Girls' aspirations, in areas such as education, employment, marriage and family, suggest that mixed and ambiguous messages convey values of equality and 'choice', while compelling girls to seek approval through notions of 'responsibility' and by 'appropriately' balancing 'feminine' and 'masculine' qualities. They also reveal how expanded opportunities have shaped girls' considerations regarding their future roles and identities.

Introduction

This paper examines Indo-Trinidadian girlhood as a contemporary experience of adolescent agency. It is based on research conducted between 1999 and 2002 in a semi-urban area of North Trinidad.[1] In this late-twentieth-century context, young Indo-Trinidadian women are increasingly responsible for their 'choices' regarding future aspirations, bodily self-regulation, and gender identities. Their expanded capacity foregrounds crucial changes to Indo-Trinidadian girls' adolescent experience over the past 50 years.

Little data exist on how Indo-Trinidadian girls perceive the intersections of ethnicity, femininity and adolescence in their lives. The significance of class, religion and generation is also under-explored. This paper attempts to address these gaps by examining these girls' 'choices', their feelings of ambivalence and the pleasure of succeeding at belonging (to divergent spaces) at the turn of the century. It primarily explores girls' experiences in terms of 'gender strategies' such as negotiation. As briefly discussed in the conclusion, the kinds of lived experiences highlighted may suggest issues and themes relevant to young women and to the Caribbean women's movement as we continue to think about future feminist organising in the region.

Emerging Adolescence

The emergence of Indo-Trinidadian female adolescence may be traced over a span of about 50 years to the contemporary period. In parallel, one may note changes to the way that Indo-Trinidadian young women's identities have been understood. For example, in early ethnographies of rural Indo-Trinidadian communities (Niehoff and Niehoff 1960; Klass 1961; Smith 1963), girls feature primarily in discussions of young women's sexuality, marriage arrangements and 'women's' responsibilities in marriage. These ethnographers described a situation of girls moving from being children to wives, and thus 'women', with little experience similar to a contemporary or western defined period of adolescence. Rather, their lives were regulated first by their status as children and second by their preparation for wifely responsibilities with little period of transition or development of alternative identities.

For girls, the liminal, interstitial period between childhood and womanhood was brief and marked by strict regulation of their mobility and sexuality. According to Klass (1961), notions of individual reputation and respectability, (caste) purity and pollution, patriarchal protection, and community honour and shame were powerful forces. They provided the foundation for conceptions of female sexuality, feminine moral imperatives and girls' ethnic identities. They were, therefore, key elements in a gendered framework that, in addition to imperatives of obedience to family and community, delimited legitimate options in girls' transition to womanhood. Behavioural codes for these girls marked points of inter-ethnic difference. Specific rules regarding reputation and respectability also marked significant intra-ethnic difference among adolescents.

Then and now, the individual experiences of these girls, their feelings about the framework of reputation and respectability, and their own conceptions of sexuality and moral imperatives remain largely 'hidden from history' (Rowbotham 1973). In the historical literature, it is noteworthy that Indo-Trinidadian 'women' were often still teenagers or in their early twenties. Theoretical contributions may therefore have inadvertently emerged from a conflation of adolescent and adult women's experiences.[2] There thus remains a great deal of opportunity for studies specifically documenting and theorising young Indo-Trinidadian womanhood. This is true also for a more thorough understanding of why, how and with what implications this group of girls has renegotiated their options in different periods and circumstances.

We first hear Indo-Trinidadian girls' voices in Vera Rubin's (1969) landmark study of adolescent aspirations in pre-independence Trinidad. Using an ethnically mixed sample, the study looked at how 'intra- and inter-ethnic group and social class differences can affect value systems and the impact the changing social order can have on individual attitudes and aspirations' (ibid., 197). This study's focus on the intersections of gender, adolescence and ethnicity (but not area of residence, class or religion) enabled a different picture and analysis to emerge.

Rubin noted that, across ethnic groups, girls' career aspirations were influenced by their knowledge of social requirements and their perception of appropriate roles. Yet, in particular, Indo-Trinidadian girls aspired to a university education and jobs requiring a university degree. The authors concluded that, against the background of traditional and changing cultural patterns, education was seen as 'a channel to a career and personal independence, rather than as preparation for the housewife's role'[3] (ibid., 95). The widening chasm between traditional expectations regarding appropriate women's roles and girls' own feeling about personal fulfilment, was informed by the 'powerful attraction' that a career offered and the changing gender norms which were opening new options for girls.

This was seen to be particularly true for these confident Indo-Trinidadian girls who were 'more anxious and willing than the others to break with traditional sex roles' that had historically limited girls' educational and employment opportunities in the multi-ethnic public sphere. Thus, by the early 1960s, Indo-Trinidadian young women were both holding to traditional imperatives while aspiring to break with a tradition of gender inequality in the Indo-Trinidadian 'nuclear family' (ibid, 136-138). This is a picture of change and fluidity in opportunities, influences, values and expectations faced by those growing up in the late 1950s and early 1960s. Such changing attitudes toward 'early marriage, parental choice of partners and traditional women's roles' were an extremely significant development.

By the 1980s, Nevadomsky's re-examination of Klass' fieldsite would confirm changing gender and generational practices. He argued that the rising age of marriage and higher levels of education were encouraging young women to 'enter marriage with rather firm notions about their roles as mother, wife and housemaker' (1984, 122). He also asserted that changes to parental roles made power relations between parents and children 'less gerontocratic' and 'more egalitarian' (1980, 51), and led to the 'restructuring of authority systems' (1983, 205). Such conclusions highlighted the generational aspect of cultural change affecting social customs and institutions. Younger Indo-Trinidadians were increasingly taking on multiple value systems and exercising their power to establish values and standards for behaviour. Together, the influence of wider urban society, social mobility, Christian and secular education, growing antipathy toward early childbearing and intruding ideas of romantic love were stimulating change and fluidity in young Indo-Trinidadian women's identities. As well, Mohammed (1997, 127) particularly highlighted a growing 'modern consciousness of the child as an individual having separate or different needs or even rights', an expanded age of sexual maturity and a liminal state as 'neither child nor adult' as key factors encouraging young women's aspirations and agency (ibid., 141).

These points suggest a burgeoning idea and time of adolescence as a phase marked by the encounter of values of different generations and groups, and girls' growing responsibility as individuals for their feelings and 'choices'. Growing acceptance (to varying degrees among, for example, different family, class and religious groups) of girls' 'personal choice' (Nevadomsky 1980, 46) was especially significant for the emergence of a contemporary experience of adolescence among young Indo-Trinidadian women. Feminist scholarship on Indo-Trinidadian women (Reddock 1986; Mohammed 1994, 36-7; Hosein 2001) suggests a departure from simply marking females' 'obedience' or 'disobedience'. Instead, women's agency should be central to study of Indo-Trinidadian femininity, identity and community belonging. From this view, evolving ideas about 'personal choice' and girls 'individuality' can be seen to establish new parameters for the construction and negotiation of (adolescent) female gender identities.

Perhaps for the first time, young people's – and young women's – generational challenges to the authority of elders and tradition could be legitimated by changing Indo-Trinidadian values and those of the wider society, and certainly among an age-based sub-grouping (Nevadomsky 1980, 45, 50). The increasing acceptance of personal choice opened a space for young women to experience more than the powerlessness of childhood and the obligations of females to parental choices and, later, to the responsibilities of marriage (Mohammed 1997, 118). More importantly, it created a distinct (and expanding) adolescent space and experience defined by a focus on development of individual identity, aspirations, desires and opinions. Thus, in the contemporary period, acceptance of adolescence as a phase of individual identity formation changed the terms within which females were bargaining with (patriarchal and generational) community expectations and traditional gender roles. Put another way, increasingly, girls were not just expected to obey, but to *choose* to obey parents and authority figures, moral imperatives and gendered sanctions. Yet, late twentieth-century adolescents could also intervene in conceptions of femininity and womanhood, and could represent a knowledgeable (generational) standpoint. The legitimacy of exercising personal 'choice', and seeking independence and fulfilment, provides a new enabling context for young women's exercise of agency. Of course, such an exercise operates within the parameters of contemporary parental, community and cultural expectations, and gendered value systems. This is, nonetheless, part of a fundamental change in the terms of Indo-Trinidadian girlhood and the transition from childhood to womanhood, over 50 years.

Framing Contemporary Adolescence

What are some of the ways to understand this contemporary experience of Indo-Trinidadian girlhood? How has girlhood been framed? Scholars writing about young women in Britain and North America have essentially focused on 'the ways that social subjects 'consent' to and negotiate their subordination' (Skelton and Valentine 1998, 13). Both these responses have consequences for girls who equally rely on supportive relationships *and* need to challenge those that 'feel false or which are conventions that require self-sacrifice or silence' (Taylor et al. 1995, 26). Similarly, Taylor (1996, 122) has argued that aspects of cultural belonging are more empowering for some girls than others. She therefore posits that explorations of non-white girls'/'girls' of colour' identity development should account for their negotiations with disparate conventions of femininity and womanhood requiring them 'to conform to their culture's beliefs and expectations while simultaneously being part of mainstream culture'. As Erkut et al. (1996) pointed out, the significance of this approach is its acknowledgement of ethnic imperatives (or cultural expectations) for girls. Belonging, which both enables the process of identity development and establishes limited identity choices, is linked to 'feeling good about who you are'.

In contrast to adolescent masculinity, Eisikovits (1998, 48-9) has described young womanhood as closely tied to conformity, self-correction, 'good' behaviour, 'serious and conservative acceptance of the responsibilities of adulthood', and 'settling down'. Thus, girls are seen to be more willing than boys to *overtly* conform to the social requirements of adulthood. Scholars such as Lykes (1985), Bush and Simmons (1987), Simmons and Blyth (1987) and Gilligan *et al* (1990) have understood this conformity in terms of the 'social individual' who develops 'in relationship'. Pastor et al. (1996, 18) have argued that, for girls and women whose lives are 'nested inside power inequities', 'recognizing and making sense of social injustice and oppression' and developing 'a keen ability to find spaces for resistance' is a fundamental part of their social individuality. Thus, while girls are seen to overtly 'conform' more than boys, female identity development is specifically related to girls' familiarity with feelings of oppression *and* desire for resistance.

Unfortunately, what also emerges is that girls 'engage in deconstructing' in isolation and with little thought to collective social transformation. The idea of 'individualistic strategies' was further nuanced by Skeggs (1994, 83-4) who suggested that young women use femininity 'tactically, when appropriate, and often in contradictory ways'. Thus, as Anyon (1982) has noted, often 'girls and women find themselves caught in cycles of resistance and accommodation where they learn that options for resistance more often than not reproduced the very oppressive cultures they think they are resisting' (Pastor et al. 1996, 20). Hey (1997, 115-6) too has concurred that the contradictions of girls' lives do not enable a 'coherent or "pure" non-contradictory feminist positioning' and advocated that, instead, we explore 'the production of competing meanings'. As she (ibid, 13) has aptly summarised, many feminist scholars see adolescence as 'a time in which girls come to learn how to take up their place in multiple and competing regimes of power' where class and race differences are 'important social markers' and heterosexuality 'confers differing (if troubling) forms of social power associated with girls' different claims upon its prestige'.

Most compelling about these approaches to different forms of girls' resistance is feminist scholars' recognition that they do not offer 'unadulterated oppositionality'. Rather, 'the seductions of cultural hegemony are shaped by girls' co-investments in intimacy and difference' and 'worked through the pleasures of belonging' (ibid, 26). This is 'the powerful coalition between dominant gender "scripts" and girls' own desire to be "normal"' – a desire, which Hey has contended, leads girls to invest in 'insider femininity' (being a "good" girl) versus 'outsider femininity' (being a 'bad' girl) (ibid, 131).

In this regard, Taylor *et al* (1996, 53) have emphasised that 'self-regard', a cultural construct referring to the 'feelings one has about oneself', can be a useful window for examining girls' identity development. As Leadbeater and Way (1996, 2) have suggested, girls' concerns revolve not just around identity formation, but also, and importantly, identity *presentation*. Here, the question is not just 'Who am I?' but 'How should I present myself, given who others think I am and who I really am?' In this way, self-regard is manifested in girls' concerns about identity presentation or enactment in everyday settings (Rotheram-Borus et al. 1996, 50). As these scholars noted, the demands of identity presentation may enable girls to express who they 'really' are only in specific ways/spaces or suppress a great deal of possibility for doing so at all.

Appropriate appearance enables girls to 'stake claims as particular beings on the public stage' (Hey 1997, 118). Feminist scholars agree that the development of feminine subjectivities, a specifically gendered process, rewards girls for presenting themselves in 'appropriately feminine' ways. In this sense, 'coming to grips with the demands of womanhood and emerging sexuality' (McRobbie 1991) is also about accepting feelings and representations of subordination, and conditions not of girls' own choosing. Yet, girls nonetheless appropriate, subvert and transform dominant meanings or create their own. Elucidating this is key to unravelling 'the inter-connection between representation and lived social relations' (Skelton and Valentine 1998, 18).

These observations about girls' overt conformity and tactical resistance, insider and outsider femininities, self-regard and identity presentation, and multiple and syncretic identities speak significantly to Indo-Trinidadian young women's experiences. Writing about Afro-Tobagonian girls, Laitinen (1997) has also highlighted the fluidity and overlap in adolescents' identities, values, choices and behaviour across various settings. As she wrote, the multiple nature of feminine identities causes shifts 'according to and in interaction with cultural and historical circumstances and may have different aspects privileged at different times by the self or others' (ibid, 60–63). With regard to past generations of Indo-Trinidadian women, Hosein (2001, 19, 37) has noted that individuals challenged particular frameworks even while upholding their 'sanctity'. In the contemporary period, Kanhai (1999, 219) has attributed young Indo-Trinidadian women's 'schizophrenia' to competing cultural demands from home, community and larger society. These writings closer to home suggest a need for nuanced analysis of how such parallels are intersected by age, generation, religion, class and ethnicity in the Trinidadian context.

Further in this paper, and following from Rubin (1969), I examine young Indo-Trinidadian women's contemporary aspirations, and the comparative ambivalences and contradictions in their lives. Mainly, I employ Patricia Mohammed's (1994) useful concept of negotiation to understand how they manage the demands and opportunities of 'competing patriarchies'[4] and their own belonging to syncretic and divergent spaces. Mohammed used the concept to explore collusions and subversions, hegemonic and resistant ideals, sites of contestation and sources of power available to Indo-Trinidadian women in the early twentieth century (ibid, 31-8). Building on Deniz Kandiyoti's (1988) concept of 'patriarchal bargaining', she examined how women 'strategize' within constraints determined by a patriarchal gender ideology. Essentially, she conceptualised negotiation as an accretional process of compromises and resistance over time and changing circumstances. For her, it occurred at both individual and institutional levels. These levels were connected by 'a continuous dialectical relationship between individual action, and group or community concerns', and were influenced by ongoing social, political and economic changes.

My own use of the concept is qualified. I suggest that late twentieth century 'patriarchal bargaining' includes both forms of negotiation *and* navigation.[5] With the expansion of notions of adolescence, individuality and personal 'choice', the forms and parameters of girls' accommodations and resistances changed. Not only do Indo-Trinidadian girls now seek individuality within gender codes and roles, but they are also able (and to some extent compelled) to move among and 'choose' from a range of competing prescriptions. The expanded legitimacy of choice is centrally important here. This is a continual process of finding the balance of identities and practices 'appropriate' to different spaces and situations. In a contemporary context of multiple and shifting demands of womanhood, I propose that these Indo-Trinidadian young women must navigate different ideals as well as negotiate the expectations of each. In other words, they work out the tensions among ideals *within and across* different spheres of their lives. This differential mediation of divergent spaces has important implications.

First, it becomes a tactic for challenging gender prescriptions with competing (now legitimate) ideals of choice and negotiation. Second, it lets girls manage to hold to ideals that they nonetheless contest in practice. For example, as I discuss below, girls do this by disconnecting feminine ideals associated with marriage and family aspirations from those associated with their education and future careers. Marriage and family are regulated by distinctly 'insider' femininities, and values of accommodation, compromise and responsibility. Somewhat in contrast, education and employment are associated with approved kinds of 'outsider femininity' (or what I call accessible aspects of 'insider' masculinity). These are associated with assertiveness, challenge to gender boundaries and the pursuit of individual self-fulfilment. In this way, these young women attempt to ensure their femininity is validated. At the same time, they aspire to compete equally and successfully take on a masculine world. In this respect, what they consider valued masculine attributes also become approved aspects of an 'insider' femininity with now hazy and shifted boundaries.

Concomitantly, these girls reproduce dualistic conceptions of reputation and respectability. Nonetheless, they simultaneously approve of aspects of 'outsider' femininity (particularly when associated with whiteness and 'modernity'). This both expands the meaning of respectability and blurs the symbolic distinctions between respectability and reputation. Femininity and respectability therefore become lived as both dualistic cultural ideals and as continuums of possible 'styles of being' (Laitinen 1997) in the everyday. As Handa (1997) concluded for South Asian girls in Toronto, these negotiations 'blur the line between good girls and bad girls and resist the definition of the "typical Indian" (sic) girls in their day-to-day practices' (ibid, 24). This is consistent with Laitinen's finding that, while adolescent females may uphold particular values, the relationship between ideals and practice is fluid and contextual. Thus, third, girls' negotiation and navigation enable them to cloud clear boundaries between 'insider' and 'outsider' femininities, and femininities and (aspects of 'insider') masculinities. As part of this process, opposed notions of appropriate and inappropriate, and respectability and reputation also develop more obscure outer limits.

Thus, young women's ideals may appear to contradict or diverge from their practices and/or they may appear to differently accommodate and resist across different spheres.[6] These gender strategies do not necessarily suggest controversy, clash or contradiction between moral values and everyday choices. I suggest that they show the tensions, multiple subjectivities and ambiguities involved in continuously having to find an 'appropriate' balance among shifting demands of representation. It is in this contemporary context that these young women seem compelled to navigate across and claim belonging to divergent value systems.

This is additionally significant for adolescent Indo-Trinidadian girls' agency because it allows them to access the pleasures of succeeding at a wider spectrum of feminine ideals. It therefore offers options for and validates a wider range of possible selves. This extends opportunities for gender bargaining and for different kinds of gender strategies. Those managing cultural and ethnic community ideals, as well as a range of others, can therefore adhere to and depart from specific kinds of demands without necessarily sacrificing social individuality and community belonging. The possibilities for choosing from among competing womanhoods frame these girls' negotiations with each. The notion of navigation rests on their legitimating of personal 'choice', even when they collude and accommodate.

Yet, the challenge of finding the 'right' balance creates feelings of ambivalence and anxiety about their ability to manage competing and overlapping imperatives. This is especially true because the messages and identities associated with modernity are themselves ambiguous and contradictory. To many young Indo-Trinidadian women, white womanhood represent or are the 'face' of modernity. The ideals of white womanhood enable Indo-Trinidadian young women to access limited status through 'reputation', re-read as modern, cool and liberal. Through an association with metropolitan whiteness, notions of modernity can therefore legitimise otherwise 'inappropriate', 'disrespectful' and 'unfeminine' adolescent Indo-Trinidadian female identities. In this way, the notion of modernity positions reputation ambiguously as both a source of status and shame. It offers options for expanding the boundaries of respectability, and for blurring gendered and ethnic dualisms. Yet, the boundaries are not so permeable that they don't exist. Even these influential white metropolitan ideals demarcate clearly 'inappropriate' aspirations and identities for girls.

In this paper, I therefore use the concepts of negotiation and navigation to explore young Indo-Trinidadian girls' contemporary aspirations. I further examine how they are mediated by ideas of self-regard, tactical resistance and conformity, and insider and outsider femininity as well as by ethnicity, class, age, religion and generation. This approach makes girls' agency and their identity 'choices' central to understanding late twentieth-century Indo-Trinidadian female adolescence.

Ambivalent Aspirations

How do young women navigate the contradictory and coalescing imperatives of insider femininity? In the following section, I explore how they both reproduce and contest such shifting ideals. As outlined earlier, I focus on their future aspirations in areas such as education, employment, marriage, children and family, and what they suggest about the kind of women girls feel they can and want to be. I also examine what their aspirations for equality and political representation suggest about their feelings about growing up as a female, and their vision for society and for women.

This section is based primarily on questionnaires returned by 126 young women between 15 and 25 years old. In 1999, I administered a survey to 114 girls in fourth and fifth form in four schools located within the area of study. The schools were chosen to encompass the range of classes, religions and backgrounds represented in the area. The schools selected were the Sanatan Dharma Maha Sabha (SDMS) run Lakshmi Girls Hindu College (LGHC) in St Augustine, the Presbyterian St Augustine Girls' High School (SAGHS), the co-educational Rafeek Memorial Trinidad Muslim League (TML) Secondary School in St Joseph and the co-educational state-run El Dorado (EL DO) Secondary Comprehensive School. Twelve young women working in retail stores also participated.

Indo-Trinidadians comprise almost three quarters of the entire sample group. Similarly, general discussions of girls' views primarily represent Hindus as they comprise 60 per cent of this group and 45 per cent of the entire sample population. In comparison, Muslims and Christians represent approximately 15 per cent and 26 per cent respectively, and 16 per cent and 40 per cent respectively of the entire sample population. In particular, Roman Catholics and Presbyterians represent 6 per cent and 11 per cent respectively of Indo-Trinidadians, and 16 per cent and 8 per cent of the entire survey group. Disaggregated by age, girls 14 to 16 years old comprise over 80 per cent of all girls in the survey.

a) Education, modernity, power

Over 70 per cent of the 35 non-Indo-Trinidadians and over 80 per cent of the 91 Indo-Trinidadians in the study's survey prioritised education, career, independence and success before marriage and family. Nonetheless, marriage and family, which are tied to ideals of respectability, remain important. Examined comparatively, Indo-Trinidadian girls seemed to primarily emphasise education and career whereas non-Indo-Trinidadians more greatly prized asserting equality and improving women's status (Table 1). For Indo-Trinidadians, education is an especially important pre-marital goal. As one young woman wrote, 'Because education is the only way to ensure that we do not become housewives, mothers and slaves. If you don't have a job, you'll have to stay home and look at kids'.

Table 1: Girls' reasons for valuing women's educational achievement

Response	Total girls	Indo-Trinidadian	Non-Indo-Trinidadian
To get qualifications, to get a job, be successful and not dependent so no one could take advantage of you	52.5%	57.5%	39.4%
To be literate	1.7%	1.1%	3.0%
To be able to educate their family	2.5%	3.4%	0%
To feel accomplishment, achievement and confidence and have goals	15.8%	14.9%	18.2%
To prove that women are equal to men, improve women's status	26.7%	22.9%	36.3%
Other	.8%	0%	3.0%
Total	100%	100%	100%

Despite different class and ethnic emphases, all 126 girls in the sample agreed that educational achievement is important for women. Essentially, it is valued for securing a good job, accessing opportunities, avoiding dependence, feeling a sense of accomplishment and confidence, proving women's sense of worth and improving women's status. Notions of 'modernity' and accompanying challenges to established gender roles inform these aspirations. Girls placed high value on participation in the 'public' and male-dominated 'working world' and judged 'success' in terms of white-collar or high-status jobs instead of reproductive responsibilities. A majority of Indo-Trinidadians in school emphasised these reasons. As a Lakshmi Girls' Hindu College student wrote,

> If women do not have an education, they would always have to depend on a man for support which is not good in these modern times. They can support themselves and feel less trapped in a limited world. (15-year-old, Indo-Hindu)

Another, this time from St Augustine Girls' High School, repeated,

> Women need to *show*[7] men that we can achieve just as much as they can. (15-year-old, Indian-white identified, Roman Catholic)

In their own way, young women appear to want to address a perceived sexual division of labour and a sense that men do not value their capacities in the 'working world'. Fundamentally, then, no girl in this sample wants to be dependent on men. Rather, these young women aspire to work outside the house, participate in society and feel a sense of accomplishment. Education is seen to facilitate this.

A majority of all groups of girls seem less willing to compromise and accommodate to access freedoms and decision-making power regarding employment, material goods, leisure, mobility and money. This desire appears to be tied to a sense of changing opportunities for women and changing conceptions of womanhood in the contemporary period. Thus, the notion that these are 'modern times' also seems to significantly legitimate aspirations regarding economic independence. As girls generally articulated, 'because women were degraded in the past and taken for granted, we need independence and wealth now that society is cosmopolitan and changing and women play an important part'. In particular, economic independence appears cast as a source of power to which girls are turning, not simply to negotiate, but to *assert* control over their lives 'so women can be equal to men, don't have to be grateful for all the things a man did for them and can't be taken advantage of because they are dependent'. It appears to primarily represent a means of challenging female powerlessness, dependence and inequity. These priorities of future economic independence and, secondly, success and recognition seem to underscore young women's educational and occupational aspirations. A Lakshmi Girls' Hindu College student similarly asserted

> Yes, I think it is important for women because right now there are not many prominent women in society and I think we should make it known that all the stereotypes are not true and we can achieve just as much and more than men can. (15-year-old, Indo-Hindu)

However, explored further, these goals highlight the confusions of navigating competing and coalescing ideals of womanhood. On the one hand, their future career goals seem to focus on challenging 'traditional' feminine roles. On the other hand, their goals also appear to conform to notions of 'inappropriate' and 'unfeminine' occupations for women. In this study, competing ideals may explain girls' desires for very high status (historically male-dominated) occupations, their fantasies of future glamour and their sense of gender 'appropriate' career aspirations.

Examined by ethnicity and religion, all groups of young women share aspirations to traditionally professional, high-status occupations such as lawyers and doctors. Their aspirations generally fell into a few main groups. These were high-status professional jobs including accountant, businesswoman and politician, less prestigious professional jobs including teacher, flight attendant and journalist, and new professional jobs including computer analyst and programmer. A relatively small number of girls aspired to jobs in a creative or artistic field as a dancer, graphic artist or fashion designer. Even less desired were technical, vocational, clerical, service, agricultural or manual/skilled trade jobs such as a 'construction worker, farmer, baker, massager or upholsterer'. Such little interest may reflect both the relatively low status of these jobs as well as a sexual division of labour and, consequently, a sexual division of career aspirations. However, together, the number of girls who aspired to be famous supermodels, actresses and singers made this group of occupations the fourth most popular.

Rubin's (1969, 85) study found a great discrepancy between girls' future career aspirations and the possibilities for achievement. This was especially true for the Afro-Trinidadian and Indo-Trinidadian students.[8] In part, Indo-Trinidadian (as well as groups Rubin termed 'Negro' and 'Coloured') students' aspirations were tempered by their expectations of fulfilling these dreams. However, the author found that even their expectations did not match their chances of achieving these goals. There has been an immense expansion, over 40 or so years, in educational and career opportunities for girls. Yet, it is still not possible for *all* girls to achieve these very high aspirations even if increasing numbers can. Nevertheless, girls' strong desire to be part of these professions has also not significantly changed.

However, the picture is more complicated. Given three choices, a single girl would not necessarily choose a high status occupation for all three options. In fact, girls' aspirations varied widely. Many desired both high-status traditional occupations such as being a lawyer or doctor and 'middle status' traditional professional occupations such as being a teacher and flight attendant. Additionally, the surprisingly high number of girls who wanted to be accountants, lawyers and politicians *as well as* supermodels and actresses highlights a playful side to girls' fantasies. It may suggest that girls' aspirations are influenced by feminine ideals and the value placed by media on glamorous sex appeal (see table 2). It is also possible that their choices reflect a combination of adolescents' idealistic and realistic aspirations, and future fantasies.

Table 2: Sample of range of occupations to which girls aspire

Occupation	School	Age	Ethnic Identity	Religion
Model, construction worker, doctor.	SAGHS	15	Indo-Trinidadian	Presbyterian/Congregational
Criminal lawyer, news reporter, politician (leader of the UNC).	SAGHS	15	Indo-Trinidadian	Presbyterian/Congregational
Doctor, lawyer, flight attendant.	TML	15	Indo-Trinidadian	Muslim-TML
Lawyer, journalist, member of Parliament.	LGHC	15	Indo-Trinidadian	Hindu-Sanatanist
Psychologist, owner of nightclub, chemist.	EL DO	15	Indo-Trinidadian	Muslim-TML
Prime Minister, lawyer, model.	EL DO	15	Indo-Trinidadian	Hindu-Kabir Panth
Lecturer within my own grasp, actress, religious dancer.	TWG	18	Indo-Trinidadian	Hindu-Sanatanist
Supermodel, actress, veterinarian.	LGHC	15	Other	Roman Catholic
Accountant manger, dancehall singer, CEO of an Inc.	TML	15	Other-mixed	Roman Catholic
Teacher, lawyer, doctor.	TWG	15	Indian-African	Hindu-Sanatanist

Girls' responses suggest that ethnicity, class and religion have some impact on their occupational aspirations. For example, girls working in Tunapuna aspired most to 'middle'-status professional jobs such as teacher, policewoman, flight attendant and manager. This suggests that their aspirations are more realistic or more limited by their participation in the working world. However, somewhat contradictorily, their second choices were most often both vocational/clerical jobs, such as being a hairdresser, accountant-clerk, secretary, customer service representative or bank clerk, *and* the highest-status professional jobs. They least often chose new professional and creative/artistic occupations. Often, these young women expressed the desire to open their own business. This suggests an entrepreneurial spirit in this group or, maybe, disgust with the idea of having to work for someone.

In this regard, many of them seem to live (and work) from day to day feeling that 'it is better to be occupied and independent'. One 18-year-old Hindu young woman, who wanted to be a 'teacher, flight attendant or hairdresser', described her job as 'hard work and later hours for underpayment (sic)'. Those girls that were happy with their jobs wrote that they 'pay me good' or 'keep me occupied, able to support myself, help pay family bills and save for the future'. Some of these young women felt comfortable with their employers and co-workers. More than one indicated that she wished she had not left school so early because it limited her ability to achieve her aspirations. A 15-year-old Indo-Hindu, dissatisfied with her job and aspiring to be 'a teacher, lawyer or doctor', explained

> Cause if I haven't drop out of school, I may have been in a better occupation, where I would be proud of myself.

Like students with greater educational and employment opportunities, young women working in Tunapuna also value independence and their own income. However, their aspirations suggest they settle for more personal, realistic, immediate and achievable goals while nonetheless maintaining fantasies of future glamour or occupational mobility.

Somewhat contradictorily, the highest sought occupations are the least attainable. They are also the most desirable because they generate the highest income, and appear to act as a potential source of independence, confidence and status. While all young women in the study valued high-status occupations and those traditionally held by men, some girls' career aspirations also conformed to a complementary gender ideology and division of labour. For example, young women who felt that females and males were better suited to different occupations argued that 'women and men have different skills and attitudes' and 'men can do jobs that women can't do' or that 'women are soft and feminine and men are tough and masculine'. However, almost three quarters of girls instead asserted, 'men and women are equal and have the same abilities'.

Yet, the explanations of some reveal contradictions, double standards and underlying ambivalence about gender roles and imperatives. For example, just less than a third of girls claimed, 'hard, manual labour, for example, being a construction worker, URP worker, garbage collector, mechanic, prostitute, pimp and stripper is unsuitable for women'. Only one wrote, 'prostitution and stripping is not for men or women because it shows no respect for yourself'. Notions of gender complementarity clearly create an unwillingness to choose the 'negative, dirty, hard and immoral jobs' considered more masculine. This reflects a double standard. Girls both feel that they should have equal opportunities and, yet, find work associated with low status and masculinity undesirable and *unfeminine*.

In comparison to jobs as security guards, watchmen and taxi drivers, 'nursing, hairdressing or housework' were seen by these girls as less suitable for men. Men are therefore seen as more suited to physical roles, industrial, technical or agricultural occupations, and those associated with mobility, risk-taking and hustling. Complementarily, young women perceived jobs in an office or as a doctor, lawyer, entrepreneur, business administrator, minister or 'anything that will uplift the nation' more suitable for women. Only one girl wrote that men were more suited to 'business'. Occupations with 'positive vibes such as being a teacher or policewoman' additionally reproduce the paradigm of femininity as service and morality. Essentially, masculinity as power (to protect) and as freedom is juxtaposed against femininity as central to the family and service of society, uplifting or beautifying, and to be protected.

Nevertheless, about 70 per cent of all groups in the study were very clear that 'women are just as capable and equal, and have the potential for becoming more or better'. Many further stated, 'men and women should be equal and have equal rights' and 'a person can become whatever he or she chooses and should not be judged by sex. In today's world, men and women are doing the same jobs, for example, men look after children and women are engineers'. Thus, despite some conformity to ideals of insider femininity, a majority of girls feel that women and men should have equal job opportunities and that, as an Indo-Presbyterian girl attending St Augustine Girls' High School stated, Everyone is equal and men should not be more important than women and in a higher class.

In summary, young women's very high aspirations may reflect a consciousness of and challenge to, what one respondent called, female 'class' difference and inequality. However, across class, ethnicity and religion, a majority of young women share also aspirations for uplifting, and 'feminine' or glamorous work. This suggests that while desires to challenge traditional limitations, and achieve equality and success in a 'man's world' are compelling, feminine ideals mediate girls' confrontation with the prevailing gender system. Their different locations mediate girls' chances of achieving their aspirations and their sense that it is legitimate to challenge gender roles and inequities. There is a great deal of ambivalence associated with 'self-regard' or feeling good about yourself even when girls believe they should take on the world.

b) *Marriage, maturity and intimate relations*

Girls' marriage aspirations contrast with their employment aspirations and point to a value system characterised by traditionally 'feminine' ideals of compromise, adjustment, responsibility and sharing. Emphasis on marital 'responsibility' and 'adjustment' is common to all girls across ethnicity and religion. These aspirations suggest that girls are trying to succeed at competing ways of valuing and expressing womanhood. However, the responses also suggest that individual choice and responsibility are important aspects of relationships. They are part of the 'mature' decisions, regarding love and motherhood, which young women feel mark the onset of womanhood. Thus, marriage appears to be very important to girls' sense of self at the same time as it involves being 'tied down to responsibilities' for others and, therefore, 'less freedom' and greater compromise regarding other aspirations.

This reflects a general tension between ideals of individual choice and traditional gendered imperatives regarding female sexuality. Their views regarding girls' 'readiness' to have sex, premarital sex and having boyfriends suggest that insider femininity still sets the terms of respectability. Yet, these are intersected by shifting conceptions of 'appropriate' sexual behaviour. Indo-Trinidadian girls' responses suggest that even while they conform to complementary gender expectations, they challenge rules regarding sexuality and value personal decisions about love, relationships and intimacy.

Essentially, Indo-Trinidadians in this study reported beginning intimate activity – holding hands, kissing and/or petting – at later ages and in lesser proportion to non-Indo-Trinidadians. Nonetheless, among Indo-Trinidadian girls, sexual activity can begin as early as 12 to 13 years old with the majority of both non-Indo-Trinidadians and Indo-Trinidadians who have had sexual intercourse having first had this experience at 17 years old. However, unlike non-Indo-Trinidadians, a majority of all groups of Indo-Trinidadian girls still believe that marriage determines readiness for sex (table 3).[9]

Table 3: Girls' views about when young women are ready to have sex

Age	Non-Indo-Trinidadian	Indo-Trinidadian	Indo-Hindu	Indo-Muslim	Indo-Christian
14 or younger	0%	0%	0%	0%	0%
15-18	17.1%	6.7%	7.8%	0%	8.7%
19-22	17.1%	7.9%	7.8%	0%	13.0%
23 or older	2.9%	0%	0%	0%	0%
When she is married	37.1%	59.6%	54.9%	61.5%	65.2%
Depends	25.7%	25.8%	29.4%	38.5%	13.0%
Total	100%	100%	100%	100%	100%

Yet, as the table below shows, less than half of Indo-Trinidadians 'strongly disapprove' or 'disapprove' of premarital sex. This suggests that, while marital sex is considered important, marriage does not confer the right to be sexually active and is not considered the only legitimate site for intimacy and sexual relations. Rather, both Indo-Trinidadian and non-Indo-Trinidadians seem to feel that 'readiness' can also reflect age, feelings and circumstances.

Table 4: Girls' view of sexual activity before marriage

Response	Non-Indo-Trinidadian	Indo-Trinidadian	Indo-Hindu	Indo-Muslim	Indo-Christian
Strongly approve	0%	2.2%	3.8%	0%	0%
Approve	5.7%	5.6%	5.8%	0%	8.7%
Disapprove	14.3%	19.1%	17.3%	15.4%	21.7%
Strongly disapprove	20.0%	22.5%	21.2%	23.1%	26.1%
Don't care	2.9%	4.5%	5.8%	7.7%	0%
Up to those involved	34.3%	38.2%	34.6%	53.8%	39.1%
It depends	22.9%	6.7%	9.6%	0%	4.3%
Don't know	0%	1.1%	1.9%	0%	0%
Total	100%	100%	100%	100%	100%

The minority of girls who disapproved of premarital sex articulated religious-based moral imperatives regarding female sexuality, and notions about the sacredness of sex within marriage. There were also fears of disease, pregnancy and abandonment. Girls who did not explicitly disapprove of premarital sex felt 'the people involved can make up their own minds about their life'. They additionally thought it was acceptable as long as 'couples' 'know if they are responsible, if that is what they want, if they are in love, if they are ready to give up their virginity to each other and are sure'. These responses are particularly significant given that 80 per cent of Indo-Trinidadian and almost 95 per cent of non-Indo-Trinidadian girls think that it is appropriate for a teenage girl to have a boyfriend. As one Indo-Trinidadian wrote, 'Why should a person wait to give her husband this "gift"?' Thus, ideals of marital sex appear to be mediated by the competing legitimacy of adolescent female desires and feelings. In other words, romantic love, the acceptability of having a boyfriend and individual feelings of 'readiness' challenge marriage as an ideal regulating adolescent girls' sexuality and intimate relations.

In 1957 and 1961, at the time of Rubin's research, marriage was still an important and expected part of growing into womanhood. For many Indo-Trinidadian girls, it was the first marker of womanhood and of 'adulthood', the second being motherhood. In the contemporary period, it seems that the significance of marriage and the age at which girls expect to marry have both changed. In this regard, over 90 per cent of Indo-Trinidadians expect to marry when they are past 21 years old and almost half as late as 28 years old. With 'romantic love' and not arranged marriages, now the norm among Indo-Trinidadians (Klass 1991), this suggests that Indo-Trinidadian and non-Indo-Trinidadian girls commonly expect to marry at later ages when individual choice and responsibility are more significant.

Nonetheless, Indo-Trinidadians felt more likely than non-Indo-Trinidadians to marry between 21 and 24 years old. As Table 5 shows, slightly more Christians than Muslims or Hindus, and a greater proportion of girls working in Tunapuna, also expect to marry at this age. A majority of all girls expected to marry before 30 years of age. This suggests an 'inappropriate' age to remain unwed may still exist. While only a minority of non-Indo-Trinidadians attending St Augustine Girls' High School seemed disinterested in marrying, no Indo-Muslims or Christians expressed this view. Marriage, therefore, still appears highly significant to Indo-Trinidadian girls' expectations regarding adult femininities.

Table 5: Age at which girls expect to marry

Age	Non-Indo-Trinidadian	Indo-Trinidadian	Indo-Hindu	Indo-Muslim	Indo-Christian
17-20	5.9%	2.2%	1.9%	7.7%	0%
21-24	26.5%	42.2%	37.7%	46.2%	52.2%
25-28	55.9%	48.9%	49.1%	46.2%	43.5%
29-40	5.9%	5.6%	7.5%	0%	4.3%
Never	5.9%	1.1%	1.9%	0%	0%
Total	100%	100%	100%	100%	100%

However, young Indo-Trinidadian women's responses also suggest that marriage has changed from a rite that confers adulthood (Klass 1961) to a symbol and expression of having attained adulthood. This may be its contemporary significance for these Indo-Trinidadians. For example, many young Indo-Trinidadian women imagine they will know they are ready to get married by their ability to make 'mature decisions' and have a 'mature relationship'. Other lesser factors include instinct and feeling, love and a sense of accomplishment of personal goals.

Interestingly, Indo-Trinidadians to a greater extent than non-Indo-Trinidadians in this study seem to emphasise needing to feel that '*I am ready* to make a commitment and can make *mature, right choices*'. Decisions regarding marriage, therefore, seem to emerge from a sense of womanhood. They may reflect a feeling of adulthood that, perhaps, now comes with autonomy, success, education or simply age. Yet, whatever their reasons for marrying and anticipated age of marriage, marriage itself seems to have remained an important rite signifying adult womanhood for the majority of Indo-Trinidadian young women. In this respect, having a mature relationship appears most significant to almost half of Indo-Trinidadian girls, but just over a quarter of non-Indo-Trinidadian young women. Similarly, while almost a quarter of Indo-Trinidadian girls want to marry after accomplishing personal goals, this was articulated by only 10 per cent of the non-Indo-Trinidadian group. Conversely, notions of romantic love dominate among almost half of non-Indo-Trinidadian girls, but just over a quarter of Indo-Trinidadians. Divergent responses suggest significant differences in the ways that girls from different ethnic groups may characterise relationships and marriage. Overall, Indo-Trinidadians more greatly emphasised 'readiness' when 'the "right" guy has a good job, seems to be able to be responsible and committed, thinks of me as an equal and individual' and 'after I accomplish personal goals, achieve self-understanding, finish school, have a career and I am then ready for family'.

With regard to religious differences, marriage appears to still determine sexuality according to imperatives of racial 'purity'. Girls' responses suggest that this imperative is virtually insignificant for non-Indo-Trinidadian girls, but especially important to Hindu and Muslim Indo-Trinidadians. However, it is noteworthy that over half of Indo-Trinidadian girls generally stated that they do not consider it important to marry within their own 'race'. Their own 'choices' may, therefore, challenge the regulatory power of Indo-Trinidadian ideals of female 'purity' as the signifier of group respectability and honour. This appears consistent with their approach to sexuality and marriage generally, and the importance they give to individual decision-making as a competing ideal.

Nevertheless, whereas girls in the study seem more willing to challenge the status quo while they are single or unmarried, marriage aspirations are marked by greater acceptance of a traditional sexual division of labour and the 'compromises' of being a wife and mother. Almost 60 per cent of young women seem willing to meet these complementary gender ideals and to believe that, because of her new responsibilities, a married woman can no longer focus on her own individual freedoms and self-development. As 40 per cent of girls further described, a woman must instead focus on 'adjustment to a new way of life and expectations, and being a wife and woman'. These young women may be attempting to differently negotiate competing aspirations and value systems. Thus, many girls may have aspirations to assert power and challenge gender roles through educational and occupational advancement while anticipating having to adjust to complementary gender ideals of wifehood and motherhood. This suggests that ideals of insider femininity still present important considerations, and that marriage and motherhood may remain quintessential exemplifiers of womanhood and femininity. As a Lakshmi Girls' Hindu College student affirmed, 'To me it is a joy treasured by us lucky enough to be part of the female population. Something that the men cannot do better than us in'. (15-year-old, Indo-Hindu)

Young women's marriage aspirations show, as they navigate divergent ideals, girls must differently negotiate a range of spheres and identities.

c) *Motherhood, womanhood and 'choice'*

As with marriage, the majority of girls in this study value childbearing and see it as important and even inevitable for women. They associate children with new experiences and responsibilities, and with opportunities for teaching others, giving love and feeling fulfilled. However, across ethnic, religious and school groups, the majority of young women think that children satisfy the most important goal of womanhood and are women's greatest (and lasting) contribution.

Over 60 per cent of all young women specifically felt that 'children complete the primary goal of womanhood and the circle of life, give a sense of being a woman and fulfil a biological need'. Additionally, almost one third wrote that having children is a 'changing time of added responsibilities for a woman, more worries and happy, sad, painful moments, now the main purpose is to take care of kids, there is added pressure and adulthood'. In this way, children are perceived as an individual female's greatest 'achievement', fulfilling both a biological, social and spiritually ordained 'purpose', and making her feel like a successful *woman*.

Motherhood, therefore, still offers a compelling source of identity and fulfilment to a majority of all girls in the study. Ideals of womanhood have shaped many of these girls' desires and ideas of themselves in the future so motherhood is associated with 'the troubles and joys' of mature adulthood and, perhaps, gives girls a sense of power through their role of raising and socialising a child 'to call your own'. Motherhood underscores womanhood and may regulate other aspects of female sexuality through the imperative of being 'the perfect role model'. However, ultimately, young women's responses suggest that they both hold and negotiate these ideals. Notably, while less than five per cent of girls 'never' want to marry, just over 15 per cent of both Indo-Trinidadian *and* non-Indo-Trinidadian young women reported not wanting children. To them, the ideals of wifehood and motherhood may not be coterminous.

The data also suggest that Indo-Trinidadians disapprove of unwed motherhood to a greater extent than non-Indo-Trinidadians. However, both groups of girls more greatly disapprove of unwed motherhood than abortion. This further emphasises the continuing significance, particularly for Indo-Trinidadians in this study, of ideals of marriage and childbirth within marriage. Yet, almost half of non-Indo-Trinidadians and just fewer than 40 per cent of (especially Hindu and Christian) Indo-Trinidadians believe that a decision regarding unwed motherhood is 'up to the people involved' and/or 'depends on the situation'. Similarly, in contrast to an average of 40 per cent of Indo-Trinidadian students, over half of the girls working in Tunapuna felt that having children out of wedlock was 'up to those involved' and/or 'depends on the situation'. This suggests that norms regarding marriage and childbirth within marriage may differ by class. In comparison, as Table 6 shows, a greater proportion of Indo-Trinidadians, and particularly Hindus, felt that the choice to have an abortion is 'up to the people involved' and/or 'depends on the situation'.

Table 6: Girls' view of abortion

Response	Non-Indo-Trinidadian	Indo-Trinidadian	Indo-Hindu	Indo-Muslim	Indo-Christian
Strongly approve	0%	2.2%	2.0%	0%	4.3%
Approve	5.9%	2.2%	3.9%	0%	0%
Disapprove	8.8%	15.7%	9.8%	23.1%	26.1%
Strongly disapprove	41.2%	37.1%	33.3%	46.2%	34.8%
Don't care	0%	0%	0%	0%	0%
Up to those involved	17.6%	19.1%	19.6%	23.1%	17.4%
It depends	26.5%	23.6%	31.4%	7.7%	17.4%
Don't know	0%	0%	0%	0%	0%
Total	100%	100%	100%	100%	100%

'Proper' wifehood and motherhood compellingly signify successful adult *womanhood* and situate forms of 'appropriate' femininity within the home and family. The above responses show that while a majority of young women may not support unwed motherhood or abortion, many often felt these decisions depended on the people and/or circumstances or were 'up to the people involved'. Thus, girls' views suggest both that they reproduce moral imperatives regarding marriage and motherhood, and contest these naturalised ideals. It therefore appears that context and competing ideals of individual negotiation and agency inform how aspirations are valued and mediated in the everyday.

c) *Equality and public participation*

Placed in wider social context, a majority of Indo-Trinidadian and non-Indo-Trinidadian young women disagreed with what they saw as different moral standards or 'double standards' regarding women's and men's behaviour and appearance. About 60 per cent of both groups treated these double standards as cause and effect of sexual discrimination, unfair judgment of women, and girls' more limited freedom. Instead, girls desire equality between women and men. Their critical 'view from below' (Mies 1983) seems to inform a revisioning of moral imperatives and complementary gender ideals. Yet, their perception that sexual equality doesn't exist also leads to ambivalent feelings about growing up female.

While almost three quarters of Christians reported feeling that men and women face different moral standards, less than a half of Muslims gave this response. Similarly, in stark contrast to the high school students, only about one third of young women working in Tunapuna felt that different standards exist. Perhaps, the views of these older and/or working girls reflect less sensitivity to gender issues, or their difference from students who may experience greater 'protection' and surveillance. However, overall, it is striking that up to 40 per cent of the entire sample reported feeling that men and women did not face different moral standards.

Table 7: Girls' views regarding whether men and women face different moral standards

Response	Non-Indo-Trinidadian	Indo-Trinidadian	Indo-Hindu	Indo-Muslim	Indo-Christian
Strongly approve	0%	2.2%	2.0%	0%	4.3%
Approve	5.9%	2.2%	3.9%	0%	0%
Disapprove	8.8%	15.7%	9.8%	23.1%	26.1%
Strongly disapprove	41.2%	37.1%	33.3%	46.2%	34.8%
Don't care	0%	0%	0%	0%	0%
Up to those involved	17.6%	19.1%	19.6%	23.1%	17.4%
It depends	26.5%	23.6%	31.4%	7.7%	17.4%
Don't know	0%	0%	0%	0%	0%
Total	100%	100%	100%	100%	100%

Almost two thirds of the girls who felt that different moral standards existed for women and men wrote that 'men get more freedom and can do what they want e.g. promiscuity and society says nothing while women get branded' or 'because of double standards, women are viewed and judged differently and expected to have higher standards'. More than 20 per cent of girls additionally felt that 'women will always be discriminated against', that 'tradition keeps women on a shorter chain than men who have more free rope' and this is 'still true in society today'. In this regard, non-Indo-Trinidadian girls appeared to disagree more (89 per cent) with these standards than Indo-Trinidadian girls (69 per cent). However, a majority of both groups nonetheless felt that 'all should be treated equal, we are all equal'.

Notions of 'modernity' seem to also inform these aspirations. As these young women wrote, women deserve more because 'in this new era, the role of women is changed and some traditions need to change also so women have equal freedom and are equally judged as men'. Thus, the girls in this study appear both aware of the goal of equality between women and men, *and* its general absence in their experience of society. Almost 90 per cent of non-Indo-Trinidadians and almost 95 per cent of Indo-Trinidadians felt that women are equal to men and should be treated as equal to men. In contrast, less than ten per cent of non-Indo-Trinidadians and less than five per cent of Indo-Trinidadians felt woman *are* treated equally.

Such mixed messages create ambivalent feelings toward growing up female. When asked for their feelings about being a woman in this society, almost 40 per cent of girls wrote of feelings of frustration and injustice, and fears of being taken advantage of, denied freedoms, discriminated against and disrespected. For them, it is an 'uphill struggle and pressure to achieve the same as men'. Girls in this group also expressed the ambivalence of being 'only sometimes glad' because 'being a woman is sometimes a privilege, sometimes a burden ....' Yet, almost a third of girls felt 'good, honoured, happy and proud' about being a young woman in this society. They privileged both the traditional role of motherhood and new opportunities for 'women's successes'. Additionally, as many as 15 per cent of girls said that they felt 'treated equally', that being a woman is 'no problem, and good' and there was nothing that they would change about being a woman in society.

On the other hand, over half of all young women in the study primarily wanted changes to men's attitudes and behaviour toward women. As well, these young women wanted 'men and women to be equal, to have the same roles, for women to do the activities they want to, to have less overprotective and strict parents of girls, and to have more freedom'. What is noteworthy is that some justify their claim to greater freedom on the basis of their sense of responsibility and discretion (read respectability). For example, one Lakshmi Girls' Hindu College student wrote, 'I would like men to be looked upon like women when they sleep around and they should have less privileges because women I think are more *responsible*'. (15-year-old, Indo-Hindu)

And, another argued that if society's views toward women changed, 'I would be allowed more freedom because I think I have the knowledge to be *discreet*'. (15-year-old, Indo-Hindu)

Young women's aspirations for women's participation in parliamentary politics similarly suggest a critical view of gender stereotypes and constraints. Their desires for greater equality in this sphere also highlight the successful mainstreaming of white, Western, liberal feminist priorities of equal rights and representation for women. However, young women's desires for greater representation are not matched by aspirations or interest in becoming involved in politics. In this regard, girls' responses suggest that they believe stepping out of 'protective discourses' (Handa 1997) can leave women too vulnerable. They also show how aspirations to challenge the status quo are regulated by discouraging, gendered realities. Thus, young women in this study may be caught between desiring social and political change and being aware of the personal difficulties and risks associated with these challenges.

More than 90 per cent of girls wanted women representatives in Parliament because 'women need representation to fight for women's rights, to hear women's voices, to balance views' and because 'women need to be part of decision-making'. As well, girls' responded that it is important to have women in Parliament for 'girl power' and because 'women can rule too, we are all leaders, Parliament needs women, so men can see we are equal, have rights and abilities, and will see who we can be'. Thus, women's participation in Parliament signifies a greater role in decision-making, greater representation of women's views and issues of women's rights, and greater expression (and proof) of female capability. It seems that Parliament appears both as a site of inequality and under-representation of women and *also* a place where young women aspire to claim, exercise and assert power. Yet, while young women overwhelmingly supported women's equality and public participation, less than 40 per cent in the study were interested in politics. This was less true for Indo-Trinidadian Christians and Muslims. However, generally, girls cited a sexual division of labour and the male-defined and dominated nature of politics as primary obstacles. These girls blamed 'men's criticism and rejection, discrimination, societal double standards and stereotyping, and not enough support and encouragement for women'.

Stepping into male terrain such as Parliament may be associated with the difficulties of successfully challenging and negotiating both the boundaries of insider femininity and masculinity. As the experience of past Attorney-General and UNC politician Kamla Persad-Bissessar showed, once within this terrain of masculinity (at times also seen as outsider femininity), it is easier to lose respectability.[10] Young women may be impressed and inspired by women who successfully defy convention, cross gender boundaries and are still accepted. However, they are clearly aware of, and discouraged, by the risks involved.

Conclusion: Navigating an Appropriate Balance

Class and ethnicity inform different desires, and provide different opportunities for asserting and accommodating values. For example, the responses from the small sample of girls working in Tunapuna suggest that they can most easily access fulfilment by meeting feminine ideals and their day-to-day aspirations. Nonetheless, throughout the study, Christian Indo-Trinidadians at St Augustine Girls' High School in particular reported views and values that overlapped with those of non-Indo-Trinidadians. This suggests that shared religious background may inform inter-ethnic commonalities.

Yet, all young women in the study overwhelmingly desired equality, autonomy and greater freedom to make their own decisions. While their educational and occupational aspirations highlight desires to assert themselves, challenge male dominance, be equal and make their own decisions, girls also articulate competing beliefs about gender-appropriate career aspirations. In very different ways, glamorous femininity and conformity to a sexual division of labour affirm a sense of femininity. Further, wifehood and motherhood appear to epitomise forms of 'female' power associated with morality, femininity and respectability.

Thus, compromise and complementarity compete with ideals of challenge and agency. Desires for equity as well as relationship and gender-appropriate identity may therefore be met by differently negotiating education and employment, and marriage and family. As well, it seems that the majority of girls maintain dichotomous notions of masculine and feminine imperatives *even* while they cross and challenge them. This may partly explain why they choose to negotiate educational and occupational success, and marriage and motherhood differently. Girls may assume that gender divisions are natural or unchangeable as a whole, while being 'tactically' adaptable in parts. It may also explain why self-regard appears linked to 'appropriately' balancing accommodation of gendered imperatives and challenge to feminine boundaries. The qualities to which girls aspire show simultaneous adherence to and departure from demands of 'appropriate' womanhood. Their identities therefore reflect a crosscutting range of reasons for which girls are valued and the pleasures of succeeding at belonging in divergent spaces.

However, ideals of maturity, individual responsibility and 'choice' appear *across* divergent value systems and point to a complex, contextualised relationship between young women's ideals and practices. This suggests that tensions among divergent ideals are worked out both across *and* within different parameters and spheres of young women's lives. As a result, there appear to be shifting combinations of assertion and accommodation 'appropriate' for different arenas of aspirations. In this regard, whatever their ideals, young women's competing emphasis on individual decision-making and responsibility makes sense. These are central to how girls in this study manage their own attempts at balance. Their more contemporary responsibility for both reproducing and contesting naturalised ideals, and their perception of women's opportunities and, yet, inequity in political, public and private spheres, understandably leads to ambivalent feelings about growing up female.

Briefly looking ahead, girls therefore appear unprepared for the future realities of the working world and the challenges of family life. Their responses seem to be premised on an assumption that equity is embedded in both spheres. They clearly expect to be able to assert, challenge or at least make decisions that reflect a sense of self. Caribbean feminists[11] working on issues such as sexual harassment note that women don't often respond in the workplace as they expect or say they would. Rather than confronting head-on, women may have to 'flirt' or leave their job, and they may become ill or frustrated. The workplace may become another sphere of femininity. The compromises of marriage and family may also not lead to feelings of joy, fulfilment or mutual respect. Compromises may not feel like choices these young women expect to make as part of a mature relationship. As they get older, these girls may have to assert themselves in their homes, and challenge expectations in ways they do not yet anticipate. Though contemporary Indo-Trinidadian girlhood is a far greater experience of agency than in the past, these adolescents' achievements may not have been their aspirations and may be far different from their expectations.

Notes

1. This study was undertaken for a Master of Philosophy (MPhil) degree at the Centre for Gender and Development Studies, The University of the West Indies, St Augustine.

2. By the end of the 1950s, marriageable girls were generally between 15 and 17 years old (Klass 1961, 120). In the Niehoffs' study, over one third of Indo-Trinidadian girls were married by 14 and the majority were married and mothers – and therefore women – by 19 years of age.

3. While Presbyterian missionaries enabled girls to access education since the turn of the century, Angela Hamel-Smith (1984, 4) points out that schooling generally institutionalised the process of gender socialisation in order to make girls better wives. While this is true, education nonetheless began to offer girls an opportunity to 'change their own self-image and expectations of womanhood and motherhood' from early in the twentieth century (Brandow 1983).

4. Mohammed described a post-indentureship system of three 'competing patriarchies' jostling for economic, political and social status and power. In this hierarchical system, 'Indian men found themselves at the lowest end of the ladder' beneath the dominant white patriarchy and the 'creole' patriarchy (ibid, 32) of the time. Reddock (1991) and others have noted Indo-Trinidadians' significant social mobility over the last decades and it is likely that the competing power of different patriarchies has become reconfigured.

5. I am grateful to Patricia Mohammed (personal communication, April 18, 2002) for helping me clarify this point.

6. Though not discussed in this paper, it should also be observed that, in areas where girls cannot directly assert, 'symbolic womanhood' - the tactical performance of masking and manipulating femininities – appears to also enable both belonging and transgressive desires, behaviours and identities.

7. Emphasis added.

8. Largely, this was due to very limited opportunities for scholarships to study after finishing high school, high costs of tertiary education, having to work either to save for further education or help support families and, more than anything else, the extremely high aspirations that these young students held (with the exception of white girls who were more inclined to become housewives and mothers).

9. The idea of virginity therefore still appears symbolically significant. In 1997, the Hindu Women's Association publicly criticised the choice to give an Afro-Trinidadian the Miss Mastana Bahar title because she was an unwed mother. They emphasised that she did not represent (Hindu) Indo-Trinidadians' continuing value for sex and childbearing within marriage. These values therefore remain tied to honour/shame and morality/immorality dualisms, to notions of duty and respect, and to the definition of Indo-Trinidadian gender and ethnic identities.

10. On a political platform during the UNC campaign leading up to the 2001 general election, Mrs Persad-Bissessar made a double-entendre about 'pipes' and the laying of 'pipes' (as part of infrastructure to provide greater household access to water). In fact, she said that the only 'pipe' she knew was Mr Bissessar's. Nonetheless, there was ensuing public debate about whether or not she had dishonoured herself and other (Indo-Trinidadian and, particularly, Hindu) women by even engaging in this sexual joke started by another male MP on the platform.

11. Discussion with Tracy Robinson (personal communication, July 25, 2003)

References

Anyon, J. 1982. 'Intersections of Gender and Class: Accommodation and Resistance by Working-Class and Affluent Females to Contradictory Sex-Roles Ideologies'. In *Gender, Class, and Education,* eds. L. Barton and S. Walker. London: Falmer Press.

Brandow, Mabel. 1983. *The History of Our Church Women, 1868–1983.* Altona: Manitoba.

Bush, D. and R. Simmons. 1987. 'Gender and Coping with the Entry into Early Adolescence'. In *Gender and Stress*, eds. R.C. Barnett and G.K. Baruch. New York: The Free Press.

Eisikovits, Edina. 1998. 'Girl-talk/Boy-talk: Sex Differences in Adolescent Speech'. In *Language and Gender: A Reader*, ed. Jennifer Coates. Massachusetts: Blackwell Publishers Ltd.

Erkut, Sumru, Jacqueline P. Fields, Rachel Sing and Fern Marx. 1996. 'Diversity in Girls' Experiences: Feeling Good about Who You Are'. In *Urban Girls: Resisting Stereotypes, Creating Identities*, eds. Bonnie J. Ross Leadbeater and Niobe Way. New York and London: New York University Press.

Gilligan, Carol, Nona P. Lyons and Trudy J. Hanmer. 1990. *Making Connections – The Relational Worlds of Adolescent Girls at Emma Willard School*. Cambridge: Harvard University Press.

Hamel-Smith, Angela. 1984. 'Primary Education and East Indian Women in Trinidad: 1900 – 1956'. Paper presented at the Third Conference on East Indians in the Caribbean: Beyond Survival. The University of the West Indies, St Augustine, Trinidad.

Handa, Amita. 1997. ' "Refs", "Fobs" and "Indian" Snobs: Using the Terrain of Dances and Fashion to Explore Gender and Race in Narratives of Second Generation Community Identity'. PhD thesis, York University, Toronto, Canada.

Hey, Valerie. 1997. *The Company She Keeps: An Ethnography of Girls' Friendships*. Buckingham and Philadelphia: Open University Press.

Hosein, Shaheeda. 2001. 'Until Death Do Us Part? Marriage, Divorce and the Indian Woman'. Paper presented at the 33rd Annual Conference of the Association of Caribbean Historians, the University of the West Indies, St Augustine, Trinidad.

Kanhai, Rosanne. 1999. 'The Masala Stone Sings: Poetry, Performance and Film by Indo-Caribbean Women'. In *Matikor: The Politics of Identity for Indo-Caribbean Women*, ed. Rosanne Kanhai. St Augustine: The University of the West Indies School of Continuing Studies.

Klass, Morton. 1991. *Singing With Sai Baba: The Politics of Revitalization in Trinidad*. Boulder, San Francisco: Westview Press.

———. 1961. *East Indians in Trinidad: A Study in Cultural Persistence*. New York: Columbia University Press.

Laitinen, Maarit. 1997. 'Becoming a Woman in Tobago: Femininity, Women's Morality and Responsibility'. In *Tobagonian Styles of Being*. MA thesis, Helsinki University.

Leadbeater, Bonnie J. Ross and Niobe Way, eds. 1996. *Urban Girls: Resisting Stereotypes, Creating Identities*. New York and London: New York University Press.

Lykes, M.B. 1985. 'Gender and Individualistic Versus Collectivistic Bases for Notions about the Self'. Journal of Personality 53: 356-83.

McRobbie, Angela. 1991. *Feminism and Youth Culture: From 'Jackie' to 'Just Seventeen'*. Basingstoke: McMillan Education Ltd.

Mies, Maria. 1983. 'Towards a Methodology for Feminist Research'. In *Theories of Women's Studies*, eds. G. Bowles and R. Klein. London: Routledge and Kegan Paul.

Mohammed, Patricia. 1997. 'The Idea of Childhood and Age of Sexual Maturity among Indians in Trinidad: A Sociohistorical Scrutiny'. In *Caribbean Families: Diversity Among Ethnic Groups*, eds. Jaipaul L. Roopnarine and Janet Brown. Greenwich, Conn: Ablex.

———. 1994. 'A Social History of Post-migrant Indians in Trinidad from 1917-1947'. PhD dissertation, Institute of Social Studies, The Hague.

Nevadomsky, Joseph. 1984. 'Marital Discord and Dissolution Among the Hindu East Indians in Rural Trinidad'. *Anthropos* 79: 113-128.

———. 1983. 'Changing Patterns of Marriage, Family, and Kinship Among the East Indians in Rural Trinidad'. *Anthropos* 78: 107-148.

———. 1980. 'Changes in Hindu Institutions in an Alien Environment'. *The Eastern Anthropologist* 33, no. 1: 39-53.

Niehoff, Arthur and Juanita. 1960. *East Indians in the West Indies*. Milwaukee: Milwaukee Public Museum Publications in Anthropology, No. 6.

Reddock, Rhoda. 1991. 'Social Mobility in Trinidad and Tobago, 1960-1980'. In *Social and Occupational Stratification in Contemporary Trinidad and Tobago*, ed. Selwyn Ryan. St Augustine: ISER.

———. 1986. 'Indian Women and Indentureship in Trinidad and Tobago 1845-1917: Freedom Denied'. *Caribbean Quarterly* 32, nos. 3 &4: 27-49.

Rotheram-Borus, Mary Jane, Steve Dopkins, Nuria Sabate and Marguerita Lightfoot. 1996. 'Personal and Ethnic Identity, Values, and Self-Esteem among Black and Latino Adolescent Girls'. In *Urban Girls: Resisting Stereotypes, Creating Identities*, eds. Bonnie J. Ross Leadbeater and Niobe Way. New York and London: New York University Press.

Rowbotham, Shiela. 1973. *Hidden from History: 300 Years of Women's Oppression and the Fight Against It*. London: Pluto Press.

Rubin, Vera and Marisa Zavalloni. 1969. *We Wish To Be Looked Upon: A Study of the Aspirations of Youth in a Developing Country*. New York: Teachers College Press.

Simmons, R. and D.A. Blyth. 1987. *Moving into Adolescence: The Impact of Pubertal Change and School Context*. Hawthorne, NY: Aldine de Gruyter.

Skeggs, Beverly. 1994. 'Situating the Production of a Feminist Ethnography'. In *Researching Women's Lives from a Feminist Perspective*, eds. Mary Maynard and June Purvis. London and Bristol: Taylor and Francis Ltd.

Skelton, Tracy and Gill Valentine, eds. 1998. *Cool Places: Geographies of Youth Cultures*. London and New York: Routledge.

Smith, Robert J. 1963. 'Muslim East Indians in Trinidad: Retention of Identity Under Acculturative Conditions'. PhD dissertation, University of Pennsylvania.

Taylor, Jill McLean. 1996. 'Cultural Stories: Latina and Portugese Daughters and Mothers'. In *Urban Girls: Resisting Stereotypes, Creating Identities*, eds. Bonnie J. Ross Leadbeater and Niobe Way. New York and London: New York University Press.

Taylor, Jill McLean, Carol Gilligan and Amy Sullivan. 1995. *Between Voice and Silence: Women and Girls, Race and Relationship*. London: Harvard University Press.

26 | MICHELLE V. DAVIS

Gender and the HIV/AIDS Epidemic in the Caribbean

Many studies done on women in the Caribbean have largely focused on women and family life and few have examined female sexuality beyond its reproductive capacity. In this paper, I intend to show that the gendered nature of the AIDS pandemic has, as Long and Messersmith (1995) argue, forced researchers and policy-makers to 'reconfigure social thought and reality, challenging traditional means of thinking and understanding illness, our bodies, and our intimate relationships to examine relations of power and inequality' (p.157).

Although women in the Caribbean continue to pursue higher education, enter managerial positions and professions and so appear to be doing well, gender inequities persist that undermine women's progress. This is best illustrated by the many acts of violence committed against women and girls. Added to this is the fact that most countries in the Caribbean report lower rates of female participation in labour markets and higher female unemployment rates than those for males. Situating this analysis within a human rights approach, I will show not only the need to challenge asymmetrical gender relations but also the obligation of states and other non-state actors to ensure the fulfilment of women's human rights.

Gender and the HIV/AIDS Epidemic

As with many economic, political and social issues, HIV/AIDS is indeed gendered. In 2002, women comprised 48 per cent of persons living with HIV/AIDS worldwide but in regions where HIV is transmitted mainly via heterosexual intercourse, more young women than young men are infected (Population Reference Bureau, 2002). Sub-Saharan Africa, South and Southeast Asia, North Africa, the Near East and the Caribbean have more young women so affected, with the rates of infected females being twice as high as those for males. Camara (2002) reports that, in 2001, the Caribbean reported close to half of one million persons living with HIV/AIDS with the Dominican Republic accounting for 27 per cent of all cases with a 2.0 per cent prevalence rate and Haiti accounting for 52 per cent of all cases with a 3.13 per cent HIV prevalence rate, while Cuba had the fastest growing rate between 2000 and 2001. He notes that, between 1982 and 2000, women accounted for 33 per cent of AIDS cases in the region. The Pan-American Health Organization (PAHO 2002) reports, however, that the gap between the number of women and men infected with HIV/AIDS is narrowing in the Caribbean, while in some countries the number of newly infected females outnumbers that of males (see appendix 1).

This may be explained by physiological factors whereby the mucosal membrane of the vagina is a large, thin area that is vulnerable to microscopic tearing, thus making young women particularly vulnerable to infection. Vaginal tissue absorbs fluids easily, including sperm, which has a high concentration of HIV. Women may also have other untreated sexually transmitted infections (STIs) which increase susceptibility to and are a known risk factor for HIV infection (PAHO 2002). As the World Health Organization (WHO 1999) states, the 'STI epidemic, with 333 million new cases a year, fuels the AIDS epidemic' (p. 29). WHO (1999) reports that 165 million cases of curable STIs occur each year worldwide among women aged 15-49. Women are more prone to infections due to the large mucosal surface of the vagina that is exposed to large numbers of pathogens during sexual intercourse and because STIs, including HIV, are more easily transmitted from men to women. Women with STIs tend to be asymptomatic and thus less likely to seek treatment, resulting in chronic infections with long-term implications for health such as infertility (WHO 1999).

The social construction of gender, however, accounts for much of the difference in rates of infection between men and women. Femininity is associated with motherhood, fertility and passivity, whereas masculinity is premised on sexual prowess, aggression and strength and fatherhood. These differing sexualities are ascribed unequal amounts of power, status, and privilege. Barriteau (1998) argues that current gender relations are associations of domination and asymmetry where men and women receive different rewards, benefits and penalties. Sexuality, both ideologically and materially, impacts men and women differently; men tend to benefit from the control of women's sexuality, including women's bodies, self-conceptions, and sexual decisions. Gender not only affects sexuality and gender relations but also social and occupational roles and men's and women's access to and control of economic and social resources. A gender analysis of HIV/AIDS points to several factors that compound and confound the issue and 'shape vulnerability to infection and the personal, social and economic impact of the epidemic. As a result, gender should be viewed as a cross-cutting issue that has implications for all aspects of the epidemic' (United Nations Division for the Advancement of Women 2000, 8).

Sexuality and Gender Relations

Weeks (1986) states that sexuality is the 'abstract noun that refers to the quality of being "sexual"' (p. 13). Sex itself has two meanings: the behaviour or action of 'natural' sex that occurs between men and women; and the biology of a person indicated by the reproductive organs. In the sixteenth century, sex meant the division of humanity into men and women but by the nineteenth century the meaning of the word had changed and referred to behaviour or action. This indicates a shift in the way that sexuality was perceived, a shift that occurred through many and often complex social processes. Weeks (1986) argues that sexuality is a product of the historical and social and thus it is not static and universal. He posits that sex became further politicised in the nineteenth century with the advent of medicine, psychology, sexology and pedagogy operating outside of the Church and aided by binary thinking that separated the body from the mind and entrenched moral and social standards even further. Sexuality is thus constructed through various social processes. Weeks suggests that one such process is the distinction between the sexes, even an antagonism; for example 'the battle of the sexes'. Another is the belief that sex is an overpowering natural or biological force located in the genitals; and lastly, the creation of a sexual hierarchy that privileges heterosexual intercourse. These views of sexuality are deeply embedded in many cultures and provide the ideological justification for uncontrollable male lust and the act of rape, the downgrading of sexual autonomy and the maligning of seeming sexual deviants.

Foucault (1985) shows that Christianity, for example, has associated intercourse with evil, sin, deceit and death and has defined legitimate sex as that which occurs within monogamous marriage with exclusively procreative functions. Women's sexuality is constrained and relegated to chastity and virginity, and to monogamous marriage. Rich (1986) contends that motherhood and heterosexuality have created prescriptions and conditions in which choices are made or constrained, where both are channelled to serve male interests. Behaviours that threaten these institutions, such as illegitimacy, abortion, and lesbianism, are considered deviant and criminal with the institutionalisation of heterosexuality telling women that they are dangerous, unchaste, and the embodiment of carnal lust. She argues that:

> It has withheld over half of the human species from decisions affecting their lives; it exonerates men from fatherhood in any authentic sense; it creates the dangerous schism between 'private' and 'public' life; it calcifies human choices and potentialities. In the most fundamental and bewildering of contradictions, it has alienated women from our bodies by incarcerating us in them (1986, 270).

Thus, women must resist male domination within heterosexual relations. Foucault (1979), however, states that there is no single, all-encompassing strategy to reduce all sex to its reproductive function, its heterosexual and adult forms and its matrimonial legitimacy. Such a perspective 'fails to take into account the manifold objectives aimed for, the manifold means employed in the different sexual politics concerned with the two sexes, the different age groups and social classes' (p. 103). Foucault's historical research shows that sexuality has assumed different forms at different times, from the homosocial groupings of Roman and Greek societies through to dominant monogamous heterosexual relations of industrial societies. Moreover, the one-dimensional assertion of sexuality, as Rich suggests, ignores the many ways that women resist this powerlessness and victimisation across cultures and time. The notion of women's sexual liberation has played a significant role in the second wave feminist movement spurred by the introduction of oral contraception and the development of analytical tools to explore the private realm and so encouraged women to take control of their sexuality whether in or outside marriage. Nonetheless, the power dynamics inherent in heterosexual relations found in many societies do in fact privilege men; thereby constraining women's abilities to negotiate safer sex practices, make use of family-planning methods, and construct positive self-conceptions of their bodies and beings.

Sexuality is at the heart of gender relations and is the site where we learn about our bodies and socially sanctioned behaviours, including sexual relations (Harcourt 1993). Harcourt continues by stating that women's sexuality is most often linked to their abilities to reproduce; women's own sexual desire is often negated by them and deemed dangerous to men. To be desired by a man and to be married are often primary goals in women's lives and their social status is often tied to these goals. 'Often it is the unspoken inequalities between the sexes based on iniquitous sexual relations within the family that prevent women from achieving their true potential' (Harcourt 1993, 25).

Women and men ascribe to particular gender norms. Ideal femininity dictates that young women should be chaste and pure and sexually innocent, so young women may not possess accurate information about sex and sexuality. Men, however, are expected to know a great deal about sex and also to be sexually experienced. This may then lead to boys not receiving proper information on sexual health since it is often assumed that they already have that knowledge. Boys and young men may not ask questions about sex and sexuality for fear of ridicule if they do not know and/or are sexually inexperienced. Girls may not seek information on sex to avoid being labelled loose.

The social shaping of gender includes the creation and maintenance of asymmetrical relations between and among men and women, where power, status and privilege are afforded to persons who ascribe to hegemonic sexualities. Jackson (1996) contends that the social shaping of sexuality is patriarchal, that 'gendered patterns of domination and submission are intrinsic to patriarchal societies and written into their cultural representations' (p. 22). She argues that sexuality is imbued with hierarchies of power and that at the apex of this hierarchy is heterosexuality, where sexual activity is defined as heterosexual, vaginal and in terms of active subject and passive object. Heterosexuality, as an institution, also dictates who performs what jobs both in and outside of the home, and the value placed on this work. In the Caribbean, much of the work around issues of HIV/AIDS has largely focused on heterosexuality and penile/vaginal sex, yet, other forms of sexuality and sexual behaviours exist. Moreover, gender inequality has not been adequately addressed. UNIFEM (2001) posits that 'women are not increasingly represented among vulnerable, infected and affected simply because they are women, but because of the discrimination and inequality that distorts and impairs virtually every aspect of their lives' (p. 2).

Most women are overwhelmingly infected through heterosexual intercourse. Power differentials that exist between men and women often constrain women from negotiating safer sex practices. PAHO notes that 64 per cent of AIDS cases in the Caribbean report heterosexual transmission (Camara 2002). Miles (1993) contends that the construction of sexuality around the notions of monogamy and trust, the 'uncontrollable' male sex-drive and the sexually responsible but chaste female, who assumes the burden for contraceptive use, together create unequal sexual relations between men and women. Femininity, often understood as a woman's ability to reproduce, contradicts safer sex practices since these behaviours may also prevent pregnancy, where childbearing is often highly valued in and by women. Also, many women find it necessary to have multiple partners and/or to engage in high-risk sexual behaviours because of financial constraints, and this increases their risk for HIV/STI infections.

Mohammed and Perkins (1999), in their study of sexual decision-making among women in Dominica, St Lucia and Barbados, found that many women in the Caribbean pride themselves on being economically independent but this does not necessarily translate into autonomy within sexual relationships. Women have to negotiate safer sex practices with their partners, something that requires specific skills and power so that they can make sexual decisions without fear of reprisal. In addition, the construction of sexuality based on the monogamous, chaste woman and the aggressive, polygamous man and his uncontrollable sex drive, forces women to meet the needs and desires of men, thus placing themselves at increased risk.

Gender-based Violence

Gender-based violence contributes to the HIV/AIDS pandemic. Women and girls are most often the victims of sexual violence, which places them at risk for HIV infection. Sexual intimacy is premised on monogamy and faithfulness, consequently if the woman suggests condom use, the male partner may see in it an accusation of infidelity and/or lack of trust. Potential negative consequences include verbal, emotional and physical abuse, ranging from name-calling to withdrawal of financial support and even violence. Many women report feeling uncomfortable or even afraid to suggest safe sex behaviours including non-penetrative intercourse and condom use because of fear of backlash from their partners. The threat of violence prevents women from accessing information on health information, HIV testing, treatment and counselling. Women also fear violence upon disclosure of HIV status and partner notification. WHO (1999) shows that gender-based violence adversely affects women's health, particularly their mental and emotional well-being and PAHO (2002) argues that children who are physically and/or sexually abused 'are more likely to exhibit high-risk sexual behaviours later in life, lowered self-esteem, and decreased ability to negotiate safer sex'.

There is a belief that married women are somehow safeguarded from HIV/AIDS and violence. However, Human Rights Watch in its report 'Just die quietly: Domestic violence and women's vulnerability to HIV in Uganda' documents widespread rape and attacks on women by their husbands. The report states that 'HIV/AIDS programmes focusing on fidelity, abstinence and condom use do not account for the ways in which domestic violence inhibits women's control over sexual matters in marriage'.[1] Women and girls' vulnerability to gender-based violence must be taken into account in HIV/AIDS programmes across the Caribbean.

Masculinity and Sexual Relations

Men are vulnerable to HIV infection mainly because of their risk-taking behaviours. In the Caribbean, masculinity is often defined by sexual prowess, multiple female partners and the fathering of many children. This masculinity, which often is not questioned and challenged, is costly. Young men start having sex earlier and have more partners than girls, yet they feel least at risk from HIV infection. In Jamaica, for example, the mean age for the initiation of sexual activity for females is 15.9 and for males 13.9 years old (Planning Institute of Jamaica 2001). In Trinidad and Tobago it is 15 for boys and 16 for girls but one year later for Indo-Trinidadian boys and girls (St Bernard 1997). Chevannes and Brown (1998) and Bailey et al. (2002) report that homophobia in parents causes them to encourage boys to engage in sex at early ages and to have many female partners as proof of their sons' heterosexuality. Girls, on the other hand, are closely supervised due to fear of rape and teenage pregnancy. Yet, girls are often pressured to have children to prove their womanhood so as not to be labelled as 'mules' – unattractive, undesirable and infertile creatures. PAHO (2002) reports that early sexual activity among boys, added to men's higher rates of substance abuse and their lower rates of health-seeking behaviours than women, put men at high risk for HIV infection.

Added to this is the fact that some men in the Caribbean have sex with men. Due to the homophobia in many communities throughout the Caribbean, men may engage in 'invisible lives', maintaining public heterosexual relationships while also having secret sexual relations with other men. Men who have sex with men may not use condoms and so put themselves and their partners at risk for STIs and HIV infection. Men must thus assume greater responsibility in the fight to prevent the spread of HIV/AIDS. This may be achieved through more male-friendly health services and programmes, more men participating in HIV/AIDS programmes and working with other men to inform and educate them about issues of masculinity and gender, including working with men who have sex with men. Men must thus critically re-examine notions of Caribbean manhood and be willing to challenge those aspects of it that are negative.

Persons Infected and Affected by HIV/AIDS

Women are increasingly burdened with the illnesses of household members since they are often the ones that tend to sick family members. Women usually assume the care of and responsibility for children orphaned or abandoned by caregivers that have died as a result of AIDS. The economic insecurity of households tends to increase where women head households, are the main breadwinners and are also HIV positive. Southern African women living with HIV/AIDS report 'endemic levels of exhaustion, grief and depression among caregivers' (UNIFEM 2003). They also tell of the sexual harassment and abuse they suffer at a time when they are most vulnerable. The significant number of female-headed households in the Caribbean, added to women's multiple roles and responsibilities, warrants immediate attention in policies and programmes in the region.

Increasingly, the HIV/AIDS pandemic is leaving children to care for family members and to head households. When primary caregivers become ill and/or pass away, the responsibility for care may be left to older children. For these children, their education is interrupted and their life opportunities are thus limited. This has tremendous repercussions for communities and states in terms of economic production and social reproduction.

Persons thought to be HIV-positive face stigma, discrimination and violence but it is women who are often viewed as carriers of the virus. The Women and HIV/AIDS prevention report of a day of dialogue (2000) reports, for example:

- commercial sex-workers are often forced to undergo mandatory HIV testing where proper health services are often not provided and without their clients also being so targeted;
- pregnant women are often included in testing programmes where the focus is placed on preventing transmission of HIV to the foetus instead of on women's health status;
- Mandatory pre- and post-natal HIV testing may be part of practices that place pressure on women who test positive to agree to abortions or sterilisation;
- Women are denied treatment.

Women within marginalised groups often face even greater vulnerability. These may be women of ethnic and other minority populations, indigenous peoples, female prisoners, gay women, commercial sex-workers, drug users and displaced women (International AIDS Vaccine Initiative 2000).

Adolescent Sexual and Reproductive Health

The sexual health behaviours of adolescents are of great concern. This group has high awareness of both HIV/AIDS and prevention methods but experiences poor translation of this knowledge into practice. Female adolescents are at a further disadvantage because they are often involved with older men with whom they cannot negotiate safer sex practices in relationships characterised by power imbalance. UNAIDS (1999b) estimates that, worldwide, one-half of all persons living with HIV/AIDS were infected before the age of 25. PAHO reports that HIV infection is growing the fastest among persons 14-25 years old in Latin America and the Caribbean. In Jamaica, girls aged 10-14 and 15-19 had two and three times respectively higher risk of HIV infection than boys. This can be attributed to the practice of girls having sexual relations with older and HIV-positive men. It can also be attributed to the high incidence of rape and sexual abuse of girls.

Another area for concern with regard to adolescent females is that of child labour. Dunn (2001) reports that the majority of children involved in commercial sex work in Jamaica are girls, with the most common activities being:

- Boys living and working on the streets and exchanging sex as a means of meeting basic survival needs;
- Girls who engaged in formal prostitution and solicited clients on the streets;
- Girls who were employed as exotic go-go dancers;
- Girls who were employed as masseuses in massage parlours;
- Girls and boys in arranged sexual encounters for economic exchange.

Factors identified as accounting for this situation include, among others, poverty, poor parenting, poor family values, peer pressure, limited education and inadequate monitoring of laws.

Factors that increase these groups' vulnerability to HIV infection include poverty, violence, lack of skills, and negative societal attitudes relating to sexual relationships (UNAIDS 1999). For example, many women feel compelled to have multiple sexual partners that may provide them with financial support. In Jamaica, the female unemployment rate remains twice that of men, although there are more females pursuing higher education. Statistics indicate that, across the Caribbean, the average female unemployment rate was often 1.5 to twice the rate for males (see table 1). The economic, social and political spheres continue to favour men and impact upon the negotiations that occur in sexual relations. In addition, adolescents' right to education, condoms and services, before and after sexual initiation, is often denied.

Table 1: Male and Female Labour Force Participation and Unemployment Rates for Selected Caribbean Countries

Country	Labour Force Participation Rates		Unemployment Rates	
	Male	Female	Male	Female
Bahamas (1999)	83.1	70.9	6.0	9.7
Barbados (1999)	74.7	61.5	7.7	13.3
Belize (1999)	79.7	39.6	9.0	20.3
Dominica (1997)	74.9	59.6	19.6	27.2
Grenada (1998)	75.6	55.0	10.5	21.2
Jamaica (1999)	73.0	56.5	10.0	22.4
St Lucia (1999)	77.0	62.0	16.0	20.3
Suriname (1998)	71.0	37.0	7.2	17.0
Trinidad and Tobago (1999)	75.0	46.6	10.9	16.8

Source: Bailey, B and Ricketts, H (forthcoming)

Sexually Transmitted Infections

A well-known risk factor for HIV is sexually transmitted infections (STIs). Allen (1997) argues that research on STIs in Jamaica and the wider Caribbean must 'examine alternative health beliefs, questions of power and resources and the social mores governing sexual activity, and how they affect knowledge, attitudes, beliefs and practices' (p. 263). This would include studying the knowledge of both the biological and social body to determine how we perceive our bodies, and how this affects our sexual relations. Surveys that measure knowledge, attitudes and practices tend to report high knowledge of HIV/STIs with high recall of the condom as a means of protection from STIs during intercourse. Many persons, however, do not use the condom consistently, especially with their regular partners and so put these partners at increased risk. A study conducted in Barbados, St Vincent and the Grenadines, Trinidad and Tobago and St Kitts and Nevis reports higher rates of condom use at last intercourse with casual partners than with regular partners, that is, 60-80 per cent versus 55-60 per cent. This same study shows higher consistent use of condoms during sexual intercourse with casual partners than with a regular partner, that is, 40-75 per cent versus 30-45 per cent (Camara 2002). There remains a dissonance between knowledge about risk and practices that decrease risk and this may be due to the social construction of sexuality based on unequal power relations, factors that are not explored in surveys. Camara (2002) reports that, in this same study, only 35-40 per cent of youth interviewed perceived AIDS as a serious threat.

There remains the need to challenge the construction of sexuality that is based on male sexual prowess and women's sexual responsibility, so that both men and women see safer sex practices as their personal responsibility. As well, individuals need to be empowered so that they can negotiate safer sex, including the ability to refuse to engage in sex. Such skills include self-confidence and knowledge allowing individuals to make informed decisions. As well, HIV/STI programmes must acknowledge the connections between financial security and sex. Many women and girls find it necessary to exchange sex for financial support for both themselves and their dependents. This is directly related to the fact that, although there are more women in the Caribbean pursuing higher education and receiving certification, the female unemployment rate continues to be higher than that of men. Thus social, economic and political arenas continue to favour men, all of which influence safer sex practices.

Gender, HIV/AIDS and Human Rights in the Caribbean

Global inequalities shape the HIV/AIDS epidemic, where it is most acute in regions marked by high incidences of poverty. A human rights approach to HIV and AIDS:

> emphasises the claims or entitlements that all people have to a full and satisfying life, in which each person is able to develop to his or her full human potential. Human rights also impose obligations on states and non-state actors to ensure that these claims are met, thus affirming democratic principles of accountability and participation. Importantly, human rights set standards for human well-being and development, and constitute important resources for the achievement of this (Division for the Advancement of Women 2000, 9).

The Division for the Advancement of Women (2000) defines human security as freedom from want and fear in addition to access to and control of resources including survival (food, water, shelter, health), safety (freedom from violence), opportunity (education, employment, information), dignity (tolerance and respect), agency and autonomy (participation in decision-making, self-determination, individual agency) (pp. 10-11).

The evolving understandings of human security encompasses a shift in emphasis from security of states to security of individuals and reinforces the obligation of states to ensure the security of all of its citizens, (DAW 2000). The right to disclosure, partner-notification and confidentiality, mother-to-child transmission, informed consent, pregnant women and abortion/termination of pregnancy, pre- and post-test counselling, breastfeeding and access to treatment must all be taken into account in a human rights perspective on HIV/AIDS in the Caribbean. Improved 'human rights literacy' that increases a person's understanding of human rights mechanisms, that is, instruments, bodies and processes that women and men may use to seek redress is critical to ensuring that individuals and groups can effectively seek protection of the human rights from states, civil society and international bodies.

The Convention on the Elimination of Discrimination Against Women, or CEDAW, adopted by the United Nations in 1979 and signed by 174 member nations, contains several articles that seek to protect women's human rights and HIV/AIDS. In article 10, the Convention states that 'State parties shall take all appropriate measures to eliminate discrimination against women in order to ensure them equal rights with men in the field of education' and specifically 'access to the educational information to help to ensure the health and well-being of families, including information and advice on family planning'.

In its General Recommendation on the Convention's article on health, the CEDAW Committee recommended that states ensure the 'removal of all barriers to women's access to health education and information in the area of sexual and reproductive health' and provide programmes for adolescents aimed at preventing and treating sexually transmitted infections, including HIV/AIDS. The General Recommendation on HIV/AIDS directs states to increase their efforts to disseminate information to 'increase public awareness of the risk of HIV infection and AIDS, especially in women and children'.

Article 5 requires state parties to take all appropriate measures 'to modify the social and cultural patterns of conduct of men and women with a view to achieving the elimination of prejudices and customary and all other practices which are based on the idea of inferiority or the superiority of either of the sexes or on stereotyped roles for men and women'. Article 10 directs that these measures must be within the ambit of education so states parties see to the 'elimination of any stereotyped concept of the roles of men and women at all levels and in all forms of education'. Article 12 states that 'State parties shall take all appropriate measures to eliminate discrimination against women in the field of health care in order to ensure, on a basis of equality of men and women, access to health care services, including those related to family planning'.

CEDAW provides one example of an international instrument that can be used by women and women's groups to agitate for increased protection from both state and non-state actors within the context of HIV/AIDS.

Conclusions and Recommendations

- Men are integral to HIV/AIDS programmes in order to treat and prevent the transmission of HIV. They must be willing to question and challenge those aspects of masculinity that hinder efforts to not only fight the epidemic but that also prevent the realisation of gender equality.
- Sex education (health and family life education) must be offered to youth both in and out of school at an age before they begin to have sex. It should also be offered to parents and caregivers.
- Caribbean states must sign, ratify legal instruments such as CEDAW and the Optional Protocol. Gender-based violence legislation needs to be put in place in order to protect and provide women with legal redress for such violations.
- Cultural practices that condone child abuse, incest and rape must be continuously challenged and far more shelters for women and girls that are abused need to be created.
- Sexually transmitted diseases and reproductive tract infections must be properly treated and diagnosed in women of all ages. In addition, the consistent and proper use of male and female condoms needs to be increased through comprehensive health programmes that include HIV prevention.
- The focus needs to move to parent-to-child transmission, which involves male partners in testing and pre- and post-test counselling as opposed to mother-to-child transmission, where women are often blamed and stigmatised for being carriers of HIV.
- More and sustained support is needed for research on microbicides and vaccines in the Caribbean.

Research is needed that examines the power dynamics inherent in sexual relations. The social construction of sexuality places men and women at risk for HIV and STIs due to assumptions regarding monogamy, male prowess and female responsibility for contraception. Other areas for research include herbal remedies and drug therapies, clinical studies into microbicides and virucides that potentially could replace or supplement the use of condoms.

Strategies that target HIV/AIDS must take a more holistic approach, linking socioeconomic and sociocultural behaviours and practices with gender issues. The present social and gender inequalities that permeate sexual relations continue to hinder interventions because projects and programmes have failed to include such analyses. The large transmission of HIV through heterosexual intercourse throughout the Caribbean helps to debunk the notion of AIDS as a disease of 'high-risk' groups as persons in supposedly monogamous relations are affected and infected with HIV. Sexual relations can no longer be seen as private issues but as political ones imbued with power imbalances, largely in favour of men. Gender analyses in policy, programmes, and projects are crucial to ensuring the redress of social, economic and gender inequalities.

Note

1. Personal e-mail communication August 15, 2003. Please see www.hrw.org/reports/2003/uganda0803 for full report.

References

Allen, C. 1997. 'Researching sexually transmitted diseases in the Caribbean'. In *Gender: a Caribbean multi-disciplinary perspective,* eds. E. Leo-Rhynie, B. Bailey and C. Barrow, 259-276. Kingston: Ian Randle Publishers and the Centre for Gender and Development Studies, The University of the West Indies, Mona.

Bailey, W., C. Branche and A. Henry-Lee. 2002. *Gender, contest and conflict in the Caribbean: lessons from community-based research.* Kingston: Sir Arthur Lewis Institute for Social and Economic Studies, The University of the West Indies, Mona.

Barriteau, E. 1998. 'Theorizing gender systems and the project of modernity in the twentieth century Caribbean'. In *Feminist Review* 59: 186-210.

Brown, J. and B. Chevannes. 1998. *Why man stay so: gender socialisation in the Caribbean.* Kingston: UNICEF and The University of the West Indies, Mona.

Camara, B. 2002. *Twenty Years of the HIV/AIDS epidemic in the Caribbean: A summary.* Caribbean Epidemiology Centre. www.paho.org/ (accessed April 4, 2003)

Division for the Advancement of Women. 2000. *The HIV/AIDS pandemic and its gender implications.* Report of the expert group meeting Windhoek, Namibia, November 13-17, United Nations Division for the Advancement of Women, World Health Organization and the Joint United Nations Programme on HIV/AIDS (UNAIDS). http://www.un.org/womenwatch/daw

Dunn, L. 2001. *Jamaica's situation of children in prostitution: a rapid assessment.* Geneva: International Labour Organization, International Programme on the Elimination of Child Labour (IPEC).

Foucalt, M. 1985. *The Foucalt Reader.* New York: Pantheon Books.

―――――. 1979. *The History of Sexuality.* New York. Pantheon Books.

International AIDS Vaccine Initiative. 2000. *Women and HIV/AIDS prevention. Report of a day of dialogue.* London: Commonwealth Secretariat.

Jackson, S. 1996. 'Heterosexuality and Feminist Theory'. In *Theorizing Heterosexuality*, ed. D. Richardson, 21-38. Philadelphia: Open University Press.

Long, L. and L. Messersmith. 1995. 'Reconceptualising risk: A feminist analysis of HIV/AIDS'. In *Women in the Third World: An encyclopedia of contemporary issues*, ed. N Stromquist, 157-163. New York: Garland Press.

Miles, L. 1993. 'Women, AIDS and power in heterosexual sex: A discourse analysis'. In *Women Studies International Forum* 16, no. 5:497-511.

Mohammed, P. and A. Perkins. 1999. *Caribbean Women at the Crossroads: The Paradox of Motherhood among Women of Barbados, St. Lucia and Dominica.* Kingston: Canoe Press, University of the West Indies.

PAHO. 2002. *Gender and HIV/AIDS in the Latin American and Caribbean region.* Women, health and development program, Pan-American Health Organization. www.paho.org (accessed April 6, 2003).

Planning Institute of Jamaica. 2002. *Economic and social survey Jamaica 2001.* Kingston: Planning Institute of Jamaica.

―――. 2001. *Economic and Social Survey Jamaica 2000.* Kingston: Planning Institute of Jamaica.

Population Reference Bureau. 2002. Women of our world 2002. Washington, DC: Population Reference Bureau Measure Communication.

Rich, A. 1986. 'Compulsory Heterosexuality and Lesbian Experience'. In *SIGNS: Journal of Women in Culture and Society* 5: 62-91.

St. Bernard, G. 1997. Aspects of family life, gender relations and ethnic background: An empirical evaluation of multi-ethnicity and youth in Trinidad and Tobago. Paper presented at Workshop on Family and the Quality of gender Relations. The University of the West Indies, Mona, March 5-6.

UNAIDS 1999 (a) *Call to action for 'children left behind' by AIDS.*

———. 1999 (b) *Handbook for legislators on HIV/AIDS, law and human rights.*

UNIFEM. 2003. *Southern African women living with HIV/AIDS voice concerns to UNIFEM.* Press release May 19. www.unifem.org/www/newsroom/press/pr-030159_SA_AIDS.html (accessed June 24, 2003).

———. 2001. *Turning the tide: CEDAW and the gender dimensions of the HIV/AIDS pandemic.* New York: UNIFEM. www.unifem.org/cedaw/turningthetide.htm (accessed April 10, 2003).

WHO. 1999. *Beijing platform for action: A review of WHO's activities (related to the 'women and health' section).* Geneva: Department of Women's Health, Health Systems and Community Health Cluster, WHO.

Appendix 1: Number of Cases of AIDS in the Caribbean, 1982-2000

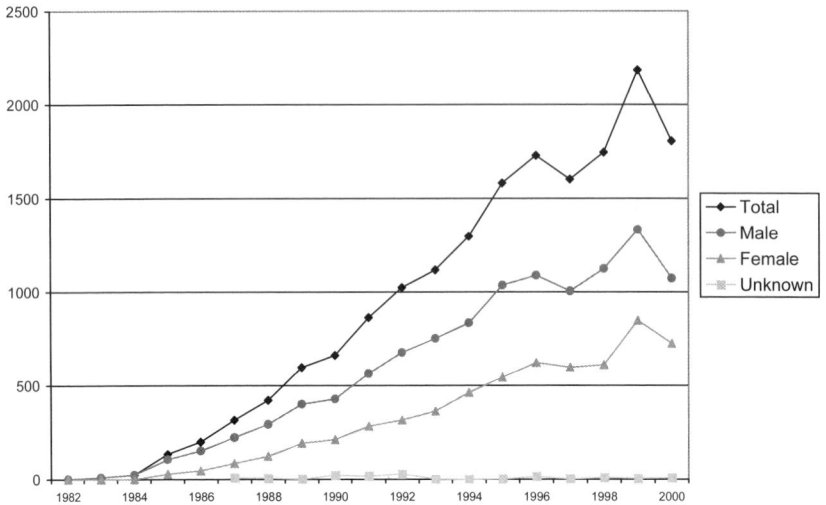

Source: Caribbean Epidemiology Division.

Setting New Agendas:
Within and Beyond the Academy

27 | MAXINE HENRY-WILSON
Presentation to the University of the West Indies

Governance, Leadership and Decision-making
Prospects for Caribbean Women

In this presentation, I will be presenting my own reflections, and somewhere in the backdrop there will be my acquaintance with the relevant literature and the scholarship. As a practitioner you sometimes wonder about the theories versus the practice. However, I have no doubt that each informs the other.

At the outset, I want to say that I think that anyone who enters politics does so with some idealism. This, I believe, is subsequently conditioned by the reality that you face on the ground on a daily basis. There are very few of us in here (I see one person) who has the experience of the practice of politics. Yesterday I spent some five hours sorting a file with requests from persons who attended my constituency clinic in the previous week. At the end of the exercise, with some exasperation, I exclaimed 'Is this what representation is about? Is this what being in the legislature is about?'

In my presentation today, I want to reflect on some of these experiences and share these reflections with you.

There is a publication by a Peruvian scholar, Cecelia Blondet, in which she cites a case study of the women in Peru who were confronted with a conundrum. They were guided by the notion that numbers was one critical variable in empowering women. Hence there was need for more women in the country's legislature as that was where crucial decisions were deemed to be made. The presumption was that numbers per se would automatically guarantee certain types of behaviour and policies. President Fujimori had made a proposal to the women vis-à-vis a quota law, and the extent to which that law would allow for more women to be in the legislature. They immediately struck a compromise with the president.

At the end of the period, however, the conclusion was that the consequence of their choice was the support of four authoritarian dictators who were women, rather than four authoritarian dictators who were men. The question is the extent to which gender is a determining factor in women giving their support to candidates for any role or responsibility. I raise that because I think that for the last three decades, much energy has been invested in the debate about our numbers – more women should be encouraged to enter representational politics. This was based on the presumption that the fact of more women in pivotal positions, in and of itself, results in a certain kind of decision-making that will further not only 'the woman's agenda', but also qualitatively better social development. Now, I don't think that that is so, and I think we have to re-look at that whole question of numbers versus ideology and philosophy.

Over the last three decades, more women have entered the political arena, certainly in the Caribbean, and I even go so far as to say that up to recently it was 'en vogue' for every political party to have a Women's Platform. The logic was that, in order to make sure that this Women's Platform had real value, it was imperative to have a quota of women candidates. Consequently, there was actually a scramble by political parties to get female candidates to enter the electoral arena. The more you had, and the more strident your women's platform, the more female votes you would garner.

I believe that three decades later, there is a lot of disillusionment among women representatives about women's representation. In the case of Jamaica in the elections of 2002, there was a decrease in the number of female candidates seeking election. Some of it was due to the vicissitudes of representational politics. I believe, however, there is a deeper cause of this.

Speaking to some of the women who were representatives (and who are no longer representatives), they almost breathed a sigh of relief 'Thank God I am out of it'. I don't want to put anybody on the spot, but there is one person who is here perhaps that could concur with that viewpoint.

In selecting women to be representatives, nothing really changed in the body politic, nor in the selection process, in the criteria that were used, in the way in which campaigning was done, and most important, in the kind of supports that women received in becoming representatives. The situation with our women was not unique in that respect; men will echo a similar call for better supports to carry out their tasks effectively. In the case of women, I think there were some very basic things.

The conduct of politics is very male in its orientation. For example, most of it is done on a Sunday. Women's domestic lives invariably suffer while they are attending to political matters on a Sunday. The campaign trail is extremely rigorous, almost to the point of being dangerous. After a while you begin to wonder 'Well, is this what I really want to do?' The norms of the campaign trail sometimes embody experiences and behaviours that are not seen as 'feminine'. I remember there was the case of a woman, who did what all men did, which was to go to the bar and drink, and it was used against her in the campaign. There are cases where you hear of women being described as very 'loose', and therefore you should not support them. But I also remember a case where a prime minister's mother declared that he had had only three girlfriends in his adult life, and how he was defamed on the radio talk-show programmes the following day because nobody believed that a man should only have three girlfriends while he/she is in politics.

I believe the most poignant comment though, on why there is so much of this disillusionment, comes from Carlene Robertson, a former Member of Parliament in Northern St Andrew. In her first speech, what they call your 'maiden address', in Parliament, she made a cry, a '*cri de coeur*', 'What is my job description? I am being asked to be everything – I must bury the dead, be the mother of all his children, give birth, make sure I am there as the midwife, be on call 24 hours, what exactly is my job description?' People laughed at her, but I think anybody who is in politics, both men and women, must ask 'What is my job description?' As a consequence of that concern to define your job description, or whether in fact you can fulfill your job description, you find that different constituencies have different ideas of support or antagonism, differing views as to the roles and responsibilities of the MP.

The task is made even more difficult because of the low capacity of our institutions. If, in response to an enquiry or request by a constituent, you send a letter to a ministry official to access a government programme, frequently the constituent receives a reaction such as 'Who is this person sending this letter, who is the MP? This is politics and I don't business with it'. On the other hand, you may get a reaction which says that we just don't have any resources to deal with the request.

In addition to being weak, our institutions often suffer from resource inadequacies. The member of parliament must then find a way to address these myriad demands. The question is *how* you can meet these demands, given the absence of such resources. Corrupt use of resources is one approach taken by some politicians, thereby, delegitimising the entire process.

Women, as do men, make choices. There are many who make alternative choices to being involved in any type of illicit, corrupt relationships and, instead, opt to build community institutions.

Our political culture is, however, a very individualistic one. It is 'what I got last time from the MP', not what structures are put in place, or whether institutions are functional. It is a part of the culture that comes, I believe, from years of being deprived of basic material resources; people give regard primarily to their own interests.

The dominance over the last two decades of the neo-liberal model of development has eroded the legitimacy of politics and the political process. The view that there is a tripartite approach to development with one partner's bona fides having been eroded over a period of time, whether by his/her doing or otherwise, leads to the political partnership being unequal. NGOs and corporate structures are deemed to be legitimate institutions – national, bilateral and multilateral. They opt to engage with the other two partners, while preferring not to respond to or have any relationship with the politician in fulfilling the representational role.

A further deficit in the representational equation is the absence of the basic supports for the parliamentarian. To be effective, there is need for social work, community organisation and project development skills. The human capital to undertake this is not available. Hence the MP is not able to respond programmatically to many of the requests by constituents.

There has been a period of dis-investment in politics and politicians, and a de-funding of political activities. Each day it is reaffirmed: It *does* take cash to build a political organisation. As we attempt to look at the future governance systems and structure, we need to decide whether we are going to continue to allow corporate donors to political organisations to dictate the agenda, the scope, and even who gets selected, or we are going to talk about monitored and accounted for state funding. I have always believed that if you want more quality women to enter politics, the state has to provide a level of funding, not just for elections, but for political organisation that can enable them to really pay attention to the in-depth organisational work that they have to do in communities. And so I believe that this issue needs to go squarely on the agenda.

The other thing is, of course, the whole notion of governance has changed. I think over the last couple of days you have probably looked at it from all dimensions and directions, but in that process of governance, many of the old practices of politics are no longer a part of the norm. Just a simple example: there was a time when the MP, call it patronage or whatever you will, would have a voice in the recommendation of a contractor or workers. People felt that the MP had some control over what happened in the constituency of which you were the representative. Now, with all the new rules about procurement, all the new rules about how you do public works to ensure accountability and performance, most members of parliament have no say in the 'who works where or who does what'.

In the former dispensation, the appointment of contractors by the member of parliament led to him or her becoming too involved in the distribution of resources. This has come to hurt political representatives. The new dispensation leads to constituents questioning 'Who is in charge, who is really taking these decisions?' When somebody calls you and says 'Well Minister, there is a whole new building going up here by the government…' and I say to them 'Well, it's the first I'm hearing about it', their response is 'Then we don't need any MP'. I fervently believe, however, that political representatives should *not* be involved in work distribution.

The response of the constituent, however, is indicative of the perception of our people. On the other hand, there is the notion as to where decision-making does actually take place and whether the representative is really peripheral to this activity. The reality is you cannot *not* be involved in the development of an area you are supposed to represent, so that when questions are referred to you, you have no informed response to their queries.

I believe that some representatives have attempted new ways of organising constituencies. In the main, however, these persons have found that it is such a long-term process, that it cannot be achieved in five years. Therefore, what invariably happens is that at the end of a period, they find that their efforts are not rewarded as they should be. So there is the time horizon in terms of how do you change that culture, and how do you work in a constituency so that you can look at the new structures, the new ways in which you deal with institutions, to prevent you, as a representative, becoming a purveyor of benefits.

With the new initiatives to create innovative community-based representational structures and the existence of relics of the old patronage systems, two virtually antagonistic structures exist parallel to each other. It is difficult, if not impossible, to have both functional simultaneously.

In terms of the future and where we need to go, I believe that one of the things that have led to women being a little disillusioned about involvement in leadership and decision-making is the reality of the warning that women's issues are no longer as relevant as they used to be.

The number of women's organisations have declined, and the supports that women need in order to have that self-confidence to enter the political arena, to be involved in the legislature, to be involved in governance, and which existed over a decade ago, are no longer there.

Therefore, even the number of female entrants into the political arena is beginning to decline. The women's movements must extend their reach once again. I know that the Jamaica Women's Political Caucus has been very useful. However, the corps of voluntary energy that is needed to sustain the caucus's efforts is not there. Further, while there may be a willingness to make a contribution to the efforts of the caucus, the invitation to enter representational politics is often rebuffed.

Women involved in political decision-making and leadership need to have access to resources. This has to be placed squarely on the women's agenda for political action so that they can be a part of competitive politics.

Some views express that the functioning of the legislature does not sufficiently relate to the day-to-day concerns, and involve the discussion of a lot of seemingly esoteric issues. I believe we have to influence the functioning of the legislature to ensure that the issues that are important to our constituents are listed on the agenda, and that women feel that they can be a part of it.

I do not believe that the issue is only about numbers. I think that we have gone far beyond that, that women need to be more involved in what have traditionally *not* been women's issues, including matters relating to the new paradigm in which we are involved, and how it makes us either better, or less ready to be representatives.

But as long as there is this feeling that there is no room for you to exercise leadership in the political arena, for you to influence decision-making, I believe that fewer and fewer women are going to be willing to take the plunge.

Thank you very much.

28 | TRACY ROBINSON

Gender, Feminism and Constitutional Reform in the Caribbean

Abstract

The Commonwealth Caribbean has entered the twenty-first century with constitutional reform firmly on regional and national agendas. This paper looks at how the constitutional reform process has been a site for the production and reproduction of gender relations and at the same time one within which relations of gender are contested and challenged. The ironies of constitutions and constitutional reform processes that speak to gender equality but not necessarily with a clear understanding of women as equal citizens, even when citizenship laws are being reviewed, are explored. The pervasive sense is that gender equality is 'not unimportant' but is not a pre-eminent concern. The paper shows how feminist engagement with the process has attempted, with only moderate success so far, to subvert this by putting the issue of women as political citizens on constitutional reform agendas.

'We need a new constitution which befits a free people at the dawn of the twenty-first century.' Ralph Gonsalves, Prime Minister of St Vincent and the Grenadines (2003)

Introduction

My concern in this chapter is how *gender* has figured in recent constitutional reform in the Caribbean. I am thinking not just about how gender justice has formed part of the reform agendas and discourse and feminist engagement with the process of reform. I am also interested in how relations of gender have been produced and reproduced in the reform processes and how they have been contested and challenged through it. This chapter proceeds from, and alongside, an earlier argument of mine – that the question of citizenship offers a critical lens to theorise 'the woman question' and to continue political work around it and, more concretely, that the constitutional reform process provides a venue to do this – one not yet consumed by the antipathy towards feminist work that is so apparent at the frontlines of gender politics in the Caribbean. Thus I see participation in the constitutional reform process as valuable, even indispensable, feminist practice in the new millennium (Robinson 2004). My aim here is not to test this theoretical claim – to say how valuable constitutional reform has turned out to be for women (that may come in later work). Significantly it is to bolster the claim and its desire to encourage greater feminist participation in a practical way by offering what is still a preliminary account of gender dimensions of this aspect of the practices and processes of the constitution.

The Commonwealth Caribbean now, more than any other time since independence, is taken with processes of constitutional reform.[1] There were dramatic constitutional post-independence overhauls in Trinidad and Tobago in 1978 and Guyana in 1980, but nothing hitherto approximates the mindedness of the last decade of many elements across the region about the need to rethink existing constitutional arrangements and the almost unwitting synchronisation of those endeavours. By the end of the nineties, the promise of constitutional reform had become *de rigueur* in election manifestos. And almost every independent Commonwealth Caribbean country has entered the twenty-first century contemplating or engaged in some structured process of constitutional reform.[2] Though lacking formal regional coordination, the process is characterised by an incipient regionalism.[3] The establishment of the Caribbean Court of Justice has placed regional aspirations squarely on national constitutional agendas. CARICOM intervention and mediation in political crises in the region have been the early stage of the constitutional reform process in countries like Guyana and St Kitts & Nevis. International agencies and organisations have been facilitating national and cross-national participation in the process, and a cadre of common regional experts have now led constitutional commissions in different territories.[4]

The widespread reform processes, perhaps more in effect than design, are a reflection on our constitutional traditions (McIntosh 2002,53). These forward-looking projects can only be understood with reference to the past. The trend of reform has been stylised in very modern ahistorical terms, a desire for 'better governance and greater equity' (OAS 2002, 5). It has been located within worldwide trends of constitutionalism, globalisation and the imperatives of greater regional cooperation in order to safeguard Caribbean sovereignty (see OAS 2002). Nevertheless, many of the prominent concerns in the debate – the establishment of a Caribbean Court of Justice, a move to republicanism and the sustainability of the Westminster model of parliamentary democracy – suggest that this period constitutes the most sustained collective questioning of the independence vision that continuity with British institutions was the best prescription for progress and future development.

These reform processes are critical acts of national and regional self-definition and collective refashioning of the Caribbean post independence generation. Ironically, at times they do not look so and seem like the antithesis of the higher order law-making exercise they are supposed to be. There is profound disappointment at the disparity between the processes' possibilities and their product. They have been marred by poor public participation and interest, partisan politicisation of the issues, contumacious disputes about race, ethnicity and territory, slim parliamentary debates and overwhelming government domination of lower houses, and piecemeal reforms that are virtually incomprehensible to the ordinary citizen. There is an image some of us have of constitutional reform as the paradigmatic act of engaged citizenship, or the venue for the most authentic of public conversations, that has not materialised with any coherence in this recent period in the Caribbean. We most likely will have to give up some of our conception of the grandness of constitution redesign or, alternatively, temper our hope that it will engender peace and consensus about national identity, to see something of the distinctiveness of this moment, even with its pervasive flaws, and what sets it apart from ordinary law making.

Ordinary law reform is attended with reasonable expedition, or at least that is the objective. The hallmark of Caribbean constitutional reform is its extended conversation, the protracted character of the debates and its unexpected turns and concerns. Agendas are carefully crafted and terms of reference constructed, but the character of a constitution anticipates subversion of these goals because the law of the constitution is a self-conscious dialogue addressing the most fundamental questions about the organisation of social and political life (Macklem 1988, 118). The process of constitutional reform in the Caribbean has been guided by text, but the immenseness of the constitution in theoretical terms makes it an invitation to broader discourse about what matters most to the nation and its citizens. The Jamaica constitutional review process, the longest running of the recent period, nicely illustrates these elements of obstinate longevity and extendable agendas. Roughly it began in 1991 with the creation of the Joint Select Committee of Parliament on Constitutional and Electoral Reform, and a Constitutional Commission the following year. That commission, which was reconstituted in 1993, held 36 meetings, hosted 13 public fora and received written submissions from 129 organisations and individuals.[5] The Joint Select Committee received the reports of the Constitutional Commissions and began meeting in 1993. That committee embarked on further consultations, holding 32 meetings and receiving 32 written submissions, and laid its report in Parliament in 1995. A bill was eventually tabled in parliament in 1999 to provide a charter of rights to replace the chapter on fundamental rights and freedoms. It was sent to a Special Select Committee of Parliament, which again held meetings – 24 over the course of two years between 1999 and 2001. The earlier commission had received submissions from, among others, the Maroons and Rastafari for constitutional recognition; now new participants and advocates, such as Jamaica Forum for Lesbians, All-Sexuals and Gays (J-Flag) entered the process.[6] In 2002, a new bill was laid in parliament to introduce a Charter of Rights in the constitution, and the debate continues. A decade of constitutional reform has not yet borne the expected amendments, but, apathy notwithstanding, its prolonged development and avenues for public participation have made it an important site for the performance of citizenship and working through and articulating the meaning of citizenship.

To return to the focus of this paper, what of *gender* in this remarkable ongoing process? The exercise of reform must be set against earlier constitution making in the Caribbean which was dominated by men. It involved some women but they did not play a central role in shaping the present constitutional vision. On the whole, the earlier processes were premised on the assumption that men were the archetypal citizens and women their subordinates. They were very concerned with manhood, meaning establishing that Caribbean men were ready to self-govern (Edmondson 1999). It is a rare acknowledgement in the constitutional reform process that 'the Constitution ... was written ... by men – unfortunately, there were no women involved' (Musa 1999). There has been a powerful call to now 'make the constitutions our own' (McIntosh 2002), but gender has hardly ever been a frame of analysing the concerns of the authority, authorship and legitimacy of Caribbean constitutions that this implies. The masculinist character of past constitution making (see Lewis 2000) has tended to be neither problematised nor entirely abandoned in the current exercises of reform, as evidenced by the inattentiveness to gender balance in the composition of the apparatuses of reform.

That said, gender talk, and other signifiers like 'cultural' and 'ethnic diversity', have provided avenues for political rectitude.[7] Women's rights, and the rights of people with disabilities, children and indigenous people, have been characterised as the 'new rights' – those that 'have gained somewhat more currency' (Guyana 1999, 184). The ambivalence and sometimes antagonism towards initiatives directed at addressing women's inequality can be contrasted with what looks like no controversy about the concept of gender equality in the constitutional reform debates. There is a suspiciously overwhelming consensus in the reform exercises on the need for a strong commitment to gender equality, but when contemplated less abstractly, there are often countervailing considerations – things that matter more at the moment – to which it gives way.

In the region family, household and neighbourhood have been viewed as separate from 'governance', Hazel Brown, coordinator of the Network of NGOs of Trinidad and Tobago for the Advancement of Women has observed (OAS 2002, 13). This is central to thinking about women's participation in processes of constitutional reform. It is a challenge to articulate how Caribbean constitutions, as the supreme law, speak to injustices women experience. The abstract articulation of fundamental rights and freedoms in the constitutions are focused on civil and political rights and do not readily touch the intractable social and economic inequities women face. Some of the gravest abuse against women is most directly at the hands of private citizens and does not fit evenly within present constitutional imagination, concerned as it is with the domain of the public, the organisation of governmental power and the responsibilities of the state to the citizen. That many feminists and women's organisations regionwide do not appear entirely convinced that constitutional reform is a pre-eminent concern for women and continue to focus their energies on otherwise addressing women's continued oppression, is not surprising. While this disjuncture between the constitutions and women's lives has generated indifference among some feminists, it has also galvanised feminist engagement with constitutional reform.

The first part of this chapter presents an overview of some the of basic concerns about gender and the texts of the present constitutions, and briefly indicates how these have been responded to in the constitutional reform processes. The second part of the chapter examines a range of issues about gender and political citizenship. I look at whether women have been viewed as political citizens integral to the process of reform itself. I also consider the feminist articulation of political citizenship as a right to be supported by positive action, and the growing feminist expression of political citizenship as a zone of responsibility for women. In the third section I examine the contradictions of what I term 'gender somethings' in the constitutional reform process. This refers to that admixture of unequivocal support, but for a principle the materiality of which is not readily discernible, and which routinely succumbs, even if not quite fatally, to elements that matter more in the moment. Gender somethings have been most clarified through their particular exclusions, such as, 'sex does not include sexual orientation'.

Contextualising Text: Gender Paradoxes of the Constitution

Constitutions must be read as a whole and with an eye to the practices and authoritative understandings that have developed around the text. The chapter devoted to the protection of 'Fundamental Rights and Freedoms' in Caribbean constitutions, commonly referred to as the Bill of Rights, has been the source of undue confidence about the place of women in the constitutional scheme. Its provisions are routinely cited in reports on the status of women in the Caribbean to illustrate that women's rights are viewed as fundamental rights and freedoms within the constitutions (see, for example, Barbados 1995, 24; Mondesire, Dunn 1995, 40). In a discussion on the accession of Barbados to the Convention on the Elimination of All Forms of Discrimination Against Women, it was suggested that 'policy and current practice provide firm evidence that the existing constitutional guarantees are adequate protection from all potential human rights violations' (Forde 1987, 3). However, the very language of the constitutions, the violence some constitutions themselves do to the idea of gender equality by their inclusion of patently discriminatory provisions in other parts of the texts, and the conservative interpretation by Caribbean judges of protection against sex discrimination (see Robinson 1998) present a more nuanced, less satisfactory image. This I will illustrate from the preambles, provisions dealing with citizenship and bills of rights of the constitutions.

Beginnings and the language of law

The body and substance of a constitution begins later, but the soul of a constitution is in the preamble. It speaks most powerfully to how a nation sees its past and its vision of its future. Though the preamble is generally not enforceable, Caribbean judges have been turning to its declarations, like respect for the rule of law, as evidence of constitutional commitments borne out in the rest of the texts.[8] It is a useful place to begin to explore the place of men and women in the constitutional scheme. The preamble is that critical moment when the authorship of the document is claimed by 'We the People' who go on to define who they are as citizens and what matters most to them. The masculine terms of the constitution is in some cases very apparent from these opening words. Ironically, nowhere is this more apparent than in the 1980 Constitution of the Co-operative Republic of Guyana, which had the most expansive constitutional protection of the rights of women found anywhere in the Commonwealth Caribbean.

The preamble of the Guyana Constitution 1980 read: 'We the People of the Co-operative Republic of Guyana are the proud heirs of the indomitable spirit and unconquerable will of our forefathers who by their sacrifices, their blood and their labour made rich and fertile and bequeathed to us as our inalienable patrimony for all time this green land of Guyana. Saluting the epic struggles waged by our forefathers for freedom justice and human dignity and their relentless hostility to imperialist and colonial domination and other forms and manifestations of oppression; …' Hearing this language – of the proud heirs (in traditional terms the male offspring entitled to inherit from their father) of the unconquerable spirit of the forefathers, who bequeathed their inalienable patrimony (technically property inherited from one's father) – the irresistible question is how do women fit in this conception of 'We the People'. As a matter of legal interpretation and, frankly, contrivance, the masculine references are said to include women. Still, we cannot miss the order of things. It is men in the first instance who are described as 'We the People', the epitome of citizen, and women come in through their relationship to the forefathers as mothers, daughters and sisters. Women are not excluded from citizenship, but that citizenship is firstly conceived in terms of women's relationship to the paradigmatic citizens, men (Robinson 1999). This implication that women are second to men as citizens stands in opposition to the very detailed and flamboyant language in article 29 of the constitution stating that men and women are entitled to equal legal status.

Around the Caribbean there has been consensus on the need for simpler, more comprehensible language in the constitutions. In addition, there has been widespread support for what the Barbados Constitution Review Commission called a formal rather than a substantive issue – that of 'gender-neutral' language in constitutions (so that 'he' and 'him' would be followed by 'she' and 'her' and so on). The Belize Political

Reform Commission in its 2000 Report said that 'Much of the attitudes we hold as people, including our biases, are reflected in our written and even official language. ... there is no longer any excuse for language in public documents to exclude women when more inclusive language is available' (Belize 2000, 130). Gender neutrality is not without difficulties. The design of 'more inclusive' language has tended to be that of neutralising gender – to say that it matters little whether we are talking about men or women. The project of the constitution should be quite different. There is an urgent need, given the past, for the constitutions to affirm that women, like men, are primary subjects of citizenship, that women are integral agents in the constitutional scheme and that their concerns and interests legitimately form part of the fabric of the constitutions. That formal inclusion of women to make woman-ness irrelevant in constitutional contexts that are already premised on women's irrelevance, only serves to reiterate the male norm.

The restorative character of gender equality, its project of rendering visible the marginalised and affirming the integrity of the historically excluded, has been negated in constitutional reform processes. In Antigua and Barbuda, women failed to persuade the Constitution Review Commission that language was a substantive concern. The commission did not support their submissions that the preamble should embrace an articulation of women's role in public life and the right to equal participation therein. The new preamble to the Guyana Constitution, as amended by the Constitution (Amendment) (No. 4) Act 2001, recognises the cultural and racial diversity of Guyana, and includes reference to the indigenous peoples, protection of the environment and endorsement of the role of young people, though not the place of women in the nation (Guyana 1999, 183). It begins: 'We the Guyanese People, Proud heirs of the indomitable will of our forebears, in a spirit of reconciliation and cooperation, proclaim this Constitution in order to: Safeguard and build on the rich heritage, won through tireless struggle, bequeathed us by our forebears...' 'Forefathers' neutralised becomes 'forebears', but women remain barely visible in this enlarged conception of citizenship and in the affirmation of the values of the nation.

Grades of citizenship

In one regard, constitutional review has begun with a gender agenda – citizenship rights. The older model constitutions – those that are found in The Bahamas, Barbados and Jamaica – and occasionally some newer ones spoke of the enjoyment of fundamental rights and freedoms regardless of sex and at the same time contained patently discriminatory citizenship laws.[9] Most notably, a child born outside the jurisdiction to a male citizen and a foreigner was given automatic citizenship. Similarly, foreign wives of male citizens were entitled to be registered upon application as citizens.[10] Female citizens did not enjoy the same citizenship rights. In Barbados, for instance, the husbands of Barbadian women were only entitled to permanent residency. There was one exception; a child born to a citizen abroad and outside of marriage acquired the citizenship of his or her unwed mother.[11] Citizenship passing through the maternal line in this case was entirely by default because, under the common law, the illegitimate child was *filius nullius*, that is, belonged to no one. The Jamaica Constitutional Commission concluded that these provisions 'either expressly or by inescapable implication transgressed the principle of equality of the sexes' (Jamaica 1993, 16).

The discriminatory provisions have had enormous practical consequences for married women and unmarried fathers and their families, especially in territories where there are strong patterns of inward migration. Most of the individuals making submissions to the Barbados Constitution Review Commission, especially those in overseas fora, were advocating reforms to the laws dealing with citizenship (Barbados 1998, 26). The commission ultimately recommended that gender discrimination be removed from all citizenship provisions, that children born of Barbadian males and females should be equally treated, and that the constitution be amended to allow the non-national spouses of Barbadian-born persons to be equally treated (Barbados 1998, 29-30).[12]

So pressing was the issue of reform in Jamaica that the Constitutional Commission's recommendation for reform was pre-empted by the enactment of the Citizenship (Constitutional) Amendment Act 1993 and later, the Citizenship (Constitutional Amendment) Act 1994. In The Bahamas, matters have evolved differently. In February 2002, the government put similar reforms to a referendum vote as required by the constitution. Opposition political parties, the church and other members of civil society campaigned against the reforms on the ground that the process was rushed and the inadequate opportunities provided for debate and public consultations. The result was a resounding no to constitutional reform. I will say more on this below.

Constitutional reforms in the area of citizenship rights have been precipitated more by pragmatic than ideological demands. The enthusiasm for constitutional reform has not evolved from an abandonment of the philosophical underpinnings of the discriminatory provisions – the assumption that men are the archetypal citizens and women their subordinates. Thus, it does not come entirely as a surprise that initiatives to make more meaningful women's political citizenship are among the most contested gender concerns in constitutional reform.

Incongruous bill of rights

Gender equality as a goal is not explicitly articulated in most Caribbean constitutions. Support for the concept is usually implied from the opening section to the chapter protecting fundamental rights and freedoms. Its typical formulation reads: 'Whereas every person … is entitled to the fundamental rights and freedoms, that is to say, the right, whatever his…sex…to each and all of the following, namely…'[13] This, the most unequivocal language in Caribbean constitutions attaching importance to protecting the rights of both men and women, is said to not give rise to an enforceable guarantee of gender equality in most constitutions where no right of access to the High Court for its infringement is provided within the constitution. That opening section has been described as merely a 'forerunner of things to come worthy of protection'.[14]

The ramifications of non-justiciability of the opening section are acute in the older constitutions. The bill of rights of most constitutions provides that discriminatory laws and discriminatory acts by public authorities violate the constitution. Discriminatory is defined as affording different treatment to different persons attributable wholly or mainly to their respective descriptions by race, place or origin, political opinions and so on. In the older constitutions, sex was not included and would not be implied.[15] The result, under the older constitutions, is that the opening section is viewed as unenforceable and the later anti-discrimination section provides no opportunities for relief. Curiously, a parallel occurs in Guyana under the 1980 constitution. The gender equality clause in article 29 is found in a chapter devoted to 'Principles and Bases of the Political, Economic and Social System'. The constitution was amended in 1989, to provide that this chapter contained only directory principles and did not give rise to any enforceable rights.[16] In another chapter protecting fundamental rights and freedoms, there is an anti-discrimination clause that, like the older constitutions, does not prohibit discrimination on the grounds of sex, and again this will not be implied.[17] The extraordinary effect, not unlike the older constitutions, is that where gender equality is generously enunciated in article 29, its inclusion is said to *mean nothing* in terms of justiciability and where gender *is not* mentioned, this time in the anti-discrimination section in article 149, its absence is said to *mean everything* (Robinson 2004).

Here, too, there has been little disputing the need for constitutional reform. The Barbados and Jamaican constitutional commissions have recommended that the anti-discrimination provision include 'gender' or 'sex' as a prohibited category of discrimination. A similar reform was proposed in The Bahamas in the ill-fated February 2002 referendum. The anomalous Guyanese position has been the subject of constitutional reforms to ensure the right to gender equality is justiciable. The reforms and others related to rights are in abeyance because of disputes about the inclusion of sexual orientation as a prohibited ground for discrimination.

What of the newer constitutions that do contain a clear prohibition of discrimination on the grounds of sex? Even these more progressive constitutions present serious challenges. The prohibition of discrimination on the grounds of sex has not been very effective because it thus far has been conservatively interpreted by the courts and the obligations it places on decision-making have not always become part of the consciousness of legislatures and policymakers. For instance, there are still reports across the Caribbean of teenage schoolgirls being deprived of access to secondary education. Laws like the Antigua and Barbuda

Sexual Offences Act 1995, which fail to provide married women with the full protection of the law against sexual violation by their husbands, continue to be enacted. Constitutional litigation is an inadequate safety valve where women's rights, and those of most other marginalised groups, are concerned. Constitutional litigation is expensive, little legal aid is available and the risk of bearing the costs if the application fails has a chilling effect on novel claims. Impecuniosity and concerns about privacy, stigmatisation and safety in small communities will militate against the women most affected by laws and policies that compromise bodily integrity and personal autonomy bringing constitutional claims.

Thus, the mantra of constitutional lawyers that courts are the 'guardians' of the constitutions – the mechanisms of holding the legislature and executive accountable for its observance – is theoretically and practically inadequate on the issue of gender equality. Not least because the courts have been slow to disrupt long-standing traditions that undermine gender equality with reference to this provision. In Saint Lucia, two teachers who were dismissed pursuant to a law that mandated the state to suspend any unmarried teacher on her first pregnancy and to dismiss her if she became pregnant a second time were unsuccessful in establishing that the law was discriminatory on the grounds of sex.[18] Only women were the objects of the legislation, there was no disciplinary action against unmarried male teachers with children. The government's justification for the law was that the ideal of a married family life must be upheld and that (presumably female) teachers are expected to set an example in the community.[19] The Saint Lucia High Court ruled that the teachers and their unions had failed to shift the presumption of the constitutionality of the law. Alternatively, even if the law was discriminatory, it was held that the restrictions on the right were constitutionally permissible. In a similar vein, in Guyana, the Court of Appeal ruled that an immigration statute that gave to Guyanese men only the right to automatically pass on 'belonger' status to their foreign spouses in no way contravened the gender-equality clause of the constitution.[20]

The misgivings about the sex-discrimination prohibition in the more 'advanced' constitutions do not end with interpretation; they extend to the scope of the prohibition. Most constitutions apply only to discriminatory laws and discriminatory actions by public authorities. They do not apply horizontally, to the actions of non-state actors. This limitation bears heavily on women who experience myriad forms of discrimination and oppression in private domains. The framers of some of the newer constitutions were mindful of this constraint. The Dominica Constitutional Conference in 1977 recommended that protection against discrimination include sex as a prohibited ground and extend to discrimination in the private sector (Dominica 1977, 4). This question was keenly debated in Jamaica, and the Charter of Rights and Freedoms (Constitutional Amendment) Bill 2002 reflects the growing trend to bind natural or juristic persons to the bill of rights, taking into account the nature of the right and the duty imposed by the right, but this has not been a feature of all other debates.[21]

A final word on the bills of rights – both newer and older constitutions in the Caribbean fail to meaningfully address social and economic rights. There is no consensus on how this should be addressed but the shortcoming has been acknowledged by almost all constitutional commissions. A useful recommendation came from the Belize Political Reform Commission in relation to childcare. The commission favoured a joint private sector and public sector approach to childcare, based on the principle that access to basic childcare for working parents should become a constitutionally guaranteed right. The suggestion was that both private employers and the state would contribute to a childcare fund that is used to set up facilities accessible to working parents.

Engendering Civic Virtue

Political citizenship in process

There is no gainsaying that the legitimacy of constitutional reform depends in good measure on citizen participation and on the existence of representative mechanisms for decision-making. The discourse of twenty-first century constitutional reform in the Caribbean invariably speaks about the need to integrate civil society into the governing process and the need for greater equity in decision-making (see OAS 2002). This neutral, ahistorical, non-specific parlance can elide gendered realities.

Baldly, of the groups traditionally excluded from power, women almost always comprise the largest (Brown and Andaiye 1999). Little in the design and execution of constitutional reform processes in the Caribbean has taken this as a pivotal point of departure for constitutional reform. Constitutional reform commissions that commenced their work with terms of reference and missives from prime ministers to seriously address gender equality were constituted with minimal representation of women.

Women were represented on constitutional commissions and special parliamentary committees dealing with constitutional reform across the region, but the commissions and committees were rarely truly representative. That the legislature, which is itself unrepresentative, is the ultimate decision-maker in most constitutional reform is an inherent impediment. The special parliamentary committees set up to receive submissions from the public and make recommendations to parliament, even when bipartisan with joint membership from both houses, plainly reflect the gender disparities already evident in the composition of parliament. The constitutional commissions, which presented greater opportunities for an equitable appointment of men and women, follow this pattern.

No women were appointed to the three-person commission in St Kitts & Nevis and the five-member commission in Grenada. One member resigned from the commission in Grenada and women lobbied vigorously and successfully for a woman to replace him. The follow-up Task Force established in St Kitts and Nevis after the commission, was made up of six men. The larger commissions elsewhere combined a collection of representatives of political parties and civil society. In Guyana, the Constitution Reform Commission created in 1999 of 20 persons included two women. In Belize, three women sat on the Political Reform Commission of 13 set up in 1999, with a fourth joining later as a replacement. In Barbados, two women were appointed to the commission of ten that submitted its report in 1998. In Jamaica, of the initial 38 commissioners appointed in 1991, ten were women. In The Bahamas, 16 men and seven women were appointed to the 2002 Constitution Review Commission. Many commissions solicited the views of women's NGOs, but women were seldom incorporated as experts in the process. The Jamaica Constitutional Commission hosted 13 public fora, 12 of the 13 keynote speakers and nine of the 13 moderators were men. There was one woman among the 14 local and foreign experts on which the Guyana Constitution Reform Commission relied.

Notwithstanding, the reform processes have not been seamless domains of male hegemony. In Belize, the Society for the Promotion of Education and Research (SPEAR) was an influential partner in the constitutional and political reform process. SPEAR launched the first comprehensive campaign to engage the nation in a sustained debate on the issue of political reform in March of 1994 with a staff that included prominent feminists like Diane Haylock, a former director of the organisation. This campaign eventually led to the establishment of the Political Reform Commission in 1999 of which another former director, Dylan Vernon, became the chair. The resignation of commission members was successfully used as an opportunity to lobby for the inclusion of women on the commissions in Grenada and Guyana. In the case of Guyana, Philomena Sahoye-Shury, a women's activist, joined the commission as a replacement and representative of PPP/Civic.

Staffing needs have opened the door for the association of a few feminists with the machinery of reform. Andaiye, well-known Guyanese feminist political activist and thinker, took on the little desired task of editing and writing the report of the Guyana Constitution Reform Commission. Others joined her in the writing, including Roxanne George of the Guyana Association of Women's Lawyers (GAWL). Editing and writing created room for dialogue with the commissioners, and, in the case of George, for further participation in the process. George, a feminist lawyer working with the government, became the legal adviser to the parliamentary committee that considered the commission's report and joined the Task Force that was created to draft the recommendations approved. She consulted with some women's groups about specific proposals and attempted to see that their concerns and views were represented in the draft she was helping to produce (George 2002, 3). These gaps of personnel in the reform process have provided sites for feminist intervention but they should not be overstated. These are only small pockets of feminist involvement that have by no means transformed the institutions engaged in constitutional reform.

Political citizenship as right

In constitutional reform, women have been treated as an interest group, a client of the state, and the maximum objective is that they be consulted and marginally represented. Entirely overlooked in the conceptualisation of constitutional reform almost everywhere in the Caribbean are the implications of political citizenship for women as well as men – the need for and right of women to become integral agents of all political decision-making, including the apparatuses for reform. Women in a number of Caribbean countries have disrupted the equanimity/complacency about concerns of gender in the constitutional reform by insisting on the existence of a relationship between gender equality and fair representation of women and men in the political process. They have advocated for positive or affirmative action to achieve equality. This has been a frontal challenge to prevailing conceptions of citizenship that continue to place men at the centre of constitutional concern.

There has been moderate success in Guyana. The hard-fought-for Guyana Elections Law (Amendment) Act 2000-15 provides, among other things, that the total number of female candidates on each party's national top-up list and list for geographical constituencies taken together must be at least one-third of the total number of persons on the national list and the lists for geographical constituencies taken together respectively. This law does not guarantee seats for the women candidates in the legislature. In Antigua and Barbuda, the Directorate of Women's Affairs made strident arguments before that country's Constitutional Review Commission about the need for the constitution to articulate the value of women's participation in public life and their right to equal participation therein, and the need for the constitution to authorise positive action to facilitate this. These were some of a number of submissions made by the directorate that the commission did not endorse and described as matters that could be the subject of further discussion (Antigua and Barbuda 2002, 119).

The question has been raised of women's participation in not just the legislative branch of government, but the executive or administrative branch. In Belize, organisations like the Belize Women's Political Caucus and United Democratic Party National Women's Organisation made submissions to the Political Reform Commission on women's participation in political and public life. The majority of the commission was not convinced that a proposal that the government be mandated to comprise public bodies with women as at least one-third of its membership was desirable. It, however, made a general statement that it was 'supportive of the general principle that women should be equally represented on public bodies and urged the political parties to commit themselves to doing this as well as ensuring greater female participation in the leadership of the parties' (Belize 2000, 131).[22] In the constitutional reform debates, feminists have yet to press similar concerns about women's participation in the third branch of government –the judiciary. In my view, the statute or treaty establishing the Caribbean Court of Justice should incorporate gender parity in the composition of the court and its personnel as a major goal, and introduce some mechanisms to achieve this, as has become the practice in newly established courts like the International Criminal Court.

The propriety of enshrining in the constitution positive action to deal with women's participation in government has been the source of enormous controversy. Among feminists and women's organisations there is no consensus on the best way of securing fair representation and participation. However, by placing women's right to participate in national life as full political citizens on the constitutional reform agenda, women have challenged prevailing conceptions of citizenship that rhetorically support 'gender equality' and continue to place men at the heart of constitutional imagination. On the other side, it has put in focus one of Caribbean feminism's persistent challenges – the relations of power among women involved in feminist work and thought. Of Guyana, Andaiye (2002) said:

> I did not find it useful that women who were demanding their own inclusion did not think it critical to be inclusive of women across class, race, etc. On what basis did we know what women not represented among us would want in a constitution? With what moral or political authority did we demand inclusion?

Constitutional reform finds the women's movement as it is, no more no less. It provides a glimpse of a women's movement challenged by its diminishing human and economic resources and the implications for feminist work of multiple axes of oppression.

Political citizenship as obligation

What is emerging from some of the conversations about constitutional reform and women's political participation, including the reflection on who and what women representatives will represent, is a fuller account of political citizenship as women's right as well as political citizenship as a 'realm of female responsibility'. This is heard in Andaiye's very poignant call to Guyanese women to participate in the constitutional reform process: 'Aren't we tired yet of being less than others all around us, and less than we could be...?' (Brown and Andaiye 1999).

As might now be sensed, feminist engagement with the constitutional reform process was at its peak in Guyana, and even here there is no evidence of an overwhelming groundswell of women interested in and participating in constitutional reform. In Guyana, the National Commission on Women (NCW) led a campaign that began in 1997 to ensure that women's voices were heard in the constitutional reform process (George 2002, 1). Jean LaRose, the representative of indigenous peoples on the Constitution Reform Commission was the NCW's vice-chair. NCW and a few women's organisations closely followed the process and the responses to the proposals made. When reports were received by the representative of the women's organisations on the commission that negotiations on certain women's rights, particularly political participation, were not going well, 'Magda Pollard[23] and an army of women literally commandeered a meeting' with the commission (George 2002, 3).

At a later stage, women's organisations requested an audience with the Oversight Committee which had the responsibility of approving the drafts produced by the special Task Force and they mobilised in significant numbers to attend the meetings of this committee to make representations. When reforms to the electoral laws were finally drafted, the agreed provision that a minimum of one-third of the candidates on the electoral list should be women was omitted. A group of women mobilised again and lobbied opposition and government members until a version of the proposed change was included in the legislation and enacted. This sustained advocacy produced agreement and legislative approval for the establishment of a Women and Gender Commission, the incorporation of human rights conventions in the constitution, including the Convention on the Elimination of All Forms of Discrimination Against Women (CEDAW), and an enforceable guarantee of gender equality.

Outside Guyana, the enthusiasm has been markedly less. The high point in Antigua and Barbuda was a Women's Constitutional Conference to mark International Women's Day on March 8, 2001. The conference educated women about the process, and principal issues, and was the beginnings of a strategy for future action and submissions to the Constitutional Review Commission. It drew over 200 women and men from government bodies, NGOs and civil society, but it has been difficult to maintain women's interest in the process. In Barbados, only about 30 of the over 200 submissions by individuals to that country's Constitution Review Commission were made by women. The list of 22 organisations specifically invited by that commission to submit memoranda included the Barbados Women's Club, the Business and Professional Women's Club, the National Organisation of Women and the Soroptimist Club of Barbados as well as professional associations dominated by women such as the Barbados Registered Nurses Association and the Barbados Secondary Teachers' Union. Only the Barbados Overseas Women's League (UK), the Soroptimists International of Barbados and the Bureau for Women's Affairs, as it was then called, made written submissions. The St Kitts and Nevis Constitutional Commission received submissions from 25 organisations and individuals, which included only two women and no women's organisations.

Apathy towards constitutional reform is not confined to women. Many view the constitution as abstract and highfalutin, irrelevant to the ordinary struggles of daily life – women more so because of male control over matters connected to it and its obsession with the public domain. Women's wariness is not entirely imprudent because the investment in securing constitutional reform is onerous precisely because the process is extended; there are so many agents to persuade and the consensus for reform must be strong enough to satisfy the requirements of entrenchment clauses in the constitutions. The reality that law in general and the reforms, if achieved, will not of themselves produce the social transformation that is typically hoped for is also sobering.

Notwithstanding, amidst keen awareness of the possibilities, frustrations and disappointments of constitutional reform processes, there still is the feminist call, albeit sometimes faint, to participation, as the performance of citizenship. This is citizenship understood as a continuous activity, a demanding process that never ends, not a momentary engagement with an eye to a final goal or societal arrangement (Dietz 1998, 391). Mary Dietz (ibid.) argues that 'only when [feminists] stress that the pursuit of … social and economic concerns must be undertaken through active engagement as citizens in the public world and when they declare the activity of citizenship itself a value will feminists be able to claim a truly liberatory politics as their own'. This logic informs not just the language with which many Caribbean feminists now advocate on women's political participation, but the less visible involvement of other feminists from the platform of broader political agendas.[24]

Gender Somethings: Idiosyncratic Ideals

Gender somethings, an uncontroversial ideal

In constitutional reform many amorphous, what I term, *gender somethings* have evolved in some measure as a self-conscious distancing from *women things*. The support from constitutional commissions for gender somethings is entirely clear: what is less discernible is substantively what is being supported. For example, the Barbados Constitution Review Commission identified greater recognition of 'gender rights' as a specific issue to be considered in the expansion of the chapter protecting fundamental rights and freedoms, and the commission likened these rights to those of the disabled and the aged. Are *gender rights* the rights *of a* gender, rights *based on* gender, or does the term connote its now technical use in the transgender movement to include the right to free expression of gender identity, to choose a gender role and to freely express it? We risk linguistic nonsense and conceptual inanity from the uncritical replacement of 'women' with 'gender'. Admittedly, as feminist intellectuals, we are part of the production of new 'gender somethings'; still it is worrying that at the policy level their wider acceptance or currency is accompanied by a growing opacity and the rendering of women and their concerns into an abstraction. As in other aspects of public discourse, *gender* is rapidly becoming disembodied in political terms.

'Gender discrimination' is among the more discernible gender somethings. Protection against discrimination on the grounds of gender has been among the least controversial of claims in constitutional reform debates. In Guyana, Mandatory Issue No. 4 considered by the commission was the elimination of discrimination in all its forms including discrimination against women (Guyana 1999, 96). The terms of reference for the Constitution Review Commission of Barbados established in 1996 included ensuring the elimination of gender discrimination in the constitution (Barbados 1998, 1). The 'gender question' has at times been given short shrift, precisely because it is deemed to be incontrovertible. At a public session held by the Barbados Constitution Review Commission in Toronto, commission member, Norma Forde, expressed reservations about the implications reform would have on Barbados and its services because 'everybody now wants to be a Barbadian' (Barbados 1997, 54-5). Another member of the Constitution Review Commission dismissed such concerns and put the issue beyond doubt: 'the door [for constitutional change of these citizenship provisions] is open and so many people are pushing against it that if anyone stands behind the open door they're in trouble' (ibid., 55).

Commitment to the principle of gender equality does not guarantee prominence far less pre-eminence. Gender equality can be affirmed while other concerns come first. What I am speaking of here is very subtle, at times almost imperceptible, because theoretically the goals are not abandoned just delayed. In Belize, the preamble to the constitution was amended to include a statement that the policies of the government must include gender equality as one of its goals, as recommended by the Political Reform Commission. The Preamble of the Constitution was first amended on February 23, 2001 to add ethnicity as an inappropriate basis for disparity, to better recognise the cultural expression of indigenous people and to more strongly recognise economic and social rights and the right to vote.[25] Gender equality as an ideal and recognition of the rights of the disabled were added later in another amendment to the Preamble on December 31, 2001.[26]

In Antigua and Barbuda, the commission relegated most of the submissions on behalf of women to a chapter at the back of the report titled 'Outstanding Issues' which included 'without comment, summaries of certain representations raised with our commissions which we were unable to endorse but which we feel could be the subject of further discussion and public debate' (Antigua and Barbuda 2002, 119). Among the matters included therein and not endorsed, were submissions that the principle of equality of men and women be explicitly embodied in the constitution and other appropriate legislation, and that there should be established a Gender Commission to monitor, investigate, research, educate, lobby, advise and report on issues concerning gender equality. In the commission's view, the present constitution was 'already an advance on those of Barbados and the United States in prohibiting discrimination on the grounds of sex' and it recommended further consideration of gender equality at the 'policy level', not that of constitutional reform (ibid., 61).

At the inaugural meeting of the Jamaica Constitutional Commission, Prime Minister P.J. Patterson specifically mentioned that all discriminatory actions, including those based on gender grounds, must be outlawed (Jamaica 1993, 5). The Jamaica Constitutional Commission 'unanimously and unhesitatingly' recommended that 'sex' be included as a prohibited ground for discrimination (Jamaica 1993, 26). An interim bill to amend the chapter protecting fundamental rights and freedoms in Jamaica in 1999 was presented to parliament. The Jamaican attorney-general was asked to explain why the bill did not execute the commission's unanimous recommendation to include sex as an unlawful ground for discrimination. He explained that the issue of gender would eventually be looked at, but was not included in the interim bill because 'we have to put into that Bill *matters which are of the utmost importance* like the right to vote, the right to hold a passport, to have fair treatment' emphasis added (Ansine 1999). He added: 'I am *not saying that gender is not important* ... it is intended that the new charter on fundamental rights will be tabled within weeks and will include the provision that has to do with discrimination on the grounds of gender' [emphasis added] (ibid).

The pecking order of interests implied from the categories, matters that are 'not unimportant' and those of the 'utmost importance', is the angle from which gender equality is being understood and supported. This notion that women can wait a little longer for their concerns to be addressed while matters of the utmost importance get dealt with, the placative tone calling for patience in getting to questions of women's rights, the hesitation or equivocation before turning to women's inclusion are all filled with hierarchical tendencies and realities. Nowhere are these complexities of advancing women's rights better noted than in The Bahamas referendum of February 2002 in which a series of 'uncontroversial' reforms to The Bahamas' old model constitution to better secure gender equality were rejected with a resounding no vote.

The country was given about a month to consider a number of proposals for constitutional reform that required a referendum vote. Some were concerned with areas like the teaching service commission, the position of an independent parliamentary commissioner and an independent boundaries commission. On gender equality and gender discrimination, the referendum question to the Bahamian voters was No. 1 and asked: 'Do you agree that all forms of discrimination against women, their children and spouses should be removed from the Constitutions and that no persons should be discriminated against on the grounds of gender, and do you approve the proposed amendments to Articles 3, 5, 8, 9, 10, 13, 14, 26 and 54 of the Constitution…?' There was no consultative constitutional reform process, the proposed reforms were the prime minister's initiative. He was very concerned with commitments under CEDAW and the place of Bahamas in the international community.

Even if, as the attorney-general said, the reforms were 'substantially non-controversial and generally agreed as being desirable' (Lundy 2002), procedurally and technically the government seriously misstepped. Criticisms of the absence of a consultative process, the haste of the reforms and the timing of the referendum close to national elections were all legitimate. Reforms to secure gender equality were to be made to eight major constitutional articles. Any one of these may have included a drafting error, and some did, or might give rise to more debate than another. For instance, in a country like The Bahamas that is very concerned about immigration, it might be agreed that men and women should have the same rights as citizens, but the debate would inevitably ask whether equality should be achieved by extending to women the rights men have, or limiting the rights men have to those enjoyed by women, or a middle ground. The government lumped all the reforms together for the voters to give one answer, yes or no. No opportunity was provided on the ballot for an intelligent electorate to affirm each of what were different and significant reforms. In a word, through this crude consolidation of varying gender concerns, it was asking voters to affirm gender somethings with all their well-intentioned opacity.

The reform proposals were designed to benefit women, yet women outside of the government machinery were completely invisible as political actors in their production. This is the ultimate paradox, and not infrequent occurrence, of pro-women laws that women play little role in developing (Andaiye 2002). Women became the abstract object of rights instigated by the state as a benevolent patriarch that did not anticipate women's place as full political citizens. From the start, despite the laudatory named objectives of the reforms, women as fully materialised subjects of decision-making were never at the centre of these proposals.

On the other side, the referendum became so otherwise politicised, that the public debate contained little expression of regret, even if the no vote could be justified in various ways. Nor was there any widespread anxiety about the injury to the national psyche of such a resounding collective decision on the question of women's rights. There were 'elated cheers [echoing] through the meeting hall [of the main opposition party] when the NO votes came in thick and fast' (Missick, Nixon 2002a). The no vote was heralded as 'a victory for common sense and democracy – and one that all Bahamians can be justly proud of' (Mackey 2002), the Archbishop described its outcome as a demonstration of maturity (Missick 2002b), the Christian Council congratulated Bahamians for so 'boldly and courageously demonstrating to the government that they … are the inheritors and successors to this family of islands' (ibid.). The then opposition leader, Perry Christie, who became prime minister in the elections in the wake of the referendum, told the public that the referendum did not mean that Bahamians rejected equality for women, just that if proposals were to be advanced, 'they must be advanced properly and carefully' (McKenzie 2002). Bahamians were assured that the new government would initiate reforms through a proper process. This no doubt will be one of the matters considered by the Constitutional Commission set up by the new government at the end of 2002. But yet again, the pervasive feeling is that women and their concerns are 'not unimportant' but 'not of the utmost importance'.

The irony of the referendum is that the very action that came to symbolise a victory for democracy and participatory governance – saying no to, among other things, gender equality – had as its foundation the formal repudiation of equal access of women to full citizenship and participation in the democracy. The tragedy that this defining moment of 'courage' and 'national pride' and 'moral integrity' should come by means of a no vote to reforms to strengthen women's rights as citizens, was largely lost. Even for feminists and women generally, there is a challenge to not reduce gender into redundancy, so that it matters only if something else does not matter more in the moment. Prominent Bahamian feminist, Marion Bethel, explained that women were torn by the referendum, 'Some said, if I vote against this referendum, I would be letting women's rights become secondary. But if I vote for it, I would be conceding that the process was appropriate. For me personally, process is very important' (Bethel 2002). In the constitutional reform process in Guyana, attempts to build consensus among women electoral candidates met resistance from the women themselves who were campaigning 'as soldiers in a highly combative "war" between the two parties' with the result that frequently 'race/party trumped gender – again' (Andaiye 2002). In the zero sum game we construct about social justice and equity, the door may be wide open to the subject of gender equality in constitutional reform, but there always seems to be a trump about to be played lurking not far behind.

Gender somethings clarified, sex does not include sexual orientation

As early as the 1986 Trinidad and Tobago Sexual Offences Act, the perverse practice developed of using statutes that had as one goal strengthening women's rights, as a location for retrenching the 'erotic autonomy' of gays and lesbians (see Alexander 1994; Tambiah 2002). The criminalisation of consensual sex between adult women therein was the imposition of gender equality with a vengeance (see Tambiah 2002). Men were already defined as buggers and so women engaged in same-sex sexual intimacy would not escape the criminal law's disciplinary purview. In 2000, Trinidad and Tobago enacted the Equal Opportunities Act. For the first time, the law prohibited discrimination in a number of settings like the workplace, on grounds that included sex. For the avoidance of doubt, the legislation states that 'sex does not include sexual orientation'. Constitutional language of the same order has been a slight more subtle. The Jamaica Charter of Rights and Freedoms (Constitutional Amendment) Bill 2002 protects the right of freedom from discrimination on the ground of 'sex, that is to say, male or female'. Gender equality and non-recognition of lesbians and gays are troublingly juxtaposed as a coherent conceptual claim within a single frame.

In the Caribbean, there has been growing advocacy for a constitutional right to freedom from discrimination on the grounds of sexual orientation. Defying norms about circumspectness and invisibility, gays and lesbians in Jamaica, under the institutional cover of J-Flag, represented themselves in writing and in person at the Special Select Committee to consider the proposed charter. The heart of their submissions was their right to citizenship. The Special Select Parliamentary Committee devoted fair attention to the submissions in its report. They were concerned about the effect accepting this would have on the institution of marriage and on parenting. The committee supported the repeal of legislation criminalising buggery but it was not prepared to support constitutional reform (Jamaica 2001). The concession was practically significant but the message of second grade citizenship was clear. The prime minister and the cabinet rejected these submissions of J-Flag, including that of the committee about decriminalising consensual sex between adult men. 'We will not be considering the issue of homosexuality …. That issue is not on the agenda of the Cabinet', the Information Minister said (Observer Reporter 2002).

This pattern, with variations, would repeat itself across the Caribbean. One of the earliest demands within the context of constitutional reform that the constitution take seriously the rights of gays and lesbians, came from Barbadian feminist historian, Melanie Newton, who was then a graduate student and the youngest member of the Barbados Constitutional Review Commission. She argued that, in recognising the right to hold religious beliefs and creeds, the constitution was recognising the right not to be discriminated against on the basis of biological factors as well as on the basis of individual choice. To her mind, there was no 'justifiable legal or ethical reason why sexual orientation should not be included in the fundamental rights provisions' (Barbados 1998, 117). Newton filed a dissenting opinion to the position of the majority. The majority considered this question under the rubric 'gender rights', and said that it was not satisfied that a 'convincing case' had been made out for the inclusion of sexual orientation as a prohibited ground of discrimination.

In Belize, the Political Reform Commission received several suggestions to include sexual orientation as a prohibited ground of discrimination and a majority of the commission in fact recommended an amendment to this effect (Belize 2000, 47). Following the Commission's Report there have been some constitutional amendments but none in relation to this recommendation. In Guyana, the Constitution Reform Commission also recommended the inclusion of sexual orientation as a prohibited ground of discrimination. The Constitution (Amendment) Act 2001, properly speaking, never became law because it was not assented to by the president. It adopted the recommendations of the commission on human rights and included an all-embracing anti-discrimination clause. The clause prohibited grounds of discrimination including race, place of origin, political opinion, colour, creed, age, disability, marital status, sex, gender, language, sexual orientation, birth, social class, pregnancy, religion, conscience, belief or culture. The proposal appears to have been 'slipped in without the broad public or ... even "interest groups" noticing' (Andaiye 2002). They did notice the words 'sexual orientation' among the array of other prohibited grounds of discrimination after legislative approval was given. Vociferous opposition ensued and in response, the president withheld his assent of the law. The result is that all the provisions relating to human rights, including gender equality, have been in abeyance.

At best, we as Caribbean feminists appear ambivalent about the rights of gays and lesbians. The issue continues to divide Caribbean feminists and feminist organisations who, at times, have been insensible to, maybe in some cases indifferent to, how legislative instruments ostensibly of women's liberation are being used to underline the marginality of homosexuals. Considerable feminist energy has been directed at the harms women experience as sexual and sexualised beings, and appropriately so. However, there is also a need for us, as part of intellectual and activist projects, to start 'theorising yes' more (Franke 2001). By that I mean devoting more attention to developing a positive theory of female sexuality and not just focussing on the dangers posed by sex (ibid.). A stronger interest in what Jacqui Alexander (1994) calls women's 'erotic autonomy' will advance our own work and our capacity to support that of others. From the identification of homophobia as a performance of masculinity, to the suggestion that we might expect to find it more where male power is threatened (Chevannes 2001, 22), and the mundane aggregation of lesbian and feminist as epithets for women, put us in mind of how ideologically wrapped up sexual orientation and gender are as sites of oppression. Analytically, we should resist treating sexual orientation as nothing more than a subset of gender, but must interrogate state action that positions these as distinct, antagonistic concerns.

Conclusion

The process of constitutional reform is a paradox of sorts. It is articulately a location to chart reconstruction, and, at the same time, is a venue in which the same contestable relations of gender are normalised. Most disquieting is how zones of equanimity reproduce unequal gender relations in terms not at odds with those in realms of strong hostility. There is arguably a more structured platform for contestation and resistance and, given the nature of the constitution, less prescription of what one can talk about than in most other present day forms of public discourse. Notwithstanding, committee and commission deliberations, report-editing and writing, executive decision-making about which reforms to proceed with first and legal drafting are all mechanisms used to re-enact power and relations of gender. Participation in its processes with change in mind, however modest, is enormously difficult, interminable work requiring careful, consistent attention to both structures and principles.

This may be exactly what citizenship is about but surely not for everyone and at all times. The centralisation of constitutional reform processes and its 'high politics' should not become a medium of privileging a narrow understanding of the political. Feminist advocacy around women's political participation must always stand short of this danger, which brings us to the pivotal position of the feminist activist as a representative of and a part of communities of women. The contours of the constitutional reform process allow us, I believe, to talk about activism as more than a facilitative *process* existing on the edge of womankind. The nature of debates about the constitution gives us an opportunity to view women's activism in its various shapes and forms as *a way in which women live*. I take the risk of the essentialist quandary in challenging the narrative that feminism is irredeemably alienated from women. Activists are not *other* women, they are women. They represent women, but equally their lives represent a way women live. We as feminists, cautious of what constitutional reform cannot give us, should still seize it as an opportunity for public dialogue and internal reflection.

Notes

1. In this article, 'Commonwealth Caribbean' is at times used interchangeably with 'Caribbean' to refer to those Caribbean territories that obtained their independence from Britain, namely: Antigua and Barbuda, Bahamas, Barbados, Belize, Dominica, Grenada, Guyana, Jamaica, St Kitts & Nevis, Saint Lucia, St Vincent and the Grenadines and Trinidad and Tobago.
2. In the last decade, constitutional commissions bearing different names have been set up in Jamaica (1992); Barbados (1996); Dominica (1997); St Kitts and Nevis (1997); Belize (1999); Guyana (1999); Antigua and Barbuda (2000); The Bahamas (2002); Grenada (2002), St Vincent and the Grenadines (2002).
3. The OAS Secretary General Cesar Gaviria put it this way: 'constitutional reform cannot be addressed in one Caribbean country without taking into consideration the economics and politics of the region as a whole' (OAS 2002).
4. Legal luminaries like Sir Fred Phillips, Dr Nicolas Liverpool, Professor Ralph Carnegie and Justice Telford Georges have been participating in constitutional reform in a number of territories.

5. The organisations ranged from and included the Adventist Youth Society, Council of Voluntary Social Services, Jamaica Chamber of Commerce, Jamaica Council of Churches, Jamaica Coalition on the Rights of the Child, Jamaica Police Federation, Jamaica (Caribbean) Society, Manchester, Maroons Federal House of Assembly, Media Association of Jamaica, National Spiritual Assembly of the Bahai's of Jamaica and Pharmaceutical Society of Jamaica.

6. Hubert Devonish, UWI lecturer, presented an intriguing submission on protection against discrimination on the grounds of language.

7. Prime Minister of Belize, Said Musa (1999), warned his Political Reform Commission: 'At every stage of your deliberations I will ask you to be sensitive to gender perspectives as well as to the fact that we are a multi-cultural nation with a policy of celebrating and respecting cultural diversity'.

8. See *Allie Mohammed v The State* (1998) 53 WIR 444; *Gairy v Attorney General* (1999) 59 WIR 174; *Shah & Lasalle v Attorney General* (1972) 20 WIR 361.

9. Caribbean constitutions can be broadly categorised into two types: the older model constitutions that came into force between 1962 and 1973 of which Jamaica, Barbados and the Bahamas remain. Then there are newer constitutions of the OECS and Belize that came into force after 1973. For these purposes we can add to the latter group the republican constitutions of Trinidad and Tobago and Guyana.

10. See Constitution of Barbados 1966, ss. 5-6; Constitution of the Bahamas 1973, ss. 8-10.

11. See Constitution of Barbados, s. 10(3).

12. The Barbados Constitution (Amendment) Act 2000-18 addresses some of the discriminatory constitutional provisions.

13. See for example, Constitution of Saint Lucia, s. 1.

14. *Girard and others v Attorney General*, (unreported) December 17, 1986, High Court, Saint Lucia (Nos. 371/1986, 372/1986), at 17. The status of this clause is still the subject of debate. Recently the Privy Council confirmed that this section does not give rise to enforceable rights under the constitution an *obiter dictum* in a Bermuda case for the reason mentioned above—the inapplicability of the redress clause to the opening section. See *Grape Bay Ltd. v Attorney General of Bermuda* [2000] 1 WLR 574. However subsequently, in the well-known *Neville Lewis* case [2000] 3 WLR 1785, the Privy Council stated clearly that the section gave rise to constitutional rights, however it failed to distinguish or overrule its dictum in the Bermuda case leaving us unclear as to how one enforces the constitutional rights that arise.

15. The rationale is that the express reference to 'sex' in the introductory section makes it clear that the omission in the anti-discrimination clause was deliberate, and that no construction, however broad and purposive, could conclude otherwise. See *Matadeen v Pointu* [1998] 3 WLR 18 at 35.

16. See Demerieux (1992, 421, n 22). This followed the case *Att-Gen v Ali* [1989] LRC (Const) 474.

17. *Nielsen v Barker* (1982) 32 WIR 254. The Guyana Court of Appeal ruled that the category of prohibited grounds was closed and sex could not be implied.

18. *Girard v Attorney General of St. Lucia*, above n. 14.

19. Complaint against the Government of Saint Lucia presented by – World Confederation of Organisations of the Teaching Profession – WCOTP, Report No. 270, (Vol. LXXIII, 1990, Series B, No. 1) http://www.oit.org.pe/sindi/english/casos/luc/luc199001.html accessed July 10 2003.
20. *Nielsen v Barker*, above n. 17.
21. The Jamaica Charter of Rights and Freedoms (Constitutional Amendment) Bill 2002, s. 2, is heavily influenced by the Republic of South Africa Constitution 1996.
22. In Belize, within the Political Reform Commission there was a fear that other groups would demand quotas. Questions were raised about the constitutionality of such a measure even though the very purpose of the reform exercise was to suggest what ought to be part of the constitution and thus constitutional. The use of criteria of physical traits as opposed to capacity and experience was challenged and some argued that women were doing well enough on their own and did not need special privileges. That this should be addressed at the political party level was another response (Belize 2000, 131).
23. Pollard is the former head of the Women's Desk at the CARICOM Secretariat and was the then chair of NCW.
24. We have few resources linguistically and ideologically to describe and understand the life and work of Caribbean feminists who have always been engaged in many political struggles and who have multiple zones of concern and activity. It is easy to overlook submissions made to the constitutional commissions by feminists such as Linnette Vassell (Jamaica) representing the Coalition for Community Participation in Governance and Keturah Babb (Barbados) representing the Caribbean Policy Development Centre (CPDC) or the advocacy of feminists within organisations such as Grenada Community Development Agency (GRENCODA).
25. Belize Constitution (Third Amendment) Act 2001-2.
26. Belize Constitution (Fourth) Amendment Act 2001-39.

References

Alexander, M.J. 1994. 'Not Just (Any)*Body* can be a Citizen: The Politics of Law, Sexuality and Postcoloniality in Trinidad and Tobago and the Bahamas'. *Feminist Review* 48 (Autumn): 5-23.

Andaiye. 2002. E-mail correspondence with Tracy Robinson. May 18 (On file with author).

Ansine, J. 1999. 'Women's rights ignored'. *The Gleaner*, March 18 (Jamaica).

Barbados. 1995. *Barbados Report to the United Nations Fourth World Conference on Women, Beijing, China, September 1995*. Bridgetown.

———. 1997. *Verbatim Transcript of Public Session of Constitution Review Commission, North York Community Hall, Ontario, Canada, 7 September*.

———. 1998. *Report of the Constitution Review Commission*. Bridgetown: Government Printing Office.

Belize. 2000. *Final Report of the Political Reform Commission*. Belize City.

Bethel, Marion. 2002. 'Interview with Marion Bethel: The Bahamas Referendum, Challenges to the Implementation of CEDAW'. *Gender Dialogue* 3 (December): 1-2.

Brown, Hazel and Andaiye. 1999. 'If in Trinidad and Tobago, why not here? Trinidad and Tobago women work and win cross party in recent elections'. *Stabroek News.* July 25 (Guyana).

Chevannes, Barry. 2001. *Learning to be a Man: Culture, Socialization and Gender Identity in Five Caribbean Communities*. Kingston: UWI Press.

Demerieux, Margaret. 1992. *Fundamental Rights in the Commonwealth Caribbean*. Bridgetown: Faculty of Law Library, UWI.

Dietz, Mary. 1998. 'Context is All: Feminism and Theories of Citizenship'. In *Feminism and Politics*, ed. Anne Phillips, 378-400. Oxford: Oxford University Press.

Dominica. 1977. *Report of the Dominica Constitutional Conference held in Marlborough House London in May 1977.*

Edmondson, Belinda. 1999. *Making Men: Gender, Literary Authority, and Women's Writing in Caribbean Narrative*. Durham: Duke University Press.

Forde, Norma. 1987. *The Convention on the Elimination of All Forms of Discrimination Against Women-Barbados a Signatory*. Unpublished manuscript. (On file at the Faculty of Law Library, UWI, Cave Hill).

Franke, Katherine. 2001. 'Theorizing Yes: An Essay on Feminism, Law and Desire'. *Columbia Law Review* 101: 181-208.

George, Roxanne. 2002. 'Women's participation in decision-making – the battle to make it a reality'. Paper presented at Workshop 'Women's Political Participation: Training in Democracy and Governance', October 26, Antigua.

Gonsalves, Ralph. 2003. 'Good Governance and Constitutional Reform in St Vincent and the Grenadines', Feature Address delivered at the formal launching of the Constitutional Review Commission, February 10, House of Assembly Building, Kingstown, St Vincent and the Grenadines.

Guyana. 1999. *Report of the Constitution Reform Commission to the National Assembly of Guyana July 17, 1999*. Georgetown.

Jamaica. 1995. *Final Report of the Joint Select Committee of the Houses of Parliament on Constitutional and Electoral Reform*. Kingston: Jamaica Printing Service.

———. 1994. *Final Report of the Constitutional Commission Jamaica*. Kingston: Jamaica Printing Service.

———. 1993. *Report of the Constitutional Commission Jamaica*. Kingston: Jamaica Printing Service.

———. 2001. *Report of the Joint Select Committee on its deliberations on the Bill entitled An Act to Amend the Constitution of Jamaica to provide for a Charter of Rights and for connected matters*. http://www.jis.gov.jm/information/Charter%20of%20Rights.hmt

Lewis, Linden. 2000. 'Nationalism and Caribbean masculinity'. In *Gender Ironies of Nationalism*, ed. Tamar Mayer, 261-281. London and New York: Routledge.

Lundy, Tameka. 2002. ' "Postpone Referendum" suggests Archbishop'. *The Bahama Journal* January 24.

Mackey, George. 2002. 'The Viewpoint – A victory for democracy'. *The Tribune*. March 2.

Macklem, Patrick. 1988. 'Constitutional Ideologies'. *Ottawa Law Review* 20: 117-156.

McIntosh, Simeon. 2002. *Caribbean Constitutional Reform: Rethinking the West Indian Polity.* Kingston: Caribbean Law Publishing.

McKenzie, Tamara. 2002. 'Bahamian Masses not "dumb and stupid" says Christie'. *The Bahama Guardian*. March 1.

Missick, Rupert and Arthia Nixon. 2002a. 'Verdict is a victory for the people, says party leader'. *The Tribune*, February 28.

Missick, Rupert (2002b). 'Church set to demand "proper" referendum from next government' March 2 (The Bahamas).

Mondesire, Alicia and Leith Dunn. 1995. *Towards Equity in Development: A Report on the Status of Women in Sixteen Commonwealth Caribbean Countries.* Georgetown: CARICOM Secretariat.

Musa, Said. 1999. Address by the Prime Minister of Belize to the First Session of the Political Reform Commission, January 13, WASA Conference Room, Belize City.

Observer Reporter, 'Government says no to gay rights advocates'. *The Jamaica Observer* January 22.

Organization of American States. 2002. *Constitutional Reform in the Caribbean: Final Report of the OAS/UNDP Conference held in Barbados January 20-22, 2002.*

Robinson, Tracy. 1998. 'Protection of Funda(men)tal Rights and Freedoms: The Invisibility of Women in Caribbean Constitutions'. Paper presented at Human Rights into the Twenty-First Century: Linking the Domestic and the International Conference, October 2-4, University of Toronto, Faculty of Law. (On file with author).

———. 1999. 'Fictions of Citizenship: Bodies without Sex and the Effacement of Gender in Law' *Small Axe* 7: 1-27.

———. 2004. 'Beyond the Bill of Rights: Sexing the Citizen'. In *Confronting Power, Theorizing Gender: Interdisciplinary Perspectives in the Caribbean,* ed. Eudine Barriteau. Kingston: UWI Press.

St Kitts & Nevis. 1998. *Report of a Constitutional Commission Appointed by His Excellency The Governor General of St Kitts and Nevis.*

Tambiah, Yasmin. 2002. *Redefining the female body politic: Women, sexuality and the state.* SEPHIS Postdoctoral Research Study, 2000-2002 (on file with author).

---

*   I am very grateful to Ms Corinne Henry for the research assistance she provided in the preparation of this paper.

29 | BARBARA BAILEY

The Caribbean Experience in the International Women's Movement
Issues, Process, Constraints and Possibilities

Introduction

The focus of this paper is an analysis of the Caribbean's involvement in the international women's movement with particular reference to the 1995 United Nations Fourth World Conference on Women (FWCW) in Beijing, China and the post-Beijing period leading up to the United Nations General Assembly Special Session (UNGASS) on women held in June 2000 in New York (popularly referred to as Beijing +5). The analysis will focus on four concerns: the process of engagement of the Caribbean at the sub-regional, regional and international levels; the evolution of issues critical to Caribbean women between the Beijing 1995 conference and the Beijing +5 meeting in 2000; the isolation of constraining factors in the process; and, the identification of opportunities for advancing the gender equality agenda beyond Beijing +5. These concerns will not be addressed sequentially because they are in fact interrelated concerns and discussion of any one aspect invariably leads to consideration of other areas.

The analysis is informed by my own engagement in the women's movement over the last two decades and therefore, in many ways, on personal reflections of the experience. The analysis nonetheless points to some of the strengths and weaknesses of the Caribbean women's movement and lessons that can inform the strengthening of the movement at national, sub-regional and regional levels as we move towards the ten-year review of the Beijing Conference in 2005.

The FWCW: Pre and Post Events

The hallmark of the Caribbean's involvement in the 1995 FWCW was the highly coordinated and well-managed preparatory process that was mounted at the national and sub-regional levels and which involved CARICOM member states. At the international level, funding from various multilateral agencies was allocated for different regions of the world and activities were orchestrated through the collaborative effort of the Caribbean Offices of the United Nations Development Fund for Women (UNIFEM) and the United Nations Economic Commission on Latin America and the Caribbean (UNECLAC), the Women's Desk at the Caribbean Community (CARICOM) Secretariat, the Women and Development (WAND) Unit of the School of Continuing Studies of the University of the West Indies and the Caribbean Association for Feminist Research and Action (CAFRA). Reflecting on the networking strategy used in the Beijing preparatory process, Massiah (2003)[1] records that

> A division of labour was worked out based on the principle of comparative advantage of the partners and the plan put into effect. The plan depended highly on collaboration and consensus building, involving governments, NGOs, members of the diplomatic community, universities and individual consultants. It embraced all language areas and all political ideologies of the region. (p. 6)

A major activity in the preparations for Beijing was the convening of a panel of consultants to assist governments in the preparation of national reports. In this regard, Massiah (2003)[2] further notes that:

> Consultants were assigned to specific territories in which they undertook baseline research to acquire the information which was required to complete the questionnaire designed by the United Nations. CARICOM and UNIFEM then recruited two consultants to put together the findings of the national reports into a regional report entitled *Towards Equity in Development: A Report on the Status of Women in Sixteen Commonwealth Caribbean Countries*. (p. 10)

In preparing this report, Mondesire and Dunn (1995)[3] found that from among the 12 areas identified by the UN as critical to improving the status of women worldwide, six were crucial to Caribbean women:

1. The inverse relationship between women's levels of education and remunerative benefits and their resulting growing impoverishment, higher levels of unemployment and engagement in unwaged work;

2. Reduction in spending on health services and the impact on women as primary caregivers in the family;
3. Women's low access to established power domains and their inability to utilise power in areas where they have an advantage;
4. Use of psychological and physical force against women;
5. Influx of migrants and the correlation to poverty;
6. Insufficient mechanisms to promote women's advancement.

Other preparatory activities included a public education programme around the 12 critical issues identified by the UN. This communication strategy involved a radio series, 'Home Front', mounted with support from United Nations Children's Fund (UNICEF), WAND and UNIFEM and a newsletter published by CAFRA, who also mounted a television series on the issues critical to Caribbean women. A workshop on negotiating skills and conference diplomacy was also mounted to equip members of national delegations with the capacity to engage in debates in an international forum and with the skills and understandings required to carry a Caribbean position forward.

Massiah (2003),[4] a leading figure in the preparatory process, notes:

> The creativity lay in the sheer size of the activity, the innovative strategy and the opportunities it offered for experimentation with the principle of networking. The risk lay in confronting the problems and conflicts which were bound to arise – and they did – when such a wide range and number of partners were involved. (p. 6)

For those involved, however, the preparatory phase leading up to attendance at the Beijing Conference proved to be an exciting and invigorating experience that did much to build both individual and institutional capacity. In fact, in an assessment of UNIFEM's work in the region between 1992 and 2001, Dunn and Sebro (2002)[5] note that the preparatory process for Beijing 'is regarded as a high point in the history of the Caribbean women's movement'. (p. 39)

At the actual Beijing conference the approach was no less highly coordinated and the networking strategy, with a clear division of labour among members of the various delegations, was carried forward at that level. Each morning there was a Caribbean caucus which provided an opportunity for progress reports on the ongoing debates in the various working committees to which persons had been deployed based on expertise as well as an in-depth understanding of the issues, particularly those related to the Caribbean priorities. These encounters allowed for feedback, for discussion of contentious issues and for clarifying Caribbean positions in relation to these issues. So even where there was a single Caribbean representative serving on a working committee, as was the norm rather than the exception, there was never any doubt that one spoke on behalf of the collective and that one had been mandated so to do.

A distinguishing feature of the Caribbean contribution to the FWCW was the strong position taken in relation to women's unremunerated work and the need to consider this with other factors in national accounts. The urgency to move to consensus on this matter was based on the recognition that:

> People in the Caribbean, especially women and children carry a heavy burden of unwaged work: among the reasons are the high proportion of female-headed, single-parent households; the entrenchment of gender-stereotyped roles; and the lack of social support for child and family care except through private arrangements mainly among women and girl children.... Counting and valuing unwaged work in official statistics is an essential basis for changing public policy on issues ranging from wages to macro economic strategy. (CARICOM 1997)[6]

Based on this conviction, the Caribbean successfully led the debate on unwaged work in terms of formulating language that reflected the need to find creative ways to measure and count women's unwaged work in national statistics and so acknowledge and recognise their valuable contribution to national development. One of the strategic objectives related to women and the economy and, more specifically, to women's economic rights and independence, included in 'The Platform for Action' therefore called on governments to:

> Seek to develop a more comprehensive knowledge of work and employment through, *inter alia*, efforts to measure and better understand the type, extent and distribution of unremunerated work, particularly work done for family farms or businesses, and encourage the sharing and dissemination of information ... including the development of methods for assessing its value in quantitative terms, for possible reflection in accounts ... consistent with core national accounts (Platform for Action #165 (g), p. 98).[7]

Following close on the euphoric success experienced by the Caribbean in Beijing, the CARICOM Secretariat initiated the development of a Post-Beijing Regional Plan of Action[8] and, in this regard, held national consultations in selected member states. These meetings involved a cross section of persons: government ministers including ministers of women's affairs, members of opposition parties, Women's Bureaux personnel, representatives of key government departments and leaders and members of women's non-governmental organisations. The Plan of Action was also informed by information contained in a number of relevant documents as well as by two regional post-Beijing meetings: a UNIFEM workshop for Ministers in charge of Women's Affairs and Heads of Women's Bureaux and a Partners of the Americas workshop which brought together NGOs which had not taken part in the preparatory process.

In the Regional Plan of Action, two major strategic objectives were identified to achieve greater gender equality and social justice in the region; *viz.*:

1. The promotion of support for gender equity among policy-makers and the broad public through the *mainstreaming of gender* in (a) the culture and organisation of relevant institutions as well as in programming and policy at national level and at the level of the CARICOM Secretariat; and, (b) in public debate and concern through expansion of the pre-Beijing communication strategy.

2. The initiation of a *process of structural reform* in specific institutions/areas beginning with:

    (a) the impact of gender socialisation on practices in education, reproductive and sexual health and rights and violence;

    (b) poverty linked to unwaged and low-waged work;

    (c) political representation; and

    (d) constitutional and/or legislative discrimination against, or lack of protection of, indigenous people and people with disabilities. (pp. 38-39)

In relation to unwaged work the plan, among other things, called for the development of a framework, methodologies and instruments for measuring and valuing unwaged work in satellite accounts in member states with technical assistance from agencies such as the International Labour Organization (ILO), the UN International Research and Training Institute for the Advancement of Women (INSTRAW) and the International Women Count Network (IWCN). It was also suggested that the bill to measure and value all unwaged work that had been passed in Trinidad and Tobago in 1996 be used as a model for developing similar legislation in other states.

The Post-Beijing Regional Plan of Action was intended to serve as a guide for member states to prepare their own national action plans and in this regard, several actions were identified in relation to government and NGOs to be pursued at national levels. Specific actions to be taken by the secretariat were also suggested in respect of gender mainstreaming at that level as well as the role the secretariat would need to assume in implementation and monitoring of the plan.

Although a multidimensional implementation strategy was outlined in the Plan of Action, which called for regional collaboration, the creation of transitional and permanent regional implementation and monitoring mechanisms, reporting mechanisms and lobbying to foster political will and commitment, for the most part, the Plan of Action was not addressed in any coordinated and deliberate way by Women's Bureaux and national governments. Several constraining factors might have accounted for this including:

1. Change in the political administration of many Caribbean countries and a concomitant change of heads of Women's Bureaux;
2. An absence of institutional leadership at the CARICOM Women's Desk;
3. In response to heightened concerns about male marginalisation, renaming of some Women's Bureaux to incorporate the term 'gender' without a clear conceptual understanding of implications of the change resulting in uncertainty of terms of reference and therefore loss of focus on issues related to women's inequality;
4. General lack of political will and limited human and financial resources, particularly in national machineries, to move the process forward;

5. Changes in the global geo-political environment and diversion of international funding to other regions of the world in response to new and emerging situations;

6. The accelerated pace of globalisation and impacts on macro-economic policy and social stability of the region.

The convergence of these factors resulted in a marked decline in the synergy experienced in the Beijing preparatory process and a sharp decline in energy, motivation and attention to the issues that had been so passionately debated and defended at the FWCW. However, in August 1997, a ministerial meeting hosted by the Government of Guyana, ECLAC, CARICOM and UNIFEM was held in Georgetown, Guyana.

At that meeting, the need to maintain the spirit of collaboration between governments and NGOs, that had been a Caribbean hallmark leading up to and at the FWCW, was reaffirmed. It was also acknowledged that, in order to advance the process towards the attainment of gender equality, social justice and development as advocated in the Regional Plan of Action, there was need to accelerate actions to promote an active and visible gender mainstreaming perspective in policies and programmes in all political, economic and social spheres through the implementation of: gender analysis and planning, the introduction of gender management systems and gender impact assessments. Specific actions related to poverty, power-sharing and decision-making, education, violence, health, the environment and human rights were also included in the Georgetown Consensus.[9]

The Beijing +5 Process: Markers along the way

Third Caribbean Ministerial Conference on Women

The UN announcement of its intention to host a Beijing+5 mid-decade meeting served as an impetus for renewed effort and revitalisation of the Caribbean women's movement since member states were being called on to review and appraise progress towards the goals of gender equality, development and peace as set out in the Beijing Platform for Action. In the Caribbean sub-region, the first marker in the review process was the Third Caribbean Ministerial Conference on Women held in Port of

Spain, Trinidad and Tobago in November 1999, hosted by the UNECLAC Sub-regional Headquarters for the Caribbean and the Secretariat of the Caribbean Development and Cooperation Committee (CDCC).

The major objectives of that meeting were to:

1. Receive a report on the review and appraisal of the implementation of the Beijing Platform for Action in the Caribbean; and

2. Receive selected country reports on progress towards gender equity related to three of the thematic areas identified as critical to Caribbean women: poverty and the economy; women in power and decision-making and institutional mechanisms for the advancement of women; and, human rights, peace and violence.

Based on information contained in 15 country reports, a paper on 'The Caribbean Subregional Review and Appraisal on the Implementation of the Beijing Platform for Action'[10] was prepared by ECLAC-CDCC and presented at this meeting. In response to the presentation it was noted that:

> *despite the progress made, ... women in the Caribbean continued to bear the brunt of responsibility for social reproduction, and for the caring of all categories of vulnerable persons ... Even whilst they had fewer opportunities for employment and had higher levels of underemployment and unemployment than their male counterparts.* (p. 5)[11]

In relation to information presented on the situation of violence against women and women's participation in the political process, it was agreed that, since Beijing, the situation had not improved and in this regard it was noted that:

> *Although increasing State resources were directed at violence against women, the combination of patriarchal gender relations and a pervasive culture of violence had meant that women's personal integrity and security appeared more threatened in the contemporary period now than in previous periods. Whilst women's participation in the political process as voters and campaigners was significant, this participation had not translated into increased numbers of women in elected office within the parliamentary system ... women remained marginal to and excluded from the process of the identification of economic development priorities.* (p. 5)[12]

Generally, information emerging from the panel presentations on the thematic areas confirmed these troubling trends. In each case, however, key strategies for moving towards greater gender equity in the sub-region were identified by discussants as well as through the ensuing general discussions from the floor and were subsequently captured in the Port of Spain Consensus[13] coming out of that meeting.

In relation to poverty and the economy, the need to implement areas of the Regional Plan of Action that address macro-economic policies aimed at economic development was reiterated in the Consensus document and measures that were required towards this end were identified (#2). A new concern that had emerged since Beijing, however, was the need to analyse the impact of globalisation and liberalisation on women living in poverty and to 'consider and take account of negative economic effects created by globalization, loss of preferential access to markets and trade embargos in policy formulation and national agreements, since these contribute to increasing levels of poverty and unemployment and to cultures of violence' (#4).

In relation to the second thematic area, women in power and decision-making and institutional mechanisms for the advancement of women, the major concerns were to 'ensure that mechanisms are established to accelerate the achievement of gender equality in political participation and representation at all levels of the electoral process, in the composition of boards, commissions and other public appointments and in the granting of national honours and awards' (#12); and the need for greater articulation between national machineries and sectoral ministries and the impact of frequent changes in political administrations were identified as factors affecting programmes spearheaded by Women's Bureaux.

The major issue raised by the panel addressing human rights, peace and violence, related to the common concern about increased incidents of violence against women which threatened to erode gains already made in this area. The new direction that emerged was the need to go beyond interventions that were mainly responsive to focus on addressing the root causes of violence and identifying institutions and cultural practices which reproduced violence. Paragraph 20 of the Port of Spain Consensus therefore called for '*research to address the root causes of violence against women*' and among other things to '*study and address the construction of undesirable forms of masculinity and the ways in which violence against men and boys in, for example, educational and penal institutions contribute to such construction'.*

Eighth Session of the Regional Conference on Women in LAC

Following close on the heels of the Port of Spain Caribbean sub-regional meeting was the Eighth Session of the Regional Conference on Women in Latin America and the Caribbean in Lima, Peru in February 2000. In contrast to the sub-regional meeting, where 19 CDCC member and associate member countries had attended, Caribbean representation at the regional meeting was disappointing with only ten Caribbean countries including Cuba and the Cayman Islands present and only in the case of Suriname was there ministerial representation.

The Lima Conference was organised around two themes, the second of which had been addressed at the sub-regional Port of Spain meeting: Gender Equity in Latin America and the Caribbean and Human Rights, Peace and Violence. In keeping with the pattern established during the Beijing preparatory process, two consultants were appointed by CARICOM to provide necessary advice with regard to focus and strategy on the Caribbean's participation in the conference as well as provide, as needed, assistance to delegations in terms of making appropriate interventions and formulating language in the negotiating process. At a pre-conference CARICOM caucus, it was suggested that positions taken in the debates should be informed by the outcomes of the sub-regional meeting as set out in the articles of the Port of Spain Consensus.

Several problems surfaced in relation to the Caribbean's participation in the Lima conference which stemmed primarily from conference logistics, the limited size of Caribbean delegations, the low level of participation on the part of some individuals, the absence of official translation facilities and constraints related to language barriers during negotiations to arrive at the Lima Consensus.

During the conference, two working groups were convened concurrently but, because of the limited size of Caribbean delegations, there was never adequate representation in either group. Most of the time in plenary sessions was devoted to receiving country reports, with little opportunity for discussion or intervention from the floor so, where required, the consultants gave assistance to helping delegations shape country reports in relation to the focus of the conference as reflected in the two sub-themes.

In this regard, the major concern was the uncritical nature of country reports which showed little evidence that activities at the national level had been guided by actions related to critical issues facing Caribbean women identified in the Beijing Platform for Action and more importantly The CARICOM Post-Beijing Regional Plan of action to the Year 2000. For the most part, the reports tended to be descriptive with little analysis of the context and framing factors, including the effects of globalisation and trade liberalisation, which either facilitated or constrained progress towards goals included in the above referenced documents. It seemed, therefore, that these documents had had little national impact in terms of shaping agendas and informing policy positions.

There was also limited participation in the negotiating process due mainly to three factors: the paucity of Caribbean representation; the lack of continuity in representation at this meeting and the earlier Port of Spain sub-regional meeting and therefore no real appreciation on the part of delegates of the critical issues and positions reflected in the Port of Spain Consensus; and, the fact that most Caribbean delegates had little experience in formulating language or in the art of negotiating to arrive at consensus while not compromising Caribbean priorities and positions.

The onus was therefore left to the consultants to manage and carry this process forward and negotiate an agreed position on behalf of Caribbean governments. In a later review of the Caribbean's participation in this meeting, the view was expressed by a government representative that the role carried out by the consultants in Lima had created some tensions, given that they were not accredited members of national delegations. It was equally acknowledged, however, that there had been little choice but to pursue this strategy, given the lack of negotiating skills among the majority of country representatives (Follow-up Meeting Beijing+5).[14]

In spite of these constraints, having the Port of Spain Consensus gave the Caribbean a competitive advantage, and, in many respects, the

Caribbean was therefore in a position to take the lead in the negotiating process. Text prepared by the regional ECLAC Secretariat was used as the starting point for negotiations, but the process was slowed down and critical time lost because, in contrast to the Caribbean, the Latin American grouping had not had a sub-regional meeting and, therefore, had no agreed position. Time was requested by those delegations to respond to the proposed draft text and as soon as a Latin American position was arrived at and negotiations were underway, CARICOM delegations had frequent meetings to agree on positions on which there should be little or no flexibility.

In the final analysis, the negotiations were severely hampered by the absence of translation facilities and the fact that negotiations occurred simultaneously with meetings of the two working groups and in open corridors outside of assigned rooms. Negotiations for the Latin American group were led by a senior staff member of the Peruvian Mission in New York whereas in the case of the Caribbean no Mission staff participated in the meeting.

In her report to CARICOM, Andaiye sums up the situation:

> While we had the Port-of-Spain Consensus as a political guide, the absence of Ministers was a serious problem: *vis-à-vis* large Latin delegations, some led by senior political figures, it weakened CARICOM both subjectively and objectively. Not only did our relative weakness frankly embolden those Latin delegations which made little effort to deal with the language difference, but our delegates lacked the ability to respond to situations as they emerged; technical officers usually do not have the authority and few have the confidence to do this. (p. 2)[15]

It was therefore gratifying that, in spite of these constraints, many of the positions put forward in the Port of Spain Consensus were acknowledged, accepted and incorporated in the Lima Consensus with little or no modification.[16]

Given the emphases of the CARICOM Regional Plan of Action and the Port of Spain Consensus, of particular importance to Caribbean delegations was the recognition in the preamble of the Lima Consensus of the changing global political environment and, in determining strategies to move the region towards greater gender equality and social justice, the need to be cognisant of the fact that 'economic globalisation, trade liberalisation, structural adjustment, external debt and the resulting migration patterns are factors which, among others, can have specific and sometimes negative impacts on the lives and situation of women, particularly those of the least economically developed regions, and can cause the dislocation of families, communities and nations'.

Common threads running through the Port of Spain and Lima Consensus documents and specific actions in the latter which underscored positions taken in the former included reaffirming the urgency to:

- Reorient public policies, placing social and gender equity at the centre of governmental concerns and achieve this systematically basing these policies on assessments of their differential impact on males and females and monitoring their implementation (# d);
- Strengthen democracy in the region through the adoption of policies and measures that facilitate women's rights to full and equal citizenship and their participation in decision-making in all sectors and at all levels, bearing in mind that democracy is based on the will of people, freely expressed to determine their own economic, political and social structures and arrangements (# j);
- Guarantee the protection of women's human rights and address violations of these rights with particular attention to all forms of gender-based violence and their root causes, including the reproduction of a culture of violence (# n);
- Promote a recognition of the social and economic contribution made by the unpaid work performed by women, predominately in the home, and urge Governments to provide them with social security coverage (# v);

Against the backdrop of a growing concern about the role of the school in gender socialisation and the increasing decline in male participation at the higher levels of Caribbean education systems which had been a major focus at the 1997 Georgetown meeting, several articles of the Port of Spain Consensus focused on gender issues in education and, among other things, highlighted the need for 'developing non-discriminatory education and training' and programmes for teacher education in an effort to 'eliminate differential expectations of the sexes that reinforce the sexual division of labour' (# 17). These were not central concerns at Lima and were therefore not reflected in the Lima Consensus. All countries represented at that conference, however, agreed that the Lima Consensus would constitute the region's contribution to the special session of the UN June 2000 General Assembly on Women to be convened as the Beijing +5 review and appraisal of the Beijing Platform for Action.

Beijing+5: A re-engineering of the issues

Prior to the 23rd Special Session of the UN General Assembly (UNGASS) entitled 'Women 2000: Gender Equality, Development and Peace for the 21st Century' held in New York, June 5 to 9, 2000, more commonly referred to as the Beijing+5 meeting, several Preparatory Committee meetings were held starting on March 13 through to June 4. In this case, CARICOM contracted only one consultant to attend the Preparatory Committee Meetings and the UNGASS who, along with the Women's Desk staff person, at various points over the time period, assisted Caribbean delegations through the negotiating process.

Over the five-year period between the FWCW and Beijing+5, the global context had changed in many ways resulting in new issues which had differential impacts on different social groups particularly in a number of developing and small island states that make up the Caribbean archipelago. Several of these challenges and their impacts on women are summed up in a Report of the Secretary General prepared for the March Preparatory Committee for the June UNGASS meeting.[17] Factors highlighted included, among others: shifts in government policy in many countries in favour of trade and financial liberalisation as well as privatisation of state-owned enterprises and lower public spending; impacts of globalisation on cultural values and lifestyles with shifts to a culture oriented towards material consumption; widening economic and social inequalities between and within countries with increased risks for many social groups; the burden of the increasing poverty disproportionately borne by women; changed patterns of migratory flows of labour involving trafficking of women and girls and illegal migration; increasing rates of female employment but in low paid, part-time jobs with little protection and security;

changing demographic trends in populations with increased numbers among both the elderly and adolescent age groups; rapid progression of the HIV/AIDS pandemic particularly in the developing world; and, increased intra-state armed conflicts creating the climate for increased trafficking of narcotic drugs and organised crime.

Essentially, however, the six issues identified as critical for Caribbean women going into the 1995 FWCW persisted up to the mid-decade review in 2000, although, in many ways, due to the changing socio-economic and political global context, the issues had been reengineered and reconfigured in terms of definition and response as reflected in stronger language and more far-reaching proposals for action. In addition, some new issues had emerged and were put on the table for debate and consensus.

By this time, the Caribbean, although not abandoning concerns about women's unremunerated work, now had a broader concern about the findings of Country Poverty Assessments and other studies which showed, among other things that, in countries for which data were available, women were at the lower end of the gender poverty gap and in many instances, female-headed households were more likely to fall below the poverty line (Andaiye 2003).[18]

In the Beijing+5 debates, language related to issues of poverty and poverty reduction was coalesced around issues of globalisation and trade liberalisation and their impacts on women's employment in relation to new, flexible and emerging forms of work and the need for adequate access to social protection systems for workers in such situations. The importance of facilitating the establishment of micro-enterprises as well as small and medium enterprises for women was also iterated (# 74b, 75).[19] Concerns about the feminisation of poverty and the recognition of gender dimensions of poverty were therefore linked to the negative social and economic impacts of globalisation and poverty eradication was seen as being dependent on 'comprehensive gender-sensitive poverty eradication strategies addressing social, structural and macro-economic issues' (#101e).

Debates around poverty extended to the economic impact of armed conflicts on women which was seen as, among other things, directing the possible allocation of funds away from social and economic development, particularly for the advancement of women, to military expenditure, arms production and acquisition. In this regard the call was for international and national actors to 'Strengthen efforts towards general and complete disarmament...so that released resources could be used for, *inter alia*, social and economic programmes which benefit women and girls' (# 99k). It is instructive to note that, although this paragraph was adopted, the United States reserved on this decision.

At Beijing+5, the positioning of issues of violence against women within the broader ambit of women's human rights reflected in the Beijing Platform for Action was reinforced. This position, that violence against women constitutes a violation of fundamental human rights requiring state action, is widely accepted by Caribbean states as reflected by the fact that, by May 1996, six countries had signed and ratified, and by November 1999, a further seven had ratified the Inter-American Convention on the Prevention, Punishment and Eradication of Violence adopted by the General Assembly of the Organization of American States (OAS) in June 1994 (Pargass & Clarke 2003).[20]

In the Beijing+5 Outcome Document, language related to actions required in respect of violence against women was stronger in terms of calling for the creation of an environment that does not tolerate any violation of the rights of women and girls and issues not mentioned in the Platform for Action including marital rape as a criminal matter, are introduced. Paragraph 69 (c) therefore calls on governments to 'treat all forms of violence against women and girls of all ages as a criminal offence' and this is followed by a call to 'establish legislation and/or strengthen appropriate mechanisms to handle criminal matters relating to all forms of domestic violence ... and ensure that such cases are brought to justice swiftly' (# 69d).

The need to 'continue to undertake research to develop a better understanding of the root causes of all forms of violence against women in order to design programmes and take measures towards eliminating these forms of violence' (# 69h) is an excellent example of the way the Caribbean was able to influence debates and consensus at the international level. This proposal, for a more radical approach to understanding and responding to issues of violence against women by addressing root causes came directly out of the Port of Spain Consensus was fed into the Lima Consensus and was incorporated into the UNGASS outcome document.

Of note is the fact that language related to identifying root causes of problems is also echoed in actions related to: 'trafficking of women and girls for prostitution and other forms of commercialised sex' (# 70a); 'increase in the drop-out rates of girls and boys at the primary and secondary education levels' and the need to 'design appropriate national programmes to eliminate the root causes and support lifelong learning' (# 95g); and, addressing 'the root causes of armed conflict' (# 99d).

The provisions related to women and health are more focused and incorporate additional issues which had gained importance over the five-year period. Health issues go beyond those addressed in the Beijing Platform of Action to include concerns related to the HIV/AIDS pandemic, sexually transmitted diseases, malaria and tuberculosis and women's mental health and the aging process. In the Caribbean, the HIV/AIDS epidemic is described as dynamic and increasing in the female population particularly among the 15-24-year-old age group (DeBique, 2003).[21] The call was therefore for governments to 'adopt, enact, review and revise ... and implement health legislation, policies and programmes ...and allocate the necessary budgetary resources to ensure the highest attainable standard of physical and mental health ... throughout their life cycle' (# 72g).

At the Beijing+5 meeting, reproductive health which remained an acutely critical issue of gender equality in the region in the period since 1995 (DeBique 2003)[22] was also addressed and a clear and comprehensive definition, in keeping with that agreed upon at the 1994 International Conference on Population and Development (IPCD) is provided in paragraph 72 (j). In the outcome document, reproductive rights are squarely located within the larger ambit of women's and girls' human rights and the need to promote 'equal relationships between women and men in matters of sexual relations and reproduction' (#72k). In this regard the need to 'design and implement programmes to encourage and enable men to adopt safe and responsible sexual and reproductive behaviour, and to use effectively methods to prevent unwanted pregnancies and sexually transmitted infections including HIV/AIDS' is highlighted in paragraph 72 (l).

A major concern for the Caribbean is with the treatment of issues related to education. The provisions and actions identified in the outcome document do not take into account the unique Caribbean reality and the anomalous situation between educational outputs and social outcomes for both sexes. In the Caribbean, as in many other parts of the world, women have increasingly been seizing opportunities for higher education. Bailey (2003),[23] however, points to the fact that increased participation and performance have not translated into economic, political or personal empowerment for the majority. Further, the high proportion of women at the tertiary level has been used to fuel a thesis of male marginalisation and to divert attention from the fact that women are still excluded from decision-making and that gender relations are, in fact, deteriorating as reflected in the high levels of gender violence women experience.

For this reason, it was very disturbing that 'the rise in the numbers of females in tertiary education in many parts of the world' and outcomes related to this phenomenon were not regarded as requiring investigation and this clause was therefore dropped from paragraph 95 (g). Another case in point is paragraph 101 (d) which addresses poverty eradication programmes and the need to 'evaluate … the extent to which access to quality education and training have an impact on the empowerment of women'. In this case, there was difficulty arriving at consensus on the reference to 'quality education and training', and for a long time, the word 'quality' was bracketed. In the long run, however, the brackets were removed and two paragraphs were merged to produce paragraph 101(d).

As a result of the persistence of the above problems, in The Beijing+5 outcome document there is a more explicit concern about gender mainstreaming as a means of achieving gender equality and both are linked to issues of women's empowerment. A framework for instituting gender mainstreaming is clearly laid down and spelt out for governments in a number of paragraphs.

Paragraph 73 (b) points to the fact that the mainstreaming process needs to start at the level of 'macro-economic and social development policies and national development programmes' (#72a) and therefore from the point of resource allocations and there is therefore the need to 'Incorporate a gender perspective into the design, development, adoption and execution of all budgetary processes, as appropriate, in order to promote equitable, effective and appropriate resource allocation and establish adequate budgetary allocations to support gender equality and development programmes which enhance women's empowerment'. In the same paragraph, the need to 'develop the necessary analytical and methodological tools and mechanisms for monitoring and evaluation' of this process is highlighted.

The onus for carrying the gender mainstreaming process forward is placed on national machineries, as reflected in paragraph 76 (b) and (c) where governments are encouraged to strengthen 'national machineries to mainstream the gender perspective to accelerate the empowerment of women in all areas and to ensure commitment to gender equality practices' as well as 'Provide national machineries with the necessary human and financial resources, ... so that gender mainstreaming is integrated in all policies, programmes and projects.

Constraining factors in the Beijing+5 process

The low level of governmental participation in the various stages of the process and a general lack of an appreciation of the points in the process where interventions are most critical are cause for concern. The large attendance of Caribbean delegates at the June UNGASS meeting was commendable but was not the best use of scarce financial resources. At that stage, many members of delegations were entering the process for the first time having not been part of the Port of Spain or Lima meetings and were therefore not in a position to make a worthwhile contribution to the debates which had been ongoing for years and weeks prior to the special session. Added to this, representation at the preparatory committee meetings was totally inadequate and there were too few persons present to service the three major working groups as well as the informal contact groups set up around selected issues such as health, trafficking and globalisation.

There was therefore little evidence of an understanding of the interconnectedness of preceding and succeeding stages of the process as marked by the various meetings leading up to Beijing+5 (see figure 1). Too many players simply stepped on and off of the stage at various points, and worst of all, at many points there were no players.

Figure 1: Flow Diagram of Beijing and Beijing+5 Process Regional Meeting

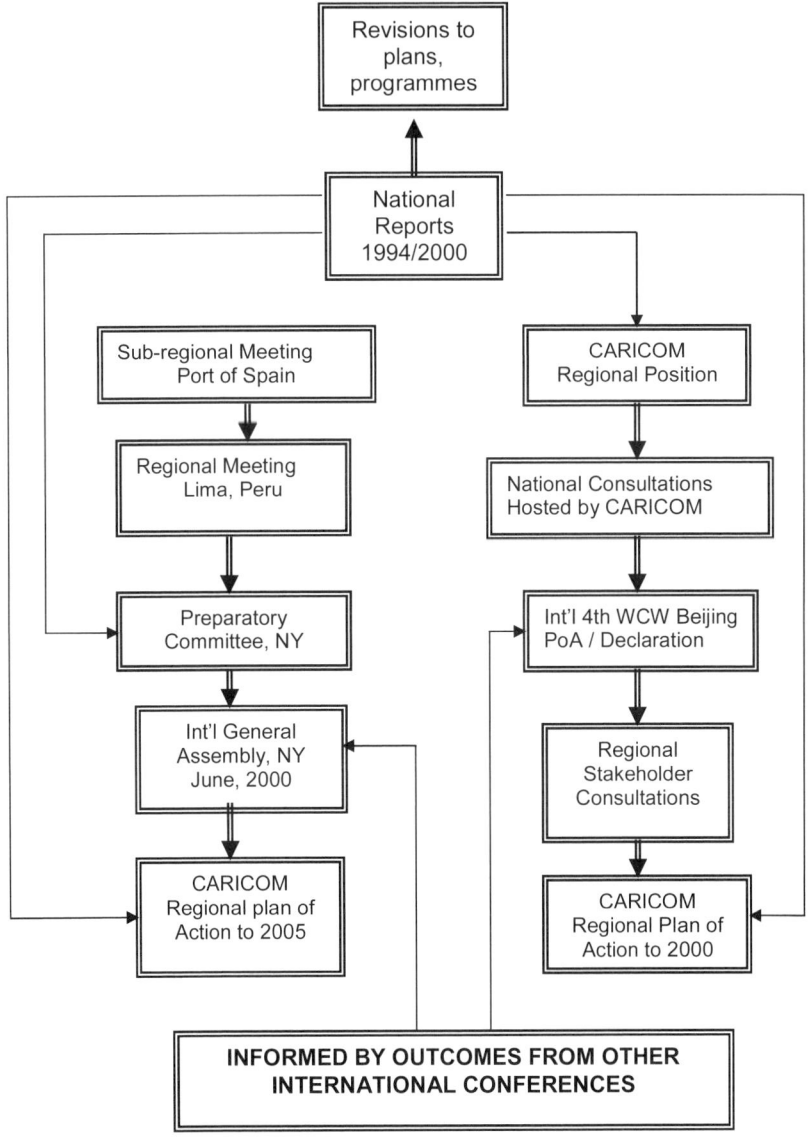

THE CARIBBEAN EXPERIENCE IN THE INTERNATIONAL WOMEN'S MOVEMENT | 645

This resulted in:

- a lack of continuity in representation from one stage of the process to the next;
- a lack of an in-depth understanding of the evolution of the issues and positions reflected in various outcome documents and the ways in which these should inform programmes, projects and policy at the national level; and,
- a low level of awareness of the constantly changing dynamics and contexts at all levels – international, regional, national – and the need therefore to be constantly reassessing the issues.

Gender relations and the problems related to these relationships are not fixed but in a constant state of flux and there is therefore the need for ongoing reassessment and strategising. An absence of these understandings poses serious challenges to any real progress towards greater gender equality in the region.

A second obstacle encountered was a lack of awareness of outcomes and language emanating from other international forums that deal with concerns that impinge on debates around gender and development issues. Of note in this regard, was language coming out of the Social Summit and the Population and Development conferences. Ongoing negotiations by the International Labour Organization (ILO) around issues of work and social protection of workers were also brought to the table in the Special Session. In many instances when consensus could not be reached, agreed language from other outcome documents was often proposed as the solution to the problem.

This raises the question of the role of Mission staff *vis-à-vis* representatives from capitals. It is obvious that, while the former have a critical role to play in the process, especially when meetings are held at headquarters, they are constrained by competing demands. The reliance on the Missions to represent governments at preparatory sessions and the extent to which this is feasible therefore needs to be reconsidered. On the other hand, these are the individuals who are most *au fait* with negotiations going on in other forums and who would, therefore, be most familiar with issues and language related to such negotiations. The flip side, however, is the need for Mission Staff to be familiar with capital perspectives and initiatives. There needs to be a greater interface between capitals and missions particularly with respect to preparations for meetings such as Beijing+5 and, in this regard, UNIFEM played a pivotal role in bringing together Mission Staff for a one-day briefing in New York prior to the start of the March Preparatory Committee meetings.

As a result of the issues outlined above, the negotiations were fraught with problems. Firstly, there were not enough persons to cover all the working groups and at one stage there were only three Caribbean representatives from capitals and one or two Mission Staff who gave fairly consistent but inadequate time to the process. A second problem was the failure of the G77 grouping to submit a position on outstanding paragraphs by the stated deadline and the breakdown of the grouping in the final days of the preparatory meetings leaving member countries free to speak as individual countries or sub-regional groups. As a result, several smaller groupings emerged and put forward independent positions during the plenary debates. The Caribbean was unprepared for this and in many instances worked through a Latin American grouping (SLAC – Some Latin American Countries). This general approach contributed to a slowing down of the negotiations since many more voices had to be accommodated in plenary sessions and, of course, there were shifting alliances to deal with, depending on the issue at hand.

In relation to gender mainstreaming, there are challenges and obstacles to overcome in implementing a gender mainstreaming strategy (GMS) in CARICOM member states. The major challenge is that of creating a critical mass of persons equipped with the knowledge base and skills and the commitment to engage in the task. This again is a process which must start with education around the critical issues, and training in using gender as an analytical tool at all stages of the programming or project cycle.

A further obstacle in implementing a GMS is having access to an adequate and accessible database to facilitate a gender analysis to inform programme and policy formulation. This, however, has been addressed in the outcome document and paragraph 113a calls for governments to

'Provide national statistical offices with institutional and financial support in order to collect, compile and disseminate data disaggregated by sex, age and other factors that are accessible to the public and to policy-makers for, *inter alia*, gender-based analysis, monitoring and impact assessment, and support new work to develop statistics and indicators, especially in areas where information is particularly lacking' (# 77a).

In addition to these specific concerns, more general factors constrained the region's engagement in the women's movement in the period leading up to the 2000 Beijing+5 New York meeting. Chief among these was the impact of the accelerated pace of globalisation and the institution of more neo-liberal trade and financial policies and practices on national economies. Fiscal constraints resulted in public sector reforms and reduced spending in a numbers of areas. Not surprisingly, there has therefore been reduced attention to women's issues and the exacerbation of the usual problems of locating and resourcing national machineries mandated to address the status of women. The net result is a sense of tokenism rather than any purposeful political will to give necessary and sustained attention to the situation of women whose success in the educational arena is often used to justify this position.

But this seeming lack of political will on the part of patriarchal gatekeepers in relation to the women's agenda has to be juxtaposed against the shift of focus, in many Caribbean countries, to issues of men and their masculinities which is not only a backlash to a perceived threat of loss of power but also appears to be a more politically correct stance given the not very well understood conceptual shift in the discourse from 'women' and 'women's equality' to 'gender' and 'gender equality'. This diversion of attention to the highly visible sex-linked pathologies of crime and violence is also driven by a sense of fear and helplessness on the part of the power brokers.

Another contributory factor in many Caribbean countries, which is not unrelated to the macro-economic situation and reduced political will, is the diversion of international funding that was available in the period leading up to the 4th WCW, to support what is now determined to be more critical and urgent needs of women in countries engaged in internal and sometimes external armed conflicts as in Afghanistan and other Islamic states where these conflicts are underpinned by political transitions, economic dislocation and weak civil society often resulting in almost virtual anarchy. Haiti seems to be the most recent of these casualties.

Massiah (2003)[24] aptly sums up the situation by posing a number of questions:

> how did a region, which was in the vanguard of commitment and action in the seventies, eighties and early nineties find itself at the turn of the century, unable to articulate a comprehensive programme of action towards the achievement of gender justice? Does it mean that women and their gender concerns are only of value at a particular historical juncture? Is it that international pressure for gender justice has declined? Does it mean that states do not have the financial resources at this time to implement the infrastructural and other requirements needed for an effective and efficient gender programme? Does it mean that gender justice is considered irrelevant to social, economic and political development? (p. 14)

Opportunities for Advancing Gender Equality

Even as we grapple with these questions several opportunities present themselves for improving on the Caribbean's engagement at the national, sub-regional, regional and international levels of the women's movement and for advancing gender equality in the region. In relation to representation at various levels of the process several issues need to be addressed. Paramount among these is the need for there to be a better understanding of the interface between meetings held at the various levels and the points at which interventions are critical if they are to influence outcomes at a subsequent stage.

This requires an appreciation of the importance of approaching the goal of gender equality as a cyclical process and the need therefore to understand the inter-connectedness of the different stages of the process and the critical importance of building in feedback mechanisms to ensure the forward and backward flow of information between and among all stages and levels of the process. The ultimate goal: to use information generated at each stage to inform action related to programmes and policy which address identified inequalities at national and/or regional levels.

Figure 2: Interface between and among stages of process

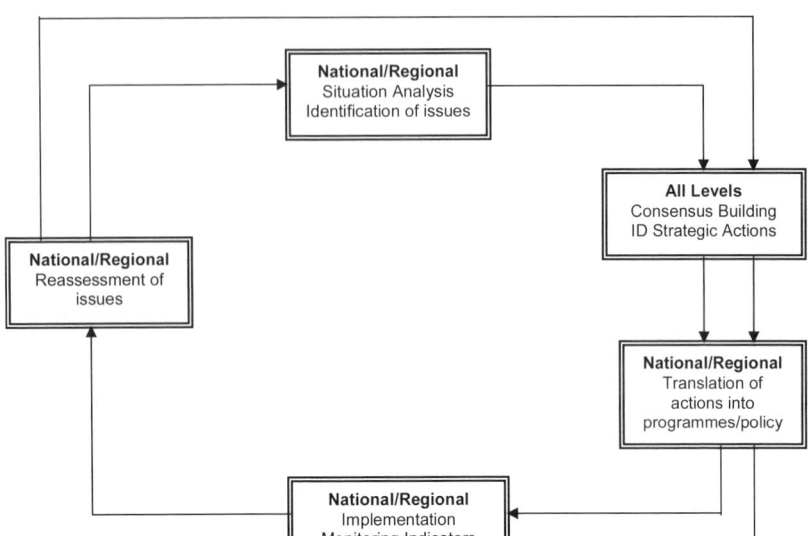

If a meaningful interface is to be created between and among all stages of the process two factors are essential. Closer attention needs to be given to the criteria used for selection of delegates to attend meetings and to participate in the process. Individuals need to be selected based on a grounded understanding of identified critical issues and should be deployed to particular working or contact groups according to expertise and understanding of the matter at hand. Related to this is the need to give more attention to succession planning to ensure continuity of representation and that newcomers to the process develop the knowledge and skills required for sustained participation.

This can only be achieved, however, if such persons are provided with opportunities for developing these understandings and the skills required for meaningful participation in the process. A regional training programme therefore needs to be developed which addresses:

(i) issues critical to Caribbean women and these need to be located in relation to wider global and regional socioeconomic and political realities;

(ii) how these issues relate to various international conventions and instruments as well as to outcomes from related forums such as the

World Conference on Human Rights (WCHR), the International Conference on Population and Development (ICPD), World Summit on Social Development. Documents relevant to these meetings should be analysed ahead of time to identify points at which Caribbean interventions would be essential to take forward outcomes from national, sub-regional and regional positions;

(iii) negotiating skills as well as the Caribbean's positioning and role in the Latin America and G77 blocks.

In the past, the Caribbean's involvement in the international women's movement has been enhanced by involving resource persons in an advisory capacity at national, regional and international levels. These persons have been chosen based on expertise in one or more of the critical issues and have been deployed accordingly. Participation of these persons has, in the past, been sustained from one level to the next ensuring an element of continuity and the presence of a Caribbean voice at all stages of the debate which has, in some measure, compensated for the more sporadic participation of national delegations. The use of this arrangement in the future is therefore endorsed but with such persons being accredited to appropriate national delegations to give authority and credence to these voices. Further, when meetings are convened at the UN Headquarters, the interface among mission staff, resource persons, members of national delegations and technical personnel from national machineries needs to be improved, possibly by involving mission staff in sub-regional meetings leading up to the New York based international meeting.

Finally, the recommendation that gender mainstreaming be used as a strategy for achieving gender equality has not only been endorsed but is also being used, with varying degrees of success, in some Caribbean countries. This strategy for achieving greater gender equality and social justice has been reiterated by CARICOM and is also the core element of the Plan of Action to 2005[25] which aims to promote an integrated, intersectoral approach to human and social development. Three areas have been selected for attention: education, with a focus on building human capital; health, with an emphasis on HIV/AIDS: and, labour in the social dialogue. In proposing the strategy, the Gender Mainstreaming Task Force, endorsed the need to locate the strategy within a rights-based social justice framework 'premised on the understanding that all groups and individuals have equal rights to the conditions that will allow them to realize their full human potential to contribute to development in its broadest sense and to benefit from its results.' (W/BUR (DC) 2002/212, Item 6, p. 12)[26]

The hope is that gender-mainstreaming will facilitate a more strategic approach to pursuing gender equality at both the national and regional levels and the shaping of policies and programmes that are responsive to the unique and different needs of men and women. The ultimate goal is:

> the building of new structures of power-sharing at the household, community, national, regional...levels, where both men and women can participate fully in developing a system of cooperation in decision-making, as equal partners in the sustainable development of their societies. (p. 38)[27]

The elaboration of a gender mainstreaming strategy, however, has to be evidence-based and is dependent on access to adequate datasets, which incorporate a range of gender sensitive quantitative and qualitative indicators. It is therefore suggested that indicators need to be identified in relation to each of the areas identified as critical to Caribbean women. This project has already begun with the publication of a set of papers which analyses the post-Beijing situation of Caribbean women in relation to the six critical issues and chronicles progress and gaps for further action.

The publication is intended to inform policy formulation and the design of programmes and projects aimed at promoting the goal of gender equality but as Massiah (2003)[28] notes in the preface to the book *Gender Equality*:

> To an increasing extent, states are seeking people with specialized knowledge and expertise to assist them in formulating policies and strategies to confront the challenges they face. Yet gender specialists and the material they produce have remained largely on the periphery of political thought and praxis in the region...it is our hope that those who guide the progress of our nations will...take the next step from paper commitment to the exercise of genuine political will. (p.xvii)

Without this political will and an informed strategic agenda which strikes at the very core of unequal relations of power between and among the genders and at reform of hierarchical structures and systems, the goal of gender equality will continue to be elusive and to be illusion rather than reality.

Notes

1. J. Massiah, Address at the Opening Ceremony of The Summer Institute in Gender and Development, Centre for Gender & Development Studies, University of the West Indies, Cave Hill, Barbados. July 6, 2003.
2. Joycelin Massiah, Preface, in *Gender Equality in the Caribbean: Reality or Illusion*, eds. G. Tang-Nain and B. Bailey (Kingston: Ian Randle Publishers, 2003).
3. A. Mondesire and L. Dunn, *Towards Equity in Development: A Report on the Status of Women in Sixteen Caribbean Countries*. (Georgetown: CARICOM Secretariat, 1995).
4. J. Massiah, Address at Opening Ceremony.
5. L. Dunn and M.J. Sebro, *Challenge and Change in the Caribbean: 1992-2001 Review of the UNIFEM Caribbean Office* Bridgetown, Barbados, 2002.
6. *Gender Equality Social Justice and Development: The CARICOM Post-Beijing Regional Plan of Action to the Year 2000* (Georgetown: CARICOM Secretariat, 1997).
7. Fourth World Conference on Women Beijing China. *Op. cit.*
8. *Gender Equality Social Justice and Development: The CARICOM Post-Beijing Regional Plan of Action to the Year 2000*. (Georgetown: CARICOM Secretariat, 1997).
9. Georgetown Consensus.
10. *The Caribbean Subregional Review and Appraisal Report on the Implementation of the Beijing Platform for Action*. ECLAC-CDCC, Third Caribbean Ministerial Conference on Women: Review and Appraisal of the FWCW Platform for Action. Trinidad Hilton Hotel, Port of Spain, October 5-7, 1999. September 1999.
11. *Report of the ECLAC/CDCC Third Ministerial Conference on Women: Review and Appraisal of the FCWC Platform for Action*. General LC/CAR/G.584. November 15, 1999.
12. *Report of the ECLAC/CDCC Third Ministerial Conference on Women: Review and Appraisal of the FCWC Platform for Action. Op. cit.*
13. *Report of the ECLAC/CDCC Third Ministerial Conference on Women: Review and Appraisal of the FCWC Platform for Action. Op. cit.*
14. Caribbean Community. Report of the Follow-Up Meeting Beijing +5. Kingston, Jamaica, December 5-8, 2000.
15. Report arising out of technical assistance provided to the CARICOM delegation attending the 8th Regional Conference on Women of Latin America and the Caribbean. February 8-10, 2000. Lima Peru. Prepared by Andaiye, February 21, 2000.
16. Economic Commission for Latin America and the Caribbean. Eighth Session of the Regional Conference on Women in Latin America and the Caribbean. Lima Peru, February 8-10, 2000. Plenary Conference Room Paper FL1/3, February 10, 2000.
17. Report of the Secretary-General. Commission on the Status of Women acting as the preparatory committee for the UNGASS. Third Session March 3-17, 2000. *Emerging issues containing additional material for further actions and initiatives for the preparation of*

the outlook beyond the year 2000. htpp://www.un.org/womenwatch/daw/csw/ecn6-2000pc4.htm

18. Andaiye, 'Smoke and Mirrors: The Illusion of CARICOM Women's Growing Economic Empowerment', in *Gender Equality in the Caribbean: Reality or Illusion*, eds. G. Tang-Nain, and B. Bailey (Kingston: Ian Randle Publishers, 2003).

19. UN General Assembly. Twenty-third Special Session. Agenda Item 10. Resolution adopted by the General Assembly. Further actions and initiatives to implement the Beijing Declaration and Platform for Action. A/RES 23/3. November 2000.

20. G. Pargass and R. Clarke, 'Violence against women: A human rights issue Post Beijing Five Year Review', in *Gender Equality in the Caribbean: Reality or Illusion*, eds. G. Tang-Nain and B. Bailey (Kingston: Ian Randle Publishers, 2003).

21. D.N. DeBique, 'Gender Equality and Women's Health in the Caribbean', in *Gender Equality in the Caribbean: Reality or Illusion*, eds. G. Tang-Nain and B. Bailey (Kingston: Ian Randle Publishers, 2003).

22. D.N. DeBique, *Op. cit.*

23. B. Bailey, 'The Search for Gender Equity and Empowerment of Caribbean Women: The Role of Education', in *Gender equality in the Caribbean: Reality or Illusion*, eds. G. Tang-Nain and B. Bailey (Kingston: Ian Randle Publishers, 2003).

24. J. Massiah, Preface. *Op. cit.*

25. *Plan of Action to 2005: Framework for Mainstreaming Gender Into Key CARICOM Programmes*. Prepared for the CARICOM Secretariat by Andaiye. Caribbean Community Secretariat. Georgetown, Guyana 2003.

26. Item 6 – Gender and Development: A Cross-Cutting Element in Human Resource Development. Working Document for the 2nd Meeting of Directors/Coordinators of Women's/ Gender Bureaux. St George's, Grenada. September 17-19, 2002.

27. CARICOM Secretariat, *Gender Equality Social Justice and Development: The CARICOM Post-Beijing Regional Plan of Action to the Year 2000* (Georgetown, Guyana: Red Thread Women's Press, 1997).

28. J. Massiah, Preface. *Op. cit.*

30 | MICHELLE ROWLEY

Bureaucratising Feminism
Charting Caribbean Women's Centrality within the Margins

I want to use this paper as a case study that allows us to explore the bureaucratic duplicity of Caribbean state-managers as they engage women's issues within the national machinery. The paper explores and exposes the stratagems used by policy makers and state managers to reinforce historical and cultural inequities of gender relations, *while* using their newly found fluency in the area of gender sensitivity and gender awareness. I highlight some of the inherent institutional and conceptual weaknesses that emerge when gender-mainstreaming models are attempted within state formations without a commensurate commitment to the political force of gender equity. I use the Trinidadian Gender Affairs Division as my entry point to examine the extent to which gender mainstreaming models all too easily facilitate the contradictory gesture of arguing that women are centrally located within planning and policy formulation as a *form of heteropatriarchal resistance* within the region's national machinery. While feminists have historically critiqued the ways in which women have been excluded from state resources, I argue that it is now equally as relevant, if not more so, to examine the *terms of inclusion* for its potentially discriminatory practices. These kinds of conversations are of critical importance because our regional Gender Bureaux remain the lead change agents within the national machinery and, as such, their legitimacy must be premised upon their capacity to envision and implement the terms of a twenty-first century gender-just Caribbean society and build coalitions of dialogue around this vision.

The proliferation of international gender-based documents, a plethora of gender indicators and the eagerness of states, particularly in the Third

World to ratify these documents, as an avenue toward increasing their credibility on the global playing field makes it difficult for issues of women's empowerment, rights and gender equality to be sidelined from the discursive landscapes of national policy discussions. Yet, how do we account for the fact that 29 years after the First World Conference on Women in 1975, Caribbean women, in reality, appear to be under the same, and in many instances even greater, threat within the planning machinery of these territories?

To this end, I analyse interview data with state functionaries throughout the Trinidadian Gender Affairs Division, the lead gender focal point within national machinery. I conducted these interviews to capture a sense of the institutional memory of the members of staff who were employed in the ministry during critical periods within the Division's development. I examine the disjuncture between the designated goals of gender mainstreaming against the enactment of these goals through Trinidad and Tobago's state manipulation of gender-sensitive rhetoric. Finally, I argue that, as the lead change agent within the national machinery, it is imperative that Gender Bureaux throughout the region strategise, and collaboratively politicise their mandate toward securing a twenty-first century gender-just Caribbean society.

Developing Gender-based Indicators of Modernity

One of the major accomplishments of the United Nations Human Development Report (HDR) has been the introduction of gender-based indicators. The HDR ranks countries within the global community based on their performance in three primary areas: life expectancy, educational attainment, and real GDP per capita. Beyond highlighting a country's performance in these key areas, the HDR's ranking is now an important part of ascribing and assessing the legitimacy of state performance in the 'modern world'. The nationalised desire for 'development' and 'developed country status' that now pervades the electoral and policy rhetoric of the anglophone Caribbean,[1] is due in no small part to the disciplinary links that have been forged between the indicators of 'development' and 'modernity'.

Instituted in 1995, the Gender Empowerment Matrix (GEM) indicates the extent to which women are able to participate in the economic and political life of their country and the Gender Development Index (GDI) assesses the gender differentials of the Human Development Index. Despite the fact that these indicators have been established to elucidate the extent of women's access and control of their country's resources, it is undeniable that they also reinstitute a degree of erasure of women's multiple and cultural realities and their localised experiences. The GDI, for example, by maintaining the Gross Domestic Product (GDP) as its measure of economic activity, masks the level of mobility that many Caribbean women have been able to achieve as a result of aggressive income generating activity as 'higglers', or micro-entrepreneurs within their informal economies.[2] Similarly, it also masks the difficulties experienced by these very women in the informal economy as they approach formalised institutions such as banks and state based micro-enterprise lending agencies.

Further, country ranking based on the HDI's composite indices (for example, longevity, GDP and educational attainment) reflects the capacity of already financially endowed states to perform well in the provision of resources to their citizens. However, the usefulness of these gender-based indicators is evident when we account for the gender differentials of development. When HDI rankings are adjusted for their responsiveness to the gender differentials of access (GDI) instructive disparities emerge between a country's economic buoyancy and women's ability to benefit from this buoyancy. An overview of the GDI adjusted ranking of countries in 1997 reflects the economic disparity and inequity women experience globally in controlling the most basic benefits that can be derived from their country's 'development'.

Of the 64 countries that were ranked in the 'High' cohort, 25 (39 per cent) dropped when adjusted for the GDI, whereas all of the 44 countries that were ranked in the low cohort of the HDI, improved in their GDI. Table 1 highlights elements of this disparity and further suggests that addressing gender inequity is not purely a function of economic prowess but an explicit commitment to addressing the terms of inequity. However, because the GDI is already based on the economic stability of a country and its capacity to provide socioeconomic opportunities, it remains true that in poorer territories where country rankings may have improved thereby suggesting that women have been able to lay claim to the terms of development, women's absolute level of access is precarious and threatened by the overall predicament of scarcity. An improved ranking therefore cannot categorically suggest acceptable standards of well-being and livelihood for women.

Table 1: Comparative HDI, GDI, and GEM Ranking for Selected Countries

Country	1995			1997			2000		
	HDI	GDI	GEM	HDI	GDI	GEM	HDI	GDI	GEM
Barbados	24	16	18	25	17	14	31	-	18
Grenada	51	-	-	54	-	-	83	-	-
Jamaica	84	65	-	83	63	-	86	67	-
Trinidad and Tobago	40	38	17	40	32	17	50	45	21
Netherlands	7	12	9	6	11	10	8	8	6
Switzerland	16	18	13	16	20	12	11	14	13
Sweden	10	3	1	10	3	2	2	5	3
USA	4	6	11	4	5	7	6	4	11

The need to read the qualitative and contextual nuances of these indicators also applies to the Gender Empowerment Measure (GEM). While the GEM indicators highlight the importance of women's access to formalised political activity, it simultaneously reinforces a mainstream private/public dichotomy of what kinds of activity constitute legitimate political activity. The intersectionality of women's lives consistently defies this binary, as such much of the important work done by community activists remains erased, invisible and at best undervalued. Women's access to the formal reins of decision-making remains an imperative toward the achievement of long-term gender equity; an indicator on which all countries in the anglophone Caribbean score abysmally (Vassell 2003). The GEM's inability to challenge the definition of 'political activity' is consequently unable to account for the work that women do within the less formalised arenas of political activities.

Caribbean political parties have also historically exploited the canvassing done by their female supporters. This activity arguably improves Caribbean women's status in their community as community managers and their roles as mediators between their communities and prospective government agents and state functionaries. However, while Caribbean women remain the primary actors in this regard, they have yet to become the benefactors of increased levels of access to formalised corridors of power (Figueroa 2003). The GEM's embrace of the private/public dichotomy of political activity is unable to elucidate the disparity that arises between these spheres. Further, by importing the private/public dichotomy of political activity, the GEM also devalues community political activism as a distinct political product within women's domain of activity and therefore constrains our ability to investigate the exigencies that must be addressed to encourage women's access to the formal reins of power.

Despite the weakness of these indices, they have initiated a new and critical lexicon on the terms of 'development'. The global discourse on women's rights within the world's nation-states is now informed and governed by, among others, four International Women's Conferences, the Convention Against the Elimination and Discrimination Against Women,[3] now ratified by approximately 170 of the world's countries, and the Beijing Platform of Action which outlines a number of activities to be achieved in 12 different strategic areas of change. The terms and content of these internationally established mechanisms of monitoring and evaluation assess the efficacy with which nation-states, themselves unequal in power, have actually implemented gender sensitive legislation, and a bureaucratic structure that facilitates the practice of gender equity.[4]

These indicators have initiated a way of scribing national identity that further incorporates and institutionalises women's bodies into a discussion on modernity, and re-invokes the historically drawn lines between the 'West and the Rest'.[5] For countries in the supposed 'Developing South' there is a shifting yardstick that marks its status as 'modern' by virtue of its ability to speak about the terms by which its female citizens exist. It is not surprising therefore that there is an increasing tendency within nation-states in the anglophone Caribbean to craft themselves (if only rhetorically) as gender-sensitive in their planning approaches. The region's state managers are invested in representing themselves as gender aware to the world community and are indeed called upon to do so through annual ranking and a number of periodic reporting to conventions ratified, as explicitly stated in the *National Report on the Status of Women* (1994)

> The Government has ratified several conventions that impact in a general way on the welfare of women.... In addition the Government in 1990 ratified the Convention on the Elimination of all Forms of Discrimination against Women....In the past twenty five years, conscious efforts have been made to repeal or amend all known discriminatory legal impediments to the advancement of women. (pp. 43-44)

These gender-related factors have become critical components of how contemporary nation-states attempt to craft an identity of international merit; a gesture that we will critique throughout this paper.

Trinidad and Tobago, like many other displaced and disadvantaged actors on the international scene, have found themselves caught in the *race of ratification*. This is a race however that must be identified for its hollowness and incapacity for operationalisation primarily because it facilitates the political rhetoric of gender sensitivity and inclusion without commitment to the infrastructural, ideological, legislative and financial implications of what it means to be a signatory to conventions that are aimed at facilitating gender equity (for example, CEDAW, Beijing Platform of Action arising out of the Fourth World Conference on Women, 1995).

As such, a huge dissonance emerges when we track the strength of the primary gender focal point within the national machinery against the ratification enthusiasm. For the same period within which many of the region's governments would have ratified documents such as CEDAW, Nairobi Forward Looking Strategies or Beijing, the institutional status of women, in many Caribbean territories experienced several transitions from Desk to Bureau to Division. However, in so far as we can identify these organisations as the barometer of the state's thinking on women and gender-equity, it is therefore particularly telling to note that these organisations have been notoriously under-funded, limited in ministerial influence, and poorly staffed both in terms of personnel and training.

These things are now well known and cannot be disputed. However, I am more concerned with the *subtleties of incapacity*. That is to say even in situations where there may have been increased financial allocations, or an increase in staffing and technical resources, what are the qualitative and unmapped elements that debilitate the extent to which the region's bureaux can effectively realise any goal of gender equity. Should we not conclude that the region's bureaux have been institutionalised to fail? Should not the region's state managers be called upon to account for this if it is indeed so?

De-centring Women: Planning and the Gender Affairs Division

In Trinidad and Tobago, 40 years after independence, we can say with some certainty that a national agenda for women's equality has been an eclectic, if not an ad hoc and reactionary, approach. The interim 40 years have been characterised by a number of political and economic upheavals. The emergence of new political actors,[6] 1970s Black Power movement, an oil boom and crisis marking both economic prosperity and depression, structural adjustment policies, an attempted *coup d'etat* and peaceful elections in the midst of ethnic diversity and rapid change have been some of the defining features of Trinidad and Tobago's first 40 years as a nation-state. This overview also gives a partial outline of the fraught political climate in which the question of women's equality would be placed on the national landscape. In this context the issues that would have been prioritised within the state machinery could be categorised as those seen to have international impact, those promoted by strong advocacy of a local feminist lobby, and, or changes in the voting demographics of any given period. The imperative to address gender equality in Trinidad and Tobago therefore emerges at the intersection between the international mandate and local feminist lobby within the nation-state.

Prior to the declaration of the International Women's Year in 1975, any approximation to women's issues in Trinidad and Tobago was largely under the purview of partisan political campaigning by the women's arm of their perspective political parties or under the framework of 'generic' legislative framework of services provided to men and women and through the dispensation of welfare services and the formulation of a social safety net.[7] The predominantly male nationalist leaders of the post-independence period adhered to a welfare approach in the provision of social good, albeit void of concerns about women's empowerment and gender equality. Therefore, while this welfare approach laid the groundwork for the development of a social consciousness and a sense of entitlement in the areas of access to health care, education and basic needs and amenities, it did very little to move women beyond their traditional roles as wives and mothers.

The UN Decade for Women 1975-1985 was a pivotal period both in terms of the institutionalisation of women's issues. This period gathered momentum and synergy due to the growing vibrancy of the women's movement, which had crystallised into a number of pressure groups that focused on advocacy for women's rights. The language employed by many of these 'second wave' activists in this decade, reflected the socialist base politics of the Left and a catalytic blend of issues such as, sexual autonomy and control of women's bodies (for example, Rape Crisis Society); social equity (CAFRA 1985) and Women Working for Social Progress (1985). During this period, the Trinidad and Tobago state was called to a degree of accountability on issues that addressed women's domestic and community management responsibilities through organisations such as the Housewives Association of Trinidad and Tobago (1975) (Reddock 1998). State managers therefore had to up the ante in terms of their response to these demands in ways that undermined the comfort found in the race of ratification. In spite of the force of a localised women's lobby, there are several structural, ideological, and conceptual flaws that compromise the credibility of the responses that have come from the state.

State-Bureaucracy and Gender Mainstreaming

At the point at which a Women's Desk was instituted (1975), the Women in Development (WID) model was the primary driving force for the approaches adopted during this period (Moser 1991). Reflecting the terms of WID, one of the main objectives of the Nairobi Forward Looking Strategies was that governments should seek to involve and integrate women in all phases of the planning, delivery and evaluation of multisectoral programmes that eliminate discrimination against women (UNECLAC/CDCC 15.03.00, 3). The competition for resources in emerging Third World states, worsened by the economic uncertainty and paralysis of the 1980s and the subsequent embrace of the IMF's market driven structural adjustment policies, all weakened the state's capacity to take effective action in this regard.[8]

The Beijing Platform for Action also repeated the demand for nation-states to account for their treatment of women's equality and act assertively in a number strategically designated areas.[9] The platform calls for the creation and strengthening of the national machinery designated to address women's empowerment and advancement. This goal has been identified in tandem with the need for these designated agencies to take the lead role in the process of gender mainstreaming and gender sensitisation within state machinery.

In Trinidad and Tobago, for example, there have been several legislative milestones with direct impact on the advancement of women, which, if taken at face value, can make a convincing argument that the state has been proactive in its efforts to improve the status of women in Trinidad and Tobago. Among some of the milestones have been the Domestic Violence Act, No. 22 (1999);[10] the Maternity Protection Act, No. 4 of 1998;[11] The Cohabitational Relations Act, No. 30 1998[12] (CEDAW Periodic Report/Trinidad and Tobago: December 2000). Further, Trinidad is one of the few Caribbean countries to submit periodic reports on the CEDAW convention, albeit approximately ten years after having initially ratified the convention.

The operationalisation of many of the conventions ratified falls within the purview of the Gender Affairs Division, which is the only state-based institution explicitly mandated to address and facilitate the holistic implementation of CEDAW's concerns and other issues related to Trinidadian women's empowerment and gender-based inequality. In keeping with their mandate to effectively 'promote Gender Equity and Gender Equality through the process of Gender Mainstreaming in all Government Policies, Programmes and Projects' the Division is designated and perceived as the lead agency in the promotion and monitoring of measures that facilitate women's advancement. An examination of any of the region's bureaux is an important indicator toward assessing the state's position on the issue of women's empowerment and equality. The Trinidadian GAD is expected to provide and receive support at two levels, through intra-ministerial networking and through the resources and capacity built into the Division itself. However, on both counts, the state's treatment of the Division mirrors the marginalised status of women in Trinidad generally. I want us to consider how the capacity of the region's Bureaux to actually realise their mandate is constrained by what I see as three important components to the production of incapacity; these are, a struggle against suspicions of 'illegality', constructed narratives of incompetence and a colonially driven bureaucratic structure that is generally hostile to change and obstructively hostile to gender equity.

The sense of 'illegality' has been part of the GAD's existence from its very inception, as evident in the following narrative given by one the project officers who would have been among the first complement of staff within the then Women's Affairs:

P.   so they hired us, they hired us ostensibly to implement the Inter-American Development Bank (IDB) plan of action which was agreed by the government. When we got there, there was politics…the policy changed….In fact when we got there the PS said we were illegal, there shouldn't be a division for women alone so he refused to deal with us. That was (name blurred on tape). I will never forget that name. So they used to give trouble about our contracts and payments and

M.   But illegal in what sense?

P.   He said he couldn't understand how the government could have a division to implement programs for women…the Women's Affairs Division. We were leaving out one half of the population. The usual M. nonsensical argument.

P.   Yeah

The term 'illegality' repeated itself throughout my interviews with the state's functionaries as a way of describing any conceptual location that did not define gender relations as a categorical attendance to the concerns of 'men and women.' Any other organisational model to this rudimentary and incorrect understanding of gender, regardless of its empirical and conceptual merit, was seen as 'illegal,' and therefore not a viable contender for accessing state resources. This lack of perceived legitimacy by state managers subsequently resulted in deliberate acts of sabotage through tardy salary payments, and contractual instability.[13]

Populist assumptions about 'gender' as categorically requiring attention to men, when enacted as the basis of policy and decision-making opens hitherto untapped resources that were previously unavailable for women. This depoliticised terminology also makes it more difficult for feminist activists to argue for women's socioeconomic, physical and political vulnerabilities. The following dialogue between myself and a former minister of government reflects the insidious hold which rudimentary 'gender' models have produced on the inside of the Gender Affairs Division and the state generally

Min. I remember I was going to a meeting in India, I think 1999, and there were a number of issues that we were going to discuss in India and there was opposition to my going to India. But I said what are the things we are going to do and when I talked about the males, because we were going to deal with that thesis on male marginalization. I think it is Miller

M.   Yes Errol Miller in Jamaica

Min. …when I mentioned that, in fact not only did I have to mention it I had to bring documentary evidence that the male marginalization thesis was being addressed in India…that allowed me to go.

This exchange reminds us that women's political success cannot merely be numerical access to the corridors of power without a commensurate concern for redressing the patriarchal institutional cultures and procedures that exist within these corridors. Here, we find that the Division's work-agenda is governed by the need to respond, negatively or positively, to the growing concerns about masculinity in the region. The growing correlation between masculinity and marginality has successfully redefined and undermined the terms against which decisions are made for women's empowerment, as well as the levels of access that women have to state resources.[14]

However, the term 'illegality' substantively extends beyond the Division's ability to procure resources for administrative expenses or work plans geared toward gender equality. The term 'illegality' reflects a stronger sense of 'un-belonging'; a malaise of organisational identity within the mechanisms of state machinery. This dimension to the idea of 'illegality' was poignantly expressed in the following exchange with one of the Division's former directors.

> ... I was a mad woman anyway and this was not an NGO this was what people would have perceived. But the key would have been to operate like an NGO inside there because of the politics of the thing, knowing fully well that you wear your masks at the critical time.
>
> M.   I want to pick up on something you said somewhat facetiously, "I'm a mad woman anyway" ... what makes you use that idea, to suggest that some of this didn't work because they perceived you as being crazy any way.
>
> (giggles) Well I said it in a pleasant way but there were lots of feelings. I did not want to manage the Division the way the public service and the Minister wanted me to manage it. I absolutely did not want to do it! My training in feminist methodology didn't allow it ... I disliked hierarchy to the bottom of my heart. But my Minister kept shouting at me to direct! "Why don't you direct?!".... I understood power well, so what I quickly had to learn to do was to wear all these different masks. So for some people on staff I cyar (can't) manage at all! And for me I'm saying I don't want to manage because I ... don't want to do it in the same way as the teachers do, as the community officers do it, the nurses do it and so on. Take off your shoes let us go down in the market street let us talk with the women on Charlotte St. let us (becoming more and more animated).

Bureaucratic cultures, by their very nature, are designed to produce dispassionate, distant similarity of procedure and function across a network of ministries. This bureaucratic culture is an oppressive force for a division such as the Gender Affairs Division, which ideologically and functionally has been designated to produce change within its counterpart agencies. Straddling this insider/outsider relationship within the national machinery produces psychologically incarcerated changed agents who are torn between the desire for gender-just change, and a predetermined organisational structure that resents and resists such change.[15]

Of course this must suggest to us that as long as the present bureaucratic structure and climate persists, there can be no political will or structural capacity to lobby and advocate for gender change on the inside of the state. The only function that is then possible, if the region's bureaux remain determined by existing bureaucratic policies and procedures of state-making, will be patronage and a reactionary implementation of ministerial political will. However, such obstacles ought not to categorically suggest the demise of state sponsored-feminism (Barriteau

2003). Regionally, Gender Affairs Bureaux have been institutionalised with overwhelming impossibilities as their inheritance, consequently, their limits and possibilities are yet to be explored. Rather, what we must envision are viable alternatives of advocacy on women's issues within state machinery.

Similarly, the reference to 'madness' is not accidental and should not be treated as such, even though the director herself dismisses her statement as a conversational filler by the use of the adjunct 'anyway' ('I was a mad woman *anyway*'). Mental instability and irrationality have a long philosophical history as the basis of women's exclusion from public life (Pateman 1992). Madness, even if used facetiously, opens up several avenues for sabotage due to supposed or imputed irrationality, and incompetence. Ascribing madness to any change-agent, inclusive of those pursuing gender concerns, sets the stage for dismissing the speaker's point of view and perspective. Madness then becomes both a silencing strategy and an indicator of how bureaucratic institutional cultures produce psychological discomfort for feminist change-agents. In addition to ascribing questionable narratives to the capacity of change agents, another important aspect in weakening the bureaux globally has been the systematic detachment of the GADs from a community of feminist activists or the further instrumentalisation of this community towards the furtherance of state goals rather than the feminists interests and the intent of their varying constituencies (von Braunmuhl 2002, 73).

Sonja Harris has questioned the extent to which gender bureaux can feasibly exist within the present bureaucratic climate. She argues that

> what is required for Women in Development or Gender and Development cannot automatically be met within the policy framework and praxis currently being pursued. This praxis is characteristically authoritarian, top-down, patriarchal, market-driven and dependent on benefits trickling down to the poor an approach long discredited in the sub-region for its poor results whereas development planning and programming are by nature – participatory, people-centred and focused on equity and sustainability' (2003,184).

Harris suggests that an endorsement of participatory democracy should override the authoritarianism that presently exists. However, it is disconcerting that the political rhetoric around 'participatory democracy' is such that 'participatory demagoguery' is often lauded as 'participatory democracy'. This is to suggest a distinction between the appearance of popular participation only as that sanctioned by the voice of the maximum leader, versus rethinking our organisational structures and bureaucratic cultures to encourage broad-based leadership, community involvement in decision-making and new ways of functioning within existing bureaucratic structures.

In the above exchange the former director, reflecting on her tenure with the Division, highlights the need to claim 'NGO status' while being located within the bureaucratic framework of the state. This is a striking observation in light of my earlier assertion that one of the challenges of this century for gender focal points in the Third World is to clarify and strategise around their terms of inclusions. Here the respondent refashions the terms of inclusion by claiming NGO status as a way of denoting an aggressive advance, that is to say, having found ourselves as feminist change agents *within* the state machinery how do we strategise to effect change? The NGO analogy I find to be an apt one, as it asserts the importance of laying hold of an insider/outsider identity within the state machinery in order to maintain a critical and confrontational stance toward advocacy. The difficult question that remains is how can GADs regionally be empowered to operationalise such a stance to their advantage?

Genderising the Planning Debate: Conceptual and Programmatic Ambiguities

Conceptual ambivalence produces programmatic hesitance and inefficient use of resources. The primary area of ambiguity with Bureaux regionally is the 'gender dilemma' that must be confronted at the most rudimentary level of 'gender mainstreaming'. The dilemma around 'woman'/'gender' in the day-to-day running of the Division's work produces a great deal more than semantic ambiguity. Rather, this dilemma supports the narrative of women's 'illegality' within national machinery and secures the propensity for gender-planning agencies to become a safe place for state misogyny to hide.

A degree of optimism had been attached to the capacity of gender mainstreaming to rid us of state based discrimination against women.

To this end, gender mainstreaming mandated that all policy, legislation, institutional frames and implementation and monitoring procedures confront and address the question of gender. A tautology if ever there was one, further bedevilled by the obscurity around who, or what is gender? Much of the confusion is to be found in the popular perception that 'who or what is gender' is asking the same question when in reality it is not. This dilemma is at the heart of the matter, each time a 'femocrat' is called upon to respond to a line minister or permanent secretary who asks 'where are the men in this project?' In essence, what is being asked here is 'who is gender, if not a categorical inclusion of men and women?' The femocrat responds that her project, plan or idea is premised not on a series of additive factors but consideration of the hierarchies (for example, class, race/ethnicity, rural/urban, levels of literacy, skills, access to information, credit, cultural biases and expectations, economic vulnerabilities and legislative jeopardy) that historically or contextually dis-empower her identified target group. Instantaneously, two different linguistic and conceptual codes collide and we recognise that 'who and what is gender?' are not only phenomenally different points of departure, but also that the power differentials involved in those who understand versus those who do not, come with dangerous effects for the region's women.

The 'gender dilemma' as it exists regionally, aborts any productive consideration of institutional responsiveness to culture and structure in order to facilitate mainstreaming approaches. In the absence of a clear conceptualisation of gender there is no sense of which categories of individuals should be addressed or how resources should be allocated by already fiscally strapped states. This conceptual ambiguity in turn compromises the legitimacy of the claims made by women, as well as the politics and purpose that informs the Division's work programme.

This 'gender dilemma' took an interesting turn in Trinidad and Tobago in 1997 when the nominal shift from woman to gender resulted in an impasse between members of the feminist NGO community and the state. This transition was more than nominal, rather it is one that generated conceptual uncertainty among staff, increased the levels of ambiguity about the Division's target group and the legitimacy of resource allocations to these various constituencies. The transition brought the 'gender dilemma' to the fore. The conceptual ambiguity among staff was palpable. One of the main points of conceptual uncertainty had to do in the most fundamental sense with what the term 'gender' meant and, by extension, how it then modified the Division's constituency and work programme. The transition was not accompanied by training or re-education and the staff was called on to operationalise a term in the daily running of their Division that had little or no meaning to them. A range of different (mis)understandings came to the fore when I asked the Division's functionaries how they felt about the Division's transition from woman to gender:

- I just thought it was so stupid. Because to me, if you want to do it, you're going to ask what informs it? So when gender, as I say exploded and it has exploded on the country…this is why we have all this conceptual unclarity and confusion.

- Well early we shifted from women to gender and I understood the gender, as a matter of fact, I had bought into the shift in the concept. Because you can't help women in isolation, *unless you talk about the men too*. I had a little um, in terms of my version of what I saw as gender, got a little um, a little opposition within the Gender Affairs Division. Because from the literature, even though the literature was saying gender you got this feel that it was saying women. (emphasis mine)

- I don't think the minister understood conceptually what was the difference between women and development and gender and development or if she understood she didn't really care. She just decided you know to attract men and get away from some of the negative vibes of women's affairs, let's do gender! It was women's affairs and then became gender affairs. She (minister) felt that in working for women and this happened a lot because of domestic violence and because a lot of policy makers were men. She felt that if you didn't use a gendered approach where men were targeted with gender training and gender information and also that men saw themselves supported by the Commonwealth because they were also changing their approach from girl and woman to gender.…A lot of people in the women's movement felt that we hadn't achieved the goals of Beijing…we hadn't arrived. They felt that we were giving ground.

These responses provide direct insight into the various arguments and positions that emerged around the shift. Despite clear evidence of dissent or disapproval of these change agents, there was an attendant narrative of disempowerment and inability to initiate change. The operationalisation of the term 'gender' reflected the super-ordinate position of the minister's mandate over and above the Division's technical expertise. There was little consideration of what the change would mean in a bureaucratic climate governed by male marginalisation rhetoric. Neither was there a sense that 'gender' was required to work in tandem with 'mainstreaming' and there was yet to be a discussion on the relationship that should exist between substance and form of mainstreaming exercises.[16]

Many of the Division's former employees felt that the enthusiasm with which the minister pursued the transition to gender was a strategy of political survival rather than 'a thing to really help women'. The minister herself in the following exchange surprisingly enough somewhat unwittingly corroborated this:

> M   Again the question of political will. Referring to your earlier statement about the importance of timing when approaching the cabinet; the importance of understanding what are the topical issues and using that as an opportunity? Do you think that the shift from woman to gender would have been in a sense, a strategy of approaching cabinet?
>
> Min. You bet, you bet! Yes, yes, because the members of cabinet are male. They largely also hold in general, the predominant views of men-women relationships. I mean not in the extreme they won't say you should beat your wife…

'Gender' as the basis of a planning can be conciliatory and aimed at appeasing, rather than challenging the assumed and traditional views among different categories of 'men-women relationships'. Women's issues, if driven by a feminist mandate that challenges the status quo, will hold a precarious and antagonistic opposition within bureaucracies. There is no easy way to lobby the state to address women's issues while residing within the institutional machinery of state. The transition from woman to gender cannot be dislocated from the Gender Affairs Division's attempt to gain greater institutional credibility via a less confrontational or overtly woman-centred approach. The discord that resulted among different feminist stakeholders such as the women's movement, and various academics, was premised on the sentiment that this transition was not in the interest of improving the status of women and served to create a situation where women's entitlement and access were being eroded.

These conceptual deficiencies neutralised the empowerment and advancement offensive that inhabits the spirit of CEDAW and the Beijing Platform for Action and also stunted the possibilities that could result from a radical use of the word gender. One of the major by-products of this transition was a heightened 'sensitivity' to the needs of males in society. Regardless of the privilege and statistical and sociopolitical dominance that Caribbean men experience generally, what became of paramount importance was the need to craft a male programmatic. This anxiety around masculinity resulted in the creation of a Male Support Unit. According to the minister who spearheaded the transition, these changes were necessary if her ministry was to respond appropriately to the perceived sense of male insecurity as expressed here:

M. How would you assess the national climate on women's issues?

Min. There are two elements I think that I caught. One is, because of the concerted effort we used to address women's issues we find the men have been feeling more insecure and to some extent marginalized and they have expressed this. I told you we had a male support group and now a unit um, so we've had to deal with the male backlash if that is the correct word ... we've even been accused of, of strengthening the woman as opposed to the man and therefore making men more insecure.

The complete disconnect between the question and the minister's response reflects exactly where the national climate is on women's issues; locked within, and submerged by a growing anxiety about masculinity. The thesis of male marginality has been on the ascendancy *as part of* the political and popular rhetoric of 'gender'. Both the currency and danger of this rhetoric are not to be underestimated. The male marginalisation model propagates the popular belief that men and women exist in an obverse relationship with each other, that is to say, acknowledging the specificities of one, simultaneously means that one ignores the demands or needs of the other.[17] In addition to the simplicity of this model, the danger of incorporating these ideas into planning and policy formulation invites a planning model that disregards the sociocultural privilege that Caribbean men hold. It distracts us from understanding the ways in which state institutions can be best poised to indeed assist Caribbean men (for example, assessing the areas of need in relation to questions of equity). Finally, it compromises the certainty with which women and ministers with perceived responsibility for women are able to hold the state accountable to women as a constituency; in sum it is an unproductive framework for anything but the reassertion of Caribbean male privilege.[18]

There is an almost inextricable relationship between conceptual murkiness and programmatic ambiguity. The 'gender dilemma' has compelled gender planners to take an apologetic stance for initiating programmes that confront women's statistical, legislative, and political marginalisation from access to and control of resources. The fact that skills-training programmes occur for 'women only' in the Gender Affairs Division is not adequate grounds on which to differentiate the Gender Affairs projects from others that may exist in other line ministries or divisions in the same ministry in which the Gender Affairs Division is located. This is no more the case than does the categorical presence of men provide adequate grounds on which to legitimise the use of the term 'gender'. The distinguishing feature must be the capacity to understand the terms of inequity and, from such a platform, envision the structural and programmatic interventions and strategies necessary to counteract inequity.

All planning for women in Trinidad and Tobago must, as a matter of priority, be ensconced in the reality that women continue to be the poorest of the poor, with unemployed female heads of households falling approximately 49 per cent below the Trinidad national income (GOTT Household Budget Survey 97/98, 5). The 'gender dilemma' has weakened all aggressive ownership of any programmatic agenda that appears to address the needs of women. However, gender planning regionally has been primarily eclectic and expedient. Therefore, programmatic functions are not always explicitly conceptualised to confront the empowerment component of gender issues within the Gender Affairs Division. This omission presents a number of anomalies and compromises the credibility of these divisions.

The Division's mandate of women's economic empowerment is cognisant of the fact that women's control over money, assets and livelihood translates into a better standard of life. The gendered component of this assumption, however, is that without adjusting the power relations in the home, community and the market place, economic empowerment in isolation will not necessarily translate into an improved status for women generally. Training carries little intrinsic value to women without a vision for the type of output that will enhance women's capabilities not as wives, not as mothers but as self-sustaining citizens.

Without a vision for women's strategic change, gender focal points will themselves fall into the trap of conceiving change via numerical indicators, that is to say how many projects and how many women.[19] The women who approach the Division to participate in a 'numerically driven' programmatic agenda fall into what we can refer to as a 'cycle of certification'.[20] In this cycle participants move from one skills training programme to the other without a directed sense of how these skills actually make a difference to the quality of their lives or their ability to challenge their lived practices of inequity.

This was immediately evident in the following respondent's narrative. Joan is unemployed with five children. She has moved back into her parent's home to care for her ailing mother and benefits from not having to pay rent but laments the loss of her autonomy. She rationalised her participation in the non-traditional training programme offered by the Division as an avenue to 'bettering' herself. More in-depth discussion revealed, however, that since graduating from the programme Joan has not been able to use the training given to her. In fact, she has not even thought seriously about how her training in electrical installation can be used.

> M. Were you satisfied with the quality of training that you received?
>
> J. Although I find they should have gone a step further. This was just the first part they should have a more advanced part to the programme.
>
> M. What about opening avenues for you to make money? How do you see that happening from the skill, because is one thing to have the skill but you have to make the skill work for you.
>
> J. Well I will need, such as, um, well like going into business?
>
> M. However, you decide.

> J.   Well I could go into a business and going into that business is like going into a contractual something and whereas I could have people working, ... now working for me. Now I know electrical, I wouldn' be able to do it but I can have a qualified person working for me so that when you do something I could go and say well yes I'm satisfied.

When asked about her projected plans to use the training there is little indication to suggest that Joan had even thought of the training in terms of self-maintenance, hence her delayed response and need for clarification. When pressed she begins to build what sounds more like an entrepreneurial flight of fancy rather than a clearly thought-out business plan, even though the curriculum of the programme requires them to think through such a business plan. In this exchange there is no clear sense of what her envisioned supervisory role will require her to provide in terms of start-up capital, or technical expertise. When asked later in the discussions to think about the usefulness of the training, her response had scaled down significantly

> J.   I went in (to the training programme) because I wanted the...ah (I) fixing meh (my) place and I would learn more about wiring and ah went in and I enjoyed it. It was good and I was glad in a sense that I did because at home I'm able, there was a cord, I watch the cord and I say but wait....it had a socket outlet on to it and I was able to take out the socket outlet, rewire it over, fix it over, take out the plug cut the wire put on a good plug and fix it and so on.

Further discussions with Joan show that she has accumulated a number of training experiences and is yet to make any of them work for her. She has done an upholstery course, an electrical installation course and is about to embark on counselling; all of them 'atypical' skills training yet none has changed her material condition.

This concern for the 'cycle of certification' was voiced by one of the employees of the Gender Affairs Division. In critiquing another of the Division's offerings, the agent noted that many of the participants were merely accumulating certificates that were of no general value

> especially in the agricultural programme they just come in to collect the stipend for three months and then they go back out there and they really don't have the funds, the infrastructure, they don't have anything to continue the programme or to continue anything they have learnt.

Structurally and conceptually, the Gender Affairs Division is the primary indicator of the state's position on women reflects a position of ambivalence and chronic disregard for the terms that inform its own *raison d'être*. Yet, skill-training remains the primary indicator of the Division's successes. In the midst of this welfarist, stipend approach to skill-training, the only programme (IADB Non-Traditional) that has incorporated a gender empowerment component has done so apologetically and that gender module remains under threat. Assessed against the lives of women such as Joan, who look to these training programmes to provide a greater sense of purpose and direction as heads of households, it is difficult to clearly point to the unique contributions that the Division makes to their lives.

Political Correctness versus Political Will: Using Women as an Electoral Resource

In a societal context where so many of the activities emerge from a welfarist modus operandi of '*what are you doing for women*' rather than addressing the more critical question of '*how are we creating systemic change for women*' these programmes secure a band-aid approach to gender equity that shows little or no awareness of the terms upon which one must plan holistically for change.

Many of these programmes are primarily adult education programmes for women; which is a critical component of women's advancement as it addresses educational imbalances that may confront women. It is the lack of feminist rationale and focus, however, that make these projects problematic. Throughout the interviews conducted with functionaries, both past and present, of the Gender Affairs Division, it became clearer that the overt project oriented work programme was governed by the need to be seen to be 'doing something for women'.

Throughout the interviews, a theme that persisted was the importance of portraying a sense of 'busy-ness'. In reality this imperative of 'busy-ness' or 'doing something for women', was reflective of a number of competing partisan interests. Rather than finding compatibility with the Division's agenda, a range of project-motivated activity designed to highlight ministerial visibility of the minister often took precedence to systemic change.

The ministers who would have had responsibility for the Gender Affairs Division, as well as the gender-based technocrats within the Division, at various stages all noted (albeit for different reasons) that the rationale behind their activities was often the need to be seen as 'doing something for women'. This modus operandi was explained by way of procuring increased ministerial recognition and credibility in the public's eye. The lack of energies given to research, strategic planning and forging a clear policy direction inevitably follows such a programmatic approach. There was, for example, a very telling response by a former employee of the GAD when asked whether a feasibility study had been conducted for one of the Division's projects:

P. Policy? It's not research driven, it's not from the bottom up. We stay in our office and the Minister may have some constituent in her head or someone who said 'you know what? I find you all should get involved in blah, blah, blah in Embacadere or somewhere, so you can do something for Embacadere, some women down there need training'. And you go and you do something for Embacadere without any kind of data informing what you're supposed to be doing.

M. and as a member of staff did you feel 'empowered' to speak back and ask why?

P. It depends, after a while you just did what you had to do. It was just easier, because you got all the licks about not being out there. She hated when we sat at our desk she said 'you all are not out there, you all are not doing the work'. And doing the work meant that you had to be in the field. Being in the field.

Gender Divisions will be unsuccessful in their mandate unless there is a clear vision of expertise, training and conceptualisation of their constituencies. Conceptually, bureaucracies are not designed to bend to political will, *in practice* however they do. The anxiety that is produced around securing subsequent political terms in office makes gender-related focal points particularly vulnerable to co-optation and instrumentalisation. Activities are therefore generated, not around demographics, need or a vision of equity, but rather, through a sense of political expediency. Planning then becomes coterminous with the political intention of the minister. Political visibility overwhelms policy direction and the demand for directionless activity heightens during election years. The extent to which a state-led vision for mainstreaming gender equity is compromised by political expediency was best expressed by one former functionary of the Division who felt, during periods of high election campaigning, as if she was transformed into a worker in her minister's campaign office, rather than on behalf of a constituency of women.

In addition to this political pressure, the historical inclusion of Caribbean women into state activity via a welfare model continues to undermine any empowerment potential. It is not surprising therefore that women's empowerment has gradually shifted into a framework of poverty alleviation programming, in support of the social services:

> We were in a ministry, a social services ministry and people wanted us to deliver. People wanted to find out what we were doing. So we couldn't be dabbling in policy which is you know…we were trying to put things in place in order to implement data. The Minister would say you all have to go out there and work. So we worked like community development officers you piloted a lot of small projects. Its disheartening because you didn't have the funds to carry through and stuff like that…

Further to the interference of partisan politics, the Division's recruiting policy further entrenches even more its programmatic redundancy within the state machinery.[21] This programmatic redundancy reflects a similar ethos, tone and programmatic content of the welfare approach that exists within the Social Services. This transference obtains for a number a reasons, among these are the long-standing institutional significance of the Social Services in Trinidad. This significance exists both in terms of institutional longevity, as well as its strategic importance to the clientilism of political parties while in government as these divisions provide an immediate interface with wider cross-section of non-party supporters through control and disbursement of community allocated state resources. Second, the category 'Caribbean woman' within the WID model was first institutionalised within a conceptual stranglehold of, 'Afro-', poor, mother, wife, widow, heterosexual and/or in need of sexual restraint. The region's bureaux must be cognisant of these historical narratives and consciously strategises programmatically to counteract them, or they too will appeal to these existing narratives of a dysfunctional, maternal or nuclear-origin modus operandi already at work within the state.

The welfarist model of social services delivery programmes to women also becomes evident in the hiring practices pursued by GADs regionally. In Trinidad and Tobago, the first wide-scale attempt at hiring staff completely dedicated to the advancement of women's issues within the state machinery came in 1994. The Division then secured a range of skills areas such as Development Studies, Agriculture, Economics and Accounting. The first director had also received post-graduate training in the area of Women and Development Studies. This combination of skills was poised to engage questions of policy, planning and gender mainstreaming as their mandate.

Much has transpired since then. However, a recent posting for vacancies within the division continues to move in the direction of social services redundancy in their call for applicants with training in the area of social work, sociology, with '[E]xperience in the delivery of training programmes and/or community work [being] desirable. Training in gender issues is required. Familiarity with the concepts and methods of gender analysis and women's studies will be a definite asset' (*Daily Express* September 20, 2002, 16). In this posting, the disciplinary skills of gender analysis appear tangential to the advertised vacancies. This oversight, while responding to an already existing institutional culture, is still inexcusable in light of, the fact that, in 1993, the Centre for Gender and Development Studies was established at the University of the West Indies. Subsequent to their establishment, the St Augustine Unit had generated undergraduate minors in Gender Studies, Gender and Development and an MPhil/PhD Programme in Gender and Development. Yet, ten years later, with an increasing pool of graduates with the capacity to conduct gender analysis, the posting that emanates from the Gender Affairs Division requires that the successful candidate be 'trained' in the area of sociology and social work but have 'familiarity' in the areas of gender relevant expertise.

A professionalised approach toward the process of gender-just policy formulation appears grim.[22] At the time of the research for this paper the GAD had begun in, conjunction with their donor (GOTT and UNDP) and executing (CGDS) agencies, to prepare the Terms of Reference for a National Gender Policy. In 2004, the preliminary aspects of this work is completed, however, prior to the start of the project a climate of scepticism already existed. One former employee of the Division captured this relationship between policy direction and political will most succinctly:

> Written policies are really a waste of time if the Minister has no intentions of carrying [them] out. To me the more effective ministries are the ministries where you have strong ministers and a strong P.S. (Permanent Secretary). It has nothing to do with the written policy. A lot of the policies that are implemented are unspoken and unwritten. It changes from year to year and from government to government and from personality to personality and that is how the Public Service operates. We don't follow any set policy. And when they come in, it depends on what are the topical issues, what are the main…I don't know, what are people clamouring about…those are the policies and what the Minister feels he or she is really hip with or bent on achieving. They could have written ten gender affairs policies. Nothing would have made a difference unless it was one that was fully sanctioned by the Minister and he or she was there for a length of time to see it implemented gradually.

The overriding ad hoc nature of policy formulation in the Trinidad and Tobago can easily lead to the same level of cynicism articulated here. Nonetheless, it is counter-productive to derail the process before commencement, and ours is the quest of strategies that can address the concern that generated this paper, namely the subtleties of incapacity.

If gender-justice is to be argued as part of the 'developmental goals' for the region, then it must emerge from the contextual realities and histories and resist the impulse to be primarily driven by reactionary and rhetorical commitment to forms of ratification. A gender-just society must take cognisance of the historical marginalisation and discriminatory practices against different constituencies and permutations of people by virtue of location (urban/rural), class, sexual preference, race and other aspects of one's identities and subjectivity.

As the lead agency, the Gender Affairs Division is of critical importance if Caribbean nation-states are to envision new subjectivities and potentials for Caribbean women and men. As the primary focal point for such change, the Gender Affairs Division must set the standard for all other line ministries. The Gender Affairs Division therefore has the Herculean task of producing a counter-discourse about all gendered categories within the state machinery, without a clear plan of how this can be achieved.

Here, Sonia Alvarez's notion of 'hybridity' is of great relevance. This term has already been alluded to in our earlier discussion around the need for GADs to politicise their insider/outsider status within the state. Alvarez uses the term 'hybridity' to speak to a Latin American phenomenon where

> Most newly professionalized feminist groups fashioned hybrid political strategies and identities – developing expertise in gender policy advocacy while retaining a commitment to movement-oriented activities aimed at fostering women's empowerment and transforming prevailing gender power arrangements. In collaboration with the 'global feminist lobby' local NGOs succeeded in pressuring many Latin American governments to enact a number of feminist-inspired reforms – such as electoral quotas to enhance women's political representation and legislation to combat domestic violence (Alvarez 1999 in von Braumuhl 2002).

Alvarez's insight suggests to us that each faction of the feminist struggle must wear multiple identities of activist, advocate and bureaucrat towards the achievement of individualised goals; hence her term 'hybrid political identities'. As we have discussed in this paper, the 'politicisation' of such a multifaceted identity cautions against embracing diluted, unproductive concepts, as well as the danger of assuming a position of comfort and collusion with state forces even under conditions of increased financial allocations, staffing. I want, in conclusion, however, to invert Alvarez's idea of multiple identities to speak also to the simultaneous importance of 'multiple responsibilities'. While 'multiple identities' speaks to a wide range of skills and capacities within an agency/agent, 'multiple responsibilities' extends these resident capacities outwards in service of other feminist organisations.

My use of the term 'multiple responsibilities' therefore suggest a refocused attention to the spheres of complementarity that exist within the Caribbean women's movement. The term therefore projects a sense of planning strategically and collectively to provide what Sonja Harris refers to as an 'organised response' to forms of contemporary popular and political biases. We tend to envision a gendered landscape that is inherently antagonistic and competitive when we do, in actuality, operate in spheres of complementarity with tremendous potential for a feminist synergistic demand of accountability and collectively devised strategies towards ensuring that state-managers remain responsive to gender justice and equity.

I maintain that, in the absence of a clearly delineated network of collective support, Caribbean women will continue to be, at best, central within the margins. In many ways therefore the objective of this paper was simply a renewed call to arms in the protection of and struggle with the GADs of the anglophone Caribbean.

Notes

1. In Trinidad and Tobago this nationalised desire for development is constructed most comprehensively in the Prime Minister's Vision 2020, a comprehensive ministerial restructuring toward Trinidad and Tobago's achievement of developed country status by the year 2020.
2. Of course the corollary of this is that we are similarly unable to address the forms of economic, physical and sexual exploitation that occur with women within the informal economy, rebounding nonetheless to increased profit margins within the household and formal economic activity (Peterson 2003).
3. Unless a country has signed the optional protocol of the CEDAW Convention there are no sanctions or inquiries that can be applied to nation-states who do not implement or enforce the terms of the CEDAW Convention. The optional protocol allows individuals or groups to place written complaints before CEDAW for any violations of the Convention. No country in the CARICOM region has signed the optional protocol. All have ratified CEDAW.
4. Equity requires that the playing field of gender relations be levelled, that is to say that resources be allocated based on declared need, rather than a predetermined fixed notion of equality which does not always take cognizance of the antecedents of inequity. Equality, I argue, cannot be achieved without an ongoing, if not preceding discussion about the question of equity.
5. Despite the fact that Afghanistan and the USA have both not signed the CEDAW convention, the representation of the veiled woman and the protection of this brown body legitimises a number of encroachments against the state to which she belongs. Liberating the brown female body has become a common trope that is used to validate increasing military offensive, civilising missions against the non-Western nation-state.
6. On Independence, the two main political parties were the People's National Movement and the Democratic Labour Party. In 1976, two new political parties emerged – the United Labour Front led by Mr Basdeo Panday and the Democratic Action Congress, led by Mr A.N.R. Robinson both emerged. The two latter parties merged in 1981 to form the National Alliance for Reconstruction. In 1988, there was a further split back into their organic parts with one half keeping the acronym NAR and the other coining the term Club 88 which eventually became the United National Congress. With the exception of the Democratic Labour Party, each of these emergent parties would have

been given the opportunity to hold the reins of power by the voting public (Ghany 1988,183).

7. I argue elsewhere for the gender biases that are embedded in this early welfare approach to planning within the Trinidad and Tobago bureaucratic landscape (2003).
8. Globalisation's encroachment on the sovereignty of the state has become a primary argument used by state-managers in deferring the importance of gender issues. However, not only are these economic conditions inherently gendered, but gender equality also requires political and legislative will to change.
9. Among the thematic concerns identified for special attention by state machinery and civil society have been women and the media, women and the environment, the girl child, reproductive health and access to health care, access to education, violence against women.
10. This Act repealed the Domestic Violence Act, No. 10 of 1991 and improved the compensatory and protective components for victims.
11. This Act guarantees paid maternity leave for 13 weeks and protection against dismissal as a result of pregnancy.
12. The implementation of this Act accords women who have lived in a common-law relation for five years or more, the right to apply for an adjustment of property on separation and child maintenance.
13. To date, the post of Director is the only position that has been permanently established within the GAD, with the present director functioning in an acting capacity.
14. Misogyny continues to be a very marketable commodity and big business if the entertainment industry stands as our gauge. However, the distillation of state-endorsed misogyny in both unwritten and embodied policy is often veiled through the cloak of 'dispassionate' and 'neutral' bureaucratic 'procedure'.
15. Ascribing 'feeling' and cognisance to a bureaucratic structure is quite apt if we remember the obvious yet overlooked fact that structures are embodied by agents, many sexist, others misogynistic, a few supportive. To ignore the politics of location in policy making perpetuates a belief in procedural neutrality, objectivity and hence the appearance of equal and favourable conditions for the region's women.
16. Gender mainstreaming as a planning procedure requires that state functionaries with responsibility for gender mainstreaming strategise in culturally and contextually relevant ways to 'market' the relevance of gender analysis both in *substance and form* to disinterested, yet critical stakeholders. While 'substance' speaks to the content of any legislation, policy, plan or project, 'form' refers to procedures of marking success (monitoring and evaluation), as well as the formation of structures that allow for participation, the naming of one's own concerns, and is responsive and *holistic* in its implementation (Kabeer 2003).
17. See both Lindsay (2002) and Barriteau (2002) for a strong critique of the male marginalisation thesis.

18. Sonja Harris (2003,182) has observed that the women's movement has not organised a sufficiently coherent response to the marginalisation debate. This is not quite accurate, there have been a number of responses by both male and female feminists in the region (see Lindsay, Barriteau, Bailey, Figueroa, Hamilton). The failure, however, is to be found in the mode of dissemination, which is yet to be as populist or as far reaching as Miller's circulation of marginalisation.
19. Harris (2003) reminds us that, in her review of regional gender bureaux, none of the agencies during the five years under review had established clear CEDAW or Beijing+5 targets e.g. women's (reproductive) health, improving the livelihood of the girl child etc. (198).
20. This term arose out of an interview with a former member of staff within the GAD.
21. Equally as important to where the Bureau is located is the number of times it gets volleyed from ministry to ministry, thereby compromising the consistency of its work programme and mandate (Harris 2003).
22. I am using the term 'gender-justice' in keeping with Barriteau's assertion that a 'policy shaped by a commitment to gender-justice and gender-equity will not discriminate nor tolerate conditions of discrimination for either sex'. However, even this understanding of gender re-imposes a dualistic understanding of gender as a dialogue between two sexes (El-Bushra 2000).

References

Alexander, Jacqui. 1994. 'Not Just (Any)Body Can be a Citizen: The Politics of Law, Sexuality and Postcoloniality in Trinidad and Tobago and the Bahamas'. *Feminist Review* 48 (Autumn): 133-149.

Alexander, Jacqui and Chandra Mohanty. 1996. *Feminist Genealogies, Colonial Legacies, Global Movements*. New York: Routledge.

Anderson, Benedict. 1983. *Imagined Communities: Reflections on the Origin and Spread of Nationalism*. London: Verso.

Barriteau, Eudine. 2003. 'Constructing Feminist Knowledge in the Commonwealth Caribbean in the Era of Globalisation'. Paper presented at the Mona Academic Conference 'Gender in the 21st Century: Perspectives, Visions and Possibilities' August 29-31. Centre for Gender and Development Studies, Regional Coordinating Unit, UWI, Mona.

Blomstrom, Magnus and Bjorn Hettne. 1984. *Development Theory in Transition. The Dependency Debate and Beyond: Third World Responses*. London: Zed Books.

Brown, Wendy. 1992. 'Finding the Man in the State'. *Feminist Studies* 18, no. 1 (Spring): 7-34.

Chevannes, Barry. 2001. *Learning to be a Man. Culture, Socialization and Gender Identity in Five Caribbean Communities*. Mona : The UWI Press.

El-Bushra, J. 2000.'Re-thinking Gender Development Practice for the Twenty-First Century'. *Gender and Development* 8, no. 1 (March): 55-62.

Ellis, Pat. 1986. *Women in the Caribbean*. London: Zed Books.

Enloe, Cynthia. 2000. *Bananas, Beaches and Bases: Making Feminist Sense of International Politics*. Berkeley, Los Angeles: University of California Press.

Figueroa, Mark. 2003. 'Challenging Gender Privileging: A Caribbean Experience'. Paper presented at the Mona Academic Conference 'Gender in the 21st Century: Perspectives, Visions and Possibilities' August 29-31. Centre for Gender and Development Studies, Regional Coordinating Unit, UWI, Mona.

Ghany, Hamid. 1988. 'Parliament in Trinidad and Tobago 1962-1987. The Whitehall Model at Work' *Trinidad and Tobago: The Independence Experience 1962-1987*. St Augustine: ISER.

Government of Trinidad and Tobago. 1995. *National Report on the Status of Women in Trinidad and Tobago*. Gender Affairs Division of Trinidad and Tobago. Prepared for the Fourth World Conference on Women Beijing, China – September 4-15.

———. 2000. *Initial, Second and Third Periodical Report of the Republic of Trinidad and Tobago, International Convention on The Elimination of Discrimination Against Women*. Ministry of the Attorney General and Legal Affairs. December.

———. 2002. Finance Committee Report, Trinidad and Tobago Hansard, Sept. 22, p. 908.

Harris, Sonja T. 2003. 'Review of Institutional Mechanisms for the Advancement of Women and for Achieving Gender Equality 1995-2000'. In *Gender Equality in the Caribbean: Reality or Illusion*, eds. Gemma Tang Nain and Barbara Bailey, 178-200. Kingston: Ian Randle Publishers.

Jones, Kathleen B. 'Towards the Revision of Politics'. In *The Political Interests of Gender. Developing Theory and Research with a Feminist Face*, eds. Kathleen B. Jones and Anna G. Jonasdottir. London: Sage Modern Politics Series.

Kabeer, Naila. 2003. *Gender Mainstreaming in Poverty Eradication and the Millennium Development Goals: A Handbook for Policy-Makers and other Stakeholders*. London: Gender Section. Commonwealth Secretariat.

Laws of Trinidad and Tobago. *Public Assistance Act, Chapter 32:03*, 1980.

Lindsay, Keisha. 2002. 'Is the Caribbean Male an Endangered Species?'. In *Gendered Realities: Essays in Caribbean Feminist Thought*, ed. P. Mohammed, 56-82. Mona: University of the West Indies Press and CGDS.

Loomba, Ania. 1998. *Colonialism /Postcolonialism*. London and New York: Routledge.

Lloyd, Anthony and Elaine Robertson.1971. *Social Welfare in Trinidad and Tobago*. Trinidad: Antilles Research Associates.

Massiah, Joycelin.1983. *Women as Heads of Households in the Caribbean: Family Structure and Feminine Status*. Paris: UNESCO.

Massiah Joycelin. 1986. Women in the Caribbean: Special Issue in *Social and Economic Studies* 32, nos. 1&2 (June).

Nussbaum, Martha C. 2000. *Women and Human Development: The Capabilities Approach.* Cambridge: Cambridge University Press.

Pateman, Carole. 1992. 'Equality, Difference, Subordination: The Politics of Motherhood and Women's Citizenship'. In *Beyond Equality and Difference: Citizenship, Feminist Politics, and Female Subjectivity*, eds. Gisela Bock and Susan James, 17-31. New York: Routledge.

Peterson, V.S. 2003. *A Critical Rewriting of Global Political Economy: Integrating Reproductive, Productive and Virtual Economies.* London and New York: Routledge Press.

Regional Assessment of Social Services Delivery Systems: Volume I of II. Main Report. May 1998. Trinidad: Kairi Consultants.

Rowley, Michelle. 2003. Crafting Maternal Citizens? Public Discourses of the 'Maternal Scourge in Social Welfare Policies and Services in Trinidad'. *Social and Economic Studies.*

Simey, T.S. 1947. *Welfare and Planning in the West Indies.* London: Oxford University Press.

Von Braumuhl, Claudia. 2002. 'Mainstreaming Gender – A Critical Revision'. In *Common Ground or Mutual Exclusion? Women's Movements and International Relations*, eds. Marianne Braig and Sonja Wolte. London: Zed Books.

31 | LINNETTE VASSELL

Feminisms, Gender Studies, Activism
The Elusive Triad

The topic I have been asked to address, 'Feminism Gender Studies, Activism: The Elusive Triad', provides an opportunity for me to formally engage in the conversation about the crisis in 'feminist' politics. At the beginning of the twenty-first century, we must engage the protracted downturn in the 'feminist' and women's movement or movements since the 1980s and our failure as women's movements to secure and sustain the goals that we have set ourselves over these many years.

The conversations around 'feminist' politics take us back some 30 years at least, to the 1970s because the issues being raised today lead us to consider, among other things, some of the key differences between women's politics or, if you prefer, 'feminist' politics of that period and in the present. These might help us to understand aspects of our present dilemma.

Particularly since the 1980s, first structural adjustment policies and now globalism have taken their toll on the lives of the majority of citizens in our various Caribbean countries, and on women and children in particular. The increase in poverty, in crime and violence, including gender-based violence which is among the top three concerns of women in CARICOM Caribbean, is directly linked to the growing vulnerability that women and children in particular experience. Our men experience alienation and emotional insecurity and in many instances blame this on women. This is part of the male backlash which also is linked to the broader context that shapes the conversation about 'feminist' politics.

There is also the matter of our own responses as women inside our organisations to these developments. The two aspects are clearly linked but I treat them separately because personal choices, including political choices, govern our responses and as in all aspects of life, we have to take responsibility for the choices we make.

Although our women's organisations and movements have come up with varying strategies in the face of the continuing crisis, we have experienced in these organisations, a weakening of our capacity since the 1980s linked to a falling off in membership; reduced and unstable financial support; a slackening of internal control and accountability systems; heightened conflicts and tensions in interpersonal relations undermining cohesiveness and effectiveness nationally and regionally.[1] In Jamaica, for example, we have seen the implosion of the Association of Women's Organisations in Jamaica (AWOJA) which was formed with much enthusiasm in 1988 through the insight and initiative of the Mona Women and Development Studies Group. The Caribbean Association for Feminist Research and Action (CAFRA) has experienced, and has thankfully survived, the bitter internal struggles of the 1990s. Throughout the Caribbean, women can do a roll call of sharp conflicts within our organisations which have not been effectively managed and so unfortunately have led to a falling-off and falling-out among activist women. Organisationally, these are some of the expressions of the crisis in feminist politics over the past 15 years.

In 1998, Joycelin Massiah posed a pertinent question in the title of her presentation at the inaugural Lucille Mathurin Mair lecture: 'On the Brink of the New Millenium: Are Caribbean Women Prepared?' Her optimistic answer was – 'Yes, I believe that they are.' She, however, added: 'Institutional weaknesses may be still endemic and tensions and difficulties may yet be unresolved within the movement itself but a solid foundation has been built and strength has (been) gained in the building.'[2]

We cannot discount the gains that have been made and this conference clearly confirms that assessment. Unfortunately, however, the unresolved issues continue to weaken us organisationally. They render us unable (at this stage) to connect the many important issues being discussed here over these two days, with the key practical challenges of 'back to school', crime and violence, unemployment, poor access to water and sanitation, that are today at the heart of concerns among the majority of women in Jamaica and the Caribbean and globally.

My own view is that the absence of a defining ideological position, one that clearly articulates what we believe, who and what we defend, and that guides our organisational work, is at the heart of the crisis in 'feminist'/women's politics today. We have failed to establish a political grounding for our actions.

I started to reflect seriously on this issue from about 1999 when, for a period of five days, 26 women from the CARICOM countries came together to examine issues of women's leadership and to participate in gender training. We identified, as a shared concern, 'the need to clarify what is the underlying ideology/the conceptual framework influencing or guiding the work of women's organisations in the Caribbean' the importance of defining 'a Caribbean feminist perspective'.[3]

This issue has sharpened in my mind over the weeks of reflecting on the contradictions encoded in this challenging topic 'feminisms, gender studies, activism: the elusive triad'. This title, emerging from the conceptual and organisational framework of this conference, classically summarises, in my view, how the crisis in feminist politics is expressed in the Caribbean today.

My contribution to this conversation is therefore aimed at articulating a way of coming to terms with the elusiveness that has characterised 'feminist politics' for nearly two decades.

An important starting point for me is to revisit our understanding of feminism. The Caribbean Association for Feminist Research and Action (CAFRA), our regional feminist organisation, has defined feminism as 'understanding the relationship between the oppression of women and other forms of oppression in the society and... working actively for change'.[4] Andaiye quotes Rhoda Reddock, one of the founders of CAFRA, as she elaborated on this definition: 'For women's movement activists' Reddock asserts, 'the challenge is therefore not simply to remove male dominance, which, by the way, oppresses men as well as women, but the overall social and economic system of which it is a part'.[5] Bell hooks presents the spirit of this perspective in her straightforward definition: 'Feminism is a movement to end sexism, sexist exploitation and oppression' elaborated in her work, *Feminism is for Everybody*.[6]

The core principle inherent in these perspectives is that the feminist struggle embraces the struggle against all forms of subordination, exploitation and social exclusion on the basis of class, gender, race/ethnicity/colour, disability, age, sexual orientation. By these definitions, feminist politics embodies the struggle against women's subordination for gender equality, for social justice and social transformation. It posits a radical engagement for radical change in power relations in society.

Do we really agree with this definition? Is our feminist politics today consistent with that definition? One way to reflect on this is to examine comparatively, some aspects of our organisational experiences in the 1970s.

There is general agreement that the period of the 1970s into the 1980s, the decade of women (1976-1985), represented a particular high point of women's struggle in the Caribbean since the re-emergence of the feminist movement of the 1960s.[7] Feminist politics of the 1970s, 'within the counter-culture of the left' sought fundamental changes in the context of contemporary political realities globally, regionally and nationally.[8] In the Jamaican context, cold war politics and the anti-imperialist democratic socialist agenda of the People's National Party under the inspiring leadership of Michael Manley, critically supported by the communist Workers' Party of Jamaica, gave a sharp edge to left politics and to the allied women's agenda. This period of the late 1970s to the mid 1980s saw the mushrooming of women's organisations; a heightened activism of women in political parties of the left and the right; a high visibility of working class/grassroots women, active in their own organisations, and also working alongside middle-strata women. There was, in this context, a strong mobilisation of women for reform. Notable among these reforms was the winning of the Maternity Leave Law of 1979 which provided benefits for working women, including Household Workers. The emergence of an active left progressive women's organisation, the Committee of Women for Progress (CWP)/Organisation of Women for Progress (OWP) (1976-1992) played a central role within the main women's movement at the time.[9]

Maxine Henry, then a lecturer in the Department of Government, University of the West Indies, Mona, presented in a 1986 seminar, a paper titled, 'Women's Participation in the Social and Political Process in Jamaica in the 1970s'. In this, she analysed aspects of feminist politics of the period:

> In 1976 a more Marxist oriented feminist movement began to emerge. This group which was called the Committee of Women for Progress promoted women's policies

and issues within a similar context to that of the PNP Women's Movement. The Committee was integrally involved in consumer affairs and in advocating egalitarian legislations, training programmes and economic opportunities for women. Their philosophical perspective was, from the outset, far more radical and definitive than that of the PNP Women's Movement. They gave at least rhetorical recognition to and promoted more fundamental structural transformation as a prerequisite for any genuine liberation of women. They unequivocally defined the causation of women's deprivations as systemic. Their pronouncements, analyses and policies uncompromisingly identified the capitalist class as the enemy. Their educational publications were stridently opposed to the *status quo*. Yet the limits of reality and the need to make the organisation viable by defining achievable goals frequently dictated that the CWP embrace reformist tactics to 'ameliorate' the plight of women. They continually collaborated with the PNP Women's Movement and other less radical women's groups on legislative and programmatic issues, eg. demands for appointment of Voluntary Price Inspectors, National School Uniform and continuation of subsidy of basic foods and for their importation through the State Trading Corporation.[10]

I am not here going to comment on the Hon. Minister of Education, Mrs Maxine Henry-Wilson's assessment of the strategy and tactics of the CWP, nor make too large the political significance and pioneering role of the CWP in the commemoration of International Women's Day since 1978 and in the struggle for the Maternity Leave Law in 1979. Those will have their place in the continuing recording of Jamaican women's history.

I am really more interested in the first part of her presentation on the organisation's ideological perspective, namely its linking of the struggle for women's rights and emancipation (as we called it) and the struggle of the whole people, including men, against exploitation and oppression.

A second aspect of the CWP/OWP ideological perspective was in the organisation's conscious and explicit bias towards poor and working women. For the organisation declared its dedication 'to raising the consciousness, organisation and upliftment of all women – but first and foremost (of) working class and grassroots women who constitute the majority, who are the most oppressed and who have the greatest potential to bring about fundamental changes for women'.[11] The first ten years of the CWP/OWP saw the membership being overwhelmingly middle class and university trained and up to 1983 located only in Kingston. However by 1989 the majority of members were working-class and rural women participating through women's clubs and as individual members in 17 groups across seven parishes. It was this broadening and emergence of working class and rural membership and leadership that justified the change in name from Committee to Organisation of Women for Progress in 1986.

These two principles of the CWP/OWP's ideology – its understanding of the need for and commitment to systemic transformation and its explicit bias towards the poor and working class – was a clearing ground for its work with other organisations. They were the well with the right-wing conservative politics from the 1980s.

Our ideological perspective was in no way refined or complete – in fact there were glaring shortcomings, due, in my view, to the uncritical (some would say slavish) adherence to Marxist-Leninist analysis fed into the organisation from the Workers' Party of Jamaica through the influence of those of us who were members of the party. We were, for example, blind to the question of racial denigration of black people and the continuing manifestations of this among women.

Our ideology of 'emancipation' spoke to class but not to the racial denigration that persisted and still persists in the society; we did not explicitly discuss interpretations of 'brown-skin attitude' politics, or the 'black-chip-on-the-shoulder politics' which, from time to time, were raised as issues of concern within 'sensitivity sessions' in the confines of the women's section of the Workers' Party which in general guided the mass organisation.[12] However, these sessions were important spaces for discussing relationship issues between and among ourselves as women; they challenged us to grapple with painful questions of attitudes and behaviour in our political practice, consistent with what we said we believed.

Another area of weakness was in terms of confronting gender relations themselves. We understood and spoke about the subordination of women but our analysis was incomplete – we did not sufficiently analyse issues of subordination within the party structure itself, although some guidelines were developed around man-woman relations, mainly from the influence of the women's section. But this issue was in general not brought into the public life of the CWP and the broader struggles of women.[13]

And we did not call ourselves feminists. To be perfectly frank, I recall that there was, among some of us as WPJ women in the CWP, some suspicion about the proposed formation of CAFRA in 1985, the fear being that the organisation might signal the formation of a radical feminist turn in the women's movement and divert the focus from the class struggle.

However, in spite of these weaknesses and inconsistencies, the CWP/OWP's clear definition of its radical goal, helped to shape the tasks of important sections of the women's movement and the strategies related to those tasks. I believe that our perspectives as women of the left-influenced women like Joan Ffrench who was among the founders of CAFRA. To my mind, CWP/OWP's practice of politics, with all its flaws, is best reflected in CAFRA's definition of feminism and its stated understanding of feminist politics.

Is there agreement among us today that feminism is about a radical engagement for radical change? I think not – not even in CAFRA itself. When it was pointed out in a CAFRA policy paper that its definition 'calls for a broader approach to the analysis of oppression and thus to the process of acting to *change* society', an influential national representative of the organisation commented: 'While I agree with this interpretation, I wonder whether the general membership would accept this.'[14] This was in 1997.

Today our title speaks about feminisms and the question arises: what perspective and practice of 'feminist' politics are encoded in the title 'Feminisms, Gender Studies, Activism: The Elusive Triad?'

Feminisms

To speak about feminisms is to recognise political differences among women who all may subscribe to some aspect of what is defined as a feminist perspective. Typically in the literature, we have seen classification of feminist theories and applications in terms of liberal/reform feminism; radical feminism; marxist/socialist feminism; postmodern feminism. Kournay, Sterba & Tong are among the texts to which students are exposed in the feminist theory course here through the Centre for Gender and Development Studies.[15] This typology has gained currency because it has provided a manageable and convenient model into which to fit the complex ways in which women have actually responded to their multiple sources of oppression. This modelling has also supported the idea of multiple feminisms.

However, the discourse around these various philosophies, especially in the context of decline of the political radicalism of the 1970s, has also shaped what bell hooks calls 'life-style feminism' – the view that there can be 'as many versions of feminisms as there are women'. Her analysis of the feminist movement in the United States from the 1980s is also applicable to the Caribbean experience today in my view: 'Suddenly', she states 'the politics was being slowly removed from feminism. And the assumption prevailed that no matter what a woman's politics, be she conservative or liberal, she too could fit feminism into her existing lifestyle'.[16] Hooks further argues that 'advancing the notion that there can be many "feminisms" has served the conservative and liberal political interests of women seeking status and privileged class power. ... The representation of feminism as a life-style or a commodity automatically obscures the importance of feminist politics. Today many women want civil rights without feminism. They want the system of patriarchy to remain intact in the private sphere even as they desire equality in the public sphere.'[17]

Conversations about feminism(s) and feminists are characterised by unclarity about what we actually mean. Caribbean women across generations refuse to call themselves feminists – from a Dame Nita Barrow, to the young women across the Caribbean who were recently interviewed by students in the CGDS Distance Studies course which I taught earlier this year. If, indeed, most of us experience problems with the word 'feminism' and 'feminist', then we have to talk about what these are and establish some basic understanding of what we mean and defend. Not to do so is to deepen the crisis of identity which is part and parcel of the crisis in feminist politics today.

So back to basics: What do we mean by feminism or feminisms? What would we then believe as feminists – if this is indeed how we name ourselves!

Gender Studies

Gender Studies, we understand much better. Through the work of the feminist movement, 'gender' has become central to our analysis and understanding of the systemic nature of women's subordination. Exploring gender reveals the unequal power relations that are inherent in relations between men and women in the economic, political and social structures of most societies. Understanding these power relations that gender encodes, has been regarded as being fundamental to the strategies to advance the struggle for women's human rights and for social transformation, consistent with the 'feminist' vision. This was seen as part of the mission of Gender Studies in the academy.

However, this mission of gender studies has been subverted within and outside the academy, engendering, to quote Peggy Antrobus, 'the fall of feminist politics in the Caribbean'.[18] In her 2000 Lucille Mathurin Mair Lecture, Antrobus defined three stages in Caribbean women's politics; the first stage,1978-81, 'putting women on the agenda'; the second, 1982-1985, 'a search for alternatives' and the third stage, 1985-1995, characterised by a 'political feminist approach…and a search for a more development (sic) paradigm'. In her view, the fall of feminist politics has come in this latter period and has been manifested through a number of strategies, including *gender mainstreaming, gender analysis, and the substitution of the word "gender" for "women" in so many programmes.*[19] Peggy does not explicitly mention the UWI, but her analysis that Gender Studies has been itself re-politicised and infused with the institutional politics of development is relevant to our work in this institution.

It is not that these gender strategies are not significant in the broad framework of feminist politics, or are in themselves unworthy of 'feminists'. It is more that Gender Studies, as an academic discipline born of feminist activism, has in many instances and places been more concerned to build its legitimacy within the academy and serve development policy than to strengthen the capacity of women to struggle for themselves outside the academy and within the movement(s).

I recall that the debate to change from 'women' to 'gender' studies here at Mona in 1992 was quite heated and seemed to express a fear that has come to pass. On the one hand, proponents for naming it 'gender' studies were of the view that this was in keeping with the increasing acceptance of women's studies within the academy, signalled among other things by the appointment of Dr Elsa Leo-Rhynie as the first Professor of Gender Studies. Gender studies was therefore politically correct and would, in addition, it was assessed, propel academic studies to be more questioning of structures, of roles and relationships of men and women in society, including, it was hoped, structures within the university the itself.

Those who called for the retention of Women's Studies expressed fears that, in a context of the male backlash and the discourse around male marginalisation, the word 'gender' would distort the focus on women's oppression in society, and would obscure the reality that needs to be eradicated, that gender relations denote unequal power relations between men and women. The fear was that feminist discourse and political engagement, which had unmasked the gender system of patriarchy and its encasement in the cultural, economic, political and social system, would be undermined by gender professionalisation, and that, as a consequence, gender studies would lose the activist mission that women's studies had established when we believed that we wanted to understand the world in order to change it.

We acknowledge the flourishing of gender studies over these ten years within the University of the West Indies as indicated by the many important papers presented at this conference. At the same time, we note the concurrent downturn in women's political activism through their own formal organisations, including the experience within the Mona UWI Women's Group itself. The question we should ponder is this – is there a disconnection of Gender Studies from its feminist and activist roots?

Which brings us to the third component of our analysis of our title: *activism*.

Activism

Activism is agency, in this context, women's agency (individual and collective) to confront subordination and oppression and to effect change and transformation. That agency for transformation can be invisible – located inside that individual woman – until it moves, if it will, into networks in family, community; in small or larger groups, to express itself in organisations, informal or formal.

Our activism as Caribbean women from the days of our enslavement and into the post-slave-colonial period, has been embodied in the lives of countless women un-named – nurturers, healers, workers fighters like Queen Nanny, and into post-slave emancipation into the present, women – black and Indian, Garifuna and Mayan, mestizo, coloured, white women standing for space and place, for autonomy and for identity about beauty and hair and clothes and Black Power and citizenship. Activism has embraced a search for comfort and balance with and within the self, about staying at roots and family and 'not forgetting where you coming from' as my mother had warned me.

While we may not know when and where it starts, we know the destiny of feminist activism; we know that activism is political agency for change; it is of the foundation of feminism and gender studies; it is the engine for change and transformation. Yet, politically, activism is subordinated in the hierarchy of the triad. Its place reflects the distancing of brain and brawn; of the academy and the community/NGOs; of theory and action. Its place in the scheme of our work and priority mirrors the marginalisation of analysis of community activism and its relationship with feminist politics as an integral issue on the agenda of this conference.

Feminist scholars Jacqui Alexander and Chandra Mohany tell us of the importance they attach in their work to linking theory and practice through their own location 'within communities of women' and to 'feminist communities in struggle'.[20] From this positioning, they express a hope that their work will establish the basis for a much wider discussion on these themes and relationships. Such connection between activist research and theorising can yield for us a new level of understanding of what political activism within community organisations can accomplish. It can make visible the work of women who are usually ignored in academic feminist theorising. Such work, also, according to Nancy Naples, helps women to reconcile their feminist and activist identities and provide lessons on the possibilities and challenges of organising across differences of race and class.[21]

It is our failure to apply our understanding of organising across differences of class and race, our failure to 'connect hierarchies' in our organising, that, in the view of Andaiye, is at the root of the problem in feminist politics in the Caribbean. She asserts, 'In the form and practice of organizing in the 1980s and later, we studiously ignored the power relations among women, thereby allowing us, women with more power (however derived) to dominate or exclude – consciously or not, deliberately or not-it does not matter'.[22]

The fact is, there was no explicit and shared agreement that the interests of poor and working class women would be primary; that examining issues of power among us would be part of our politics.

Community activism (not the same thing as outreach) has been divorced from feminist theorising. Research and teaching is an example of this lack of specific commitment to a radical ideological position. Yet women seem to be calling for this. According to CAFRA, a 'recurrent theme in Caribbean feminism' is 'the extent to which feminism does not have a grassroots orientation'.[23] This is indeed a matter of continuing concern among women across the Caribbean, including young women.

Other issues of exclusion relate to the marginal space allowed the experience of East Indian women in the movement, and we could add of Garifuna and Mayan women, Carib and other indigenous women, and white women as well as to lesbians. Weaknesses include black women's experience from a perspective of racial exclusion in the historical and contemporary setting; nor has it spoken to activism, mediated by race and ethnicity. However, problems of exclusion are not at root questions of strategy, but of political perspective, of ideology. They point to a perspective that is not grounded in the foundational tenets of feminism that are inherent in the CAFRA definition of feminism. They are reflective of the 'knot around power' which Eudine Barriteau challenged us to confront in recentring Caribbean feminism,[24] because we are not sure whether and how we can or should confront power relations that exist for example, among women.

There are those among our academic colleagues who insist that the demarcation between gender studies and community-based activism is false because academic research and teaching themselves constitute 'scholarly activism'. This may well be the case. The question is – what do we use to judge and who is to judge? Could the present generation of students point to an answer? According to Patricia Mohammed, the teaching of Gender Studies at the campus level introduces many students 'to the feminist movement and to feminism which to them appears to be another dying ism along with socialism, Marxism, communism and (in) this day and age, perhaps idealism itself'.[25]

One way to judge is to ask: are our students being 'touched moved and inspired' to take action? Another is to evaluate the extent to which we are at all engaged in activist research defined as 'empowering the powerless, exposing the inequities of the status quo, and promoting social changes that equalize the distribution of resources'. In Francesca Cancian's view, 'researchers will be more effective in challenging inequality insofar as they emphasize major changes in equalizing power, as opposed to improving services for the disadvantaged within the existing power structure, and they incorporate collective action into their research instead of restricting themselves solely to academic analysis, i.e. they include "practice" as well as "theory".'[26]

To my mind, another way to judge whether our academic research and teaching are activist is to determine whether they perpetuate the false separation between the academy and the community and whether the research is done *on* women or *for* women.

Now to summarise the examination of the crisis in feminist politics from the imagery of the 'elusive triad', we must recall that a triad refers to a 'group of three'; for example, in relation to music, three notes in a chord – typically the first, third and fifth notes of the musical scale (doh, me, soh). Sung together, played together, there is balance, integration, concord, harmony. But being elusive means that balance, integration and harmony are 'difficult to find, catch or remember' to quote the Oxford dictionary's meaning of elusive.

Our title therefore clearly alerts us to the fact that, despite the commendable achievements we celebrate, there remains a disconnection in our understanding and application of feminism, gender studies and activism as core principles and pillars of feminist politics, as a radical engagement for change. In other words, our politics, that should support the struggle for women's emancipation and social transformation, is characterised by discordance. Put yet another way, we are not sure where we are going or where we want to go or should be going and therefore unsure of how to build coherence in our politics as women.

Defining an Ideological Position

First, to say that where the movement goes and its ideological position, are a matter of choice – personal, individual choice about what each of us stands for, defends and will do in terms of our political engagement in the women's or feminist struggle. We have to move from this to a situation in which our organisations come to an agreed position on whether our project is directed to continuing our search for liberal reforms within the existing framework of globalism in which the majority of women and men are actually getting more vulnerable and marginalised or whether it is directed to radical change and social transformation of existing systems and relations.

This conference celebrating the achievements of ten years of the CGDS, must be a marking for the continuation of these conversations on the meaning of our political engagement as women and feminists and how we move forward.

Holding an Explicit Bias towards the Poor

I believe that the grounding of our ideological position should be derived from our understanding that the struggle of women globally for self-definition and self-determination, and that freedom from oppression, is linked to that of men whose potential as human beings, is also linked to the search for economic and social justice, for transformation in our societies.

As Caribbean women, our history and culture must inform the course of our struggle, and that is why we must also commit and hold an explicit bias towards the interests of the poor – the grassroots women and men and children in our region in the urban and rural areas whose potential continues to be blighted by poverty, injustice and under-privilege and a history of exclusion.

Take the case of the over 30 per cent of working women who make their living in Jamaica as domestic workers. In the main, many of us here, as employers, are part of the system that blights their prospects, as a recent report on the Jamaica Household Workers' Association attests. I am curious to find out, *inter alia*, why in four years (1998-2002) only 96 household workers applied for maternity leave and what, as employers and political activists, we can do to open the spaces for the economic and social advancement of women in this occupational category as for ourselves. I believe that until we commit to the strengthening of the organisational capacity and autonomy of domestic workers, individually and collectively, we cannot, as women of the middle strata, begin to effectively grapple with questions of relations among ourselves – a matter of great concern among women.

Partnership with Community

But libratory political activism will not and cannot become a force in the work of our organisations unless it is established and shaped through our transformational interaction with the broader community. Whether and how we engage with poor communities is a choice for the CGDS, as for other sections of women's movements. However, the CGDS in particular, coming out of this conference, is encouraged to seriously reflect on and determine its vision and goal and design mechanisms to build stronger relations for accountability, responsiveness to and partnership with the agenda of the wider community of women's and feminist organisations across the region.

A related aspect of this activist thrust should be to determine the ideological line of march for the CGDS itself within the academy into the next decade through a process that engages students and faculty within the academy and engages partners and potential partners, and women's and men's organisations in the wider community.

This will require that we get back to the basics of explorations and consciousness-raising among women and men which should be combined with organisation-building, with special attention to the rebuilding of the Mona campus women's group.

How can we 'touch, move and inspire' our students to take action on these issues? How can we engage in activist research that is 'empowering the powerless, exposing the inequities of the status quo, and promoting social changes that equalize the distribution of resources';[27] research done not *on women* but *for women* and their families? That is a challenge of our time.

Confronting Internalised Oppression

We must seek renewal in our relationships with each other; we must start by critically looking at ourselves individually. This means that wherever we are, we have to become more self-critical and more committed to renewal in all aspects. We need spaces and mechanisms that help us to be more sensitive and honest and forthright in our dealings with one another. Our research urgently needs to look at these relationship issues also.

We have to get our own house, our own organisations and movements in order against the bad-minded competitiveness, the long-run malice-keeping, the 'judgementalism', the gate-keeping that lets in our friends and keeps out others – traits and practices that are in all of us and show up themselves – despite our best efforts.

This in my view calls for a new kind of leadership: transformational leadership. This is leadership that engages the power that is in all of us to make the transformation that we all say we want to make; leadership that builds on the power to create with others, not power over others. Being a part of such a process will bring the passion to end the crime and violence, including sexual violence being inflicted on us by our own sons…and brothers…and partners.

Transformational Leadership

Transformational leadership does not demand conformity, but seeks to build on what each brings. For some of us see it as a disgrace that so many women and children do not, in our countries, have access to basic rights and services like potable water and decent sanitation; others of us want to be part of the movement to get our countries to feed ourselves by a revolution in agriculture; some of us might want to focus on what others of us see as a human rights agenda; others might focus on welfarism.

Regardless of the definitions and labelling, transformational leadership must be directed towards creatively linking the multiple women's and feminist agendas that seem to pull us into so many directions, to enable us to grasp the common links that unite us in order to move forward in the interest of the majority of women and men and to promote gender and social equity.

Coming out of this present conference, we need to move to examine these issues before we get swamped and busy on the next 'event'. That is why it is important to see this conference as part of the process towards the new agenda for CGDS and the wider community.

There is much to do and, Sisters and Brothers, many of us are beginning to wonder how any of this fits into the next research project, into the next book...into making more money. And there is nothing bad about any of that, but Friends, the truth is, this is also a time to get back to base and to strengthen our commitment to lift as we ourselves climb. So let us think on it, but more so, let's do it. Our future depends upon it.

Notes

1. *A Profile of Civil Society in Jamaica*. Prepared by Janet Cupidon Quallo for the Inter-American Development Bank (IDB), Jamaica. May 2003, pp. 23-24.
2. Joycelin Massiah, 'On the Brink of the New Millenium: Are Caribbean Women Prepared?' *The 1998 Lucille Mathurin Mair Lecture*. Centre for Gender and Development Studies, University of the West Indies.
3. See Women in Development Europe (WIDE) and the Association of Women's Organisations in Jamaica (AWOJA) *REPORT, Caribbean Regional Workshop*, April 18-24, 1999, p. 38. Other concerns were 'having space for personal development; to a revival of women's groups and women's movements; the declining representation of males in higher education; and conflicts among women and within women's organisations.'
4. Carol Narcisse, 'Gender and Societal Transformation: A Policy Document of the Caribbean Association for Feminist Research and Action' (CAFRA, 1996), 46.
5. Andaiye, 'The Angle You Look From Determines What You See: Towards a Critique of Feminist Politics in the Caribbean', *The Lucille Mathurin Mair Lecture 2002* (Centre for Gender and Development Studies, University of the West Indies, 2002), 9-10.
6. bell hooks, *Feminism is for Everybody: Passionate Politics*, (Cambridge, MA: South End Press, 2000)
7. See Rhoda Reddock, 'Women Organisations and Movements in the Commonwealth Caribbean: The Response to Global Economic Crisis in the 1980s', *Rethinking Caribbean Difference. Feminist Review* No. 59, (Summer 1998): 57-71. Also Patricia Mohammed, *Stories In Caribbean Feminism: Reflections on the Twentieth Century*. Fifth Anniversary

Lecture, Centre for Gender & Development Studies, University of the West Indies, St Augustine, 1998.
8. See Amelia Valcarcel, 'The collective memory and challenges of feminism'. Women and Development Unit, ECLAC, Santiago, Chile, 2002.
9. The Committee of Women for Progress was renamed Organisation of Women for Progress in 1986.
10. Maxine Henry, 'Women's Participation in the Social and political Process in Jamaica in the 1970s'. Department of Government, University of the West Indies, 1986.
11. Organisation of Women for Progress. *3 Year Development Plan, 1989-1992.*
12. See Linnette Vassell, 'Women and Political Parties'. (Presentation at) WAND, Barbados, 1988.
13. See some perspectives on CWP/OWP from Judith Soares, 'Women and Revolutionary Politics: The Case of the Workers Party of Jamaica', in *Forging identities and pattern of development in Latin America and the Caribbean*, ed. Harry P. Diaz et al. (Toronto: Canadian Scholars Press, 1991), 157-167.
14. See Carol Narcisse, and Ann-Marie Bonner, 'Comments on Gender and Societal Transformation Prepared by Carol Narcisse', May 10, 1997.
15. Janet A. Kourany, James P. Sterba and Rosemarie Tong, *Feminist Philosophies: Problems, Theories and Applications* (New Jersey: Prentice Hall, 1992).
16. hooks, *Feminism is for Everybody,* 5-6.
17. Ibid., 114.
18. Peggy Antrobus, 'The Rise and fall of Feminist Politics in the Caribbean Women's Movement 1975-1995', *The Lucille Mathurin Mair Lecture 2000.* Centre for Gender and Development Studies, University of the West Indies, 2000.
19. Antrobus, 'The Rise and Fall of Feminist Politics', 25.
20. M. Jacqui Alexander and Chandra Mohanty, *Feminist Genealogies, Colonial Legacies, Democratic Futures* (New York and London: Routlege, 1997), xx.
21. Nancy A. Naples, 'Women's Community Activism and Feminist Activist Research', in *Community Activism and Feminist Politics.* (New York and London: Routlege, 1998), 1-27.
22. Andaiye, 'The Angle You Look From', 11.
23. CAFRA News, 2002.
24. Violet Eudine Barriteau, 'Issues and Challenges of Caribbean Feminisms'. Key Note Address – Caribbean Feminisms Workshop: Recentering Caribbean Feminism . June 17, 2002. University of the West Indies, Cave Hill Campus.

25. Patricia Mohammed, *Stories In Caribbean Feminism: Reflections on the Twentieth Century*. Fifth Anniversary Lecture, Centre for Gender & Development Studies, University of the West Indies, St Augustine, 1998, p.24.
26. Quoted in Naples, 1998, p. 24.
27. Quoted in Naples, 1998, p. 24.

List of Contributors

Peggy Antrobus, a visionary force in the feminist struggle and a key figure in the setting up of the Women's Bureau in Jamaica and the Women and Development Unit in the School of Continuing Studies, UWI, Cave Hill, holds a BA in Economics from the University of Bristol and a PhD in Education from the University of Massachusetts, Amherst. She is a founding member of Development Alternatives for Women of a New Era (DAWN), serving as its General Coordinator from 1990-1996. She was a 1998 Dame Nita Barrow Distinguished Visitor at the OISE, University of Toronto, and has published widely on women and gender studies, development policies, economics and human rights. She has served as consultant and policy adviser to various international agencies and Caribbean governments.

Barbara Bailey is Professor and Regional Coordinator of the Centre for Gender and Development Studies (CGDS), University of the West Indies (UWI). She was formerly specialist lecturer in Curriculum Studies in the School of Education, UWI, Mona, Jamaica. Professor Bailey's recent teaching and research focus has been on Gender and Education Studies, with particular emphasis on the relationship of educational outputs to outcomes in the economic, social and political spheres for both genders. She has published several related articles, including 'Gender and Education in Jamaica: What About the Boys?' published in the UNESCO monograph series, *Education for All in the Caribbean: Assessment 2000*. Professor Bailey has been part of the International Women's Movement for the past two decades.

Wilma Bailey is Professor of Medical Geography at the Mona Campus of the UWI where she teaches courses in Bio-geography, and Health and Society. While seconded to The Sir Arthur Lewis Institute for Social and Economic Studies (SALISES), Professor Bailey was Chief Investigator in a Ford-funded project on reproductive health. So far, 13 published monographs and papers have been based on this project. These include 'Gender and the Family in the Caribbean', 'Gender, Contest and Conflict in the Caribbean', 'Street Culture' and the 'Decay of Community'. The research team received the Principal's Award for distinguished research for 2002. Her current research focus is on HIV/AIDS and education, gender differentials in education and health utilisation.

V. Eudine Barriteau is Senior Lecturer and Head of the Centre for Gender and Development Studies, UWI, Cave Hill Campus, Barbados. She is the author of *The Political Economy of Gender in the Twentieth Century Caribbean* (2001). She has published several articles including 'Confronting Power and Politics: Feminist Theorizing of Gender in Commonwealth Caribbean Societies' in *Meridians: Feminism, Race, Transnationalism* 3:2 and 'Women Entrepreneurs and Economic Marginality: Rethinking Caribbean Women's Economic Relations' in *Gendered Realities: Essays in Caribbean Feminist Thought* (2002) edited by Patricia Mohammed. She is currently coordinating three Research Projects that collectively examine Caribbean political economy and social change from the perspective of gender. She is the inaugural Dame Nita Barrow Women in Development Fellow, OISE, University of Toronto.

June Ann Castello, a trained teacher, has a Bachelor's degree as well as an MSc in Gender and Development Studies. She has worked in education for many years both as a teacher and as an administrator. She is currently employed as a Lecturer in the UWI's Mona Unit of the CGDS, teaching courses in Gender and Caribbean Culture, Men and Masculinities in the Caribbean and (at the graduate level) Sex, Gender and the Family. Her research interest is gender and religion

Suzanne Charles, who holds a BSc (Hons.) degree as well as the Dip IR and MSc, is currently attached to the Mona Unit, CGDS, UWI, as a Research Assistant. Her research interests include the feminist agenda in International Relations, Caribbean (homo)sexuality, the creation of an authentic Caribbean self identity and child rearing practices.

Carolyn Cooper is Professor of Literary and Cultural Studies at the UWI's Mona Campus where she teaches Caribbean, African and African-American literature. She also coordinates the university's embryonic Reggae Studies Unit, an academic project she initiated. Professor Cooper is the author of *Noises in the Blood: Orality, Gender and the 'Vulgar' Body of Jamaican Popular Culture* (1993) and *Border Clash: Jamaican Dancehall Culture at Large* (forthcoming, 2004).

Michelle V. Davis is currently a CUSO co-operant/Research Assistant at the Regional Coordinating Unit, CGDS at the UWI, Mona. Her work at the centre includes acting as one of two researchers for the United Nations Development Fund for Women's (UNIFEM's) Transformational Leadership Programme and the 'Root Causes of Gender-Based Violence in Jamaica' research project. She is also co-authoring a chapter on teen life in Jamaica for Greenwood Publishers, contributing to a gender-training module for use in the Caribbean, and a study guide for the course, Research Methods and Interactive Skills. She has worked in the area of HIV/AIDS for the past seven years and in several countries, including Jamaica where she is a member of the Education Sub-Committee of the National AIDS Committee.

Marjan de Bruin is the new director of CARIMAC (Caribbean Institute of Media and Communication) and the first woman to be appointed to that position. She has been with CARIMAC for 16 years, most of them as head of the Print Journalism Department. Before coming to Jamaica, she was editor of a Dutch weekly. She holds a PhD in Social Psychology from the University of Amsterdam.

She is currently vice president of the International Association of Media and Communication Research (IAMCR) and editor of its journal. Her publications include articles in refereed journals, monographs and a forthcoming book (*Identities at Work*, co-edited with Professor Karen Ross, Hampton Press, USA). She is on the Editorial Board of *Feminist Media Studies*.

Leith L. Dunn, a social scientist, holds a PhD from the London School of Economics and Political Science, a Bachelor's degree (Hons.) in Languages and Social Sciences and an MSc in Sociology and Social Psychology from the UWI. She has been a part time lecturer at the UWI Mona for a number of years, teaching at the Caribbean Institute of Media and Communication, the Regional Coordinating Unit of the CGDS and the University Hospital of the West Indies. She also served as acting regional coordinator for the CGDS Regional Coordinating Unit for the 2000-2001 academic year. Dr Dunn has conducted child labour studies in several Caribbean countries for the ILO and has completed several research publications on child-related issues for international agencies and organisations. She served as an adviser to the Commonwealth Foundation between 1988 and 1999 and as a member of the Commonwealth Observer Group for the 2002 Presidential elections in Zimbabwe. Along with Hopeton Dunn, she has co-authored *People and Tourism: Issues and Attitudes in the Jamaican Hospitality Industry* (2002).

Fay Durrant assumed the positions of Professor and Head of the UWI Department of Library and Information Studies in August 2000. She was an elected director of the Association of Caribbean States for a three-year term from 1997 to 2000, and senior programme specialist at the International Development Research Centre (IDRC) 1989–1997. She is a member of the ACURIL Executive Council, the Executive Committee of the Library and Information Association of Jamaica (LIAJA), the board of the Jamaica Sustainable Development Network (JSDN), the Archives Advisory Committee and the Board of the National Library of Jamaica. She also served as a member of the Board of the National Library and Information System (NALIS) of Trinidad and Tobago from 1999 to 2000.

Her recent work includes: 'Knowledge Management in the context of E-government' presented at the Caribbean Regional Ministerial Consultation and High Level Workshop on E-Government, Information and Communication Technologies which was published in *Public Sector Management* (December 2001) and the *Telecentres in Jamaica* report for the Jamaica National Commission for UNESCO (February 2002).

Mark Figueroa is a lecturer in the Department of Economics, UWI, Mona. His research interests include aspects of the relationship between the economy and its sociocultural and natural environment. In the early 1980s, he was a founding member of the UWI's Women's Studies Group at Mona. More recently, he has written a number of papers on gender and socioeconomic outcomes focusing especially on the relationship between historic male privileging and the changing patterns of gender achievement in education. In exploring what he has called the dialectic of gender privileging, he has provided an alternative to those perspectives that have been linked to concepts of male marginalisation and male victimisation. His publications include: 'Making Sense of Male Experience: The Case of Academic Underachievement in the English-speaking Caribbean' in *IDS Bulletin* 31:2 (April 2000) and 'Gender Privileging and Socio-Economic Outcomes: The Case of Health and Education in Jamaica' in *Gender and the Family in the Caribbean* (1988) edited by Wilma Bailey.

Maxine Henry-Wilson is currently the Minister of Education, Youth & Culture, having been appointed to this position in October 2002. She holds an undergraduate degree from the UWI and graduate degrees from UWI and Rutgers. She has lectured at the UWI, has been Minister of State in the Ministry of Finance and Planning, served as Minister Without Portfolio and Minister of Information in the Office of the Prime Minister. She has also served as a Government Senator, specifically, as Leader of Government Business in the Upper House. She is also the Member of Parliament for South Eastern St Andrew. She is married with a daughter.

Gabrielle J. Hosein is currently a PhD student in the Department of Anthropology at University College, London. She completed her MPhil at the CGDS at the UWI, St Augustine Campus with a thesis titled 'Gender, Generation and Negotiation among Young Indian Females in Trinidad'. She has been involved in stimulating feminist activism among young women in Trinidad over the last few years. She is also a Trinidadian performance poet and has recorded with a group of young female performers who perform under the label "10 Sisters".

Elsa Leo-Rhynie, Professor of Gender and Development Studies at the UWI, was appointed Pro Vice Chancellor and Chair of the Board for Undergraduate Studies at the UWI in August 2002. Prior to this, she served as Deputy Principal of the Mona Campus, Regional Coordinator of the CGDS, UWI, Executive Director of the Institute of Management and Production, and lecturer and senior lecturer in the Faculty of Education for ten years. Professor Leo-Rhynie has carried out research and published extensively in the areas of gender, education and training. She has directed projects for government and international agencies, and has also successfully undertaken consultancy assignments across the Caribbean region. She sits on a number of boards and foundations involved in education, and chairs the Dudley Grant Memorial Trust that advocates on behalf of early childhood education in Jamaica.

Linden Lewis is Associate Professor of Sociology at Bucknell University. He has written extensively on issues of gender, race, labour and globalisation in the Caribbean. He is Editor of the forthcoming anthology, *The Culture of Gender and Sexuality in the Caribbean* that will be published by The University Press of Florida. His work has appeared in such journals as *Feminist Review, Race and Class, Beyond Law* and the *Journal of Black Studies*. He has also contributed numerous book chapters to anthologies on gender, nationalism and politics.

Joycelin Massiah has for four decades been involved in every aspect of Caribbean society. A Demographer, she received her training at the UWI where she enjoyed an illustrious career, including being the first female professor appointed in the Faculty of Social Sciences. Her pioneering work on women in the Caribbean has had far-reaching effects on Caribbean scholarship in the field of women and development and on women's rights activism in the region. She has been the Regional Programme Director of the UNIFEM Caribbean Office for the past ten years. Her dynamic leadership there contributed to a successful outcome for the Caribbean at the 4th World Conference on Women in Beijing in 1995. Among her many awards have been the Gold Crown of Merit, the third highest award of Barbados, in 1998, and the sixth CARICOM Triennial Award for Women in 1999.

Hermione C. McKenzie, Sociologist and Senior Lecturer in the UWI Mona's Department of Sociology, Psychology and Social Work, is a graduate of the London School of Economics and Brandeis University.

She has published widely on issues relating to gender, family, family planning, education and social development policies. She has prepared numerous reports for government, statutory and private sector organisations on issues ranging from family planning and community development to socioeconomic development in Jamaica and the wider Caribbean. She has served as a member of several organisations such as the Jamaica Council of Voluntary Social Services. She has contributed significantly to the women's movement in the Caribbean, serving as a member of the Jamaican delegation to the UN's 'End-of-Decade Conference' on Women in Nairobi in 1985 and as former convenor of the Women's Studies Working Group at the UWI, Mona.

Errol L. Miller has been Professor of Teacher Education in the Institute of Education, UWI, Mona since January 1981. He is a former Principal of Mico Teachers' College, Past President of the Jamaica Teachers' Association, former Permanent Secretary of the Ministry of Education and, from 1984 to 1989, Independent Senator in the Jamaican Parliament. He is the author of several books on gender including: *Marginalisation of the Black Male*, *Men at Risk*, and *The Prophet and the Virgin: The Masculine and Feminine Roots of Teaching*. He has also written numerous articles and book chapters on the issues of gender, education and the family. Professor Miller is chairman and member of several Boards related to public service in Jamaica and the Caribbean and is the current Chairman of the Electoral Advisory Committee in Jamaica. He has been the recipient of a number of awards and honours for public service and contribution to education in the Caribbean including two Fulbright Fellows for Senior Academics to Universities in the United States, the Jamaican national honour, Commander of the Order of Distinction, and the UWI's, Vice Chancellor's Award for Excellence.

Patricia Mohammed, former head of the Mona Unit of the CGDS, is Senior Lecturer at the CGDS, UWI, St Augustine Campus. She has been involved in both feminist activism and scholarship for over two decades. Her academic publications include *Gender Negotiations among Indians in Trinidad, 1917–1947* (2001) and the edited collection *Gendered Realities* (2002). She was also guest editor of *Rethinking Caribbean Difference*, a Special Issue of *Feminist Review* (Routledge

Journals Summer 1998), co-author with Althea Perkins of *Caribbean Women at the Crossroads* (1998) and co-editor with Catherine Shepherd of *Gender in Caribbean Development* (1988). She has published numerous essays in journals and books, magazines and newspapers. She recently completed a two-year Mona Campus Research fellowship with a manuscript entitled 'Imaging the Caribbean', which is to be published in book format as well as a documentary film.

Jeanette Morris holds an MA from the University of Edinburgh, an MSc from Georgetown University, and an MA Ed and PhD from the UWI. She is a senior lecturer in the School of Education at the UWI's St Augustine Campus and has been Head of the School for the past five years. She lectures in the Teaching of Modern Languages and Qualitative Research Methods. She was a former coordinator of the Women and Development Studies group at St Augustine. Her research interests and publications are in the areas of gender and education, foreign language education and qualitative research methods.

Velma Pollard is a retired Senior Lecturer who taught in Language Education in the Department of Educational Studies in the Faculty of Arts and Education, UWI, Mona. Her major research interests have been Creole Languages of the Anglophone Caribbean and the Language of Caribbean Literature and Caribbean Women's Writing. She has published a handbook: *From Jamaican Creole to Standard English: A Handbook for Teachers* (1994) and a monograph, *Dread Talk: The Language of Rastafari* (1994, 2000). Dr Pollard is involved in creative writing and has published poems and stories in regional and international journals and anthologies. Her novella, *Karl*, won the Casa de las Americas prize in 1992. Her other creative publications include *The Best Philosophers I Know Cant Read and Write* (2001), *Homestretch* (1994), *Considering Woman* (1989) and *Crown Point and Other Poems* (1988).

Rhoda Reddock is Professor and Head of the CGDS at the UWI's St Augustine Campus. She has a PhD in Applied Social Sciences from the University of Amsterdam, is an activist in the Caribbean Women's movement and a founding member of the Caribbean Association for Feminist Research and Action (CAFRA). She has numerous publications including *Women, Labour and Politics in Trinidad and Tobago: A History* (1994) which was named a CHOICE Outstanding Academic Book for 1996; (ed) *Ethnic Minorities in Caribbean Society* (1998); (co-edited with Shobhita Jain) *Plantation Women: International Experiences* (1998) and (co-edited with Christine Barrow) *Caribbean Sociology: Introductory Readings* (2001). Her research interests include Caribbean women's history, race/ethnicity, class and gender and masculinities and sexualities. In 2001, Professor Reddock received the 7th Triennial CARICOM Award for Women and the UWI Vice Chancellor's Award for Excellence in Teaching, Research, Outreach and Administration.

Tracy Robinson is a Lecturer in the Faculty of Law, UWI, Cave Hill Campus. She teaches Gender and the Law, Family Law, Constitutional Law and Administration of Trusts and Estates. She is the editor of the *Caribbean Law Bulletin*, a journal devoted to examining contemporary legal issues in the Caribbean region. Her publications cover areas including family law reform, citizenship, domestic violence and sexual harassment.

Michelle Rowley received her PhD in Women's Studies from Clark University, Worcester, MA. Her doctoral dissertation is entitled 'The Politics of (M)Othering: Maternal Centrality and Afro-Trinidadian Women's Subjectivities'. Her present research interests include issues of reproductive rights, gender planning and policy formulation, and cultural constructions of Caribbean femininity. She is currently on staff at the CGDS, UWI, Cave Hill Campus.

Verene A. Shepherd, Professor of Social History at the UWI, is the second woman to hold a professorship in the Mona History Department, the first being Elsa Goveia. She has contributed to the advancement of Women's History in the History Department, helping to develop the course 'Women and Gender in the History of the English-speaking Caribbean' which she has taught since 1993. She chaired the organising committee of the first ever gender history symposium held at the UWI in 1993 (in which the CGDS collaborated) out of which came *Engendering History: Caribbean Women in Historical Perspective* (1995). She compiled *Women in Caribbean History* (1999) on behalf of the Mona

History Department's Social History Project, which she directed from 1993-1996; and, while a Board member of the CGDS, initiated the idea of the Lucille Mathurin Mair Lecture Series. She has authored two books focused on the Indian diaspora in the Caribbean and has edited/ co-edited seven other books including *Working Slavery, Pricing Freedom: Perspectives from the Caribbean, Africa and the African Diaspora* (2002) and *Slavery without Sugar: Diversity in Caribbean Economy and Society Since the 17th Century* (2002).

Grace Sirju-Charran has been a Lecturer in Botany in the Department of Plant Science, UWI, St Augustine Campus since 1978. She gained a BSc (Gen. Double First Class Honours) in Chemistry and Botany from the UWI, St Augustine in 1971 and the PhD in Agriculture from the UWI in 1978. She has been the recipient of several awards and fellowships including the UWI Cable and Wireless Fellowship-Distance Education and a Senior Fulbright Award, University of Minnesota, St Paul's Campus. Her current research involves, among other things, Gender Issues in Agriculture and Science and Technology. She was a member of the Board of Government of the National Institute of Higher Education (Research and Technology) – NIHERST – between 1994 and 1997. She has also been a member of the Women in Caribbean Agriculture, Advisory Committee of the Caribbean Association of Feminist Research and Action (CAFRA) and Coordinator of the Women and Development Studies Group (WDSG) UWI, St Augustine.

Orville W. Taylor is Lecturer in Sociology at the University of the West Indies, Mona, and received the first PhD in Sociology from Florida International University. A member of the (American) Association of Black Sociologists, he has written several articles and book chapters on the subject of race, the African Diaspora and labour studies and has presented more than 20 conference papers in both Spanish and English. An external collaborator with the International Labour Organization (ILO), and former Senior Director of Industrial Relations in the Ministry of Labour and Social Security in Jamaica, he is a specialist in international labour standards and has produced several country and regional reports. His most recent publications are the co-edited *Tourism and Change in the Caribbean and Latin America* (2002) and an edited special issue of

IDEAZ entitled, *Re-Thinking and Re-Searching our Blackness* (2003), both published by Arawak Publishers and 'Globalization, Racism and The Terrorist Threat: An Afro-Caribbean Response' in Malveaux and Green's controversial, *Paradox of Loyalty: An African American Response to the War on Terrorism* (2002), launched on Black Entertainment Television (BET). His *Thirty Years of Industrial Conflict in Jamaica* is forthcoming.

Winsome Townsend holds an MSc in Agricultural and Rural Development, a Postgraduate Diploma in Science Education, and a BSc in Natural Sciences – Pure and Applied Chemistry. She is employed to the National Environment and Planning Agency as its Director of Policies, Programmes and Projects. She has served at the Jamaica Agricultural Development Foundation as Research Associate and at the Scientific Research Council as a Senior Technical Information Officer. She has studied gender issues in environmental change and her master's thesis was titled 'Identifying the Prospects of an Environmental Organisation Becoming More Gender Responsive'. Mrs Townsend has had vast experience in the fields of project management, policy analysis and environmental and sustainable development. She enjoys reading and excursions into the countryside.

Linnette Vassell, MPhil History, a graduate of the UWI, Mona, where, from the 1980s into the 1990s she taught Caribbean History, including Women's History, is part of that generation of women who have been associated with the struggle for women's rights in the region since the 1970s. She was the first coordinator of the Committee of Women for Progress (CWP) a left wing activist organisation formed in 1976 which was among the pioneering organisations for the struggle for maternity leave with pay for women. She is also a member of Caribbean Association for Feminist Research and Action (CAFRA), Gender and Water Alliance, a global network of organisations, and the Board of the Small Business Association of Jamaica. Linnette Vassell is currently involved in graduate teaching at the UWI Mona's CGDS. Her publications include: 'Power, Governance and the Structure of Opportunity for Women in Decision-Making in Jamaica' in *The Construction of Gender Development Indicators for Jamaica* (PIOJ/UNDP/CIDA, 2000) edited by Patricia Mohammed; 'Colonial Gender Policy in Jamaica, 1865-1944' in *Before and After 1865:*

Education, Politics and Regionalism in the Caribbean (1998) edited by Brian Moore and Swithin Wilmot; 'Women of the Masses: Daphne Campbell and "Left" Politics in Jamaica in the 1950s' in *Engendering History*, and *Voices of Women in Jamaica 1898-1939*, a compilation of writings and speeches of women (1993), edited by Verene Shepherd, Bridget Brereton and Barbara Bailey.

Saskia E. Wieringa, PhD, joined the Institute of Social Studies in The Hague in 1981, to run the first MA of the Women and Development Programme. Besides lecturing, she coordinated the research programme on Women's Movements and Organisations in five countries and one region (the Caribbean). She has been involved in setting up women's studies in various countries, for example, in the Caribbean, Sudan, Yemen, Namibia and Bangladesh. She is, at present, General Coordinator of the Gender and Women's Studies Institutes Network in Asia (GWINA), co-coordinator of Kartini, Asia-European Network of Women's Studies, and the President of the International Association for the Study of Sexuality, Culture and Society (IASSCS). Her present research focuses on women's empowerment in the face of HIV/AIDS in Indonesia. She has recently designed the African Gender and Development Index, for the Economic Commission for Africa. She has published widely, on gender policy, women's movements and sexuality. Her latest books are (with Evelyn Blackwood) *Female Desires; Women's Same Sex Practices Cross-culturally* (1999), which received the Ruth Benedict Award, and *Sexual Politics in Indonesia* (2001).

The keynote address at the Mona Academic Conference 2003 was delivered by the Hon. Mia Mottley and is here reproduced as the Foreword.

Mia Amor Mottley, QC, MP and Attorney-General of Barbados, was elected to the Barbados Parliament in September 1994 as part of Prime Minister Owen Arthur's new Barbados Labour Party Government. Prior to that, Miss Mottley served as one of two Opposition Senators in the Senate of Barbados between 1991 and 1994 while serving as Shadow

Minister of Culture and Community Development and on a number of Joint Select Committees on various areas, such as praedial larceny and domestic violence.

In 1996 and again in 1997 she served as chair of the CARICOM Standing Committee of Ministers of Education. She is also a member of the National Security Council of Barbados and the Barbados Defence Board. She is currently General Secretary of the Barbados Labour Party. An attorney-at-law with a law degree from the London School of Economics specialising in advocacy, she became a member of the Local Privy Council in January 2002. She was also admitted to the Inner Bar of Barbados, becoming the youngest ever Queen's Counsel in Barbados.

Index

'A Life Free of Violence': campaign, 17
Abortion: Indo-Trinidadian adolescent girls' attitude to, 554; and women's rights, 112
Academic leadership (Jamaica): women and, 140–142, 146–147, 158
Adolescent experience: of Indo-Trinidadian girls, 529–533
Adonis complex: male body image and the, 143, 160–161
Afro-Tobagonian girls: and identity development, 535–536
Andaiye: and constitutional reform in Guyana, 607, 609
Angier: interpretation of the body by, 518
Anthropomorphism: in scientific research, 486–487
Antigua and Barbuda: ILO conventions ratified by, 322–323; and gender equality in constitutional reform, 614
Antigua and Barbuda Constitution Review Commission: and gender equity in language, 600
Antigua and Barbuda Sexual Offences Act (1995): and married women, 604; and women's participation in constitution reform, 611
Antiquity: class and upward mobility in, 122; gender and patriarchy in, 109–113
Antrobus, Peggy, 705; and feminist politics, 20–21, 22
Aristotle: interpretation of the body, 285
Artistic interpretation of history, 491–500
Association of Women's Organisations in Jamaica (AWOJA), 688; establishment of, 405
Attribution theory: definition of, 224–225

Babymother: dancehall culture in, 264; erotic disguise in, 278; robber bridegroom theme in, 276–278
Bailey, Professor Barbara, 705; and male performance in education, 15
Bailey, Wilma, 706
Bahamas, The: and gender equality, 615–617; ILO conventions ratified by, 322–323
Bahamas constitutional reform, 602
Banana industry: globalisation and the Caribbean, 186–187
Barbados: educational system, xxvii; globalisation and, 443, 444; ILO conventions ratified by, 323–324; social partnership in, xxv; unemployment and gender in, 445, 446
Barbados Constitution Review Commission: and freedom from discrimination, 619; gender and citizenship in the, 602 and gender equality, 612, 613; and gender equity in language, 599; women's participation in, 606, 611
Barbados Mulatto Girl, 500
Barriteau, V. Eudine, 706; and feminist activism, 54–55; feminist scholar, 8–9, 11; on social feminism, 11–12, 20
Beach boy: and sex tourism, 246–247, 251–254
Beach Policy for Jamaica (2001, Draft), 352–353
Beauty: colour and female, 515–516; defining, 519–521; women and the burden of, 521–525
Beauty industry: globalisation and the, 200–208, 523–524; and the oppression of women, 524

Beauty Queens on the Global Stage: Gender Contests and Power, 203
Beijing Platform for Action (PFA): gender issues in the, 14, 17, 18, 24; and gender mainstreaming, 357; and women's advancement, 663; and women's unwaged work, 629, 630–631
Beijing + 5 process, 632–635, 639–649
Belize: ILO conventions ratified by, 325–326; unemployment and gender in, 445
Belize Reform Commission: and gender equity in language, 599–605
Belize Women's Political Caucus: and women's participation in government, 608–609
Berden, Mia: and the development of women's studies, 375–376, 377
Bharose, Jennifer: and cultural influence of the USA in T&T, 190–191
Bill of rights: gender equity and language in the, 602–605
Biodiversity conservation: in Jamaica, 352
Biology as destiny, 484–486?
Birth of Venus: history-based commentary on, 491–493
Black feminists: and the concept of patriarchy, 101; philosophy of, 10–12
Black male body: and sex tourism, 244–248, 251–254
Black masculinity: under slavery, 76–78
Black power: beauty contests and, 201–202, 203
Black Skin, White Masks, 273; and black identity, 515
Black women: eighteenth and nineteenth century images of, 494–500
Bluest Eye, The: and black self-image, 515–516
Body: Christianity and the, 282; consciousness and the, 242–248; dancehall and the female, 281, 263; defining the 281–282, 510–511, 516; feminism and the, 287–289; and self-image, 514–516; sexuality and the black male, 244; in Western philosophy, 284, 285–287

Body of Christ: liberation theology and the, 296–299
Body Dysmorphic Disorder: beauty industry and, 525
Body image: beauty industry and black, 201
Bollywood: USA influence and, 210–212
Boundaries: crossing, 486–487; gender and, 486–488; in scientific research, 480–481; shifting, 482–483
Bridgens, Richard: slave images by, 496
Brunias, Agostino: slave images by, 497–500
Bureau of Gender Affairs, 13
Bureau of Women's Affairs, 13; Caribbean, 22; in Jamaica, 356

Cambridge 'A' Level Examinations: gender and performance in, 90
Canadian International Development Agency (CIDA): and gender mainstreaming, 358
Capitalism: the body and, 243–244
Career aspirations: of Indo-Trinidadian adolescent girls and, 543–547
CAFRA News, 7
Caribbean: beauty contests, 203–206; feminist theories, 11; gender equity in the, 455–459; globalisation and the, 185–187; research on gender and ICTs, 472
Caribbean Association of Feminist Research and Action (CAFRA), 688, 689, 693; and globalisation, 454
Caribbean body: race and the, 512
Caribbean Community (CARICOM): and constitutional reform, 593–620; evolution of, 336–337; and feminist scholarship, 23, 28, 30, 44–45, 50; and gender issues, 19, 337–341; women and, xx–xxi, 12
Caribbean Court of Justice (CCJ): establishment of the, 593; and gender equality, 609
Caribbean culture: globalisation of, 193–195

Caribbean Examination Council (CXC): and access to secondary education, 83; gender and performance in the, 84, 90; and history education, 64–79
Caribbean feminism: emergence of, 11, 40
Caribbean Free Trade Association (CARIFTA): establishment of the, 336
Caribbean literature: working mothers in, 361–366
Caribbean masculinity: and identity, 63–64
Caribbean women: and HIV/AIDS, 565–573
Caribbean Women's Association (CARIWA), 42–43
CARICOM Declaration of Labour and Industrial Relations Principles, 338
CARICOM Declaration of 1995: and the rights of women workers, xvi
CARICOM Plan of Action: gender and the, 12
CARICOM Single Market Economy (CSME): creation of a, 336, 337
CARIMAC: research on women and media, 220–222
Carnival: and Caribbean culture, 273
Cartesian theory: of the body, 286, 510–511, 516
Castello, June Ann, 706
Centrality: defining, 106–109
Centre for Gender and Development Studies (CGDS) (UWI), 45; establishment, xi–xii, 5; and gender policies, 19
Charles, Suzanne, 706–707
Charter of Civil Society: and working conditions, 338
Charter of Rights and Freedoms (Constitutional Amendment) Bill 2002 (Jamaica), 605
Children Guardianship and Custody Act (1958, Jamaica), 343
Church: and gender issues, xxviii
Christianity: and the body, 282, 285, 289–294

Citizenship (Constitutional) Amendment Act (1993, Jamaica), 601
Citizenship rights: constitutional reform and, 601–602
City states: patriarchy and, 115–118
Civil society: and the nation state, 119–121
Clarke, Roberta: and women's rights, 15
Class: and male marginalisation, 240
Claypole and Robottom: and gender, 68, 72, 73; representation of males in texts by, 78
Columbus, Christopher: artistic representation of landing of, 492–493
Commercial sex work: Jamaican adolescent girls and, 573
Commission on the Status of Women (CSW), xii; creation of the, 22
Committee of Women for Progress (CWP, Jamaica), 46, 690, 691–693
Communication: globalisation and, 181–182, 184, 187–189, 191; and the international women's movement, 184–185
Computer access: in the Caribbean, 472–474
Constitutional reform: gender and, 592–593; gender issues in, xx, xxiii; women's participation in Caribbean, 606–610
Constitutional Reform Constitution (Guyana): and freedom from discrimination, 619
Convention for the Elimination of all Forms of Discrimination Against Women (CEDAW), 23; and HIV/AIDS, 577; T&T and the ratification of, 663
Cooper, Carolyn, 707
Cooper, Laura Facey: statue, 248–249, 253
Council on the Affairs and Status of Women in Guyana (CASWIG, Guyana), 43
Cricket: and Caribbean cultural identity, 207–208
Crime: inner-city males and, 170–171

Cultural belonging: and identity development, 533, 535
Cultural hegemony: and the interpretation of beauty, 520–21, 523
Cultural imperialism: concept of, 188, 193. *See also* Cultural hegemony
Cultural representation: and gender ideologies, 189–190, 200–206
Cultural values. *See* Values
Culture: globalisation and the domination of USA, 187–189, 190–195, 200–212; patriarchy and popular, 257–258
Curriculum: gender and, 84
Custody legislation (Jamaica): women and, 343–344

Dancehall culture: the body in, 281; female body in, 262–264; masquerade in, 264, 266–275
Dancehall Queen: dancehall culture in, 264–266, 275–276
Danger: defining, 163
Davis, Michelle V., 707
DAWN: and feminist activism, 50–51; and globalisation, 48, 49
de Bruin, Marjan, 707
Decolonisation: and gender, 73–74
Descartes: philosophy of the body, 286
Development: in the Caribbean, 399; and education, 61; women and economic, 447–451
Digital Opportunity Task Force, 467
Directorate of Women's Affairs (Antigua and Barbuda): and women's participation in politics, 608
Discrimination: CARICOM and freedom from, 339–340
Discriminatory laws: and gender equality, 602–604
Disguise. *See* Masquerade
Division for the Advancement of Women: and HIV/AIDS, 576–578
DNA research: and reductionism, 485–486
Domestic violence: and sexual decision making, 570

Dominant social groups: and privilege, 122–125
Dominica: ILO conventions ratified by, 326–327; school drop-out and repetition rates in, 91
Dookham, Isaac: and gender, 68, 73
Draft National Biodiversisty Strategy and Action Plan (2001, Jamaica), 352
Draft Watershed Policy (2003, Jamaica), 351
Dress: and identity, 266
Drop-out rates: female, 91; male, 91
Dunn, Leith L., 708
Durrant, Fay, 708

Economic independence: identity and female, 541–547
Education: Beijing +5 and, 643–644, 647–649, 652; and development, 61; and gender, 62; gender in CARICOM programmes of, 12; male performance in, 15
Educational achievement: Indo-Trinidadian adolescent girls attitudes to, 540–542
Edwards, Bryan: use of The Voyage of the Sable Venus from Angola to the West Indies, 495
Electoral process: women in the Jamaican, 137–140
Emancipation: representation of males under, 71: representation of women under, 72
Emancipation Park sculpture (Jamaica): and the black male body, 282, 248–249, 253
Employment: and gender in the Caribbean state, 443–447; ICTs and opportunities for, 469–471
Enslaved men: marginalisation of, 164
Enslaved women: role of, 164; role in resistance, 78–79
Environment: the body and, 516
Environmental management: gender and, 348
Environmental Management Systems (2001, Jamaica), 354

Equal (Pay for Men and Women) Act (EEPMWA, 1975) (Jamaica), 339
Equal opportunities Act (T&T): and gender equality, 618
Equal remuneration: CARICOM and, 339–341
Equal Rights Act (2000, T&T), 339
Erotic disguise: dancehall, 263; motherhood and, 264–266, 275–276
Ethnicity: academic performance and, 93; and beauty, 524; Caribbean feminism and, 41
European Union: studies on gender and ICTs, 471
Exclusionary process: and patriarchy, 127–128; practised by dominant groups, 124

Family: black males and, 70
Fanon, Franz: and black identity, 515
Fantasy: in dancehall culture, 264, 272–275
Fatherhood: inner-city male attitudes to, 168, 170
Female body: Christianity and the, 282–283; feminism and the, 287, 290–291, 293–294; male control over the, 510–512
Female DJ: body language of the, 262
Female employment: UWI and, 412
Female sexuality: in dancehall culture, 262, 267–270, 274; defining, 568
Female unemployment: and HIV/AIDS in Jamaica, 574
Family structures: gender and Caribbean, 449–451
Femininity: defining, 112; Indo-Trinidadian adolescent girls and violation of, 537; redefining, 143–152
Feminisation: of teaching and male underachievement, 82–83, 91–92, 93–94
Feminism: and the body, 287–289; defining, 36–39, 40, 689, 693–694; definition of, 9
Feminist activism: and the beauty industry, 201; Caribbean, 16, 27–29; in CARICOM, 50; defining, 36, 38–39; differences between scholarship and, 30–32, 52; and gender studies, xxi, xxvii; in Jamaica (1970s), 690–691; and society, xiii–xiv, 52; weakening of, 688–689
Feminist conscientisation: process of, 39–40
Feminist environment: Caribbean, 19–21, 26
Feminist scholarship: academic, 10; defining, 30; definition of, 6–10; definition of terms in, 21; globalisation and, 451–455; role of, 27–29, 50; and society, xiii–xiv; and the UWI, 51–53
Feminist theory: Caribbean, 11–18
Feminists: and Caribbean constitution reform, 607–612; sexual orientation and Caribbean, 620; and women's studies, 376–380
Figueroa, Mark, 709
Folk culture: shape shifting in Jamaican, 266
Francois, Elma, 41
Freedom: women and access to, 71
Freedom from discrimination: CARICOM and, 339–340

Garvey, Amy, 41
Gattens: interpretation of the body, 516–518, 519
Gender analysis: in history textbooks, 74–75
Garvey Movement: and Caribbean feminism, 42
Gender: and academic performance, 83–85; concepts, 11; and constitutional reform, 596–597, 602–610; debate on the term, xi, 6, 11, 12; defining, 105–106, 111, 612; and education system, 62, 82; and history education, 68; and HIV/AIDS, 387, 564–579; and poverty, 387; scientific research and, 480–488; and sexuality, 568–571

Gender Affairs Division (T&T): and gender mainstreaming, 668–676; programme, 663–668
Gender analysis and power relations, 383
Gender and Development (GAD): emergence of, 23; strategy, xiii, 5, 12
Gender-based indicators: development of, 656–661
Gender Equality in the Caribbean: Reality or Illusion, 19
Gender Development Index (GDI), xii; defining, 657–661
Gender Dialogue, 7
Gender discrimination: constitutional reform and, 613
Gender Education Training Manual, 15
Gender Empowerment Matrix (GEM): defining, 656–661
Gender Empowerment Measure, xii
Gender Environment and Development (GED) framework, xvi, 348
Gender equality: and access to information, 168; and the Barbados Constitution Review Commission, 613; in the Caribbean, 455–459; CARICOM and, 337–344, 346; opportunities for advancing, 649–652; and representation of women in politics, 608
Gender identity: concept of, 223–224, 225, 226, 230; sexuality and, 283
Gender ideologies: and cultural representation, 189–190, 200–206
Gender justice: Constitutional reform and, xxiii, 5
Gender mainstreaming: defining, 357; Gender Affairs Division (T&T) and, 668–676
Gender Management Strategy (GMS), 14–15
Gender participation: in Jamaican politics, 135–137
Gender-privileging: challenging, 150–152; leadership roles and male, 146–147
Gender relations: in news production, 228–230; state and, 254
Gender rights: defining, 612

Gender stereotyping: curriculum choice and, 84–89
Gender studies: controversy in, xiv; UWI and, xi, 407–408
Gender training: ISS and, 391–393
Genealogy: and patriarchy, 104, 118–119, 126
Gene: research, 484–486
George, Roxanne: and constitutional reform in Guyana, 607
Girvan, Norman: definition of globalisation, 182–183
Global feminism, 22–24, 50
Globalisation: and the beauty industry, 200–206, 523–524; and the Caribbean, 185–187; defining, 179–185, 188–189; and cultural hegemony, 520; and feminism, 27–28, 48, 50; and feminist scholarship, 451–455; and male marginalisation, 451–455; sports and, 206–210; and women-in-development discourse, 447–451
Goodison, Lorna: and the sewing machine, 361–363
Gordon, Shirley: and gender, 68
Governance: women and, 586
Grenada: ILO conventions ratified by, 327–328; unemployment and gender in, 444
Gross philosophy: of the body, 285, 286
Guyana: and gender equality, 617; ILO conventions ratified by, 328–330; women's movements in, 43
Guyana constitution: gender equality and discriminatory laws in, 604; gender in preamble of the, 599, 600; women's participation in the review of the, 606; and women's political participation, 607, 609–610
Guyana Constitution Reform Committee: women's participation in, 607
Guyana Elections Law (Amendment) Act 2000, 608

Hairstyles: in dancehall culture, 267–270
Hegemonic masculinity: challenge to Caribbean, 238; definition of, 63; history and, 64; slavery and, 76–79
Henry-Wilson, Maxine, 709
Heterosexuality: and power, 569–571
Hindu Women's Organisation (T&T), 46
History: and the male marginalisation thesis, 164
History education: and gender, 68–79; and male identity, 64
HIV/AIDS: Beijing +5 and, 642–643; and the Caribbean body, 248–251; and gender, 29, 30, 387; and gender relations, 564–579; and risk environment, 165–166, 169; women and, xix, 5
Homophobia: ISS and, 387
Homosexual: tourism, 245–248
Homosexuality: and constitutional reform, 620
Hoscin, Gabrielle J., 709
Human Development Index (HDI): Caribbean and the, 442; defining the, 656–661
Human rights: and HIV/AIDS, 576–578
Human vs nature thesis, 510

ILO Convention 100: on equal remuneration, 335, 340
ILO Convention 111: on discrimination, 335
ILO Declaration on Fundamental Principles and Rights at Work, 334–335
ILO Night Work Convention, 342–343
Identity: body image and male, 143–146, 148–149, 160–161; Caribbean feminism and, 41; Caribbean masculinity and, 63, 165; and dress, 266; and gender, xiv, xv; religion and cultural, 199–200; and sexuality, xv–xvi; shifting, 227–228, 229, 230, 264, 266. *See also* Cultural identity, National identity, Shape shifting

Identity development: and educational achievement, 540–541; and personal choice among Indo-Trinidadian adolescent girls, 532–533; self-regard and, 535
Indian films: USA influence and, 210–212
Indo-Trinidadian girls: and identity development, 529–558
Information and communications technologies (ICTs): defining, 168–169; and gender equity, 166–168
Information Society Technologies: European Union programme on, 471
Insider femininity: concept of, 537
Institute of Social and Economic Research (ISER): and women's studies, 403–404, 431
Institute of Social Studies (ISS): and gender studies, xvii, 373–393; and the UWI, 407–408
International Decade for Women (1976–1985), 23, 44, 49, 50, 399
International Labour Organization (ILO): Caribbean ratification of, 321–332; establishment of the, 334; and the rights of women workers, xvi, 303–304
International Monetary Fund (IMF): definition of globalisation, 181, 183
International women's movement: Caribbean involvement in the, 626–652
International Women's Year (1975), 23, 43, 44, 399
Internet use: gender and, 471, 473–475
'Interpretation of the Landing of Columbus on the Island of Guanahana, October 12, 1492', 493

Jamaica: constitutional review process in, 595–596, 606; electoral process in, 137–140; environmental management in, 349–350; Equal Pay for Men and Women Act (1975), 339, 340–341; gender and political leadership in, 135–137; HIV/AIDS in, 573–574; ILO

conventions ratified by, 330–331;
unemployment and gender in, 445;
women's movements in, 41–42, 43, 46;
women workers in, 340–342

Jamaica Charter of Rights Freedoms (Constitutional Amendment) Bill 2002: and gender equality, 618

Jamaica Constitutional Commission: and gender equality, 614

Jamaican folk culture: shape shifting in, 266

James, C.L.R.: on cricket and cultural identity, 207–208

JFLAG: and freedom from discrimination, 618

Journalism: gender relations in, 228

Judeo-Christian philosophy: the body in 285, 289–284

Junior Secondary Schools: gender and education in T&T, 86–89

Justice: gender, xii, 5

Kartini: establishment of, 382–383

Kingston: gender relationships in inner-city, 163

Knowledge needs: meeting women's, xviii

Labour: the body and, 243, 255; gender and, 67, 72; globalisation and the exploitation of, 184, 185; slavery and the division of, 76–78

Labour force: CARICOM female, 340

Labour force participation: gender and, 444–447

Labour market: Caribbean women in the, 195–198

Labour Movement: and Caribbean feminism, 42

Labour standards: CARICOM, 338; international, 335

Language: and gender equity in the Guyana constitution, 599

Leadership: gender in, xii; women and, xx. *See also* Political leadership

Legislation: on equal pay, 339–341; and participatory government, xxvi; and violence against women, 15–16

Leo-Rhynie, Elsa, 710

Lewis, Linden, 710

Liberal feminists: philosophy of, 10

Liberation theology: the body and, 297; defining, 294–295; and feminism, 295–296

Lycklama, Geertje: and the development of women's studies, 378–380, 389

Maintenance Act (1881, Jamaica), 343

Mair, Lucille Mathurin: and women's issues in the UN, 22–23, 43; and the Women's and development Studies Unit, 407–408; and women's studies, 402

Male control: evolution of, 510–511, 513

Male-body image: changing, 143–146, 148–149, 160–161

Male dominance: history education and the representation of, 66–67

Male gaze: concepts, 265

Male gender-privileging: leadership roles and, 146–147

Male marginalisation thesis, 78–79; economics and, 237, 239, 254–255; emergence of the, 16, 62–63; feminisation of teaching and the, 82, 83, 90, 91; globalisation and, 446–447, 451; history and the, 164; and the labour market, 344–345; studies on the, 412; lower classes and the, 127; and women's issues, 672–673

Male sexuality: and power, 513

Male socialisation: academic performance, 92–93

Male Support Unit (T&T): establishment of the, 672–673

Male underachievement: feminisation of teaching and, 82–83, 91; gender stereotyping and, 84–86, 92–93

Mandela, Nelson: and gender justice, xxiii

Marginalisation: defining, 106–109; of males, 196–198

Marriage: Indo-Trinidadian adolescent girls attitude to, 550–552

Masculinity: Caribbean, 165; defining, 236, 238; education system and, xiv, 12; redefining, 143–152; and sexual relations, 571–572, 575; sports and, 206–210
Masquerade: in Caribbean culture, 273, 276; in dancehall culture, 264, 267–275
Massiah, Joycelin, 710
Maurice Committee: and secondary education for girls, 85
McKenzie, Hermione C., 711
Media: cultural representation in the global, 190–194, 200–206
Media production: gender and, 217–219
Men at Risk: definition of patriarchy in, 102; masculinity in, 106
Men's rights: and the Caribbean State, 443–444
Metrosexual: defining, 143, 148
Miller, Errol L., 711
Mind vs body: philosophy, 510–511
Modernity: Indo-Trinidadian adolescent girls attitude to, 556–558
Mohammed, Patricia, 711–712; feminist scholar, 9
Morris, Jeanette, 711
Morrison, Toni: and black self-image, 515–516
Mother/daughter relationship: in dancehall culture, 276–277
Motherhood: dancehall and the eroticisation of, 276; Indo-Trinidadian adolescent girls attitude to, 552–554
Moyne Commission: and gender, 73
Mulatto women: images of, 499–500

Nation state: patriarchy and the, 118–131
National Commission on the Status of Women (Barbados), 43
National Commission on Women (NCW, Guyana): and constitutional reform, 609
National Environment and Planning Agency (NEPA): and gender mainstreaming, 358

National identity: and sport, 208–210
National Land Policy (1996, Jamaica), 351
National System of Protected Areas (1997): policy on, 352
Nature vs nurture debate, 479, 481, 484
News: portrayal of women in the, 219
News production: gender and, 217–220; gender relations in, 228–230
NGO Forum: and the UN World Conference on Women, 398–399
Noise: defining inner-city, 170–174
Non-governmental organisations (NGOs): and governance, xxvi, 5; work of women's, 17–19

Ocean and Coastal Zone Management in Jamaica (2001), 353–354
Oppression: feminine concepts of, 101–102
Organisation of Women for Progress (OWP), 690, 691–693
Organisational identity: concept of, 226, 229, 230
Outsider femininity: concept of, 537–538

Participatory government: constitutional reform and, xxvi
Partnership process: among dominant social groups, 122–124; and patriarchy, 126–127
Patriarchal bargaining: concept of, 536
Patriarchy: challenge to, 49; defining, 36, 101–105; and female beauty, 521–523; genesis of, 510; masculinity and, 238, 255–258; social construction of, 109–131
Peer pressure: inner-city males and, 172–173
People's National Party (PNP, Jamaica): and the women's movement, 47
Personal choice: Indo-Trinidadian adolescent girls and, 532–533
Planning Institute of Jamaica (PIOJ): and gender mainstreaming, 358; and women's issues, 28

PNP Women's Auxiliary (Jamaica), 46, 47–48
Police: education programme to combat violence against women, 17–18
Political leadership: gender and, 135–137
Political Reform Commission (Belize), 607; and freedom from discrimination, 619; and gender equity in constitution reform, 613
Politics: Indo-Trinidadian adolescent girls aspirations towards participation in, 557–558; women representatives in, 587–591
Pollard, Velma, 712
Post-Beijing Regional Plan for Action: obligations of the, 630–632
Post-modern feminists: and gender, 102
Post-slavery. *See* Emancipation
Poverty: gender and, 387; women and, 350, 673–674
Poverty reduction: Beijing +5 and, 640–641
Power: class structure and, 122–123; and gender, 449; gender and sexual division of, 111, 112–113; male marginalisation and loss of, 164; and male sexuality, 513; and male-privileging, 147
Power relations: and gender analysis, 383
Pre-emancipation history: and gender, 68
Pre-menstrual syndrome (PMS): and the female body, 511–512
Preferential trade arrangements: globalisation and the removal of, 186
Professional identity: concept of, 226, 229, 230
Pregnancy: WHO study on inner-city attitudes to, 166–170, 173
Primary schools: gender and drop-out and repetition rates in, 91
Public education programme: to combat violence against women, 17–18; and HIV/AIDS, 577–579
Public participation: in the Jamaica constitutional review process, 595–596

Race: and control over the Caribbean body, 512–515; and male marginalisation, 241–242; and self-image, 267–274
Racial classification: genesis of, 514
Radical feminism: and concept of patriarchy, 101
'Recentring Caribbean Feminisms', 7, 20
Reddock, Rhoda, 713; feminist scholar, 8, 9, 11; on social feminism, 11
Reductionism: defining, 483
Regional Conference on Women in Latin America and the Caribbean (2000), 635–649
Regional cooperation: constitutional reform and, 594–595
Religion: and cultural identity, 199; and power, 114–115, 116–118
Repetition rates: female, 91; male, 91
Research: on gender and ICT issues, 469–473
Resistance: gender and, 69, 78–79
Risk: defining, 163–164; men as, 165; unprotected sex and, 169
Risk environment: development of urban, 165–174
Robber bridegroom theme: in *Babymother* and *Dancehall Queen*, 276–277, 278–279; in Caribbean folk culture, 266–267
Roberts, Audrey Ingram: gender analysis by, 14
Robertson, Dr. Paul: on gender and education, 62
Robinson, Tracy, 713
Role-play: in dancehall culture, 273
Rosehall (St Vincent): Women in Rural Development project, 53
Rowley, Michelle, 713

Saint Kitts and Nevis: ILO conventions ratified by, 331
Saint Lucia: gender equality and discriminatory laws in, 604; unemployment and gender in, 444, 445

'Santa Cruz River 2' (Cazabon), 502
Schooling. *See* Education system
Scientific research: boundaries in, 480–481; crossing boundaries in, 486–487; influences on, 480; shifting boundaries in, 482–483
Scott, Gloria: and the promotion of women's issues, 23, 44
Secondary education: gender and, 83
Secondary Education Modernisation Programme (SEMP): in T&T, 86–89
Self-image: beauty industry and black female, 267–275; black women and, 514–516
Self-regard: and identity development, 535, 539
Sewing machine: and the economic liberation of Caribbean women, 361–366
Sex: risk and unprotected, 169, 173–174
Sex trade: and tourism, 244–254
Sexual activity: gender and, 571–572, 575; Indo-Trinidadian adolescent girls attitude to, 547–550
Sexual decision making: women and, 569–570
Sexual equality: Indo-Trinidadian adolescent girls perception of, 555–558
Sexual exploitation: beauty industry and, 525–526; of enslaved women, 494–498; under slavery, 70; women's role in, 276
Sexual harassment: in media, 228
Sexual orientation: and freedom from discrimination, 618
Sexuality: black male body and, 244–254; Christianity and, 282, 290; defining, 283–284, 566; and gender relations, 565–566
Sexually transmitted infections (STIs): 575–576
Shape shifting: in dancehall, 26; in Jamaican folk culture, 266
Shepherd, Verene A, 713–714
Singer, Isaac: and the invention of the sewing machine, 362

Sirju-Charran, Grace, 714
SISTREN Theatre Collective (Jamaica), 46
Skin-bleaching: self-image and, 270–274, 515
Slave imagery: in eighteenth and nineteenth century art, 495–500
Slavery: black masculinity under, 76–78; and control over the Caribbean body, 512–514; family and, 70; gender division of labour under, 68; marginalisation of men under, 164
Social benefits: of beauty, 521
Social change: factors affecting, 113–114
Social identity: concept of, 223–224, 225–226
Social justice: and governance, xxiv
Social mobility: obstacles to, 122
Social partnership: in Barbados, xxv
Socialisation: cultural values and, xxviii–xxx; of males in risk environments, 166
Socialist feminists: philosophy of, 10, 11
Society: constructing an equitable, 106–109; evolution of modern, 114–126; gender and patriarchy in, 109–113, 121–122
Society for the Promotion of Education and Research (SPEAR, Belize): and political reform, 607
Spinoza: philosophy of the body, 287
Sport: gender and, 206–210
St. Vincent and the Grenadines: unemployment and gender in, 444
State: and gender relations, 254–256
Status of men: in Caribbean society, 236–258
Status of women: globalisation and the, 195–198
'Status of Women in the Jamaican Family Structure', 397
Structural adjustment policies: and feminism, 48–49
Student enrolment (UWI): gender and, 159
Subject choice: gender and, 84
Sustainable Development Network: and gender equity, 469–473
Symposium on Caribbean Masculinities, 7

Symposium in Honour of the Work of Peggy Antrobus, 7

Taylor, Orville W., 714–715
Teacher education: gender and, 93–96
Telecentres: use of, 473–474
Teenage pregnancy: attitudes to, 278
Tertiary education: gender and performance in, 84
Textbooks: gender in, 66–68; and gender stereotyping, 89; history, 65–66; representation of males in, 66
Third World feminism, 50
Tourism: sex, 244–248, 251
Townsend, Winsome, 715
Trade union movement: and gender, 73
Training: in computer technologies, 473–475
Triangle of empowerment: concept of, 374–375, 376, 378, 389–393
Trinidad and Tobago (T&T): cultural influence of the USA in, 190–191, 200–206, 208–212; drop-out and repetition rates in, 91; gender equality in, 661–662; gender and secondary education in T&T, 86–89; ILO conventions ratified by, 331–332; religion and identity in, 199–200; unemployment and gender in, 444; women's movements in, 46
Trinidad and Tobago Sexual Offences Act: and gender equality, 617–718

UN Decade for Women (1976–1985), 399; and women's issues in T&T, 662
UN Fourth World Conference on Women (FWCW): 23–24; CARICOM and the, 627–632
UN Human Development Report (HDR): and gender-based indicators, 656–661
UN International Research and Training Institute for the Advancement of Women (INSTRAW): research on gender and ICTs, 470

UN World Conference on Women (Mexico, 1975), 454; Jamaica's participation in, 397, 398
Unemployment: inner-city males and, 170
United Democratic Party National Women's Organisation: and women's participation in government, 608–609
United Nations: and status of women, xii; and women's rights, 22–24
United Nations Development for Women (UNIFEM), 8
United States of America (USA): and the beauty contest industry, 200–202; globalisation and the cultural domination by the, 187–189, 191, 192, 195, 200–212
University of the West Indies (UWI): and feminist scholarship, 51–54; gender and leadership in the, 140–142, 146–147, 158; and gender studies, xi, 407–414; and the ISS, 373, 374, 379, 382; and women's organisations, 454; and women's studies, 398
Untitled Brunai painting, 500
Unwaged work: CARICOM and women's, 629, 640
Urban risk environments: development of, 165–175

Values: gender and cultural, xxiii
Vassell, Linnette, 715–716
Venus: image in slavery, 494–499
Violence against women: Beijing +5 and, 641–642; in the Caribbean, 15–16, 17; patriarchy and, 256–257
Voting patterns: gender and, 156
The Voyage of the Sable Venus from Angola to the West Indies: critiques of, 494

War: and patriarchy in, 111–112; 116–118
Washing Day Dominica, 503
Washing Day in Jamaica (Forrest), 502
Washing Day at Port Antonio (Duperly), 503
Washing in a stream in Saint Lucia (Mohammed), 503

Washing Day at the White River (Jas Johnson), 502
Watershed management: in Jamaica, 351–352
Weber, Max: definition of patriarchy, 102
West India Washerwoman, 497
West Indian women: images of, 500–505
Western philosophy: the body in, 284–287
Western Sector Policy (Jamaica), 354–355
White feminists: and concept of patriarchy, 101
Wieringa, Saskia E., 716
Woman selling fruit and vegetables in Kingstown (Mohammed), 504
Women: academic leadership by, 140–142; and the burden of beauty, 521–523, 524–526; and constitutional reform, 592–610; in dominant groups, 122–124; globalisation and the exploitation of, 184; feminist movement and the behaviour of, 26–27; and freedom, 71; globalisation and the status of Caribbean, 195–198; and HIV/AIDS, xix, 5, 564–573; in the Jamaican electoral process, 137–140; images of mulatto, 499; women and nature, 518; images of West Indian, 500–505; in politics, 587–591; 608–610; and poverty, 350; represented in the news, 219; and resistance, 69; and shelter, 351; in sports, 206–210; and work, 303–317
Women in the Caribbean Project (WICP), 399; findings of the, 400–401, 405; philosophy, 11
Women and Development (WID), 23; strategies in T&T, 662
Women-in-development: and globalisation, 447–451, 453
Women and Development Unit (WAND): 7; and Beijing +, 18; establishment of, 399, 402; role of the, 45–46, 52–56
Women and development studies: international, xii; ISS and, xvii; UWI and, xi, xvii–xviii

Women and Development Studies Programme: establishment of, 402, 404–408
Women and Development Studies Unit: establishment of, 406
Women and gender studies: development of, 375–380; and the ISS, 373–393
Women and health: Beijing +5 and, 642–643
Women in Rural Development (St Vincent), 53
Women workers: in Jamaica, 340–342; status of Caribbean, xvi, xxix
Women's Auxiliary (Jamaica), 43
Women's Bureau (Jamaica): establishment of the, 398
Women's Desk (T&T): establishment of the, 662
Women's liberation. *See* Status of women
Women's Organisations: Caribbean, 42–46; globalisation and, 453–455
Women's political participation: and constitutional reform, 607–612
Women's rights: globalisation and, 454–459
Women's status: in the Caribbean, 454–455, 456–459
Women's studies: development of, 374, 375–380; global reach of, 388–390; integration of, 384–386; principles of, 380–383
Women's Studies Working Group (Mona), 402–404
World Conferences on Women (UN), xii
World Conferences for Women, 23
World Health Organization (WHO): study on men's attitude to relationships and pregnancy, 163, 166
World Trade Organization (WTO): and Caribbean economy, 443; and globalisation, 183
Work: gender and, xvi
Working mothers: the sewing machine and, 361–366